Beginning Adobe Animate CC

Learn to Efficiently Create and Deploy Animated and Interactive Content

Tom Green
Joseph Labrecque

Apress®

Beginning Adobe Animate CC: Learn to Efficiently Create and Deploy Animated and Interactive Content

Tom Green
OAKVILLE, Ontario, Canada

Joseph Labrecque
Thornton, Colorado, USA

ISBN-13 (pbk): 978-1-4842-2375-8
ISBN-13 (electronic): 978-1-4842-2376-5
DOI 10.1007/978-1-4842-2376-5

Library of Congress Control Number: 2017934517

Copyright © 2017 by Tom Green and Joseph Labrecque

This work is subject to copyright. All rights are reserved by the Publisher, whether the whole or part of the material is concerned, specifically the rights of translation, reprinting, reuse of illustrations, recitation, broadcasting, reproduction on microfilms or in any other physical way, and transmission or information storage and retrieval, electronic adaptation, computer software, or by similar or dissimilar methodology now known or hereafter developed.

Trademarked names, logos, and images may appear in this book. Rather than use a trademark symbol with every occurrence of a trademarked name, logo, or image we use the names, logos, and images only in an editorial fashion and to the benefit of the trademark owner, with no intention of infringement of the trademark.

The use in this publication of trade names, trademarks, service marks, and similar terms, even if they are not identified as such, is not to be taken as an expression of opinion as to whether or not they are subject to proprietary rights.

While the advice and information in this book are believed to be true and accurate at the date of publication, neither the authors nor the editors nor the publisher can accept any legal responsibility for any errors or omissions that may be made. The publisher makes no warranty, express or implied, with respect to the material contained herein.

Managing Director: Welmoed Spahr
Editorial Director: Todd Green
Acquisitions Editor: Louise Corrigan
Development Editor: James Markham
Technical Reviewer: Thomas Benner
Coordinating Editor: Nancy Chen
Copy Editor: Kezia Endsley
Compositor: SPi Global
Indexer: SPi Global
Artist: SPi Global
Cover image designed by Freepik

Distributed to the book trade worldwide by Springer Science+Business Media New York, 233 Spring Street, 6th Floor, New York, NY 10013. Phone 1-800-SPRINGER, fax (201) 348-4505, e-mail orders-ny@springer-sbm.com, or visit www.springeronline.com. Apress Media, LLC is a California LLC and the sole member (owner) is Springer Science + Business Media Finance Inc (SSBM Finance Inc). SSBM Finance Inc is a **Delaware** corporation.

For information on translations, please e-mail rights@apress.com, or visit http://www.apress.com/rights-permissions.

Apress titles may be purchased in bulk for academic, corporate, or promotional use. eBook versions and licenses are also available for most titles. For more information, reference our Print and eBook Bulk Sales web page at http://www.apress.com/bulk-sales.

Any source code or other supplementary material referenced by the author in this book is available to readers on GitHub via the book's product page, located at www.apress.com/9781484223758. For more detailed information, please visit http://www.apress.com/source-code.

Printed on acid-free paper

This book is dedicated to Jim Babbage and Doug Winnie, who, for the past 10 years, have embarked on our annual Excellent Adventures across North America where deep conversation or silence around a campfire is the mark of an "Excellent Friendship".

A small dedication to those designers, developers, and digital artists around the world who never abandoned what they love—instead choosing to persevere and adapt— toward our present victories.

Contents at a Glance

About the Authors xix

About the Technical Reviewer xxi

Acknowledgments xxiii

Introduction xxv

■Chapter 1: Learning the Animate CC Interface 1

■Chapter 2: Graphics in Animate CC.. 57

■Chapter 3: Symbols and Libraries 123

■Chapter 4: Interactivity Basics 181

■Chapter 5: Audio in Animate CC 249

■Chapter 6: Text in Animate CC 281

■Chapter 7: Animation 313

■Chapter 8: The Motion Editor and Inverse Kinematics 391

■Chapter 9: Animate CC and the Third Dimension... 457

■Chapter 10: Video 477

■Chapter 11: Components and External Media 519

■Chapter 12: Optimizing and Publishing Animate CC Projects 563

Index 589

Contents

About the Authors xix

About the Technical Reviewer xxi

Acknowledgments xxiii

Introduction xxv

■Chapter 1: Learning the Animate CC Interface 1

Getting Started 2

Creating a New Animate CC document 3

    Managing Your Workspace 5

Setting Document Preferences and Properties 7

    Document Preferences 8

    Document Settings 9

    Zooming the Stage 10

Exploring the Panels in the Animate CC Interface 13

    The Timeline 13

The Properties Panel 21

    The Tools Panel 25

    The Library Panel 27

    Creative Cloud Library 28

Using Layers 28

    Layer Properties 29

    Creating Layers 30

    Adding Content to Layers 32

    Showing/Hiding and Locking Layers 34

CONTENTS

Grouping Layers 35

Where To Get Help 35

Your Turn: Building an Animate CC Movie 36

Adding the Mountains and Playing with Color 39

Using Trees to Create the Illusion of Depth 40

Using a Motion Tween To Create a Twinkling Star 43

A Moon Over Lake Nanagook 45

Breaking the Stillness of the Night at Lake Nanagook 50

Testing Your Movie 52

Moonrise Over Lake Nanagook 53

You Have Learned 56

Chapter 2: Graphics in Animate CC 57

The Tools Panel 58

The Selection and Subselection Tools 60

The Free Transform Tool 63

The Gradient Transform Tool 66

Object Drawing Mode 69

Drawing in Animate CC 71

The Pencil Tool 71

The Paint Brush Tool 75

The Brush Tool 77

The Eraser Tool 80

The Pen Tool 81

Your Turn: Drop a Pin 85

Dropping the Pin 86

Working with Color in Animate CC 88

The RGB Model 89

The HSB Model 89

The Hexadecimal Model 89

The Color Palette and the Color Picker 90

| Creating Persistent Custom Colors | 91 |
| Creating Color Palettes with Creative Cloud Libraries | 94 |

Your Turn: Playing with Color ... 95
Using Bitmap Images in Animate CC ... 100
Working with Bitmaps Inside Animate CC ... 102

Your Turn: Tracing Bitmaps in Animate CC ... 103
Tracing an Image ... 103
Optimizing the Drawing ... 105

JPG Files and Animate CC ... 107
Using GIF Files in Animate CC ... 109
Working with GIF Images ... 110
Working with GIF Animations ... 111
Importing Photoshop Documents into Animate CC ... 112
Importing Illustrator CC Documents into Animate CC ... 115
Importing Sketch 3 Documents into Animate CC ... 120

You Have Learned ... 122

Chapter 3: Symbols and Libraries ... 123

Symbol Essentials ... 124
Symbol Types ... 127
Graphic Symbols ... 127
Button Symbols ... 128
Movieclip Symbols ... 129
Editing Symbols ... 131

9-Slice Scaling ... 132
How 9-Slice Scaling Works ... 132
Your Turn: Frames for an Olive Seller ... 135
The 9-Slice "Gotchas" ... 137
Sharing Symbols ... 140
Creative Cloud Libraries ... 142

Filters and Blend Modes 146
Applying Filters 147
Applying a Drop Shadow Filter 147
Adding Perspective 149
Playing with Blends 152

Managing Content on the Stage 157
Aligning Objects on the Stage 159
Stacking Order and Using the Align Panel 161
Using the Align Panel 165

Masks and Masking 166
A Simple Mask 167
Creating a Masked Animation 169

Your Turn: A Sunny Day on Catalina Island 173
Adding the Clouds 175

What You Have Learned 179

Chapter 4: Interactivity Basics 181

Using Code in Animate 182
The Actions Panel 182
Code Editor Preferences 187
The Code Snippets Panel 189
JavaScript and ActionScript 190

General Programming Concepts in Animate CC 191
Classes 192
Properties 193
Setting Properties with Code 198
Methods 199
Events 202

Additional Coding Fundamentals 206
Syntax 206
Capitalization Matters 206
Semicolons Mark the End of a Line 207

Mind Your Keywords	207
Commenting Code	207
Dot Notation	209
Scope	211
Variables	212
Data Types (ActionScript)	213
Operators	216
Conditional Statements	219

Working with JavaScript, HTML5 Canvas, and CreateJS 223

How to Read the CreateJS Documentation	224
JavaScript Troubleshooting	225
Using Additional JavaScript Libraries	226

Working with ActionScript and the Flash Platform 228

Class Files and the Document Class	229
ActionScript Syntax Checking	230
How to Read the ActionScript 3.0 Reference for the Adobe Flash Platform	233

Using ActionScript and JavaScript 236

Your Turn: Pause and Loop with JavaScript 236

Pausing a Timeline	237
Looping the Timeline	240
Using Movieclips to Control the Timeline	241
Using Code Snippets	242
Adding a Snippet to the Code Snippets Panel	245

What You Have Learned 247

Chapter 5: Audio in Animate CC 249

Animate CC and Audio Formats 250

Bit Depth and Sample Rates	251
Animate CC and MP3	252

Adding Audio to Animate CC 253

Importing an Audio File	253
Setting Sound Properties	254

CONTENTS

Using Audio in Animate CC 257
    Choosing a Sound Type: Event and Stream 257
    Removing an Audio File from the Timeline 260
    Getting Loopy 261
    Adjusting Volume and Pan 262
    Splitting Stream Audio Along the Timeline 265

Your Turn: Adding Sound to a Button 267

Controlling Audio with JavaScript 268
    Playing a Sound from the Library 268
    Using a Button to Play a Sound 270
    Playing a Sound from Outside of Animate CC 271
    Turning a Remote Sound On and Off 272
    Adjusting Volume with Code 273
    Your Turn: Storm Over Lake Superior 275

What You Have learned 279

Chapter 6: Text in Animate CC 281

Fonts and Typefaces 282

Adobe CoolType 284
    CoolType to the Rescue 285
    Typefaces and Fonts 286
    Using Adobe Typekit 286

Using Google Fonts 290

Working with Device Fonts 291

Embedding Fonts 293

Your Turn: Working with Text 296

A Word About TLF Text in Animate CC 298
    Dealing with Older Documents Using TLF 299

Creating Text with JavaScript 300

Creating Text with ActionScript 303

CONTENTS

Your Turn: Scrollable Text in HTML5 Canvas 307
- Rolling Your Own Scroller 307

What You Have learned 311

Chapter 7: Animation 313

Before We Start 314

Shape Tweening 315
- Scaling and Stretching 315
- Modifying Shape Tweens 320
- Altering Shapes 322
- Shape Hints 326
- Altering Gradients 330

Classic Tweening 332
- Rotation 332
- Classic Tween Properties 334
- Scaling, Stretching, and Deforming 335
- Easing 338
- Custom Easing 341

Using Animation 349
- A Closer Look at the Timeline Panel 349
- Onion Skinning 350
- Modifying Multiple Frames 353
- Combining Timelines 355
- Motion Guides 361
- Tweening a Mask 364
- Tweening Filter Effects 366

Programmatic Animation 368
- Copying Motion as Data 369
- Using the Keyboard to Control Motion 372
- Creating Random Motion 381
- Advanced Random Motion Using JavaScript 384

What You Have Learned 388

CONTENTS

Chapter 8: The Motion Editor and Inverse Kinematics 391

Animating with the Motion Editor 392
- Getting Acquainted: Scaling and Moving 393
- Applying Easing 399
- Easing with Graphs 400

Managing property keyframes 408
- Changing Duration Proportionally 411

Motion Paths 412
- Manipulating Motion Paths 412
- Motion Tween Properties 416

Motion Presets 417

Inverse Kinematics (IK) 421
- Using the Bone Tool 421

Putting Some "Spring" in Your Bones 432
- Applying Joint Translation 434
- Animating IK Poses 442
- Using the Bind Tool 444
- Your Turn: Animate a Fully Rigged IK model 449

What You Have Learned 454

Chapter 9: Animate CC and the Third Dimension 457

A Brief Lowering of Expectations 457

Understanding the Vanishing Point 458

Using the 3D Rotation Tool 459
- The 3D Translation Tool 461
- How to Set a Vanishing Point 461
- How to Use the 3D Translation Tool 464
- Using the 3D Center Point to Your Advantage 465
- Be Aware of Depth Limitations 468

CONTENTS

The Camera Tool in Animate CC.. 471
    How to Use the Camera 473
    How to Move the Camera 474
What You Have Learned... 476

Chapter 10: Video 477

Video on the Web and Beyond 478
    The MP4 and WebM Video Formats 478
Encoding Video 479
    Using Adobe Media Encoder... 479
    How to Use the Basic Video Settings 482
    How to Set the Video Bitrate... 483
    How to Encode the Audio Track 484
    Using the Animate CC Video Wizard.. 486
Video Playback with ActionScript 3.0 Documents.. 489
    Using the ActionScript 3.0 FLV Playback 2.5 Component 489
    Playing Video Using Raw ActionScript 492
Video with HTML5 Canvas Documents... 494
    Using the HTML5 Canvas Video Component 495
Creating Captions and Adding Accessibility 498
    WebVTT and HTML5 Canvas Documents 498
    WebVTT and ActionScript 3.0 Documents 504
Your Turn: Custom HTML5 Canvas Video Controls 510
Bonus Round: Create a Cinemagraph in Animate CC 513
    How to Create an Animated GIF 516
What You Have Learned... 518

Chapter 11: Components and External Media 519

Building Content with UI Components.. 519
    Working with ActionScript 3.0 UI Components 520
    Working with HTML5 Canvas UI Components 529

CONTENTS

Building a Slideshow with XML 534
- Image Files and XML Structure 535
- Assembling the UI Components 538
- Slideshow Functions 542

Building a MP3 Player with JSON 547
- MP3 Files, Image Files, and JSON Structure 547
- Assembling the UI Components 551
- Sound Playback Functions 554
- Additional Customization Options 558

What You Have Learned 560

Chapter 12: Optimizing and Publishing Animate CC Projects 563

Animate CC, Flash Player, and the Internet 563
- This "Internet" Thing 564
- Enter the World Wide Web 565
- Bandwidth 565

Project Delivery 567

Project Profiling 568
- Simulating a Download 569
- Optimizing Elements in an Animate CC Project 570

Publishing and Web Formats 573
- Flash Player 573
- HTML 574
- JavaScript 574
- Cascading Style Sheets (CSS) 574
- Images 575
- Audio 575
- Video 575

Publish Settings for ActionScript 3.0 Documents 575
Publish Formats 577
Publish Settings for HTML5 Canvas Documents 580
Publish Formats 581
What You Have Learned 587

Index 589

About the Authors

Tom Green is currently a Professor of Interactive Multimedia through the School of Media Studies and IT at the Humber Institute of Technology and Advanced Learning in Toronto, Canada. He has written numerous books on Adobe Technologies for Apress, is the Graphics Software Expert for About.com, and has written hundreds of tutorials for several magazines and web sites. Tom is an Adobe Community Professional and an Adobe Education Leader. He has spoken and lectured at more than 50 conferences and universities internationally, including Adobe Max and FITC, and at over a dozen universities in China, including the Beijing Central Academy of Fine Arts and Shenzhen Polytechnic. In his spare time, you catch him hiking a local trail or paddling across a lake in Northern Ontario.

Joseph Labrecque is primarily employed by the University of Denver as a senior interactive software engineer specializing in the creation of expressive desktop, web, and mobile solutions. His work incorporates a strong focus on the Adobe Flash platform alongside more general web standards initiatives involving the use of HTML5, CSS, JavaScript, and related technologies. He is also the proprietor of Fractured Vision Media, LLC, a digital media production company, technical consultancy, and distribution vehicle for a variety of creative works. Joseph authors video courses and written works through organizations which include Lynda.com, Peachpit, Pluralsight, Apress, and more. Joseph is an Adobe Education Leader and Adobe Community Professional.

About the Technical Reviewer

Thomas Benner is an Adobe Community Professional, Adobe Education Leader, and Adobe Certified Expert in Flash, Photoshop, and Illustrator. He has extensive experience teaching web design and development, vector and raster graphics, interactive multimedia, animation, digital presentation, and programming. He has been on the Graphic, Web, and Interactive Design faculty at the Art Institute of Austin for the past eight years. He is an innovative designer, animator, developer, programmer, and instructor who loves training others. He is always seeking an opportunity to develop outstanding training materials, utilizing the Adobe Creative Cloud and Apple Macintosh software with a focus on integrating various applications (Photoshop, Illustrator, Animate, Dreamweaver, Muse, Premiere, After Effects, and Behance) for effective desktop and screen publishing workflows.

About the author of the book

Acknowledgments

In a previous incarnation of this book, back when the subject was Flash CS3, I said, "Working with a co-author can be a tricky business. In fact, it is a lot like a marriage. Everything is wonderful when things are going well, but you never really discover the strength of the relationship until you get deep into it." Strange as it may sound, working with Joseph has been wonderful.

I have known Joseph for too many years to count and our paths have crossed as Adobe Education Leaders, a rather extensive series of jointly-written articles around Animate CC for Adobe and at various conferences where we presented. I have always enjoyed Joseph's company as well as his dry sense of humor and a way of explaining the intricacies of code that is awesome to witness. In fact, when I stepped away from Flash for a couple of years, Joseph became one of the strongest advocates for Animate CC out there. There were many times when I would gently tell him, "Dial it back, Joseph. Flash is dead." I am so glad he never listened because, when asked by Apress if I would undertake this title, I didn't have to think twice about who my co-author would be.

Next up is our beloved editor, Nancy Chen, who was relentless in her efforts to bring this book to life. It is an odd relationship between an editor and an author because there seems to be this perception that it is adversarial. In fact, it is just the opposite and and I am grateful to have that relationship with Nancy.

Another group of people who unwittingly had a profound influence on this book are my students and two colleagues—George Paravantes and David Neuman—at Humber. George and David always look at process and tools when it comes to development and much of the mobile stuff in these pages was sparked by conversations we had. My students were unwitting beta testers. I tried out many of the exercises in this book during our weekly classes and they rather forcefully let me know whether my idea worked or where I needed to start again.

Finally, writing a book of this size means I hole up in my office and generally become moody and difficult to live with as I mull over an exercise or the order of a chapter. How my wife and life partner, Keltie, puts up with it, I'll never know but it does tend to all work out in the end.

—Tom Green

I would first like to acknowledge Tom for bringing me into this project and for allowing me to run wild with some of the assets and exercises we came up with. Throwing together Serbian vampires, Ernest Hemingway, aural alter-egos, and the preparation of fine absinthe into a discussion on Animate CC, ActionScript, and HTML5 Canvas makes for a great authoring experience!

I'd also like to mention Ajay Shukla and Rich Lee at Adobe, who are both widely responsible for the revival of Flash Professional (as Animate CC) and the ongoing successes we all share.

Finally—as always—a thank you to my wife Leslie and our daughters Paige and Lily for dealing with my seemingly constant occupation with ongoing extra-familial activities.

—Joseph Labrecque

Introduction

This book marks the fifth time in 10 years that I have written a book for Apress about Animate CC when it was still known as Flash. The first book was the scariest because the "Foundation Flash ..." series was one of Apress' premiere titles and best sellers. It was both frightening and exhilarating to be the author and, I must admit, it was one heck of a lot of fun. Then Steve Jobs stepped in with his infamous rejection of the Flash Player on the iOS platform and ... that was that. In fact, one of the most memorable conversations I had with my editor at the time was when I had wrapped up the Flash CS5 title and he said, "Well, this is probably the last Flash title we will ever publish."

Here we are again and I can't help but thinking, "Isn't it funny how things turn out?"

This software has had some pretty dark years and in many respects, it needed them. Flash, now Animate CC, was software looking for a market and really not succeeding. That started turning around a couple of years ago when Adobe started slowly turned the application toward the HTML5 universe, removing a lot of bloat—Device Central is a good example—and stripping it down to its current incarnation with a sparkly new name —Animate CC. That is the subject of this book.

This book is quite a bit different from previous editions because waltzing between HTML5 Canvas and ActionScript 3.0 documents creates some pretty interesting challenges when it comes to things like what code snippet to use or what video format to use in the video chapter. Then it occurred to both of us that that we were asking the wrong questions. The question should have been, "What do you need to know and why." That was when we realized, "Nothing has really changed, just how we talk about it." Thus, the tone of this book is friendly and inviting, and there isn't a ton of what we call "techie talk."

One thing we did notice as we started planning the exercises is that Animate CC is one seriously cool, mobile prototyping tool. This explains the numerous exercises that demonstrate a technique but the explanation takes place in an Android or iOS interface. As one of the authors has been saying for over two years, "You can't talk about motion. You have to show it." Animate CC has all of the tools you need to do just that and in less time than you may think.

One other aspect of this book is that we had a huge amount of fun developing the exercises and examples in this book. The word "fun" is important because if learning is fun, what you learn will stay with you. Explaining 9-slice scaling is a lot more fun when applied to a Chinese Olive Seller. Explaining how to "swap" movieclip instances is more understandable when you drop an anvil on a rabbit's head. Nested movieclips become more real when explained in the context of a Hostess Twinkie. Want an Animate CC quick start? Welcome to Lake Nanagook.

As you may have guessed, we both continue to exhibit a sense of joy and wonder with Animate CC and we hope some of that rubs off on you as well.

Book Structure and Flow

This is not a typical software book. There is no common project that runs throughout the book. Instead, each chapter contains a number of exercises and examples designed to give you experience with the core concepts of Animate CC. Then, in several chapters, we turn you loose with a "Your Turn" exercise.

INTRODUCTION

We start by taking you for a walk through the Animate CC interface, pointing out important areas and showing how they work. We finish up our stroll on the shores of Lake Nanagook and create a scene with a moonrise and howling wolves. Chapter 2 introduces you to working with the graphic tools and finishes with showing you how you can bring your Illustrator, Photoshop, and Sketch 3 work into Animate CC.

Chapter 3 introduces you to the all-important Symbols and Library features in Animate CC. In this chapter, you learn about 9-slice scaling by meeting an olive seller in Guangzhou, China. We show you how filters work by adding a realistic drop shadow to a dancing fool; you discover how to use the Animate CC Library and your Creative Cloud Library as repositories for reusable content, including "bunny bits". We then turn you loose on Catalina Island off the coast of California to bring clear skies to a foggy day.

At this point in the book, you have been exposed to the fundamentals of Animate CC and the time has arrived to dig into the coding aspect of the application. This is the focus of Chapter 4 and is ideal for those of you who have never used ActionScript 3.0. Chapter 5 starts by explaining how to use audio in Animate CC and finishes up with you creating a rather intense rainstorm. Chapter 6 reinforces the message that "text isn't the grey stuff around your graphics". We show you how it is both serious and fun and how to use two of the most extensive type libraries out there—Adobe Typekit and Google Web Fonts—right from Animate CC.

Chapters 7 and 8 are extensive overviews of the animation features of Animate CC. In these two chapters, you will be dropping an anvil on a rabbit's head, banging hammers, fixing a neon sign, learning about bones with bones, and animating an fully rigged Inverse Kinematics model.

Chapter 9 is devoted to the 3D aspects of Animate CC. In this chapter, you use a vanishing point to put an image on a wall-mounted computer screen, opening and closing doors and setting an astronaut loose in space by using the new camera feature of Animate CC. Chapter 10 moves into the realm of video in Animate CC. Here, you will learn how to create and deploy video in your HTML5 Canvas and ActionScript 3.0 projects. We even show you how to create a cinemagraph in Animate CC.

Chapter 11 is a rather extensive look at many of the HTML5 Canvas and ActionScript 3.0 components that are packaged with Animate CC, along with an overview of XML and JSON data structures. We finish up by answering the inevitable question, "How do I deploy my Animate CC projects?"

Finally, Joseph and I are no different from you in that we, too, are learning more about what you can and can't do in Animate CC. Although we may be coming at it from a slightly different level than you, the constant stream of updates and feature additions to Animate CC makes this a pretty exciting time for us as we discover where Animate CC fits into the mobile, app development, and web design fields.

Our final words of advice are these:

"The amount of fun you can have with Animate CC should be illegal. We'll see you in jail!"

CHAPTER 1

Learning the Animate CC Interface

Welcome to Adobe Animate CC. We suspect you are here because you have seen a lot of the great stuff that Animate CC can do and it is now time for you to get into the game. We also suspect you are here because you discovered that Animate CC is more complex than you originally thought. The other reason you may be here is because you were a former Flash Professional user and you need to get a handle on this new stuff in relatively short order. Whatever your motivation, both authors have been in your shoes at some point in our careers, which means we understand what you are feeling. So instead of jumping right into the application . . . let's go for walk.

What we'll cover in this chapter:

- Exploring the Animate CC interface
- Using the Animate CC stage
- Working with panels
- Understanding the difference between a frame and a keyframe
- Using frames to arrange the content on the stage
- Using layers to manage content on the stage
- Adding objects to the Library
- Testing your movie

If you haven't already, download the chapter files. They can be found at http://www.apress.com/us/book/9781484223758.

These files are used in this chapter:

- 01_Magnify.fla (Chapter01/Exercise Files_CH01/Exercise/01_Magnify.fla)
- 02_Ad.fla (Chapter01/Exercise Files_CH01/Exercise/02_Ad.fla)
- 03_Timeline.fla (Chapter01/Exercise Files_CH01/Exercise/03_Timeline.fla)
- 04_Properties.fla (Chapter01/Exercise Files_CH01/Exercise/Properties.fla)
- 05_Layers.fla (Chapter01/Exercise Files_CH01/Exercise/Layers.fla)
- 06_MoonOverLakeNanagook.fla (Chapter01/ExerciseFiles_CH01/Exercise/Garden.fla)
- Nanagook.mp3 (Chapter01/ExerciseFiles_CH01/Exercise/FliesBuzzing.mp3)

© Tom Green and Joseph Labrecque 2017
T. Green and J. Labrecque, *Beginning Adobe Animate CC*, DOI 10.1007/978-1-4842-2376-5_1

CHAPTER 1 ■ LEARNING THE ANIMATE CC INTERFACE

We are going to take a walk through the authoring environment—called the Animate CC interface—and point out the sights to give you an opportunity to play with some of the stuff we will be pointing out. By the end of the stroll, you should be fairly comfortable with this tool called Animate CC and have a fairly good idea of what tools you can use and how to use them as you start creating Animate CC movies.

As we go for our walk, we will also have a conversation that will help you understand the fundamentals of the creation of an Animate CC movie. Having this knowledge right at the start of the process will give you the confidence to build on what you have learned. So let's start our walk right at the beginning of the process . . . the Start page.

Getting Started

A couple of seconds after you double-click the Application icon to launch Animate CC, the Start page, shown in Figure 1-1, opens. This page, which is common to all of the CC applications, is divided into six discrete areas.

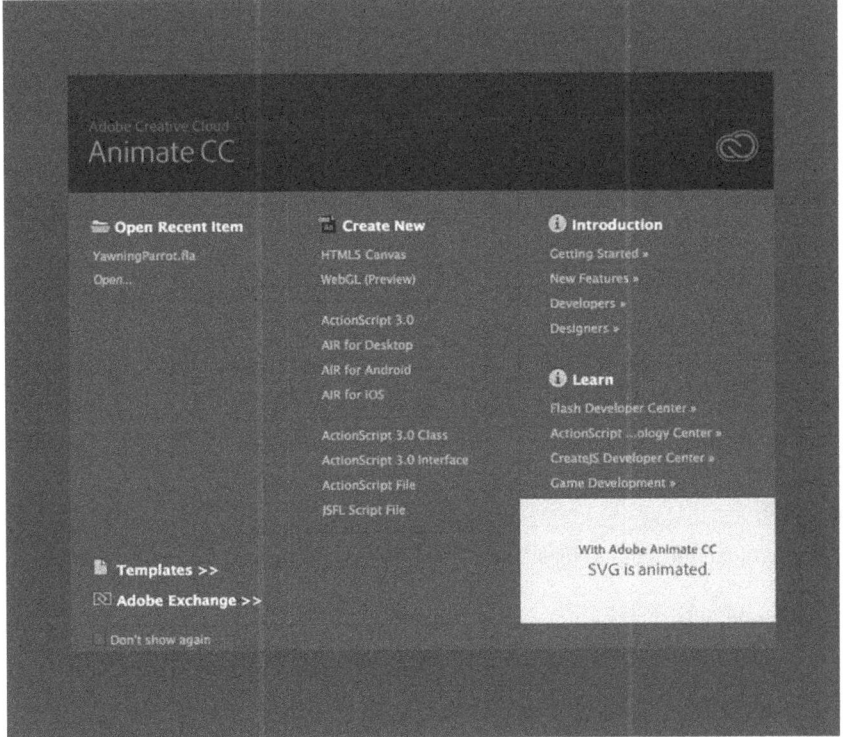

Figure 1-1. The Start page

- **Open Recent Item:** The documents listed are the ones opened recently. Provided you haven't moved them to another location or deleted them, clicking one will open it. Clicking Open will let you browse for files not contained in the list.

- **Create New:** The middle area is where you can open a variety of new documents. It is broken into three distinct sections for a reason: They reflect the three major document types you can create. In this book we will only be dealing with ActionScript 3.0 and HTML5 Canvas documents. HTML5 Canvas can use detailed artwork, graphics, animations, and practically everything else that can be created in Animate CC. The other choice is WebGL (Web Graphics Library), which allows you to to render plug-in free graphics on any compatible browser. The two groups below it are for specific types of documents ranging from the code-only ActionScript 3.0 document to the three AIR plug-ins that allow you to package your Animate CC projects into apps. The final four types are specific code-based options.

You may have noticed that the name is officially WebGL (Preview). The current version of Animate CC only supports basic animations and has a limited set of interactivity features. Thus it is a work in progress.

- **Introduction:** Each item here will launch a browser that takes you to a series of Animate CC tutorials that address the category you clicked.

- **Learn:** This area provides you with a series of Animate CC help documents that will allow you to explore, in greater depth, topics and techniques aimed at the category you selected.

- **Templates:** This category is a bit misleading. Double-clicking one of the choices actually opens the New from Template dialog box. The purpose of these templates is to give you the opportunity to dissect a variety of sample documents.

- **Adobe Exchange:** Click this and you are taken to a web page that gives you the opportunity to purchase or download a variety of plug-ins and extensions for Animate CC.

Creating a New Animate CC document

Let's continue our stroll through Animate CC by creating a new Animate CC document. To do this, simply click the HTML5 Canvas button in the Create New area of the Start page. This opens the interface shown in Figure 1-2.

CHAPTER 1 ■ LEARNING THE ANIMATE CC INTERFACE

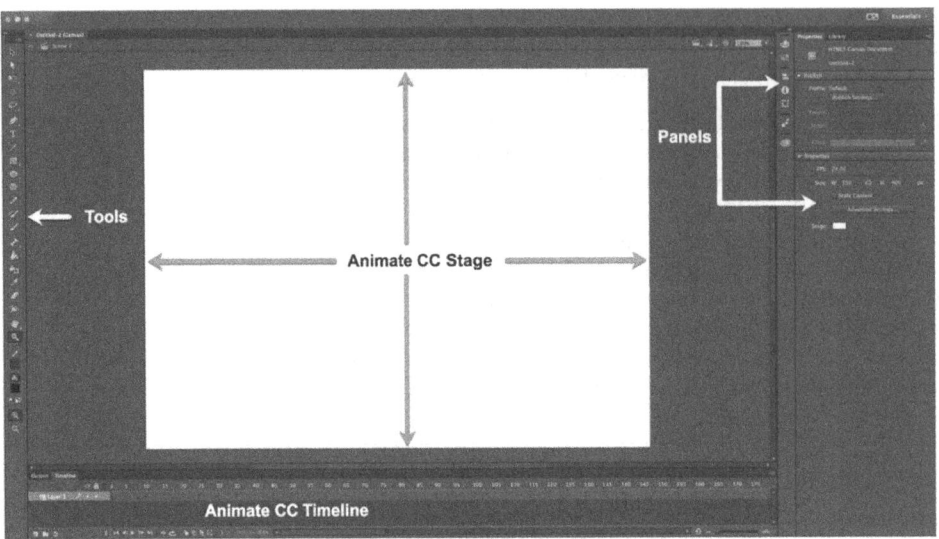

Figure 1-2. *The Animate CC authoring environment*

This interface is the feature-rich authoring environment that is the heart and soul of Animate CC. Let's now step into that big white area on the screen and take a moment to look around. The **stage**, that large white area in the center of the screen, is where the action happens. A good way of regarding the stage in relation to Animate CC is this: if it isn't on the stage, the user isn't going to see it. There will be instances where this last statement is not *exactly* true, but we'll get into those later in this book.

On the far-right edge of the screen is a set of tools that allow you to draw, color, and otherwise manipulate objects on the stage.

To the right of the stage are the panels. Panels are used to modify and manipulate whatever object you selected on the stage or to even add an object to the stage. These objects can be text, photographs, line art, short animations, video, or even interface elements called **components**. You can use the panels and the menus to change not only the characteristics of the objects but also how the objects behave on the stage. Panels can be connected to each other (**docked**), or they can float freely in the interface (**floating**) and can be placed anywhere you like. To move a panel simply, click the Panel tab and drag it to a new location. If you see a blue line, the panel will dock to that location.

From our perspective, one of the more indispensable panels is the Properties panel. We'll talk about this a little later, but as you become more comfortable with the application, this panel will become a very important place for you. In fact, we can't think of any chapter in this book where we don't refer to this panel.

At the bottom of the interface is the Timeline panel, which longtime Animate CC users simply refer to as the **timeline**. This is the place where the action occurs. As you can see, the timeline is broken into a series of boxes called **frames**. The best way of regarding frames is as individual frames of a film. When you put something on the stage, it will appear in a frame. If you want it to move from here to there, it will start in one frame and move to another position on the stage in another frame a little farther along the timeline. The box with the vertical red stem draped over the timeline is called the **playhead**. Its purpose is to show you the current frame being displayed. When an Animate CC movie is playing through a browser or being tested, the playhead is in motion, and the user is seeing the frame where the playhead is located. This is how things appear to move in Animate CC. Another thing you can do with the playhead is drag it across the timeline while you are creating the Animate CC movie. This technique is known as **scrubbing** the timeline and has its roots in film editing.

Managing Your Workspace

As you may have surmised, the Animate CC authoring environment is one busy place, and if you talk to any Animate CC developer or designer, he or she will also tell you it can become one crowded place as well. As you start creating Animate CC projects, you will discover that screen real estate becomes a valuable commodity because it fills up with floating panels and other elements. Thus you need to know how to mange the panels. Here's how:

- **Collapse panels:** At the top of Panels area on the right side of the screen is an icon that looks like a double arrow (see Figure 1-3). Click it, and the panels will collapse and become icons. If you click the arrow above the panel, the Tools panel changes from a series of Tool icons to a single icon. The process is called *panel collapse,* and it is designed to free up screen space in Animate CC. There are three views for panels: fully expanded, partially collapsed showing the icon and panel name, completely collapsed to just the icon.

Figure 1-3. Panels can be collapsed to give you more screen space

- **Show collapsed panels as icons only:** Sometimes you need the extra interface room taken up by the panel's name. Roll the mouse pointer to the left or right edge of the panel strip. When the mouse pointer changes to a double-sided arrow, click and drag to expand and show the panel's name, or shrink to the width of the icons in the strip.

CHAPTER 1 ■ LEARNING THE ANIMATE CC INTERFACE

- **Open and close drawers:** Click an icon, and the contents of that panel will fly out, as shown in Figure 1-4. Click it again, and it will slide back. These panels that fly out and slide back are called *drawers*.

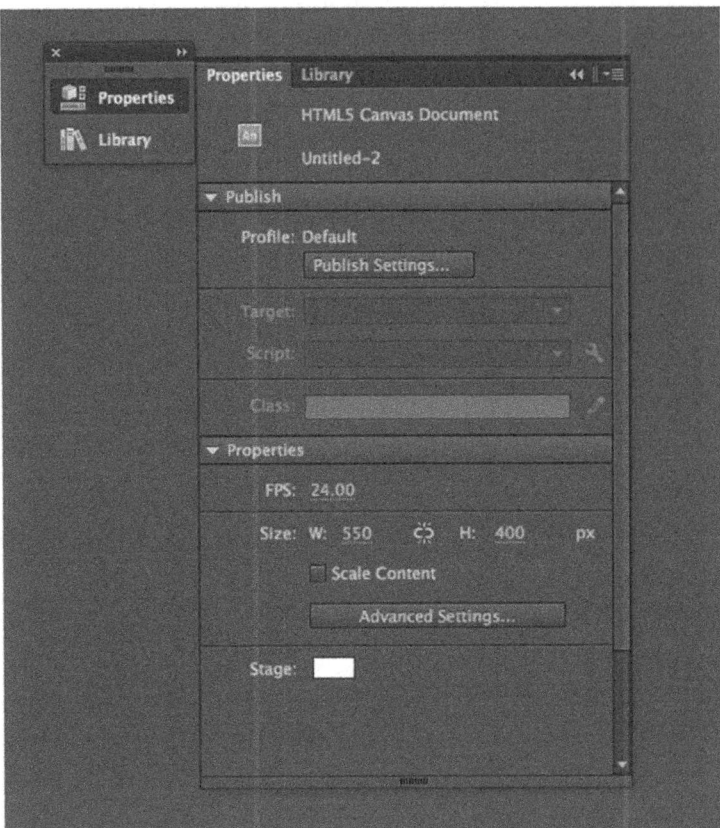

Figure 1-4. Click a panel icon, and the contents slide out. Click the icon again, and they slide in

- **Minimize panels:** Another method of buying screen real estate is to minimize panels you aren't using. Double-click the tab with the panel's name, and the panel collapses upward. Double-click it again, and it expands to its original dimensions.
- **Close panels:** Right-click (Windows) or Control+click (Mac) a panel, and select Close from the context menu. This not only closes the panel but also removes it from your workspace. To get it back, simply open the Window menu and click the name of the panel you closed to restore it.
- **Add panels to sets:** A collection of panel icons, as shown in Figure 1-5, is called a *panel set*. To create a customized panel set, drag one panel icon onto another panel. When you release the mouse, the panel will expand to include the new panel added. To remove a panel from a set, just drag the panel icon to the bottom of the stack.

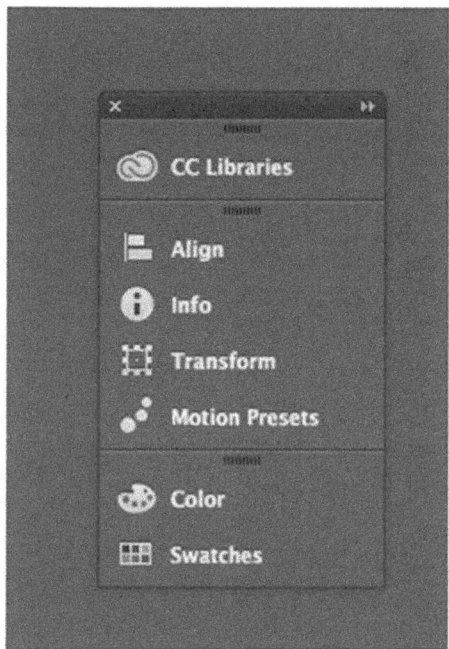

Figure 1-5. *A typical panel set*

To save your customized workspace, select Window ➤ Workspace ➤ New Workspace and enter a name for your custom workspace into the New Workspace dialog box. Click OK to add the workspace. If you want to delete one of your workspaces, select Window ➤ Workspace ➤ Manage Workspaces. When the Manage Workspaces dialog box opens, select the space to be deleted and click the Delete button.

Speaking of workspaces, at the top right of the Animate CC interface is a drop-down list of "prerolled" workspaces that came with the application. The default is Essentials. If you click and hold down that button, a drop-down list of the choices appears. If you want to return the workspace to its "out-of-the-box" look, select the Reset Essentials item in the menu.

Now that you have learned to become the master of the work environment, let's take a look at how you can also become the master of your Animate CC document as we wander over to the Preferences and Properties areas of Animate CC.

Setting Document Preferences and Properties

Managing the workspace is a fundamental skill, but the most important decision you will make concerns the size of the Animate CC stage and the space it will take up in the browser. That decision is based on a number of factors, including the type of content to be displayed and the items that will appear in the HTML document beside the Animate CC movie. These decisions all affect the stage size and, in many respects, the way the document is handled by Animate CC. These two factors are managed by the Preferences dialog box and the Document Properties panel.

CHAPTER 1 ■ LEARNING THE ANIMATE CC INTERFACE

Document Preferences

To access preferences, select Edit ➤ Preferences (Windows) or Animate CC ➤ Preferences (Mac). This will open the Animate CC Preferences dialog box. There is a lot to this dialog box, and we'll explore it further at various points throughout this book. For now, we are concerned with the general preferences in the Category area of the window. Click General, and the window will change to show you the general preferences for Animate CC, as shown in Figure 1-6.

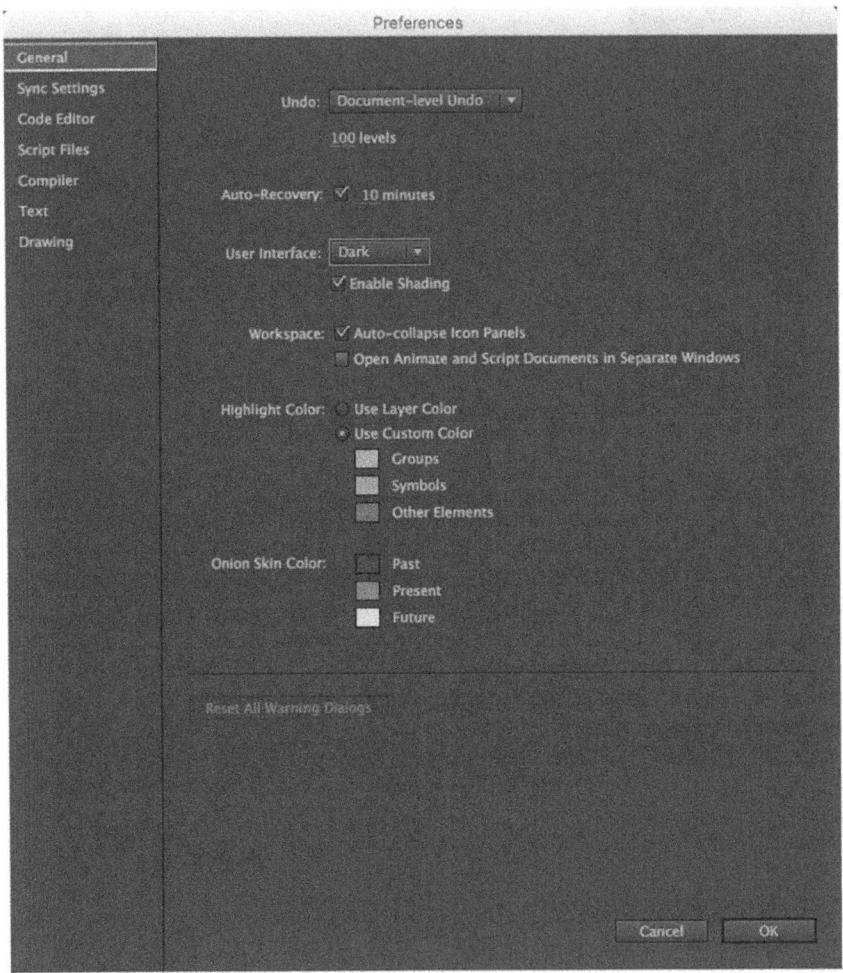

Figure 1-6. *The General preferences can be used to manage not only the workspace but also items on the stage*

CHAPTER 1 ■ LEARNING THE ANIMATE CC INTERFACE

If you examine the selections, you will realize they are fairly intuitive. You can change the interface from dark to light, how many Undo levels are available to you and even the colors that will be used to tell you what type of object has been selected on the stage.

Now that you know how to set your preferences, let's take a look at managing a document's properties. Click the Cancel button to close the Preferences dialog box. When it closes, let's wander back to the stage and explore how a document's properties are determined.

Document Settings

To access the Document Settings dialog box, use one of the following techniques:

- In the Properties panel, click the Advanced Settings button in the Properties area—not the Publish area. This will open the Document Settings dialog box shown in Figure 1-7.

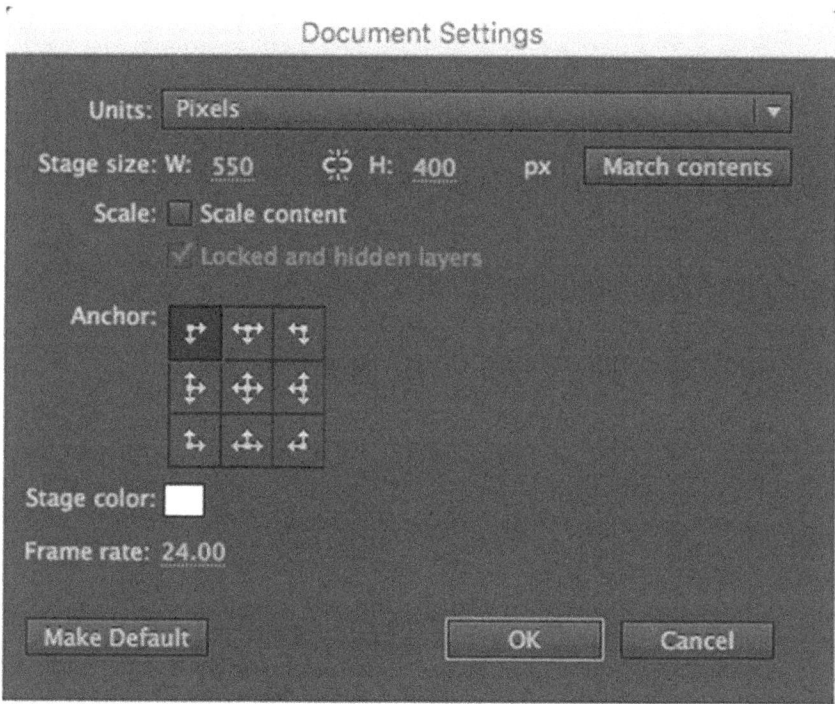

Figure 1-7. *Set the stage size through the Document Settings dialog box*

- Select Modify ➤ Document.
- Press Ctrl+J (Windows) or Cmd+J (Mac).
- Right-click (Windows) or Control+click (Mac) the stage and select Document Properties from the context menu.

9

As you have just seen, there are a number of methods you can use in Animate CC to obtain the same result. In this case, it is opening the Document Settings dialog box. Which one is best? The answer is simple: whichever one you choose.

Now that the Document Settings dialog box is open, let's look around. The Dimensions input area is where you can change the size of the stage. Enter the new dimensions and press the Enter (Return) key. If you enter a value, you may need to press the the Enter or Return key twice. Once to accept the new entry and a second time to close the dialog box, or click the OK button, and the stage will change. The Match Contents button is commonly used to shrink the stage to the size of the content on the stage.

The Anchor area is not what you may think. Each selection determines how the stage will scale when the dimensions of the stage are changed, not the content.

For example, if you change the Dimensions setting to a width of 400 pixels and height of 300 pixels, set the Background color option to #0033CC, select the Center anchor, and click OK, the stage will shrink to those dimensions and change color to the blue chosen. The changes, as shown in Figure 1-8, are also reflected in the Properties panel.

Figure 1-8. Changes made to the document properties are shown in the Properties panel

Zooming the Stage

There will be occasions when you discover that the stage is a pretty crowded place. In these situations, you'll want to be sure that each item on the stage is in its correct position and is properly sized. Depending on the size of the stage, this could be difficult because the stage may fill the screen area. Fortunately, Animate CC allows you to reduce or increase the magnification of the stage through a technique called **zooming**. (Note that zooming the stage has no effect on the actual stage size that you set in the Document Settings dialog box.)

To zoom the stage, click the Magnification drop-down menu near the upper-right corner of the stage. The drop-down menu shown in Figure 1-9 contains a variety of sizes ranging from Fit in Window to 800% magnification. For example, click the 400% option, and the stage will most likely fill your screen, as shown in Figure 1-10. Just keep in mind that you are not scaling the image on the stage. You are actually magnifying the stage and its contents. Click the 25% option, and you will see not only the stage but the entire pasteboard (that gray area surrounding the stage) as well.

CHAPTER 1 ■ LEARNING THE ANIMATE CC INTERFACE

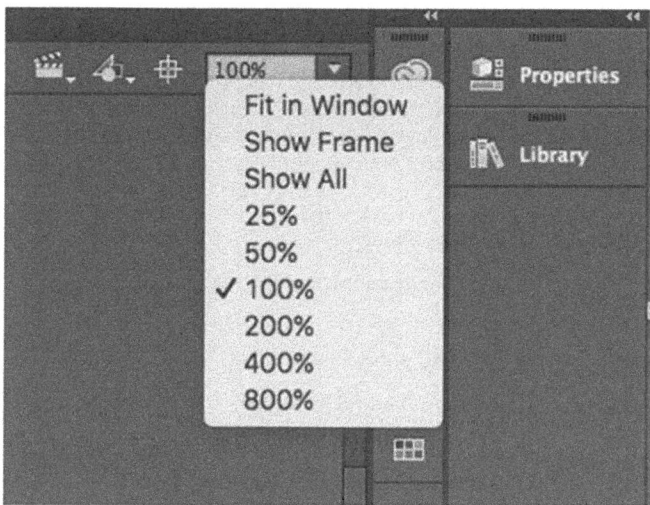

Figure 1-9. *Select a zoom level using the Magnification drop-down menu*

Figure 1-10. *Selecting a 400 percent zoom level brings you close to the action*

11

CHAPTER 1 ■ LEARNING THE ANIMATE CC INTERFACE

If you want more zoom, you can get a lot closer than 800 percent. Select View ➤ Zoom In or View ➤ Zoom Out to increase the zoom level to 2000 percent. If you want a real bird's-eye view of the stage, Zoom Out allows you to reduce the magnification level to 8 percent. For you keyboard junkies, Zoom In is Command/Ctrl+= and Zoom Out is Command/Ctrl+ -. If you are a control freak, you can enter your own value. Just keep in mind the maximum zoom level is 2000 percent, and the minimum zoom level is 8 percent.

If you want a side-by-side comparison in which one image is at 100 percent view and the other is at 400 percent or 800 percent, follow these steps:

1. Open the `Magnify.fla` file in the `Chapter 1 Exercise` folder.

2. Select Window ➤ Duplicate Window. The current document will appear in a separate tab.

3. Set the new window's magnification level to 400% and press the Enter key.

4. Undock the 100 percent window, as shown in Figure 1-11, and let it float.

Figure 1-11. *Duplicating a window gives you a bird's-eye view and a detailed view of your work simultaneously*

5. Select the image in the floating window by clicking the image and dragging it around the stage. You will see that the zoomed-in version in the docked window also moves. This is a really handy feature if precise positioning of elements on the stage is critical.

6. Click each window's close button to close the window. Don't save the changes.

Exploring the Panels in the Animate CC Interface

At this point in our stroll through the Animate CC interface, you have had the chance to play with a few of the panels. We also suspect that by this point you have discovered that the Animate CC interface is modular. By that we mean that it's an interface composed of a series of panels that contain the tools and features you will use on a regular basis, rather than an interface that's locked in place and fills the screen. You have also discovered that these panels can be moved around and opened or closed depending on your workflow needs. In this section, we are going to take a closer look at the more important panels that you will use every day. They include the following:

- The timeline
- The Library panel
- The Properties panel
- The Motion Editor
- The Tools panel
- The Help panel

The Timeline

Here's the secret behind how one becomes a proficient Animate CC designer: ***master the timeline, and you will master Animate CC.***

When somebody visits your site and an animation plays, Animate CC treats that animation as a series of still images. In many respects, those images are comparable to the images in a roll of film or one of those flip books you may have played with when you were younger. The order of those images on the film or in the book is determined by their placement on the film or in the book. In Animate CC, the order of images in an animation is determined by the timeline.

The timeline, therefore, controls what the users see and, more importantly, when they see it. To understand this concept, let's go for a walk in a Canadian forest while the leaves are falling from the trees.

At its most basic, all animation is movement over time, and all animation has a start point and an end point. The length of your timeline will determine when animations start and end, and the number of frames between those two points will determine the duration of the animation. As the author, you control those factors.

For example, Figure 1-12 shows you a simple animation. It is a leaf that falls from the top of the stage to the bottom. From this, you can gather that the leaf will move downward when the sequence starts and will continue to its final position at the bottom of the stage once it has twisted in the middle of the sequence.

CHAPTER 1 ■ LEARNING THE ANIMATE CC INTERFACE

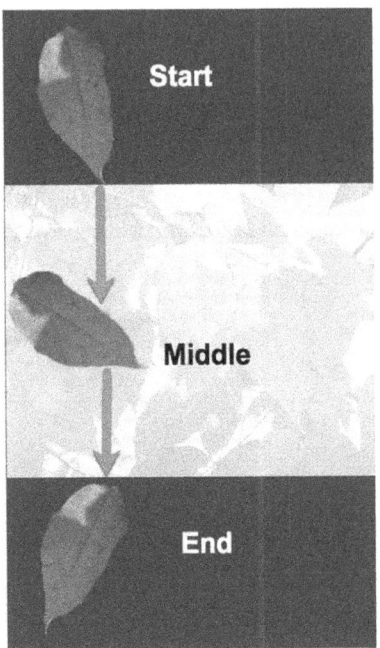

Figure 1-12. *A simple animation sequence*

So, where does time come into play? Time is the number of frames between the start and middle or middle and end points in the animation. The default timing in an Animate CC movie—called **frame rate**—is 24 frames per second (fps). In the animation shown in Figure 1-13, the duration of the animation is 48 frames, which means it will play for 2 seconds. You can assume from this that the leaf's middle location, where it twists, is the 24th frame of the timeline. If, for example, you wanted to speed up the animation, you would reduce the length of the timeline to 12 frames; if you wanted to slow it down, you would increase the number of frames to 72 or decrease the frame rate. If you want to see this animation, open the `Timeline.html` file in the `01_Complete` folder.

CHAPTER 1 ■ LEARNING THE ANIMATE CC INTERFACE

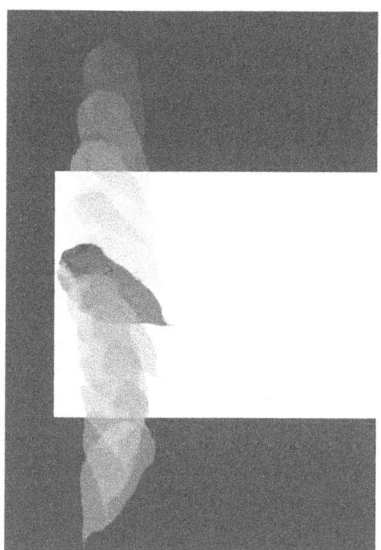

Figure 1-13. Animation is a series of frames on the timeline

So much for a walk in the woods; let's wander over to the timeline and look at a frame.

Frames

If you unroll a spool of movie film, you will see that it is composed of a series of individual still images. Each image is called a **frame**, and this analogy applies to Animate CC.

When you open Animate CC, your timeline will be empty, but you will see a series of rectangles—these are the frames. You may also notice that these frames are divided into groups. Most frames are gray, and every fifth frame is numbered (see Figure 1-14), just to help you keep your place. Animate CC movies can range in length from 1 to 16,000 frames, although an Animate CC movie that is 16,000 frames in length is highly unusual.

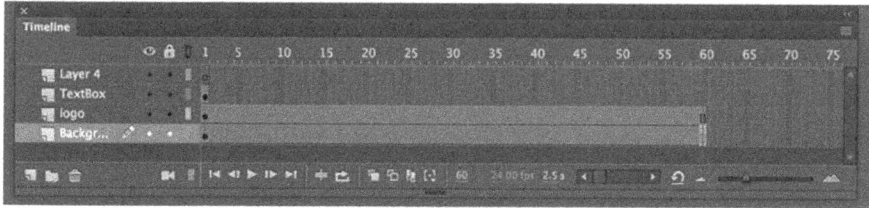

Figure 1-14. The timeline is nothing more than a series of frames

15

CHAPTER 1 ■ LEARNING THE ANIMATE CC INTERFACE

A frame shows you the content that is on the stage at any point in time. The content in a frame can range from one object to hundreds of objects, and a frame can include audio, video, code, images, text, and drawings either singly or in combination with each other.

When you first open a new Animate CC document, you will notice that frame 1 contains a hollow circle. This visual clue tells you that frame 1 is waiting for you to add something to it. Let's look at a movie that actually has something in the frames and examine some of the features of frames:

1. Open the 02_Ad.fla file located in the Chapter 1 Exercise folder. When the file opens, you will see a basic banner ad for a local garden center. There is a text box, in frame 1, sitting at the bottom of the stage and a logo at the top. You should also note the solid dot in the background, TextBox, and Logo layers. This indicates that there is content in Frame 1 of each of those layers The empty layer above them has a hollow dot, which indicates there is no content in that frame.

2. Place the mouse pointer on any frame of the timeline and right-click (Windows) or Control+click (Mac) to open the context menu that applies to frames (Figure 1-15).

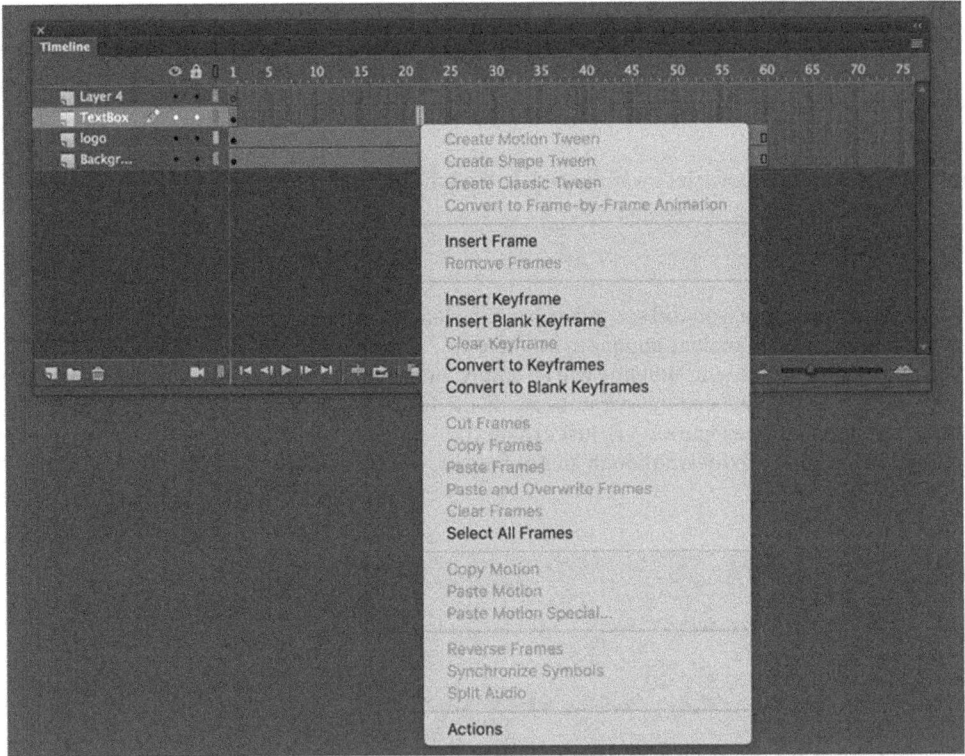

Figure 1-15. The context menu that applies to frames on the timeline

CHAPTER 1 ■ LEARNING THE ANIMATE CC INTERFACE

As you can see, quite a few options are available to you. They range from adding motion to the timeline to adding actions (code blocks) that control the objects in the frame. We aren't going to dig into what each menu item does just yet, but rest assured, by the time you finish this book, you will have used each menu item.

3. Place the mouse pointer at frame 30 of the TextBox layer, open the context menu, and select Insert Keyframe. Repeat this step at frame 60 as well. What you will notice is that the timeline changes to the series of gray frames and three black dots, as shown in Figure 1-16. These gray frames represent a span of frames separated by keyframes.

If you prefer to use the keyboard, place the mouse pointer at frame 30 and press F5. With that frame selected, press F6. The F5 command adds a frame, and F6 converts the selected frame to a keyframe. If you just want to add a keyframe, select frame 30 and press F6.

An obvious question at this point is, "So, guys, what's a keyframe?" Remember when we talked earlier about animations and how they had a start point and an end point? In Animate CC, those two points are called *keyframes*; any movement or changes can only occur between keyframes. In Animate CC, there are two types of keyframes: those with stuff in them (indicated by the solid dot shown in frame 1 of Figure 1-16) and those with nothing in them. The latter are called *blank keyframes*, and they are shown as frames with a hollow dot. The first frame in any layer, until you add something to that frame, is always indicated by a blank keyframe.

Figure 1-16. *The timeline contains three keyframes*

To navigate to specific frames in the timeline, you drag the playhead to the frame. It is the red rectangle with the line coming out of it.

4. Move the playhead to frame 1 and drag the TextBox to the left of the stage and on to the pasteboard.

17

5. Drag the playhead to frame 30, use the Selection tool to click the TextBox on the stage, and move the TextBox over to the middle of the stage. As you moved the object, you may have noticed there was a "ghosted" version of the leaf on the screen. This feature was introduced in Flash Professional CS4. It gives you a reference to the starting position of the motion.

As mentioned earlier in the chapter, the technique of dragging the playhead across the timeline is called *scrubbing*. As you scrub across the timeline, you will also see the values in the Current Frame and Elapsed Time areas at the bottom of the timeline change. This is quite useful in locating a precise frame number or a specific time in the animation.

---

6. Drag the playhead to the keyframe in frame 60 and drag the object to the bottom-right edge of the stage.

7. Scrub the playhead across the stage. The TextBox doesn't do much other than "pop" to its new positions as you encounter the keyframes. Let's fix that right now.

8. Right-click (Windows) or Control+click (Mac) between the first two keyframes of the TextBox layer and select Create Classic Tween from the context menu. An arrow will appear between the two keyframes. Scrub across the timeline again, and the object's movement is much smoother. Repeat this step for the next two keyframes.

    A *tween* is how simple animations are created in Animate CC. Animate CC looks at the locations of the objects between two keyframes, creates copies of those objects, and puts them in their positions in the frame. If you scrub through your timeline, you will see that Animate CC has placed copies of the object in frames 2 through 30 and in frames 31 through 60 and then puts them in their final positions to give the illusion that the TextBox is moving.

    That was interesting, but we suspect you may be wondering, "Okay, guys, do tweens work only for stuff that moves?" Nope. You can also use tweens to change the shapes of objects, their color, their opacity, and a number of other properties. We'll get to them later on in the book.

9. Drag the playhead to frame 30 and click the TextBox on the stage. Drag it toward the center of the bottom of the stage. If you scrub through the timeline, you will see it move quite a distance to the right. This tells you that you can change an animation by simply changing the location of an object in a keyframe.

10. You may have noticed that the logo vanishes. Let's fix that. Right-click on frame 60 of the Logo layer and select Insert Frame from the Context menu. This technique is ideal for objects that don't move.

11. Close the file without saving it.

Using the Motion Editor

As you get deeper into working with Animate CC, you will find there is a reason why the Timeline and Motion Editor are inseparable: motion is created in the timeline and manipulated in the Motion Editor. Make a change in one, and it is instantly reflected in the other.

In previous versions of Animate CC, the Property Inspector, which is now the Properties panel, could be used to change the properties of an animation. This would include techniques such as "ramping" the speed of an animation, called **easing**, or even changing how an animation occurs such as adding or removing rotation. This is still true for shape tweens and classic tweens, but the true power of motion is realized in the Motion Editor which, in Animate CC, is no longer a separate panel on the timeline.

Although we are going to get deeper into using these features later in this book, now would be a good time to stroll over to it and take a peek. Open the 03_Timeline.fla file. When the file opens, the first thing you will notice is there is an icon beside the layer name. This "zooming square" icon indicates the layer is a tween layer. The term **tween** indicates that something is changing at some point in the layer—we'll get into tweening in more detail later. The other thing you may have noticed is that there are no arrows between the keyframes. The tween span is indicated in blue, and because of the icon, the use of the arrow is not necessary. The dotted line you see on the stage indicates a tween path.

If you are an After Effects user, you may be looking at that tween path and thinking, "Nah, it can't be!" Yes, it is a motion path, and just like with an After Effects motion path, you can adjust that path by clicking and dragging one of the dots. Each dot represents a frame of the animation.

Drag the playhead across the timeline, and you will see the leaf gently tumble downward as you move the playhead from left to right. To see the Motion Editor, as shown in Figure 1-17, right-click anywhere on the Leaf timeline and select Refine Tween from the Context menu or simply double-click anywhere on the timeline. The Motion Editor shows you what properties have changed between the keyframes. In this case, it is Location and Rotation.

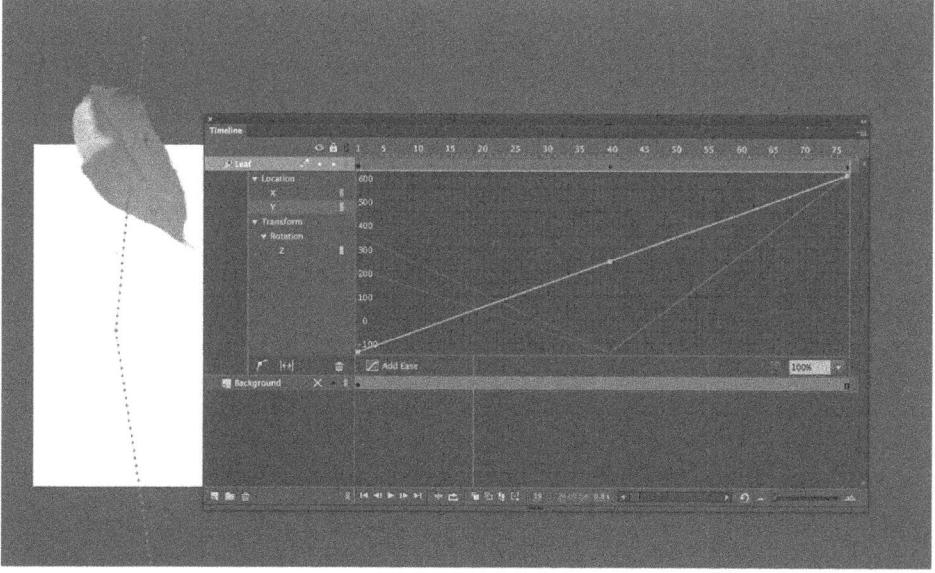

Figure 1-17. *A motion layer, tween path, and the Motion Editor*

The horizontal scale is time and the vertical scale shows you the property change of that object over time. Each line on the graph is color-coded and reflects a particular property change. For example, the Motion Editor is showing the Y motion (Downward) that starts just over 100 pixels above the stage—thus the negative value—and, over the 75 frames of the timeline, stops about 600 pixels below the top of the stage. Right in the middle is another keyframe.

Time for a history lesson. Back in 2000, one of us attended FlashForward. That event is regarded by many of the old Animate CC hands as being Animate CC's "Woodstock." It was at this conference that Adobe introduced LiveMotion. LiveMotion used the same timeline as the Motion Editor. At the time, we (and many people at the conference) thought the timeline was a "sweet" idea. Eight years later—three years after it purchased Macromedia (which owned Flash)—Adobe added this feature and it is now in Animate CC.

See those triangles beside the property names in Figure 1-17? If you click one, it rotates down, and the area is revealed. Those triangles are called *twirlies*, and the term used to describe clicking one of them to reveal the contents of the area is named "Twirl Down". We will be using these terms quite extensively when we talk about the Motion Editor.

At the bottom of the Motion Editor there are four icons, as shown in Figure 1-18. They have a specific purpose:

- **Add Anchor Point:** When you select this and click anywhere on one of the graph lines, you are adding a new keyframe.
- **Fit to View:** Click this and the Motion Editor grows or shrinks.
- **Trash Can:** This one is dangerous. Click it and you remove the tween for the selected property.
- **Apply Easing:** Click this and you can apply a number of "eases" designed to give motion a more natural feel.

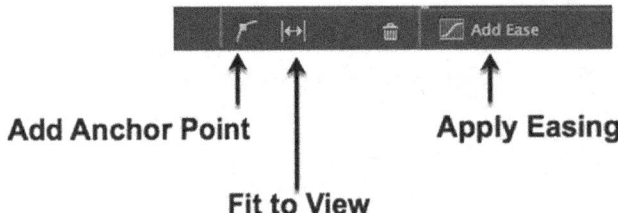

Figure 1-18. You can manage the look of the Motion Editor

CHAPTER 1 ■ LEARNING THE ANIMATE CC INTERFACE

The Properties Panel

We have been mentioning the Properties panel quite a bit to this point, so now would be a good time to stroll over to it and take a closer look. Before we do that, let's go sit down on the bench over there and discuss a fundamental concept in Animate CC: everything has **properties**.

What are properties? These are the things objects have in common with each other. Tom and Joseph share the Author property of this book. We are both males. We both have a common language property, English, but we also have properties we don't share. For example, our location properties are Denver and Toronto. Joseph has longer hair than Tom. At our most basic, we are humans on the planet Earth. In Animate CC terms, though, we are objects on the stage. Click the Joseph object, and you will instantly see that, even though he and Tom share similar properties, they also have properties that are different. The properties of any object on the Animate CC stage will appear in the Properties panel, and best of all, any properties appearing in the panel can be changed.

The panel, as shown in Figure 1-19, is positioned, by default, to the right of the screen. You can move it elsewhere on the screen by simply dragging it into position and releasing the mouse. There are locations on the screen where you will see a shadow or darkening of the location when the panel is over it. This color change indicates that the panel can be docked into that location. Otherwise, the panel will "float" above the screen.

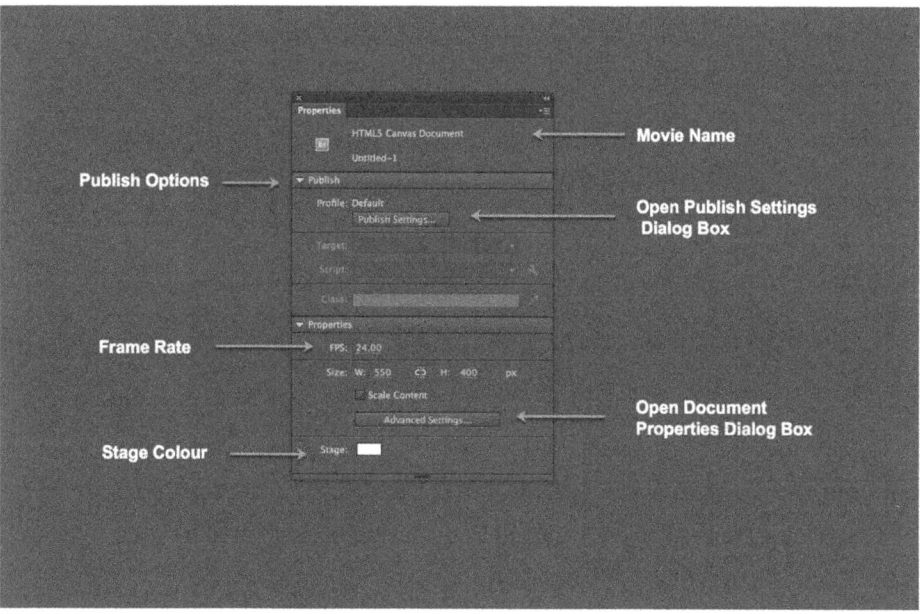

Figure 1-19. *The Properties panel*

21

CHAPTER 1 ■ LEARNING THE ANIMATE CC INTERFACE

When an object is placed on the stage and selected, the Properties panel will change to reflect the properties of the selected object that can be manipulated. For example, in Figure 1-20, a box has been drawn on the stage. The Properties panel shows you the type of object that has been selected and tells you that the stroke and fill colors of the object can also be changed. In addition, you can change how scaling will be applied to the object and the treatment of the red stroke around the box.

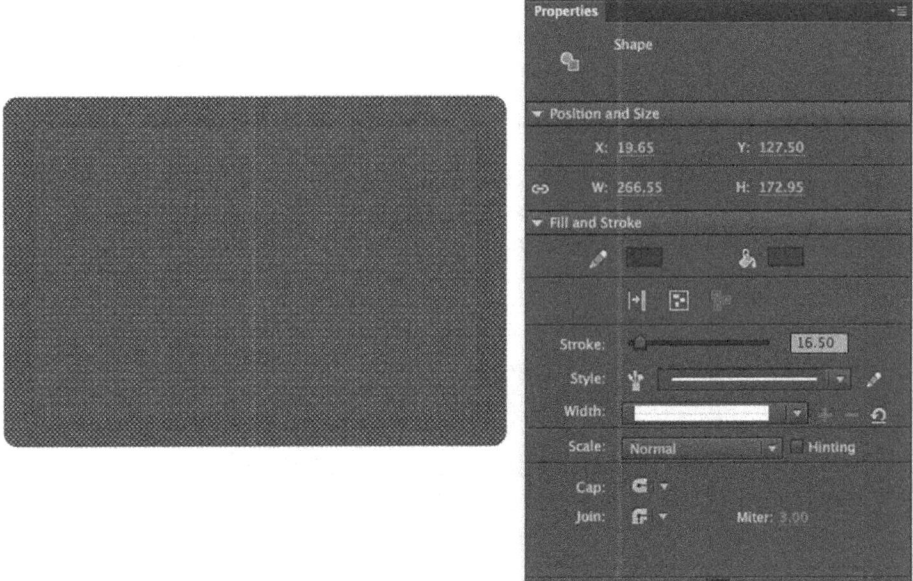

Figure 1-20. The Properties panel changes to show you the properties of a selected object that can be manipulated (in this case, the size, location, and stroke and fill properties of the box on the stage)

Let's experiment with some of the settings in the Properties panel:

1. Open the file named 04_Properties.fla in the Exercise folder. When the file opens, you will see an image of the Summer Palace in Beijing over a black background and the words Summer Palace, Beijing at the bottom of the stage.

2. In the Tools panel, click the Selection tool, which is the solid black arrow at the top of the Tools panel (Figure 1-21).

Clicking tools is one way of selecting them. Another way is to use the keyboard. When you roll the mouse pointer over a tool, you will see a tooltip containing the name of the tool and a letter. For example, the letter beside the Selection tool is V. Press the V key, and the Selection tool will be highlighted in the Tools panel.

22

CHAPTER 1 ■ LEARNING THE ANIMATE CC INTERFACE

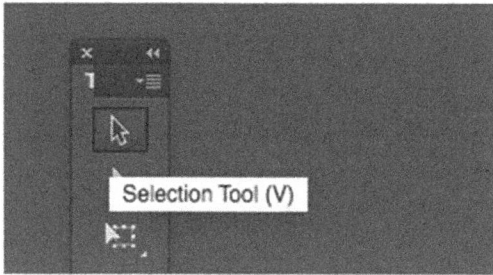

Figure 1-21. *Click a tool or use the keyboard to select it*

3. Using the Selection tool, click once in the white area of the stage. The Properties panel will change to show you that you have selected the stage and can change its color.

4. In the Properties panel, click the Background Color chip to open the Color Picker, as shown in Figure 1-22. Click the medium gray on the left (#999999), and the stage will turn gray. You have just changed the color property of the stage.

Figure 1-22. *Color and stage dimensions are properties of the stage*

23

CHAPTER 1 ■ LEARNING THE ANIMATE CC INTERFACE

5. Click the text. The Properties panel will change to show you the text properties, as shown in Figure 1-23, that can be changed. Click the color chip to open the Color Picker. When it opens, click the white chip once. The text turns white.

Figure 1-23. *Color is just one of many text properties that can be manipulated*

6. Click the black box surrounding the image. The Properties panel will change to tell you that you have selected a shape and that the fill color for this shape is black. It also lets you know that there is no stroke around the shape. In the Position and Size areas are four numbers that tell you the width, height, and X and Y coordinates of the shape on the stage. Select the Width value and change it from 500 to 525. Change the Height number from 380 to 400. Finally, change the X and Y values for the selection to 5 and 23, as shown in Figure 1-24. Each time you make a change, the selected object will get wider or higher.

If you are an After Effects user, then seeing properties as links (or, as they are known in Animate CC, *hot text*) is not new. If you want to quickly change any value, simply click and drag a value to the left or the right. As you drag, the numbers will change, and the selected object on the stage will reflect these new values.

CHAPTER 1 ■ LEARNING THE ANIMATE CC INTERFACE

Figure 1-24. *The size and the location of selections can also be changed in the Properties panel*

The Tools Panel

The Tools panel, as shown in Figure 1-25, is divided into four major areas:

- **Tools**: These allow you to create, select, and manipulate text and graphics placed on the stage.
- **View**: These allow you to pan across the stage or to zoom in on specific areas of the stage.
- **Colors**: These tools allow you to select and change fill, stroke, and gradient colors.
- **Options**: This is a context-sensitive area of the panel. In many ways, it is not unlike the Properties panel. It will change depending on which tool you have selected.

CHAPTER 1 ■ LEARNING THE ANIMATE CC INTERFACE

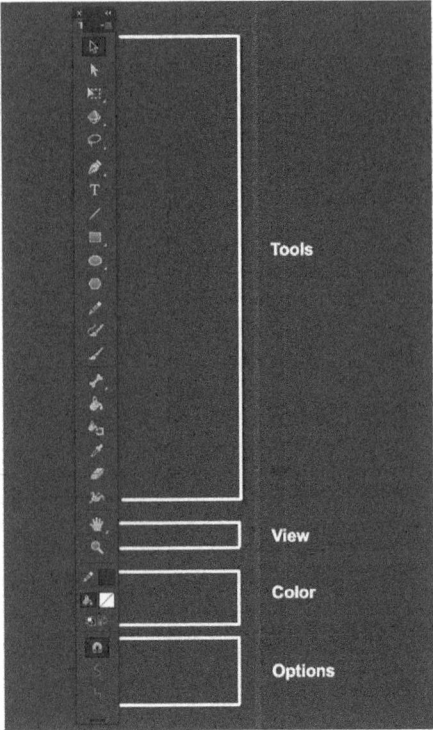

Figure 1-25. *The Tools panel*

If there is a small down arrow in the bottom-right corner of a tool, this indicates additional tool options. Click and hold that arrow, and related tools will appear in a drop-down menu, as shown in Figure 1-26.

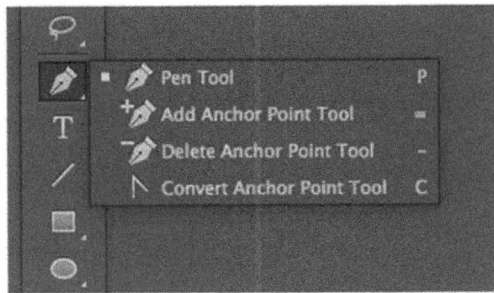

Figure 1-26. *Some tools contain extra tools, which are shown in a drop-down list*

The Library Panel

The Library panel is one of those features of the application that is so indispensable to Animate CC developers and designers that we simply can't think of anybody who doesn't use it . . . religiously.

In very simple terms, it is the place where content, including video and audio, that is used in the movie is stored for reuse later in the movie. It is also the place where symbols and copies of components that you may use are automatically placed when the symbols are created or the components are added to the stage.

Let's wander over to the Library and take a look. If the `Properties.fla` file isn't open, open it now. Click the Library icon on the right side of the screen, or click the Library tab if the panel isn't collapsed. The Library will fly out, as shown in Figure 1-27. Inside the Library, you will see that the Summer Palace image is actually a library asset. Drag a copy of the image from the Library to the stage. Leave it selected and press the Delete key. Notice that the image on the stage disappears, but the Library item is retained. This is an important concept. Items placed on the stage are, more often than not, instances of the item and point directly to the original in the Library.

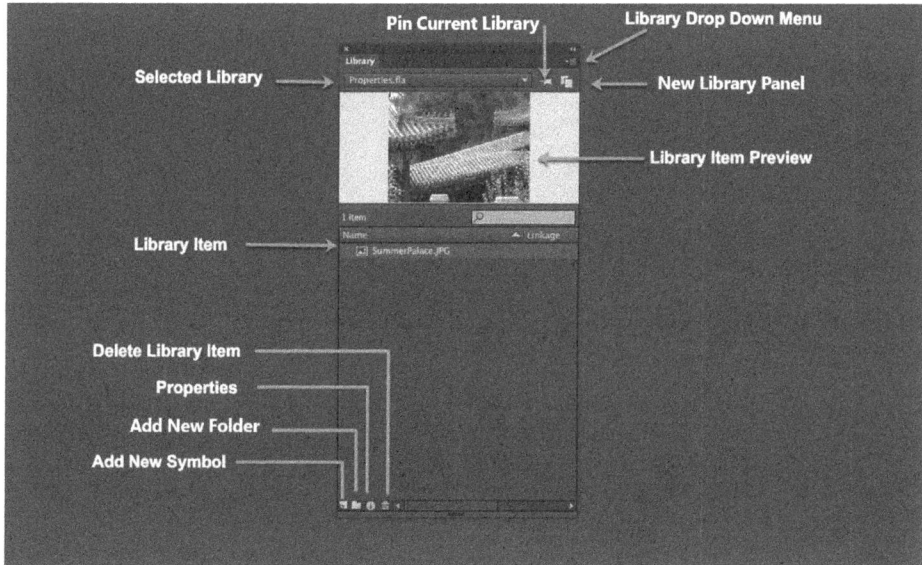

Figure 1-27. *The Library panel*

To collapse the Library panel, click the stage. Panels, opened from icons, are configured to collapse automatically. If, for some reason, you want to turn off autocollapse, select Edit ➤ Preferences (Windows) or (Animate CC ➤ Preferences) to open Preferences. Click General and deselect Auto-Collapse Icon Panels when the preferences open. Another way of opening and closing the Library is to press Ctrl+L (Windows) or Cmd+L (Mac).

Creative Cloud Library

If you are using Adobe Animate CC then you also have a Creative Cloud account. Your Creative Cloud account lets you create a Library of assets from many of the Creative Cloud Desktop and Mobile apps. For example, you can create personal and shared libraries to keep track of logos, icons for web layouts, video clips, or your go-to brushes and color themes for illustrations. Your Library items are automatically synced to your Creative Cloud account, so you can work with them wherever you are, even if you're offline.

Your Creative Cloud library is available to you in Animate CC. To access it and use the items in your personal or team's Creative Cloud Library, click the Creative Cloud panel icon in the panels. As shown in Figure 1-28, your panel opens and you can drag items from it to the Animate CC stage. Items that can't be used in Animate CC are grayed out and items that can be used in Animate CC are lit up.

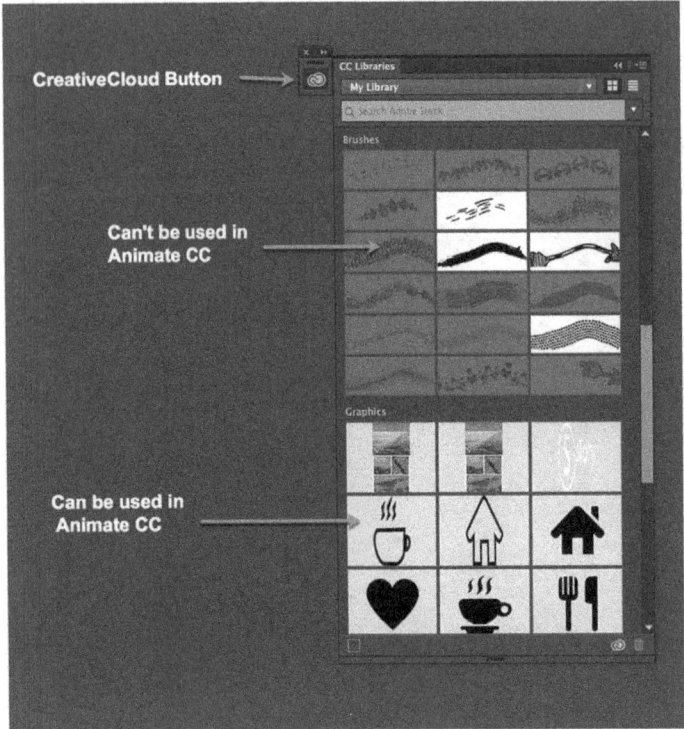

Figure 1-28. The Creative Cloud Library panel

Using Layers

The next stop on our walkabout is found under the stage: the layers feature of the timeline. There are a few things you need to know regarding layers:

- You can have as many layers in an Animate CC movie as you need. They have no effect on the file size.
- Use layers to manage your movie. Animate CC movies are composed of objects, media, and code, and it is a standard industry practice to give everything its own layer. This way, you can easily find content on a crowded stage. In fact, any object that is tweened must be on its own layer.

- Layers can be grouped. Layers can be placed inside a folder, which means you can, for example, have a complex animation and have all the objects in the animation contained in their own layers inside a folder.

- Layers stack on top of each other. For example, you can have a layer with a box in it and another with a ball in it. If the ball layer is above the box layer, the ball will appear to be in front of the box.

- Name your layers. This is another standard industry practice that makes finding content in the movie very easy.

Screen real estate is always at a premium. If you need to see more of the stage, double-click the Timeline tab to collapse the layers. Double-click the Timeline tab again, and the layers are brought back.

Layer Properties

Layers can also be put to very specific uses, and this is accomplished by assigning one of five layer properties, as shown in Figure 1-29, to a layer. Although they are called **properties**, they really should be regarded more as layer modes than anything else. We will be covering these in great depth in Chapters 3, 7, and 8, which focus on animation, but this is a good place to start learning where they are and what they do. The modes, accessed by right-clicking (Windows) or Control+clicking (Mac) a layer name and clicking Properties, are as follows:

- **Normal layer:** This is the layer you have been working with at this point in the book. Objects on these layers are always visible, and motion is more or less governed by the Motion Editor. You can always identify a normal layer; its icon looks like a folded sheet of paper.

- **Mask layer:** The shape of an object on a masking layer is used to hide anything outside the shape and reveals only whatever is under the object. For example, place an image on the stage and add a box in the layer above it. If that layer is a masking layer, only the pixels of the part of the image directly under the box will be seen. The icon for a mask layer is a square with an oval in the middle of it.

- **Masked layer:** If you have a mask layer, you will also have one of these. Like Siamese twins, mask layers and masked layers—any layer under a mask—are joined together. The icon for a masked layer looks like a folded sheet of paper facing the opposite direction as the icon for a normal layer. In addition, the layer name for a masked layer is indented.

- **Folder layer:** The best way of thinking of this mode is as a folder containing layers. They also provide quick access to layer groupings you may create. The icon for a folder layer is a file folder with a twirlie. Click the twirlie, and the layers in the folder are revealed. Click the twirlie again, and the layers folder collapses, hiding the layers.

- **Guide layer**: A guide layer contains shapes, symbols, images, and so on, that you can use to align elements on other layers in a movie. These things are handy if you have a complex design and want a standard reference for the entire movie. What makes guide layers so important is that they aren't rendered when you publish the animation. This means, for example, that you could create a comprehensive design (or *comp*) of the Animate CC stage in Photoshop CC, place that image in a guide layer, and not have to worry about an overly large set of files being published and bloating the project with unnecessary file size and download time. The icon for a guide layer is a T-square.

CHAPTER 1 ■ LEARNING THE ANIMATE CC INTERFACE

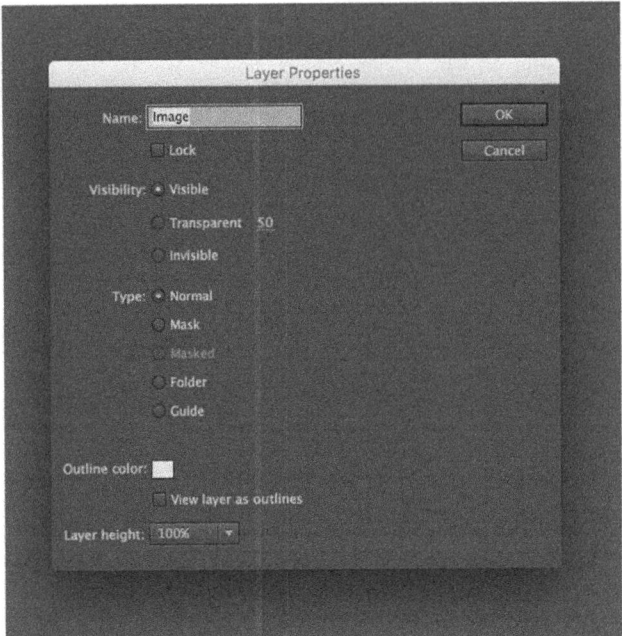

Figure 1-29. *The Layer Properties panel*

By default, Animate CC omits layers that are hidden—we get into hiding layers in a couple of minutes—when the file is eventually published.

Creating Layers

Let's start using layers. Here's how:

1. Open the 05_Layers.fla document. When it opens, you will see the garden and a couple of butterflies, as shown in Figure 1-30. If you look at the timeline, you could logically assume this is a simple photograph sitting on a single layer named Garden.

2. Open the Library. You will notice that there is an object named Butterfly contained in the Library. That object is a movieclip. We'll get into movieclips in a big way in Chapter 3.

CHAPTER 1 ■ LEARNING THE ANIMATE CC INTERFACE

Figure 1-30. *We start with what appears to be a photograph of flowers and butterflies*

3. Click the keyframe in the Garden layer. Three objects—the two Monarch butterflies and the image—are selected. What you have just learned is how to select everything on a layer. Click the pasteboard to deselect the objects.

4. Each object should be placed on its own layer. Click the New Layer button—it looks like a page with a turned-up corner—directly under the Garden layer strip. A new layer, named Layer1, is added to the timeline.

5. Select the Garden layer by clicking it and add a new layer. Notice how the new layer is placed between Garden and Layer 1. This should tell you that all new layers added to the timeline are added directly above the currently selected layer. Obviously, Layer 2 is out of position. Let's fix that.

6. Drag Layer 2 above Layer 1 and release the mouse. Now you know how to reorder layers and move them around in the timeline. Layers can be dragged above or below each other.

7. Add a new layer, Layer 3. Hold on—we have four layers and three objects. The math doesn't work. That new layer has to go.

31

CHAPTER 1 ■ LEARNING THE ANIMATE CC INTERFACE

8. Select Layer 3 and click the Trash Can . Layer 3 will now be deleted, and now you know how to get rid of an extra layer.

9. Double-click the Layer 1 layer name to select it. Rename the layer Butterfly. Now that you know how to rename a layer, select File ➤ Revert to revert the file to its original state. It's now time to learn how to put content on layers.

Adding Content to Layers

Content can be added to layers in one of two ways:

- Directly to the layer by moving an object from the Library to the layer
- From one layer to another layer

Let's explore how to use the two methods to place content into layers:

1. Create a new layer, name it Butterfly01, and drag the Butterfly movieclip from the Library to cover the flower, as shown in Figure 1-31, in the bottom-right corner of the stage. The hollow dot in the layer will change to a solid dot to indicate that there is content in the frame. When moving objects from the Library to the stage, be sure to select the layer, sometimes called a *target layer*, before you drag and drop. This way, you can prevent the content from going in the wrong layer. Let's now turn our attention to getting the two other butterflies into their own layers.

Figure 1-31. *Objects can be dragged directly from the Library and added to specific layers*

CHAPTER 1 ■ LEARNING THE ANIMATE CC INTERFACE

2. With the Shift key held down, click the two butterflies in the center and upper-left corner of the stage. This will select them, and the blue box around each one indicates they are movieclips.

3. Select Modify ➤ Timeline ➤ Distribute to Layers, or press Ctrl+Shift+D (Windows) or Cmd+Shift+D (Mac). The butterflies will appear in the new Butterfly layers that appear under the Garden layer. Rename these layers Butterfly02 and Butterfly03, and move them, as shown in Figure 1-32, above the Butterly01 layer.

Figure 1-32. *Multiple selections can be placed in their own layers using the Distribute to Layers command*

The next technique addresses a very common issue encountered by Animate CC designers: taking content from one layer and placing it in the exact same position in another layer. This is an issue because you can't drag content from one layer to another.

4. Click the Butterfly movieclip in the center of the stage and press Ctrl+X (Windows) or Cmd+X (Mac) to cut the selection out of the layer.

33

CHAPTER 1 ■ LEARNING THE ANIMATE CC INTERFACE

5. With the layer still selected in the timeline, select Edit ➤ Paste in Place. A copy of
    the butterfly will appear exactly where you cut it.

Whatever happened to a simple paste command in the Edit menu? The Paste in Center command replaces it. It has always been a fact of Animate CC life that any content on the clipboard is pasted into the center of the stage. The name-Paste in Place-simply acknowledges this.

Showing/Hiding and Locking Layers

We are sure the three icons—an eyeball, a lock, and a hollow square (shown in Figure 1-33)—above the layers caught your attention. Let's see what they do.

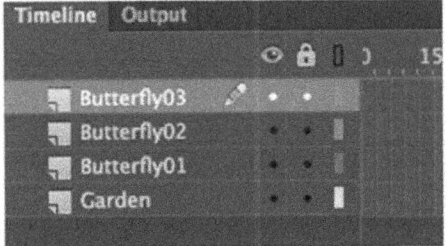

Figure 1-33. *The Layer Visibility, Lock, and Show All Layers As Outlines icons. Note the Pencil icon in the Butterfly03 layer, which tells you that you can add content to that layer.*

Click the eyeball icon. Notice that everything on the stage disappears, and the dots under the eyeball in each layer change to an *x*. This eyeball is the Layer Visibility icon, and clicking it turns off the visibility of all the content in the layers. Click the icon again, and everything reappears. This time, select the Butterfly02 layer and click the dot under the eyeball. Just the butterfly in the center of the stage disappears. What this tells you is that you can turn off the visibility for a specific layer by clicking the dot in the visibility column.

When you click a layer, you may notice that a pencil icon appears on the layer strip. This tells you that you can add content to the layer. Click the Butterfly03 layer, and you'll see the pencil icon. Now, click the dot under the lock in the Butterfly02 layer. The lock icon will replace the dot. When you lock a layer, you can't draw on it or add content to it. You can see this because the pencil has a stroke through it. If you try to drag the Butterfly movieclip from the Library to the Butterfly02 layer, you will also see that the layer has been locked because the mouse pointer changes from an arrow to a circle with a line through it. Also, if you try to click the butterfly on the stage, you won't be able to select it. This is handy to know in situations where precision is paramount and you don't want to accidentally move something or, god forbid, delete something from the stage.

Okay, we sort of "stretched the truth" there by telling you that content can't be added to a locked layer. ActionScript and JavaScript are the only thing that can be added to a locked layer. This explains why many Animate CC designers and developers create an ActionScript-only layer—usually named scripts or actions—and then lock the layer. This prevents anything other than code from being placed in the layer.

The final icon is the Show All Layers As Outlines icon. Click it, and the content on the stage turns into outlines. This is somewhat akin to the wireframe display mode available in many 3D modeling applications. In Animate CC, it can be useful in cases where dozens of objects overlap and you simply want a quick "X-ray view" of how your content is arranged. With animation, in particular, it can be helpful to evaluate the motion of objects without having to consider the distraction of color and shading. Like visibility and locking, the outlines icon is also available on a per-layer basis.

You can change the color used for the outline in a layer by double-clicking the color chip in the layer strip. This will open the Layer Properties dialog box. Double-click the color chip in dialog box to open the Color Picker. Then click a color, and that color will be used.

Grouping Layers

You can also group layers using folders. Here's how:

1. Click the Folder icon in the Layers panel. A new unnamed folder—Folder 1—will appear on the timeline. You can rename a folder by double-clicking its name and entering a new name.

2. Drag the three Butterfly layers into the folder. As each one is placed in the folder, notice how the name indents. This tells you that the layer is in a folder.

3. Next, remove the layers from the folder. To do so, simply drag the layer above the folder on the timeline. You can also drag it down and to the left to unindent it.

4. To delete a folder, select it and click the Trash Can icon.

Step away from the mouse and put your hands where we can see them. Don't think you can simply select a folder and click the Trash Can icon to remove it. Make sure that the folder is empty. If you delete a folder that contains layers, those layers will also be deleted. If this happens to you, Adobe has sent a life raft in your direction. An alert box telling you that you will also be deleting the layers in the folder will appear. If you see that Alert click Cancel instead of OK.

Where To Get Help

In the early days of desktop computing, software was a major purchase, and nothing made you feel more comfortable than the manuals that were tucked into the box. If you had a problem, you opened the manual and searched for the solution. Those days have long passed. This is especially true with Animate CC, because as its complexity has grown, the size of the manuals that need to be packaged with the application also grew. In this version of Animate CC, the user manuals are found in the Help menu. Here's how to access Help:

Select Help ➤ Animate Help or press the F1 key. If you are a Mac user, press F1. The Help resource that opens in your browser (see Figure 1-34) is one of the most comprehensive sources of Animate CC knowledge on the planet; best of all, it's free.

CHAPTER 1 ■ LEARNING THE ANIMATE CC INTERFACE

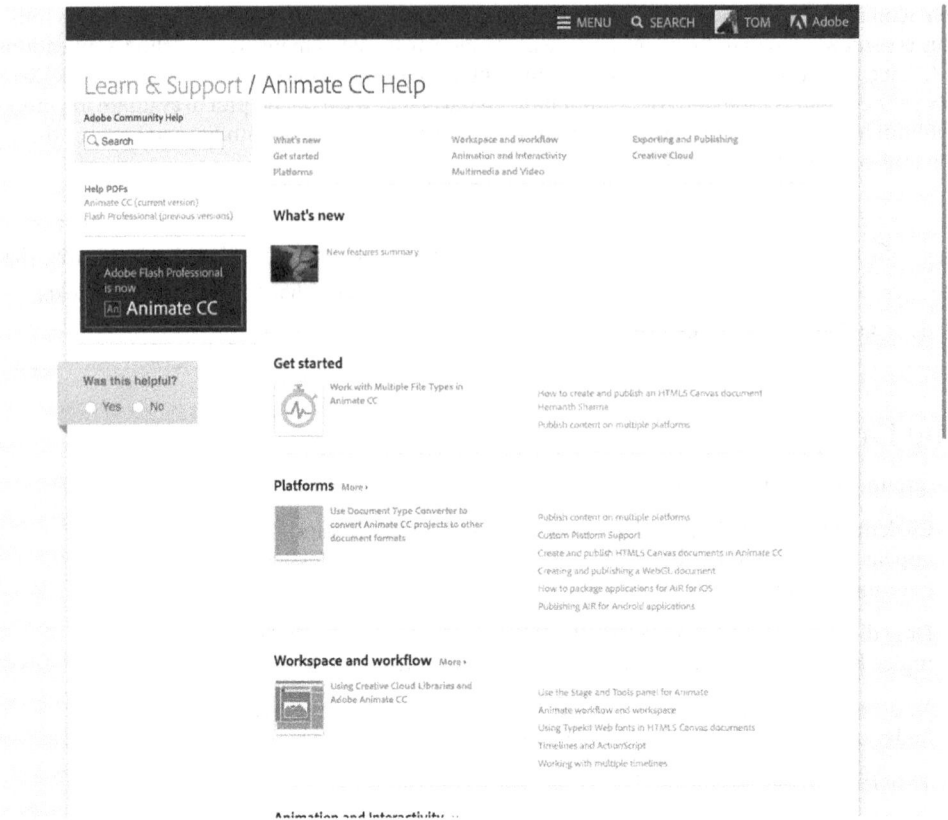

Figure 1-34. *The Animate CC Help is extensive*

The page is divided into two areas. On the left side you can enter your criteria for very specific topics. Underneath it is a link to a 482-page PDF version of the Animate CC docs, which you can download directly to your computer. The right side of the window allows you to choose a more general topic.

So much for the walkabout. It is time for you to put into practice what you have learned.

Your Turn: Building an Animate CC Movie

In this exercise, you are going to expand on your knowledge so far. We have shown you where many of the interface features can be found and how they can be used, so we are now going to give you the opportunity to see how all of these features combine to create an Animate CC movie.

You will be undertaking such tasks as the following:

- Using the Property Inspector to precisely position and resize objects on the stage
- Creating layers and adding content from the Library to the layers
- Using the drawing tools to create a shape

CHAPTER 1 ■ LEARNING THE ANIMATE CC INTERFACE

- Creating a simple animation through the use of a tween
- Testing an Animate CC movie

  1. Open the MoonOverLakeNanagook.fla file.
  2. When the file opens, show the Library panel, if it isn't already in view, by selecting Window ➤ Library or pressing Ctrl+L (Cmd+L). As you can see, you are starting with a blank stage, a few movieclips shown in Figure 1-35, an audio file, and a graphic symbol.

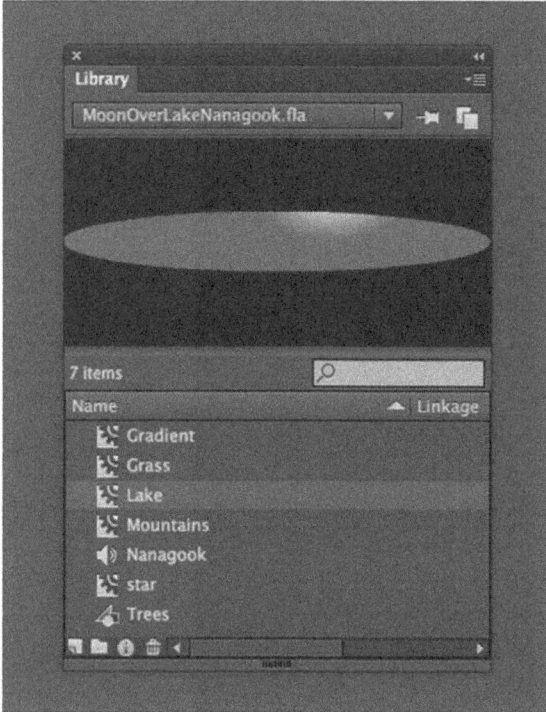

Figure 1-35. *The assets are in place. It is your job to turn them into a movie*

  3. The specifications for the project state the stage is to be 400 pixels wide by 300 pixels high. It also calls for a dark blue stage color to give the illusion of night. Click the Properties tab and change the Width value to 400 and the Height value to 300.
  4. Click the Stage color chip to open the Color Picker. Select the color text and change it from #FFFFFF to #000066 (dark blue). Click OK to accept the changes and close the dialog box. The stage will shrink to its new size and be colored a dark blue. The new size and color will now appear in the Property Inspector, as shown in Figure 1-36.

CHAPTER 1 ■ LEARNING THE ANIMATE CC INTERFACE

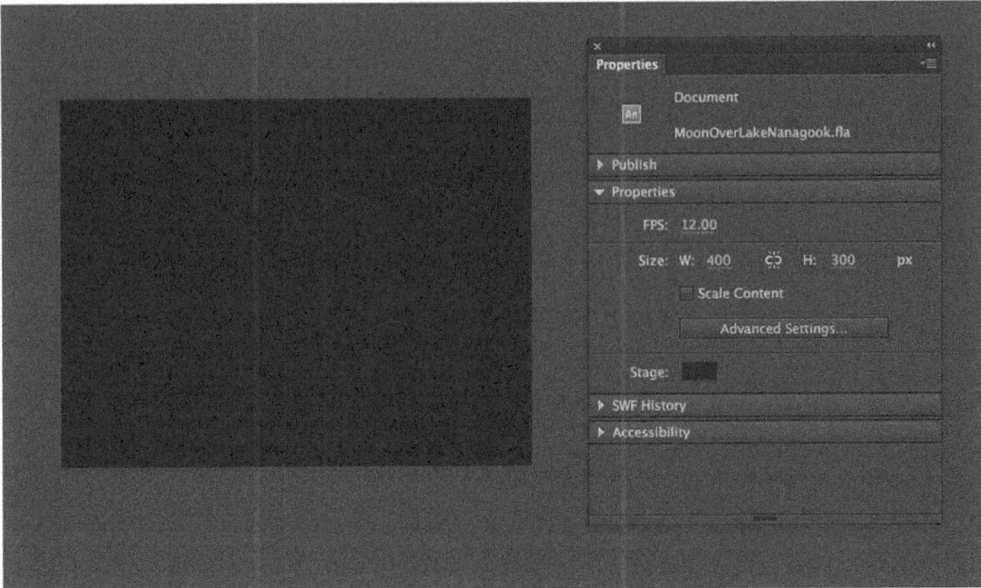

Figure 1-36. *The stage is set*

5. Rename Layer 1 to Gradient by double-clicking the layer name and entering that text. Drag the Gradient movieclip from the Library to the stage.

Though using your eyes for object placement on the stage is a great way to get stuff into position, your eyes aren't as precise as Animate CC. The gradient needs to completely cover the stage and not hang out on the pasteboard (the non-stage work area) by even one pixel. Here's how you do that:

1. Click the gradient on the stage to select it. In the Property Inspector, set its X and Y values to 0. The object will align itself with the upper-left corner of the stage.

2. Click frame 60 of the Gradient layer and press the F5 key. What this does is add 59 new frames to the timeline; you can tell this because the layer expands to the 60th frame and a rectangle (indicating the new span of frames) is shown at the end of the layer. This gradient is going to be animated later in the exercise.

   When Animate CC measures the location of an object on the stage, it uses the upper-left corner of the stage as its 0,0 point. The actual position of the object is based on something called its *registration point*. In the case of this gradient, the registration point of the symbol also happens to be its own upper-left corner, which is why the X and Y values of 0 cause it to fit neatly on the stage. If the registration point of the gradient were changed to 200,150—that is, down and in from its own upper-left corner—the gradient would end up being positioned partly on the pasteboard and partly on the stage. The symbol's registration point is indicated by the + sign you see inside the symbol.

3. Lock the layer by clicking the black dot under the Lock icon on the timeline. This is a good habit to develop. Animate CC projects, including this one, can get fairly complex in a relatively short time. By locking the layer, you are ensuring that you don't accidentally move the background later on in the project.

Adding the Mountains and Playing with Color

With the stage prepared and the sky in place, you can now turn your attention to adding the assets to the movie. The scene involves mountains, trees, grass, a lake, and the moon. What this tells you is that the objects farthest away need to be placed near the bottom of the layering order. This means that the mountains are the next piece of content to be added.

1. Add a new layer to the main timeline and name it Mountains.

2. With the new layer selected, open the Library and drag the Mountains movieclip onto the stage.

3. With the mountains selected on the stage, in the Property Inspector, set the X value to -34 and the Y value to 203. The mountain range will sit at the bottom of the stage and hang off of both sides of the stage. There is, of course, one great big problem: the mountains are black and they have been placed against a black background. Let's fix that.

4. Select the mountains on the stage and, in the Color Effect area of the Property Inspector, select Tint from the Style drop-down menu. The Property Inspector will change to show you a color chip, a tint percentage, and the RGB color of the selected object.

    If you remember what we said earlier, everything on the stage, including the stage itself, has unique properties, including its color. Changing the tint of a selected object allows you to manipulate the color property of that object. The original Library asset's color is not affected.

5. Click the color chip, and when the Color Picker opens, select the dark gray color directly under the black chip on the left side of the picker (#333333). The mountains become a lot more distinct, but they are now too obvious.

6. With the mountains still selected, move the Tint slider until the value is 49% (as shown in Figure 1-37). If you are a power user, feel free to simply double-click the value and enter 50.

CHAPTER 1 ■ LEARNING THE ANIMATE CC INTERFACE

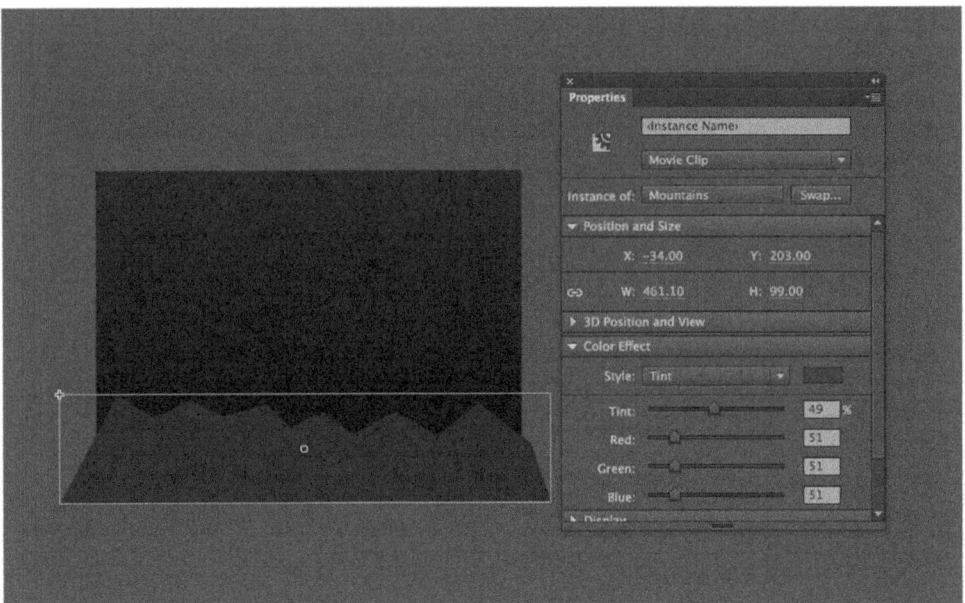

Figure 1-37. *Objects can have their color properties manipulated*

   7. Now is a good time to save your work. Select File ➤ Save As, and when the Save As dialog box opens, navigate to the Exercise folder for this chapter and rename the project. Click OK to close the dialog box.

If you have been using Animate CC for a while, we are willing to bet you missed something rather significant when you added the new layer. Did you happen to catch that the frame span of the new layer matched that of the Gradient layer? In the past, any new layer started off as a single frame and you pressed the F5 key to add a frame to create the span.

Using Trees to Create the Illusion of Depth

The mountains are in place and are faintly visible against the night sky. Let's add some depth to the scene by adding a couple of trees. Here's how:

   1. Create two new layers, named Tree1 and Tree2.

   2. Taking turns, drag one copy apiece of the Trees symbol to the stage while each tree layer is selected. This puts each tree on its own layer. You may notice that the icon for the Trees symbol is different from the other symbols in the Library. This icon indicates that the tree is a *graphic symbol*. Graphic symbols can be created with the various drawing tools in Animate CC—which is the case with this tree— and also make good containers for imported photographs.

Graphic symbols' timelines are locked in step with the timeline they're in, unlike movieclip symbols, whose timelines run independently. This explains why graphics are the de facto symbol for JibJab-style animation (www.jibjab.com/). Complex nested symbols can be scrubbed in this way for testing in the timeline, whereas movieclips only show nested animation when published. More on this in Chapters 7 and 8. A symbol placed on the stage is called an *instance*.

3. Select the tree on the lower of the two tree layers. Use these values to precisely place the selected tree on the stage, resize it, and darken it:

   - X: 49
   - Y: 178.5
   - W: 65
   - H: 105
   - Color Effect: Tint
   - Tint Color: # 000000 (black)
   - Tint Amount: 40%

   The tree gets smaller, moves to the left side of the stage, and darkens. Resizing the image and darkening it is what gives the illusion of depth in this scene.

4. Select the remaining tree and use these values in the Property Inspector:

   - X: 76
   - Y: 161
   - W: 68
   - H: 123
   - Color Effect: Tint
   - Tint Color: # 000000 (black)
   - Tint Amount: 25%

   The tree gets a bit smaller, moves to the left side of the stage, and, due to the low tint amount, becomes a bit brighter than the tree behind it (as shown in Figure 1-38). The reason for this is that it will be lit by the moon, which you will create in a couple of minutes.

CHAPTER 1 ■ LEARNING THE ANIMATE CC INTERFACE

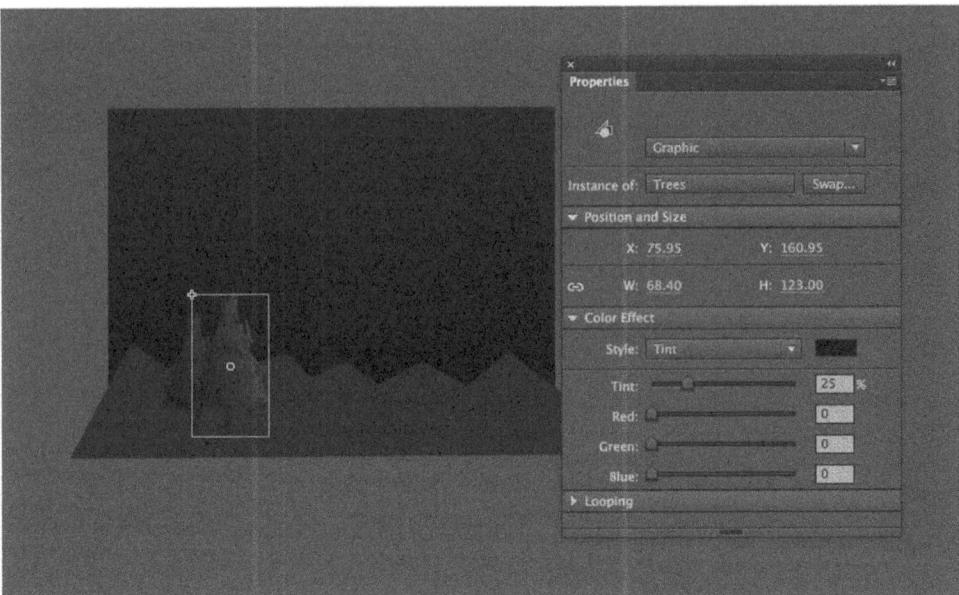

Figure 1-38. *Location and size are other properties that can be manipulated using the Property Inspector*

Let's finish the scene by adding the grass and the lake.

5. Add a new layer named Grass. With this new layer selected, drag the Grass movieclip from the Library to the stage. Set its X and Y coordinates in the Property Inspector to -306.6 and 268.9, respectively.

What's with the decimals? This is deliberate. You need to know how to input values as well as scrub the values. You may have noticed that, when you scrub values, the numbers don't have decimals. If precise placement of objects on the stage is "mission critical," you need to know how to accomplish this task. But isn't a decimal value smaller than a pixel? You bet it is, but we're dealing with vector graphics here.

---

6. Add a new layer named Lake. With this new layer selected, drag the Lake movieclip from the Library to the stage. Set its X and Y coordinates in the Property Inspector to -282 and 274, respectively.

So far, so good. It is starting to look like Lake Nanagook (see Figure 1-39), but we need to add two more elements—the moon and a twinkling star—to make it a bit more realistic. We obviously need the moon because it is reflected in the lake, and a twinkling star is a subtle bit of eye candy that will make the scene that much more interesting and catch the viewer's attention. Let's start with the star.

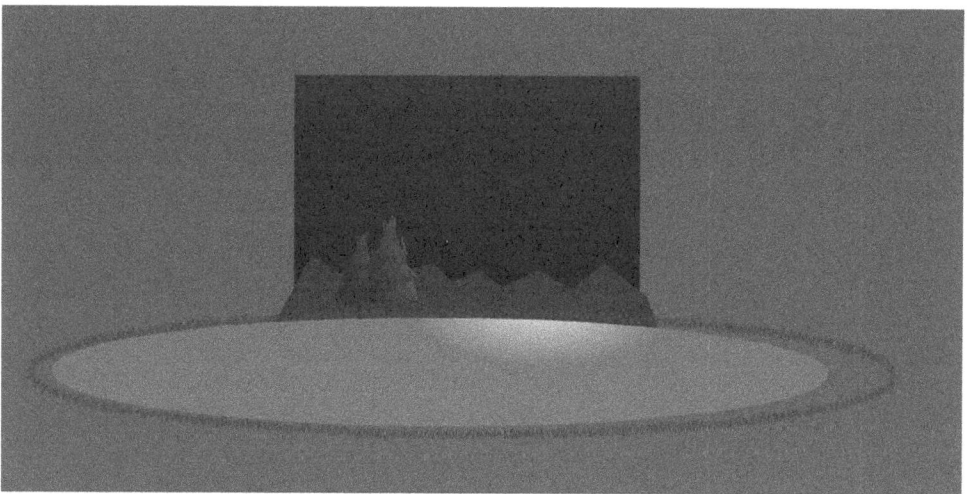

Figure 1-39. *The project is starting to come together*

Using a Motion Tween To Create a Twinkling Star

One of the steady messages running throughout this chapter is that we, as Animate CC designers, are illusionists. In this exercise, you will discover how to create the illusion of a star twinkling in the night sky. Here's how:

1. Open the Library and double-click the star movieclip to open it in the Symbol Editor. When the movieclip opens, you will see that it is composed of a layer named diamond. The shape on the stage was created using the Rectangle Primitive tool, making the sides concave and filling the shape with #FFCC00, which is a gold color.

   If the shape is too small, select the Magnifying Glass tool on the Tools panel and click and drag it across the star. This is how you can precisely zoom in on an object on the stage.

2. Right-click on the diamond layer and select Duplicate Layers from the context menu. You now have a new layer named diamond copy. Rename this layer diamond2.

3. Move the playhead back to frame 1 and double-click the star. This will select the star in the diamond2 layer.

4. In the Properties panel change its Fill Color, in the Fill & Stroke area, to #FFFF99, which is a faint yellow color.

5. With the star in the diamond2 layer selected, right-click (Ctrl+click) the star to open its context menu. Select Convert to Symbol and, when the New Symbol dialog box opens, name the symbol star2 and select Movie Clip from the Type drop-down. Click OK to accept the change. You have to convert the rectangle primitive in the diamond2 layer to a symbol in order to apply the sort of tween you're about to do. Note that converting a symbol from a shape or primitive already in place keeps everything positioned where it was.

CHAPTER 1 ■ LEARNING THE ANIMATE CC INTERFACE

Rotating a Movieclip Using the Transform Panel

The illusion of a twinkling star in the sky is actually quite simple to accomplish. You have to do nothing more than have the star rotate 360 degrees in a clockwise direction, and best of all, it only requires a couple of mouse clicks. Let's get busy:

1. Right-click (Ctrl+click) on any frame in the diamond2 layer to open the context menu. When the menu opens, select Create Motion Tween. The span will turn blue.

2. Select Window ➤ Transform to open the Transform panel or click the Transform panel button in the panels area to open the panel. When it opens you will see you can either Scale or Rotate selected object.

3. Scrub the playhead to frame 60 and, with the Transform panel open, change the rotate value to 360, as shown in Figure 1-40. Positive values will rotate an object in a clockwise direction whereas negative values will rotate the object in a counter-clockwise direction.

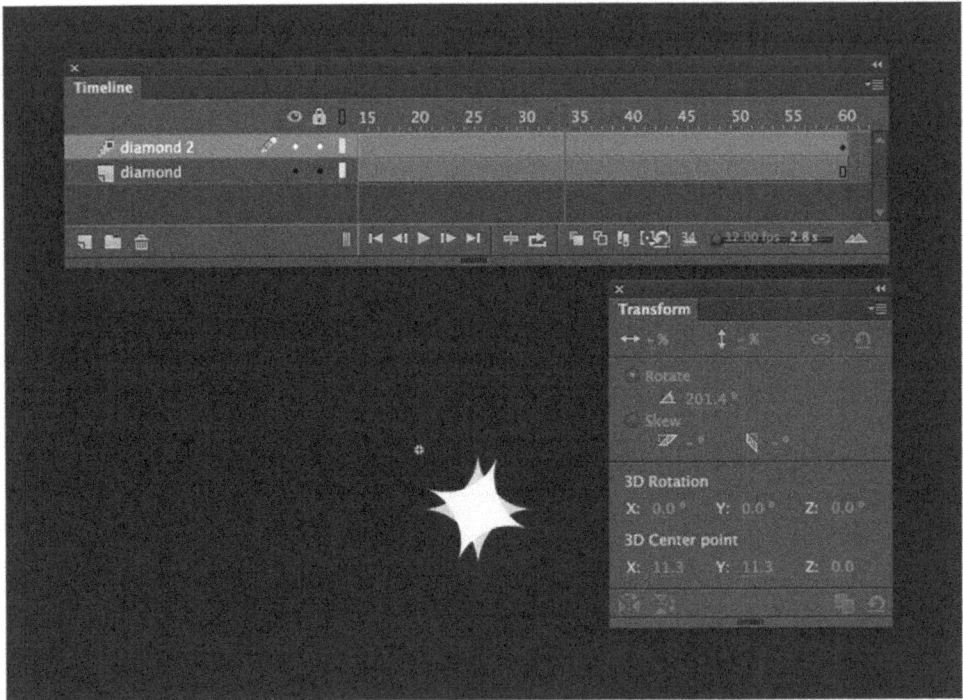

Figure 1-40. Putting a star in motion

4. Scrub across the frames to see the rotation.

5. Zoom the stage to the 100% view and click the Scene 1 link on the top left of the stage to return to the main timeline. Save the project.

A Moon Over Lake Nanagook

At this point, we have essentially handed you the assets and let you put them in place and otherwise manipulate them. It is now your turn to go solo and create the moon that rises over Lake Nanagook.

1. Select Insert ➤ New Symbol. This will open the New Symbol dialog box. Name the symbol Moon and select Movie Clip as its Type. Click OK. The dialog box will close and the Symbol Editor will open.

So far we have used the term *movieclip* and not put a space between the two words. Why then is the term broken into two words in the dialog box? The use of the single word has developed into a standard throughout the worldwide community when writing about Animate CC. The split word in the dialog box is actually one of the very few references you will see from Adobe using this terminology, which has its roots back in an early release of Animate CC.

---

2. Rename Layer 1 to bg. Add a new layer named shadow. The shadow layer should be above the bg layer.

3. In the Tools panel, click the Oval tool to select it.

4. Open the Properties panel and click the Stroke Color rectangle—called a *color chip*—to open the Color Picker. Set the Stroke color to red. (#FF0000). Click the Fill color chip and select a light blue. While you're there, give the Stroke a value of 3 to help it show up better.

5. Select the first frame of the bg layer and, with the Oval tool selected, click the stage and drag out a circle. Switch to the Selection tool and double-click the circle to select both the fill and the stroke. In the Property Inspector, change the circle's width and height values both to 120, making a perfect circle, and set the X and Y coordinates to 0. This is your moon—or the beginnings of it.

6. With the moon still selected—again, you've selected both the stroke and the fill—copy it to the clipboard.

7. Select the first frame in the shadow layer and paste the shape from the clipboard into this layer.

8. With the newly pasted shape still selected, move it upward and to the left, so that it overlaps the bottom layer, but both circles show. These shapes should look something like what you see in the movies when a character looks through binoculars.

9. Click the Show All Layers as Outlines button to temporarily display both circles as outlines. The intersection between the two shapes should look like football or rugby ball. Click the Show All Layers as Outlines button again to exit the outlines mode. Click the red stroke on the shape in the shadow layer to select it. Press the Delete key to remove it. You now have a solid blue circle over another circle that has a red stroke (as shown in Figure 1-41).

45

CHAPTER 1 ■ LEARNING THE ANIMATE CC INTERFACE

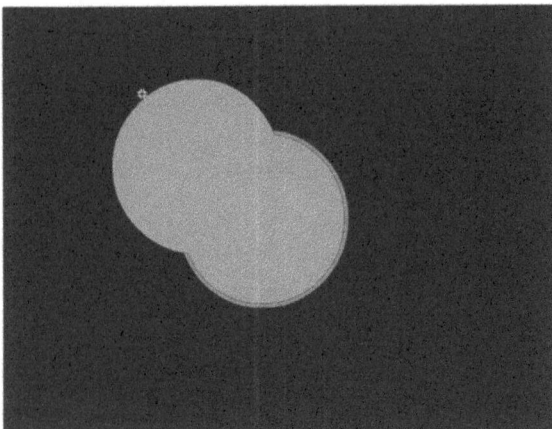

Figure 1-41. *The moon shadow starts out as a couple of circles*

10. Select the red stroke around the circle in the bg layer and cut it to the clipboard. Select the shadow layer and select Edit ➤ Paste in Place.

11. What has happened here is that the stroke you just pasted into the shadow layer has actually cut the football shape for you. The reason this is possible is because you turned off Object Drawing mode in the Properties panel.

12. In the shadow layer, click the portion of the blue circle that is outside of the stroke. Press the Delete key. Now select and delete the stroke itself. If you turn off the visibility of the bg layer, you will see that you have created the shadow shape. Let's make it a true shadow.

13. Click the football shape to select it and then open the Color panel by selecting Window ➤ Color.

14. Set the fill color to #0066FF and reduce the alpha value to 36%. Turn on the visibility of the bg layer. You will see that you indeed have a shadow (as shown in Figure 1-42).

CHAPTER 1 ■ LEARNING THE ANIMATE CC INTERFACE

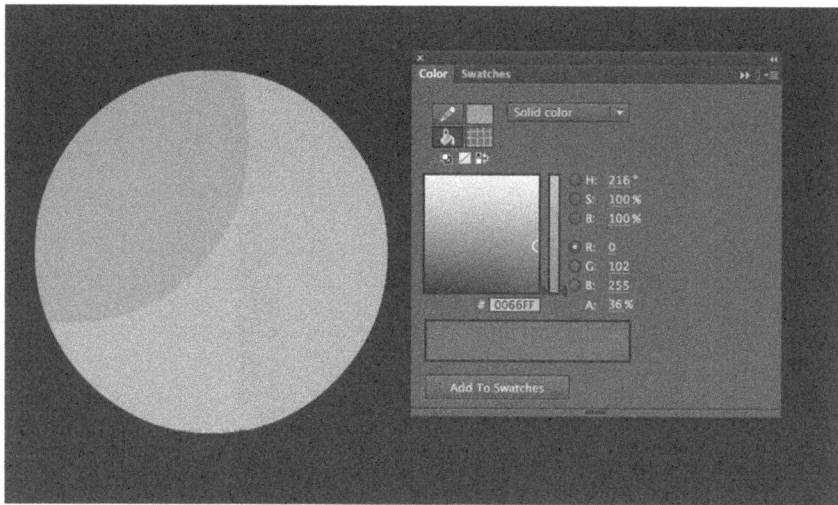

Figure 1-42. *The shadow is created by using the Color panel*

The final step in the process of creating the moon is to add a gradient fill in order to give the moon a bit of a glow. Follow these steps:

1. Select the circle in the bg layer and open the Color panel.

2. Select Radial gradient from the Type drop-down. The moon turns into a black-and-white radial gradient. The gradient colors are shown in the strip—called a "ramp"—and there are two color stops under the ramp indicating the colors used. These stops are called *crayons*.

3. Click the black crayon to select it. Change the hex color under the Color Picker to #C4DDEE.

4. Click the white crayon and change its color to #93BDE0. The moon takes on a faint glow, thanks to the similar colors in the gradient (see Figure 1-43).

47

CHAPTER 1 ■ LEARNING THE ANIMATE CC INTERFACE

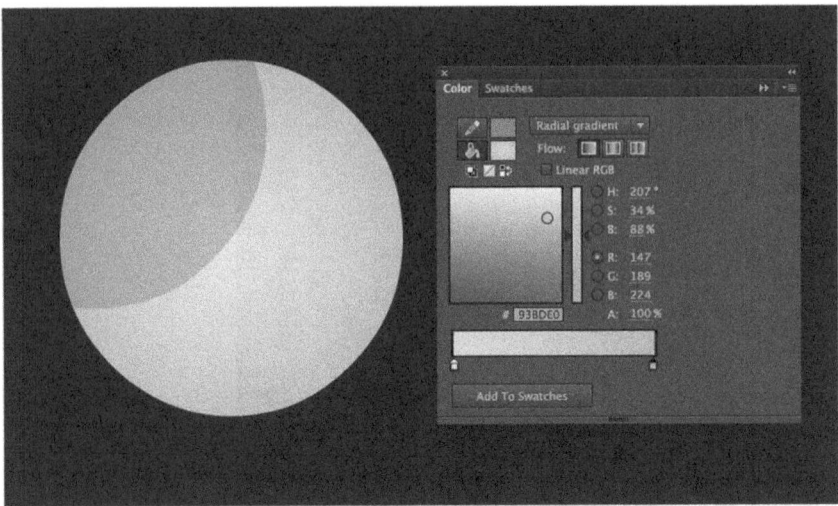

Figure 1-43. *Add a radial gradient through the Color panel*

5. Click the Scene 1 link to return to the main timeline.

6. Add a layer named Star and another named Moon. These layers should appear above the others.

7. Add the star symbol to the Star layer and set its X and Y coordinates to 219 and 42, respectively.

8. Add the moon symbol to the Moon layer and set its X and Y coordinates to 241 and 43, respectively.

Next, let's really make the moon and the star glow in the sky over Lake Nanagook. Let's add a glow effect to both of them. Here's how:

1. Select the star on the stage and click the Filters twirlie on the Property Inspector to open the Filters area.

2. Click the + sign to see the Filters list. Select the Glow filter.

3. Use these settings in the Glow filter:

    - Blur X: 14
    - Blur Y: 14
    - Strength: 418%
    - Quality: High
    - Color: #93BDE0

4. The star looks like it is about to go into supernova. Let's make it a bit smaller.

5. With the star selected on the stage, set its width and height values in the Property Inspector to 13.

CHAPTER 1 ■ LEARNING THE ANIMATE CC INTERFACE

6. Select the moon on the stage and apply the following Glow values:

- Blur X: 26
- Blur Y: 26
- Strength: 70%
- Quality: High
- Color: #93BDE0

The moon and the star in Figure 1-44 now look like they belong together in the sky.

Filters can only be added to movieclips, text fields, and buttons.

---

7. Save the project.

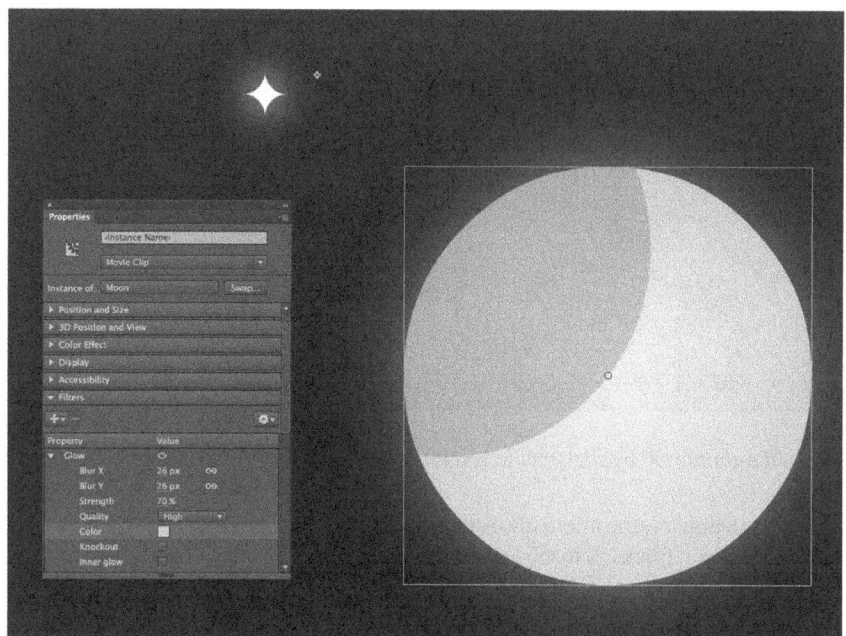

Figure 1-44. *Adding a filter to a movieclip*

CHAPTER 1 ■ LEARNING THE ANIMATE CC INTERFACE

Breaking the Stillness of the Night at Lake Nanagook

If we are going to have an outdoor scene, it only makes sense to add some outdoor sounds to the mix. Fortunately, adding audio to an Animate CC file is not terribly complicated.

1. Add a new layer and name it Audio.

2. Open the Library and locate the Nanagook audio file.

3. Double-click the sound file in the Library to open the Sound Properties dialog box. Click the Advanced button (shown in Figure 1-45) to reveal all of the features of this panel.

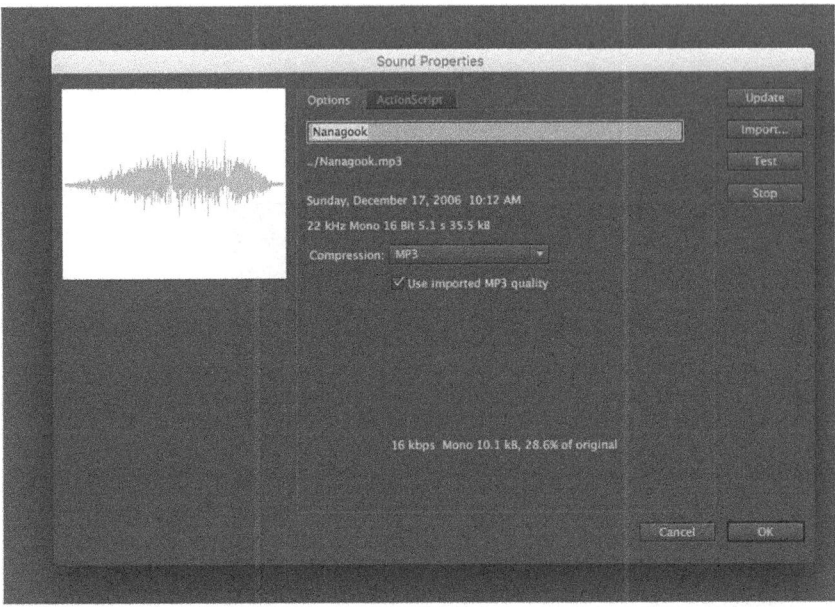

Figure 1-45. *Preview sounds in Animate CC by clicking the Test button*

4. Click the Test button to preview the audio file. Ahh, the sounds of crickets and wolves howling in the night. Click OK to close the dialog box.

5. With the Audio layer selected, drag the sound file from the Library onto the stage. When you release the mouse, the audio waveform appears in the layer.

   Dragging a sound file from the Library to the stage isn't the only way to get an audio file to the timeline. In many respects, what we've shown is not exactly regarded as a best practice because audio files can be big, and when they are in the Library, they can seriously increase the file size and take an inordinate amount of time to load if viewed online. We have a whole chapter, Chapter 5, devoted to audio best practice, so for now, let's content ourselves with getting sound into the presentation and getting it to play.

6. Click anywhere on the sound's waveform in the Audio layer, and you will see the Property Inspector change to show the sound properties (open the Sound twirlie, if you need to).

CHAPTER 1 ■ LEARNING THE ANIMATE CC INTERFACE

7. Click the Sync pop down and select Stream from the menu (as shown in Figure 1-48).

8. Scrub across the timeline and you will hear the audio file. This is possible because of the Sync change you made in Step 7. Drag the playback head to frame 1 and press the Return (Enter) key. The sound will start playing, but it abruptly ends at frame 50. This is because the audio was originally recorded for a slower movie frame rate.

9. Scroll the timeline so you can see frame 130. Click into the Audio layer at frame 130 and drag downward without lifting the mouse—until you hit the Gradient layer. This selects the last frame of all your layers. Press the F5 key. This adds enough frames to every layer so that the sound has enough room to play completely.

10. Save the file.

Picking up a pattern here? Get into the habit of saving the file every time you do something major to your movie. This way, if the computer crashes, you won't have a lot of extra work in front of you trying to reconstruct the movie up to the point of the crash.

You may have looked at Figure 1-46 and thought, "Hey my audio layer doesn't look like yours." Good eye. Layers can also be made larger. To do this, right-click (Ctrl+click) on a layer's name to open the context menu. Select Properties to open the Layer Properties dialog box shown in Figure 1-47. Select 200% in the Layer height drop-down list or enter your own value. Click OK to accept the change.

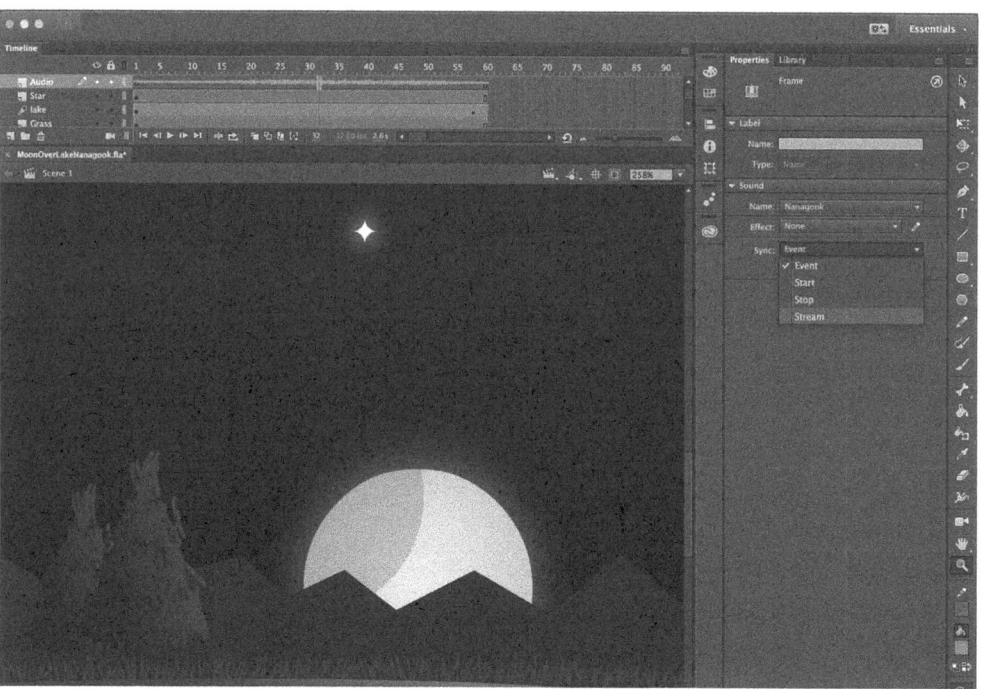

Figure 1-46. *Audio on the timeline, and the sound properties in the Property Inspector*

51

CHAPTER 1 ■ LEARNING THE ANIMATE CC INTERFACE

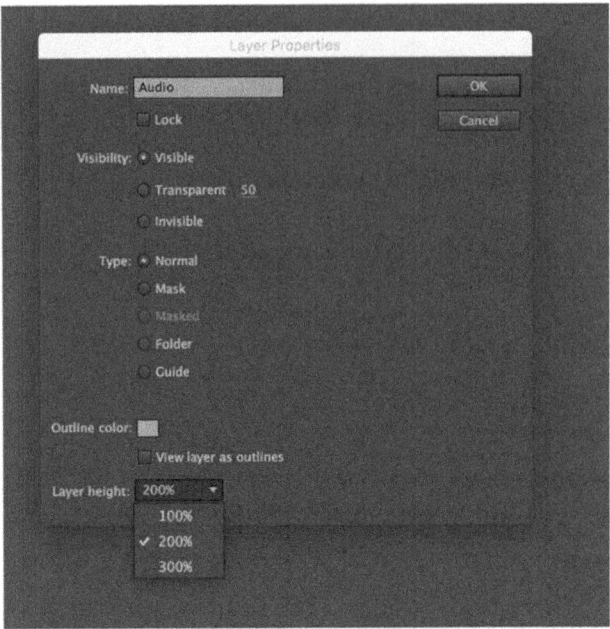

Figure 1-47. Even layers have their own properties

Testing Your Movie

You have created the animation and scrubbed through the timeline, and everything looks like it is in order. Now is a good time to test your movie in Flash Player. We can't understate the importance of this step in your workflow. The procedure, as one of the authors is fond of telling his students, *"Do a bit. Test it. Do a bit more. Test it."* The reason for this is that Animate CC movies can be quite complex. Each element you add to your movie adds to the complexity of the movie. Developing the habit of regularly testing your work, regardless of how simple it may be, will point out mistakes, errors, or problems in the work that you've just completed.

What it comes down to is this: do you really want to burrow through a complex movie, and even more complex code, searching for an issue, or do you want to catch it early? Here's how to test an Animate CC movie:

1. Press Ctrl+Enter (Cmd+Return). You will see an alert box telling you that the movie is being exported, and the movie will open in Flash Player (as shown in Figure 1-48). What you should see is the star twinkling in the sky—and all of the stuff outside the boundaries of the stage has been trimmed off.

CHAPTER 1 ■ LEARNING THE ANIMATE CC INTERFACE

Figure 1-48. *Testing a movie in Animate CC Player*

If you insist on using a menu, select Control ➤ Test Movie ➤ In Animate.

If you open the folder where you saved the FLA file, you will see that a SWF file has also been added to the folder.

Moonrise Over Lake Nanagook

We've been gently reminding you that Animate CC involves the art of illusion. The other thing you need to know is that Animate CC developers are fanatics about detail. They pay close attention to their environment and then try and mimic it in their projects.

In this final piece of this exercise, we are going to get you up close and personal with that last statement. The plan is to have the moon rise into the night sky. On the surface, that sounds like a no-brainer: tween the motion of the moon between its start position and its finish position. Not quite.

This is a night scene, and if there is no moon, things are quite dark. They only light up when the moon is in the sky. If you look at Lake Nanagook, you can see there is a problem. The lake already contains the reflection of the moon. The lake should be dark and only start to light up as the moon rises in the sky. The other issue is the trees. They, too, are lit by the moon and they should be dark and start to light up as the moon rises.

53

CHAPTER 1 ■ LEARNING THE ANIMATE CC INTERFACE

Although this may all sound rather complex, it can all be handled by the Property Inspector. Follow these steps to start yourself on the path to becoming a fanatic about detail:

1. The first issue is the moon itself. It is in a higher layer. This means that if you animate the moon in its current position, it will appear to rise in front of Lake Nanagook. Drag the Moon layer down to just above the Gradient layer. Now the moon will rise behind the mountains.

2. Turn off the visibility of the Lake layer. You will need to see what you are doing, and the lake will hide the starting point of the moonrise.

3. Right-click (Ctrl+click) the Moon layer and select Create Motion Tween. Select the Moon layer and drag the playhead to frame 1. Open the Properties Panel and, using Position and Size area of the Property Inspector, set the moon's position to 230 on the X axis and 305 on the Y axis.

4. Drag the playhead to frame 60, then select the Moon and drag it to the top of the stage. With the Moon still selected, set the X and Y coordinates to 241 and 43 (the original position of the moon). If you scrub across the timeline—either in the Timeline panel or the Motion Editor—the moon rises from behind the mountains.

5. Want to earn some "bonus marks"? How about we have the moon travel through an arc to its final position? Lock the Mountains layer. The reason you did this is that you are going to manipulate the motion path—the series of dots—to create the arc and you don't want to move the mountains by accident.

6. Click on one of the dots where the path crosses the edge of the mountain range and drag it to the left. A couple of things happened. When you rolled the cursor over the path, an arc appeared under the arrow. This tells you the path can be changed. The other thing that happened is, when you dragged the path, it bent in the direction you were dragging. This tells you motion paths can be thought of as vectors.

When you release the path, it becomes a dotted line again, as shown in Figure 1-49. Scrub the playhead across the animation and the moon follows a gentle arc as it moves into the night sky.

CHAPTER 1 ■ LEARNING THE ANIMATE CC INTERFACE

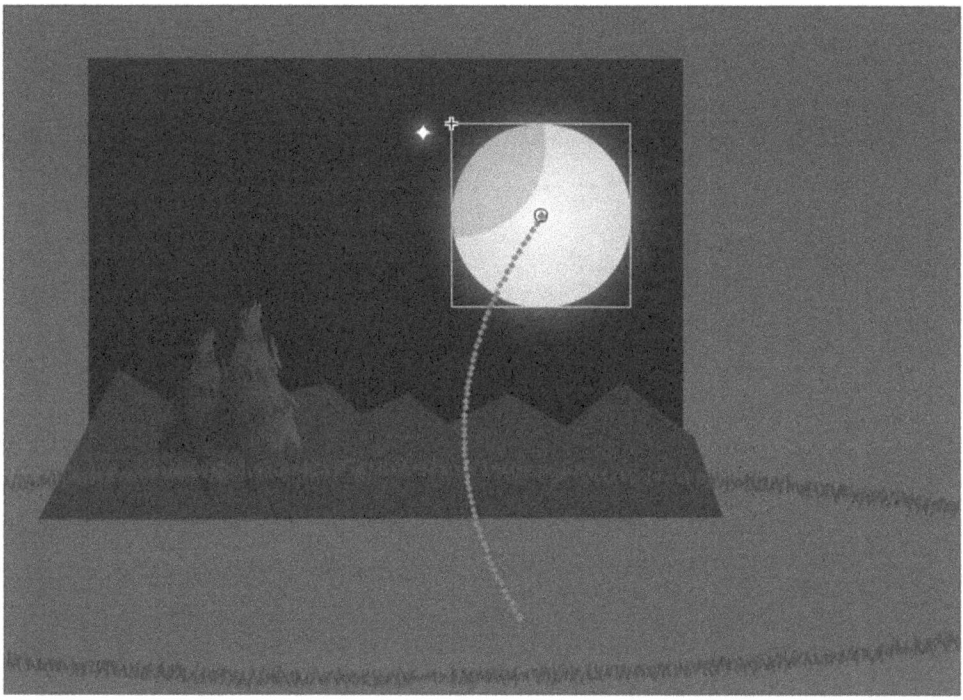

Figure 1-49. *Manipulating a motion path*

Lighting Up Lake Nanagook

Obviously, if the moon is behind the mountains when the movie starts, the lake and trees shouldn't be "lit up". Let's have them become distinct as the moon rises. Here's how:

1. Unhide the Lake layer on the Timeline panel and right-click (Ctrl+click) to select Create Motion tween. Drag the playhead to frame 1.

2. Click once on the lake on the stage and open the Properties panel. Twirl down Color Effect and select Brightness from the drop-down. Reduce the Brightness value to -100. This will turn the lake black because you have essentially removed all of the color from the lake.

3. Drag the playhead to frame 58 and increase the Brightness value to 0%, as shown in Figure 1-50. The lake returns to its original color state. Scrub across the timeline and the reflection of the moon in the lake becomes brighter as the moon arcs across the night sky.

CHAPTER 1 ■ LEARNING THE ANIMATE CC INTERFACE

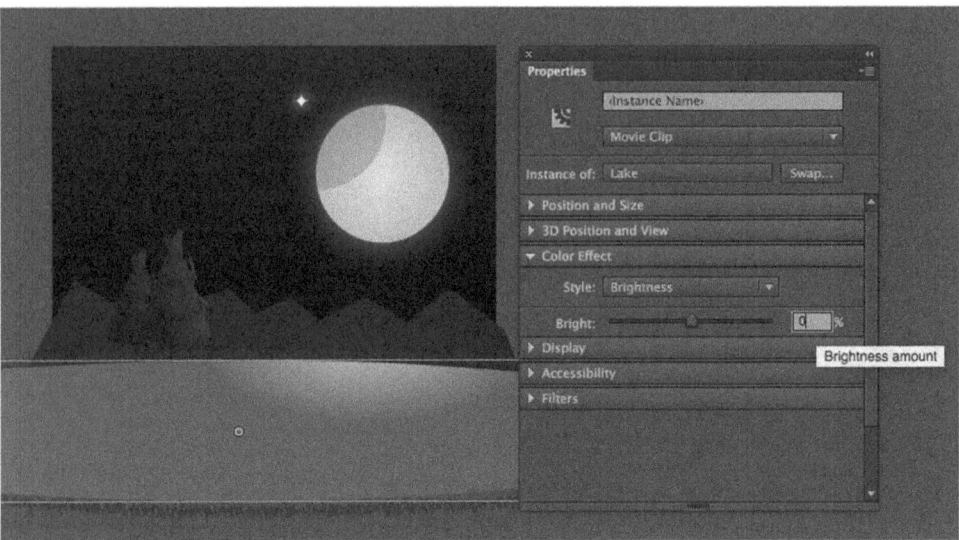

Figure 1-50. Color effects can also be tweened

Return to the Timeline panel and perform these steps with each tree layer in turn:

1. Select first frame of the Tree1 layer to select the tree on the stage.
2. Open the Properties panel and select Tint from the Color Effects. Set the Tint value to 50%, which darkens the tree.
3. Add a Motion tween, drag the playhead to frame 58 and, with the tree selected, reduce the Tint to 0% to return it to its original value.
4. Save and test the movie. It should look a lot more realistic . . . and you have concluded your introductory walk through Adobe Animate CC.

You Have Learned

- How to customize your Animate CC workspace
- A number of ways to manipulate objects on the Animate CC stage
- How to dock, undock, and minimize panels
- The importance of the Property Inspector in your daily workflow
- The difference between a frame and a keyframe
- The process involved in using frames to arrange and animate content and the properties of content on the stage using the Timeline and Motion Editor
- How to add, delete, nest, and rearrange layers
- How to test an Animate CC movie

That's a lot of stuff you've learned by taking a casual stroll through Animate CC. In the next chapter, you'll learn how to use the tools to create content in your movies, and how Photoshop and Illustrator are important elements in your workflow.

CHAPTER 2

Graphics in Animate CC

In the previous chapter, we handed you a bunch of images and essentially said, "Here, you toss them on the stage." In this chapter, we dig into how those objects were created, and in fact you are going to be drawing trees, drawing the moon, creating Venetian blinds, and playing with Chinese dancers and T-shirts, among other things. We will be using Illustrator and Photoshop and playing with JPEG and GIF images. There's a lot to cover. Let's get started.

What we'll cover in this chapter:

- Animate CC graphic fundamentals
- Using the drawing tools
- Managing and working with color
- Working with fills, strokes, and gradients
- Tracing bitmap images
- Image file formats and Animate CC
- Importing Illustrator documents into Animate CC
- Importing Photoshop documents into Animate CC

If you haven't already, download the chapter files. They can be found at

http://www.apress.com/us/book/9781484223758

These files are used in this chapter:

- 01_FreeTransform.fla
- 02_PinDrop.flaObjectDrawing.fla
- 03_Image Fill.fla
- 04_Trace.fla
- 05_JPGCompression.fla
- 06_Gif.fla
- River.jpg
- Mascot.ai

Before we start, let's take a look at what you have to work with.

Graphics in Animate CC come in two flavors: vector or bitmap. **Vector images** are usually created in a drawing application such as Illustrator. When you draw an object on the Animate CC stage, you are using the drawing tools to create a vector image. **Bitmap images** are created in such applications as Photoshop or another image editing application.

At its heart, Animate CC is a vector drawing and animation tool. The great thing about vectors is their relatively small file size compared to their bitmap cousins. The other thing to keep in mind is Animate CC's roots were as a vector animation tool (FutureSplash) for the Web. When it was introduced, broadband was just establishing itself, and the ubiquitous 56KB modem was how many people connected to the Internet. In those days, size was paramount, and vectors, being extremely small, loaded very quickly.

What makes vectors so appealing is they require very little information and computing power to draw. In very simplistic terms, a circle of 100 pixels in diameter contains five points—four on the circle and one in the center—and those points are used in a mathematical calculation that results in the diameter of the circle. The computer might also need to know whether there is a stroke around the circle and whether the circle is being filled with a solid color. If you assume the circle is yellow and the stroke is 1 point wide and colored black, this circle needs only a small amount of data: the five points, fill color, stroke width, and stroke color.

Its bitmap counterpart is treated a lot differently. Instead of requiring a limited amount of information to draw the circle, each pixel's location in the circle is charted and remembered. Not only that, but each pixel will require four units of color information to produce the red, green, blue, and alpha values for that pixel. On top of that, the computer also needs to map and draw each pixel in the background the circle is sitting on. This means producing a simple yellow circle requires thousands of bits of information, which explains why bitmap images add weight to project's file size.

All is not "sweetness and light" with vector images. Some of this art can be phenomenally complex with thousands if not millions of anchor points.

Vectors are also device independent. This means they can be scaled to 200% and still maintain their crisp edges. Scale a bitmap by that percentage, and the pixels become twice their original size. The image degrades because the pixels are "tied" to the device displaying them, which in this case is a computer monitor. If you've ever printed a photograph and seen a series of blocks in it, as if a mesh had been laid over the image, you've experienced what can happen when a device-dependent format is handled by another device.

What types of graphic objects can Animate CC use? Animate CC uses four types of graphic objects:

- **Shapes**: These are usually vector drawings created using the Animate CC drawing tools or files imported into Animate CC from Illustrator CC.

- **Drawing objects**: These are another sort of shape you draw using the Animate CC drawing tools. They behave differently from shapes when combined in the same layer, thanks to Object Drawing mode, which you learn about later in this chapter.

- **Primitives**: These are created by using the Rectangle Primitive and Oval Primitive tools in the Tools panel. These are vector shapes with a difference: they can be modified in non-destructive ways even after they are drawn.

- **Bitmaps**: These are raster images usually created in Photoshop CC and imported into Animate CC.

So much for the raw material—let's dig into Animate CC's drawing tools.

The Tools Panel

The Tools panel, shown in Figure 2-1, is where all of your drawing tools are located. Used along with Animate CC's Properties panel, effects, blends, and color panels, Animate CC's drawing tools put a pretty powerful and high-end graphics package at your disposal.

CHAPTER 2 ■ GRAPHICS IN ANIMATE CC

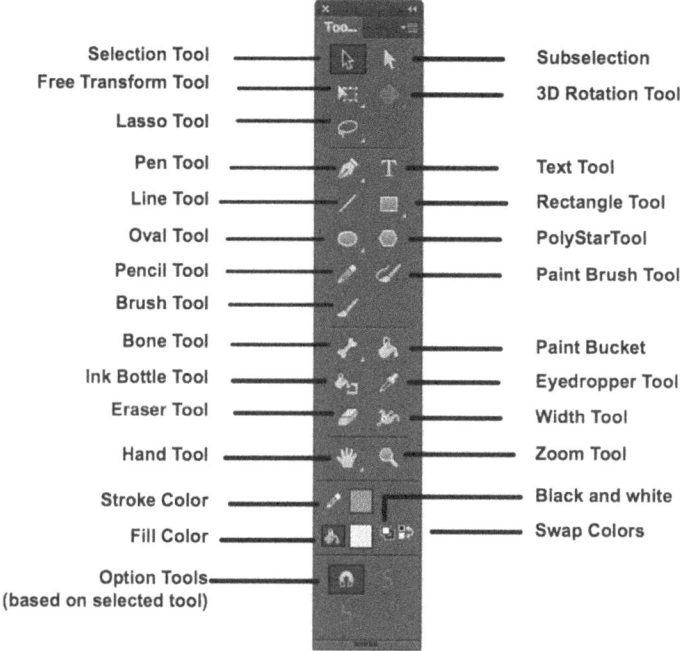

Figure 2-1. *The Animate CC Tools panel*

The tools can be roughly grouped into six distinct categories. The groupings, from top to bottom, are Selecting, Drawing, Color Modification, and Color Selection, Viewing, and Options.

- **Selecting**: The first two tools and the Lasso tool allow you select objects, select points within objects, or even select a piece of an object. The 3D Rotation and Free Transform tool, thematically, fit better into the Modification grouping.

- **Drawing**: The Nine tools in this section—Pen tool to Brush tool—can be used to draw images, create graphics and text elements, and draw shapes and lines.

- **Modification**: These six tools—Bone tool to Width tool along with the Free Transform and the 3D Rotation tools—allow you to select strokes and fills, manipulate shapes and angles, choose a specific color, or even remove a color or piece of an object. For example, you use the Ink Bottle tool to change the color of a stroke around a circle and the Paint Bucket tool to fill the circle or change its fill color. These four tools are traditionally used in conjunction with the Color Modification tools.

- **Viewing**: The Grabber Hand, Rotation, and Zoom tools allow you to move around the stage or zoom in on it while you are working.

- **Color Modification**: The four tools in this section—Stroke Color to Swap Color—allow you to change the stroke and fill colors of selected shapes or set the colors used by other modification tools.

- **Options**: The options change based on the tool selected. For example, select the Lasso tool and the Options disappear.

59

Certain tools—the Lasso, Free Transform, 3D Rotation, Pen, Rectangle, Oval, Bone, and Hand tools—have a small triangle at the bottom right, as shown in Figure 2-2. Clicking this triangle opens a drop-down menu that offers you a subselection of related tool choices. Color chips open the Color Picker.

Figure 2-2. *Certain tools have similar tools attached to them*

The Selection and Subselection Tools

The odds are almost 100% that the Selection and Subselection tools are the ones you will use most frequently in your everyday workflow. Coupled with the Free Transform and Gradient Transform tools and you have the tools that are used, at least once, in practically any Animate CC design situation.

1. Open a new Animate CC ActionScript 3.0 document. Click the Rectangle tool and make sure the Object Drawing button (the circle in the top left of the Options area at the bottom of the toolbar) is deselected. We aren't going explain why at this point because we have devoted a section of this chapter to this very subject. Draw a rectangle on the stage. Choosing a color for the stroke and fill is not important right now.

2. Switch to the Selection tool by either clicking it or pressing the V key. When you roll the tool over the square, a cross with arrows appears under the cursor. This means you are hovering over an object that can be moved by clicking and dragging.

3. All tools can be selected using the keyboard. If you roll the cursor over a tool, a tooltip will appear and the letter between the brackets is the key that can be pressed to select the tool (see Figure 2-3). If you find tooltips annoying, open Preferences ➤ General and deselect Keyboard Shortcuts in the Sync Settings area.

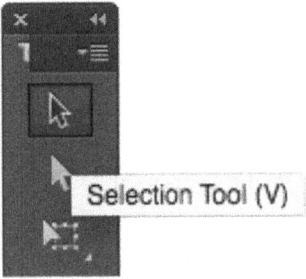

Figure 2-3. *Select a tool and the tooltip will appear*

CHAPTER 2 ■ GRAPHICS IN ANIMATE CC

4. Click the square and drag to the right. Holy smokes, you just pulled the fill out of the square (see Figure 2-4). Press Ctrl+Z (PC) or Cmd+Z (Mac) to undo that last action.

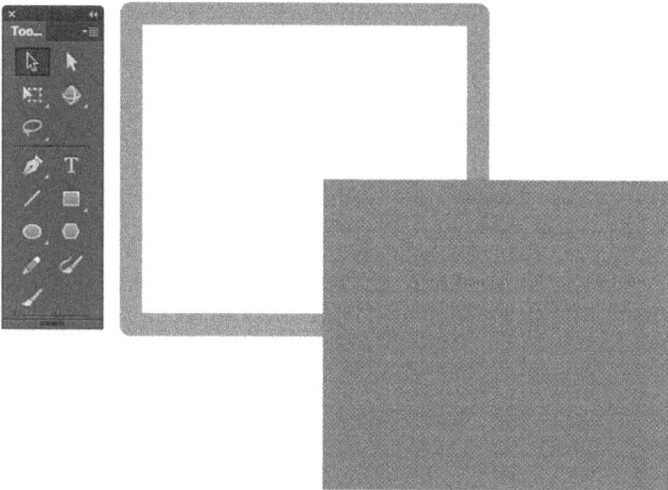

Figure 2-4. *Selections in Animate CC aren't always what they seem*

You have just discovered that Animate CC regards all objects you draw as being composed of two things: a stroke and a fill. If you are an Illustrator or Photoshop user, this may strike you as being a bit odd because in a vector universe separating the stroke from its fill is not a common behavior. Give us a minute, and we'll ease you back into more familiar territory. We have a square to move.

5. To select the entire square, you have two choices. The first is to double-click the item. The second is to "marquee" the stroke and the fill by drawing a selection box around the object. To draw your selection box, click outside the rectangle near one of its corners, and then drag toward the opposite corner. Go ahead, try both methods of selection, and drag the square. You'll see the whole square move this time.

6. Now that you know objects drawn on the stage are actually composed of a stroke and a fill, we'd like to mention a third approach to selecting and moving them as a unit. Marquee the object and select Modify ➤ Group. Now, when you click the object, it is regarded as a single entity and can be dragged at will.

    The Selection tool can be used for more than simply dragging around the stage. You can use it to also modify the shape of an object. The square on the stage, as you know, is composed of two things—a stroke and a fill. This means they can not only be moved around the stage, but can also be reshaped and still retain their crisp strokes and fills. Let's try it out.

7. Select your object on the stage and select Modify ➤ Ungroup. Deselect the shapes. Place the tip of the cursor on one of the strokes around the square. Do you see the little quarter circle, as in Figure 2-5, below the arrow? That symbol indicates you can reshape the stroke and/or the fill.

61

CHAPTER 2 ■ GRAPHICS IN ANIMATE CC

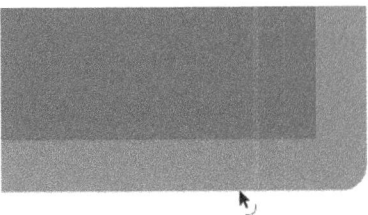

Figure 2-5. *The curvy shape under the cursor means the stroke can be reshaped*

Click and drag the stroke. When you drag the stroke, it actually bends. This tells you that the stroke is anchored, and, as in Illustrator or Photoshop, if you drag a point on a line between two anchor points, the line changes its shape. The stroke uses the location of the point where you released the mouse as the apex of the curve. The other thing you may have noticed is, as shown in Figure 2-6, the fill also updates to reflect the new shape.

Figure 2-6. *Both the stroke and the fill change to reflect the new shape*

8. Select the Subselection tool or press the A key to switch to this tool. Double-click one of the corner points for the curve you have just created. The points and the handles, as shown in Figure 2-7, become visible. You can further adjust the curve by either moving the handles or the points. These handles are only available on curves.

CHAPTER 2 ■ GRAPHICS IN ANIMATE CC

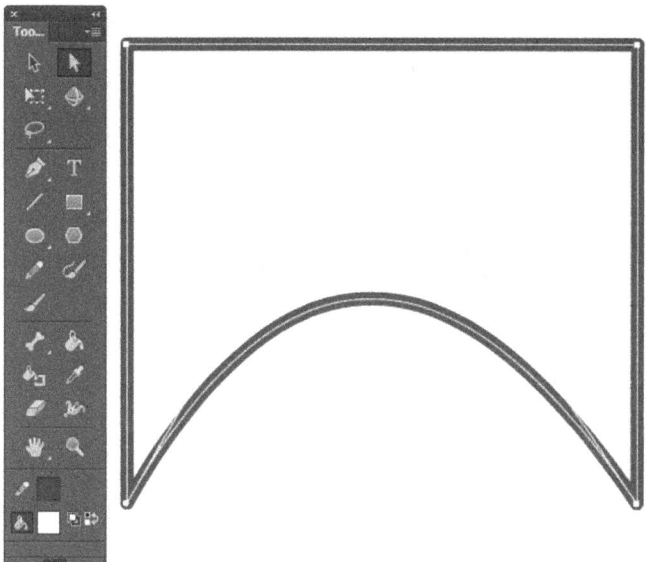

Figure 2-7. *Change a shape by dragging a handle or corner point*

Another tool that allows you to manipulate objects on the stage is the Free Transform tool, which we look at next.

The Free Transform Tool

If there is such a thing as an indispensable drawing tool in Animate CC, this one may just be it. What it does is scale, skew, and rotate objects on the stage. Here is how to use it:

1. Open the 01_FreeTransform.fla file in the Chapter02/Exercises folder. When it opens you will see a card from an Android interface on the stage. The card is a movieclip. If you test the movie using Ctrl+Enter (Cmd+Return), you will see the card move onto the stage.

Don't for a moment think Animate CC is strictly an animation application. As you can see, it can be used to prototype motion and interactivity for mobile projects.

---

2. Select the movieclip in frame 1 of the timeline and select the Free Transform tool by either clicking it or pressing the Q key. The selected object sprouts a bounding box with eight handles and a white dot in the center.

3. Roll the cursor just outside of each of the corner handles. Notice how, as in Figure 2-8, the cursor develops a rotate icon. This tells you that if you click and drag a corner, you can rotate the object. Try it out—you should also see a ghosted representation of the original position of the movieclip, which is a handy feature to ensure that the rotation is correct.

63

CHAPTER 2 ■ GRAPHICS IN ANIMATE CC

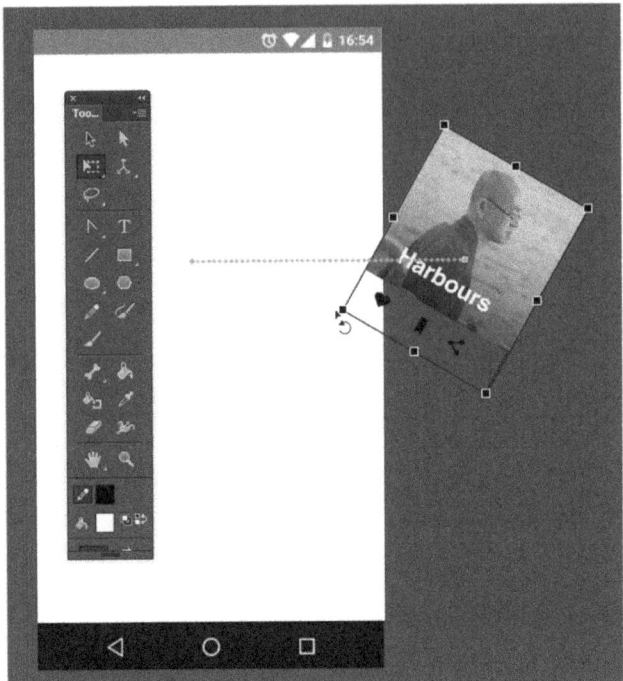

Figure 2-8. *Rotating an object using the Free Transform tool*

4. Test the movie. The movieclip has rotated. This tells you that it isn't only objects that can be transformed. Symbols with tweens and motion and other movie elements can also be transformed with this tool. Close the SWF to be returned to the Animate CC stage and let's try something else.

5. This time place the cursor on the bounding box. The cursor changes to split arrows. This tells you that clicking and dragging will skew (or slant) the object in the direction in which you drag. Go ahead, give it a try.

6. Now place the cursor directly over one of the handles. It changes to a double-headed arrow, meaning you can scale the object from that point.

    The key to mastering the Free Transform tool is to master that white dot. It is the transformation point of the object. Rotations use that dot as a pivot, and any of the other transformations applied using this tool are based on the location of that dot when you hold down the Alt key.

7. Click the white dot and drag it over the upper-left corner handle. Rotate the object using the handle in the lower-right corner. The rotation occurs around that white dot. Undo the change and this time scale the object using the bottom-right corner. Again, as shown in Figure 2-9, the upper-left corner is used as the anchor point for the transformation.

CHAPTER 2 ■ GRAPHICS IN ANIMATE CC

Figure 2-9. *The transformation point is moved to the upper-left corner of the image*

8. Now try another skew. With the white dot close to one of the corners, place the cursor on the bounding box to see the split arrows icon. Click and drag, and then hold down the Alt key and drag again. See the difference? Do the same with a scale transform.

To constrain the proportions of an object when using the mouse to scale the object, hold down the Shift key before you drag the handle. You can use Shift at the same time as the Alt key, as described previously, to both constrain and use the white dot as a pivot.

Applied a couple of transformations and don't want to use them? To remove transformations, select Modify ➤ Transform ➤ Remove Transform or press Ctrl+Shift+Z (PC) or Cmd+Shift+Z (Mac). All transform actions applied to the object will be removed. One other thing about this you may have noticed. If you have motion or there is a tween changing the location of the transformation point, moves the entire animation to a new location on the stage based upon the new location of the Transformation point.

65

CHAPTER 2 ■ GRAPHICS IN ANIMATE CC

The Gradient Transform Tool

To the novice, gradients in Animate CC can be a little tricky. The reason is you can create the colors in the gradient, but moving them around and changing their direction is not done at the time the gradient is created. This is done using a separate tool.

Let's try a couple of gradient exercises:

1. Open a new ActionScript 3.0 document. Select the Oval tool, deselect the stroke, and draw a circle on the stage. (To draw an object without a stroke, open the Stroke color swatch panel and select the swatch with a diagonal red line through it.)

2. With the circle selected, change the width and height values of the circle to 120 and 120 in the Properties panel.

3. Click the Fill Color chip to open the Color Chip panel and select the blue gradient, shown in Figure 2-10, at the bottom of the panel.

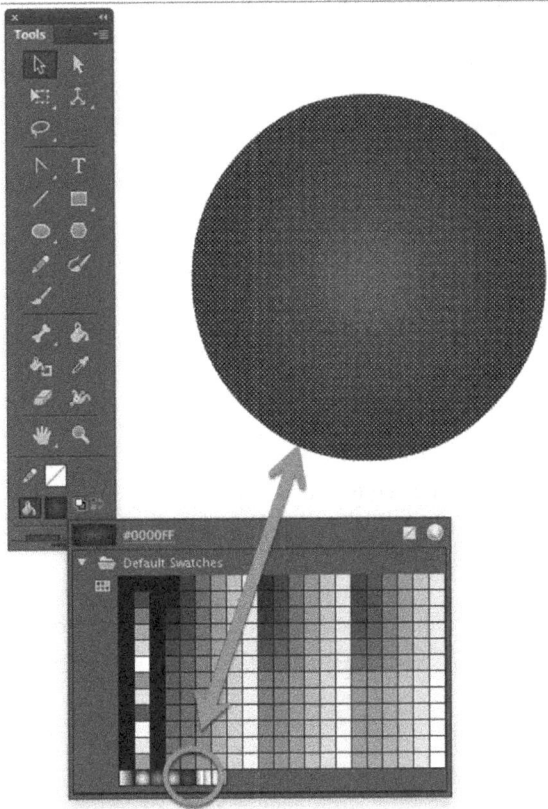

Figure 2-10. Selecting a preset gradient using the Fill color in the Tools panel

66

CHAPTER 2 ■ GRAPHICS IN ANIMATE CC

There are a couple of ways to change this gradient in order to position the centered highlight elsewhere in the graphic. The first is to use the Paint Bucket tool. This tool simply fills a selected shape with the color in the Fill color chip, but it does something really interesting when the color is a gradient. Follow these steps:

4. Choose a gradient and click the Paint Bucket tool to select it (or press the K key to switch to this tool).

5. Click in the bottom-left corner of the circle. The center of the gradient moves to the point where you clicked the mouse, as you can see in Figure 2-11. How this occurred is the paint pouring out of the tool's icon is the hot spot for the tool. The center of the gradient will be the point where the "pour" is located.

Figure 2-11. *The tip or "pour" point of the Paint Bucket's icon is its hot spot*

6. Click again somewhere else on the shape to move the center point of the gradient.

    The other technique for changing a gradient is to use the Gradient Transform tool, which is more precise than using the Paint Bucket.

7. Click and hold on the Free Transform tool to open the drop-down menu. Select the Gradient Transform tool from the menu. Alternatively, simply press the F key to switch from the current tool to the Gradient Transform tool.

8. Click the object on the stage. When you do, it will be surrounded by circle, a line will bisect the selection, and three handles will appear, as shown in Figure 2-12. The circle represents the area of the gradient fill.

CHAPTER 2 ■ GRAPHICS IN ANIMATE CC

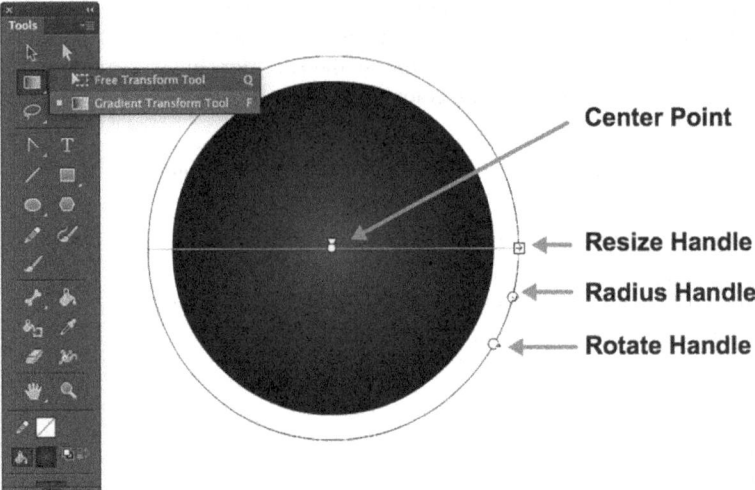

Figure 2-12. *The Gradient Transform tool allows you to precisely control a gradient*

Let's look at each of these controls:

- **Center point**: This is actually composed of two features. The white dot is the center point of the gradient and can be moved around in the usual manner. The triangle, which can only move along the line, determines the focus of the center point.

- **Resize handle**: Dragging this handle resizes and distorts the gradient without affecting the shape of the filled object.

- **Radius handle**: Moving this one inward or outward resizes the gradient proportionally.

- **Rotate handle**: Drag this handle, and the gradient rotates around the center point. The effect can be quite subtle with a radial gradient, but you'll see a difference if you squeeze the gradient into a lozenge shape with the resize handle.

Now that you know how to use the tool on a radial gradient, give it a try on a linear gradient. Here's how:

1. Select one of the linear gradients from the Fill color chip in the Tools panel.

2. Select the Rectangle tool and draw a square. Click the square with the Gradient Transform tool.

3. As you can see in Figure 2-13, the same controls are in place. This time, two lines, which indicate the range of the gradient, appear. If you click the resize handle and drag it downward toward the top of the box, the colors in the gradient become more compressed. The rotate and center point handles work in the same manner as their radial gradient counterparts.

CHAPTER 2 ■ GRAPHICS IN ANIMATE CC

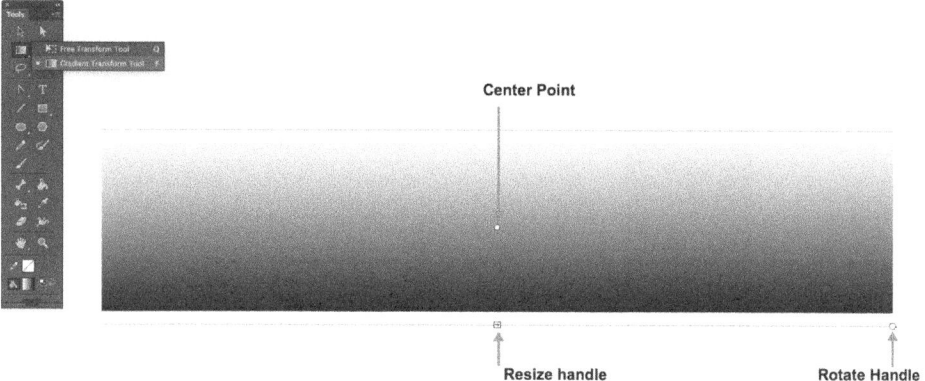

Figure 2-13. *The Gradient Transform tool can be used on linear gradients as well*

Object Drawing Mode

Introduced in Flash 8, the addition of the Object Drawing mode feature was greeted with wild cheering and dancing in the streets. Well, it didn't exactly happen that way, but a lot designers became seriously "happy campers" when they discovered this feature.

Prior to the release of Flash 8, shapes that overlapped each other on the stage was for many, a frustrating experience. If one shape was over another—in the same layer—and you selected and moved it, it would cut a chunk out of the shape below it. This is not to say it was flaw in the application. This behavior is quite common with painting applications. In Animate CC, once you understand the "one piece eats the other" phenomenon, it becomes a great construction tool. It can be much simpler to throw down a base shape and purposefully "take bites" out of it to achieve a complex figure than to draw the same figure from scratch. Object Drawing mode uses the opposite concept. You get the best of both worlds and the choice is yours.

When you select a drawing tool, the Object Drawing icon, shown in Figure 2-14, appears in the Tools panel. Click it, and the oval you are about to draw will be drawn as a separate object on the stage and will not automatically merge with any object under it, even on the same layer. Let's see how it works:

69

CHAPTER 2 ▪ GRAPHICS IN ANIMATE CC

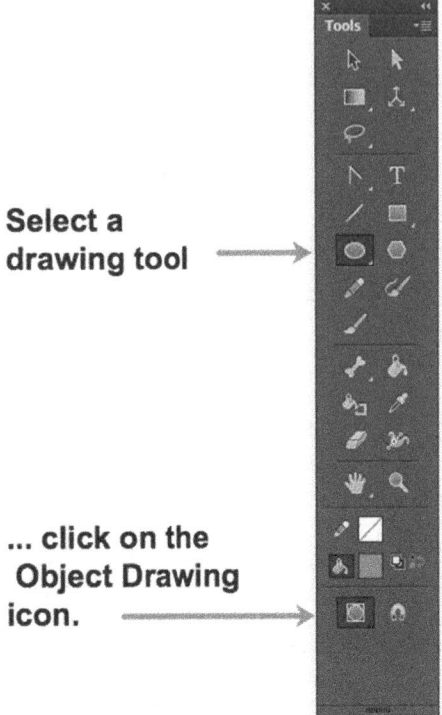

Figure 2-14. *Select Object Drawing mode to turn on this feature*

1. Open a new ActionScript 3.0 document and, when it opens, select the Rectangle tool and draw a rectangle on the stage.

2. Select the Oval tool, turn off the stroke in the Tools panel, and draw a circle over the shape on the stage.

3. Select the circle and drag it off of the shape. When you release the mouse, you will see that your circle has bitten off a chunk of the shape.

4. Select the Oval tool, click the Object Drawing mode button in the Tools panel or turn it on in the Properties panel, and draw another circle over the shape. Drag it away and nothing happens, as shown in Figure 2-15. Hooray for Object Drawing mode.

70

CHAPTER 2 ■ GRAPHICS IN ANIMATE CC

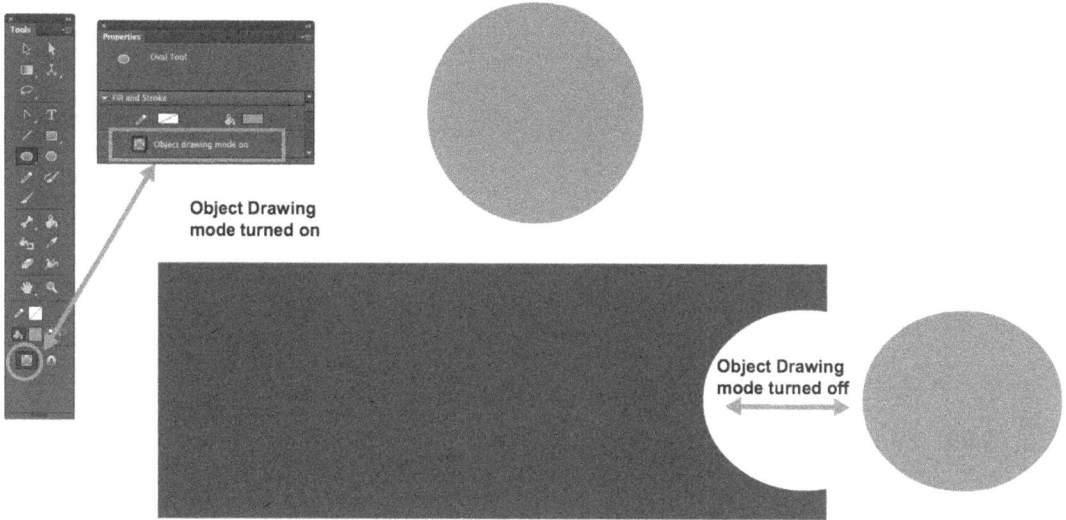

Figure 2-15. *The effects of having Drawing Mode turned on or off*

When you drew that second circle, Animate CC offered you a visual clue that you were in Object Drawing mode. When you selected the shape, it was surrounded by a bounding box.

Here's a little trick you can use to edit a single object in Object Drawing mode: Double-click the second circle you just drew. Everything but the object you just double-clicked fades, and the words Drawing Object appear beside the Scene 1 link. This allows you to edit the object in place without disturbing anything else on the stage. To return to the stage, click the Scene 1 link or double-click outside of the shape to go back a layer.

Drawing in Animate CC

In this section, you review the five primary drawing tools:

- **Pencil**: Use this tool to draw freeform lines and shapes. It is also draws strokes.
- **Paint Brush**: Use this tool to paint vector-based strokes.
- **Brush:** Use this tool to paint in fill colors.
- **Eraser:** The opposite of the brush tool. It erases and removes rather than fills.
- **Pen:** Use this to draw Bézier curves.

The Pencil Tool

Think of the Pencil tool as being a mechanical pencil with a huge number of leads and colors, all of which are available with a simple click. Select the Pencil tool and the Properties panel changes (Figure 2-16) to allow you to set properties for the lines you will draw, such as line thickness, style, and color.

CHAPTER 2 ■ GRAPHICS IN ANIMATE CC

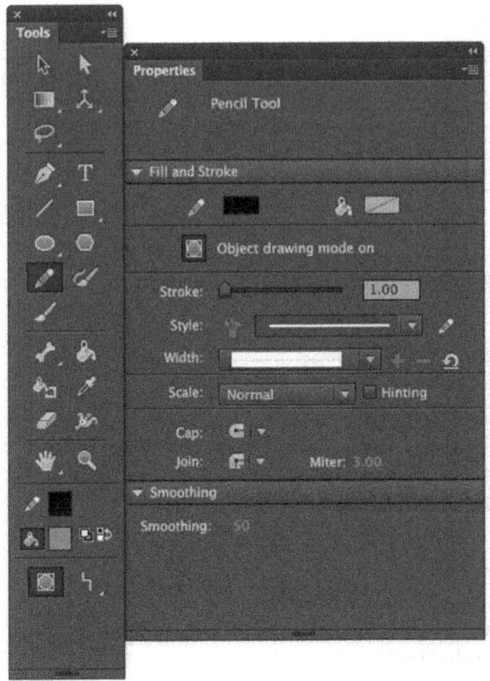

Figure 2-16. *The Pencil tool and its properties*

This tool also has a modifier that appears at the bottom of the Tools panel. Click it, and a drop-down menu gives you three modes to choose from (Figure 2-17). These modes are important because they control how the line behaves when you draw. Also, when you select this tool, you can choose to use the Object Drawing mode.

Figure 2-17. *The Pencil tool has three drawing modes*

72

Let's try out the modes:

1. Open a new Animate CC document and select the Pencil tool or press the Y key.

2. Using the Pencil tool, draw three squiggly lines. Use one of the following three modes for each line. The results, shown in Figure 2-18, will be slightly different for each mode. Here's what the modes do:

   - **Straighten mode**: Use this if you want curves to flatten.

   - **Smooth mode**: Use this mode to round out kinks or otherwise smooth awkward curves.

   - **Ink mode**: This mode gives you exactly what you draw. If you use this mode, make sure that Stroke Hinting in the Properties panel is selected. This will ensure crisp, nonblurry lines.

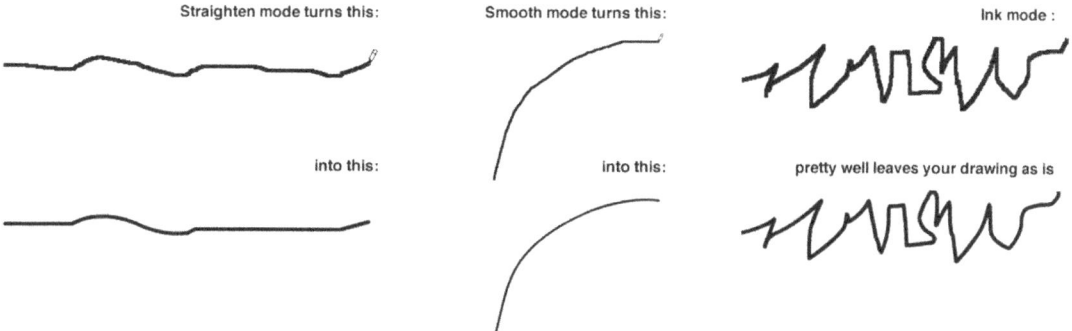

Figure 2-18. *The Smooth and Straighten modes can remove awkward angles*

3. Switch to the Selection tool and click the top line. Notice how you selected just a piece of it. The lines you draw with the Pencil tool are vectors.

4. Deselect the line segment and this time roll the mouse over the line. When you see a small curve appear under the mouse, click and drag. This tells you that you can change the shape of the lines you draw by simply moving their segments. Roll over a corner point and you will see an angular bracket cursor. This indicates you can move the anchor point.

5. Double-click one of the lines and change the thickness and line type from the drop-down menu in the Properties panel or click the Pencil icon in the Style area to open a window that lets you choose a stroke style and a thickness. As shown in Figure 2-19, your choices are solid, dashed, dotted, ragged, stippled, and hatched.

CHAPTER 2 ■ GRAPHICS IN ANIMATE CC

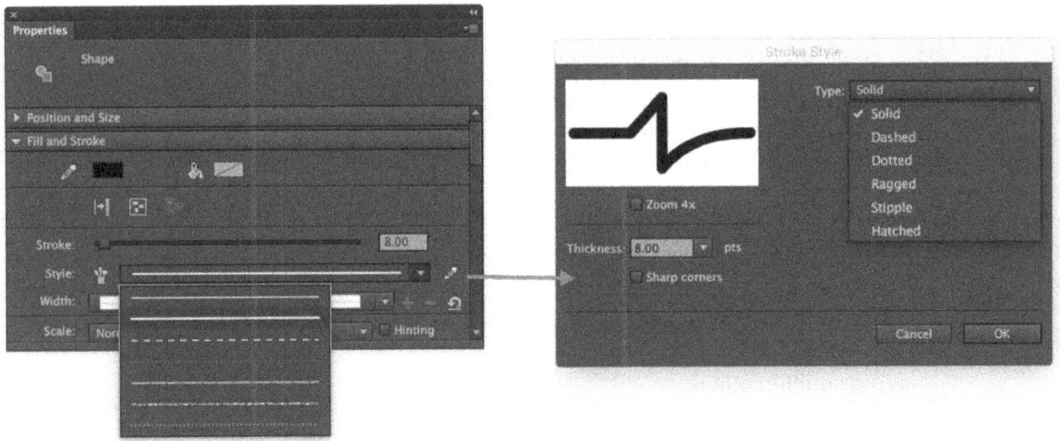

Figure 2-19. *Choose a line style in the Properties panel*

   6. Draw a circle using the Pencil tool in Smooth mode. Select the shape, and in the Tools panel, click the Smooth button. Notice how the awkward edges of your circle become rounded. Now click the adjacent Straighten button a couple of times. Your awkward circle actually becomes a round circle. Double-click one of your lines. The Pencil options change to show you separate Straighten and Smooth buttons. Click the Smooth and Straighten buttons to see how they work on nonclosed shapes. As you can see, these buttons work independently of the Straighten and Smooth options available through the Pencil tool's drop-down menu.

Animate CC has preferences that will help you with your drawing chores. If you select Edit ➤ Preferences (PC) or Animate CC ➤ Preferences (Mac), you will open the Preferences panel. Click the Drawing category at the bottom of the list and the panel will change to show you how Animate CC handles the drawing tools, lines, and shapes. The Recognize shapes drop-down list can be set to take your hand-drawn approximations of circles, squares, triangles, and the like and replace them with truer shapes, as if drawn by the Oval or Rectangle tools.

CHAPTER 2 ■ GRAPHICS IN ANIMATE CC

The Paint Brush Tool

When Adobe announced the introduction of Vector Brushes in Animate CC, both authors were seriously happy campers. Prior to the introduction of Vector Brushes, brushes were treated in much the same way they are in Photoshop. A brush would lay down colored pixels and, if you wanted to animate that shape, you were in for quite a bit of extra work. The other pain point for us was the limited number of brush shapes that ranged from round to square, and the Brush only worked with fills.

The Paint Brush tool offers you a huge workflow boost because because it uses vectors. What makes this tool really neat is that objects created with this brush can be animated. As well, any brushes saved to your Creative Cloud Library, including those created in Adobe Capture, can now be used as a brush in Animate CC.

When you select the Paint Brush tool or press the Y key to select the tool, a number of options will appear on the Properties panel, as shown in Figure 2-20. This panel is where the full power of the Paint Brush tool is contained. The properties are:

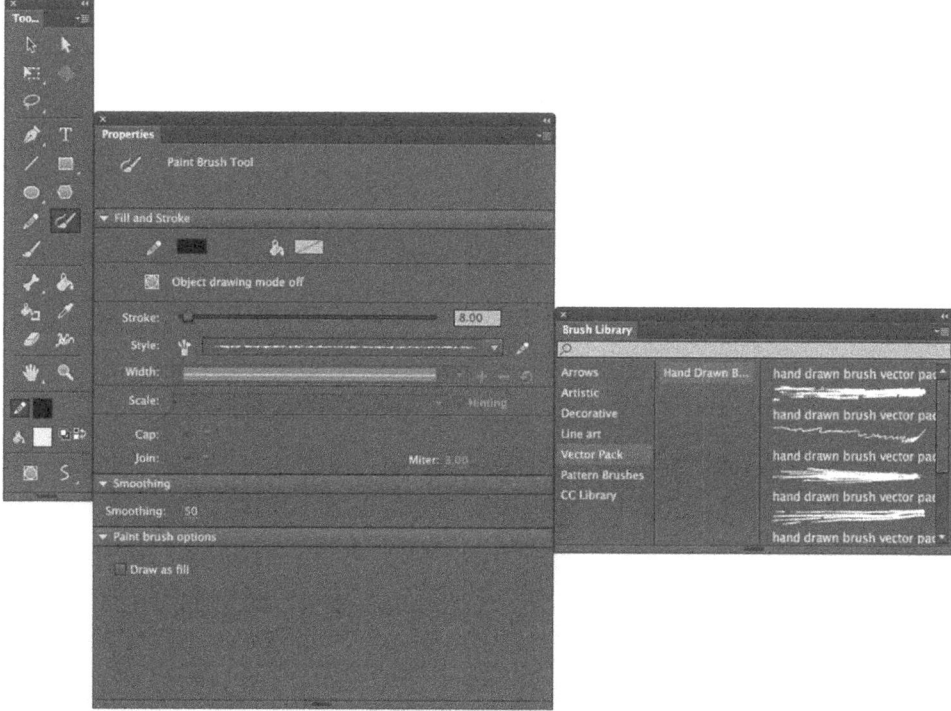

Figure 2-20. *The Paint Brush tool's properties*

75

CHAPTER 2 ■ GRAPHICS IN ANIMATE CC

- **Object Drawing:** You have seen this earlier in the chapter. It's the button that toggles Object Drawing on and off.
- **Stroke:** Determines how thick the brush stroke will be.
- **Style:** This area is where the magic happens. Click the Paint Brush Can and you open your brush library. From here you can choose any brush style, ranging from those included with Animate CC to brushes you may create in other applications on the desktop, tablet, or mobile device and are saved to your Creative Cloud Library. The line style drop-down lets you choose the type of stroke to be applied. Click the Pencil button and the Stroke Style panel opens.
- **Width:** This drop-down lets you choose the stroke style from straight to tapered.
- **Smoothing:** This option determines the amount of smoothing and sharpness applied to an object drawn with the Paint Brush tool. In many respects, it is the same as the Smooth mode of the Pencil tool.

Let's see how this works:

1. Open a new Animate CC document and click once on the Paint Brush tool to select it.
2. Open the Properties panel. Make sure Object Drawing mode is off and set the stroke to 43 pixels.
3. Click the Paint Brush Holder button to open the Brush Library panel.
4. Click once on the Vector Pack category and click once on the Handrawn Brushes category that appears. A series of hand-drawn brushes will appear on the right.
5. Double-click on one of the brushes and the brush will appear in the Style preview. If you click the preview, the drop-down will show you that the brush has been added to the Brush Styles, as shown in Figure 2-21.

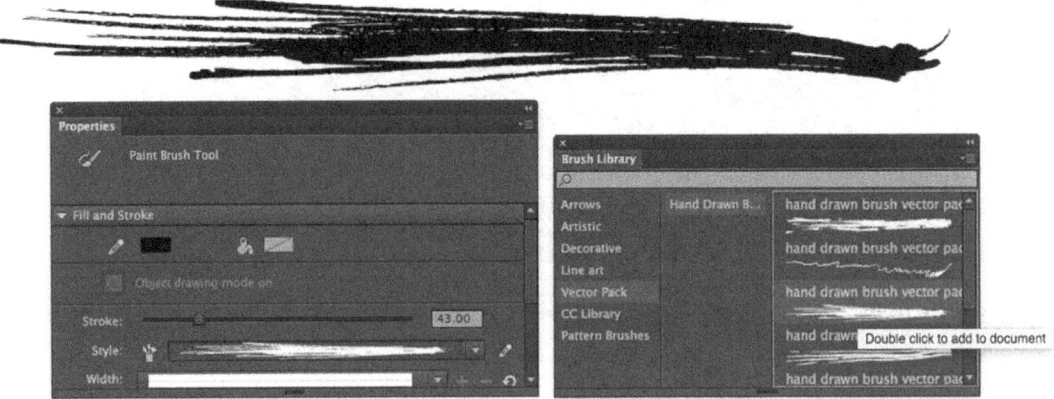

Figure 2-21. *A brush from the Brush Library is used*

CHAPTER 2 ■ GRAPHICS IN ANIMATE CC

6. Click and drag the brush across the stage.

7. Switch over to the Subselection tool—the hollow arrow—and click once on your brush stroke. The resulting path with handles tells you these are indeed vectors.

8. Click on a control point and drag it around the page. Notice how the shape of the brush stroke changes.

The Brush Tool

You have discovered that all objects drawn on the stage are separated into strokes and fills. The Pencil and the Brush tools follow that separation. The Brush tool feels quite similar to the Pencil tool in how it is used. The difference between the two is subtle but also quite profound.

When you select the Brush tool or press the B key to select the tool, a number of options will appear at the bottom of the Tools panel and the properties panel will change, as shown in Figure 2-22.

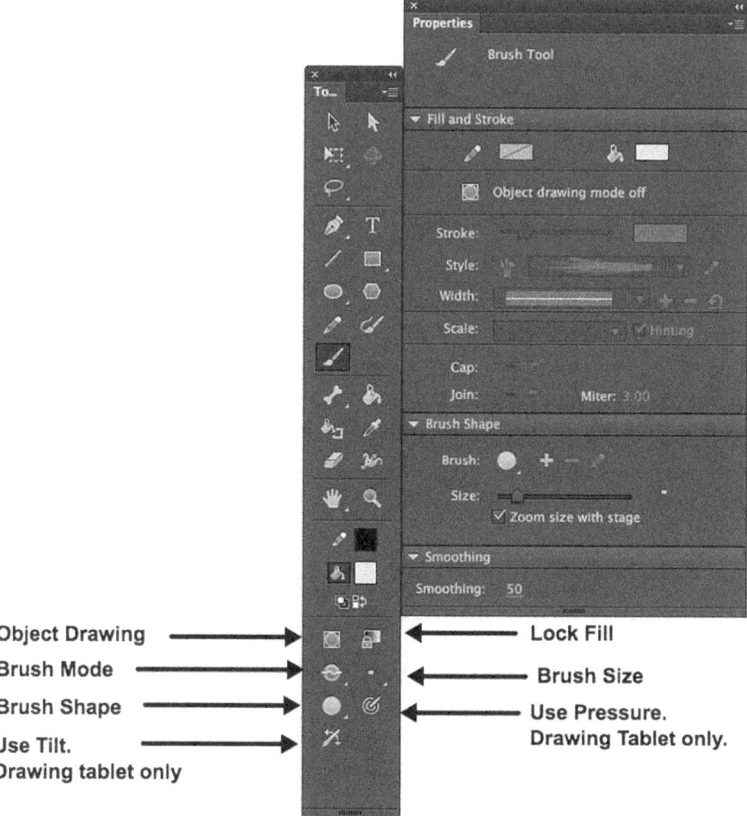

Figure 2-22. The Brush tool's options and properties

CHAPTER 2 ■ GRAPHICS IN ANIMATE CC

- **Object Drawing:** You have seen this earlier in the chapter. It's the button that toggles Object Drawing on and off.
- **Lock Fill:** Select this to fill multiple objects with a single gradient or some other fill. This can be useful in cases where the gradient implies a highlight, as the "lighting" will be applied evenly across all selected objects.
- **Brush Mode:** This controls how the strokes are painted, and the drop-down menu contains the following five modifiers:
  - **Paint Normal:** Paints over anything on the screen, provided they are on the same layer and not in Object Drawing mode. These caveats apply to the other mode options as well. If your content is a drawing object, use Modify ➤ Break Apart to turn it into a shape. When you finish, you can put it all back together as a single object by selecting Modify ➤ Combine Objects.
  - **Paint Fills:** Paints the fills and leaves the stroke alone.
  - **Paint Behind:** Paints only on the empty areas of the layer.
  - **Paint Selection:** Paints only on the selected areas of the object.
  - **Paint Inside:** Paints only inside the area surrounded by a stroke. This mode only works if the Brush tool starts inside the stroke; otherwise, it acts like Paint Behind.
- **Brush Shape:** Offers you a series of brush shapes.
- **Brush Size:** Use this to change the width and spread of the brush strokes.
- **Brush Shape:** This drop-down menu offers a number of brush shapes ranging from round to square.
- **Use Pressure and Use Tilt:** These two appear only if a tablet is attached to the computer. They allow you to use the pressure and angle settings of a graphics tablet's pen. This is a piece of hardware with a special drawing surface and "pen" that translates your actual hand motions into drawings on the screen.

The final control is the Smoothing option on the Properties panel. This option determines the amount of smoothing and sharpness applied to an object drawn with the Brush tool. In many respects, it is the same as the Smooth mode of the Pencil tool. Try it out:

1. Select the Brush tool and select a fill color.
2. Turn off Object Drawing mode and make sure the Brush mode is set to Paint Normal.
3. In the Properties panel, set the Smooth value to 0 and draw a squiggle on the screen.
4. Set the Smooth value to 50 and draw another squiggle on the screen. Repeat this step with a value of 100. As you can see in Figure 2-23, the edges move from rough to smooth flowing. Just be aware that high values tend to remove the curves from your drawings.

CHAPTER 2 ■ GRAPHICS IN ANIMATE CC

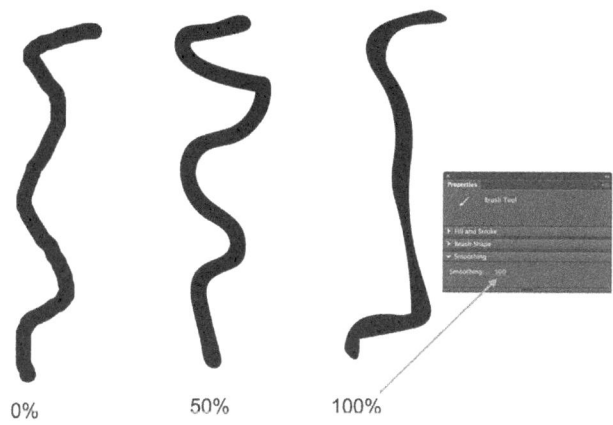

Figure 2-23. Smoothing brush strokes

If these strokes don't look all that different from each other, take a look at Figure 2-24. The number of vector points used to create the object reduces significantly as the Smoothing value increases. To see for yourself, select the Subselection tool and click on the edge of each scribble. The vector points become visible. Remember, vector points require processing power to draw on the screen at runtime. Which will appear quicker: The squiggle on the left or the one on the right?

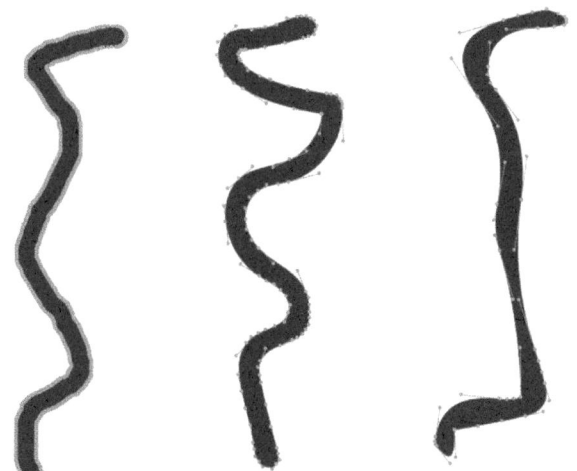

Figure 2-24. Smoothing reduces a haze of points on the left to a manageable number toward the right

CHAPTER 2 ■ GRAPHICS IN ANIMATE CC

The Eraser Tool

The Eraser tool is quite similar to the Brush tool, only it erases rather than paints. Select the Eraser tool or press the E key, and the following three modifiers, shown in Figure 2-25, appear in the Tools panel:

- **Eraser Mode:** There are five choices in this drop-down menu, and they match those in the Brush tool.
- **Eraser Shape:** The choices in this drop-down menu let you select from a number of shapes for the eraser.
- **Eraser Faucet:** Select this to erase an entire fill or line with one click. The hot spot is the tip of the arrowhead.

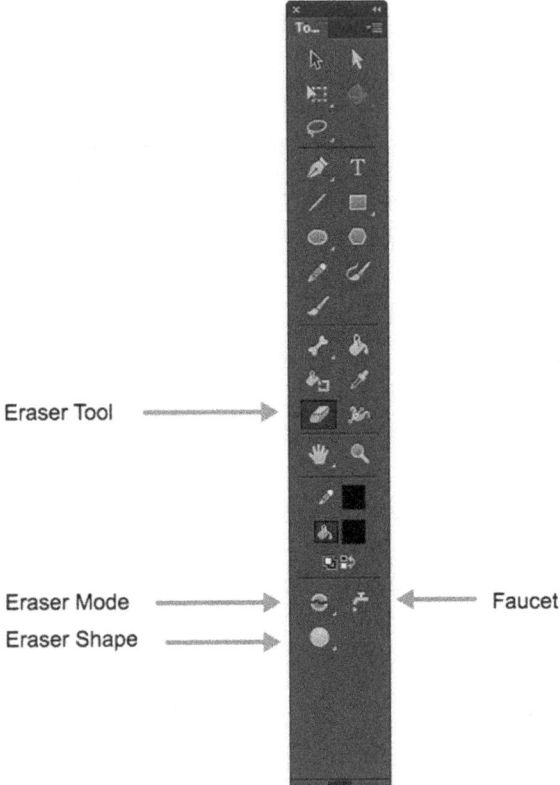

Figure 2-25. The Eraser options

Here's a quick way to erase the contents of an entire layer: double-click the Eraser tool to clear your layer.

The Pen Tool

If you use Illustrator, Photoshop, or some other vector-based drawing tool, you are accustomed to using the Pen tool. The interesting thing about this tool is its roots aren't found in the graphics industry. It started out as a solution to a tricky problem faced by the auto industry in the 1970s.

Computers were just starting to be used in some areas of car design, and the designers faced a rather nasty problem: they could draw lines and simple curves, but squiggles and precise curves were completely out of the question. The solution was to use a calculation developed by the mathematician Pierre Bézier to produce what we now know as **Bézier curves**.

A simple curve is composed of a number of points. A Bézier curve adds two additional pieces of data called **direction** and **speed**. These two data bits are visually represented by the handle that appears when you draw a curve with the Pen tool. Here's how to create a Bézier curve:

1. Select the Pen tool or press the P key. When you place the cursor on the stage, it changes to the pen and a small asterisk appears next to it.

2. Click and drag. As you drag, you will see three points on the line, as shown in Figure 2-26. The center point, called the **anchor point**, is the start of the curve, and the two outer points, called **handles**, indicate the direction and degree of the curve.

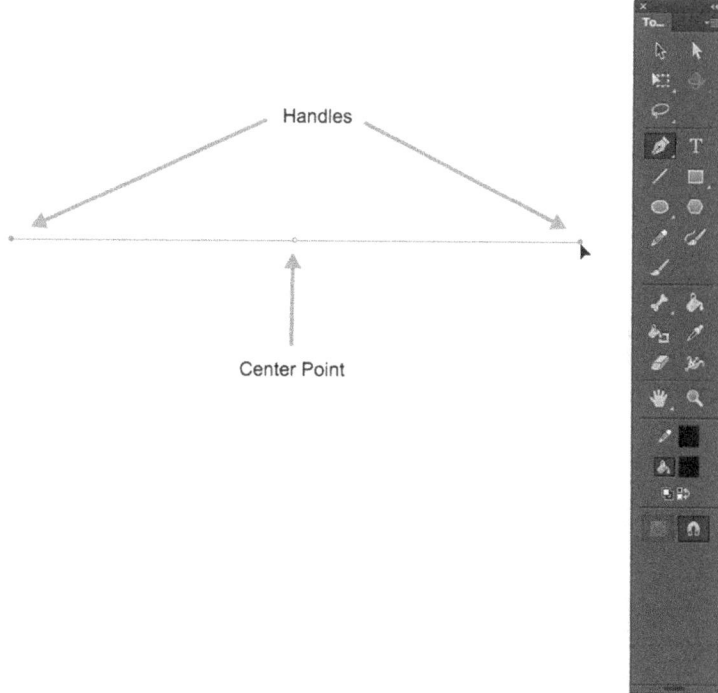

Figure 2-26. *The start of a Bézier curve*

CHAPTER 2 ■ GRAPHICS IN ANIMATE CC

3. Roll the mouse to another position on the screen and click and drag the mouse. As you drag, the mouse handles and the curve get longer and the curve follows the direction of the handle, as shown in Figure 2-27.

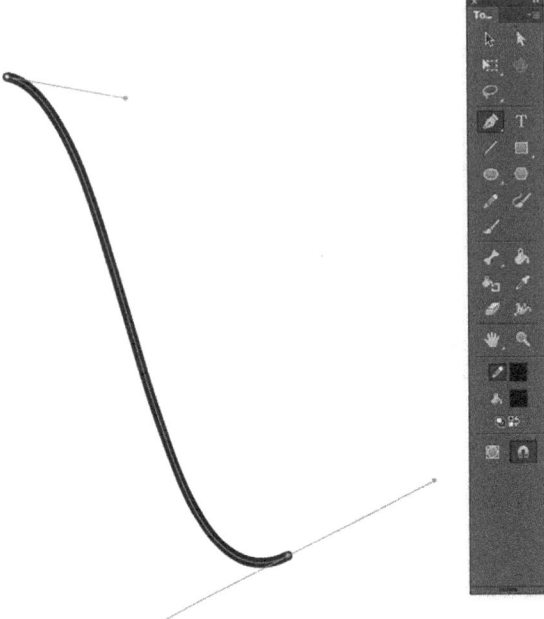

Figure 2-27. *The curve shape changes based on the length and direction of the handle*

4. Click and drag a couple more times to add a few more points to the shape.

5. Roll the mouse over the starting point of the shape. Notice the little *o* under the Pen tool, as shown in Figure 2-28? This tells you that you are about to create a closed shape. Click the mouse.

CHAPTER 2 ■ GRAPHICS IN ANIMATE CC

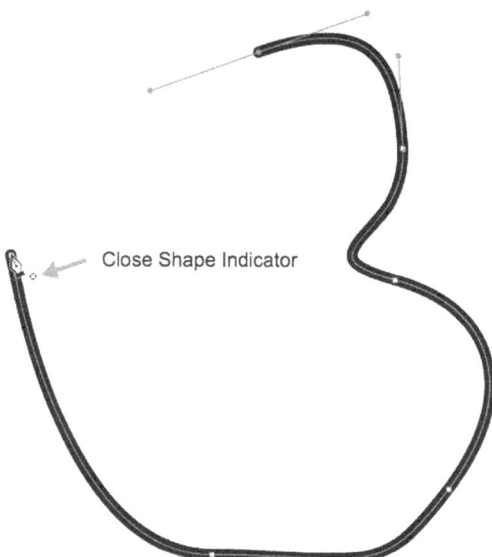

Figure 2-28. *The shape is about to be closed*

There are a couple of other options available to you with the Pen tool that will allow you to edit your curves. If you click and hold the Pen tool in the Tools panel, you will see, as shown in Figure 2-29, three extra choices:

- **Add Anchor Point:** Select this tool and click anywhere on the line to add an extra point.

- **Delete Anchor Point:** Click an anchor point to remove it. The shape will change.

- **Convert Anchor Point:** Click an anchor point, and the point will be converted to a corner point. To get your curve back, click the point with the Convert Anchor Point tool.

CHAPTER 2 ■ GRAPHICS IN ANIMATE CC

Figure 2-29. *The Pen tool choices*

You can, however, access the functionality of each tool from the main Pen tool itself. Here's the wrapped-up-in-one approach:

- **Adding an anchor point**: Using the Pen tool, hover over an existing line. Note how the normal *x* under the cursor becomes a +. Click to add a new anchor.
- **Deleting an anchor point**: Hover over a corner point, and you'll see the cursor acquire a little -. Click to delete the anchor. Hover over a normal anchor, and you'll have to click twice: once to convert the anchor to a corner point, and the second time to delete it.
- **Converting an anchor point**: Well, you just saw this in the previous bullet point. But note the Alt/Option key temporarily converts the Pen tool into the Convert Anchor Point tool.

CHAPTER 2 ■ GRAPHICS IN ANIMATE CC

Your Turn: Drop a Pin

It's time for you to put what we have shown you into practice. In this little exercise you are going to drop a navigation pin onto a Google map to indicate the location of an animal hospital. Let's get to work:

1. Open the 02_PinDrop.fla file. When it opens you will see an iPhone and a map. The plan is to have a pin point to the North Oakville Animal Hospital on the map.

2. Open the Library. As you can see, the elements of this project are contained in the iPhone folder. If you click once on the NavPin movieclip, the preview shows you there is nothing there. You need to make it.

3. Double-click the NavPin movieclip icon to open it. When it opens, you will see a blank stage with a + sign in the center of the stage. The + sign is showing you the upper-left corner or 0, 0 point of the symbol.

4. In the Tools panel, turn off the stroke by clicking the color chip to open the Color Picker and clicking the "No Color" icon—the square with the diagonal red line.

5. Open the fill color and change change the color to red: FF0000.

6. Select the Oval tool and, with the Shift and Alt/Option keys pressed, draw a circle. Holding down those modifiers draws a perfectly round circle from the center outward.

7. Switch to the Subselection tool and click once on the edge of the circle. This will show you points that make up the vector shape. Seeing as how we are more interested in the shape rather than the fill, click the Show all Shapes as Outlines button on the timeline. You now see just the circle and the points, as shown in Figure 2-30.

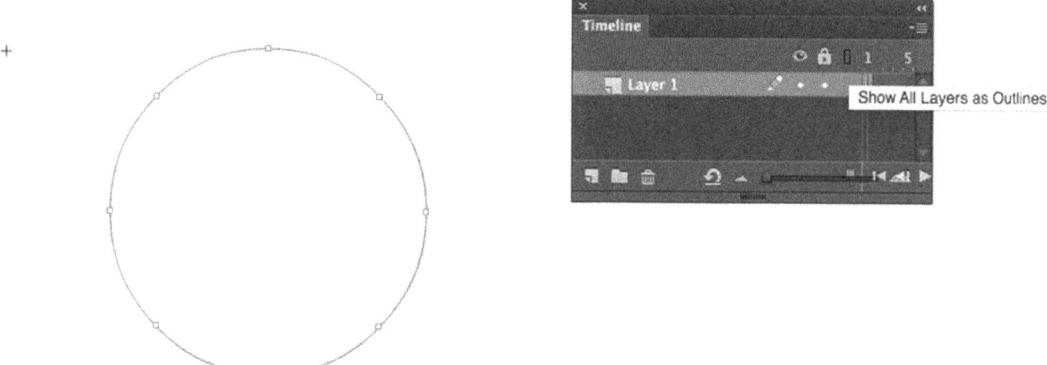

Figure 2-30. *Showing the outlines gives you a clear view of the selected object*

85

CHAPTER 2 ■ GRAPHICS IN ANIMATE CC

A pin isn't a circle. The shape looks like an ice cream cone. This tells you the circle needs to be edited so that two of the three bottom anchor points need to go and the bottom of the circle needs to become a sharp point.

8. Switch to the Pen tool, open its drop-down, and select the Delete Anchor Point tool. Click once on either side of each anchor point at the bottom of the circle to remove them.

9. Switch to the Convert Anchor Point tool and click once on the bottom anchor point. The two lines leading to it become straight lines. What you did was tell Animate the point you just clicked is not a curve it is a corner.

10. Switch to the Subselection and, with the Shift Key held down, drag the bottom point downward until the shape resembles that shown in Figure 2-31. To ensure there is no right or left movement as you drag, another technique is to press the Shift-Down Arrow to move the point downward. Click the Outlines button again to return to the red pin.

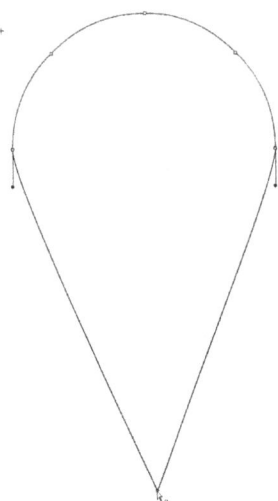

Figure 2-31. *The Pin shape is created*

11. Add a new layer to the Pin's timeline and select the Oval tool.

12. Change the Fill color to white and draw a small white circle in the new layer that is within the top of the Pin. Click the Scene 1 link to return to the main timeline.

Dropping the Pin

The plan is relatively simple: The pin will drop from the upper-right corner of the interface and land just above the Animal Hospital. That may sound simple, but there are three serious considerations involved:

- How long will the motion last?
- Will it move in a gentle arc or straight into its final position?
- How do you get the pin to move from behind the iPhone graphic but above the map?

CHAPTER 2 ■ GRAPHICS IN ANIMATE CC

Answering those questions will result in an animation that is more natural. Let's get started:

1. With the Shift key held down, select Frame 40 of the Phone, Status, and Map Layers.

2. Right-click and select Insert Frame from the Context menu. You have just dealt with the time issue. This movie plays at 24 frames per second and, by adding frames to those three layers, the animation will last just a bit longer than 1.5 seconds.

3. Lock the Map, Status, and Phone layers. You do this because you don't want to accidentally move those elements as you create the motion for the pin drop.

4. Select the Phone layer and add a new layer named Pin.

5. Drag the playhead back to frame 1 and, with the Pin layer selected, drag the NavPin movieclip on to the stage, as shown in Figure 2-32.

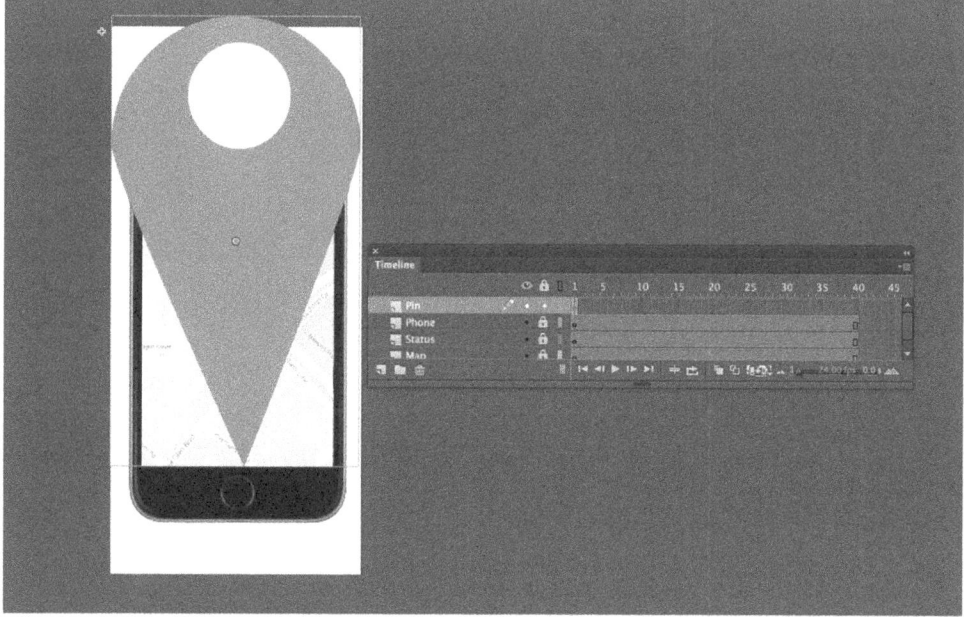

Figure 2-32. *The NavPin movieclip is added to the stage*

> Obviously the pin is too large. Select the Free Transform tool and click on the pin. With the Shift key held down, scale it down to a more appropriate size.

6. Switch to the Selection tool and drag the pin to the upper-right corner of the phone.

7. Right-click on the first frame of the first layer and select Create Motion Tween.

87

CHAPTER 2 ■ GRAPHICS IN ANIMATE CC

8. Drag the playhead to frame 40 and then drag the pin so its point is directly over the Animal Hospital. You will see the path.

9. Place the cursor over one of the dots in middle of the path and drag it to create a curve, as shown in Figure 2-33.

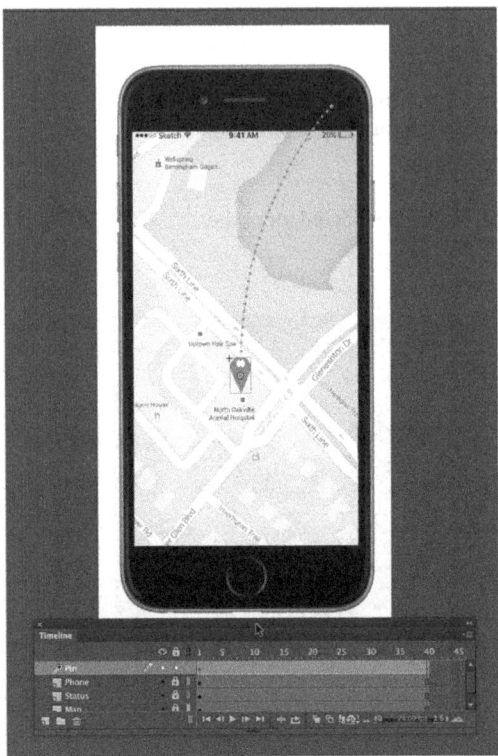

Figure 2-33. *The motion of the pin follows an arc*

10. To move the pin under the phone, drag the Pin Layer on the timeline under the Phone layer. Test your animation by pressing the Return/Enter key.

Working with Color in Animate CC

So far you have spent some time filling objects or strokes with either a solid or a gradient color. The purpose of this section is to dig a bit deeper into the color models available to you as an Animate CC designer and to show you a couple of really snazzy color techniques you can use in your day-to-day workflow. What we aren't going to do is get into color theory or take color down to its molecular level. Entire books have been written on those subjects.

In Animate CC, you have three basic color models available to you: **RGB**, **HSB**, and **Hexadecimal**. Let's briefly look at each one.

The RGB Model

The **RGB model** is the computer color model. Each pixel on your computer monitor is composed of a mixture of red, green, and blue lights. The value for each color is actually based on the old black-and-white model for computers where there were 256 shades of gray that were able to be displayed. The values started at 0 and ended at 255. The best way to imagine this is to think of 0 as being "no light," which means the color is black. This means 255 is pure white. When it comes to the RGB model, each pixel can have a color value that ranges from 0 to 255. If you are looking at a pixel with values of 0 for red, 0 for green, and 255 for blue, you can assume the pixel is pure blue.

The HSB Model

The letters in the **HSB model** represent hue, saturation, and brightness. Hue is the color, saturation is the amount of the color or its purity, and brightness is the intensity of the color. (Note that Animate CC uses the other term for brightness: Luminosity.) The ranges for each value differ in this model. Hue goes from 0 to 360; that's one of 360 degrees around an imaginary wheel of color. Red starts at 0 (the same as 360). Green is one third of the way around the wheel, 120. Blue is two thirds around, 240. To see your secondary colors, shift your travel around the wheel by 60 degrees: yellow is 60, cyan is 180, and magenta is 300. Saturation and brightness are percentages. That pure blue value from the RGB model would here be hue: 240, saturation: 100, luminosity: 100.

The RGB and HSB color modes are shown when you open the Color panel. Make a change to one and it is made in the other.

The Hexadecimal Model

The **Hexadecimal model** is the one commonly used on the Web. In this model, the red, green, and blue values for a pixel can either be a letter ranging from A to F, a number from 0 to 9, or a combination of the letters and numbers. In the case of a blue pixel, the hexadecimal value would be #0000FF.

The six characters in any hexadecimal color are actually three pairs of values: red, green, and blue. We humans, with ten fingers, count in decimal notation. We start with nothing and keep adding 1 to the "ones column" until we hit 9—that's a range of ten values, 0 to 9. Add one more, and the ones column can't go any higher, so it resets to 0, while the "tens column" advances by 1.

Computers aren't so simple. They have 16 fingers on each hand, so their ones column goes from 0 to 15. Columns can only hold one character at a time, so after 9, the value 10 is represented by . . . a letter—the letter A. 11 is represented by B, and so on, until 15, which is F. Add one more, and the ones column can't go any higher, so it resets to 0, while the tens column—actually, the "sixteens column"—advances by one. If your brain hasn't already turned to jelly, good, because even though this doesn't feel normal to us humans, it's not so hard.

That 1 in the sixteens column and 0 in the ones column look like 10, but in hexadecimal notation, that value is 16. 17 would be 11, 18 would be 12, and so on. A 10 in the ones column, as you now know, would be A. So what we would call 26—that is, a 1 in the sixteens column and a 10 in the ones column—would be 1A. Follow that through, and you'll see that FF refers to what we call 255 (that's 15 in the sixteens column, a total of what we call 240, plus a 15 in the ones column).

So hexadecimal notation is just another way to represent a range from 0 to 255 in each of the primary colors.

CHAPTER 2 ■ GRAPHICS IN ANIMATE CC

The Color Palette and the Color Picker

When you click a color chip in Animate CC, the current Color palette, shown in Figure 2-34, opens. The color chips are all are arranged in hexadecimal groupings. As you run your cursor across them, you will see the hex value for the chip you are currently over. The colors on the left side of the Color palette are referred to as the **basic colors**. These are the grays and solids used most often, though we still aren't clear on how the bright pink and the turquoise at the bottom of the common colors made the hit parade.

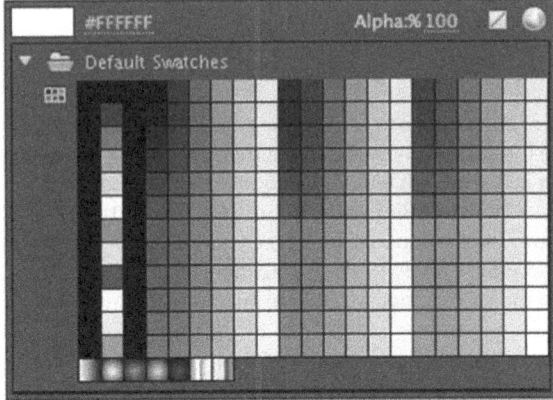

Figure 2-34. *The current Color palette*

There is a reason for the pink and turquoise colors being there. The left-hand column in that Color palette goes like this, from top to bottom: six even distributions of gray, from black to white; then the three primaries (red, green, blue); and finally the three secondaries (yellow, cyan, magenta). These colors, by the way, follow this hex pattern: red, #FF0000; green, #00FF00; blue, #0000FF; yellow, #FFFF00; cyan, #00FFFF; magenta, #FF00FF.

Another really useful feature of this panel is the ability to sample color anywhere on the computer screen when you change the stroke or fill colors. When the Color palette opens, your cursor changes to an eyedropper and, if you roll the cursor across the screen, you will see the hex value of the pixels you're over appearing in the Hex edit box, and the color will appear in the Preview box. This is a relatively dangerous feature because if you click the mouse over a pixel on your screen, that will be the selected color.

The Color Wheel in the upper-right corner, when clicked, opens the Animate CC Color Picker shown in Figure 2-35, which sort of looks like the Northern Lights gone haywire. This pane, called the Color window, contains all of the color you can use in your movies. Click a color, and you will see its RGB and HSB values as well as a preview of the color chosen. You can adjust that color by moving the Luminance slider up or down.

CHAPTER 2 ■ GRAPHICS IN ANIMATE CC

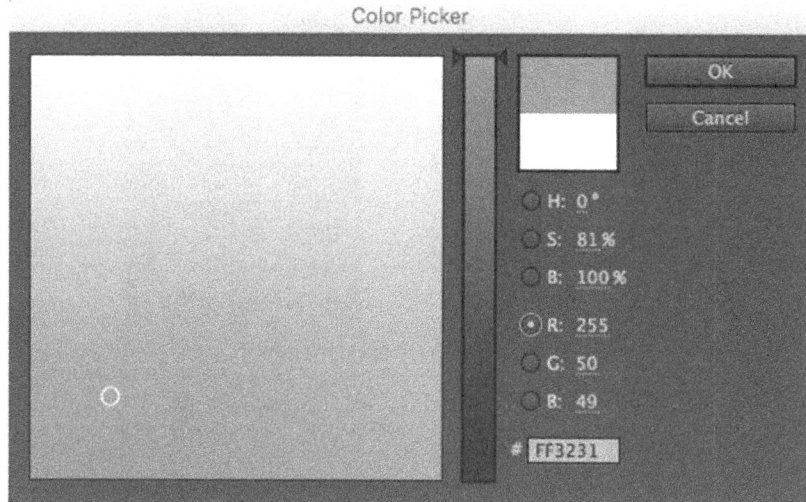

Figure 2-35. *The Animate CC (PC) Color Picker*

How many individual colors are available to you in the Color window? The answer is over 16 million. One of the authors once answered this question, and the student that asked the question remarked, "Is that all?" The author told him that was one seriously large number of crayons in his box, and the student responded," What if I want more?" The author thought about that one for a couple of seconds and asked the student to imagine a crayon box with 16 million crayons. "If you have a box of crayons, are they all given a color name on the label?" asked the author. The student replied, "Of course." The author then said, "Okay, you have in your hands a box containing 16 million crayons. None are labeled. Start naming them." That ended that discussion.

How do we get 16 million colors? First off, the exact number is 16,777,216. At rock bottom, computers use base 2 notation (aka binary), and millions of colors is referred to as being **24-bit color**. Each pixel is comprised of three primary colors, and each color is defined by 8 bits (8 to the 2nd power is 256—aha, a number we already understand!). So that's where the 24 comes from: 3 times 8, which is the same as saying 256 to the 3rd power (256 ~TMS 256 ~TMS 256 —or 2 to the 24th power).

So you have a chosen a bunch of custom colors and are ready to use them in all of your projects? Not quite. They aren't automatically saved when you close Animate CC. If you create a bunch of custom colors and then close Animate CC, they will be gone—forever—when you return to Animate CC. The question, therefore, is how do you save your custom colors?

Creating Persistent Custom Colors

Saving custom colors in Animate CC is not exactly up there in the category of "dead simple." After you have created your custom color, you need to add it to the main Color palette and then save it as a color set. Here's how:

1. Open the Color panel and select the Fill color. Then select Solid Color as the fill type. Create this color—#B74867 (dusty rose)—and make sure it is now the Fill color by pressing the Enter key.

2. Click the Add To Swatches button, as shown in Figure 2-36, and the color is added to the Swatches panel.

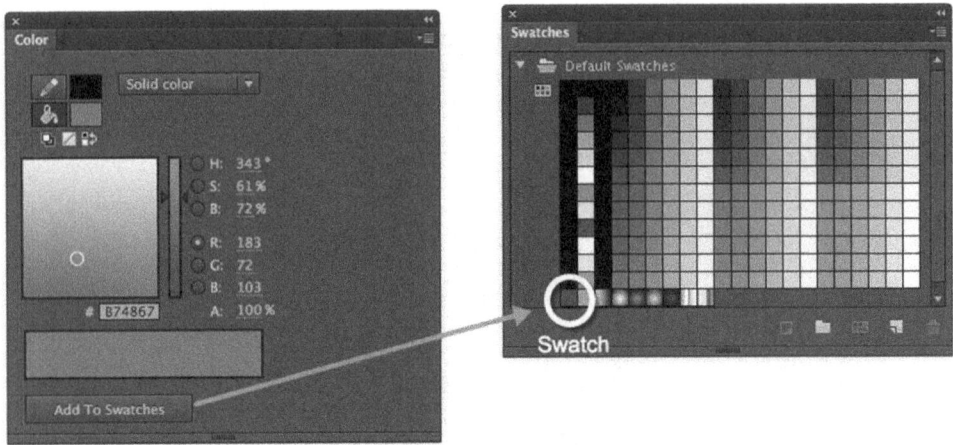

Figure 2-36. *You start by selecting Add To Swatches from the panel menu*

Let's assume you have created a series of custom colors to be used in a web or mobile project. There is a way to save the swatch collection. Here's how:

1. Open the Swatches panel by selecting Window ➤ Swatches or pressing Ctrl+F9 (PC) or Cmd+fn+F9 (Mac).

2. When the panel opens, click the panel menu, shown in Figure 2-37, and select Save Colors. The Save As dialog box will open.

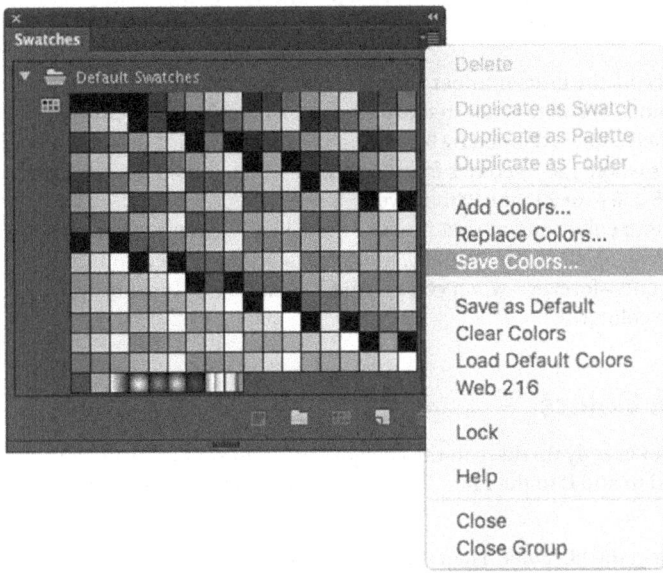

Figure 2-37. *Saving a swatch collection*

CHAPTER 2 ■ GRAPHICS IN ANIMATE CC

If you pay attention to the Save As dialog box, you will notice the file is being saved as an **Animate CC Color Set** or *.clr file.

3. Name your file myFirstSet.clr and, as shown in Figure 2-38, save it to C:\Program Files\Adobe\Adobe Animate CC 2017\Common\First Run (PC). On a Mac, it is a bit different. You need to first hold down the Option key before opening the Library. Then the path is <Hard Drive> / Users / <User Name> / Library/ Application Support / Adobe Animate CC 2017 / en / Configuration / Color Sets (Mac). Click OK to create the CLR file and close the dialog box.

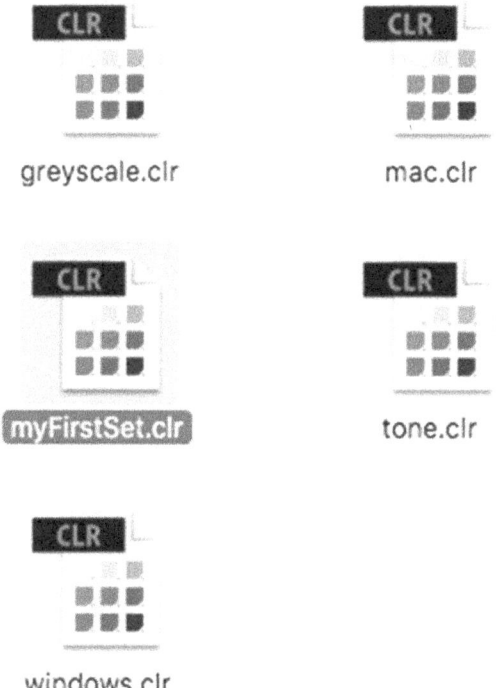

Figure 2-38. A color set

You don't have to use the Animate CC application folder for these. Just put them in a location where they will be handy. Some Animate CC Designers stick them in their My Documents folder, and others put them in the project folder.

4. To load the color set, simply open the Swatches panel and select Add Colors from the panel menu. Navigate to the folder containing the set and double-click it to add the set to Animate CC.

Yes, we agree that is a lot of work. Is there an easier way? In fact, there is. Why not do what the print guys do and attach a color swatch directly to the file? Let's assume you have a client who has six specific corporate colors that must always be used. Create a movieclip containing squares filled with those colors, and then simply put that movieclip on the pasteboard, which is the grey area just outside the stage that doesn't show in the published SWF by default. Anytime you need the color, select the Eyedropper tool and sample it. If you are really lazy, don't add it to the pasteboard and simply sample the color using the Library Preview pane. If you use the colors in a lot of projects, you might even consider adding it to a shared library along with the client's logos and other common elements used in the client's Animate CC projects.

Creating Color Palettes with Creative Cloud Libraries

A few years ago, Adobe introduced a small web-based color picker named *Kuler*. The whole premise behind the application was to give designers the opportunity to freely share custom color schemes with each other. Needless to say, the application was a hit and it was quietly been added to practically every Adobe application that contains a color palette. When Adobe created its Touch Apps, Kuler was "discontinued" and added as the Colors feature of Adobe Capture shown in Figure 2-39.

Figure 2-39. *The Colors feature of Adobe Capture*

CHAPTER 2 ■ GRAPHICS IN ANIMATE CC

The really neat aspect of Capture is the color themes you create can be saved to your Creative Cloud Library, which makes these themes available to you in Animate CC. Here's how to use them:

1. Open a new Animate CC document and, with the Rectangle or Oval tool, draw a shape on the stage.

2. Click the Creative Cloud button in the panels to open the CC Libraries. If you don't see the button, select Window ➤ CC Libraries.

3. Scroll to the Color Themes area of the Library. You will know you are there because you will see a series of color swatches. Roll the cursor over the swatches and, as shown in Figure 2-40, the swatches will have names. If you place the cursor over one of the swatches, a tooltip appears showing you the Hexadecimal and RGB values of that color.

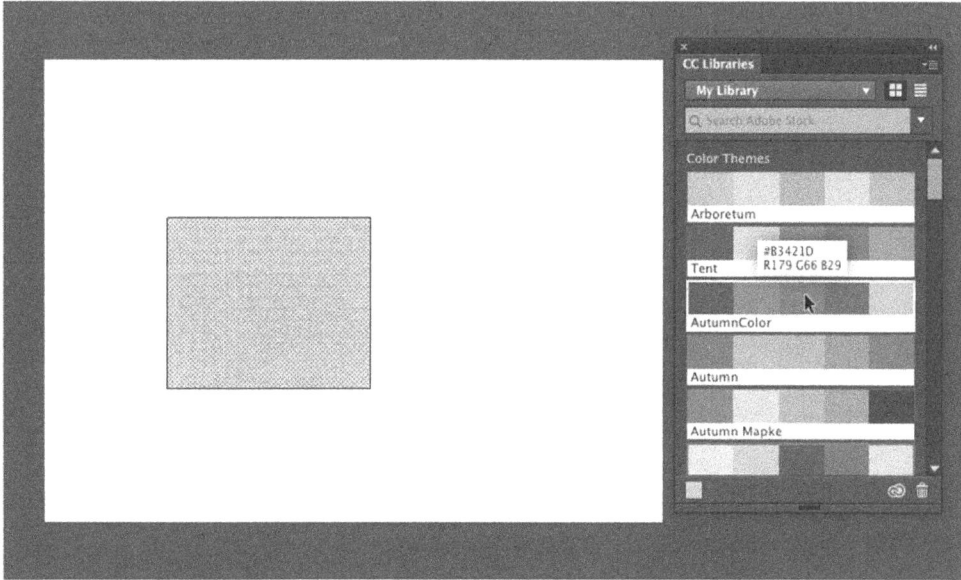

Figure 2-40. *The color themes in a Creative Cloud Library*

4. With the shape selected, click on one of the color swatches. That color is applied to the shape.

5. To save the color to the current swatches, open the Color panel and click the Save To Swatches button.

Your Turn: Playing with Color

Here are a few tricks you can do with color. Two involve the standard use of a tool, but the other is right up there in the realm of "waaay cool".

CHAPTER 2 ■ GRAPHICS IN ANIMATE CC

The first trick involves a gradient. Did you know Animate CC allows you to create a variety of gradient effects with the click of a mouse? Here's how:

1. Open a new ActionScript 3.0 document and create a big rectangle filled using the leftmost gradient in the bottom-left corner of the Fill Color Picker.

2. Switch to the Gradient Transform tool and resize the fill so it is much smaller than the rectangle. When you shorten the gradient, the black and white areas of the gradient become larger. This is because Animate CC is filling the rectangle with the end colors. This process is called **overflowing**.

3. Open the Color panel and click the middle chip in the Flow area of the panel.

The Flow Options for gradients are only available to ActionScript 3.0 documents.

These choices, from left to right, are as follows:

- **Extend the default:** The two last colors in the gradient extend to fill the shape.

- **Reflect:** The overflow area of the rectangle will be filled with repeating versions of the gradient. Every other version is mirrored/reflected. Select this, and the rectangle looks like stacked pipes (see Figure 2-41).

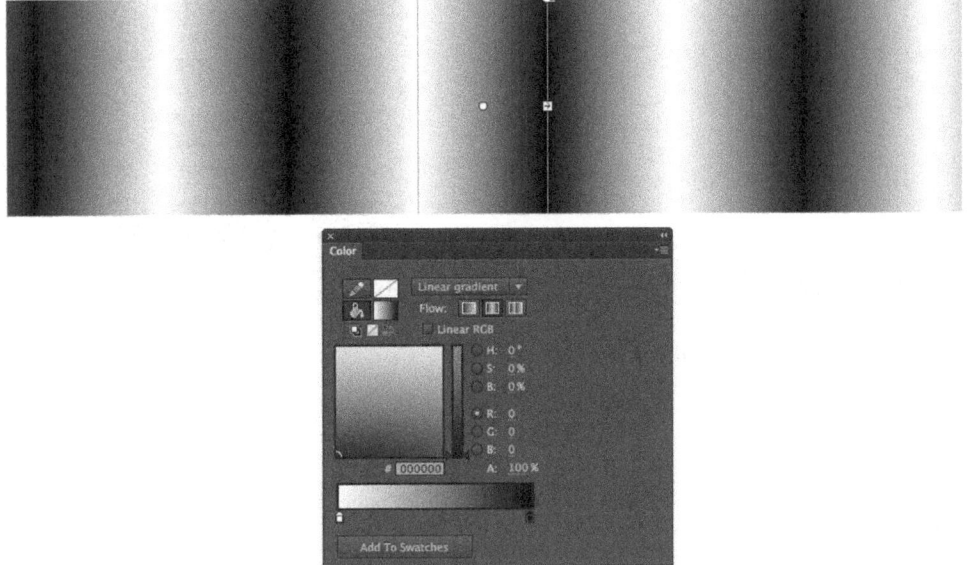

Figure 2-41. The Reflect overflow

- **Repeat:** The gradients aren't reflected, they are repeated. The result is the "venetian blind" look.

CHAPTER 2 ■ GRAPHICS IN ANIMATE CC

If you really want to rock and roll with this technique, change the gradient type to Radial, reduce the size of the gradient with the Gradient Transform tool, and select the Repeat option. As shown in Figure 2-42, the result resembles the "Looney Tunes" logo background.

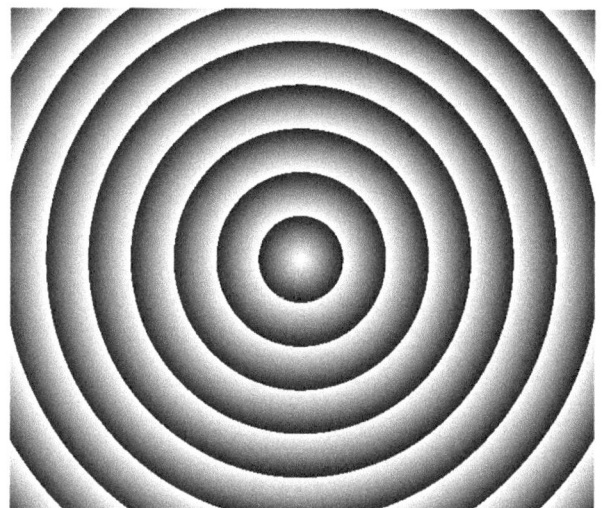
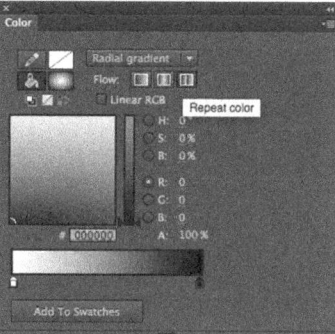

Figure 2-42. *That's all folks*

The next technique is one a lot of Animate CC designers tend to overlook: using an image, not a gradient or a solid color, to fill an object. There are two methods of accomplishing this, and they each have a different result. Let's try them:

 1. Open the `ImageFill.fla` file and select the PolyStar tool under the Oval tool.

 2. Before you merrily start dragging, open the Properties panel and click the Options button at the bottom. The Tool Settings dialog box, shown in Figure 2-43, opens. From there, you select Star from the Style drop-down and click OK.

CHAPTER 2 ■ GRAPHICS IN ANIMATE CC

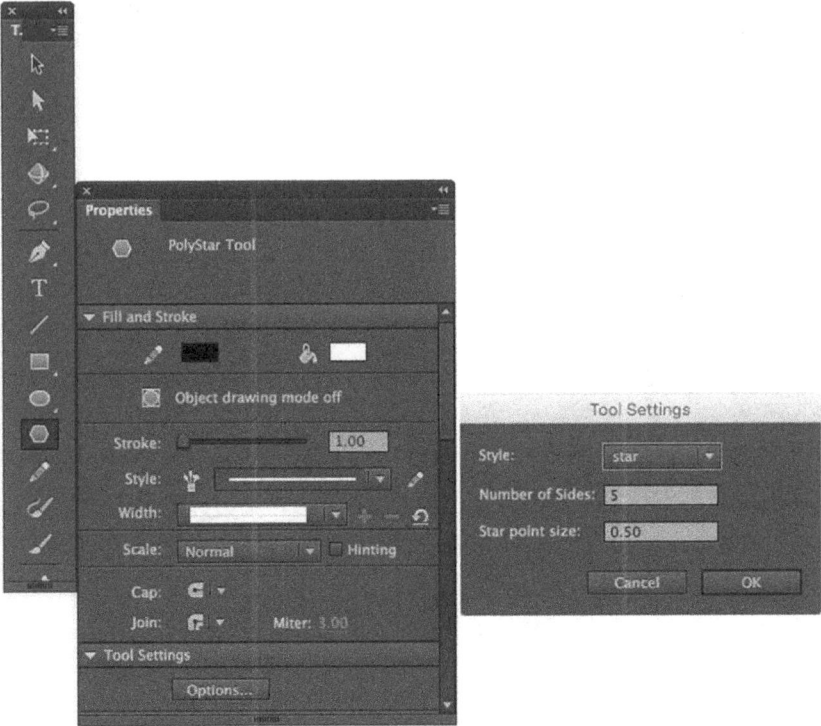

***Figure 2-43.** Select the PolyStar tool, click the Options, choose Star, and then you can build a universe*

3. Set the Stroke color to None and the Fill Color to White. Draw your star.

4. Open the Color panel and, as shown in Figure 2-44, select Bitmap Fill from the drop-down as the fill type. In cases where the file does not yet contain imported images, an Import to Library dialog box will open at this point. In this sample file, an image of the Flatiron Building in Toronto already exists in the Library panel, so you'll see the Import button instead.

CHAPTER 2 ■ GRAPHICS IN ANIMATE CC

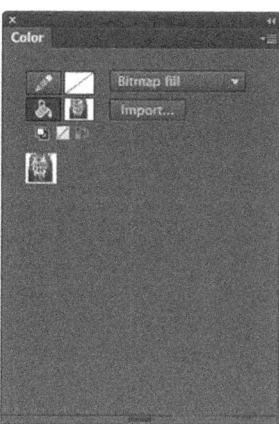

Figure 2-44. Bitmap images can be used to fill objects

5. Click the Import button, if you like, to import an image of your own. If you go this route, use the Import to Library dialog box to navigate to an image. Select the image and click OK to close the dialog box. Of course, you're welcome to use the already-imported Building.jpg. If you take a look at the Fill chip in the Color panel, the image is in the chip and in the Fill area of the Tools panel.

6. Select the Gradient Transform tool to adjust the tiled image in various ways. Given the minuscule size of the tiles, you may want to zoom in first.

Here's the second method:

1. Add your image or the one we supplied in the Library to the stage. Click the photo on the stage and select Modify ➤ Break Apart or press Ctrl+B (PC) or Cmd+B (Mac). The image looks crosshatched.

2. Select the Eyedropper tool and click once in the photo. The image will appear in the Fill color chip of the Tools panel.

3. Draw a shape, select the Paint Bucket tool, and then click in the shape. The image will fill the shape.

CHAPTER 2 ■ GRAPHICS IN ANIMATE CC

Figure 2-45. *Another way of using a bitmap as a fill*

This technique is a handy way of masking a static image that could be used in a mobile prototype or web page.

Now that you have finally had a chance to use a bitmap, let's take a closer look at how such images are used in Animate CC.

Using Bitmap Images in Animate CC

At this point in the book, you have been working with vectors. Though we have been telling you they are the most wonderful things in the Animate CC universe, we are sure our photographer friends are not exactly happy campers. Let's face it—you are going to be using bitmaps in your workflow. You can't avoid them, and they are just as important as vectors. In fact, Adobe has really improved how Animate CC manages images and integrates with Photoshop and Illustrator.

In this final section of the chapter, we are going to look at how you can use bitmap images in your workflow. We are going to talk about the image formats you can use; cover how to import images from Photoshop, Sketch, and Illustrator into Animate CC; and even show you how to convert a bitmap image to a vector image in Animate CC. Let's start with the formats that can be imported.

As an Adobe application, it is not surprising that Animate CC can import the following formats:

- **AI:** Adobe Illustrator. This is the native Illustrator file format. This format allows Animate CC to preserve the layers in your Illustrator document. The good news is the Illustrator-to-Animate CC workflow has had its molecules rearranged and turned inside-out—in a good way.

- **SVG:** Scalable Vector Graphics. Think of SVG graphics as vector drawings for the masses that can appear anywhere. They can be created in Adobe Illustrator and output in the SVG format. The format is a mass of XML-code which computers just adore. In fact, if you open your iPhone or Android device the odds are about 100% the icons you see are, in fact, SVG graphics.

- **GIF:** Graphic Interchange Format. This is the former standard for imaging on the Web. The upside of this format is the real small file size. The downside is the color palette is limited to 256 colors. These files come in two flavors: transparent and regular. The increasing use of Animate CC banner ads, with their strict file size requirements, has resulted in a resurgence of this format on web sites.

- **PNG:** Portable Network Graphic. Think of PNG files as a combination vector/bitmap file. This format supports variable bit depth (PNG-8 and PNG-24) and compression settings with support for alpha channels.

- **JPEG or JPG:** Joint Photographic Experts Group. This is the current standard for web imaging, and any image arriving in Animate CC will be converted to this format when the SWF is published.

- **PDF:** Portable Document Format. PDF is a cross-platform standard used in the publishing industry.

- **EPS:** Encapsulated PostScript. Think of this as a raw vector file.

- **PSD:** Photoshop Document. This is the native Photoshop file format. A PSD image usually contains multiple layers. Again, the workflow between Animate CC and Photoshop CC has undergone a profound change for the better.

A bitmap or raster image is nothing more than a collection of pixels. The reason bitmap images have taken a bit of a "bum rap" in the Animate CC community is because the image file needs to map and remember the location of each pixel in the image. The result is a large file size, which tends to go against the grain in a community that chants: "Small is beautiful. Small loads fast."

Use bitmaps when you need photos or lifelike images, when you need a screenshot, or when you need pictures of drawings or artwork. In fact, a good rule of thumb is to look at a bitmap image and ask, "Could I draw this in Animate CC?" If the answer is yes, you might want to consider that route instead.

The best advice we can give you about bitmaps is to make them as small as possible—a process called **optimization**—in the originating application. For example, Photoshop contains an Optimize panel, shown in Figure 2-46, which allows you to compare the effects of various image settings upon an image. In Illustrator, see if you can reduce the number of points in your shapes, and make sure you have removed all of the stray points that aren't connected to anything or serving any purpose in your artwork. In Photoshop, reduce the image size to fit the image size in Animate CC. These applications were designed to perform these tasks; Animate CC wasn't.

CHAPTER 2 ■ GRAPHICS IN ANIMATE CC

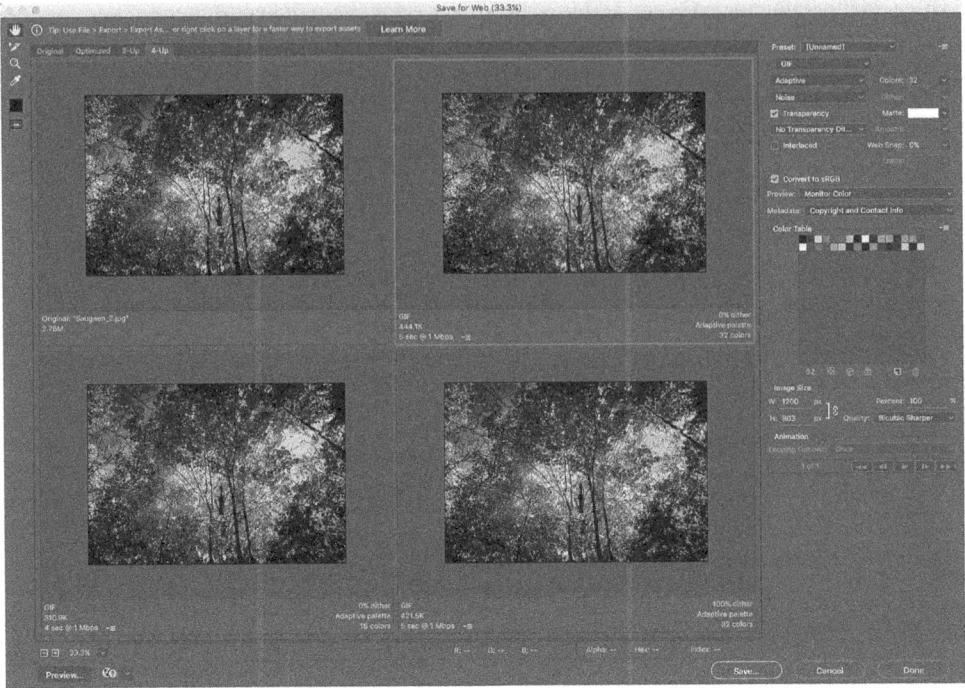

Figure 2-46. *4-Up image optimization in Photoshop allows you to balance quality against image size*

Working with Bitmaps Inside Animate CC

The decision is final. You need to use a bitmap and place it in Animate CC. Then you discover the color is all wrong or something needs to be cropped out of the image. It needs to be edited. How do you do it? Follow these steps:

1. Open a new Animate CC document and select File ➤ Import ➤ Import to Stage. When the Import dialog box opens, navigate to the `River.jpg` file.

2. Select the file and click Open to close the Import dialog box. The image will appear on the stage and in the Library, as shown in Figure 2-47.

CHAPTER 2 ■ GRAPHICS IN ANIMATE CC

Figure 2-47. *Images imported to the stage are automatically placed in the Library*

   Do not delete the image from the Library. This is the original bitmap, and deleting it will ripple through an entire project. If you screw something up on the stage, delete the image on the stage.

3. Right-click (PC) or Ctrl+click (Mac) the image in the Library to open the context menu.

4. Select Edit With. This will launch the Open dialog box, allowing you to navigate to the application folder containing the application you will be using to edit the image. If you select Photoshop, the image will launch in Photoshop. When you make your changes, select Edit ➤ Save. When you return to Animate CC, the change made in Photoshop CC will be reflected both in the image on the stage and in the Library. This process, for those of you who might be interested, is called "roundtripping".

Your Turn: Tracing Bitmaps in Animate CC

Tracing converts an image to a series of vectors. On the surface, this sounds like a win/win for everybody. Not quite. Yes, you get a vector image with all the benefits of scalability and so on, but you also inherit a whack of potential problems along the way.

Tracing an Image

There are no hard-and-fast rules in this area, so it is best to experiment. Let's fire up the Bunsen burner:

1. Open the `04_Trace.fla` file. You will see two images of temple painting from a small temple in the Chinese village of Hougou.

2. Click the image and select Modify ➤ Bitmap ➤ Trace Bitmap to open the Trace Bitmap dialog box. Specify the values shown in Figure 2-48.

103

CHAPTER 2 ■ GRAPHICS IN ANIMATE CC

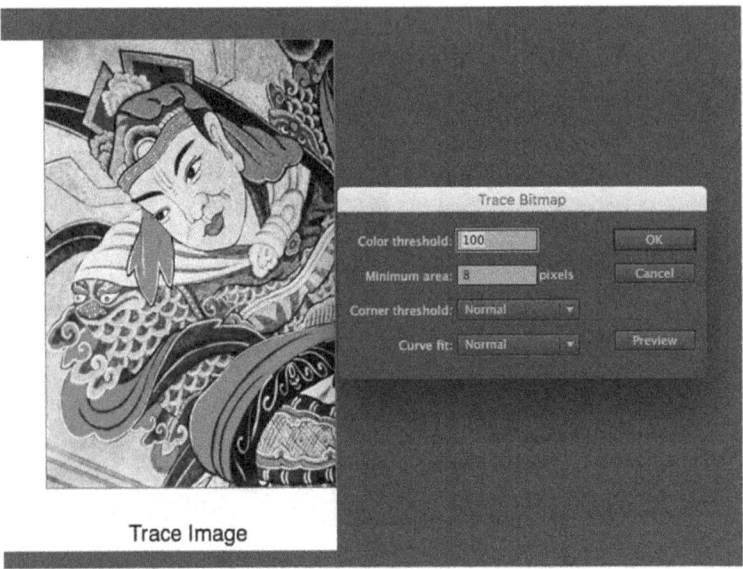

Figure 2-48. *The Trace Bitmap dialog box*

The settings aren't all that mysterious:

- **Color threshold:** The higher the number, the more colors are considered a match and the fewer the vectors. Set this value to 100.

- **Minimum area:** The number entered here defines the smallest size for a vector shape. If you want a really detailed image, use a low number. Just keep in mind: the smaller the number, the more the shapes, the larger the file size. In fact, extremely complex vectors can, and often do, carry a greater file size penalty than the bitmap images they're based on. Set this value to 8 pixels.

- **Corner threshold:** This value determines how much a line can bend before Animate CC breaks it into corners. The fewer the corners, the smaller the file's size. (Picking up a theme here?)

- **Curve fit:** Think of this as being a smoothing setting. Select Pixels, and you get a very accurate trace. Select Very Smooth, and curves really round out. Again, the fewer the curves, the smaller the file size.

3. Click the Preview button to see the effect of your choices, as shown in Figure 2-49.

Figure 2-49. *A traced bitmap is on the right and the original image is on the left. Note the loss of minor detail*

  4. Click Cancel.
  5. Now you'll see what happens when you use even closer tolerances. Select the image on the right of the stage and open the Trace Bitmap dialog box. Specify these values:
     - Color threshold: 15
     - Corner threshold: Many corners
     - Curve fit: Pixels
  6. Click the Preview button. The progress bar will take a bit longer this time, and when it finishes, the difference between the original image and the vector image is not readily evident. Click OK to apply the changes.

You are about to find out that there is indeed a major difference between the original bitmap and the traced image. The difference becomes evident when you optimize the image.

Optimizing the Drawing

In Animate CC, optimizing a drawing means you are reducing the number of corners in a traced image and smoothing out the lines in the traced image to give you a smaller and less precise image. Though you can optimize any drawing you have in Animate CC, this technique is best applied to traced images. Here's how:

  1. Change to the Selection tool and marquee the image you traced. Select Modify ➤ Shape ➤ Optimize to open the Optimize Curves dialog box shown in Figure 2-50.

CHAPTER 2 ■ GRAPHICS IN ANIMATE CC

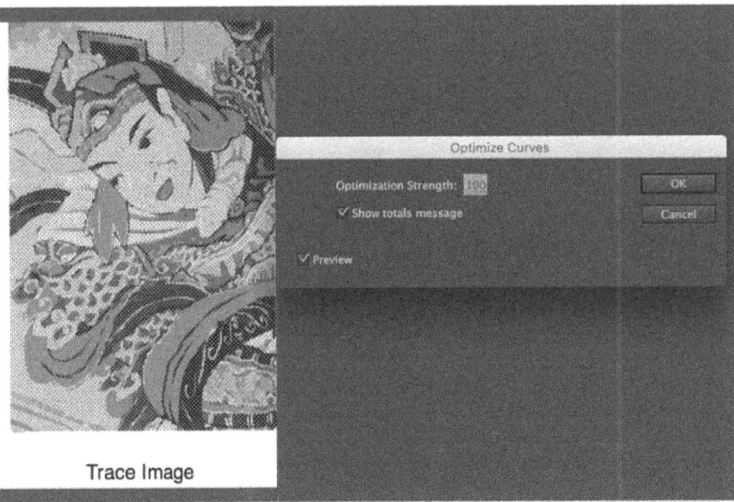

Figure 2-50. *The Optimize Curves dialog box lets you reduce the size of a traced image*

2. Change the Optimization Strength value to the Maximum value of 100 and click OK. The process starts, and when it finishes, you will be presented with an Alert box telling you how many curves have been optimized (see Figure 2-51).

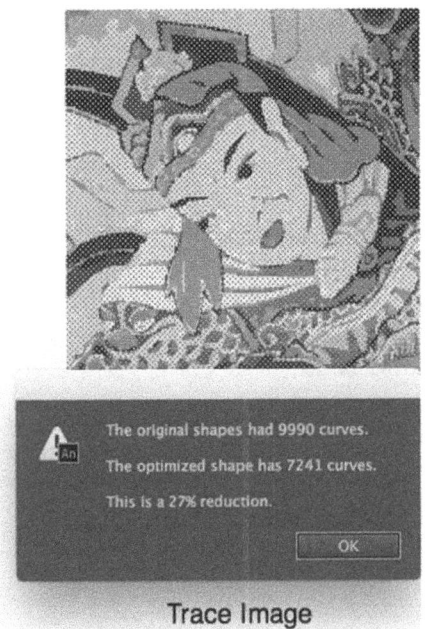

Figure 2-51. *A 27% curve reduction leads to a hefty file size reduction*

106

The downside is the image loses a lot of its precision, and some of the curves become spiky because Animate CC converted all the pixilated smoothness to vectors. If you click Cancel and repeat the process on the second image but only move the Smoothing slider to the midpoint, the process will take a lot longer than the previous one, and the curve reduction will be minimal. This is because you essentially created a high-resolution vector image, so there are a lot more curves to check out. The bottom line here is the decision regarding using a bitmap, tracing it, and optimizing the curves is up to you.

JPG Files and Animate CC

The JPG, or JPEG, file format is the one used for photos. As mentioned earlier, JPEG stands for Joint Photographic Experts Group and is a method of compressing an image using areas of contiguous color. The file size reductions can be significant with minimal to moderate image quality loss. This explains why this format has become a de facto imaging format for digital media. In this exercise, you are going to learn how to optimize a JPG image in Animate CC.

Before you do this, it is extremely important you understand that the JPG format is **lossy**. This means each time a JPG image is compressed in the JPG format, the image quality degrades. The point here is you have to make a decision regarding JPG images before they arrive in Animate CC. Will the compression be done in Photoshop, or will Animate CC handle the chores? If the answer is Animate CC, always set the JPG Quality slider in Photoshop to 100% to apply minimal compression. If you don't know where the image came from or what compression was used, don't let Animate CC handle the compression.

1. Open the 05_JPGCompression.fla file in the Chapter02/Exercises folder. When it opens, you will notice the movie contains nothing more than a single JPG image, and the stage matches the image dimensions. In short, there is no wasted space that can skew the results of this experiment.

2. Double-click the image in the Library to open the Bitmap Properties dialog box shown in Figure 2-52.

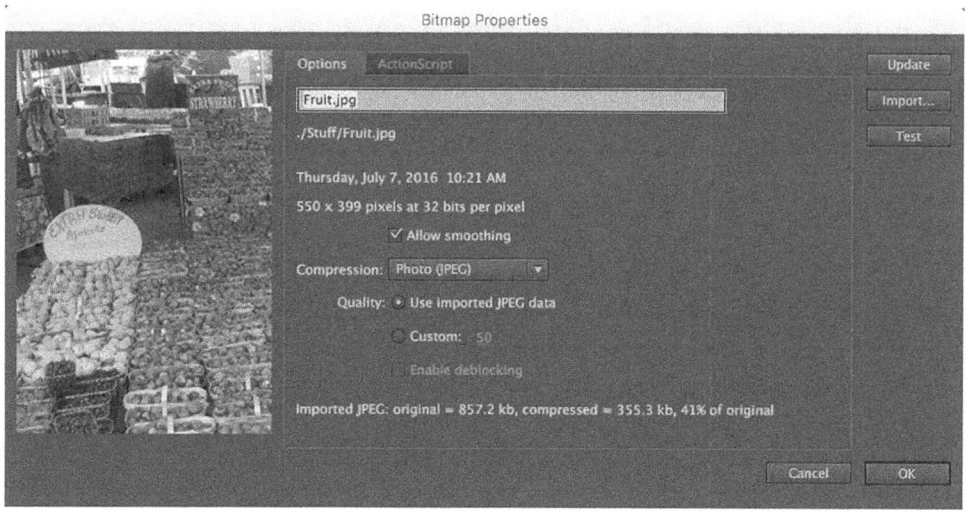

Figure 2-52. *The Bitmap Properties dialog box*

Be aware that any changes made in the Bitmap Properties dialog box ripple through the entire movie and will override the defaults used in the Publish dialog box.

Let's examine the Bitmap Properties dialog box. To start, the image on the left side is the preview image. As you start playing with some of the settings, this image will show you the final result of your choices. This is a good thing because changes you make in this dialog box are only visible when the project is playing; they won't be reflected in the image on the stage. The other areas are:

- **Name:** The name of the file. If you want to rename the file, select it and enter a new name. This only changes the name by which Animate CC knows the file—it does not "reach outside of Animate CC" and rename the original image.

- **Path, Date, Dimensions:** Fairly self-explanatory. There will be the odd occasion where this info will not be displayed. The reason is the image was pasted in from the clipboard.

- **Update button:** If you have edited the image without using the Edit with feature, clicking this button will replace the image with the new version. This button will not work if you have saved or moved the original image to a new location on the computer. To "reconnect" such a broken link, respecify the image file's location with the Import button, explained next.

- **Import button:** Click this, and you open the Import Bitmap dialog box. When using this button, the new file will replace the image in the library, and all instances of that image in your movie will also be updated.

- **Allow Smoothing option:** Think of this as anti-aliasing applied to an image. This feature tends to blur an image, so use it judiciously. Where it really shines is when it is applied to low-res images because it reduces the dreaded jaggies.

- **Compression drop-down menu:** This allows you to change the image compression to either Photo (JPEG) or Lossless (PNG/GIF). Use Photo (JPEG) for photographs and Lossless (PNG/GIF) for images with simple shapes and few colors, such as lineart or logos. To help you wrap your mind around this, the image in the dialog box uses Photo (JPEG) compression, and if you click the Test button, the file size is about 2.4KB. Apply Lossless compression and click the Test button, and the file size rockets up to 142KB.

- **Use Imported JPEG Data option:** Select this check box if the image has already been compressed or if you aren't sure whether compression has been applied. Checking this avoids the nasty results of applying double compression to an image.

- **Quality option:** If you deselect the Use Imported JPEG data check box, you can apply your own compression settings. In fact, let's try it.

3. Make sure your compression setting is Photo (JPEG) and that you have deselected the Use Imported JPEG Data check box. Change the Quality value to 10% and click the Test button. The image in the Preview area, shown in Figure 2-53, is just plain awful. The good news is the file size, at the bottom of the dialog box, is 6.9KB.

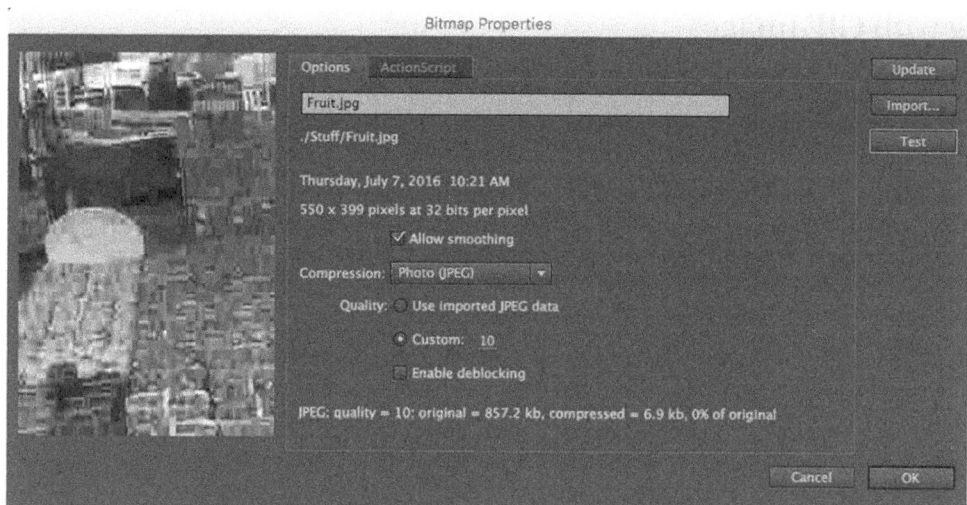

Figure 2-53. *At 10% quality, the image is terrible*

4. Change the Quality setting to 40% and click the Test button. Things are a little better, but the text in the banner a bit looks pixelated, and the file size has increased.

5. Change the Quality value to the normal 80% value used by imaging applications and click the Test button. The text issue is resolved but the file size has increased again. As you are seeing, there is an intimate relationship between the Quality setting and file size.

6. Knowing the quality between 50% and 80% is a vast improvement, let's see if we can maintain quality but reduce the file size. Set the Quality value to 65% and click the Test button. The difference between 65% and 80% is minimal, but the file size has reduced to 3KB. Click OK to apply this setting and close the dialog box.

Using GIF Files in Animate CC

There was point a few years back where many web and Animate CC designers were preparing to celebrate the death of the GIF image and the GIF animation. The reason was simple: in a universe where bandwidth is plentiful and every computer on the planet is able to display 16-bit color, the limited color range and small file size of a GIF image that made the format so important were irrelevant. GIF images were developed at a time when computer screens had a limited color depth—monitors that could only display 256 colors—and dial-up modems. Then a funny thing happened on the way to the wake; GIFs arose from their deathbed. The reason was banner advertising.

Ad agencies and their clients were discovering the Web really was a viable advertising medium and that Animate CC was a great interactive tool for ads. The problem was, standards for banner advertising appeared on the scene, and the agencies discovered they had a file size limit of 30KB. This tended to go against the grain and, as they grappled with the requirement for small files, they rediscovered the GIF image and the GIF animation.

This isn't to say you should use the GIF format only in banner ads. It can be used in quite a few situations in which size is a prime consideration.

CHAPTER 2 ■ GRAPHICS IN ANIMATE CC

Working with GIF Images

Here's how to use GIF images and GIF animations in Animate CC:

1. Open the 05_GIF.fla file in the Chapter02/Exercises folder. When the file opens, open the Library. There are two GIF files in the Library.

2. Drag the Figurines image from the Library to the stage. Notice how you can see the stage color behind the image. This image is a transparent GIF. When it comes to GIF transparency, you have to understand it is an absolute. It is either on or it is off. There are no shades of opacity with this format. GIFs may contain up to 256 colors, and one of those colors may be transparent.

3. Drag the FigurinesNoTrans file to the stage and place it under the image that's already there. This image is a GIF image with no transparency applied.

4. Select the image you just dragged onto the stage and press the Ctrl+B (PC) or Cmd+B (Mac) combination to break the image apart. Hold on, that isn't right. Only the figurines in the image break apart (see Figure 2-54). That is an expected behavior. Remember what we said in the previous step? The background in a GIF image is either on or off. If it is on, it can't be removed in Animate CC.

Figure 2-54. *Transparent and regular GIFs are treated differently in Animate CC*

CHAPTER 2 ■ GRAPHICS IN ANIMATE CC

When you break apart an image like the above Figure, here's what's really going on. That image is simply translated into a shape with a bitmap fill. It is the same thing as drawing a shape and filling it with that bitmap. This is why file size is identical between the white and transparent versions of this image. The GIF is the same in all respects—except that the color slot in one file's color table is white and in the other file's color table is transparent. But both GIFs have the same number of colors and weigh the same.

5. To "get rid of" the white background, you can select the Magic Wand tool and click somewhere in the white background to select it and then press the Delete key.

6. Close the file and don't save the changes.

Working with GIF Animations

Animated GIFs are a bit different. They are a collection of static images—think of a flip book—that play, one after the other, at a set rate, all stored inside a single GIF file. These flip book "pages" can be imported either directly into the main timeline (not a good idea) or into a separate movieclip. Here's how:

1. Open a new Animate CC document and create a new movieclip named AnimatedGif. The Symbol Editor will open.

2. Select File ➤ Import ➤ Import to Stage, and when the Open dialog box appears, locate the Counterforce.gif file, select it, and click the Open button.

3. When the import is finished, you will see that each frame of the animation has its own Animate CC frame and each image in the animation, as shown in Figure 2-55, has its own image in the Library.

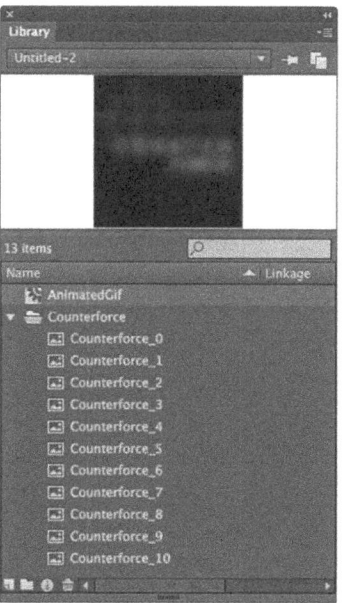

Figure 2-55. *Importing GIF animations into a movieclip*

111

CHAPTER 2 ■ GRAPHICS IN ANIMATE CC

4. Press the Enter key to test the animation or click the Scene 1 link to return to the main timeline, add the movieclip to the stage, and test the movie.

A good habit to develop is to place the images in the Library in a folder. This way your library doesn't end up looking like what your mom would call "a pig sty."

Importing Photoshop Documents into Animate CC

It is a fact of life that Photoshop is becoming a de facto imaging standard for web and mobile design. One of the common approaches is to design these interfaces and projects using multiple layers in the Photoshop document and then saving the resulting .psd document to retain the layers. One of the really neat aspects of Animate CC is you have the ability to import these .psd documents with their layers intact. This means you can easily add interactivity and motion to your designs, such as the one shown in Figure 2-56, without a cumbersome back and forth between Photoshop CC and Animate CC. Here's how:

Figure 2-56. *We start with a .psd image*

1. Open a new Animate CC document. When the New Document dialog box opens, click on the Templates button. Select Advertising from the Category list and 728 x90 Leaderboard from the Template list, as shown in Figure 2-57. Click OK to open the template.

112

CHAPTER 2 ■ GRAPHICS IN ANIMATE CC

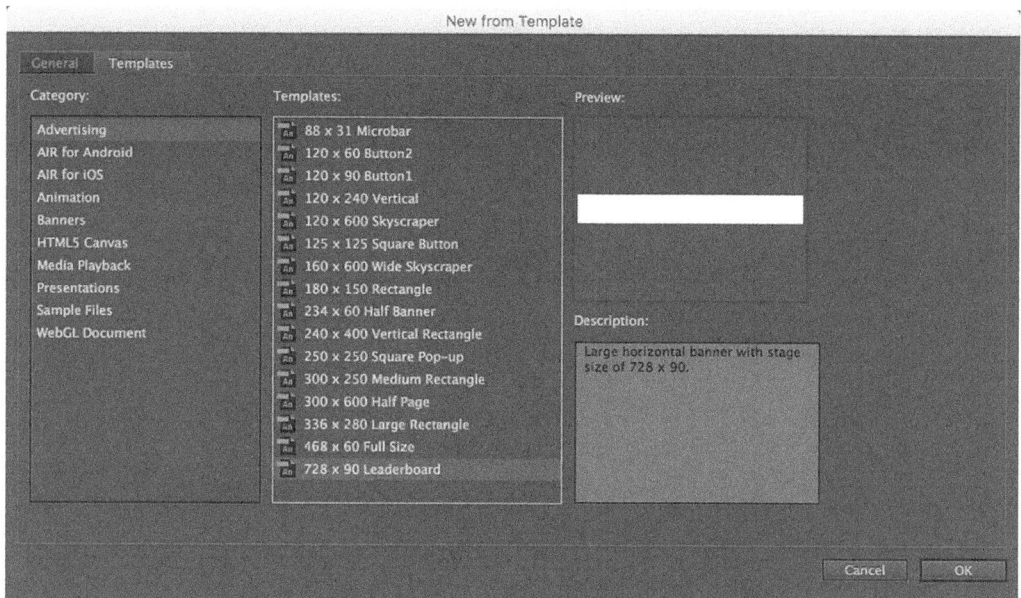

Figure 2-57. *Opening an Animate CC template*

2. Select File ➤ Import to Library and navigate to the Banner.psd image in the Chapter02/Exercises folder.

3. When you click the Open button, the dialog box will close and the Import "Banner.psd" to Library dialog box, shown in Figure 2-58, will open.

113

CHAPTER 2 ■ GRAPHICS IN ANIMATE CC

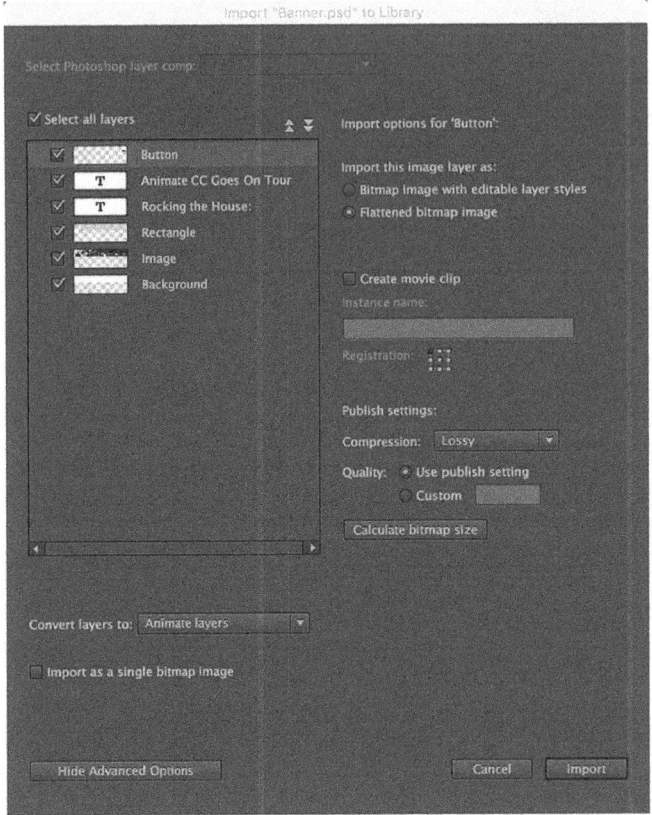

Figure 2-58. *The Import dialog box*

Let's review the options:

- **Select All Layers:** You choose which layers in the .psd document are to be imported.

- **Convert layers to:** You have three choices. You can choose to bring all of the selected layers into Animate CC as individual layers on the timeline. If you want to flatten them into one layer and still retain the images, select Single Animate Layer.

- **Keyframes**: This choice puts each layer on the timeline as a keyframe.

The options on the right determine how each imported layer is to be treated. They are context sensitive. For example, if you select a text layer you can treat the text in that layer as editable.

- **Import as a Single Bitmap Image:** Click this check box to flatten the image.

- **Bitmap image with editable layer styles:** This creates a movieclip with a bitmap inside and any supported blend modes, filters, and opacity are maintained. Blend modes that cannot be reproduced in Animate are removed. The object must be converted to a movieclip.

- **Import as Flattened bitmap image:** Rasterizes the text into a bitmap to preserve the exact appearance of the layer in Photoshop.

- **Create Movie Clip:** The selected layers are converted to movieclips when imported into Animate.

- **Instance name:** Specifies the name of the imported instance.

- **Registration:** Lets you set the registration point for your movieclip.

- **Compression:** Lets you choose lossy or lossless compression formats. Lossy **compresses** the image in JPEG format.

- **Use Publish Setting:** To use the default compression quality specified for the imported image, select Use Publish Setting.

- **Custom:** To specify a new quality compression setting, select the Custom option and enter a value between 1 and 100 in the Quality text field.

- **Calculate Bitmap Size:** To calculate the size of all the bitmaps to be imported, select all the layers and click Calculate Bitmap Size.

4. Go with the default values for this example. Click Import to import the image into Animate CC.

5. When the import finishes, you will see the Photoshop Asset folder in the Library. Open it, and you will see that Animate CC has created a folder for the page just imported. If you open that folder, you will see the various layers.

Importing Illustrator CC Documents into Animate CC

Animate CC lets you import Illustrator CC AI files directly into Animate CC and generally allows you to edit each piece of the artwork when it is in Animate CC. The Illustrator File Importer also provides you with a great degree of control in determining how your Illustrator artwork is imported into Animate CC. For example, you can now specify which layers and paths in the Illustrator document will be imported into Animate CC and even have the Illustrator file be converted to an Animate CC movieclip.

The Animate CC Illustrator File Importer provides the following key features:

- Preserves editability of the most commonly used Illustrator effects such as the Illustrator effects and blend modes that Animate CC and Illustrator have in common.

- Preserves the fidelity and editability of gradient fills.

- Imports Illustrator symbols as Animate CC symbols.

- Preserves the number and position of Bézier control points; the fidelity of clip masks, pattern strokes, and fills; and object transparency.

- Provides an improved copy-and-paste workflow between Illustrator CC and Animate CC. A copy-and-paste dialog box provides settings to apply to AI files being pasted onto the Animate CC stage.

- You can import Illustrator artboards, which makes creating mobile prototypes a relatively easy process.

CHAPTER 2 ■ GRAPHICS IN ANIMATE CC

To many Animate CC designers, that list is "nirvana," but there are two critical aspects of the Illustrator-to-Animate CC workflow that you must keep in mind:

- Animate CC only supports the RGB color space. If the Illustrator image is a CMYK image, do the CMYK-to-RGB conversion in Illustrator before importing the file into Animate CC.

- To preserve drop shadow, inner glow, outer glow, and Gaussian blur effects in Animate CC, import the object to which these filters are applied as an Animate CC movieclip. In Animate CC, these filters can be applied only to movieclips.

Let's import an Illustrator drawing to see what is causing all of the joy. The file we will be using, Mascot.ai, contains a number of Illustrator layers and paths (see Figure 2-59). One path—in the Head layer—contains a drop shadow.

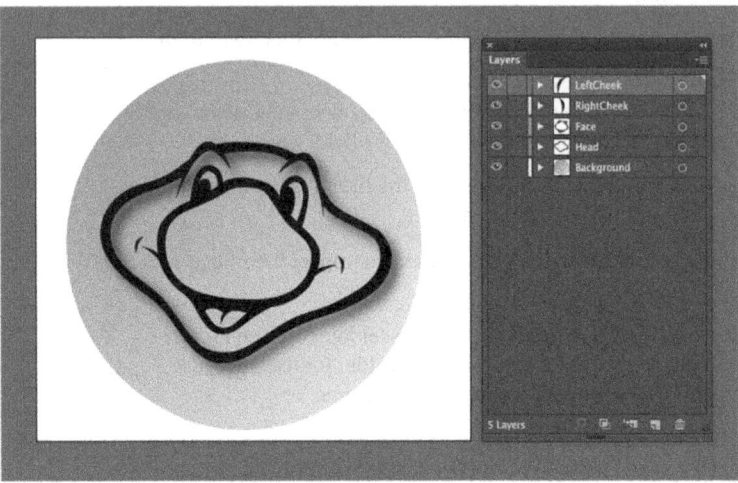

Figure 2-59. *The Illustrator file for this example contains a number of layers and paths*

The authors would like to thank Mischa Plocek for the use of the `Mascot.ai` file. Mischa is an Animate CC developer/artist based in Zurich, Switzerland and his work can be seen at www.styleterrorist.com.

Follow these steps to import an Illustrator CC document into Animate CC:

1. Open a new Animate CC document and import the `Mascot.ai` file into the Animate CC Library. The Import dialog box, shown in Figure 2-60, will appear. Keep in mind the Head layer contains a drop shadow and, as you can see, Animate CC will automatically import that layer as a movieclip in order to retain the drop shadow.

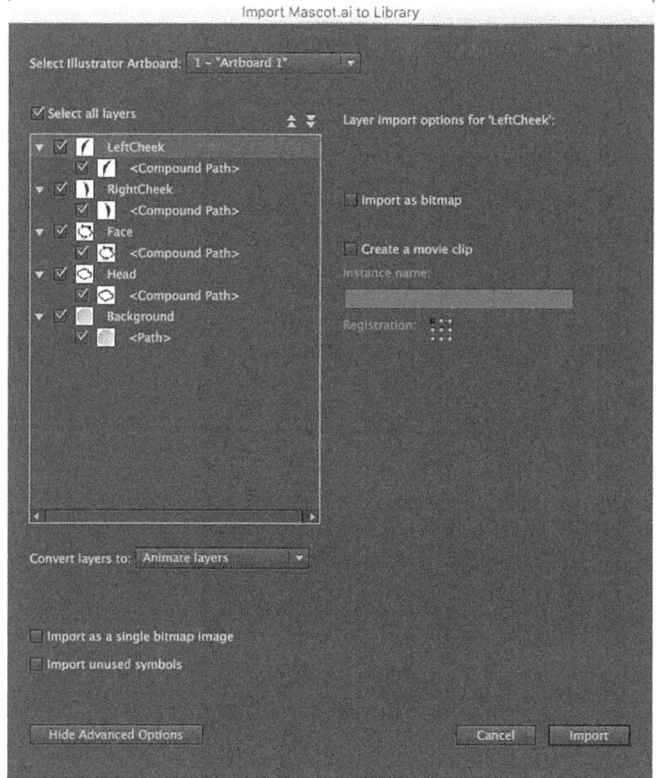

Figure 2-60. The Import dialog box used for an Illustrator image

If you select File ➤ Import to Stage, the Import dialog box will contain a couple of choices not shown here. You will be asked if you want the images in each layer to be placed at their original position in the Illustrator document and you will also be asked if you want to trim the stage to the dimensions of the Illustrator document.

CHAPTER 2 ■ GRAPHICS IN ANIMATE CC

2. Select the remaining layers, not the paths, and select Create a Movie Clip, as shown in Figure 2-61. Don't bother with instance names because there is no need for ActionScript here. The Convert Layers To drop-down menu allows you to convert your Illustrator layers to Animate CC layers or to a series of Animate CC keyframes (this is handy if they are animated), or to put the whole image into one Animate CC layer. You can also import unused symbols created in Illustrator or flatten the image and bring it in as a bitmap.

Figure 2-61. *Selected Illustrator layers can be converted to movieclips*

The Import Unused Symbols option may be a bit confusing. Illustrator allows you to create symbols, and these symbols can be imported directly into Animate CC from Illustrator. You will learn how this works in the next chapter.

---

3. Click Import. When the import process finishes, open the Library, as shown in Figure 2-62. The image has been directly imported to the Library, but each of the layers has its own folder containing the movieclip you created in the Import dialog box.

118

CHAPTER 2 ■ GRAPHICS IN ANIMATE CC

Figure 2-62. *The Illustrator image in the Animate CC Library*

At the top of this section, we mentioned how developers would simply copy Illustrator documents and paste them into Animate CC to avoid "issues." This can still be done, but when you paste the drawing into Animate CC, the dialog box shown in Figure 2-63 appears.

Figure 2-63. *Pasting a drawing from Illustrator to Animate CC will bring up this dialog box*

You are most likely looking at the Mascot image in the Library and thinking, "That's all well and good but how do I get the dang document onto the Animate CC stage and play with it?" Here's how:

1. Drag the `Mascot.ai` file from the Library on to the Animate CC stage.
2. Double-click the image on the stage. When the Symbol Editor opens, you will see the image is actually composed of the movieclips in the `Mascot.ai.Assets` folder from the Library and that each movieclip is on a separate named layer.

119

CHAPTER 2 ■ GRAPHICS IN ANIMATE CC

Importing Sketch 3 Documents into Animate CC

We wind up this overview of Animate CC's graphics features with the import of Sketch 3 images into Animate CC. Sketch 3 from Bohemian Coding is a Macintosh-only application that is becoming a de facto assembly application for the create of mobile interfaces. It is also becoming an integral tool in the UI design process as motion and prototyping assume an increasingly prominent role in the mobile workflow.

Although there are no "importers" designed to bring Sketch 3 documents into Animate CC, there are a couple of ways of bringing your work into Animate. To demonstrate, we have created a very basic iPhone interface in Sketch 3 that contains layers on a Sketch artboard (Figure 2-64). If you have Sketch 3, get started by opening the Nevada Sketch file.

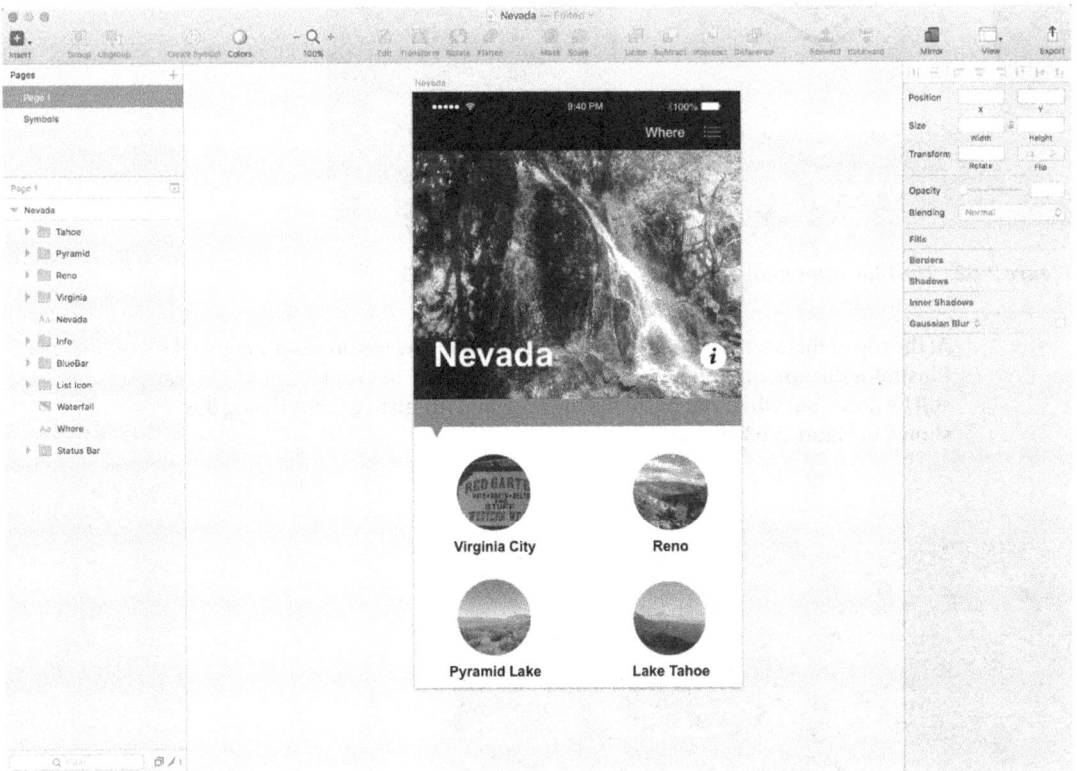

Figure 2-64. *A very simple iPhone interface is ready to go in Sketch 3*

So how do you get all of the stuff in the Sketch document into Animate CC? Here's one way:

1. Click once on the Nevada artboard in the Sketch Layers panel. The Properties panel will light up, as shown in Figure 2-65.

CHAPTER 2 ■ GRAPHICS IN ANIMATE CC

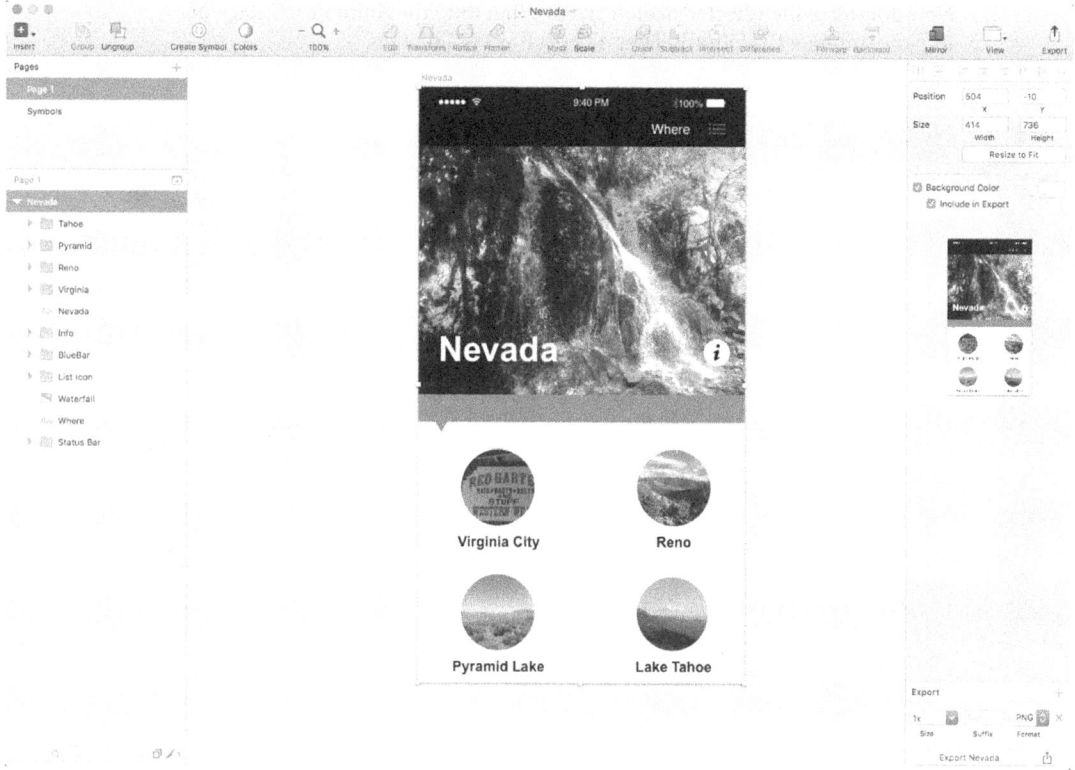

Figure 2-65. *Exporting a Sketch 3 artboard*

    2.   In the Export area, set the size to 1x and the format to PNG.

    3.   Click the Export Nevada button and, when the Save As dialog box opens, navigate to where you want the file kept and click OK. What this does is export a flattened PNG.

If you want to create a simple click-through prototype, this works, but if you want to add interactivity or motion to the elements on the artboard, a flattened.png file is out of the question. Here's how to resolve this issue:

    1.   Select all of the layers in the Sketch document and click Make Exportable in the Properties. This will open the Export Options dialog box.

    2.   Select 1x as the size and PNG as the format. Click the Export Layers button. This will open the Export dialog box.

    3.   Export the layers to the NevadaExport folder in the Chapter02/Exercises folder.

From there, you will need to import the files into Animate CC and reassemble the interface.

Oaky, that seems like a lot of work. Are you up for a "dirty cheat"? Here's what you do:

    1.   Open a new Animate CC document with the same dimensions as the Sketch artboard.

    2.   Go back to your Sketch file and, with the Shift key held down, select all of the layers.

CHAPTER 2 ■ GRAPHICS IN ANIMATE CC

3. Now drag all of the selected Sketch layers either onto the Animate CC stage or into the Animate CC Library. They all arrive as PNG images.

Figure 2-66. *Drag and drop Sketch 3 layers into Animate CC*

You Have Learned

This has been a fairly intense chapter but, along the way, you have learned the following:

- How to use the drawing tools in the Tools panel
- The process of creating and customizing gradients
- How to create custom strokes and fills
- The various color features in Animate CC and how to create and save a custom color
- How to trace a bitmap in Animate CC
- The process of importing and optimizing graphics in Animate CC
- The use of the new Illustrator and Photoshop File Importers in Animate CC
- How to import Sketch 3 documents into Animate CC

We aren't going to deny this has been a pretty intense chapter. Even so, all of the topics covered here will ripple through the remainder of this book. Most important of all, you learned how graphic content is created, added to Animate CC, and optimized in Animate CC. The next step is making that content reusable in Animate CC movies or available to different Animate CC movies. That is the subject of the next chapter. See you there.

CHAPTER 3

Symbols and Libraries

Symbols, the topic of this chapter, are one of the most powerful features of Animate CC. This is because they allow you to create reusable content. You only need one copy of a symbol. Once it is on the stage, that symbol can then be manipulated in any number of ways without those changes affecting the original piece of content.

What we'll cover in this chapter:

- Creating and using symbols
- Creating, using, and sharing libraries
- Adding filters and blends to symbols
- Grouping and nesting symbols
- Using rulers, stacking, and alignment to manage content on the Animate CC stage
- Creating masks

If you haven't already, download the chapter files. They can be found at
http://www.apress.com/us/book/9781484223758
Files used in this chapter:

- 01_GraphicSymbol.fla (Chapter03/Exercise Files_CH03/ 01_GraphicSymbol.fla)
- 02_ButtonSymbol.fla (Chapter03/Exercise Files_CH03/ 02_ButtonSymbol.fla)
- 03_MovieClip.fla (Chapter03/Exercise Files_CH03/ 03_MovieClip.fla)
- 04_SymbolEdit.fla (Chapter03/Exercise Files_CH03/ 04_SymbolEdit.fla)
- 05_9Slice.fla (Chapter03/Exercise Files_CH03/05_9Slice.fla)
- 06_Olives.fla (Chapter03/Exercise Files_CH03/ 06_Olives.fla)
- 07_9Slice_Gotcha.fla (Chapter03/Exercise Files_CH03/07_ 9Slice_Gotcha.fla)
- 08_9Slice_Gotcha_02.fla (Chapter03/Exercise Files_CH03/ _089Slice_Gotcha_02.fla)
- 09_9Slice_Gotcha_03.fla (Chapter03/Exercise Files_CH03/ 09_9Slice_Gotcha_03.fla)
- 10_SharedLibrary.fla (Chapter03/Exercise Files_CH03/10_SharedLibrary.fla)

CHAPTER 3 ■ SYMBOLS AND LIBRARIES

- 11_Filter.fla (Chapter03/Exercise Files_CH03/11_Filter.fla)
- 12_Blend.fla (Chapter03/Exercise Files_CH03/12_Blend.fla)
- 13_NuttyProfessor.fla (Chapter03/Exercise Files_CH03/ 13_NuttyProfessor.fla)
- 14_Stacks.fla (Chapter03/Exercise Files_CH03/ 14_Stacks.fla)
- 15_AlignPanel.fla (Chapter03/Exercise Files_CH03/15_ AlignPanel.fla)
- 16_SimpleMask.fla (Chapter03/Exercise Files_CH03/16_ SimpleMask.fla)
- 17_Wall.fla (Chapter03/Exercise Files_CH03/ 17_Wall.fla)
- 18_Catalina.fla (Chapter03/Exercise Files_CH03/18_Catalina.fla)

Symbols are also the building blocks of everything you will do in Animate CC (other than ActionScript or JavaScript). They are inevitably created when you come to the realization that the piece of content you are looking at will be used several times throughout a movie. In fact, the same content may appear in a number of movies, or even have a single use, such as a movieclip that plays a particular video or sound. The most important aspect of symbols is that they keep the file size manageable. The end result is fast load times and users who aren't drumming their fingers on a desk waiting for your movie to start.

Symbol Essentials

Reduced to its basics, a symbol is something you can use and reuse. It could be an image, an animation, a button, or even a movie used within the main movie. When a symbol is created, it is placed in the Library, and any copy of that symbol on the stage at any point in the movie is said to be an **instance** of that symbol. Let's create a symbol and start examining how these things work. Follow these steps:

1. Open a new HTML5 Canvas document in Animate CC. When the document opens, select the Rectangle tool and draw a rectangle on the stage.

2. Right-click (PC) or Cmd+click (Mac) on the shape and select Convert to Symbol from the context menu (as shown in Figure 3-1). You can also select the object on the stage and press the F8 key or select the object and choose Modify ➤ Convert to Symbol.

CHAPTER 3 ■ SYMBOLS AND LIBRARIES

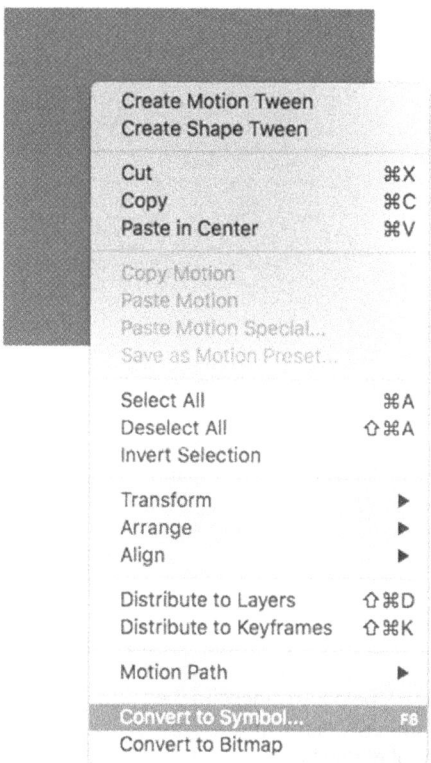

Figure 3-1. Creating a symbol

3. When the Convert to Symbol dialog box opens, name the symbol Box and select Movie Clip as its Type (see Figure 3-2). Click OK. The dialog box will close and the new symbol will appear in the Library.

125

CHAPTER 3 ■ SYMBOLS AND LIBRARIES

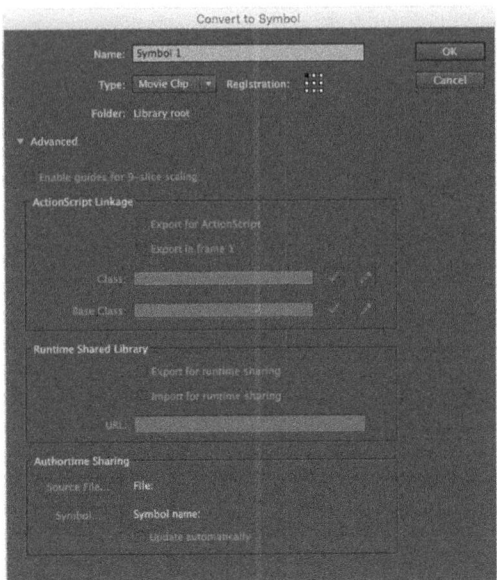

Figure 3-2. The Convert to Symbol dialog box

If you are new to Animate CC, you may notice a section labeled Advanced in the Convert to Symbol dialog box. When you click it, a number of extra options will open. Let's look at each option in the Convert to Symbol dialog box:

- **Name**: The name you enter here will be the name for the symbol as it appears in the Library.

- **Type**: You select the symbol type here. Symbol types will be explained in even greater depth in the next section.

- **Registration**: Each of the nine dots represents a possible location for the symbol's registration point. The registration point (also known as the transformation or pivot point) is used for alignment with other objects on the stage and for movement along a motion guide.

- **Folder**: Click this choose the Library folder where the symbol will be found.

- **Enable guides for 9-slice scaling:** Select this, and the guides for this special scaling will appear. We'll deal with this important topic in a separate section of this chapter.

- **Linkage**: You can use ActionScript to pull symbols and other assets out of the Library and either put them on the stage or use them for another purpose, such as playing audio. To do this, you need to assign an instance name, called a *linkage identifier*, for ActionScript to be able to find it in the Library. The Linkage check boxes allow the symbol to be used by ActionScript and to load the symbol into the first frame of the movie when the movie plays.

- **Runtime Shared Library:** This area allows you to share symbols with other Animate CC movies or to import symbols from other Animate CC movies into your project. This used to be bundled into the Linkage area but Adobe, recognizing that symbols are the cornerstones of Animate CC, has made this its own little configuration in Animate CC.

- **Authortime Sharing:** This area allows you to identify external content in a shared library or elsewhere to be used as a symbol. This comes into play in cases where you've dragged an asset from one FLA into another project.

4. Click OK. If you look at the box on the stage, you will see it is now surrounded by a thin blue line. This tells you the object just selected is a symbol. The Properties panel will also change to show that you have, indeed, selected a symbol.

5. Open the Library and drag another copy of the symbol to the stage. Click the symbol to select it. Select the Free Transform tool and scale and rotate the object. As you can see, changing one instance of a symbol does not affect any other instance of that same symbol on the stage.

6. Close the project without saving it.

Symbol Types

You have three basic symbol types to choose from: graphic, button, and movieclip. Each one has specific capabilities, and the type you choose will be based on what needs to be done. For instance, say you have a logo that will be used in several places throughout a movie and not be required to move. In this case, the graphic symbol would be your choice. If the need is for a racing car zooming across the screen with the engine sounds blasting out of the user's speakers, then the movieclip symbol is the choice. Need a button? Well that one is a bit obvious. Let's briefly review each symbol type.

Graphic Symbols

Graphic symbols are used primarily for static images or graphic content used in a project. They can also be used as the building blocks for complex animations. Although we say they are primarily static, they can be put into motion on the main timeline or the timelines of other symbols. One major advantage of graphic symbols is if they are animated, the individual instances of the graphic symbol can start at different points in the animation. For example, a Christmas animation with a falling snowflake graphic symbol can have the snowflakes all falling at different points in the animation (even though they are all instances of the same symbol), which makes the animation look much more realistic.

Graphic symbols, unlike their movieclip cousins, do not play independently of the timeline they are in. This is why they need a matching number of frames on the parent timeline in order for each frame of the graphic symbol to display. For example, if a graphic symbol animates over 60 frames, and you want it to be on the main timeline for half of its life, then you would need to allocate 30 frames on the main timeline for this task. That may sound a little convoluted. We agree and have provided a small movie that shows you what we mean:

1. Open the `GraphicSymbol.fla` file. When it opens, you will see a bronze Mao statue on the timeline that has a duration of 10 frames. Scrub across the timeline and the statue moves a short distance to the right.

2. Double-click the graphic symbol icon—Mao—in the Library, and when the Symbol Editor opens, you'll see that the animation has a length of 60 frames.

3. Click the Scene 1 link directly above the stage and pasteboard to return to the main timeline. This brings you back to the main timeline.

4. Select frame 60 on the main timeline and add a frame by pressing the F5 key or through the application menu by choosing Insert ➤ Timeline ➤ Frame (not a keyframe, just a frame). Scrub across the timeline. This time, the statue moves all the way across the stage because it is matching the movement of the symbol's nested animation.

5. Insert a frame at frame 61 of the main timeline. Because the statue's internal timeline loops back to frame 1 after frame 60, the statue pops back to the left side of the stage. If you keep inserting frames, you will eventually finish with a loop. This is an extremely useful technique to know. If you were to have a bird with flapping wings you can have the wings flap inside the graphic symbol's timeline while the main timeline manages the motion of the bird flying from side to side.

6. Select the statue on the stage and open the Properties panel. Twirl down the Looping area. The drop-down menu for the Options value lets you choose from Loop, Play Once, and Single Frame. The field labeled First lets you choose which frame of the graphic symbol's timeline to display first. We'll dig into this interesting feature in Chapter 7.

7. Close the file without saving the changes.

Button Symbols

Button symbols are rather interesting in that they are able to do a lot more than you may think. Button symbols have a four-frame timeline in which each frame is the state of the button (up, over, down, and hit), as shown in Figure 3-3. The button states can be created using graphic symbols or movieclips, drawn directly into the frame using the tools, or even use imported images. Let's look at a typical button:

1. Open the 02_ButtonSymbol.fla file and select Control ➤ Enable Simple Buttons. If you roll over the button and click it, you will see that the button changes in relation to whether it has been clicked or rolled over, and whether the mouse is off of the button.

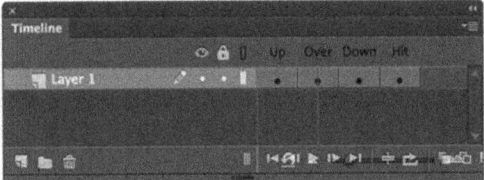

Figure 3-3. *The button symbol timeline*

If you use the Enable Simple Buttons menu item, do your sanity a favor and deselect it after you have tested the button. This menu item puts the button into its "live" state, meaning that you can't move it to another location on the stage.

2. Double-click the button symbol named Button in the Library. When the Symbol Editor opens, you will see that each state of the button is in its own keyframe. Select the Hit keyframe.

3. Select the Rectangle tool and draw a large square or rectangle.

4. Click the Scene 1 link, turn on Enable Simple Buttons and drag the mouse across the stage. The Over state will appear even though the mouse pointer is not over the button. This is the hit state coming into play. The area of the shape determines the active area for an event. This should tell you that you can have a button composed only of a hit state. If you do, what you have created is a *hotspot*, sometimes referred to as an invisible button, on the stage.

5. Close the movie and don't save the changes.

You can add layers to a button symbol. A common use of this feature is adding a sound to a button. For example, you could have something explode only when the mouse is over a button. Reopen the `ButtonSymbol.fla` document and drag the BlowUp button to the stage and try it out. The explosion sound is on the Audio layer of the symbol and is only triggered when the mouse is over the button on the stage.

Movieclip Symbols

Movieclips can be thought of as movies within movies. These symbols, unlike their graphic counterparts, actually run independent of the timeline in which they are placed. They can contain code, other symbols, and audio tracks. Movieclips can also be placed inside other movieclips—the term for this is **nesting**—and they have become so ubiquitous and useful among Animate CC designers that they are, in many cases, replacing graphic and button symbols on the stage.

A major aspect of their timeline independence is movieclips continue to play even if the parent timeline is stopped, which explains why they are often placed in a single frame on the main timeline. In cases where, for example, a movieclip fades in over a period of time, it may extend across a number of frames to accommodate this effect but, technically, movieclips need only a single frame on whatever timeline they are placed into. The other major feature of movieclips is that they can be controlled using either JavaScript or ActionScript. We are going to get into this in a big way later on in the book. In the meantime, let's explore that concept of timeline independence:

1. Open the `03_MovieClip.fla` file. If you look at the timeline, you will see that the car starts moving in frame 6 and is off the stage by frame 45.

2. Open the Library panel, and you will see the car is actually composed of several symbols. The Car graphic symbol doesn't contain a rear wheel. Why is it a graphic symbol? It is simply a picture. The Rear movieclip contains the wheel, which is rotated over a series of frames in its timeline. Why is this one a movieclip? The answer is the rotating wheel on the movieclip's timeline.

CHAPTER 3 ■ SYMBOLS AND LIBRARIES

3. Double-click the Racer movieclip in the Library to open the Symbol Editor. You will see that the car is composed of two layers, and each layer contains a symbol. This is what is meant by "nesting." Movieclips can be placed inside of other movieclips. This is also true of graphic symbols, but again, the key difference, in terms of animation, is that the timelines for the movieclips aren't controlled by the main timeline. Notice that each symbol resides in a single frame of its own layer. Even though the Rear movieclip gets one frame of the timeline, it still spins when you test the movie.

4. Click the Scene1 link to return to the main timeline. Select the car and open the Properties panel. You will see that the Racer movieclip, Figure 3-4, is used for the animation.

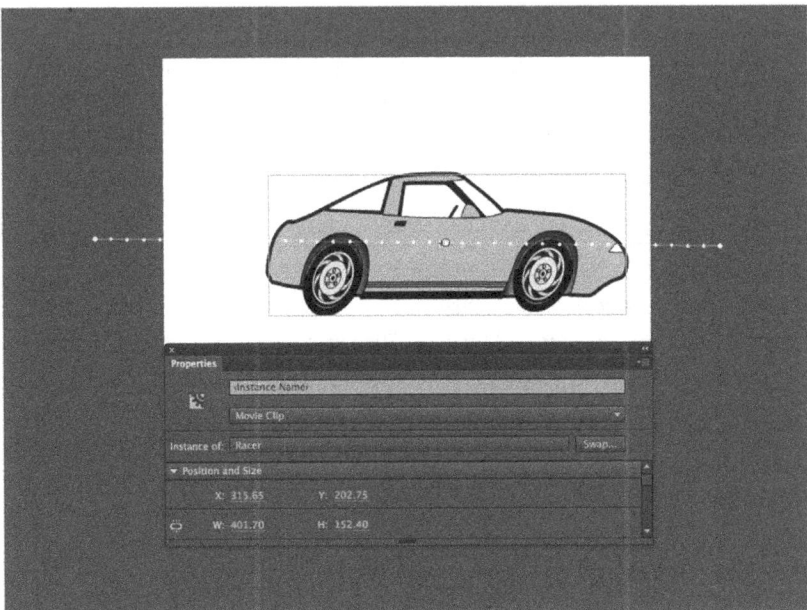

Figure 3-4. *The Racer movieclip is selected on the stage*

5. Scrub the playhead across the timeline. You'll see that the car gets larger and smaller, thanks to a tween. The key aspect of this is that movieclip properties can be changed, and in the case of nested movieclips, this change is reflected throughout the entire symbol, including the movieclips nested inside the main movieclip.

Yes, we agree this is not exactly a well-designed piece. In fact, one of the authors saw it and said, "Dude, what's with that?" Sometimes the technique is more important than the actual content. This is an important concept for those of you who are new to Animate CC: get it to work, understand why it works, and then start playing with it. Everything you do in Animate CC starts with a basic concept, and everything else in the movie builds on that concept. For example, Joshua Davis, one of the more influential characters early in the history of the Animate CC community, started one project by simply watching how a series of gray squares rotated on the Animate CC stage. Once he got the squares to rotate in a manner that worked for him, he simply swapped out the squares for shapes he had drawn in Illustrator.

Editing Symbols

There will be occasions where you will want to edit a symbol. This is where the Symbol Editor becomes an invaluable tool. There are two ways of opening the Symbol Editor:

1. Open the 04_SymbolEdit.fla file in the Chapter03/Exercise Files_CH03 folder.

2. Open the Library and double-click the Circle movieclip symbol in the Library. The Symbol Editor will open. This technique is also known as *entering the timeline* of a symbol. Click the Scene 1 link to return to the main timeline.

3. Double-click the squashed circle on the stage. This will also open the Symbol Editor, but, as you may have noticed, the other instances of any symbol on the stage are visible but look to be dim. If you try to select the instance of the Box, you will notice you can't. This technique, called *editing in place*, allows you to see how the change to a symbol or instance affects, or works with, the rest of the content on the stage.

    The edit in place technique often provides the Animate CC designer with a helpful sense of context. The other important aspect of this technique is that changes you make to the symbol on the main timeline—such as changing the size or color of the squashed circle—are only reflected in the symbol's timeline thanks to the edit in place context. If you double-click the Circle movieclip in the Library, you will see that it isn't squashed. What you can learn form this is that certain properties of symbol instances can be manipulated on the timeline without affecting the original symbol in the Library.

4. In the Symbol Editor, you can make changes to the symbol. Click the circle to select it and, in the Tools panel, change the fill color to a different color. When you do this, both instances of the circle symbol on the stage will change color.

5. Close the file without saving the changes.

6. What you can gather from this is that instances of symbols on the stage can be changed without affecting the original symbol in the Library. Change the symbol (from within the Library) in the Symbol Editor. That change is applied to every instance of the symbol in the project.

9-Slice Scaling

Until the release of Flash 8, designers essentially had to put up with a rather nasty design problem. Scaling objects with rounded or oddly shaped corners was, to put it mildly, driving them crazy. No matter what they tried to do, scaling introduced distortions to the object. The release of Flash 8 and the inclusion of 9-slice scaling solved that issue. To be fair, there are still a few quirks with this feature but it was so welcome, this feature is now appearing in Illustrator CC. The best part of this addition is that symbols created in Illustrator and are destined for Animate CC can have 9-slice scaling applied to them that carry over into Animate CC as well.

As we pointed out at the start of this chapter, 9-slice scaling is applied to movieclips when the Convert to Symbol dialog box opens. If you create a movieclip and decide to apply this feature later on during the production process, select the movieclip in the Library and right-click (Ctrl+click) the symbol to open the context menu. Select properties and add 9-slice scaling by selecting this option at the bottom of the symbol Properties dialog box. Movieclips with 9-slice scaling applied will show a grid in the Library panel's preview window.

How 9-Slice Scaling Works

What the heck is 9-slice scaling?

That question is not as dumb as it may sound because it can be a hard subject to understand. What happens is that the symbol in question—in Animate CC it can only be a movieclip—is overlaid with a 3-by-3 grid. This grid divides the movieclip into nine sections (or slices), and allows the clip to be scaled in such a way that the corners, edges, and strokes retain their shape.

Figure 3-5 shows the actual grid that Animate CC places over the object. The object is broken into the nine areas. The eight areas surrounding the center area—the area with the 5—will scale either horizontally or vertically. The area in the middle—area 5—will scale on both axes. The really interesting aspect of this feature is that each section of the grid is scaled independently of the other eight sections.

Figure 3-5. *The 9-slice scaling grid*

CHAPTER 3 ■ SYMBOLS AND LIBRARIES

The best way of understanding how all of this works is to see it in action.

1. Open the 05_9Slice.fla file. When it opens, you will see two movieclips on the stage. The upper movieclip doesn't have 9-slice scaling applied; the lower one does (see Figure 3-6). The key to both of these objects is they are the identical size and the stroke width around both shapes is also identical.

Figure 3-6. *You start with two movieclips on the stage*

2. Click the upper movieclip, open the Transform panel (Window ➤ Transform), and change the Horizontal scaling value to 300%. When you press the Enter/Return key, the shape scales along the horizontal axis, but as you can see, the corners flatten out and distort, and the stroke gets fatter.

3. Click the lower movieclip, open the Transform panel, and change the Horizontal scaling value to 300%. When you press the Enter/Return key, the shape scales along the horizontal axis, and the corners don't distort (as shown in Figure 3-7). You can see why by looking at Figure 3-5. The areas numbered 2, 5, and 8 are scaled horizontally, and the corner areas are unaffected.

133

CHAPTER 3 ■ SYMBOLS AND LIBRARIES

Figure 3-7. *Both movieclips are scaled at 300 percent along the horizontal axis; the movieclip without 9-slice scaling is distorted*

Additionally, the guides are adjustable. They can be moved, which allows you to control how the scaling will be applied. Here's how:

1. Double-click the 9Slice movieclip in the Library to open the Symbol Editor. You will see the grid.

2. Roll the cursor over one of the slice guides, and it will change to include a small arrow pointing to the right if you are over a vertical guide, or pointing downward if you are over a horizontal guide (see Figure 3-8).

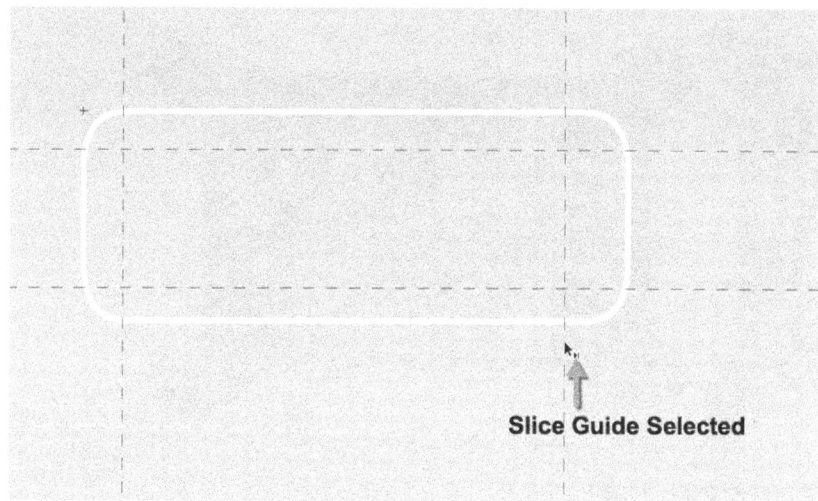

Figure 3-8. The guides can be repositioned

3. Click and drag the selected guide to its new position. When you release the mouse and return to the main timeline, you will see the change in the Library's preview window. Close the file without saving.

So far, so good. You have applied the slice guides to a geometric object. Okay, we hear you. You are probably muttering, "Not exactly a real-world project." We thought about that and agree with you. What about occasions where the corners are irregular? Let's go visit an Olive seller in Guang Zhou to give you some "real-world" experience with that issue.

Your Turn: Frames for an Olive Seller

When we approached this exercise, the question was, "What could we put in a picture frame that would be memorable?" Flowers and other images are interesting, but really don't make the point. Then one of the authors said, "How about a picture of an Olive Seller?" The reply was, "Yeah, right." To which the author who made the original suggestion said, "No. No. No. There is a guy in Guang Zhou, China who sells olives on the street. He wears a rooster suit and blows a horn. Maybe we can use it?"

1. Open `Olives.fla`. When the file opens, you will notice that the images don't exactly fit their frames (see Figure 3-9). Let's fix that.

CHAPTER 3 ■ SYMBOLS AND LIBRARIES

Figure 3-9. The picture frames don't fit the images

2. Select the Frame movieclip in the Library and enable 9-slice scaling. Open the movieclip in the Symbol Editor and adjust the guides to match those shown in Figure 3-10. Note that the guides are positioned to encompass the extent of each corner olive.

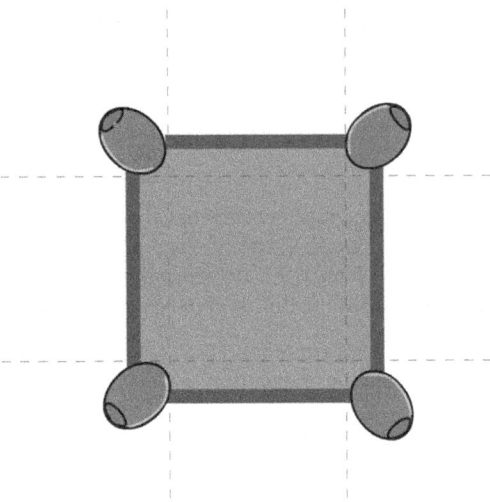

Figure 3-10. Applying 9-slice scaling and adjusting the guides

3. Click the Scene 1 link to return to the main timeline.

4. Select the Free Transform tool and adjust the picture frames to fit the image, as shown in Figure 3-11. Even though each photo has its own width, the same symbol can now be used to neatly frame these different dimensions.

Figure 3-11. *9-Slice scaling allows you to put a frame around the Olive Seller*

Now that you have seen how 9-slice scaling works, how it is applied, and how to use it, don't get lulled into thinking it is especially easy to use. That is a real danger with books of this sort, where everything appears rosy, wonderful, and trouble-free. In many cases, it is. In this one, it isn't.

When we started working on Olive Seller's picture frame, things started "blowing up". The corner images started distorting when they shouldn't have. This caused us to halt the process and really dig into this particular feature. The next section gives you the un-rosy, "it ain't all that wonderful and easy to use" run down regarding what we discovered about 9-slice scaling. Thankfully, our pointers should help you steer clear of the mines.

The 9-Slice "Gotchas"

You need to know that there are a handful of interesting "gotchas" involved with 9-slice scaling that must target an ActionScript 3.0 (AS3) document.

The first gotcha concerns the area in the middle of the 9-slice grid, which scales across both the horizontal and the vertical axes. If you have content in the center area of the grid (area 5), such as a gradient, text, or image, it will distort if the scaling is uneven. Take a look for yourself.

Open the 07_9Slice_Gotcha.fla file, select the Sign Up button on the stage, and drag out a corner. Notice how the text distorts. This is because the text is in the area 5 slice (see Figure 3-12). Depending on your needs, this makes 9-slice symbols useful only as background borders, layered behind content that simply must not be distorted.

CHAPTER 3 ■ SYMBOLS AND LIBRARIES

Figure 3-12. *The center area of a symbol containing 9-slice scaling scales on two axes. The area in the middle will distort.*

The second involves maintaining the integrity of any drawings or objects used in the corners and you can see this if you open 08_9Slice_Gotcha_02.fla. Shapes, drawing objects, primitives, or graphic symbols can be used. Movieclips or rotated graphic symbols, such as the graphic symbol of the olive originally destined for the frame's corners, can't be used. That would be easy enough to remember, but an interesting quirk rears its head with graphic symbols: if you use graphic symbols that are rotated, they will not display correctly as specially scaled 9-slice elements in the Animate CC interface. Rest assured, they work just fine when you test or publish them—you just can't see that they're working until you do that".

You can see what we are talking about in Figures 3-13 and 3-14. Instead of the drawing of the olive, it was placed into a graphic symbol, which was then rotated to meet the design. When we applied the 9-slice scaling to the movieclip, the result was Figure 3-13. The boxes and olives looked like something had gone horribly wrong.

CHAPTER 3 ■ SYMBOLS AND LIBRARIES

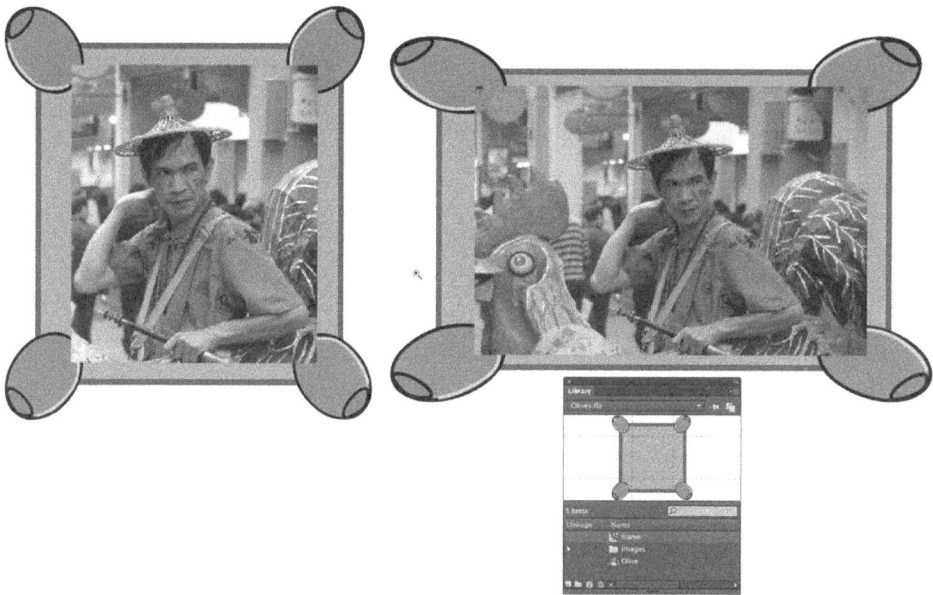

Figure 3-13. *Rotating a simple graphic symbol can cause issues*

When the movie was tested in the Flash Player, as shown in Figure 3-14, everything looked normal.

Figure 3-14. *Testing in the Flash Player. Problem? What problem?*

139

CHAPTER 3 ■ SYMBOLS AND LIBRARIES

Stretching objects along the horizontal axis is another issue that will jump up and bite the unwary. Figure 3-15 demonstrates this. We started with nothing more than a rounded rectangle with a square in the upper-left corner. If you open 09_9Slice_Gotcha_03.fla, you will see that a shape, a drawing object, a primitive, a graphic symbol, a movieclip, and an imported bitmap representing the square. These objects were all wrapped in a movieclip to which 9-slice scaling is applied.

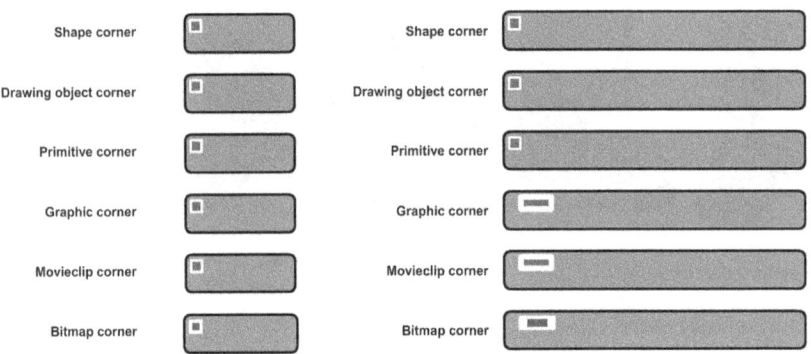

Figure 3-15. *Horizontal scaling can introduce distortions*

We did nothing more than select the Free Transform tool and stretched the selection along the horizontal axis. The results were, to be gentle, rather surprising.

The bottom line is: Use 9-slice scaling with care. The idea is a good one, but don't go nuts with it. Keep it simple! Avoid nesting symbols in the corners and sides. If you insist on using bitmaps, bear in mind that they'll stretch in ways that may not be predictable. We encourage you to experiment on your own, but by all accounts, the simpler, the better".

It is okay to rotate symbols that are not movieclips in 9-slice corners, but they look correct only when your FLA is configured for ActionScript 3.0. You can do this by selecting File ➤ Publish Settings and selecting ActionScript 3.0 in the Script drop-down menu.

Sharing Symbols

One of the really useful features of symbols in a Library is that they are available to files other than the current movie. Symbols in an Animate CC Library can be shared with other Animate CC movies. This is extremely helpful if you are working on a number of movies and need to use the same symbol or symbols in numerous documents.

Animators make extensive use of this feature. An animator will, for example, create a character composed of a number of symbols—eyes, arms, legs, and hands, for instance—that are used to put the character in motion. As the animations are built in a given movie, the animator will use symbols that were created in a separate character library movie instead of redrawing them. Here's how to use symbols from another movie:

1. Create a new ActionScript 3.0 document and open the new document's library. As you can see, it is empty.

2. Select File ➤ Import ➤ Open External Library (Ctrl+Shift+O [PC] or Cmd+Shift+O [Mac]), as shown in Figure 3-16. When the Open dialog box appears, navigate to the Chapter03/Exercise Files_CH03 folder and open 10_SharedLibrary.fla.

CHAPTER 3 ■ SYMBOLS AND LIBRARIES

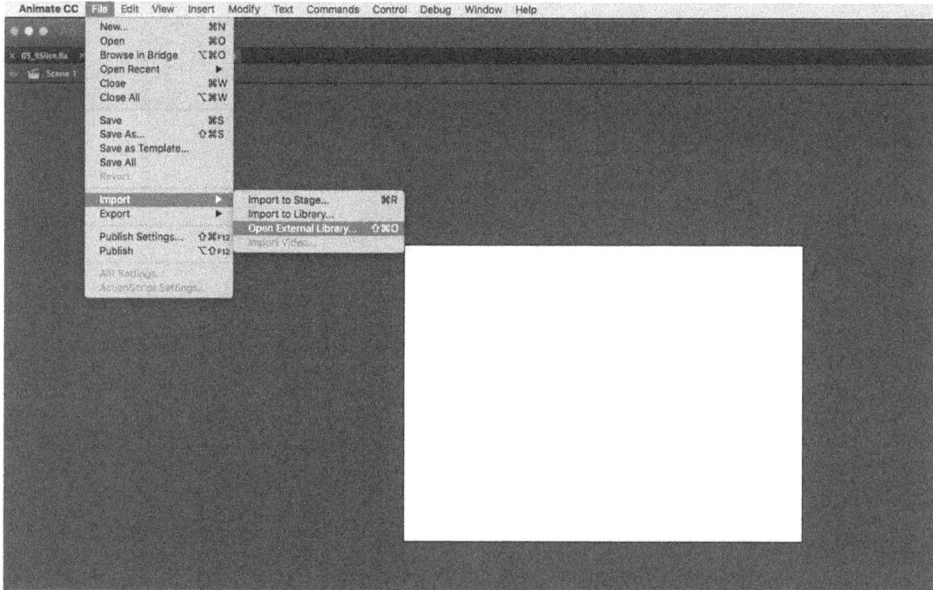

Figure 3-16. *Importing a library from one Animate document into another*

There is another method for accessing libraries. If you have an Animate CC document already open, click the drop-down menu in the Library panel and you will be presented with a list of currently open documents. Select a document from that list and its library is made available to you.

---

3. The library for the selected movie will open, but there are a couple of things missing from it. There is no drop-down menu, the pushpin is missing, and the Open New Library buttons are missing. All of these are visual clues that the SharedLibrary.fla file isn't open.

4. Drag the Street symbol to the empty library. When you release the mouse, the symbol and the bitmap will appear in the empty library and become available for use in the movie (see Figure 3-17).

141

CHAPTER 3 ■ SYMBOLS AND LIBRARIES

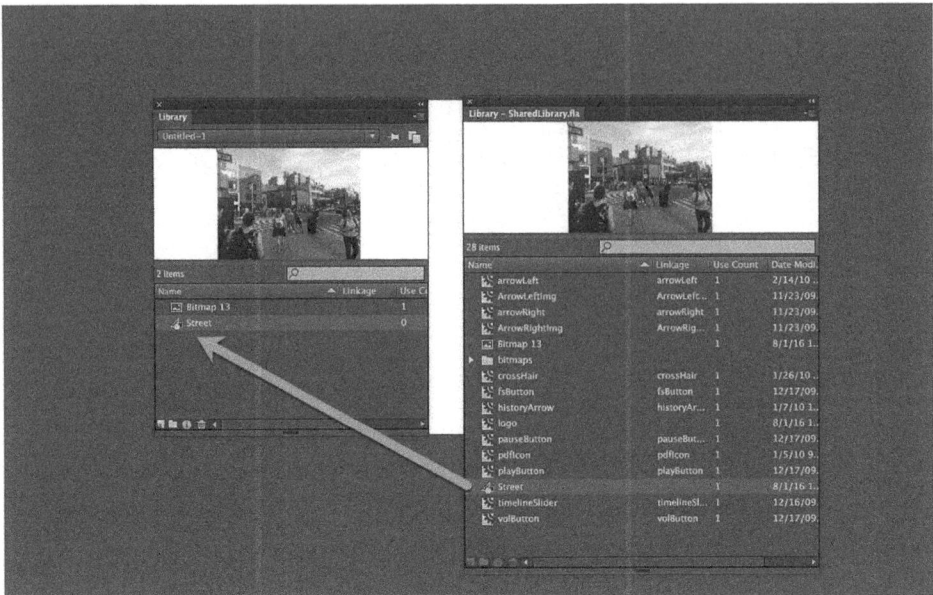

Figure 3-17. *Drag a symbol from the imported library to the empty library*

You can also share font symbols between movies when targeting ActionScript 3.0 document types. We'll get into that subject in Chapter 6.

Creative Cloud Libraries

When Adobe swung over from a boxed-software sales method to the Creative Cloud subscription model, they also introduced Creative Cloud Libraries. The fascinating aspect of these libraries is that anything—colors, characters, styles and so on—you create in an Adobe desktop or mobile application can be saved to a Creative Cloud Library and used in any Adobe application that syncs with them. It should come as no surprise that Animate CC was among the first to receive this feature.

To access your Creative Cloud Library, select Window ➤ CC Libraries or click the CC Libraries icon in the panels, as shown in Figure 3-18.

142

CHAPTER 3 ■ SYMBOLS AND LIBRARIES

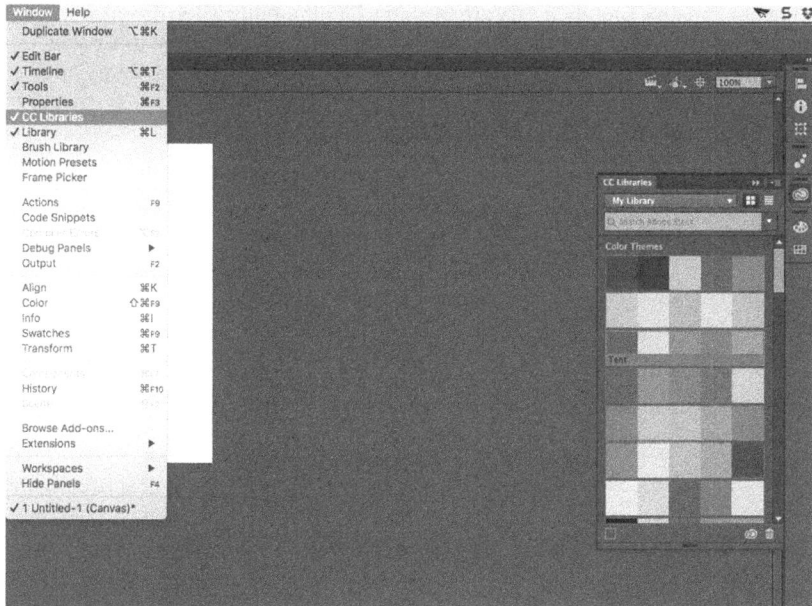

Figure 3-18. The Creative Cloud Library is selected and opened

To add an item to your Animate CC project, you simply drag the item from the Library and drop it onto the stage or into the Library. From there you can convert it to a symbol. The dialog box that appears simply asks how you want to treat the imported Library item. All you have to do is make your choice and click OK.

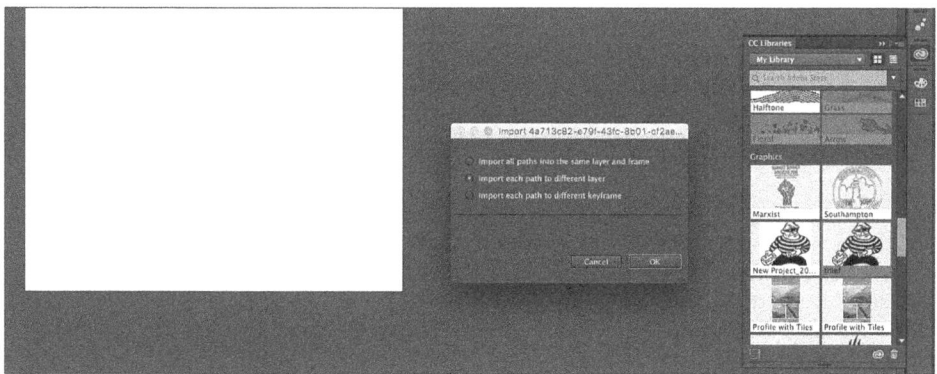

Figure 3-19. CC Library items can be dropped onto the Animate CC stage

143

CHAPTER 3 ■ SYMBOLS AND LIBRARIES

Multilayer PSDs added to your Creative Cloud Library are treated a bit differently when dropped into Animate. The Import dialog box (Figure 3-20) asks how you want to treat the layers. Again you make your decision as to how to treat the item and click Import. The item will be added to the document library and you can start using it.

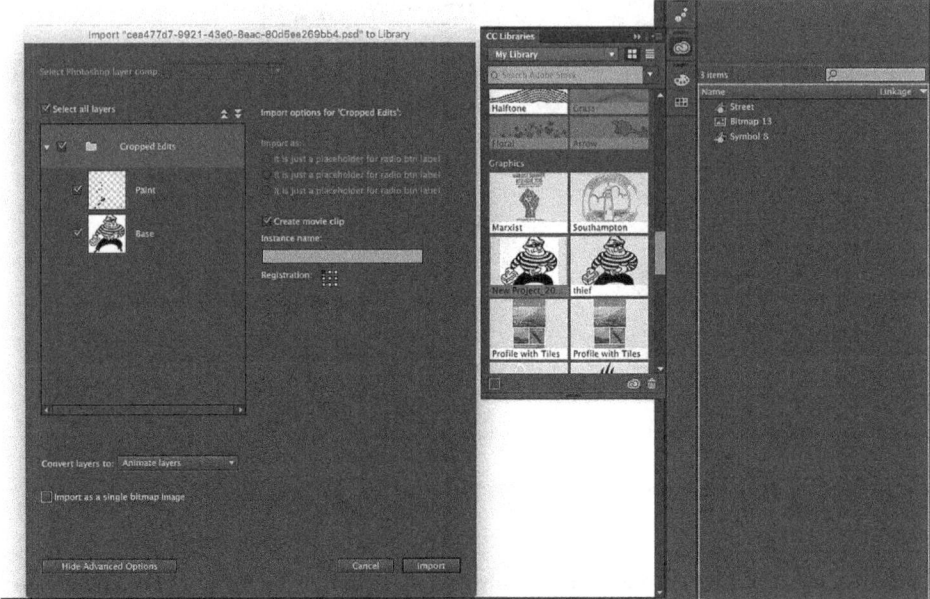

Figure 3-20. *A CC Library item is added directly to the project library*

When a CC Library item is added to an Animate Library, the library name, not the document name, travels with it. If you see something like "cea477d7-9921-43e0-8eac-80d5ee269bb4.psd" in your project, simply double-click the name and change it.

If you are in a team-based environment, you can share libraries. In your Creative Cloud account, you can create a new Library and, once you name it, open your Libraries in the web view of the application, and select Collaborate (Figure 3-21) from the drop-down. You will then be prompted to add the email for the team member and to add a short message. Once they accept the invitation they can open the Library and either directly edit the content or simply view it. The beauty of this is, once an asset is added to a shared folder, it is instantly available to anyone on the Collaboration list.

144

CHAPTER 3 ■ SYMBOLS AND LIBRARIES

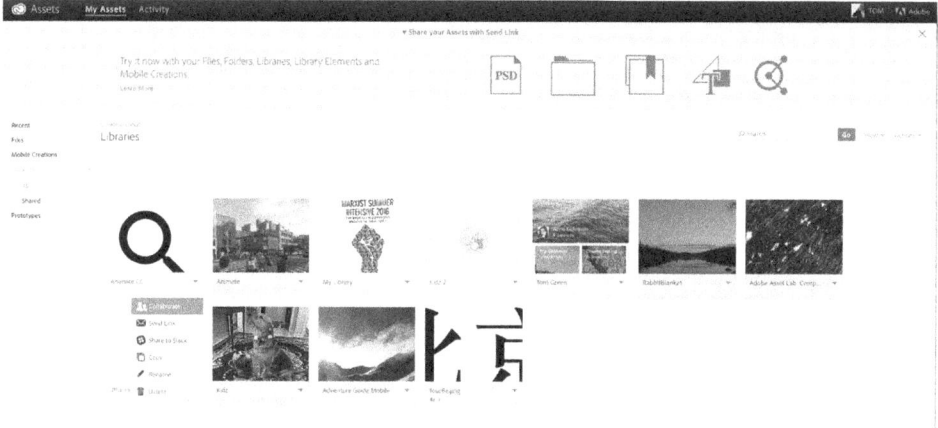

Figure 3-21. *Creative Cloud libraries can be shared with the project team*

A WORD FROM THE BUNNIES

Jennifer Shiman has created what is arguably one of the funniest sites on the Web (www.angryalien.com/). Unfortunately, she has retired the bunnies but left the site up, which is a good thing. On a regular basis, she would release an Animate CC movie that used the following premise: The movie is a 30-second synopsis of a popular film and the actors are bunnies. Drawing and animating each bunny would be a daunting task. Jennifer's solution is the use of a shared library containing all of the "bunny bits" needed to create the animations (see Figure 3-22). This is what Jennifer says about how she does it:

145

CHAPTER 3 ■ SYMBOLS AND LIBRARIES

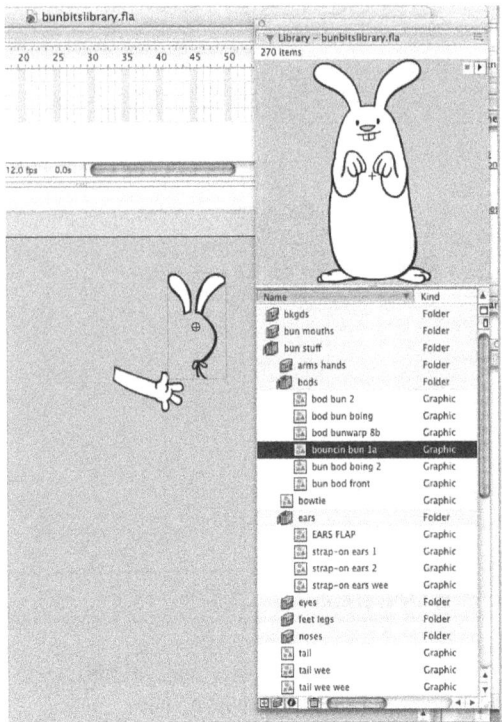

Figure 3-22. *Shared libraries help Jennifer manage complex animations*

This is my library of "bunny bits," which I incorporate into each of my 30-Second Bunnies Theatre cartoons. I've compiled a bunch of the symbols I use most commonly in animating the bunnies, and I grouped them into folders. For instance, within the "bun mouths" folder are subfolders of different mouth shapes for lip sync; mouths smiling and frowning; mouths in color and black and white; mouths of differing line thickness. The "bkgds" folder contains background symbols I frequently use, such as standardized clouds, grass, and trees. At the beginning of production, I'll open the bunny bits library and drag the folders into the library of my current cartoon file. Then I import the additional artwork specifically pertaining to that cartoon.

During the course of production, if I create new bunny-related artwork I want to use in future files (such as a new version of a bunny mouth shape or a bunny arm position I'll use often), I drag those symbols into the bunny bits library file. It saves time to have one central location for these types of reusable elements.

Filters and Blend Modes

The introduction of filters and blend modes in Flash 8 was a direct response to designers looking for more eye candy. Since then they have become indispensable tools for animators and designers.

Applying Filters

In the years prior to Flash 8, designers were quite comfortable using Photoshop filters or Fireworks Live Effects. Back in those days, if you needed to add a blur, drop shadow, or glow you would leave Flash, open an imaging application containing the needed effect, export a PNG and import the bitmap into your Flash project. If the effect wasn't quite right, you made the round trip again. Those days are over and, thankfully, these same filters have become a part of Animate CC. The ability to use filters directly in the Animate CC authoring environment (and animate them, to boot) has handed you a quick-and-easy method to create some fascinating visual effects.

The filters that are available in Animate CC are as follows:

- **Drop Shadow**: Places a gray or colored shadow beneath an object, which gives it the appearance of floating over the background.
- **Blur**: Takes the subject out of focus, making it look smudged or out of the depth of field.
- **Glow**: Creates a faint glowing outline around an object by following its curves.
- **Bevel**: Gives an object a 3D look by creating shadows and highlights on opposite edges.
- **Gradient Glow**: Quite similar to the Glow filter, except that the glow follows a gradient of colors from the inside to the outside edges of the object.
- **Gradient Bevel**: Comparable to the Bevel filter, except that a gradient is applied to the shadow and the highlights of the bevel.
- **Adjust Color**: Allows you to adjust the brightness, contrast, hue, and saturation of an object.

Before you start playing with them, understand that filters can't be applied to everything you see on the stage. Filters can only be applied to buttons, text, and movieclips. This makes a lot of sense because the bulk of the movieclips that will receive a filter arrive in the Library as either bitmaps from Photoshop or as line art from Illustrator. As you saw in Chapter 2, they inevitably get imported as movieclip symbols. Even neater, if an imported image has transparent areas, the filter—such as a drop shadow—is applied only to the opaque edges of the symbol.

The filters available to you depend on the document you are applying them to. If the project is a Canvas document, the Bevel, Gradient Glow, and Gradient Bevel filters will be grayed out. ActionScript 3.0 documents can use all of the filters.

There are also three filters that can be applied only through the use of ActionScript: Color Matrix, Displacement Map, and Convolution. Their use is out of the scope of this book, but check out the ActionScript resources in the Help menu for explanations and demonstrations of how to use these filters.

Applying a Drop Shadow Filter

In Animate CC, you can apply filters using a couple of methods. The most common is to select the object on the stage and then click the Filters twirlie on the Properties panel. Filters can also be applied through ActionScript.

CHAPTER 3 ■ SYMBOLS AND LIBRARIES

To get started, let's get creative with a simple drop shadow:

1. Open the `11_Filter.fla` file. You will see that a cartoon of one of the authors has been placed over an image of a couple of people asleep on a park bench in Paris (see Figure 3-23). The cartoon is a `Photoshop.png` image that was imported into the Library as a movieclip.

Figure 3-23. *We start with a Photoshop image imported into Animate CC*

The authors would like to thank Chris Flick of Capes & Babes (`http://www.capesnbabes.com/`) for allowing us to use this caricature of Tom.

---

2. Select the character on the stage and click the Filters twirlie in the Properties panel. Click the Add Filter button, it is the + sign, to open the Filters drop-down menu. Select Drop Shadow.

3. The Properties panel will change to show the various options for this filter and the selection on the stage will also develop a drop shadow using the current default values for the Drop Shadow filter.

4. Change the Blur X and the Blur Y values to 8 to make the shadow a little bigger and change the Distance value to 11 to make the shadow a bit more pronounced. Also change the Quality setting to High. The shadow should now look a lot better (see Figure 3-24).

CHAPTER 3 ■ SYMBOLS AND LIBRARIES

Figure 3-24. *The filter is applied to the selection*

The lock joining the Blur X and Blur Y values ensures that the two values remain equal. Click the lock if you want the Blur X and Blur Y values to be different.

The first rule of "Flash Physics" states: For every action, there is an equally opposite and ugly implication. Selecting High quality results in a great-looking shadow. The ugly implication is that this setting requires more processing power to apply. This is not a terrible thing if the image is static. For objects in motion, however, keep the setting at Low.

The result is acceptable, but we can do a lot better than what you see. The problem is the shadows in the image. Notice how they are at a different angle than the one used for the character? Let's fix that.

Adding Perspective

What we are going to do is make this effect look a little more realistic. Applying the Drop Shadow in the previous steps resulted in a character that looks flat and has no perspective. Yet, if you closely examine the image, the shadows all move away from the character in the foreground. In this exercise, you are going to add the perspective. Follow these steps:

1. Select the object on the stage, select the Drop Shadow filter in the Properties panel, and then click the visibility icon—it looks like an eyeball—to turn off the Drop Shadow filter. With the object selected on the stage, copy it to the clipboard.

2. Add a new layer, give it a name, and with the new layer selected, select Edit ➤ Paste in Place. A copy of the character is pasted into the new layer. Turn off the layer's visibility.

149

CHAPTER 3 ■ SYMBOLS AND LIBRARIES

You also have the ability to copy the contents of a particular frame in the timeline. Right-click (PC) or Ctrl+click (Mac) the frame or sequence of frames and select Copy Frames from the context menu. You can then select the frame where the content is to be placed, open the context menu again, and select Paste Frames.

3. Within the Tom layer, select the character on the stage and apply a Drop Shadow filter. Use these settings:

- Blur X: 30
- Blur Y: 7
- Strength: 70% (this is an opacity value)
- Quality: High
- Angle: 87 degrees
- Hide Object: Selected

What you should see is nothing more than a somewhat transparent shadow on the image due to your selecting Hide Object (see Figure 3-25). This opens you up to some rather creative applications. For example, just a shadow appearing over something adds a bit of a sinister feeling to a scene.

Figure 3-25. *Hiding the object allows you to only show the shadow*

4. To add the perspective, select the object with the Free Transform tool and scale, rotate, and skew the selection.

5. Turn on the visibility of the hidden layer. Select the shadow on the stage and, using the arrow keys, move the shadow to align with the foot that is on the ground.

6. Select the copy on the stage and turn on the visibility of the drop shadow. This time leave the values alone, but select High as the Quality setting, and select Inner shadow. The character takes on a bit of a 3D look to go with the shadow he is casting, as shown in Figure 3-26.

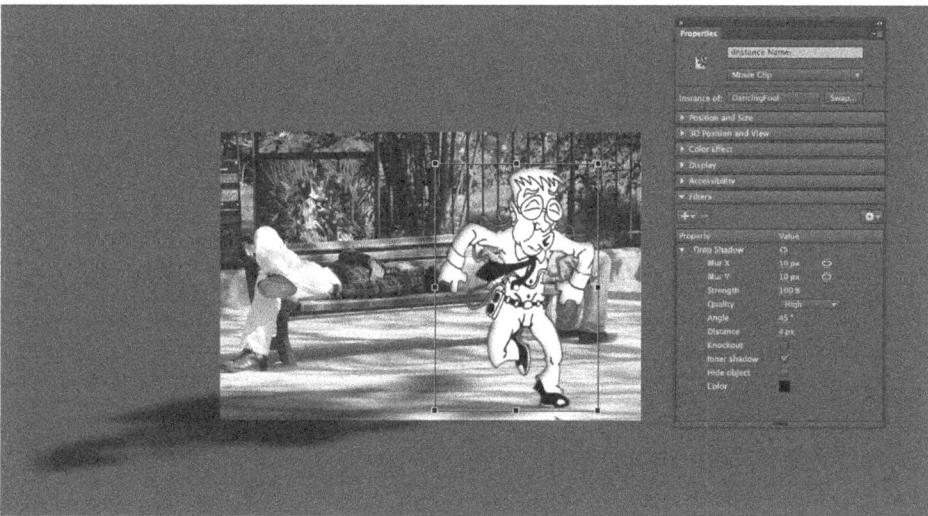

Figure 3-26. *Apply an inner shadow to add some depth*

Some Filter Facts

Before we move on to applying a blend, here are a few things you should know about adding and using filters:

- You can apply multiple filters to an object. The character can, for example, have the Drop Shadow, Glow, and Bevel filters applied to it. If you need to remove one, select the filter name and click the Trash Can in the Filters area.

- You cannot apply multiple instances of a filter to an object. You saw this in this exercise. Each movieclip has a Drop Shadow filter applied to it.

- Filters do result in a hit on the user's processor. Use them judiciously.

- Filters applied to layers in Photoshop will be visible in Animate CC, but will not be editable in when the image is imported into the project library or to the stage.

- The number of available Filters for a project will depend upon the Animate CC project document type.

- Filters can be applied to objects using ActionScript.

Playing with Blends

The blend modes operate quite differently from the filters. If you are a Photoshop user, you may already be familiar with the concept. In applications like Photoshop, such modes are commonly used to manipulate the colors of pixels to create new colors based on combinations with underlying pixels.

The blending modes in Animate CC are as follows:

- **Normal:** No blend is applied and the selection isn't affected. Use this one to remove a blend.
- **Layer:** Allows you to stack movieclips on top of each other with no effect on their color.
- **Darken:** Compares the foreground and background colors and keeps the darkest one.
- **Multiply:** Multiplies the base color value by the blend color value and divides the result by 256. The result is inevitably a darker color.
- **Lighten:** The opposite of darken with the result always being a lighter color.
- **Screen:** The inverse of the blend color is multiplied by the base color. Think of this as being the opposite of Multiply resulting in a lighter color.
- **Overlay:** Multiplies or screens the colors depending on the base color. The base color is not replaced. Instead, it is mixed with the blend color to reflect the lightness or darkness of the original color.
- **Hard Light:** Mimics the effect of shining a bright light through the selection. If the blend color is darker than 50% gray, the image is darkened as if it were multiplied. This is another way of adding shadows to a selection.
- **Add**: The blend and base colors are added together, resulting in a lighter color.
- **Subtract:** The blend and the base colors are subtracted from each other, resulting in a darker color.
- **Difference:** Depending on their brightness values, either the base color is subtracted from the blend value or vice versa. The result looks like a color film negative.
- **Invert:** Inverts the base color.
- **Alpha:** The blend color is converted to an alpha channel, which, essentially, turns transparent.
- **Erase:** The base color, including those of the background image, are erased.

Blend modes, once you grasp that they are math-driven, work like this: the pixel colors values are considered from two separate layers of an image and mathematically manipulated by the mode to create the effect. An excellent example of this manipulation is the Multiply mode. This mode will multiply the color values of a pixel in the source layer with the color values of the pixel directly below it in the destination layer. The result is divided by 256, and is always a darker shade of the color. In Animate CC, these calculations are performed on overlapping movieclips or buttons on the stage.

When applying a blending mode in Animate CC, keep in mind that it is not the same task as it is in Photoshop. Animate lets you place multiple objects in a layer. When a blend mode is applied to a movieclip or button in Animate CC, it is the object, which could be a photo, directly under the movieclip or button, which will supply the base color for the change in the movieclip, or the button.

Blends are extremely powerful creative tools in the hands of an artist. Although they can only be applied to movieclips and buttons, applied judiciously, the blend modes can provide some rather stunning visual effects.

CHAPTER 3 ■ SYMBOLS AND LIBRARIES

Be careful with using blends. They can all be applied to ActionScript 3.0 documents. If you are using an HTML5 Canvas document, you can only apply the Add Blend mode.

To apply a blend mode, you simply select the movieclip to which it is to be applied and select the mode from the Blend drop-down menu in the Properties panel. Let's look at a few of the blend modes and learn some blend fundamentals along the way.

1. Open the 12_Blend.fla file. When the file opens, you will see that we have put two movieclips on the stage (see Figure 3-27). The movieclips are also in separate layers named Source and Destination. In this example the Source layer contains some text filled with a neutral gray color. The Destination layer contains an image of autumn leaves that were blurred using the Gaussian Blur filter in Photoshop. Those layers have been given those names for a reason: *blending modes are applied in a top-down manner*. This means that the effect will do the manipulation using the source layer's pixels and apply the result to the movieclip on the destination layer. That's right, anything visible under the source (including the stage) and will be affected by the change.

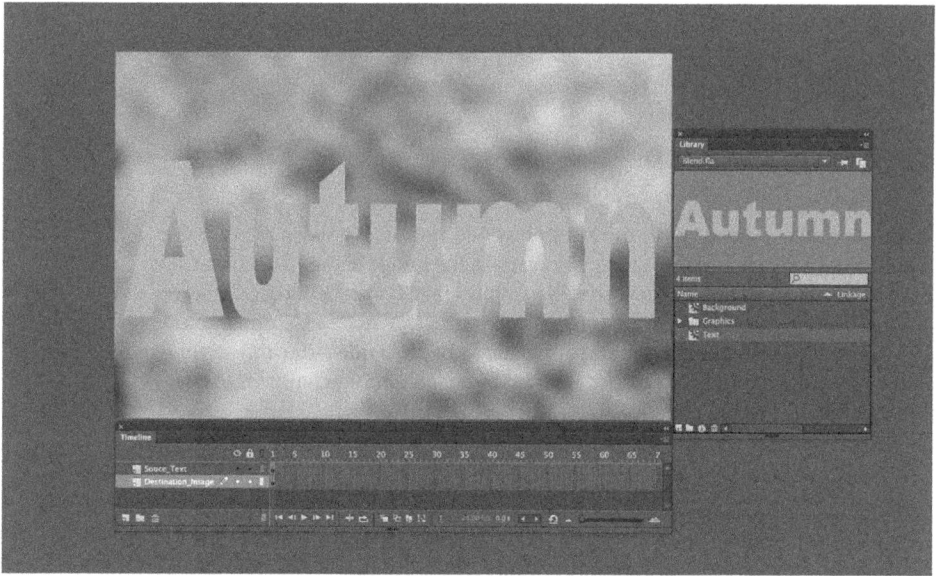

Figure 3-27. *The pixels in the Source layer—the text—are used to create the effect with the pixels in the destination layer—the blurred autumn leaves*

153

CHAPTER 3 ■ SYMBOLS AND LIBRARIES

2. Select the movieclip in the Source layer—the text—and click the twirlie in the Display area of the Properties panel, select Normal from the Blending drop-down menu, as shown in Figure 3-28. The Normal mode does not mix, combine, or otherwise play with the color values.

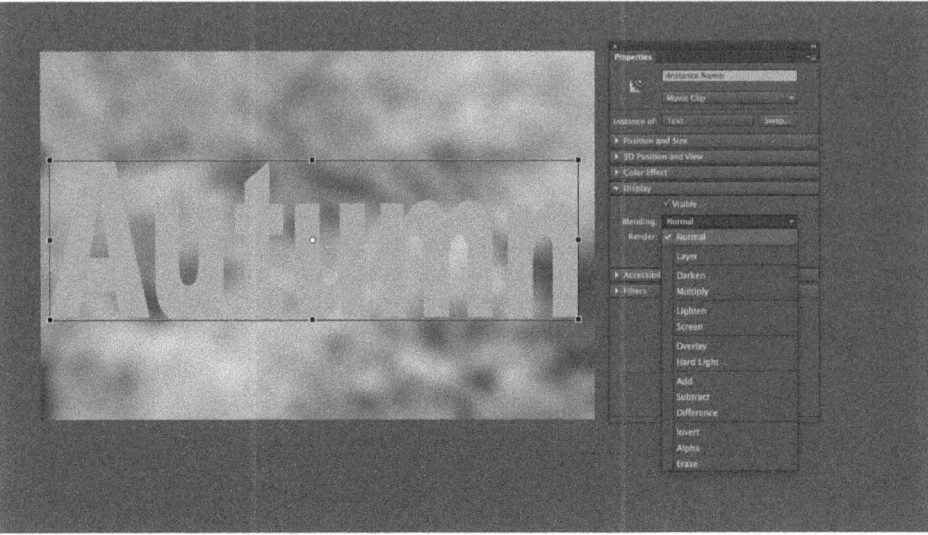

Figure 3-28. *Blend modes are applied through the Properties panel*

3. With the text still selected, apply the Multiply mode. As you can see in Figure 3-29, the colors have mixed and the darker colors make the image darker. The important thing to notice here is how the medium gray of the stage is also being used where the Source image overlaps only the stage. If you return the mode to Normal, select the image in the Destination layer and apply the Multiply mode—the image will darken due to the dark gray color (#606060) of the stage. Nothing happens to the text in the Source layer.

CHAPTER 3 ■ SYMBOLS AND LIBRARIES

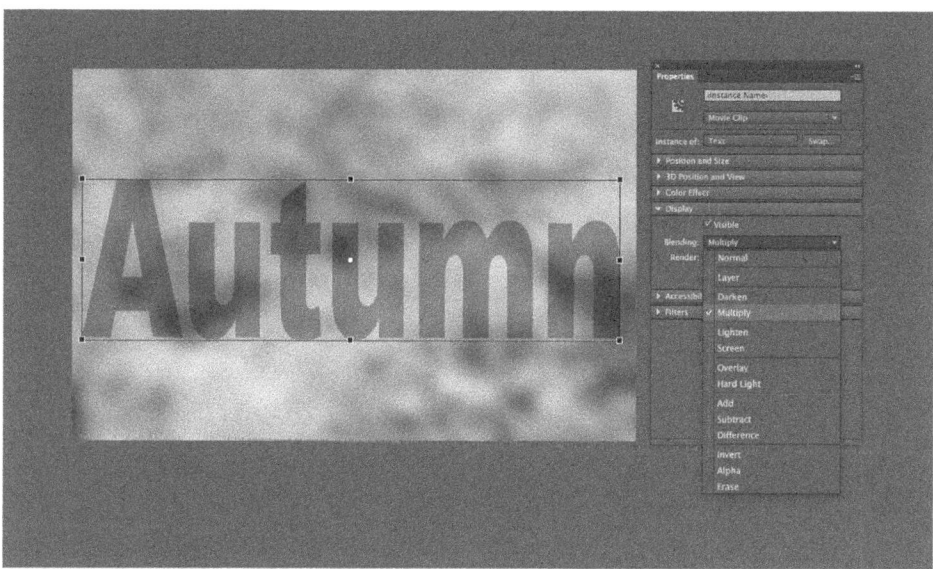

Figure 3-29. *The Multiply mode*

4. Set the blend mode of the Destination layer to Normal. Select the text in the Source layer and apply the Lighten mode. In this example, shown in Figure 3-30, the lighter color of both the Source and Destination images is chosen. As you can see, the lighter pixels in the Destination image are replacing the darker pixels in the Source image.

CHAPTER 3 ■ SYMBOLS AND LIBRARIES

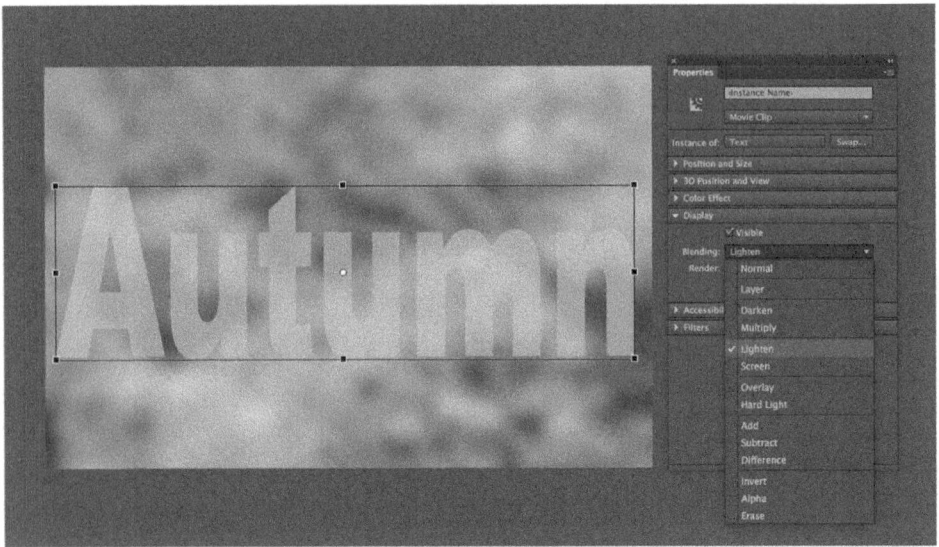

Figure 3-30. *The Lighten mode*

5. Finally, select the image in the Source layer and apply the Difference mode. This mode is always a surprise. This one works by determining which color is the darkest in the Source and Destination images, and then subtracting the darker of the two from the lighter color. The result, shown in Figure 3-31, is always a vibrant image with saturated colors.

CHAPTER 3 ■ SYMBOLS AND LIBRARIES

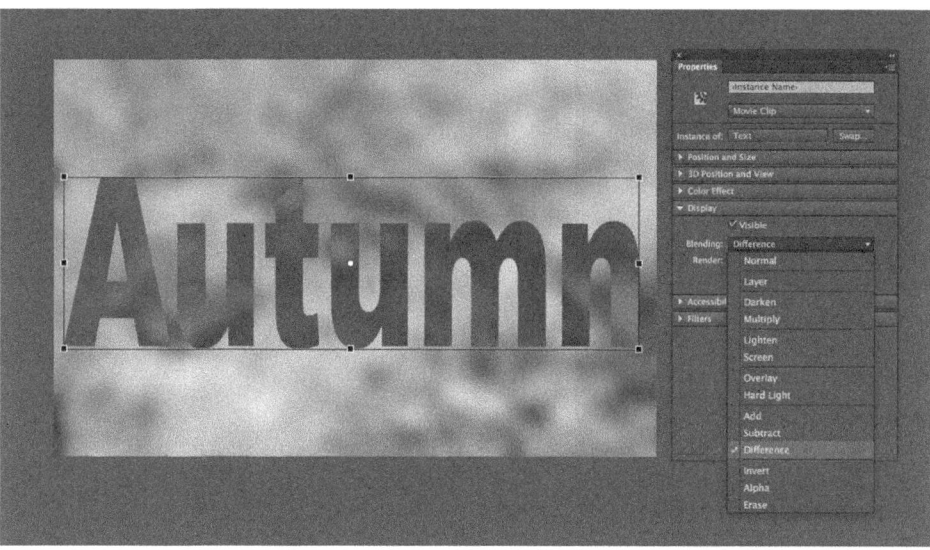

Figure 3-31. The Difference mode

Managing Content on the Stage

Now that you have had some fun, playtime is over. It is time to get back to the serious issue of managing your work. Though we have talked about using folders in layers and in the Library, we really haven't addressed the issue of managing the content on the stage.

As we have been telling and showing you, you can determine the location of objects on the stage by dragging them around. We look upon that practice, in many respects, as attempting to light your BBQ with an atom bomb. You will light the BBQ, but taking out the neighborhood is a lot less precise than striking a match and lighting a burner. This why we have been doing it by the numbers. We enter actual values into the Properties panel or use menus to precisely place items on the stage and then resize and otherwise manipulate content. The time has arrived to stop shoving the content around and manage it instead.

We'll start by showing you how to group content:

1. Open the 13_NuttyProfessor.fla file in the Chapter03/Exercise Files_CH03 folder. When the file opens, head over to the Library and open the Professor movieclip.

2. Click the Professor layer, and you will see that the drawing is composed of quite a few bits and pieces (see Figure 3-32). If you wanted to move that drawing over a couple of pixels, you would have to select each element to be moved. There is an easier method.

157

CHAPTER 3 ■ SYMBOLS AND LIBRARIES

Figure 3-32. *Lineart, in many cases, is the sum of its parts*

3. Select Modify ➤ Group or, if you are a keyboard junkie, press Ctrl+G (PC) or Cmd+G (Mac). The pieces become one unit, as indicated by the square bounding box surrounding them.

4. Deselect the group by clicking the stage, and then click the image of the professor on the stage. Again, you will again see the box indicating that the selection is grouped, and you will also be given the same information in the Properties panel, as shown in Figure 3-33.

Figure 3-33. *A group is indicated both on the stage and in the Properties panel*

5. To ungroup the selection, select Modify ➤ Ungroup, or press Ctrl+Shift+G (PC) or Cmd+Shift+G (Mac).

6. Close the file without saving the changes.

Aligning Objects on the Stage

Now that you know how to make your life a little easier by grouping objects, let's turn our attention to how objects can be aligned with each other on the stage. Reopen the NuttyProfessor.fla file and click the Scene 1 link to return to the main timeline. You will see the movieclip and some text on the stage.

The first technique is the use of Snap Align. You can switch on this very handy feature by selecting View ➤ Snapping ➤ Snap Align. When Snap Align is switched on, dragging one object close to another object will show you a solid line. This line shows you the alignment with the stationary object.

Click the words on the stage and slowly drag them toward the bottom-left corner of the movieclip. You will the "ghosted text" showing you the original location of the object and the Snap Align indicator line (see Figure 3-34) telling you that left edge of the text is aligned with the left edge of the movieclip. By dragging the text up and down the indicator line, you can align objects at a distance. Release the mouse and the text will snap to that line.

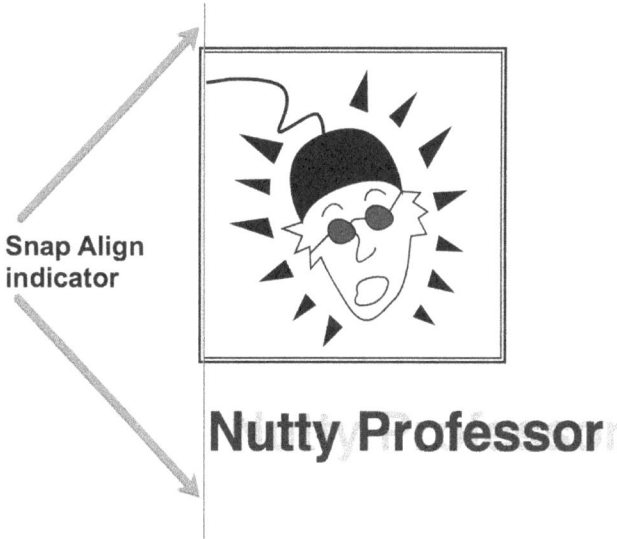

Figure 3-34. Using Snap Align

Snapping to the Grid

You can also align objects on the stage through the use of a grid. If you are creating mobile prototypes for iOS and Android devices, grids become very important. This is a handy way of precisely positioning objects on the stage. You can turn on the grid by selecting View ➤ Grid ➤ Show Grid. When you release the mouse, a grid will appear on the stage. This grid is what we call an "authortime" feature. That means that the grid won't appear when you publish the project.

CHAPTER 3 ■ SYMBOLS AND LIBRARIES

You can also edit the grid by selecting View ➤ Grid ➤ Edit Grid. The Grid dialog box, shown in Figure 3-35, will appear. Here you can change the color of the grid lines, determine if items snap to the grid, and change the size of the squares in the grid. The Snap accuracy drop-down menu lets you choose how snapping to the grid lines will be managed by Animate CC.

Figure 3-35. *Adding a grid and managing it on the stage*

Take another look at the Grid dialog box in Figure 3-35 There is a Show Over Objects option which was added in Flash Professional CS4. This option allows you show the grid over everything on the stage, meaning you now have the ability to be super accurate in snapping objects to grid lines. As we said in the previous edition of this book, this option is "super cool". Hide the grid before you move to the next section.

Aligning with Guides

Another method for aligning objects or placing them in precise locations on the stage is to use guides. You can add guides by dragging them off of either a horizontal or a vertical ruler. The ruler isn't shown by default in Animate CC; to turn it on, select View ➤ Rulers. At 100 percent view, the rulers are divided into five-pixel units. If you need even more precise placement, zooming in to 2,000 percent view allows you to work in units of .5 pixels.

To add a guide, drag it off of either the horizontal or vertical ruler and, when it is in position, release the mouse. To remove a guide, drag it back onto the ruler.

Once a guide is in place, you can then edit it by selecting View ➤ Guides ➤ Edit Guides. This will open the Guides dialog box (see Figure 3-36), which is quite similar to the Grid dialog box. The Snap accuracy drop-down menu allows you to determine how close an object needs to be to a guide before it snaps to the guide. You can also choose to lock the guides in place. Locking guides once they are in position is a good habit to develop. This way, you won't accidentally move them.

CHAPTER 3 ■ SYMBOLS AND LIBRARIES

Figure 3-36. *Rulers, guides, and the Guides dialog box*

If you need to turn off the guides, select View ➤ Guide ➤ Show Guides; reselect it to turn them on again. If you no longer need the guides, you can remove them with a single click of the mouse by selecting View ➤ Guides ➤ Clear Guides.

Snapping in a Guide Layer and to Pixels

Finally, you can snap objects to items in a guide layer—not to be confused with the guides we just discussed—and even to individual pixels.

Snapping to an object in a guide layer is nothing more than a variation of the Snap to Objects, except the layer in question has been converted to a guide layer by right-clicking (Ctrl+clicking) on the layer name and selecting Guide. What's the difference? As you saw in Chapter 1, the lines drawn in a guide layer aren't included in the final project.

Snapping to pixels is best-suited to ultra-precise positioning and control freaks. This is extremely useful with the placement of bitmaps through Snap to Bitmap and text fields. In fact, you won't even see the pixel grid until you have zoomed in at least 400%. The pixel grid is not the same grid we demonstrated earlier.

Stacking Order and Using the Align Panel

Layers are effective tools for managing content, but there is another related concept you need to be aware of: **stacking**. When multiple objects are in a layer, the objects also have a front-to-back relationship with each other, appearing to be placed on top of each other, which is called the **stacking order**.

161

CHAPTER 3 ■ SYMBOLS AND LIBRARIES

Symbols, drawing objects, primitives, text fields, and grouped objects can be stacked. Everything else essentially falls to the bottom of the pile in the layer. To accomplish this, each new symbol or group added to a layer is given a position in the stack, which determines how far up from the bottom it will be placed. This position is assigned in the order in which the symbols or objects are added to the stage. This means that each symbol added to the stage sits in front, or above, the symbols or objects already on the stage. Let's look at this concept:

1. Open the `14_Stacks.fla` file. You will see four photos on the stage and, if you look at the timeline, they are all on the same layer.

2. Drag the objects on top of each other and you will see, as shown in Figure 3-37, a stack. The location of each object in this stack is a visual clue regarding when it was placed on the stage.

Figure 3-37. Objects stacked in a layer

Stacking order is not fixed. For example, suppose you wanted to move the bread image to the top of the stack and move the stairs image under the fountain image. Here's how:

1. Select the bread image on the stage and select Modify ➤ Arrange ➤ Bring to Front. The image moves to the top of the stack. This tells you that the Bring to Front and Send to Back menu items are used to move selected objects to the top or the bottom of a stack on the layer on which they are located.

2. Right-click (Ctrl+click) on the stairs image to open the context menu. Select Arrange ➤ Send Backward, as shown in Figure 3-38. The stairs move under the fountain image. This tells you that the Bring Forward or Send Backward menu items can be used to move objects in front of or behind each other. What you have also learned is the Arrange menu is available in the Modify menu or by opening an object's context menu.

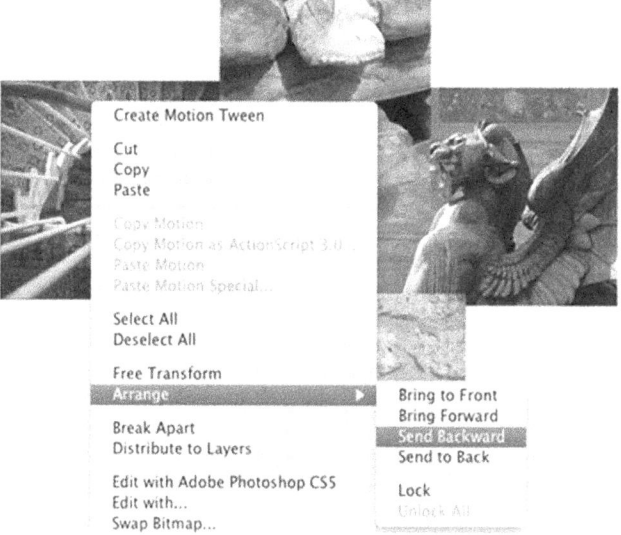

Figure 3-38. *You can also use the context menu to change the stacking order of selected objects*

Throughout this book, we have talking about the use of layers to manage content. Obviously, stacking objects on top of each other flies in the face of what we have said. Not so fast. There is an incredibly useful menu item that actually allows you to bring a bit of order to the chaos.

1. Select all the items on the stage.

2. Select Modify ➤ Timeline ➤ Distribute to Layers. When you release the mouse, the order of the objects in relation to each other doesn't change, but each object has been removed from the original layer–Layer 1–and is now on its own named layer, as shown in Figure 3-39. This is extremely useful, for example, when you import Photoshop Layer folders as movieclips and then you see that you need to break them into layers in Animate CC.

CHAPTER 3 ■ SYMBOLS AND LIBRARIES

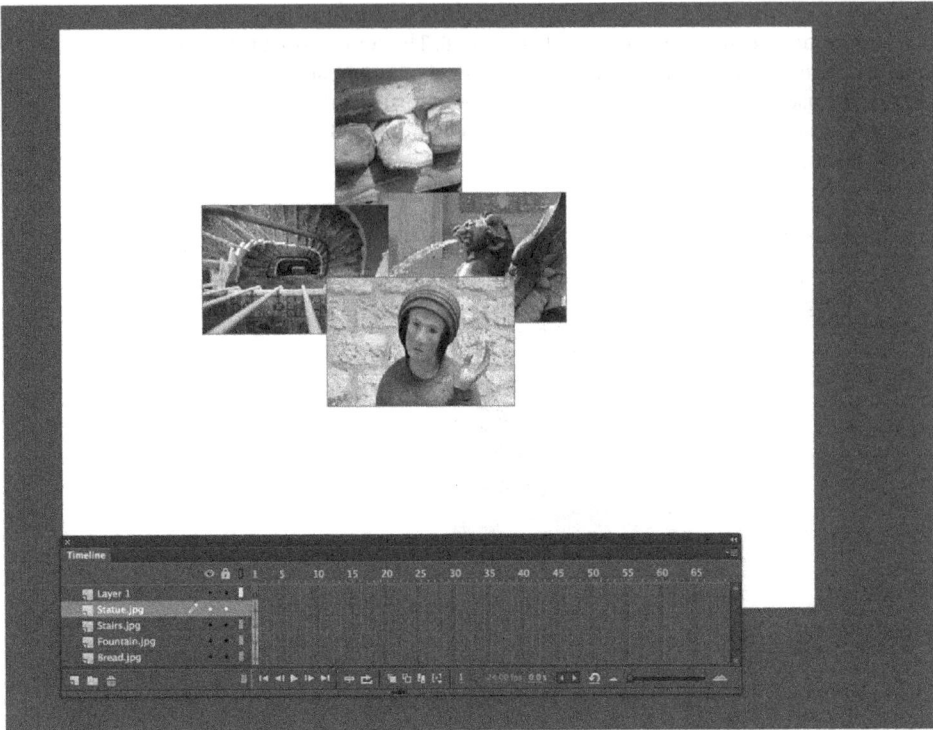

Figure 3-39. *Distribute to Layers places each selected object on its own layer*

3. Close the file and don't save the changes.

   Now that you see what you can do with this powerful menu item, you also need to understand some rules regarding its use:

   - Symbols, shapes, drawing objects, primitives, text fields, and grouped objects will be placed on their own individual layers.

   - For symbols, layer names are based on either the instance name in the Properties panel or the symbol name in the Library. If the symbol name and the instance name are the same, instance names take precedence.

   - For text fields, the name of the layer is based on the text content—or the text field's instance name in the Properties panel. Again, instance names take precedence.

Using the Align Panel

The Align panel allows you to line up and center objects, and otherwise bring order to chaos with a click or two of the mouse.

You can access the Align panel either by selecting Window ➤ Align or pressing Ctrl+K (Cmd+K) to open the panel shown in Figure 3-40. When the panel opens, you are presented with a number of alignment options—there are 17 options available and a button labeled Align to Stage. The Align to Stage option allows you to either align or distribute objects with each other or, if it is selected, align or distribute them with the stage.

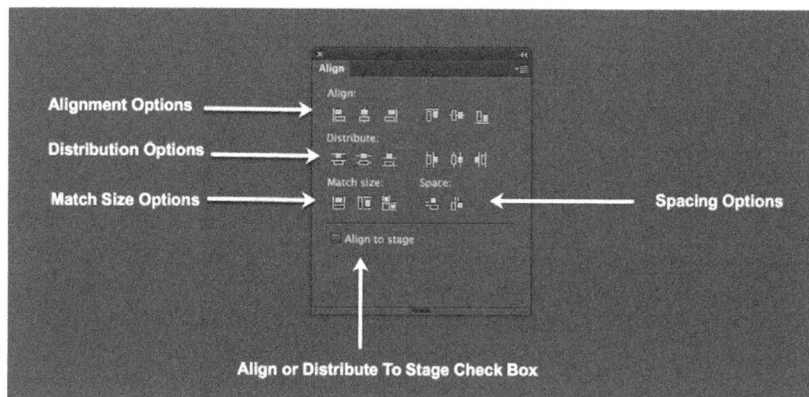

Figure 3-40. The Align panel

Let's see how all of this works:

1. Open the 15_AlignPanel.fla file in the Chapter03/Exercise Files_CH03 folder. As you can see, the file consists of a number of button components scattered across the tab bar at the bottom of the screen. Open the Align panel.

2. Select all the components, and, being sure the Align to Stage check box is not selected, click the Left Align button in the panel. The buttons all line up along their left edges. Undo the change.

3. This time, first click the Align Vertical Center button and the components line up. With the centers lined up, click the Vertical Spacing button in the Space options, and the components will be spaced evenly on the vertical axis (see Figure 3-40). Click the Distribute Horizontal Center button to even out the spacing.

Now let's use the panel to create that tab bar at the bottom of the stage.

1. Click the Align to Stage check box on the Align panel.

2. Select all the buttons and click the Align Left Edge button. The buttons will pile on top of each other on the left side of the stage.

CHAPTER 3 ■ SYMBOLS AND LIBRARIES

3. With the buttons still selected, click the Distribute Horizontal Center button. The buttons spread out along the bottom of the tab bar, as shown in Figure 3-41. Not bad . . . two clicks and you have a button bar.

Figure 3-41. *The tab bar buttons are neatly lined up*

Masks and Masking

Before we turn you loose on a project, the final subject we will be examining is the issue of masking in Animate CC. As you know, masks are used to selectively show and hide objects on the project stage. The value of a mask is, in many respects, not clearly understood by Animate CC designers. They tend to regard masking as a way to hide stuff. They see it as an overly complicated method of doing something that could be more easily done in an imaging application. This is not exactly incorrect, but what they tend to miss is the fact that masks in Animate CC can be animated and can even react to events on the stage. For example, one of the authors connects a webcam to his computer, and using Animate CC, is able to broadcast himself peering out of billboards in Times Square, waving at people walking by in Piccadilly Circus in London, or looking out of the porthole of a sensory deprivation tank. When the camera is not connected, the images revert to their normal states.

Here you will learn to create a simple mask and a masked animation. Finally, you'll tackle creating a soft mask, an exercise designed to pull together much of what you have discovered in this chapter.

A Simple Mask

In this exercise, we are going to show you the basic steps involved in a creating a mask in Animate CC. Once you have the fundamentals under your belt, you can apply what you have learned in a rather creative manner. Let's start:

1. Open the `16_SimpleMask.fla` file.
2. Create a new movieclip symbol named Wildlife and open the symbol in the Symbol Editor.
3. Change the name of Layer 1 to Sheep. Drag the `Sheep.jpg` image to the stage and set its location to 0,0.
4. Add a new layer named Mask.
5. Select the Oval tool and, being sure the Stroke is turned off in the Properties panel, draw out a circle that is 80 x 80 pixels.
6. Right-click (PC) or Cmd+click (Mac) on the Mask layer to open the Layer context menu. Select Mask. When you release the mouse, the image of the sheep will look like it is circular. You should also notice that the appearance of the layers has changed, and that they are locked (see Figure 3-42). The icon beside the Mask layer name (the rectangle with a cutout) indicates that the layer is a mask, and the indent for the Sheep layer name indicates that it is the object being masked.

CHAPTER 3 ■ SYMBOLS AND LIBRARIES

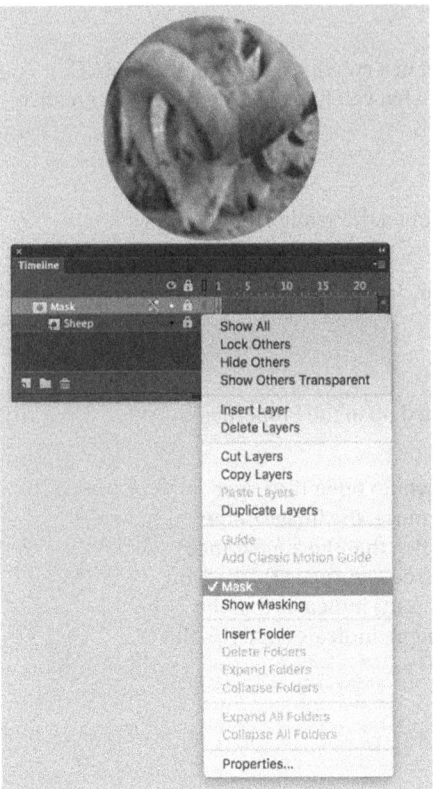

Figure 3-42. *Applying a mask*

What you see is the image showing through the circle in the Mask layer, with the stage color visible. One thing you need to know about masks is that you need to be careful dragging other layers under them. Do that, and they, too, will be masked—depending on how you are doing the dragging. The following steps explain what we're getting at:

1. Add a new layer above the mask and name it Square. Select the Rectangle tool and draw a rectangle on this new layer.

2. Drag the Square layer under the Sheep layer, making sure the layer is indented in the timeline by giving the layer a slight tug to the right. When you release the mouse, the circle and the square are visible. Click the Lock icon in the Square layer, and the square will disappear because it is under the photograph.

   The locks turn the masks on and off and allows you to edit or manipulate the content in the layers, including the masks. When you finish making your changes, click the locks to reapply the mask. When all layers are locked (the masked layers and the mask), the mask goes into a preview mode.

3. Unlock the Square layer and drag it back above the Mask layer. This time, drag the Mask layer above the Square layer. When you release the mouse, you will see that both the Mask and Sheep layers have moved above the Square layer, and that the shape in the Square layer is visible.

CHAPTER 3 ■ SYMBOLS AND LIBRARIES

4. Drag the Square layer below the Sheep layer again, this time keeping to the left. When you release the mouse, the Square layer is no longer associated with the mask. This is an alternative method of toggling between the Normal and Masked (or Mask) layer options seen when you right-click (Ctrl+click) a layer and select Properties.

5. Delete the square layer, return to the main timeline, and place the Wildlife movieclip on its own layer in the top card, as shown in Figure 3-43.

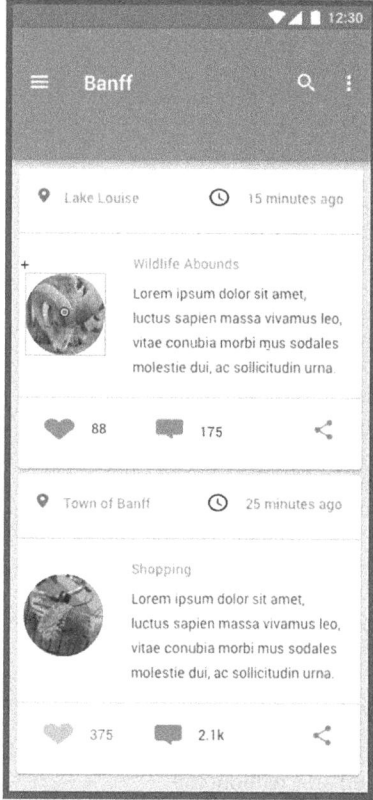

Figure 3-43. *Masks can be added to any symbol that has a timeline*

Now that you understand the fundamentals, let's get a little more complex.

Creating a Masked Animation

The art of Animate CC is, in many respects, the art of illusion. In this exercise, you'll create the illusion of the Dancing Fool from the Drop Shadow example earlier in the chapter sliding across six panels on a wall in Adobe's San Jose Headquarters building. The problem to contend with is the fact the panels are large and each panel has its own shape. How do you get the Dancing Fool to slide out from behind one panel, across a few more and slide behind another as he exists the stage?

You think a bit differently.

CHAPTER 3 ■ SYMBOLS AND LIBRARIES

The effect you want to create is shown in Figure 3-44. Instead of using the panels as the mask, you need to use the colored area in each panel as the mask. The following steps show you how to accomplish this.

Figure 3-44. *The Dancing Fool slides across colored panels*

1. Open the `17_Wall.fla` file. All of the items you will need for this exercise are located in the Library.

2. Add a new layer named Mask. Select the Magnifying Glass tool and zoom in on six panels in the middle of the image.

3. Select the Pen tool and draw a shape that matches the colored area without the triangle with the dot in the bottom-right corner of each panel. Fill each shape with Black by clicking inside it with the Paint Bucket tool.

4. Holding down the Shift key, select each of the shapes you have just drawn, and convert the selection to a movieclip named Mask.

5. Open the Mask movieclip in the Symbol Editor. Change Layer 1's name to Panels, and add a new layer named DancingFool to the timeline. Drag the DancingFool layer under the Panels layer.

6. Select frame 1 of the DancingFool layer and drag a copy of the DancingFool movieclip to the stage. Place the movieclip to the left of shapes in the Panels layer, as shown in Figure 3-45.

Figure 3-45. *The assets are in place, and you can now move on to creating the movie*

With the assets in place, you can now concentrate on creating the animation. The plan is to have the pictures rise up in the window and then sink back down out of view. Here's how you do that:

1. Select frame 80 of the Panels layer and insert a frame.

2. Select frame 80 of the DancingFool layer and add a frame. Right-Click (PC) or Control+Click (Mac) anywhere between the two frames and select Create Motion Tween from the Context menu.

3. Select frame 80 of the DancingFool layer and move the movieclip to the right of the panels. You will see a keyframe in frame 80 of the DancingFool layer and the Motion Path shown in Figure 3-46.

CHAPTER 3 ■ SYMBOLS AND LIBRARIES

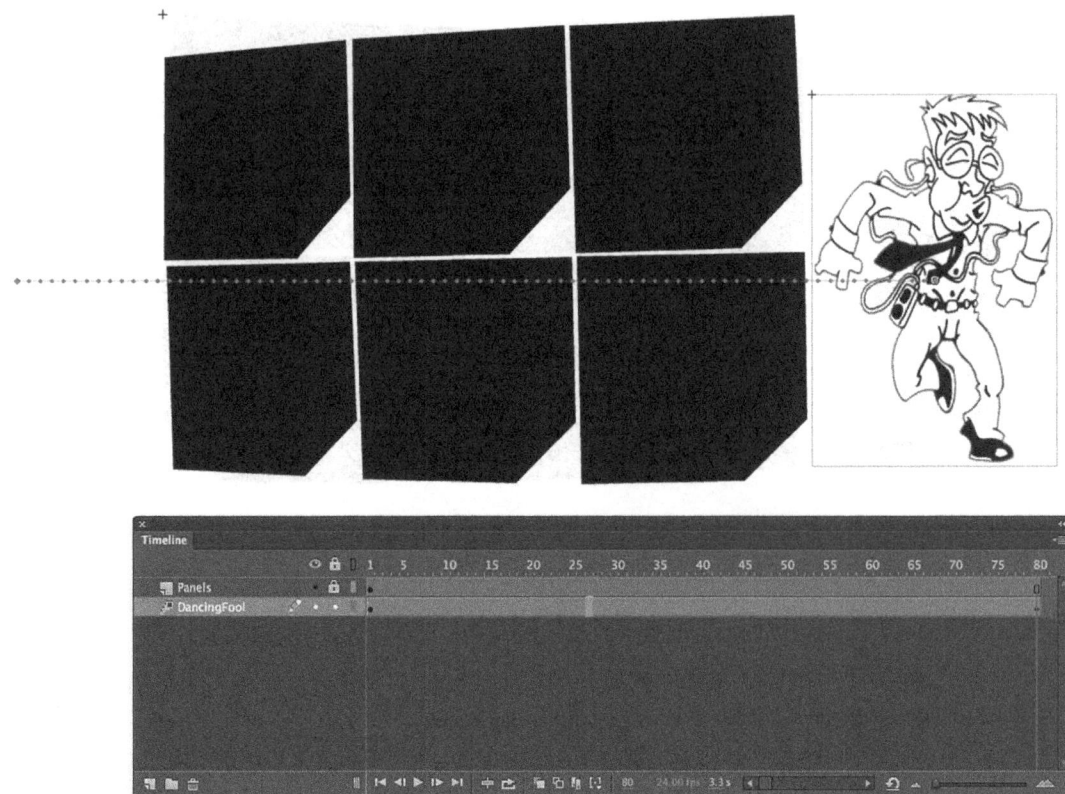

Figure 3-46. *The assets are in place, and you can now move on to creating the movie*

4. Right-click (Ctrl+click) on the Panels layer and select Mask from the context menu. If you scrub across the timeline, you will see the mask you just applied.

5. Click the Scene 1 link to return to the main timeline. The Mask movieclip just created is the white dot shown in Figure 3-47 and it's located just above the panels being masked.

CHAPTER 3 ■ SYMBOLS AND LIBRARIES

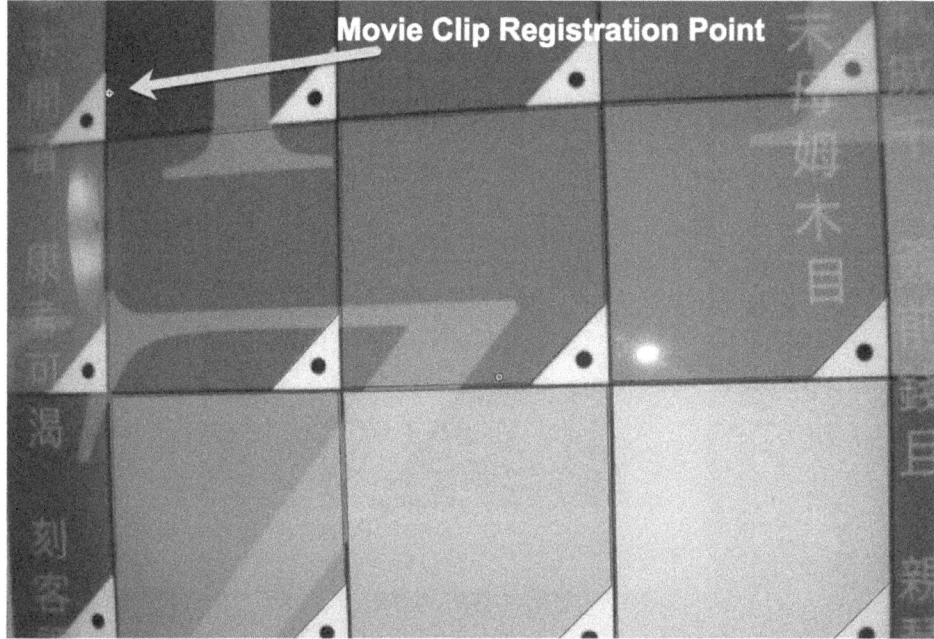

Figure 3-47. *The movieclip with the mask appears as a white dot on the main timeline*

6. Save the movie and test it.

Your Turn: A Sunny Day on Catalina Island

In this final exercise we are going to let you turn a fog bank rolling in on Catalina Island just west of Los Angeles into a blue sky with clouds. Here's how:

1. Open `18_Catalina.fla`. You will see, as shown in Figure 3-48, the foggy image is already on the stage and the clouds image is in the Library.

CHAPTER 3 ■ SYMBOLS AND LIBRARIES

Figure 3-48. *You can do amazing stuff with only two images and Animate CC's tools*

The plan for this project is simple. Replace the fog bank in the sky with the clouds image and, to give it a bit of eye candy, put the clouds in motion. You may be thinking why not simply pop open Photoshop, pull out the fog, heave in the clouds, and save it as a .psd or .jpg image? The answer is sometimes all you get is a .fla and you don't have the extra time to manipulate the image elsewhere. Also, this is as good a time as any for you to start getting comfortable with the tools in Animate CC.

2. There is obviously a lot more stage than there is image. Click the stage, and in the Properties panel, click the Advanced Settings button to open the Document Settings dialog box. Click the Match Contents button to shrink the stage to the size of the image and click OK.

If you are designing Animate CC movies and the stage is larger than the stuff on it, get into the habit of reducing the stage size. Wasted space, in the Animate CC universe, translates into increased download times. Remember, when you think Animate CC, think small.

3. Add a new layer to the timeline and name it FogMask. Move it above the Catalina layer.

4. Select the Pen tool in the toolbox. Turn off the Fill and draw a shape that follows the tops of the mountains and covers the bottom of the image, as shown in Figure 3-49.

CHAPTER 3 ■ SYMBOLS AND LIBRARIES

Figure 3-49. *Draw a shape that covers the mountains and the harbor*

5. Select the Paint Bucket tool and fill the shape with a color of your choosing.

6. Right-click (Ctrl+click) the FogMask layer and convert it to a mask. The clouds will disappear and the harbor will reappear.

Adding the Clouds

With the fog bank masked out, you can now turn your attention to the sky and make the day a lot brighter.

1. Add a new layer named Clouds and drag it under the mask layers.

2. Drag the Clouds.jpg image from the Library into the Clouds layer. Line the right edge of the clouds image against the right edge of the stage.

    As you can see in Figure 3-50, there is a problem. The clouds image is huge and you have no idea where the top of the stage is located. This is a "non-issue" if your intention is to go no farther. All of the excess will be "trimmed off" when you test the movie because content that isn't on the stage isn't visible at runtime. We intend to put the clouds in motion so let's solve the issue:

175

CHAPTER 3 ■ SYMBOLS AND LIBRARIES

Figure 3-50. The clouds are added

1. Select the Clouds layer and add a new layer named CloudsMask above it.
2. Turn off the visibility of the Clouds layer to turn off the image, which lets you see the top of the stage.
3. Select the CloudsMask layer and draw a rectangle that covers the white area of the stage.
4. Turn on the visibility of the Clouds layer, select the image, and convert it to a movieclip.
5. Turn the CloudsMask layer into a mask. As shown in Figure 3-51, the image is looking a lot better.

Figure 3-51. *Two masks and the day is looking brighter*

Putting the Clouds in Motion

In this, the final part of the exercise, we are going to put the clouds in motion. There are several ways of doing this but the issue we will be dealing with has to do with something one of the authors tells his students: "Pay attention to the world around you." In the case of the clouds, the image is flat and the clouds won't look quite right because, even though they can move sideways or up and down, they will still look flat. Instead, let's have the clouds move toward the viewer. Here's how:

1. Scrub over to frame 200 of the main timeline and add a frame to all of the layers. This tells you the animation will occur over 200 frames.

2. Unlock the Clouds layer, right-click anywhere in the Clouds layer's timeline, and select Create Motion Tween.

3. Select the Clouds movieclip on the stage and select Window ➤ Transform. This opens the Transform panel.

CHAPTER 3 ■ SYMBOLS AND LIBRARIES

We are going to get a lot deeper into the Transform panel in Chapter 9. For now, though, pay attention to the 3D Rotation settings. These settings allow you to rotate objects on the X, Y, and Z axes in 3D space.

4. With Frame 1 of the Clouds movieclip selected on the stage, set the X value in the Transform panel's 3D Rotation area to 60 degrees. The clouds will "tilt," as shown in Figure 3-52. Close the Transform panel.

Figure 3-52. *Tilt the clouds to add a degree of realism*

5. With the Clouds movieclip still selected, move the playhead to frame 200.
6. Click once on the Clouds movieclip and, in the Properties panel, twirl down the 3D Position and View area.
7. In the 3D Position and View area change the Z value to -300.
8. If you scrub across the timeline, the clouds will look like they are moving toward you.
9. To complete the effect, lock the Clouds layer to reestablish the mask. If the clouds seem to be hanging off either side of the stage, click the Clip content outside of the stage button to trim off the excess.
10. Save and test the movie. The cloud motion (Figure 3-53) looks a lot more realistic.

Figure 3-53. *The small value change on the Z axis makes the clouds move lazily across the sky*

Bonus Round

The purpose of this exercise was to not only let you play with the tools but to reinforce the fact that the more subtle effects are, more often than not, the most effective ones. Still you can have a blast with this exercise. Here's just one idea:

Slide another copy of the Clouds movieclip into a new layer under the masked clouds. If you unlock the masked Clouds layer, select it and apply a variety of blends from the Properties panel. You can get a number of different effects, ranging from a softer sky (Overlay) to a post nuclear blast sky (Subtract). Have fun.

What You Have Learned

- How to create and use symbols in Animate CC animations and movies
- How to create and share libraries among Animate CC movies
- The power of filters and blends
- A variety of methods for managing onstage content
- How to create and use a mask
- How to use masks and the 3D tools in Animate CC to create a realistic sky

In the next chapter, you will be exposed to the coding aspects of Animate CC.

CHAPTER 4

Interactivity Basics

To create interactive content within an Animate project, some basic programming knowledge is necessary. Animate makes it possible to build code-driven content across nearly all of the various target platforms it supports. This is not to say our intention is to turn you into a programmer outright, but an understanding of the JavaScript and ActionScript languages and the fundamentals of coding will make your day-to-day life easier.

Here is what we'll cover in this chapter:

- Using the Actions panel
- Understanding the fundamentals of programming
- Commenting code
- Creating and using variables
- Using data types, operators, and conditionals
- Using the Code Snippets panel
- Working with JavaScript and ActionScript
- Getting help

The following files are used in the exercises in this chapter (located in Chapter04/Exercise Files_CH04/):

- Instance.fla
- Events.fla
- Twinkle.fla
- PauseTimeline.fla
- CarRace.fla
- AddSnippet.fla
- CodeHint.fla

Additionally, we've provided completed versions of several exercises for your reference in the Exercise folder.

The source files are available at http://www.apress.com/us/book/9781484223758.

Using code in either JavaScript or ActionScript is a lot like owning a car. Our hunch is that most of you own one, or have at least thought about owning one. We also suspect that some of you (including at least one of the authors) find the mechanics of a car so mystifying or just plain difficult to deal with that you prefer to let a mechanic handle routine maintenance. Others of you won't be happy unless the hood is up and you're covered in grease up to your elbows. Whichever way you lean, it's hard to argue against acquiring at least the basic skills necessary to change the oil and maybe fix a flat tire. You never know when you'll be stuck on the side of the road with poor or nonexistent cellular service!

CHAPTER 4 ▪ INTERACTIVITY BASICS

This chapter gives you an introduction to programming as it relates to Animate and the primary target platforms it supports. We trust the following information will guide you past the first few mile markers.

Using Code in Animate

Creating interactive content using older versions of Animate (back when it was called Flash Professional) was relatively easy to explain. We were only ever dealing with ActionScript as our programming language and there was no need to differentiate between how to do go about things across platforms with the exception of certain functionality being present in AIR, which didn't exist in Flash Player. Things are a bit more complicated now that we have the additional HTML5 Canvas and WebGL document types, because they do not use ActionScript at all—they both use JavaScript.

To further complicate matters, HTML5 Canvas uses the CreateJS JavaScript libraries—which thankfully mimic much of the syntax of ActionScript—and WebGL uses a completely separate syntax altogether. The result of all this, is that we are dealing with two separate languages with at least two implementations of one of those languages. You might imagine this can get confusing rather quickly!

There is good news though... it's not all that bad. In fact, the CreateJS libraries, as you will see, were crafted with ActionScript in mind. Even to the point where simple timeline navigation commands are basically identical between the two platforms.

So, where did these languages come from, being that they are so similar? JavaScript is the de facto language used when dealing with the native web browser and ActionScript is used when creating content for Flash Player and AIR. Before Macromedia joined the Adobe family, it looked at the programming languages used for web interactivity and realized JavaScript was predominant. Rather than add yet another language, the decision was made to stay within the parameters of something called the ECMA-262 specification. This makes ActionScript a close cousin of JavaScript, so if you're already comfortable with that, you may find ActionScript encouragingly familiar and should be able to easily work within both languages.

ECMA International (formerly the European Computer Manufacturers Association) is an industry standards association that governs a number of specifications for data storage, character sets, and programming languages, including specs for C++ and C#. It's something like the World Wide Web Consortium (W3C), which manages the specifications for HTML, XML, and CSS.

So much for history. Let's roll up our sleeves and get covered in electrons up to our elbows by getting to know the interface for working with code within Animate: the Actions panel.

The Actions Panel

Let's take a look at what the Actions panel has to offer. Create a new ActionScript 3.0 Animate document. When the document appears, select Window ➤ Actions or press F9 (fn+F9) to open the Actions panel. As shown in Figure 4-1, this panel has two distinct zones: the Script Navigator and the Script pane.

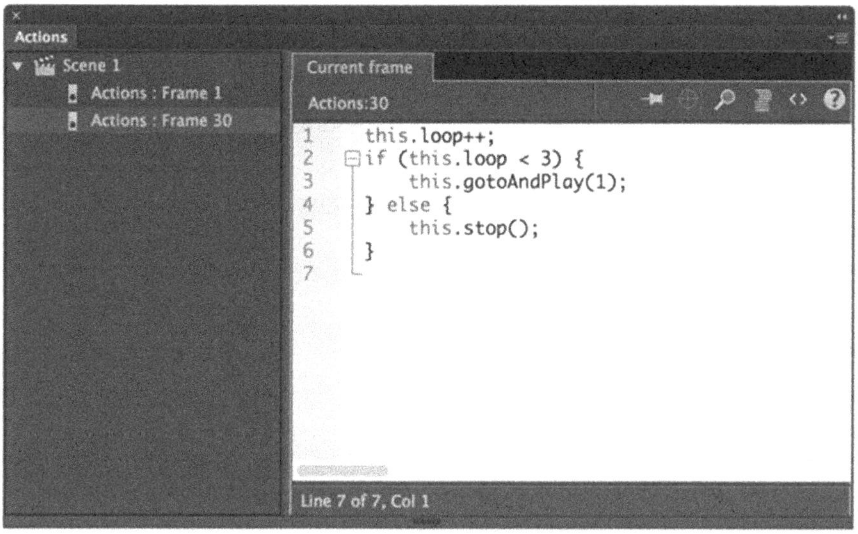

CHAPTER 4 ■ INTERACTIVITY BASICS

Figure 4-1. *The Actions panel with some code placed in it*

While there are many other ways of writing code for an Animate project, the Actions panel is the most direct method, as it is completely integrated within Animate itself. It has evolved through significant changes since its introduction in Flash 4, and it even reveals a handful of new features since Flash 8. With the original release of Flash Professional CC, the application we know today as Animate was completely rewritten and a new version of the Actions panel was born. Engineers at Adobe integrated a well-known open source code editor into the application to more easily support multiple languages. Because of this, you can write either ActionScript or JavaScript directly within your Animate project, depending on the chosen target platform!

Script Navigator

Code may be placed in any keyframe on any movieclip timeline—though it is preferable for all code to exist on the main timeline, if possible. The script navigator area shows which frames have scripts, and it allows you to quickly jump to the desired code. Sometimes within an Animate project, you will have most of your code on a single keyframe, but have additional code scattered across the project on various keyframes of the main timeline or even nested in different movieclip symbol instances. The Script Navigator makes it much easier to see where all your code lives, and to jump to those specific scripts with ease.

Selected scripts may be "pinned" beneath the Script pane. Each pinned script is displayed as a new tab, which provides an alternative navigation method.

Script Pane

The Script pane is the high-traffic zone of the Actions panel, because it's where you type your code. Along the top of the pane, you'll find the following buttons for working with your code (see Figure 4-2).

- **Pin Script:** Pins the current frame script to the tabbed interface so that you can quickly jump between scripts without needing to navigate to different areas of the timeline or even within different symbol instances.

183

- **Insert instance Path and Name:** Helps you set an absolute or relative target path for an action in the script.
- **Find:** Let's you find and replace text in your code.
- **Format Code:** Sweeps through your code to correct its posture, based on your own formatting preferences.
- **Code Snippets:** Summons the Code Snippets panel directly from the Actions panel.
- **Help:** Access web-based documentation for Animate.

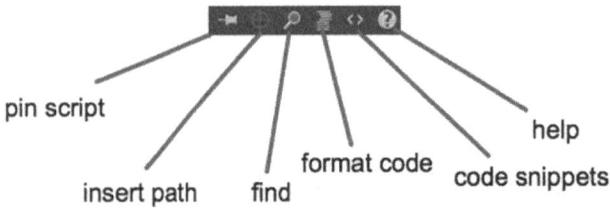

Figure 4-2. *The Script pane buttons*

Actions Panel Context Menu

The Actions panel's context menu, shown in Figure 4-3, will appear if you perform a right-click within the code editor. Many of its choices repeat functionality already discussed—such as Format Code or View Help—but a good handful of choices show features unavailable anywhere else. These include the ability to toggle code folding, comment or uncomment a selection, and toggle or remove breakpoints when debugging ActionScript.

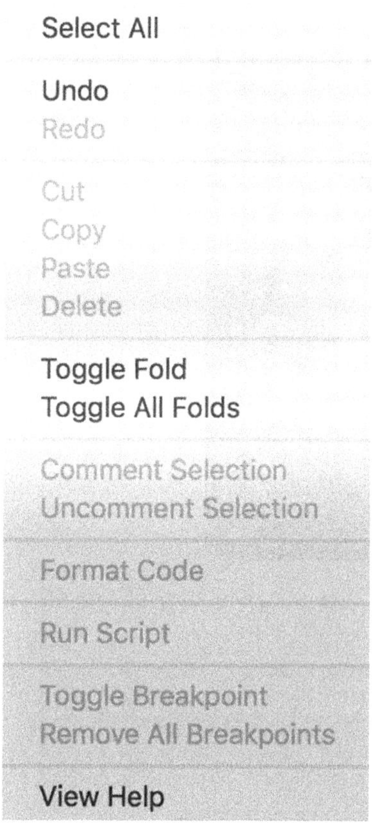

CHAPTER 4 ■ INTERACTIVITY BASICS

Select All

Undo
Redo

Cut
Copy
Paste
Delete

Toggle Fold
Toggle All Folds

Comment Selection
Uncomment Selection

Format Code

Run Script

Toggle Breakpoint
Remove All Breakpoints

View Help

Figure 4-3. The Actions panel context menu

Edit and View Menu Items

There are even more settings and commands to be found in the application menu. If you choose Edit or View with the Actions panel open and focused, you will get additional choices that impact your code experience.

185

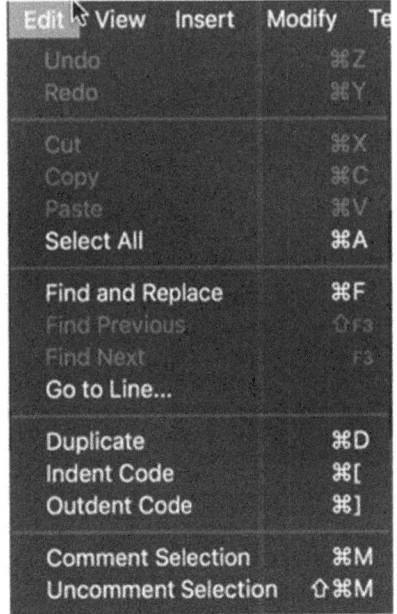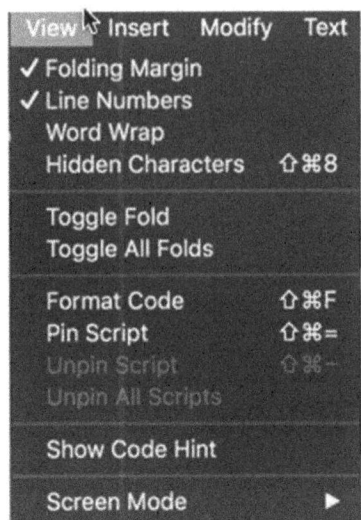

Figure 4-4. The Edit and View Menu options

Within the Edit menu, with the Actions panel active, you will find:

- **Find and Replace:** Opens the Find and Replace toolbar within the code editor.
- **Find Previous/Find Next:** Allows quick transversal of found terms with the Find and Replace toolbar active.
- **Go to Line:** Allows you to jump to a specific line of code in the current frame script.
- **Duplicate:** Duplicates the entire line of code indicated by the position of the cursor.
- **Indent Code/Outdent Code:** Quickly performs the indent or outdent of selected lines of code.
- **Comment Selection/Uncomment Selection:** Allows the quick commenting or uncommenting of the selected lines of code.

Choosing the View menu with the Actions Panel active will reveal the following:

- **Folding Margin:** When using the code folding feature of the Actions panel, the fold indicators are displayed within the margin by the line numbers. Enabled by default.
- **Line Numbers:** Will show or hide line numbers for being displayed. Enabled by default.
- **Word Wrap:** Lines of code that extend past the width of the code editor will wrap to the next line with this option enabled.
- **Hidden Characters:** When enabled, will display non-visual items like tab indents or line breaks as symbols within the code editor.

- **Toggle Fold/Toggle All Folds:** Allows the quick toggling of any folded code.
- **Format Code:** Just like the code toolbar option of the same name, formats your code in conformity with your defined code edit preferences.
- **Pin Script/Unpin Script/Unpin All Scripts:** Allows the management of pinned scripts in a similar way to what is available through buttons in the Script pane.
- **Show Code Hint:** Displays the code hint menu in the code editor if the cursor is positioned at an appropriate term.

A really good habit to develop is to keep Line Numbers selected in the View menu. Code can get very long, and if there is a mistake, your debugging environment (whether Animate itself or the web browser) usually tells you the line number where the mistake can be found.

Code Editor Preferences

There is another aspect to editing code within Animate that isn't entirely obvious from within the Actions panel, but is immensely important as it sets a lot of the underlying rules through which any code is handled through the editor. The aspect we are referring to is the Code Editor settings found in the application Preferences dialog box.

We've already seen how to adjust Animate preferences in Chapter 1, but didn't go too deeply into the Code Editor portion of the preferences dialog box. We will do so now—as we now hold the proper context. To access this dialog box, choose Preferences from the application menu. Once the Preferences dialog box is open, Click the Code Editor option from the left column to reveal both the Editing Options and Format Code sections.

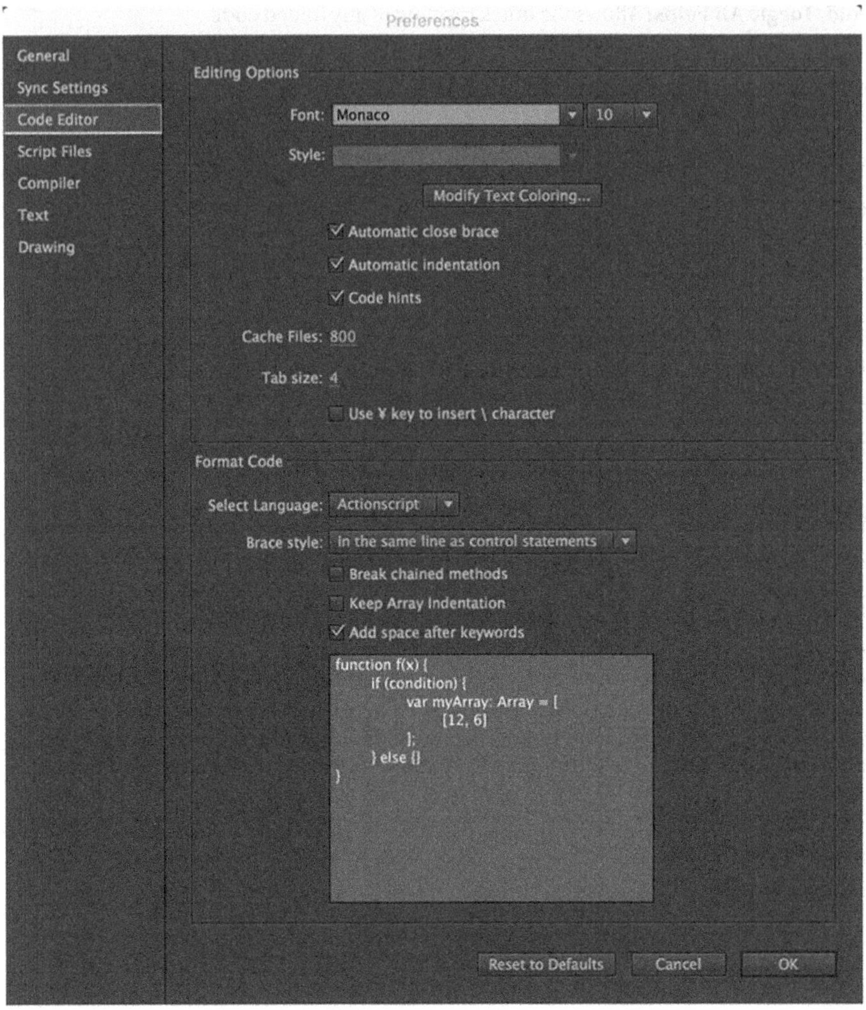

CHAPTER 4 ■ INTERACTIVITY BASICS

Figure 4-5. Code Editor Preferences dialog box

Editing Options

In this portion of the Code Editor Preferences dialog box, the options define the look and behavior of certain aspects of the coding experience in Animate. You can choose font family and size for display within the Actions panel and even modify the coloring used in the code editor for various aspects of the code itself, and the surface background.

There are also options to determine whether Animate will automatically close braces or not when a beginning brace is created, automatic indentation of functional code blocks, and the use of code hinting within the editor as you type your scripts.

CHAPTER 4　INTERACTIVITY BASICS

While it's true that there are certain conventions and code styles that teams and organizations may adopt—when using Animate as an individual—these options allow you to conform the code editing options to whatever choices you are personally comfortable with.

Format Code

The Format Code section defines rules for formatting both ActionScript and JavaScript code within the editor. The languages can be switched through the Select Language drop-down, which determines which formatting options directly beneath apply to each specific language. Switching between language selections will preserve the selections already made for that language, so no fear in losing your settings when switching back and forth. From here, you can determine the brace style, whether to break chained methods to a new line or not, handle array indentation, and decide whether or not to insert spaces directly after keywords.

An important thing to keep an eye on—no matter which language you are defining formatting rules for—is the small preview area below which will preview your code formatting options. Using this, you can determine how your code will be formatted without needed to even leave the preferences dialog box.

The Code Snippets Panel

Code snippets are pieces of code you save and reuse on a regular basis. They are a fairly regular feature in most code editors, and the editor environment within Animate is no exception. The Code Snippets panel ships with sets of snippets for ActionScript, HTML5 Canvas, and WebGL document types. It's a great way to learn how to go about performing common coding tasks in your Animate projects.

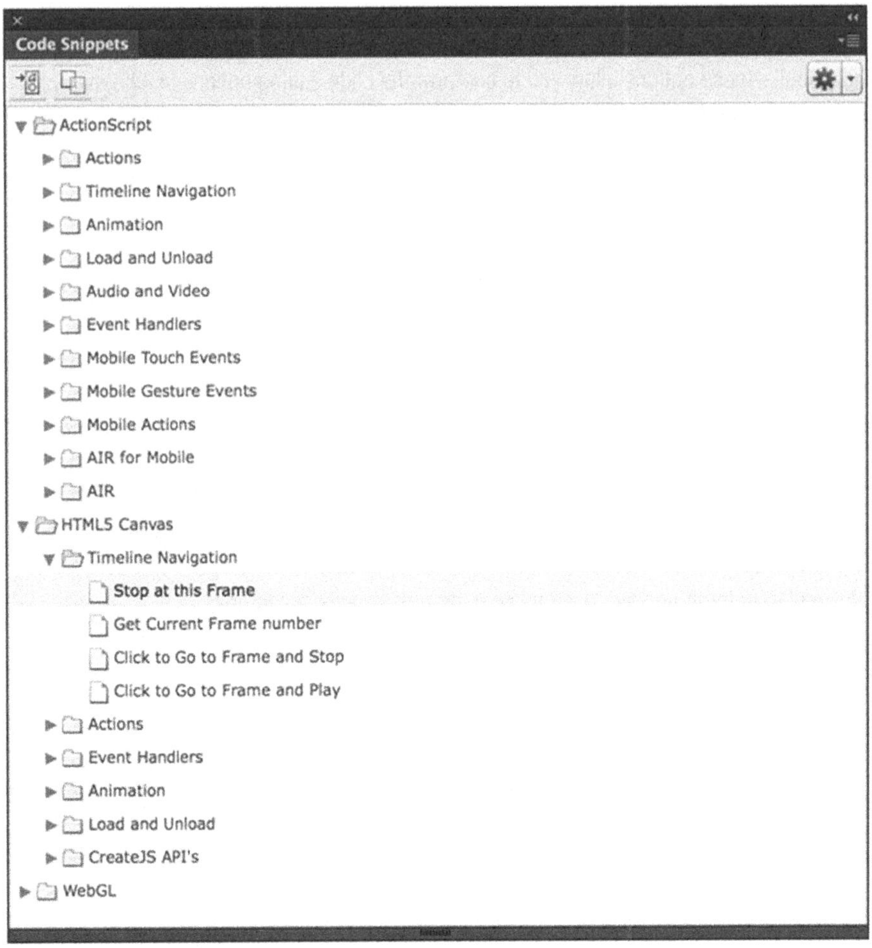

CHAPTER 4 ■ INTERACTIVITY BASICS

Figure 4-6. Code Snippets panel

Not only can you use any of the snippets that are built into Animate—but as is the case with most snippet mechanisms—you can define and store your own custom sets of snippets. We'll explore code snippets in greater detail later on in this chapter.

JavaScript and ActionScript

Depending on your chosen target platform, you are likely going to be using either JavaScript or ActionScript within your project. This chapter (as the whole of this book) will focus on working with ActionScript 3.0 and HTML5 Canvas document types, as these are the most common and mature target platforms used within Animate. Additionally, you will find that the code used to perform simple tasks for each of these platforms is nearly identical, making it fairly straightforward to work with code examples across both platforms.

Even though we are able to target completely different platforms from Animate CC, it is important to keep in mind that the primary difference really comes down to interactive elements and the code behind it all. When using HTML5 Canvas, you'll be writing code in JavaScript employing the CreateJS libraries and targeting the native HTML `<canvas/>` element. When dealing with ActionScript 3.0 document types, you'll be using ActionScript and produce either a `.SWF` to run within Flash Player, an .AIR bundle to run within the AIR runtime, or even a native app for Windows, macOS, iOS, or Android. The creation and use of assets and .FLA document structure and workflow remains nearly identical no matter what the target platform is, making it simple to share assets, animations, and more across different project types.

JavaScript using CreateJS and ActionScript are so very similar in basic syntax within Animate that there is little need to actually go into much difference in the syntax and specific code examples that follow—but when there are important distinctions, they will be noted.

General Programming Concepts in Animate CC

Your first step in using any sort of code within Animate, and possibly the most important, is to think in terms of objects. This concept is fundamental to both ActionScript's object-oriented environment or the use of JavaScript and its implementation through CreateJS. This concept ties the whole structure to an elegant, unifying metaphor. So, what is an object? Well, that's just it: you already know what an object is! An object is a thing—something you can look at, pick up, and manipulate with code.

The Animate interface allows you to "physically" manipulate certain objects—movieclips, text fields, and so on—by means of the Free Transform tool, the Properties panel, and other tools and panels. But that's only the tip of the iceberg, and merely one way of looking at the "reality" of the parts of an Animate project.

In code, objects aren't physical things, but if you place yourself mentally into Animate territory, you'll find it helpful to imagine them that way. With any form of programming, you're dealing with an abstract world. In this world, objects "live" in the parallel universe determined by the binary information stored in your project. That information may be governed by tools and panels, or by the code you write, or both.

This fact is one of the most beautiful and unique things about Animate itself. This environment is the perfect union between designer and programmer roles. You can be as creative and animated as you wish using all the visual tools Animate provides, and you are free to experiment and extend these very same assets and concepts through use of a dynamic and extensive coding environment.

Every movieclip in your project is an object. So is every text field and button. In fact, everything you use, interactive or not, is an object. For visual elements, this is generally an easy concept to grasp—you can see them on the stage—but it goes further. Things you might not think of as objects, such as the characteristics of a filter effect or changes in font settings, can be described in terms of objects. Even nonvisual notions—such as math functions, today's date, and the formula used to move an object from here to there—are objects. Thinking of these in this way may seem disorienting at first, but the concept should ultimately empower you, because it means you can manipulate everything of functional value in your project as if it were a tangible thing. The best part is that all objects are determined by something called a *class*. In many respects, classes provide a kind of owner's manual for any object you encounter, which is a big tip on how to approach the documentation.

It is important to keep in mind that classes are a bit different between the two languages. In JavaScript, classes are not actually classes in the traditional programming sense, whereas when using ActionScript, you are using a more traditional class model. This will change with upcoming versions of JavaScript set to adopt something closer to the ActionScript model of classes, bringing the two languages even closer together.

Before we move on to the owner's manual, let's look at two objects: Joseph and Tom. The authors of this book, in object terms, are human beings. We'll refine this analogy in just a moment, but for now, let's say our class is Male. You can look at either one of us and say, with certainty, "Yep, those are two guys." But drill deeper, and you'll discover that even though we are of the same class, we are also quite different, which is where the owner's manual comes into play.

Classes

Think of a class as a sort of blueprint or recipe for a given object. If you're a fan of pizza, all you need is a single pizza recipe, and you're good to go. As long as you follow the recipe, every pizza you make will be as good as the one that came before it. Some pizzas will be larger than others, some will be square, some round, and the toppings will certainly change, but there's no mistaking what's on your plate. It's the same with objects.

A movieclip symbol is defined by the `MovieClip` class in ActionScript or when using JavaScript—CreateJS also has an equivalent `MovieClip` class. Any given movieclip will have its own width and height, and it might have a longer or shorter individual timeline, but all movieclips have dimensions, and all movieclips have a timeline. Along the same lines, every type of object has its own unique qualities. These are generally defined by some combination of three facets:

- Characteristics the object has
- Things the object can do
- Things the object can react to

In programming terms, these facets are known respectively as properties, methods, and events. Collectively, these are called members of a class. This also explains why even though Joseph and Tom fit into the class Male, we are also different. We feature the same properties across the board—height, drivers license, Moose Lodge membership, and, say, hair—but each has his own unique values for those properties. For example, Tom's Moose Lodge membership expires next year, but Joseph's has only begun. Someday, one of us might have the value bald for his hair property—but not yet. In fact, Joseph's hair property would have quite different values from Tom's even now. It's the same with methods and events.

It's time to refine the analogy in which Joseph and Tom are instances of the Male class. Both of the authors have pets, and it's immediately clear these pets aren't instances of the Male class. So, let's reshuffle our thinking a bit.

In a broader sense, the authors are instances of a class that could be called Human. That means our pets aren't part of our class, which is obvious. But here is where it gets interesting. As it turns out, the Human class, in turn, fits into an even broader category called Mammal, which fits into a broader category still, called Vertebrates, then Animal, and so on. The broader you go, the more the members of these groups have in common. It's when you get narrower—down to the Human branch, for example—that specifics come into play. Mammals, for example, don't lay eggs (with very few exceptions!); they feed their young milk, and so forth. This distinguishes mammals from other vertebrates, such as fish or amphibians; and yet, as vertebrates, all backbone animals at least have a spine in common, which explains how our pets and their authors can share a class.

It works the same way in ActionScript or in JavaScript with CreateJS. The MovieClip class defines movieclip symbols no matter what the programming language. You learned about movieclips in Chapter 3, but at the time, we didn't clue you in to the fact that movieclips belong to a larger family tree. The reason we withheld this information earlier is because the ancestors of movieclips are available only in code, not something you can create with drawing tools. Just as Human is a sort of Mammal... in ActionScript, MovieClip is a sort of Sprite... and in CreateJS, MovieClip is a sort of Container. Where mammals—the authors and their pets—are a particular sort of vertebrate, the Sprite class is a particular sort of DisplayObject. The list continues. Further down the family tree, taking the ActionScript example even further, the DisplayObjectContainer class is simply one branch of the InteractiveObject class, which itself is a particular branch of the DisplayObject class.

Here is a visual to clarify this across all three models we've discussed:

Real World: Mammal ➤ Vertebrate ➤ Human

ActionScript 3.0: DisplayObjectContainer ➤ Sprite ➤ MovieClip

JavaScript/CreateJS: DisplayObject ➤ Container ➤ MovieClip

You can see in this simple example how while MovieClip is the class you will be working with most often in either language, since it is exposed directly within the Animate interface, the ancestors of that class can differ somewhat. This is simply due to platform differences and the different ways in which JavaScript and ActionScript are constructed at their core. You likely needn't worry about such low-level differences until you feel proficient enough to expand beyond the basics.

If your eyes are already starting to glaze over, don't worry. You won't see a quiz on this stuff—not in this book. The important part is that you get a general sense that classes define only the functionality that's specific to the type of object they represent. The Mammal class wouldn't define what a spine is, because all mammals are vertebrates—along with fish and amphibians—so it would be redundant for each group of animal to restate that definition. All of these animals share a spine, and therefore all of their classes rely on the definition of "spine" from the Vertebrate class, from which they all inherit information. Bearing that in mind, let's take a closer look at properties, methods, and events.

Do you want to know the name of the absolute rock-bottom object—the class used as the starting point of all classes, inherited by them all? You'll smile when you hear it. The mother of all objects is...the Object class. Both ActionScript and JavaScript have an Object class and it is basically the same thing in both languages.

Properties

Properties might be the easiest class members to conceptualize, because they seem the most concrete. For example, Joseph and Tom both live in cities, but the value of our city property is different. Joseph's city value is Denver; Tom's is Toronto. Now wrap your mind around a movieclip on the Animate stage. That movieclip symbol clearly exists at a particular position on the stage. Its position is apparent during authoring because you establish it yourself, perhaps by dragging the movieclip by hand or by setting its coordinates with the Properties panel. To access these same properties with either JavaScript or ActionScript, you'll need to be able to call the movieclip by name, so to speak. This is where instance names come into play.

CHAPTER 4 ■ INTERACTIVITY BASICS

Instance Names

As you learned in Chapter 3, you may drag as many instances of a symbol to the stage as you please. So that an instance is set apart from the others—at least in terms of code access—each instance needs a unique instance name to identify it. Recall that the two authors are unique instances of the Human class. You tell us apart by giving each of us an instance name.

A symbol's given name in the Library and its instance name are not the same thing, so they can overlap if you like. But the instance name must be unique from other instance names in the same scope. What's scope? We'll touch on this later in the "Scope" section of this chapter, but think of scope as the environment's take on the concept of point of view. Joseph and Tom can both have a pet named Poe, and those names do count as unique from the point of view that refers to each dog as "Joseph's pet Poe" and "Tom's pet Poe." But there's another point of view—in Tom's head, for example—that simply refers to the dog as "Poe." From Tom's point of view, he can have only one dog by that name; otherwise, he won't know which of his dogs is which. In the same manner, two movieclips on the main timeline can't share the same instance name.

In general, there are a few rules and conventions for instance names: use lowercase letters (not a number or an uppercase letter) for first character, never use spaces, and generally, special symbols are a bad idea.

You name an instance through the appropriately named Instance Name field of the Properties panel. Once a movieclip has an instance name, you can access its `MovieClip` class members in terms of that particular movieclip instance. Here's how:

1. In your Chapter 4 exercise folder, open `Instance.fla`—this is an ActionScript 3.0 document.

2. Rename Layer 1 to Poe add a new layer named `Actions`. Then lock that new layer.

A standard practice in Animate development is to put scripts in a separate, locked layer named actions, scripts, or some other meaningful description. This way, all the code is in one place, and nothing else but scripts can be added to the layer. This has become an "unofficial" practice throughout the industry.

---

3. Open the Library and drag a copy of the `Poe.jpg` image into the content layer.

4. Convert the image to a movieclip symbol named Poe so that it appears in the Library by that name. Select the movieclip instance on the stage and give it the instance name poe in the Properties panel (as shown in Figure 4-7).

CHAPTER 4 ■ INTERACTIVITY BASICS

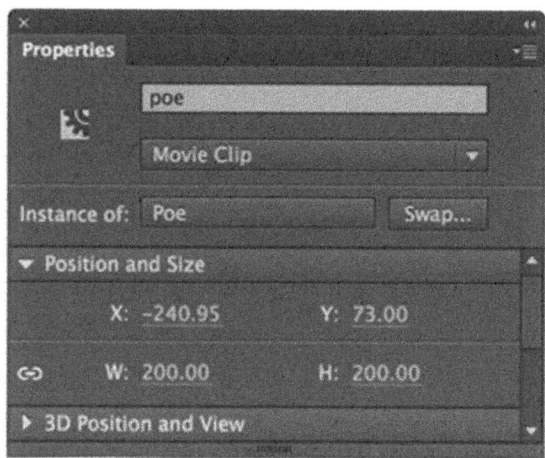

Figure 4-7. Instance names are added in the Properties panel

5. Use the Selection tool to drag the poe instance to the upper-left corner of the stage—not flush with the corner, just in the vicinity. Note its X and Y coordinates as indicated by the Properties panel. You're about to see ActionScript tell you these same figures.

6. Open the Actions panel by selecting Window ➤ Actions. Select frame 1 in the scripts layer. This directs the Actions panel to that frame—this is where your script will be stored. Type the following ActionScript into the Script pane:

   trace(this.poe.x, this.poe.y);

7. Close the Actions panel and test your movie.

After the SWF has been created, locate the Output panel, which will have opened automatically (it should appear in the area where the timeline is docked, but you can always show and hide it by selecting Window ➤ Output). In the Output panel, you'll see two numbers, as shown in Figure 4-8. They will be the same numbers you noted in your Properties panel. These numbers appear as a result of the trace() function you just typed. They are the horizontal and vertical coordinates—the MovieClip.x and MovieClip.y properties—of the poe instance of the MovieClip class. In fact, they match the X and Y coordinates shown in the Properties panel.

195

Figure 4-8. *The poe movieclip on the stage within the FLA shows its coordinates in the Properties panel. In the SWF, it shows its coordinates in the Output tab thanks to the trace() function.*

How does this work? The trace function accepts something called parameters, and these parameters affect the way the trace function acts. Whatever values you place between its parentheses, separated by a comma, are displayed in the Output panel. In this case, the two parameters are poe.x and poe.y. Like methods, functions are coding keywords that do things, but functions aren't associated with a class. We'll show you some additional examples of functions later in the chapter.

You'll find the trace() function to be a useful tool in experimenting with ActionScript and when troubleshooting your code. Its sole purpose is to display information normally under wraps, such as the value of an object property, an expression, or a variable. When using JavaScript, you can use console.log() in much the same way, displaying the results in the browser console. In actual practice, you might use a movieclip's position or the value of a property of an object to determine the outcome of some goal. For example, you might want a movieclip to stop being draggable after it has been dragged to a certain location on the stage. You wouldn't need the trace() or console.log() function to accomplish such a task, but it could certainly help you test your code along the way.

CHAPTER 4 ■ INTERACTIVITY BASICS

So that's how to accomplish this task using ActionScript, but what about JavaScript in an HTML5 Canvas document? Let's give that a look.

1. With the `Instance.fla` (ActionScript 3.0 document) still open, go to the Commands menu item and choose Convert to Other Document Formats.

2. In the dialog box that appears, choose HTML5 Canvas from the drop-down and click OK. Notice that the file is saved as a new FLA with _Canvas appended to the filename.

3. Open the Actions panel and locate the `trace()` function from before. Notice that Animate has commented it out? It now appears gray within the Script pane. This is because ActionScript will not be able to run within a HTML5 Canvas project. We need to convert this to JavaScript and will use the ActionScript as a guide!

4. Beneath the commented ActionScript, insert the following JavaScript code:

   `console.log(this.poe.x, this.poe.y);`

5. Now test your movie. The web browser will open and display the movie, just as you saw previously with the SWF. To actually see the console output, you will need to open the developer tools for your browser and view the Console.

6. To give an example of this, if using Google Chrome, you will access the option menu in the upper right and choose More Tools ➤ Developer Tools.

7. From here, click the Console tab and witness the same expected behavior!

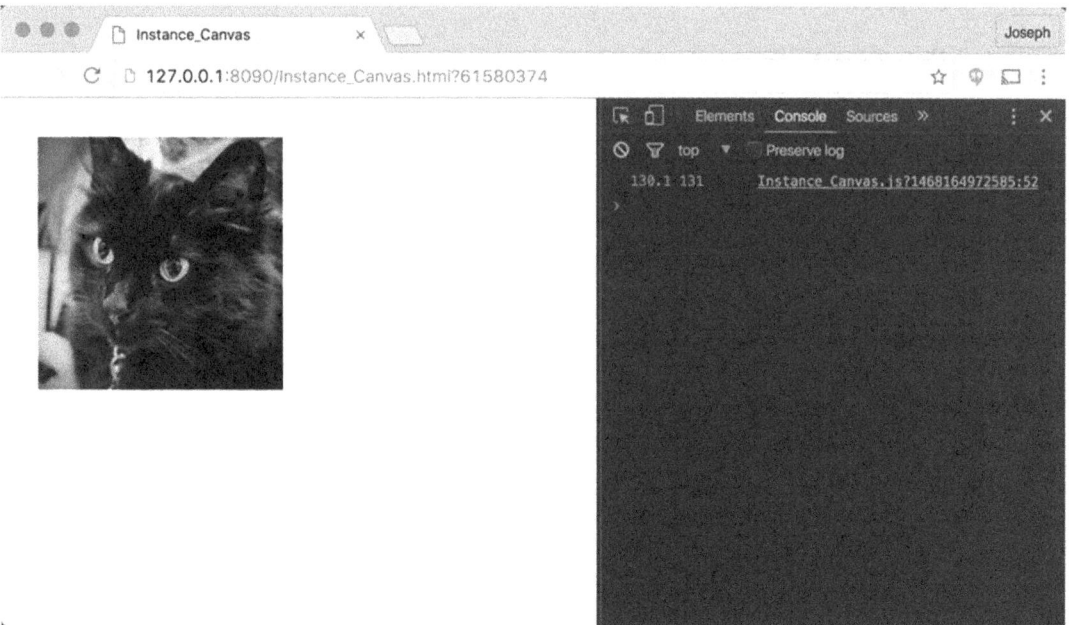

Figure 4-9. *The poe movieclip on the stage shows its coordinates in the Properties panel. In the browser, it shows its coordinates in the Console tab thanks to the console.log() function.*

You may have noticed that the X and Y positions differ between both the SWF and the HTML Canvas content. This is because in CreateJS, X and Y coordinates are always calculated based on the transform point of the object, which is located in the center of this movieclip.

For interest's sake, the X and Y properties of this movieclip don't originate with the `MovieClip` class. This is where the concept of inheritance, touched on earlier, comes into play. Movieclips certainly aren't the only objects that can be positioned on the stage. The same is true of button symbols, text fields, and many other objects. The classes that define these objects, many in their own offshoot branches of the family tree, all inherit X and Y properties (and more, besides) from a particular ancestor class. For instance, if you look up the `MovieClip` class entry in the ActionScript 3.0 Reference for the Adobe Flash platform, you might not see the X and Y properties at first. The documentation features headings for properties, methods, and events, and each heading has a hyperlink that lets you see inherited functionality. We'll talk more about the documentation in the "How to read the ActionScript 3.0 Reference for the Adobe Flash Platform" and "How to read the CreateJS Docs" sections later in this chapter.

Setting Properties with Code

In addition to being retrieved, or read, in this manner, many properties (but not all) can also be set via code. Here's how:

1. Save your current file to preserve your work thus far.

2. Select frame 1 of the scripts layer, if it isn't already selected, and return to the Actions panel. Delete the existing line of code. Enter the following new lines and test your movie again:

   ```
   this.poe.x = 300;
   this.poe.y = -50;
   ```

This time, you'll see the image positioned at 300 pixels in from the left and 50 pixels past the top of the stage, just as if you had placed it there yourself.

Changing the code and then testing it at this point may seem a bit mundane in these simple examples. There is a very good reason why we are doing this. What you have been doing is changing the code and adding to it. Whether using JavaScript or ActionScript, things can get pretty complex. This is why now would be a good time to get into the habit of "Do a bit. Test it." This way, if there is a problem or an unexpected result, you can easily fix it because you know exactly where the change was made.

There are dozens of `MovieClip` properties, and we mentioned that not all are settable. One example is the `MovieClip.totalFrames` property, which indicates the number of frames in a movieclip's timeline. Another is `MovieClip.stage`, which indicates the stage on which a given movieclip exists. Some things simply are what they are. The documentation tells you at a glance what the full set of an object's properties is and which of them are read-only. Later in the chapter, we'll discuss how to best approach the documentation, but for now, let's keep rolling.

Methods

Methods are the "verbs" of an object—things the object can do. You can spot them right away, because they usually end in parentheses (()), which is the punctuation that actually runs the method or function in question. Staying with the Joseph and Tom metaphor, both of us can walk, but Joseph may decide to take a left turn at the corner, while Tom takes a right. Like functions, methods can accept parameters that alter the way the method is carried out.

As with properties, each unique object type has its own set of methods and properties. The Text (JS) or TextField (AS3) class, for example, provides for the selection of text in various ways. These methods are absent in the MovieClip class for either language, which makes perfect sense because movieclips do movieclip things and text fields do text things. The Graphics class provides for the programmatic drawing of stroke and fill. It makes equally good sense that its methods are unique to itself and that neither it or text fields can send the playhead to the frame of a movieclip's timeline.

Let's keep exploring our movieclip instance, because movieclips are arguably the most important object in Animate to learn. Why? Because the main timeline itself is functionally identical to a MovieClip instance, which makes the main timeline and stage of your projects equivalent to movieclip symbols. If you're interested in controlling the main timeline, you'll want to know where to look for the necessary methods, and those are found in the MovieClip class. The main point is that if you're planning to send the playhead from frame to frame on the main timeline, it means you're using a timeline, which means you're using the equivalent of a MovieClip class.

As you learned in previous chapters, timelines have frames. By default, the playhead runs along those frames, displaying whatever visual assets they contain. In other words, the natural tendency of a movieclip is to move, rather than stand still. As you'll see, the MovieClip class provides methods to stop the playhead, send it to a specified frame (skipping frames in between), and stop or play from there, plus plenty more. These methods are generally identical whether using an ActionScript 3.0 or HTM5 Canvas document type.

1. Save the original Instance.fla ActionScript 3.0 document file as Instance4.fla. Make sure to use the original ActionScript 3.0 based document for this as we will be using ActionScript for this example.

2. Delete the existing three lines of code and close the Actions panel for now.

3. Click frame 50 of the Poe layer. Select Insert ➤ Timeline ➤ Frame, which displays the poe instance over a span of 50 frames.

4. Right-click (Windows) or Control+click (Mac) anywhere inside the span of frames and select Create Motion Tween from the menu that appears.

5. In frame 50, use the Selection tool to reposition the box instance to the right side of the stage, and use the Free Transform tool to increase its size. Notice a small diamond appears on that frame? This indicates a keyframe and change in property.

6. Test your movie. You should see the poe instance move from the left side of the stage to the right, increasing in size as it goes. So far, this is nothing new. This is the same sort of tweening done in Chapter 1.

    In the previous section, we referred to the poe instance to access its MovieClip properties. Here, we could access its methods in essentially the same way—and we will in the next section, "Events"—but for the time being, let's refer to the main timeline instead. Ah, but wait a moment! The main timeline doesn't have an instance name. How is this going to work? The solution depends on a special, flexible keyword: this. The meaning of the this keyword changes depending on context and it differs a bit when working with JavaScript or ActionScript. Since your code is in a keyframe of the main timeline, it refers, in this context, to the main timeline.

CHAPTER 4 ■ INTERACTIVITY BASICS

The this keyword is one of a small selection of special statements in ActionScript and CreateJS JavaScript that stand apart from all the classes that make up either language's objects. When you see this in code, recognize it as a reference to the timeline in which it appears or to the object in which it appears. It will generally refer to the current scope, but be aware that this concept is much more cloudy when using JavaScript.

7. Click in frame 1 of the scripts layer and open the Actions panel.

8. Type the following ActionScript and test your movie:

    ```
    trace(this);
    ```

9. The movie will animate as before, but this time you'll see a new message in the Output panel: [object MainTimeline]. Bingo!

If you were using an HTML5 Canvas document and wanted to view this within the browser console, you would need to use the following syntax: console.log(this); You then could see all the members that apply to that scope as displayed via an object identified in the console as lib.Instance4. This is the CreateJS equivalent to MainTimeline, which can be expanded within the console and all of its members examined in detail.

As the movie naturally loops, the message will repeat itself whenever the playhead enters frame 1. So, because you know the main timeline contains a movieclip, you now have your reference to a MovieClip instance. At this point, you simply follow that reference with a dot and refer to the desired MovieClip method.

10. Replace the existing code with the following ActionScript and then test your movie:

    ```
    this.stop();
    ```

11. Test your movie. This time, the movie stays put at frame 1. Visually, that's pretty boring, but the fact is, you just used ActionScript to direct the course of a SWF! Let's do something a little more interesting.

12. Comment out the existing ActionScript by putting two forward slashes at the beginning of line 1.

    ```
    //this.stop();
    ```

    For some of you, the term *commenting* might seem a bit odd. In fact, commenting is a standard coding best practice. The most common use for comments is to let others (or even a future-you) know what something does. For example, your comment for the previous line would be as follows:

    ```
    // This code stops the timeline on frame 1
    ```

    Don't forget to add the slashes. Omit them, and Animate's Output panel will give you this rather cryptic message:

    Scene 1, Layer 'Layer 1', Frame 1 1071: Syntax error: expected a definition keyword (such as function) after attribute This, not code.

That message translates to this: "I don't have a clue what this is." Use code coloring as your visual clue. If a comment is gray, it is a comment. We get deeper into this subject later in this chapter.

What's code coloring? Certain words, phrases, and other terms that Animate recognizes will be colored black, blue, green, violet, or gray. The words `this` and `stop` are reserved and are violet by default, though you can customize these colors by selecting Edit (Animate) ➤ Preferences ➤ Code Editor and then choosing Modify Code Coloring. Gray is the default color for commented code, which is nonfunctional as long as it remains a comment. Keep an eye on the code color. If the word `stop`, for example, is not blue in an ActionScript document, you may have a problem (maybe a typo); however, the word `stop` when using JavaScript will remain black even though it is valid. As you can imagine, code coloring is especially helpful with longer words and expressions.

13. Click frame 50 of the Actions layer and add a blank keyframe (Insert ➤ Timeline ➤ Blank Keyframe). Select this keyframe and notice that the Actions panel goes blank. That's because no code exists on this frame. You're about to add some.

14. Type the following ActionScript into this frame:

    `this.gotoAndPlay(25);`

    The keyword `this` isn't always needed when using ActionScript, but if you're using JavaScript it is nearly always necessary in order to apply correct scope to your instruction. If you drop the reference to `this` in ActionScript based examples, Animate still understands that you're referring to the timeline in which the code appears. If you're using JavaScript within an HTML5 Canvas document, you will likely always need to use `this` as scope works differently in JavaScript— you have to be very explicit!

15. Test your movie. You'll see that, because the ActionScript in frame 1 is commented out, it's ignored.

The playhead breezes right on past frame 1. When it reaches frame 50, the `MovieClip.gotoAndPlay()` method is invoked on the main timeline, and the movie jumps to frame 25, where it eventually continues again to 50. At frame 50, it will again be invoked and send the playhead to frame 25, and the cycle will repeat—sort of like a dog chasing its tail. The only difference between ActionScript and a dog is that a dog will eventually stop. The only way to stop this movie is to quit Flash Player.

What makes the playhead jump to frame 25? The number inside the method's parentheses determines that. Like the `trace` function we used earlier, some methods accept parameters, and `MovieClip.gotoAndPlay` is one of them. If you think about it, the idea is reasonably intuitive. A method like `MovieClip.stop` doesn't require further input. Stop just means "stop," but `gotoAndPlay` wouldn't be complete without an answer to the question "go where?"

To be fair, it isn't always obvious when parameters are accepted. In fact, in many cases, when they are, they're optional. Some methods accept many parameters; others accept none. What's the best place to find out for sure? The answer, once again, is the documentation. Seriously, it's your quickest source for definitive answers to questions about class members. When working across both ActionScript and JavaScript, trying to sort out which properties and methods are the same, which are slightly different, and which simply are unique—the documentation for either platform is invaluable.

Events

Events are things an object can react to. Events trigger functions, which may invoke other methods and/or property changes. They cause objects to either do something or have their properties change. Yell at Joseph, and he will turn his head in your direction. Push Tom to the right and, if he is walking, he will veer in that direction. It is no different in code. Events represent an occurrence, triggered either by user input, such as mouse clicks and key presses, or by Flash Player or the native web browser, such as the playhead entering a frame or the completion of a sound file. Because of this dependence on outside factors, your response to events—called *event handling*—requires an additional object.

It's something like you see in physics: for every action (event), there is a reaction (event handling)—and it applies only if you want your project to do something when an event occurs. On its own, an Animate document doesn't actively respond to anything. You have to tell it to respond. At this point, you may want to roll up your pant legs a few twists, because we're going to wade a little deeper here.

Event handling in ActionScript 3.0 requires an instance of the Event class or one of its many derivatives, including MouseEvent, ScrollEvent, TimerEvent, and others listed in the Event class entry of the ActionScript 3.0 Reference for the Adobe Flash platform. Events in JavaScript are a bit different, as they require no specific class imports, but are rather constructed with string references. In either case, the handling itself is managed by a custom function, written to perform the response you want to see when the event occurs. Before this begins to sound too complex, let's return to the movieclip instance.

1. Open Events.fla in your Chapter 4 exercise folder. This is an HTML5 Canvas document, so we will be using JavaScript.

2. Double-click the box instance on the stage to open the Symbol Editor.

3. Select frame 2 and select Insert ➤ Timeline ➤ Blank Keyframe to add a blank keyframe.

4. Use the Oval tool to draw a circle that is approximately 75 x 75 pixels in frame 2. If you like, use the Properties panel to adjust these dimensions precisely and to position the shape at coordinates 0,0.

5. Test the movie. You will see the box instance animate from left to right, increasing in size. However, that second frame inside box's timeline causes it to naturally loop, fluttering between the square and circle—something like an abstract artist's impression of a butterfly. It's a neat effect, but let's harness that and make it act in response to the mouse instead.

6. Click the Scene 1 link to return to the main timeline.

7. Select frame 1 of the Actions layer and open the Actions panel.

8. Type the following JavaScript:

    ```
    this.box.stop();
    ```

9. Test your movie. You will see that the fluttering has stopped, and only the square shape (the first frame of the box instance) is visible on the stage, even though the main timeline continues, which means the box moves to the right and increases in size. This happened because you invoked the MovieClip.stop() method on the box instance, which told that movieclip—as opposed to the main timeline—to stop. Now let's use the mouse to manage some events and make this even more interactive.

10. Open the Actions panel and click at the end of line 2 of the code. Press the Enter (Windows) or Return (Mac) key and add the following code block:

```
stage.enableMouseOver(20);
this.box.addEventListener("click", clickHandler);
this.box.addEventListener("mouseover", mouseOverHandler);
this.box.addEventListener("mouseout", mouseOutHandler);
this.box.cursor = "pointer";

function clickHandler(e) {
      console.log("You just clicked me!");
}
function mouseOverHandler(e) {
      e.currentTarget.gotoAndStop(1);
}
function mouseOutHandler(e) {
      e.currentTarget.gotoAndStop(0);
}
```

That may seem like an awful lot of complicated code, but it really isn't. We'll go over it in a moment.

11. Test the movie. You'll see that the cursor now controls the action. In fact, just place the cursor in the path of the box moving across the stage and watch what happens.

If you get errors or the code doesn't work, don't worry. You can use the Event.fla file provided in the Chapter 4 Complete folder. We'll talk about checking for coding mistakes a little later in the chapter.

In the code, you are essentially telling your project to listen for a series of mouse events (the three addEvent Listener() lines) and do something in response to them (the three blocks of code beginning with the word function). The events happen, regardless. It's your call when you want to handle an event. The next three lines do just that. Let's dissect the first line, which will illuminate the other two.

In plain English, the line first tells the box to listen up (this.box.addEventListener) and then says, "When the mouse clicks (click) the object on the stage with the instance name box, perform the action called clickHandler."

It's a lot like visiting the local fire station. Let's assume you're in a fire station for the first time. Suddenly, there is a bell sound and the firefighters slide down a pole, jump into their suits, and pile onto the truck. The truck, with the firefighters aboard, goes roaring out of the front door of the station. This is all new to you, so you just stand there and watch. The firefighters, trained to react to the bell (addEventListener), did something completely opposite from what you did. The difference is that the firefighters knew what to do when the bell rang. You did not. The firefighters knew what to listen for—a bell and not the phone or an ice cream truck driving past (either one of which could be considered an event)—and they knew what to do when that event occurred (execute an event handler). What you are doing with this movie is telling your Animate project how to behave when the bell rings (click), when the phone rings (mouseover), or when the ice cream truck arrives (mouseout). Speaking of which... The very first line we added, stage.enableMouseOver(20), enables mouseover and mouseout events in an HTML5 Canvas project.

CHAPTER 4 ■ INTERACTIVITY BASICS

If you were using an ActionScript 3.0 project in Flash Player, this line would not be necessary. The whole reason for its existence is that it enables certain mouse listeners that are considered very "expensive" in terms of events monitoring in the web browser. The number you enter tells your project at what frequency you want to monitor for these events, somewhat offsetting the expense. A value of 20 is the default frequency and means that the mouse position is tracked 20 times per second. Depending on your project and needs, the frequency may need to be adjusted.

You might be curious why the function references—clickHandler, mouseOverHandler, and mouseOutHandler—don't end in parentheses in the first three lines. They're functions, right? Functions and methods are supposed to end in parentheses. Well, this is the exception. It's the parentheses that kick a function or method into gear, and you don't want the functions to actually do anything quite yet. In those three lines, you're simply referencing them. You want them to act when the event occurs, and addEventListener() does that for you. (Incidentally, the addEventListener() method does feature parentheses in those lines precisely because that method is being asked to perform immediately: it's being asked to associate a function reference to a specific event.)

The fifth line essentially tells your project to treat the box like a button:

this.box.cursor = "pointer";

This means the user is given a visual clue—the cursor changes to the pointing finger shown in Figure 4-10—that the box on the stage can be clicked.

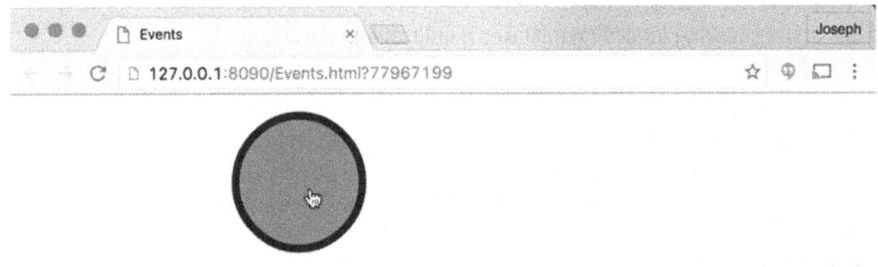

Figure 4-10. *The mouseOverHandler function changes the box into the circle.*

CHAPTER 4 ■ INTERACTIVITY BASICS

The remaining functions tell the project to put some text in the browser console if the box is clicked, to go to frame 2 of that movieclip (showing the circle) when the mouse moves over the box, and to go to frame 1 of that movieclip (showing the square) when the mouse moves off it.

So you might be asking, if we are going to frame 2 and frame 1 when these events are triggered, then why are we passing the values 0 and 1 into the gotoAndPlay() function calls? Even though we are going to frame 1, in the case of our mouseout event function, CreateJS uses a frames system that begins with an index of 0. In that case, 0 is frame 1, 1 is frame 2, 3 is frame 4, and so on. Animate will even notify you of this fact when you compile your project with the following message, which will always appear in the Console panel:

```
Frame numbers in EaselJS start at 0 instead of 1. For example, this affects gotoAndStop and
gotoAndPlay calls.
```

When using an ActionScript 3.0 document, this is not a factor as a frame value of 1 really and truly corresponds to frame 1, a value of 2 means frame 2, 3 is frame 3, and so on. A frame value of 0 means nothing within an ActionScript 3.0 document, so don't use it there!

The expression e being passed through the function represents the mouse event itself that gets fed to the event handler automatically. When we refer to e.currentTarget, it is referring to the box instance itself. If we attempted to access the box instance from within our JavaScript event function, the scope would be completely different from what it is outside of that function and the project would have no idea what box refers to. Both JavaScript and ActionScript allow direct access to the instance that was interacted with by accessing the target and currentTarget properties of the event itself as exposed through e. Really quite handy to have such access!

Here is all the code for reference:

```
this.box.stop();
stage.enableMouseOver(20);
this.box.addEventListener("click", clickHandler);
this.box.addEventListener("mouseover", mouseOverHandler);
this.box.addEventListener("mouseout", mouseOutHandler);
this.box.cursor = "pointer";

function clickHandler(e) {
    console.log("You just clicked me!");
}
function mouseOverHandler(e) {
    e.currentTarget.gotoAndStop(1);
}
function mouseOutHandler(e) {
    e.currentTarget.gotoAndStop(0);
}
```

There exist a number of useful properties on any event that you can tap into and monitor using the `nativeEvent` property of the event itself. One is called `shiftKey`, which lets you know if the Shift key was pressed while the mouse event was dispatched. To see this in action, revise the `clickHandler` function so that it looks like this:

```
function clickHandler(e) {
        console.log("You just clicked me!");
    if (e.nativeEvent.shiftKey == true) {
        console.log("The Shift key was pressed while that happened.");
    }
}
```

As you can see, the event object is referenced by the arbitrarily named e parameter. This object features a number of properties, which can be accessed by referencing the object first (e), followed by a dot (.), and then naming the desired property (`shiftKey`). If the value is true—because the user is holding down Shift while clicking—then a second output statement is sent to the browser developer console. Test the movie again and see for yourself. Pretty neat!

The `MouseEvent` entry of the ActionScript 3.0 Reference for the Adobe Flash platform lists a number of properties for this class and include the very same `shiftKey` property. As you can see, JavaScript and ActionScript are not that much different to work with after all.

Additional Coding Fundamentals

Now that you understand the idea of objects and what can be done with them, let's look at how to write valid code. We'll begin with the most basic language rules.

Syntax

Just like English, any programming language has a set of grammatical rules that governs its use. In English, for example, sentences begin with a capital letter and end with a period, exclamation point, or question mark. Of course, it gets much more complicated than that, but we assume you know most of the important stuff, even if you don't have an English degree. Whether using either ActionScript or JavaScript, grammar is called syntax, and it's easier than you might think. In fact, there are two major rules when working with the supported programming languages in Animate. The first rule of grammar is this: capitalization matters.

Capitalization Matters

ActionScript and JavaScript are both case-sensitive languages. If you want to know which frame a movieclip is currently on, you must reference its `MovieClip.currentFrame` property, spelled just like that—not `currentframe` or any other combination of uppercase and lowercase letters.

If the thought of memorizing arbitrary capitalization has you worried, have no fear. Both languages follow a manageably small set of conventions. As a general rule of thumb, just imagine a camel. Those humps will remind you of something called *camel case,* a practice in which spaces are removed from a group of words, and each letter that begins a new word (other than the first word) is capitalized. So "current frame" becomes `currentFrame`, "track as menu" becomes `trackAsMenu`, and so on. Notice that the initial letter receives no capitalization.

Add to this the observation that class names begin with a capital letter. The class that defines text fields is `Text` or `TextField` (depending on the language), the class that defines movieclips is `MovieClip`, and the class that defines a blur filter effect is `BlurFilter`. Still camel case, but with an initial cap.

Constants are the exception to this rule, because they always appear in full uppercase, with underscores where the spaces should be. For example, in the `StageDisplayState` class for ActionScript, the constant that refers to "full screen" is `FULL_SCREEN`, and the constant that refers to "normal" is `NORMAL`. When you define your own constants within ActionScript projects, it is recommended to take this same syntactical approach to naming.

Semicolons Mark the End of a Line

As you've already seen, every line of code terminates with a semicolon (;). Adding semicolons is optional, but if you omit them, Animate will make the decision on your behalf as to when a given statement has ended. ActionScript is much more forgiving than JavaScript in this regard. It's better to place them yourself, as it is best when designing assets or writing code to be as precise as possible in your intention.

Mind Your Keywords

Certain words belong to you, and certain words belong to the language. The ones that aren't yours are called keywords or reserved words. You've run into some of these already. For example, `function` is a keyword that means something to Animate (it declares a function); the term `true` is a Boolean value that tells you whether something is true; the term `this` gives you a reference to the current scope. These words aren't part of the class structure that defines the language's objects, but they're essential to the language, so you can't commandeer them for your own uses. For example, you can't create a custom function named `new()`, because new is used to create instances of a class in the case of ActionScript (as in, `var mc:MovieClip = new MovieClip();`). As you can likely guess, it is the same situation with JavaScript (as in `var mc = new createjs.MovieClip();`).

What, only three rules of syntax? Truthfully, no. But these three rules will help you ward off some of the most common beginner errors. Offshoots of the syntax concept are discussed in the following sections.

Additionally, the Actions panel provides help in the form of code coloring. Correctly typed keywords are often displayed in color, as opposed to plain old black and white, which is reserved for words and so on that aren't in Animate's dictionary. In fact, different categories of the code are colored in different ways. You may configure these colors as you please, or turn them off completely, under the Code Editor user preferences (select Edit (Animate) ➤ Preferences ➤ Code Editor.

Commenting Code

Now that you are aware of the major grammar rules, you should also be aware of a coding best practice: commenting.

In the previous exercise, we asked you to enter a lot of code. We are willing to bet that when you first looked at it on the page, your first reactions was, "What the hell does this stuff do?" A major use of commenting is to answer that question. Many developers heavily comment their code in order to let others know what the code does and to make it easy to find all of the functions in the code.

A single-line comment always starts with a double backslash (//), which tells the Animate compiler or web browser's JavaScript interpreter to ignore everything that follows in the same line. If we had added comments to the earlier code, you might not have wondered what was going on. For example, doesn't this make your life easier?

CHAPTER 4 ■ INTERACTIVITY BASICS

```
// Tell the box what events to listen for and what to do and
// when an event is detected

this.box.addEventListener("click", clickHandler);
this.box.addEventListener("mouseover", mouseOverHandler).bind(this);
this.box.addEventListener("mouseout", mouseOutHandler);

// Treat the box as though it were a button to let user know it is live

this.box.cursor = "pointer";

// Put a message in the browser console panel when the object is clicked

function clickHandler(e) {
    console.log("You just clicked me!");
}

// Go to frame two and show the ball movieclip
// when the mouse is over the box

function mouseOverHandler(e) {
            e.currentTarget.gotoAndStop(1);
}

// Go to frame one and show the box
// when the mouse is outside of the object

function mouseOutHandler(e) {
            e.currentTarget.gotoAndStop(0);
}
```

You can even put the two slashes at the end of a line of code, followed by your comment, if you like:

```
someObject.someProperty = 400; // These words will be ignored
```

You may also use a comment to temporarily "disable" or "hold back" a line of code. For example, you might want to experiment with a variety of possible values for a property. Single-line comments make it easy to switch back and forth. Just copy and paste your test values, commenting each one, and remove the slashes for the desired value of the moment.

```
//someObject.someProperty = 400;
someObject.someProperty = 800;
//someObject.someProperty = 1600;
```

You can comment whole blocks of code by using a block comment. Rather than two slashes, sandwich the desired code or personal notes between the special combination of /* and */ characters. Regardless of how you do them, comments are easy to spot in code: they are gray.

```
/*
someObject.someProperty = 400;
someObject.someProperty = 800;
someObject.someProperty = 1600;
*/
```

You'll be happy to know that commenting code in either JavaScript or ActionScript uses the exact same syntax. No matter which platform you are targeting, all you need to remember is the single-line (//) and multi-line (/* */) commenting syntax for either target platform.

Dot Notation

Objects can be placed inside other objects, just like those Russian stacking dolls, matryoshka. Actually, that analogy gives the impression that each object can hold only one other object, which isn't true. A better comparison might be folders on your hard drive, any of which might hold countless files and even other folders. On Windows and macOS systems, folders are usually distinguished from one another by slashes. In ActionScript and JavaScript, object hierarchies are distinguished by dots. As you have already seen, class members can be referenced by a parent object followed by a dot, followed by the desired member; child object, property, method, etc.

Nested movieclips can be referenced in the same way, because, after all, movieclips are just objects. All you need is a movieclip with an instance name.

Junk food is a great example of this concept. Imagine a nested set of movieclips in the main timeline that, combined, represent the Hostess Twinkie in Figure 4-11. The outermost movieclip is made to look like the plastic wrapper. Inside that is another movieclip that looks like the yellow pastry. Finally, the innermost movieclip represents the creamy filling.

Figure 4-11. Real-world dot notation

If each movieclip is given an instance name that describes what it looks like, the innermost clip would be accessed like this from a keyframe of the main timeline:

`plasticWrapper.yellowCookie.creamyFilling`

CHAPTER 4 ■ INTERACTIVITY BASICS

Note the camel case. Because `creamyFilling` is a `MovieClip` instance, it contains all the functionality defined by the `MovieClip` class. If the innermost movieclip—`creamyFilling`—has a number of frames in its own timeline and you want to send the playhead to frame 5, you would simply reference the whole path, include another dot, and then reference a relevant `MovieClip` method, like this:

`plasticWrapper.yellowCookie.creamyFilling.gotoAndPlay(5);`

This linked series of objects is known as a *path*. The extent of a path depends on the "point of view" (scope) of the code that refers to it. In Animate, this point of view depends on where the code itself is written. In this case, it's written inside a keyframe of the main timeline, and you're aiming for the innermost object; therefore, the full path is required. If the code is written inside a keyframe of the innermost movieclip's timeline—then the `this` keyword would suffice. The `creamyFilling` instance would simply be referring to itself:

`this.gotoAndPlay(•);`

It wouldn't make sense to mention `yellowCookie` or `plasticWrapper` in this case unless you needed something in those movieclips. From the point of view of `creamyFilling`, you could reference `yellowCookie` via the `MovieClip.parent` property, like this:

`this.parent;`

But bear in mind, it's usually best to keep your point of view in the main timeline. Why? Well, when all of your code is on one place—in the same layer or even in the same frame—it's much easier to find six months from now, when you have to frantically update your movie.

The most important thing to realize is that you're the one in control of what you build. If it's easier for you to drop a quick `MovieClip.stop` method into some keyframe of a deeply nested movieclip—as opposed to "drilling down" to it with a lengthy dot-notated path—then do that. Just keep in mind that paths are fundamentally important, because they serve as the connection between objects.

If you want to see how movieclips are nested using dot notation, open `twinkie.fla`. We have constructed the image on the stage as a series of movieclips from the Library. This is the code in the scripts layer:

`trace(plasticWrapper.yellowCookie.creamyFilling);`

This essentially asks, "What is the object at the end of the path?" If you test the movie, the Output panel will tell you the object is a MovieClip.

If you consult the `MovieClip` class entry in the ActionScript 3.0 Reference for the Adobe Flash platform, you'll find the built-in class members that ship with Animate. Obviously, it won't list whatever instance names you might assign on your own. This example works because the `MovieClip` class is a dynamic class, which means you can add members to it right in timeline code. Not all classes are dynamic; in fact, most are not. Similarly, when using JavaScript and CreateJS, you can reference the `MovieClip` class in the CreateJS documentation to view all of the built-in members.

Scope

Movieclips aren't the only objects that can be nested. And just as plasticWrapper, yellowPastry, and creamyFilling in the previous example each has its own point of view, so do all objects. These points of view can be thought of as special compartments that manage the availability of variables, class members, and other information to the code currently being executed.

If you trace x, for example, from the scope of creamyFilling—that is, if you put code inside a keyframe of the creamyFilling timeline that says trace(x);—you'll get the horizontal position of that movieclip in relation to its parent, yellowPastry. You won't get the position of any other movieclip, and that makes sense. creamyFilling's scope reports its own x value when asked because that scope looks into its own private world first. When it sees that it has such a property, it says so. If creamyFilling didn't have an x value, its scope would look "up the chain" to yellowPastry and try to find an x value there. This tells you that outer scopes are visible to inner scopes, but it doesn't go the other way around.

Here's a quick hands-on example that uses JavaScript instead:

1. Create a new Animate HTML5 Canvas document, and rename Layer 1 to Actions.

2. In frame 1, open the Actions panel and type the following JavaScript:

    ```
    var loneliestNumber = 1;
    console.log(loneliestNumber);
    ```

3. Test the movie in your browser and open the developer console. You'll see 1 displayed within the browser console. You've created a numeric variable named loneliestNumber, set it to 1, and traced its value. Return to Animate.

4. Beneath the existing JavaScript, add the following new code:

    ```
    function quickTest() {
    console.log(loneliestNumber);
    }

    quickTest();
    ```

5. Test the movie again. You'll see 1 in the console twice: once from the original trace and once from the trace inside the custom quickTest() function. Return to Animate.

    The idea is a bit harder to grasp, but try to wrap your head around the notion that quickTest() is an instance of the Function class. Remember that everything is an object! Just like creamyFilling is a MovieClip instance nested inside yellowPastry, this is a Function instance nested inside the main timeline. Because quickTest() doesn't have its own loneliestNumber value, it looks outside its own scope to find that value in the scope of its parent.

6. Replace the existing JavaScript altogether with this variation:

    ```
    console.log(loneliestNumber);

    function quickTest() {
    var loneliestNumber = 1;
    console.log(loneliestNumber);
    }

    quickTest();
    ```

7. Test this movie one last time. You'll see an error in the web browser console:
   `Uncaught ReferenceError: loneliestNumber is not defined.`

This time, the variable is declared inside the function. The function's scope can see it, but the main timeline's no longer can. Why? Outer scopes can't look in; the process moves only from inside out. You got an error because, when the main timeline looks into its own private world, it doesn't see anything named `loneliestNumber`. There's nothing above it that has that value either, so it gives up.

You've seen that scope has the potential to trip you up with variables. Now let's dig deeper into variables.

Variables

Variables are often described as buckets. It's not a bad analogy. Like buckets, variables are containers that temporarily hold things. Like buckets, variables come in specific shapes and sizes, and these configurations determine what sorts of things, and how many of them, a given variable can hold. In fact, variables are practically the same as properties.

A great way of understanding the concept of a variable is to consider a trip to the local market. You pay for a bunch of radishes, a bag of quinoa, a box of chocolates, a sack of coffee beans, and a package of paper towels. The clerk puts them in a bag, you pay for them, pick up the bag, and walk out of the store. If someone were to ask you what you carrying, the answer would be "groceries." The word describes all of the objects you have purchased, but it doesn't describe any item in particular, and the contents of your bag certainly might change. The word *groceries* is a suitable placeholder.

Essentially, variables are properties that aren't associated with a particular class, which means you can create a variable in any timeline and access it from that timeline without needing to refer to an object first. The formal term for creating a variable is declaring a variable. This is done with the var keyword, like this:

```
var badKitty = "Poe";
```

or this:

```
var groceries = new Array("radishes", "quinoa", "chocolates", "coffee", "toweling");
```

From that point forward, the variable `badKitty` is a stand-in, or placeholder, for the phrase "Poe," referring to the one of the author's extremely naughty pets. If you type `console.log(badKitty);` after the variable declaration, you'll see Poe in the browser console. The variable `groceries` is a placeholder for an instance of the Array class, which lets you store lists of things.

To summarize, the var keyword dictates, "All right folks, time for a variable." `badKitty` and `groceries` are arbitrary names provided by you, used to set and retrieve the contents of the variable. If you're using ActionScript, you can also provide strict data types to each variable. It isn't completely necessary but would help detect any problems that exist in the code even before it is run. Here is an example of the same code, using ActionScript:

```
var badKitty:String = "Poe";
var groceries:Array = new Array("radishes", "quinoa", "chocolates", "coffee", "toweling");
```

The `:String` or `:Array` part is interesting. Although not strictly necessary, its presence declares the variable as efficiently as possible, as explained in the next section. Just because we said the class declaration is not "strictly necessary," not using data typing is not suggested or recommended—by using it you are letting Animate know exactly what you mean, and in return Animate can help you by giving you more accurate code hinting in the Actions panel and better error reporting in the Output panel when something goes wrong. Understand though that this only works with ActionScript because JavaScript is a loosely-typed language and does not support the use of strict data type declarations such as this.

Finally, the equality operator (=) sets the value of the variable. In the first example, its value is set to a string, delimited by quotation marks. In the second, the variable value is an array, with its elements in quotation marks, separated by commas, and enclosed in parentheses.

One of the authors (it was Tom!), in order to get his students to understand variable naming, tells them they can use any name they want, and then he creates a variable named `scumSuckingPig`. A few years back, Macromedia asked for a videotape of one of his lessons, and not even thinking while the camera was rolling, he wrote "scumSuckingPig" on the white board, pointed to it, and asked the class, "What is this?" Thirty voices answered, "a variable." To this day, those Macromedia people who saw the tape never forget to mention this to him.

You pick the names for your variables, but remember the third grammar rule: you can't name your own variable after an existing keyword in any language. That makes sense—how is the runtime or interpreter supposed to know the difference between a variable named `trace` and the `trace()` function? It would be a good idea to familiarize yourself with the appropriate documentation for whichever platform you are using when writing code to avoid any such collisions. Also, your variable names can contain only letters, numbers, dollar signs ($), and underscores (_). If you decide to use numbers, you can't use a number as the first character.

Data Types (ActionScript)

Arguably, data types are just another way to describe classes. When used with variable declarations, however, they provide a useful service. Specifying a variable's data type not only helps you avoid code errors but, in ActionScript 3.0, can also reduce memory usage, which is always a good thing. Many of the people who have been using ActionScript 3.0 for some time have discovered that this also is a factor in the speed of playback in Flash Player and AIR. Adobe is not shy about claiming speed boosts of an order of magnitude, and we aren't disputing that claim.

As mentioned in the preceding section, data types can only be assigned when using ActionScript as a target platform. This is one of the big advantages to using ActionScript, as the compiler will let you know immediately when there is a problem due to data type inconsistency. JavaScript does not have any sort of capability to employ data types and so this feature cannot be used on any platforms that built on the core JavaScript language.

Thanks to the way Flash Player is built, strongly typed variables in ActionScript 3.0 can reduce memory usage because they allow variables to be only as big as they need to be. When it creates a variable, what's actually going on is that Flash Player asks the computer to set aside a certain amount of memory (RAM) to hold whatever information needs to be stored in the variable. Some data types require more memory than others, and when ActionScript knows what type you intend to use, it requests the minimum amount necessary.

Another important result of using data types is that you avoid coding errors. The more Animate knows about your intentions, the better it's able to hold you accountable for them. If a variable is supposed to hold a number and you accidentally set it to a bit of text, Animate will let you know about it. Mistakes like that happen more often than you might think, and to be honest, it will happen to you. Let's make a mistake and see how Animate reacts.

1. Create a new Flash ActionScript 3.0 document and save it as DatatypeError.fla. Rename Layer 1 to Textfield.

2. Use the Text tool to draw a text field somewhere on the stage. Select the text field and use the Properties panel to set its type to Input Text (as shown in Figure 4-12). Give it the instance name input.

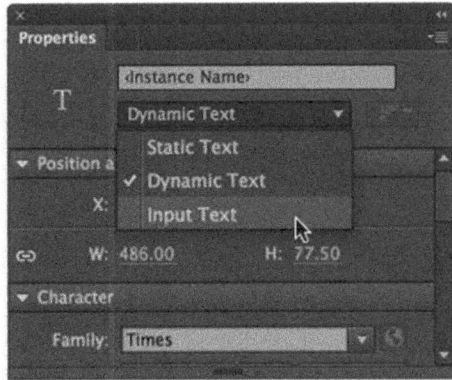

Figure 4-12. Setting the text field to Input Text.

3. Create a new layer and name it Actions. Select frame 1, and open the Actions panel. Type the following ActionScript into the Script pane:

```
var num:Number = 0;
num = input.text;
```

Another way of writing the first line would be as follows:

```
var num:Number = new Number(0);
```

The keyword new is normally used when creating new instances of complex data types, such a Sound object or a NetStream used to play a video. Less complex data types, including simple stuff like numbers and strings, really don't require the new keyword for them to be instantiated.

4. Test the SWF and keep your eye on the Compiler Errors tab in the Properties panel group. You'll see a helpful error warning that lets you know the num variable, a Number data type, doesn't like the idea of being fed a String data type, which is what the TextField.text property provides (see Figure 4-13).

CHAPTER 4 ■ INTERACTIVITY BASICS

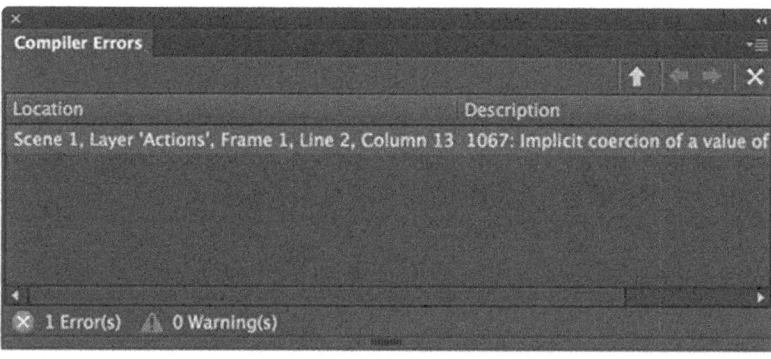

Figure 4-13. Trying to call a text string as numbers results in an error, thanks to data typing.

You can double-click the error in the Compiler Errors tab, and it will take you to the exact line in the Actions panel that contains the error.

5. For extra credit, use the Number() function to convert the string to a number on the fly. This is known as casting.

   ```
   var num:Number = 0;
   num = Number(input.text);
   ```

Besides indicating the sort of variable something is, data typing can also specify the return value of functions and methods. If a function returns a string, for example, it can (and should) be typed like this:

```
function giveMeThree():String {
         return "iii";
}
trace(giveMeThree());
```

Many functions don't return anything, which means they get to use :void.

```
function manipulateAMovieclipSomewhere():void {
// movieclip manipulation code here
// notice the function doesn't return anything
}
manipulateAMovieclipSomewhere();
```

215

For further detail on available data types, have a look at "The ActionScript 3.0 Reference" for the Adobe Flash platform.

Operators

"Hello, operator? Connect me with Grand Central, will ya?" Actually, that's not the sort of operator we're talking about here. Whether you are a casual programmer making things move from here to there or a hardcore coder, you will use operators—they can't be avoided.

In both ActionScript and JavaScript, operators are special characters—usually punctuation but sometimes words—that evaluate or change the value of an expression. Some of those most commonly used look and act just like mathematical symbols. For example, the addition operator, +, adds numbers together; the subtraction operator, -, subtracts them. The multiplication and division operators, * and /, multiply and divide numbers, respectively. These are appropriately called arithmetic operators. Let's use our old friend trace to see these in action.

Create a new ActionScript 3.0 document type, enter the following ActionScript into a keyframe and test your movie to see the results of these simple math problems:

```
trace(5 + 5);
trace(7 - 2);
trace(5 * 5);
trace(7 / 2);
```

The Output panel shows 10, 5, 25, and 3.5, as you would expect. The thing about operators is they deal with complexity in a very different manner than they deal with simplicity. For example, consider this:

```
trace(5 + 5 / 2 * 3 - 1);
```

Now, what number would that expression produce? If you answered 14, you are wrong. The answer is 11.5, and it is vitally important to your sanity that you understand how Animate arrives at this answer. The result depends on something called operator precedence. Generally speaking, expressions are evaluated from left to right. However, certain calculations take priority over others. This is the concept of precedence. The rule is simple: multiplication and division take priority over addition and subtraction. A good way to remember this is to think of how multiplication and division problems quickly reach higher (or lower) numbers than addition and subtraction do. Let's slowly walk through that calculation to help you grasp the precedence concept.

In the preceding expression, various pairings are considered in the order in which they appear, and operator precedence determines which pairings are evaluated in which order. For example, the first pairing is 5 + 5, and, sliding over one "slot," the next pairing is 5 / 2. Between those first two pairings, the division operation wins. Under the hood, the division is done before the addition, and the "new" expression reads as follows:

```
5 + 2.5* 3 - 1
```

Now the process starts again. The first two pairings at this point are 5 + 2.5 and 2.5 * 3. Of those, which one wins? Multiplication. The process continues, with the "newest" expression now reading as follows:

```
5 + 7.5 - 1
```

Here, the pairings have been simplified to 5 + 7.5 and 7.5 - 1. Neither trumps the other in this case, so the 5 is added to 7.5, making 12.5; and 12.5 has 1 removed, which leaves 11.5.

```
5 + 7.5 - 1
12.5 - 1
11.5
```

As you can see, precedence can get pretty complex. Thankfully, there happens to be a way to override the natural precedence of operators. Unless you aim to specialize in operators (and there's nothing wrong with that), we recommend that you use parentheses to group expressions. For example, 3 + 5 * 4 is 23, because 5 * 4 takes priority and evaluates to 20, and then 3 plus 20 is 23. However, (3 + 5) * 4 is 32, because (3 + 5) now takes priority and evaluates to 8, and then 8 times 4 is 32.

Here's another way of wrapping your mind around precedence. It's one of those tricks you learn in high school, and the good ones stick. Although the word doesn't mean anything on its own, the acronym PEMDAS (Please Excuse My Dear Aunt Sally) is easy to remember. It spells out the order of operations:

P: Parentheses

E: Exponents

D: Division

M: Multiplication (D and M in the order they appear)

A: Addition

S: Subtraction (A and S in the order they appear)

Thanks to Adam Thomas for the tip!

The addition operator also works for text, in which case it does what's called *concatenation*, which is a fancy word for joining things. For example, the concatenation of the strings "Ab" and "sinthe" is the complete word Absinthe, as illustrated here:

```
trace("Ab" + "sinthe");
// Outputs the value Absinthe, which is a string
```

Numbers concatenated with text become text, so be careful of your data types!

```
trace(5 + 5); // Outputs the value 10, which is a number
trace(5 + "5"); // Outputs the value 55, which is a string
```

Even though the 55 in the output generated by that second line looks like a number, it's actually stored by Animate as a string of two characters that, by coincidence, happen to be numerals.

Another operator you'll see frequently is the assignment operator (=), which we've already used several times in this chapter. The assignment operator assigns a value to a variable or property. It is an active thing because it changes the value. In the following lines, the value of the looseChange variable is updated repeatedly:

```
var looseChange = 5;
looseChange = 15;
looseChange = 99;
```

Here, it happens with a string:

```
var author = "Penelope";
author = "Tom";
author = "Joseph";
```

In plain English, the assignment operator could be described as "equals," as in "looseChange now equals 99" (hey, that's almost a dollar!) or "author now equals Joseph."

Contrast this with the equality operator (==), which is used for checking the value of a variable. Don't confuse the two! When you see something like this:

```
if (looseChange = 67) {
            // buy some quinoa
}
```

you're actually changing the value of that variable, looseChange, to 67. When you want to see if it is an exact match for 67, use this:

```
if (looseChange == 67)
```

If you want to check for any number but 67, use the inequality operator (!=, think of it as "not equal to"), like this:

```
if (looseChange != 67) {
            // buy something else
}
```

These are examples of a group called comparison operators (as well as conditional statements, which are discussed in the next section). These particular comparison operators are narrow, though. The equality operator seeks a very specify value, not a range. The inequality operator seeks a very specific value too, just from the opposite angle.

What if you don't know the exact value you're looking for? As often as not, you'll find yourself in a position to make decisions on whole sets of numbers. Think of it in terms of those restriction signs at the theme park: "You must be at least 42 inches tall to ride this roller coaster." They're not looking for people exactly 3.5 feet tall; they're looking for people greater than or equal to that number. Animate code offers quite a few ways to compare values in this manner, including the following:

< (less than)
> (greater than)
<= (less than or equal to)
>= (greater than or equal to)

In the next section, you'll see some of these in action. But be aware there are plenty more operators than we've touched on here.

Conditional Statements

One of the cornerstones of programming is the ability to have your code make decisions. Think about it. You make decisions every day. For example, if you want to visit the authors of this book, you have a decision to make: do I go to Canada to visit Tom, or to the United States of America to visit Joseph?

Both JavaScript and ActionScript provide a handful of ways to make this determination, and the most basic is the `if` statement. An `if` statement is structured like this:

```
if (condition is true) {
       do something
}
```

Thus, in programming terms, the decision to visit an author might look somewhat like this (remember, == checks for equality):

```
if (visitTom == true) {
       bookflightToCanada();
}
```

The condition between the parentheses can be relatively simple, like this:

```
if (fruit == "apple") {}
```

This might mean something like "if the fruit is an apple" (hand it over to Snow White). On the other hand, it might be a little more complex, such as the following:

```
if (beverage == "absinthe" && sugar == "cube" || sugar == "syrup"){}
```

This may seem to mean "if the beverage is absinthe and the sugar is in the form of a cube or as syrup" but actually means something quite different. In the preceding expression, two new operators, && and ||, represent "and" and "or," respectively. Because of the way precedence works, the expression hinges on the ||. We're checking whether the beverage is absinthe and the sugar is in cube form (both must be true) or simply if the sugar is in syrup form. As stated, the full expression doesn't actually care what the beverage is (if there even is a beverage). Contrast that with this:

```
if (beverage == "absinthe" && (sugar == "cube" || sugar == "syrup")){}
```

In the revision, the nested parentheses group the || elements together, and the full expression now requires that beverage not only be present but be absinthe and that sugar be present and be either in the form of a cube or syrup.

As you may have guessed by now, the only decision an `if` statement ever makes is whether something is true or false (a Boolean value). Let's just jump in and take a look at this concept.

In the following example, you're going to make a draggable star that dims when it's moved too close to the moon. The determination will be made by an `if` statement. Here's how:

1. Start a new ActionScript 3.0 document. Change the name of Layer 1 to Sky.

2. Select the Polystar tool to draw a polygon or star.

3. Before you draw the shape, click the Options button in the Properties panel to open the Tool Settings dialog box. In the Style drop-down, list select Star, as shown in Figure 4-14. Click OK and then set the Stroke to None.

CHAPTER 4 ■ INTERACTIVITY BASICS

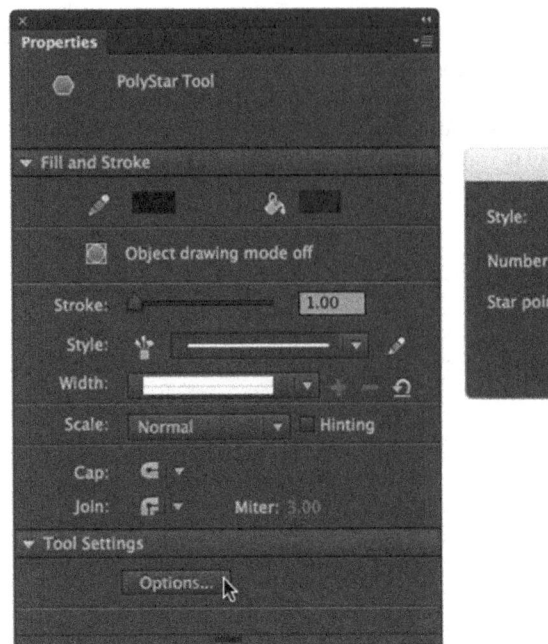
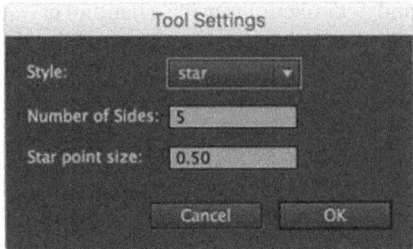

Figure 4-14. *Click the Options button in the Properties panel in order to draw a star.*

Click and drag to create the star shape. Convert this shape into a movieclip named Star and give it the instance name star. Position it on the left side of the stage.

Use the Oval tool to draw a circle with no stroke and filled with the solid color or gradient of your choice. Convert it into a movieclip named Moon and, in the Properties panel, give it the instance name moon. Position it on the right side of the stage.

Create a new layer and name it Actions. Select frame 1 of the Actions layer, open the Actions panel, and type the following ActionScript:

```
star.addEventListener(MouseEvent.MOUSE_DOWN, mouseDownHandler);
star.addEventListener(MouseEvent.MOUSE_UP, mouseUpHandler);

star.buttonMode = true;

function mouseDownHandler(e:MouseEvent):void {
    star.startDrag();
    star.addEventListener(MouseEvent.MOUSE_MOVE, mouseMoveHandler);
}

function mouseUpHandler(e:MouseEvent):void {
    star.stopDrag();
    star.removeEventListener(MouseEvent.MOUSE_MOVE, mouseMoveHandler);
}
```

```
function mouseMoveHandler(e:MouseEvent):void {
    if (star.x > moon.x) {
            star.alpha = 0.4;
    } else {
            star.alpha = 1;
    }
}
```

4. Test your movie. When the SWF opens, drag the star, and see it turn semitransparent when you drag it to the right of the moon, as shown in Figure 4-15.

Figure 4-15. *An opaque star turns semi-transparent when dragged to the other side of the moon*

We've used what may look like a lot of code, but there really isn't a whole lot that's new. Just as you saw earlier in the "Events" section, you're calling the star instance by name and assigning a couple event listeners: one for when the mouse is down (the user presses the mouse button) and one for when the mouse is up (the user releases the mouse button). This time, we are using ActionScript in place of JavaScript and the buttonMode property is used to supply a visual clue that star is clickable.

The function that handles the MouseEvent.MOUSE_DOWN event does an interesting thing. First, it invokes the MovieClip.startDrag method on the star instance. This causes the movieclip to follow the mouse. (If you poke around the documentation, you'll find that the startDrag method is inherited from the Sprite class when used in ActionScript. This inheritance business happens with either ActionScript or JavaScript, but does so with differing ancestral trees.) Second, it adds a new event listener to the star instance—this time

CHAPTER 4 ■ INTERACTIVITY BASICS

for an event that occurs while the mouse is moving. Just like the other event handlers, this one has its own function, and that's where the `if` statement appears. The event handler assigned to `MouseEvent.MOUSE_UP` stops the dragging and tells star to stop listening for the `MouseEvent.MOUSE_MOVE` event. So, pressing down starts the dragging, and letting go stops it. That's pretty straightforward.

If we were using HTML5 Canvas and JavaScript here, this logic is even more straightforward. In CreateJS, you can use the "pressmove" event to combine what we've seen in ActionScript into one single event. Within the event handler we then position the coordinates of the star instance to match those of the mouse cursor on the stage. Check it out:

```
this.star.on("pressmove", onMousePress);
function onMousePress(e){
    e.currentTarget.x = e.stageX;
    e.currentTarget.y = e.stageY;
};
```

The third event handler is where the decision making occurs. An if statement evaluates the expression `star.x > moon.x` by asking whether star's horizontal position is greater than moon's horizontal position. The answer, as you know, can only be `true` or `false`. This question is asked every time you move the mouse inside the SWF. When the star instance moves beyond the right side of the moon instance, as determined by the registration point of each movieclip, the comparison expression evaluates to true. In this case, the `MovieClip.alpha` property (or transparency) of the `star` instance is set to 0.4 (40 percent), which makes it partially see-through.

Now, try one more thing with your open SWF file. While the SWF is open, drag the star back to the left side of the moon. It's still semitransparent! With the current `if` statement, the opacity of star is reduced the first time its path crosses that of moon, but once dimmed, it will never go back. Depending on your goals, that might suit you just fine, but if you want the star to repeatedly change between both transparencies, you need to add an `else` clause to your `if` statement. An `else` clause essentially says, "Do this other thing if the condition is not met."

Close the SWF and update your `mouseMoveHandler()` function to look like this:

```
function mouseMoveHandler(evt:MouseEvent):void {
    if (star.x > moon.x) {
            star.alpha = 0.4;
    } else {
            star.alpha = 1;
    }
}
```

Now, when the expression inside the `if` statement evaluates to `false`—that is, when star's x property is no longer greater than moon's x property—star's alpha property is set back to 1 (100 percent).

In cases where you want to test several conditions in a row, you may want to consider a switch statement. From a practical standpoint, switch and if do the same thing, so it's really up to you which you use. Compare the two to settle on which looks cleaner or more compact to you. Here's an example that demonstrates the use of both (note that `else` and `if` can be combined in the same line):

```
var favoriteColor = "deep purple";
if (favoriteColor == "red") {`
    // do something reddish
} else if (favoriteColor == "blue") {
    // do something blueish
} else if (favoriteColor == "green") {
```

```
        // do something greenish
} else {
        // do something else, because no one guessed
}

var favoriteColor = "deep purple";
switch(favoriteColor) {
    case "red":
    // do something reddish
    break;
case "blue":
    // do something blueish
    break;
case "green":
    // do something greenish
    brcak;
default:
    // do something else, because no one guessed
}
```

What are all those break statements? In the context of switch statements, break tells your code to ignore the rest of the list by exiting from the switch statement as soon as it matches one of the case values.

The best part about conditional statements in Animate? They can be used between both ActionScript and JavaScript using the exact same syntax shown directly. The only difference is that with ActionScript, you have the choice as to whether you'd prefer to strongly type your favoriteColor variable to a String or not.

Working with JavaScript, HTML5 Canvas, and CreateJS

When working in an ActionScript 3.0 document type, we can be assured that either Adobe Flash Player or Adobe AIR is going work exactly as expected. When targeting HTML5 Canvas or some other platform outside of Adobe's control… all bets are off. When working in HTML5 Canvas, you are at the mercy of the web browser manufacturers; Apple, Google, Mozilla, and the like. You can view this as a good thing or a bad thing, but it is very much a thing that you must be aware of either way.

There are always going to be differences and inconsistencies between the various web browsers and the platforms they support. For instance, think of Google Chrome running on a high-powered MacBook Pro in comparison to the Mozilla Firefox browser running on a mid-range Android device. There is bound to be a great number of differences when it comes to both web standards implementation and feature set.

In the past, Adobe Flash Player broke down all such incompatibilities and differences and truly leveled the playing field when implementing features across browsers in a consistent and feature-rich way. But of course, Flash Player is not supported within mobile browsers and support varies between desktop systems as well.

So if we cannot rely on Flash Player for a consistent experience, then what are we to do? This is where libraries like CreateJS come into play. Aside from doing a nice job packing complex features into a nice, reusable package—these libraries also go far in implementing features in a way that works around any such browser inconsistencies and are more often than not already tested against all major browsers and platforms.

How do we know what is supported and what isn't? The CreateJS documentation is a great place to start.

CHAPTER 4 ■ INTERACTIVITY BASICS

How to Read the CreateJS Documentation

While Animate CC does have a nice set of code snippets with examples of how to use JavaScript within an HTML5 Canvas document, they only scratch the surface of what is available to us. Let's have a look at the official documentation for the CreateJS libraries. You can find the documentation over at the CreateJS web site at http://createjs.com, or directly at http://createjs.com/docs.

Once the documentation loads in the browser, you'll be able to choose from the particular library you wish to read documentation about. There are four different libraries that work together, making up the whole of CreateJS. These four libraries are as follows:

> **EaselJS:** A JavaScript library that makes working with the HTML5 Canvas element easy.
>
> **TweenJS:** A JavaScript library for tweening and animating HTML5 and JavaScript properties.
>
> **SoundJS:** A JavaScript library that lets you easily and efficiently work with HTML5 audio.
>
> **PreloadJS:** A JavaScript library that lets you manage and coordinate the loading of assets.

Each has its own set of documentation, though you will likely find EaselJS to be the most useful starting point as many of the others are handled directly through the Animate CC publish process. Once within the documentation for EaselJS, you are able to view specific API classes along with all the properties, methods, and events associated with each documentation entry. There is a handy search along the left side column along with the ability to filter members based on whether they are inherited, protected, private, and even deprecated. Everything is here, along with contextual example code and integrated links to related members.

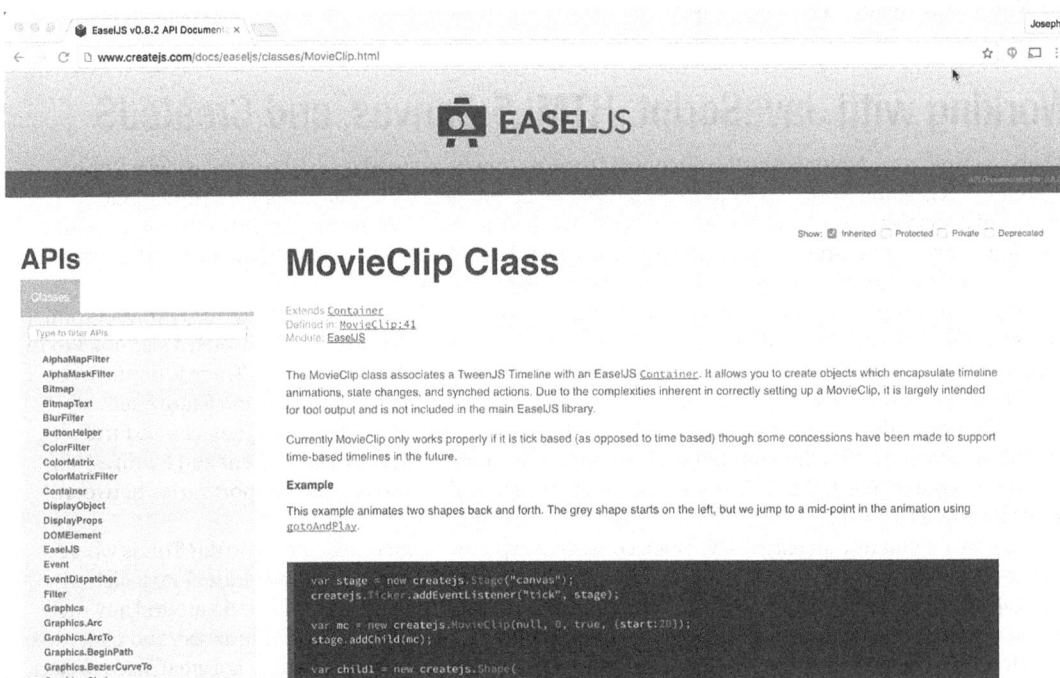

Figure 4-16. *The CreateJS documentation*

224

CHAPTER 4 ■ INTERACTIVITY BASICS

Native JavaScript Documentation

Of course, with CreateJS being a library built on JavaScript itself, we are also able to use native JavaScript functions, properties, and events within our HTML5 Canvas projects. There is nothing special you need to do to enable this, but you might benefit from some reference documentation.

There are a number of resources you can use to view basic JavaScript documentation—many provided by browser manufacturers and related entities. The authors have found one of the more useful resources such as this to be the one provided by Mozilla at

https://developer.mozilla.org/en-US/docs/Web/JavaScript/Reference

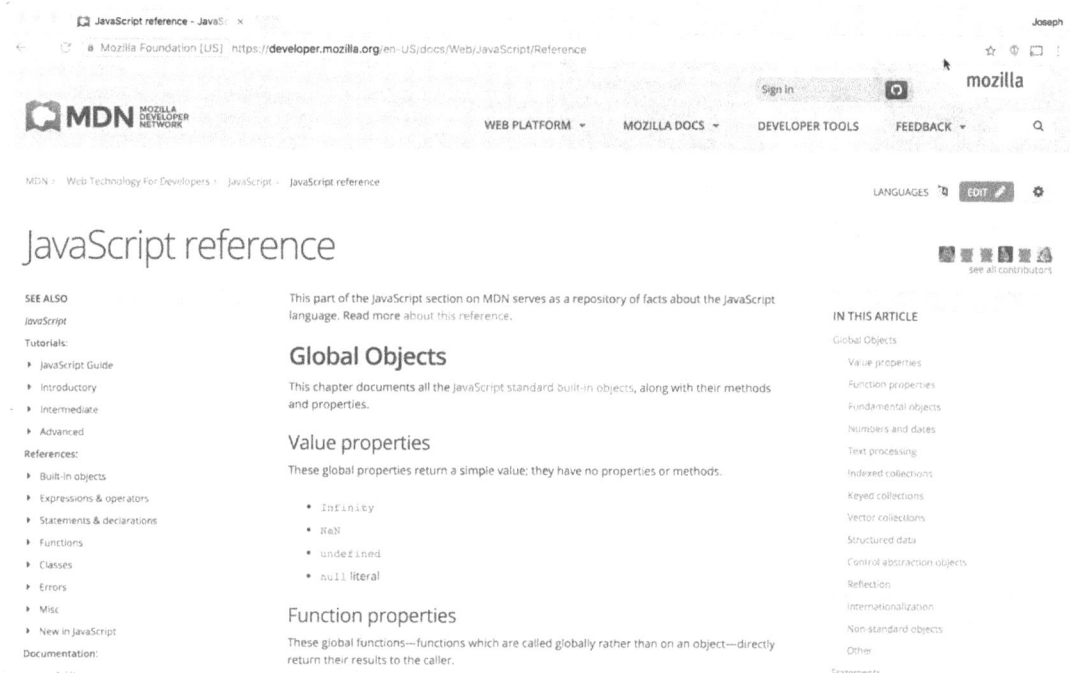

Figure 4-17. *The Mozilla Developer Network JavaScript reference*

Not only is there a full reference for every object in JavaScript, but you will also find some basic guides and additional resources to explore.

JavaScript Troubleshooting

While troubleshooting and debugging ActionScript is fairly simple—due to an integrated debugger within Animate itself—when debugging HTML5 Canvas documents thing are a bit more complicated. This is primarily because we are targeting the native web browser and so need to use that specific platform to troubleshoot or code. This is a lot simpler than it sounds though, even though ActionScript has a leg up in this department due to the tight integration with Animate CC.

The best tool you have to troubleshoot JavaScript is already on hand and is built directly into your web browser.

CHAPTER 4 ■ INTERACTIVITY BASICS

To access the browser console (as seen in Figure 4-18), all you need to do is activate the developer tools while testing your project. This mechanism varies by web browser, but one of the simplest ways to access the developer tools in most browsers is to simply right-click on some web content and choose the option from the contextual menu which appears. In Google Chrome, for instance, you can choose the Inspect option that appears.

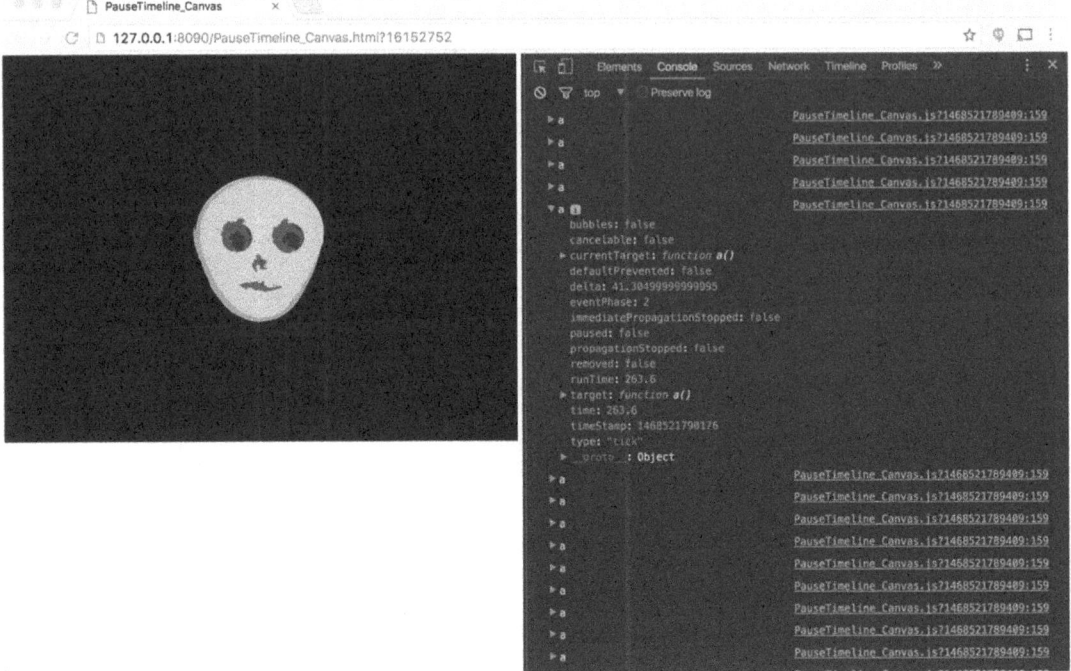

Figure 4-18. Troubleshooting within the browser

Once within the developer tools, there should be an option to view the console. This will normally appear as a tab. The browser console will display any errors, warnings, and logged data to the console for you to inspect. Using a command like `console.log()` and passing in an object to inspect, you will see the value for that object print out in the console (for simple objects like strings and numbers), or a hierarchical tree display for more complex objects like arrays and functions.

Using the console in this way, you can quickly see how the actual data compares with what is expected. If there is a problem, you can use this tool to tweak your project code and work through it.

Using Additional JavaScript Libraries

While having access to everything contained in the CreateJS libraries is absolutely wonderful, what happens if you need additional functionality that isn't present in that core library? Of course, since you can also use vanilla JavaScript in an HTML5 Canvas document, you can just write all the code yourself. However, depending on the complexity of situation at hand, this can easily become a project unto itself. If there is a library out there that already does exactly what you need, why wouldn't you use it within your project?

Okay, fine—we need to use an additional JavaScript library in our project. The question becomes, how do I go about doing this?

HTML5 Canvas Templates

The first thing to do if you want to create a template of your own is to export the default template in order to modify it to your liking. To do so, from the Advanced tab in Publish Settings, click the Export button and save the HTML file on your machine for editing. You will be prompted by Animate CC to give this file a name and location on your hard drive.

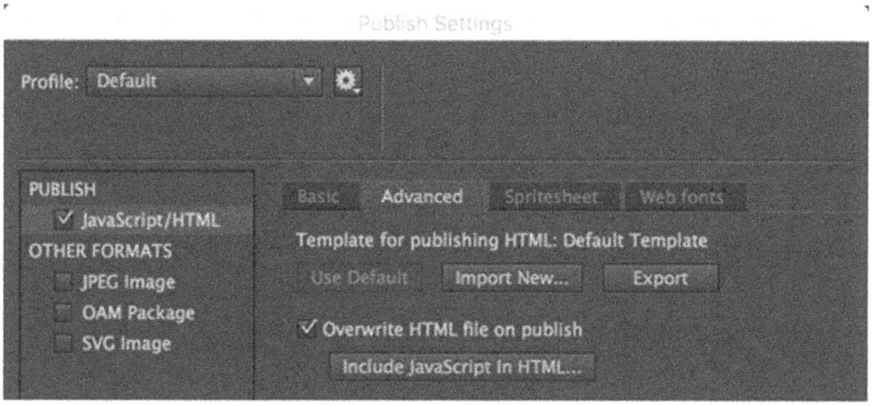

Figure 4-19. *Export a template*

With the default template exported, you will now be able to open it up in Adobe Dreamweaver, Brackets, or any text editor of your choosing to customize the HTML, JavaScript, and CSS . Perhaps you want to center your HTML5 Canvas content or add other elements like headers and descriptive text. This is all possible using templates.

Editing the Template

Now that you have the Template file open within an editor, you can make whatever modifications you wish. This includes the addition additional script tags, which include third-party libraries such as jQuery. One thing to make note of before we move on is the availability of special tokens with the HTML template, which can be used when customizing. For instance, tokens such as $BG, $WT, and $HT can be used in conjunction with custom logic and elements to adjust for sizing and background colors within your template.

Here is a short list detailing some of these tokens and what they represent:

$CANVAS_ID The ID of the Canvas element within your HTML document.

$TITLE The title of your project document.

$BG The background color of the stage defined within the FLA.

$WT The width of the stage defined within the FLA.

$HT The height of the stage defined within the FLA.

These tokens are available for use within any template and will be replaced by their appropriate values upon publication. Other tokens exist as well and can be explored within the exported HTML Template file.

Importing the Custom Template

When you are finished editing, save your HTML and return to Animate CC and the Advanced Publish Settings. Simply click the Import New button and locate the edited HTML file to use it in your project. The selected template is now clearly indicated within the dialog box.

Now, whenever you test or publish your HTML5 Canvas document, it will employ your custom template in place of the default. If at any time you wish to use the default template again, simply click the Use Default button.

Publish Profiles

What if you have a number of templates that you wish to switch between when publishing your content? It would be a pain to have to import template files every time you need to switch. This is where Publish Profiles come into play.

To establish the template just created as part of a profile, you can click the gear icon and choose to Create Profile.

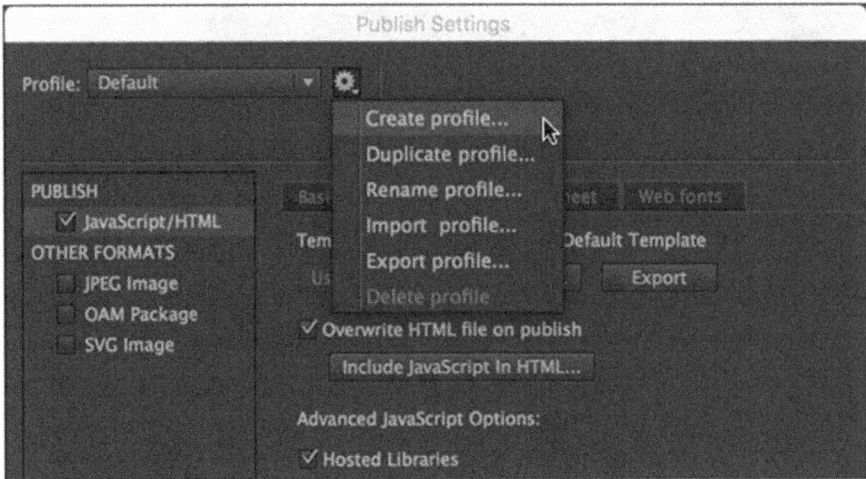

Figure 4-20. *Exporting and Importing HTML5 Canvas templates*

Working with ActionScript and the Flash Platform

When Animate first appeared on the scene (first as FutureSplash Animator, later as Flash Professional, and now Animate CC), web designers were quite content to populate sites with small movies that moved things from here to there. The result was the rise of bloated Flash movies and, inevitably, the infamous Skip Intro button. But once ActionScript was introduced into the mix, Flash started its march forward.

Today, Animate is a mature application, and Animate CC remains somewhat tied to what Adobe has designated the Flash Platform, an umbrella term that includes industrial-strength programming tools, runtimes, SDKs, and the like. Just as how Animate can produce a variety of output formats for different platforms, Flash Player and AIR projects are no longer the exclusive property of the Animate authoring environment. Adobe Flash Builder also produces content for Flash Player and AIR. They're fundamentally the same as those projects built in Animate but ActionScript 3.0 and Apache Flex are geared toward programmers who normally work in applications like IntelliJ IDEA or FDT—not at all the domain of artsy types! As you have seen in the preceding chapters, Animate can still be used to move things from here to there. On one hand, you have an animation tool for building scalable, lightweight motion graphics for various output formats, and many Animate designers are increasingly using the application to create broadcast quality animations for even film and television.

On the other hand, even without an external development environment like Flash Builder, Animate developers have plenty of room to spread their wings. They use the platform for everything from building data-rich applications to fully realized games and interactives. In between is a wealth of content ranging from rich banner ads to MP3 players, from viral e-cards to video-enhanced corporate multimedia presentations. How far you go, and the directions you take, are up to you—that's an exciting prospect! These are all possible thanks to ActionScript.

Put simply, ActionScript brings your Adobe runtime based projects to life. No matter how impressive your sense of graphic design, the net result of your artistry gets "baked," as is, into a published SWF. What's done is done, unless you introduce programming to the picture. With the use of ActionScript, your opportunities extend beyond the bounds of the Animate interface. You can program movies to respond to user input in orderly or completely random ways.

ActionScript also has a pragmatic side. You can reduce your project file size and initial download time by programming movies to load images, audio, and video from external, rather than embedded, files. You can even make things easier for yourself by loading these files based on information stored in XML and JSON documents.

ActionScript 3.0 is the latest and most mature incarnation of the programming language used by Animate. Previous versions of the application supported ActionScript 2.0 as well; however, this is no longer the case. It is still possible to download and install Flash Professional CS6 from Adobe, as this is the final version that included support for ActionScript 2.0 projects.

Class Files and the Document Class

With all this talk of objects and classes, you may be wondering if it's possible to create classes of your own. The answer is yes and is squarely in the realm of "advanced ActionScript not covered in this book." Still, be aware that ActionScript allows you to come up with completely new objects of your own design.

In Animate, classes are stored in external text files and imported as needed during the compile process. There are many benefits to writing code in this way, not the least of which is that classes allow you to separate your visual design from your programming design. An experienced programmer might, for example, program a game in a series of classes—a `SpaceShip` class, a `LaserBeam` class, and so on—which would allow new laser beam objects to be created as needed, regardless of which Library assets might be used to visually portray those lasers. Artwork could be given to a designer and later "married" with the code with relative ease, because external class files aren't spread among dozens of keyframes.

It is, in fact, entirely possible to produce a heavily coded SWF without any ActionScript touching the FLA at all. This is accomplished via something called the document class.

Create a new ActionScript 3.0 document and click somewhere on the stage or work area to put the Properties panel into stage mode. You'll see a Class field in the Publish area of the Properties panel, as shown in Figure 4-21. This field allows you to associate a class file with the Animate document. Technically, it's how you can redefine the main timeline, making it more than just a movieclip (or configuring it to be a Sprite and then optionally making it more than just a sprite).

Note the small button with the little wrench icon to the right of the Script drop-down in the Properties panel. Click this, and you will be taken to the Advanced ActionScript 3.0 Settings dialog box. You can also open this panel by selecting File ➤ ActionScript Settings.

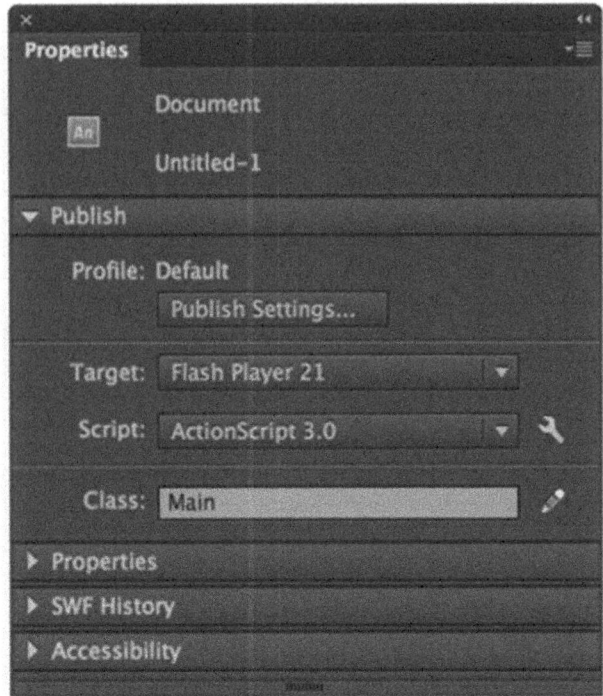

Figure 4-21. *Document class files are accessed through the Publish area of the Properties panel*

Think of a document class as the main script that creates all the other ActionScript objects necessary to do the developer's bidding. In prior versions of the ActionScript language, this sort of association wasn't possible. Developers could get close, by typing a line or two of ActionScript into frame 1 and importing the main class there, but ActionScript 3.0's document class concept allows a fully programmed FLA file to be code-free in the FLA itself.

ActionScript Syntax Checking

Being that ActionScript is a strongly-typed, compiled programming language, it is relatively easy to discover syntax errors when you publish your project. These errors could be due to a mismatched data type, broken syntax, a misspelling in a class name, property, or method… or any number of additional errors that occur when human being write code.

For example, create a new ActionScript 3.0 document and type the following into the Actions panel on frame 1:

```
var str:String = 7;
```

No need to use any visual assets in this example. Go head and test your SWF by selecting Control ➤ Test Movie. As soon as you do, the Compiler Errors panel pops up. As you may have expected, you receive a "type mismatch" error (see Figure 4-22). It's worded a bit differently, but the gist is the same.

CHAPTER 4 ■ INTERACTIVITY BASICS

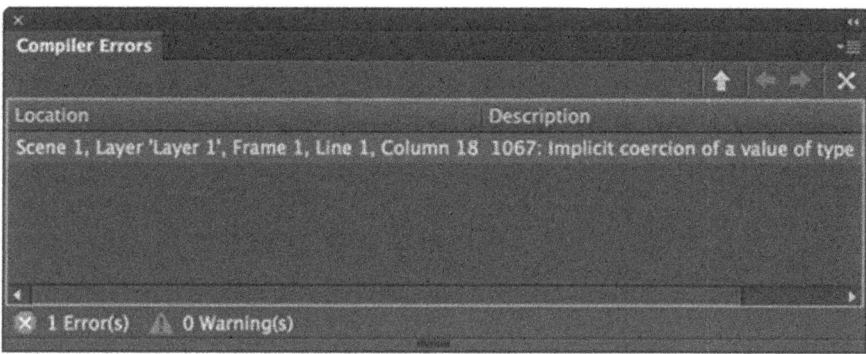

Figure 4-22. Syntax is automatically checked when a movie is tested

The trouble with testing a movie in order to "proof" your syntax becomes clear as soon as your movie takes on any complexity. There will be times you simply want to "check your bearings" in place, without having to go to the trouble of generating a SWF file.

Delete the existing code in your ActionScript 3.0 document and type the following into the Actions panel in frame 1:

```
var d:Date = new Date();
d.setMillennium(3);
```

As you do, you'll see some code hinting when you get to line 2. Thanks to the strongly typed variable d in line 1 (the strong typing is provided by the :Date suffix), Animate knows that d is an instance of the Date class. As a courtesy, the Actions panel gives you a context-sensitive drop-down menu as soon as you type the dot after the variable. The drop-down menu suggests Date class members (see Figure 4-23).

Type s, and the drop-down menu jumps to class members that start with that letter, such as setDate(), setFullYear(), and so on.

Type as far as setM, and you'll see setMilliseconds(). At this point, you're going to be a rebel. Rather than go with any of the suggestions, type setMillennium(3); to complete line 2 of the code shown previously. As you can see from the drop-down menu, the Date class features no such method. Because of this, we realize that there is something wrong. In fact, if we check the documentation, we will find that no such method exists. If we were to Test Movie, we would receive another compiler error.

231

CHAPTER 4 ■ INTERACTIVITY BASICS

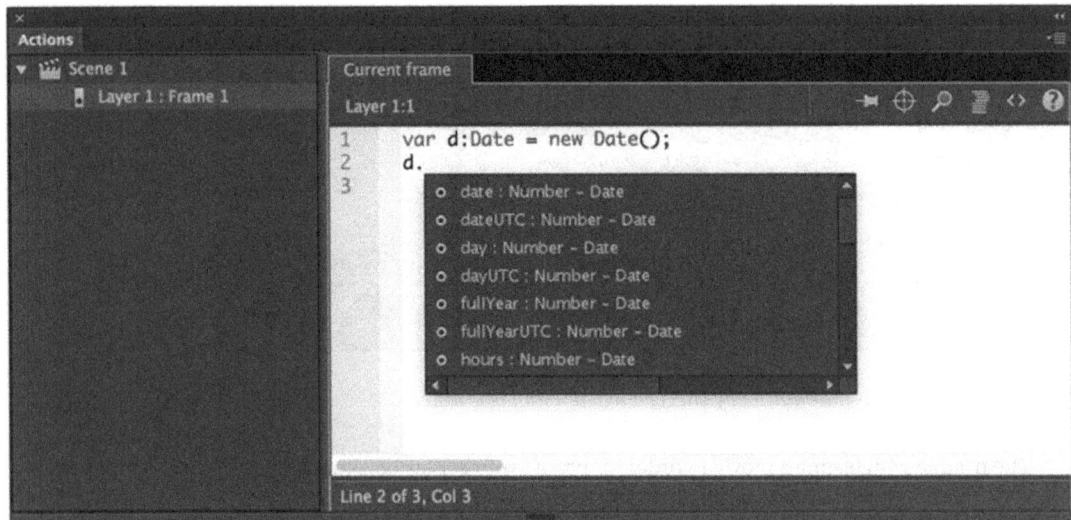

Figure 4-23. *Using strongly typed variables gives you useful code hints*

Let's perform one more example. Delete the last two characters in your code so that it looks like this:

var d:Date = new Date();
d.setMillennium(2000

Perform another Test Movie command. Are you holding your breath? Go ahead and exhale. Ahhh, the Compiler Errors panel fires up and gives you a message, which reads as, 1084: Syntax error: expecting rightparen before end of program. Sure, it sounds a little stilted. You can imagine it intoned by the colossal WOPR computer from the 1980s nerd classic *WarGames*, just before it asks Professor Falken about a nice game of chess. But it's an error message, and that's a good thing. Click OK to close the panel.

What can you learn from this? If you have a missing parenthesis or bracket, such as in this expression:

```
if ((2 + 2) == 4) {
  trace("Yes, 2 + 2 is 4.");
} else
  trace("Oddly, it isn't.");
}
```

you'll be warned about it by the compiler. In the preceding code, the else clause is missing a curly bracket ({) to its right. This sort of error reporting, even if it's all you get, is a positive asset. In the words of our mothers, "Be thankful for what you have." To that, we add this: if you need a bit of something to lean on in your programming, use the resources at hand. They include the ActionScript 3.0 Reference for the Adobe Flash Platform and code hinting, at the very least.

So, tuck your feet, pretzel-like, beneath you, and then up again over your legs. This is the lotus position. It encourages breathing and good posture and is said to facilitate meditation. Don't lose heart! The very best syntax checker is sitting closer than you think—it's right there between your shoulders.

How to Read the ActionScript 3.0 Reference for the Adobe Flash Platform

Have you ever had to give a presentation in front of a room full of people? If you're not used to that, it can be pretty nerve-wracking. In spite of hours of preparation, people have been known to draw a complete blank. The authors have seen many newcomers to Animate and the Flash Platform react in the same way to the documentation, especially when faced with the ActionScript 3.0 Reference for the Adobe Flash Platform. You may have been following along just fine in this chapter—nodding your head, because things seem to make sense—but then, when you find yourself sitting in front of an empty Animate document...gosh, where to begin?

You may be feeling a sense of the old "dictionary catch-22"—how are you supposed to look up a word to find out how it's spelled, if you don't know how it's spelled?

Let's get you past this bit of stage fright.

Getting Help

There are several places where you can access the documentation. If you are working in the Animate interface, select Help ➤ Animate Help. If you have the Actions panel open and want to quickly jump to code-specific documentation, select Help from the panel's upper-right menu (see Figure 4-24).

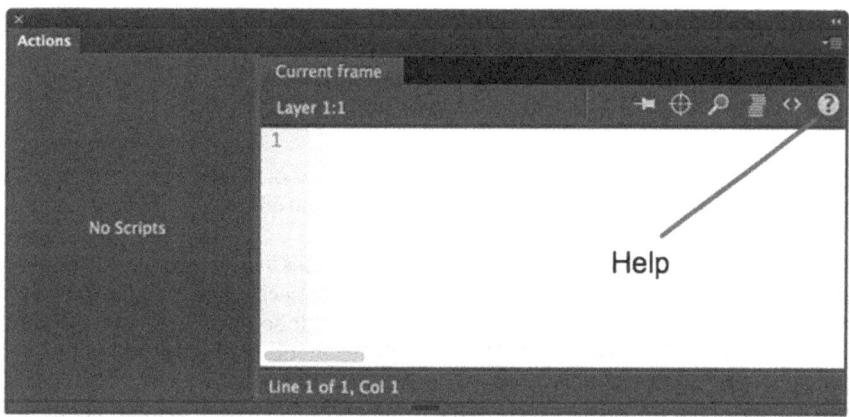

Figure 4-24. *Access help through the Actions panel's menu*

This brings you to the sections on the Actions panel within the online help resource for Animate CC. From this web-based resource, you can branch off to a number of other useful references and resources. The most useful of these, when considering ActionScript, is the ActionScript 3.0 Reference for the Adobe Flash Platform. This resource can be located directly at the following address:

http://help.adobe.com/en_US/FlashPlatform/reference/actionscript/3/index.html

The language reference should appear as seen in Figure 4-25. From here you can filter based on the version of the runtimes, by specific products, and more. The most important thing to note is that you have complete access to the packages and classes contained in ActionScript 3.0 and are able to access the complete documentation for each and every class as part of the language.

CHAPTER 4 ■ INTERACTIVITY BASICS

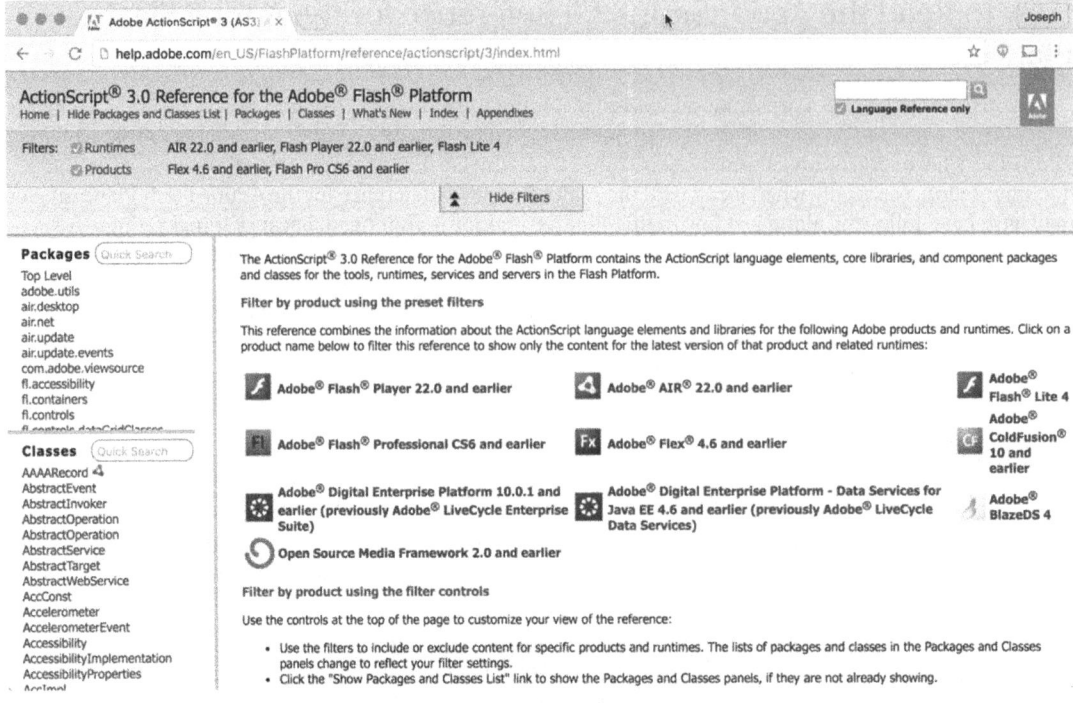

Figure 4-25. *The ActionScript 3.0 Reference for the Adobe Flash platform*

Choosing a specific class provides access to wealth of knowledge in terms of related classes, properties, methods, events, and even specific code examples that you can learn from and adapt to your particular projects.

Take the MovieClip class, for example. As one of the more complex classes in ActionScript, and one with a direct visual tie-in to what happens on the stage within an Animate project, this should provide a good introduction to how to go about using this resource. Go ahead and locate some methods you are most familiar with like gotoAndPlay or stop. Notice in gotoAndPlay how there is a robust description for the method, including the parameters it accepts along with example code? Not every single method will have as much information as this, it all depends on the method or property and how much there is to say about it!

Unsure about the properties and methods of a specific class? Give the ActionScript 3.0 Reference for the Adobe Flash Platform a look and browse what is available. You may even find something useful that you were not aware of going in.

Search Tactics

Browsing the ActionScript 3.0 Reference for the Adobe Flash platform is a good thing. We heartily encourage the practice. Flip open a section, even at random, and dig in; there's always plenty to learn, even for the expert. That said, busy schedules often mean that spare moments come at a premium. The reference's search field can be a speedy assistant when your manager is breathing down your neck.

Your number-one strategy at all times is to reduce the number of places you need to look. If a filter is available, use it to filter the products or runtimes in which you're interested. If a product filter is available, make sure to filter results for Animate only, as opposed to Animate and Flash Builder. This prevents the reference from looking at items you don't need, which means you won't need to wade through unnecessary search results, including results that might steer you down a very wrong path.

For the last several versions of Animate, advanced developers have had access to something called the Flash JavaScript API, also known as JSFL. This special language is different from ActionScript altogether, because it allows the Animate interface itself to be manipulated programmatically. For example, you can automate repetitive tasks with JSFL or even build new drawing tools from scratch. But this language can be used only with the authoring environment and Animate documents, not SWF or HTML files. The last thing you want to do is search and discover some exciting "new feature" in JSFL and spend hours trying to figure out why it doesn't work in your movie.

Take the time to learn two important descriptive ActionScript terms. Write them on a sticky note, if you like, and keep it taped to your monitor. Why? Because a number of ActionScript keywords match common English words used in everyday language. You won't get anywhere searching the word `if`, for example, because although if is an important ActionScript statement, it's also used all over the place in help documents that have nothing do with programming. If you want to see the entry on `if`, `if..else`, and the like, look up the sort of ActionScript an `if` statement is: a conditional. Here's that helpful two-item cheat sheet:

Conditionals, which include if, if..else, switch, and so on

Operators, which include <, >, +, -, and tons more practically impossible to find otherwise

Perhaps the biggest tip we can give you is this: think in terms of objects. Sounds familiar, right? We hit that topic pretty hard early in the chapter, so why is it coming up again here? Well, remember that objects are defined by classes, and the class entry gives you all the owner's manuals you'll need. If you're dealing with a movieclip instance, think to yourself, "Which class would define this object?" Nine times out of ten, the answer is a class of the same name. Search MovieClip or `MovieClip` class, and you're ushered pretty quickly to the `MovieClip` class entry.

A class entry will show you the properties, methods, and events relevant to any instance of that class. No more hunting and pecking! If you're dealing with a text field and stumble across a question, search `TextField`. If you're having trouble with audio, look up the `Sound` class. If your problem involves any of the user interface components—such as `CheckBox`, `ColorPicker`, or `ComboBox`—look up the class for that component. The only common object whose class name doesn't match the item it represents is the class that defines button symbols. In ActionScript 3.0, button symbols are instances of the `SimpleButton` class. (There's always an exception, right?)

Remember that properties are an object's characteristics, methods are things the object can do, and events are things it can react to. When you get to the desired category, make sure to show the inherited members in that category or you will not be viewing the full list and may miss what you are looking for!

Using ActionScript and JavaScript

You are going to be using ActionScript and JavaScript (depending on the specific project or example) throughout the rest of the book. Ideally, if you have made it to this point of the chapter, you should feel pretty confident about facing it. In fact, once you have coded a few projects, you will actually be able to read code. Once you arrive at that point, you are on your way to mastering the application.

Animate has come a long way from its vector animation roots and has improved significantly with ActionScript 3.0 JavaScript via CreateJS. It's a more powerful set of languages than have ever been included in a creative application of this nature. The really neat thing about each language is it is relatively accessible for navigational programming of the sort used in presentations, banner ads, and other interactive projects you may undertake.

Here's a recap of our recommendations:

- Get into the habit of creating a Scripts or Actions layer in the main timeline and movieclip timelines, if you choose to add code to nested symbols. When everything has its place, it's easier to find, which means it's easier to update.

- Take a pragmatic approach. Hard-core programmers may insist that you put all your code in a single frame, or better, in external files. In complex situations, that may be the best way to go. When you're ready to undertake complex coding and the circumstances require it, go for it. In the meantime, don't lose any sleep over doing this the old-fashioned way in Animate, which amounts to little snippets of code among many keyframes. Remember, nobody cares how it was done. They only care that it works.

- Strongly type your variables when using ActionScript 3.0 as this helps the compiler help you!

- Use comments to leave footnotes through your code. Even if you are the only one working on your files, you'll appreciate your efforts later, when the client asks for a change. Comments help you get your bearings quickly.

- Use the `trace` function in ActionScript or the console.log function in JavaScript to help yourself see where you are in a published project.

The coding languages within Animate have matured to the point where there are a lot of people making a very good living from writing code. If code isn't your thing, learn it anyway. The odds are almost 100 percent that you will eventually work with a programmer, and being able to speak the language will make your design efforts even smoother.

With the advice out of the way, let's look at some practical uses for code within Animate by applying it to a number of historically popular requests on the Adobe support forums. We will be using JavaScript and HTML5 Canvas for these examples, but you should be able to easily convert the code presented into ActionScript for use within an ActionScript 3.0 document as well.

Your Turn: Pause and Loop with JavaScript

People often want to know how to pause the main timeline for a certain amount of time before moving on, and they often want to know how to loop a movie a certain number of times before stopping at the end. Let's wire them up.

In the publish settings for an HTML5 Canvas document, there is also a check box you can select to enable automated pausing of the timeline0 once the playhead reaches the end. The example we are working with is more complex and customized though.

Pausing a Timeline

Here's an example of how a small bit of JavaScript can really make your life easier. Let's say you're building an image-based presentation in which numerous photos advance from one to the next. You have 20 of these on the main timeline and have added visual interest by tweening the symbols' alpha property to make each photo fade in and out. Your instructions are these: after an image fades in, make it hold for five seconds before moving on. Assuming your movie frame rate is the default 24 fps, you'll need 120 frames for each hold. Considering the 20 photos, that's a lot of frames! And what are you going to do when the boss says, "Ehh, you know what? Change the pause to 10 seconds"? That's a lot of manual keyframe wrangling. As soon as you redo those tweens, just watch...your boss will come back with, "Sorry, make it 3 seconds." (We guarantee something like this will happen to you in a real-life office setting. Really, it will.)

The key to a quick solution is understanding Animate's wristwatch. If you have an analog wristwatch, the minutes are marked around the dial, and the second hand ticks around the face. Animate doesn't have a second hand; it has a millisecond hand. And the watch face is not divided into minutes or seconds; it sports 1,000 little division marks. This gives you quite a bit of control, which is a good thing.

You've already seen how Animate can pay attention to mouse-related events. You've seen event handlers for mouse clicks, rollovers, and the like. Now, you're going to see an event handler for a timer-related event. In this exercise, you are simply going to tell Animate, "When you hit this point on the timeline, hang around for five seconds (actually, 5,000 milliseconds) before moving on."

1. Open the `PauseTimeline.fla` file. If you scrub the playhead across the timeline, images in each layer fade in and fade out.

2. Click frame 1 of the Actions layer and open the Actions panel. Enter the following code into the Script pane:

   ```
   var timelinePause;
   var root = this;
   createjs.Ticker.on("tick", onTick);
   ```

   We're declaring a variable, `timelinePause`, which will eventually reference the `window.setTimeout` method. We also set a variable called root equal to the current scope. We do this so that later on, within other functions, we'll be able to easily refer to the main movie scope and the child objects within it without a lot of hassle. Finally, we set up the CreateJS Ticker response handler.

   The Ticker in CreateJS is a really useful aspect of the HTML5 Canvas document type and you should definitely become more familiar with it – as it is the core heartbeat of any HTML5 Canvas project. In fact, even if you do not add an event listener as we've done here, the Ticker still exists in every project and will run, in frequency, based on the current FPS of the document.

237

CHAPTER 4 INTERACTIVITY BASICS

3. Next, add in the following JavaScript in that same frame, below the previous variable declarations:

```
function startTimer() {
    timelinePause = window.setTimeout(timerHandler, 5000);
}
function timerHandler(e) {
    root.play();
    createjs.Ticker.paused = false;
}
```

We declare a function here called `startTimer`. This is something we can invoke at any time throughout the life of our movie in order to set a controlled delay. The `setTimeout` method is sort of like a trigger. It nudges other functions into action at a given (and adjustable) delay. The mechanism that actually creates the delay accepts two parameters—a function reference and a delay. The function that's called when the delay is complete is called `timerHandler`, and the delay itself is set for 5000 milliseconds. Within this function, we set the root timeline to play (as it will be paused when we invoke `startTimer`) and unpause the Ticker as this has been paused as well. Where do we do all this pausing? Inside the `onTick` function—we'll get to that in a moment.

We can also create a timeout such as this without any reference whatsoever. However, declaring a new timeout with a reference object allows us to manipulate, and even stop, a timeout from executing later on very easily. You can almost think of it like giving an instance name to a movieclip instance on the stage, allowing you control over that object.

---

4. Add the following new JavaScript function after the existing code:

```
function onTick(e) {
        if(!e.paused) {
                switch(root.currentFrame) {
                        case 5:
                                startTimer();
                                root.stop();
                                createjs.Ticker.paused = true;
                        break;
                        case 14:
                                startTimer();
                                root.stop();
                                createjs.Ticker.paused = true;
                        break;
                        case 23:
                                startTimer();
                                root.stop();
                                createjs.Ticker.paused = true;
                        break;
                }
        }
}
```

238

This is the function called by the CreateJS `Ticker`. First, the function checks to see whether the `Ticker` has been `paused` or not. If it has, then everything else is ignored until it is unpaused. If it hasn't been paused, then we proceed to a `switch` statement.

We pass in the `currentFrame` property of the `root` reference (which is basically the main timeline). This property let's us know what frame the playhead is currently at. We check to see whether we are at any of the frames where we'd like to delay the transition: 5, 14, 23. When any of these three frames are encountered, we start the delay by invoking `startTimer()`, we stop the `root` timeline, and pause the ticker. This will effectively pause the timeline on each of the specified frames for five seconds.

So why bother pausing the ticker? Because if our project FPS is set to 24 – this means that the playhead will move across 24 frames every second and the potential is there for the ticker to fire off multiple times while on one of the specified target frames. We cannot have the startTimer code and all the rest firing off multiple times per frame! That would cause a lot of problems for us... so we simply pause the Ticker and then unpause when ready. Very organized. Very elegant.

Here's the complete breakdown. When you test this movie, the playhead begins in frame 1. When it encounters the JavaScript there, it takes note of its instructions and sets up a number of variables and event handlers with associated functions. Then it notices a graphic symbol with an alpha set to 0 and renders that. Since nothing tells the playhead to stop, it continues to frame 2, and so on. Until it hits frame 5, the playhead doesn't see anything new, code-wise, so it continues updating the alpha of the symbol in each frame.

In frame 5, it sees the Ticker event logic encounters a MovieClip.stop method. "Sure thing," says Animate, and stops the main timeline. It also sees `startTimer()`, which tells Animate to invoke the delay method as declared in frame 1. Five seconds later, the delay dispatches its event, which is handled by the timerHandler function, and the playhead restarts. This then goes on and on indefinitely.

CHAPTER 4 ■ INTERACTIVITY BASICS

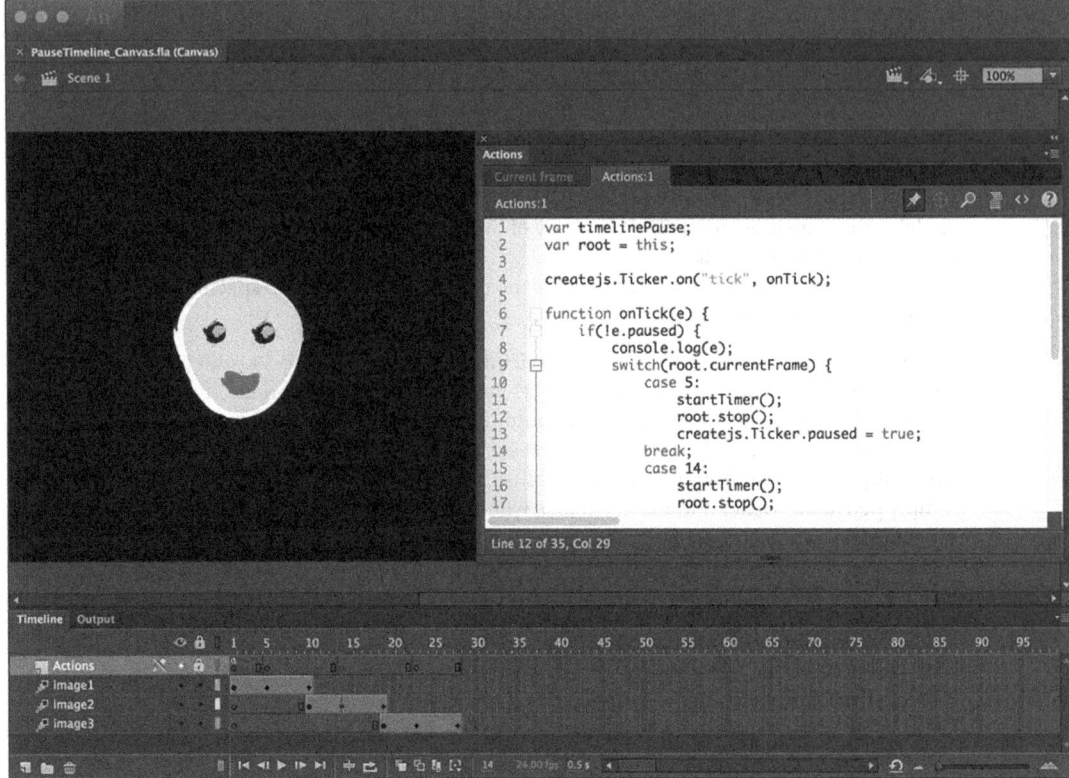

Figure 4-26. *Pausing the Animate timeline*

> 5. Test your movie to verify that each image pauses for five seconds. After frame 28, the timeline naturally loops and the process repeats.

Has the boss told you yet to change the delay interval? Easy. Just revise the 5000 parameter in frame 1 to some other number—10 seconds would be 10000, 2.5 seconds would be 2500. This updates the delay across the board.

Any way you slice it, using JavaScript has considerably reduced the horizontal expanse of your timeline, and timing changes are easy to make.

Looping the Timeline

We've all seen banner ads that play two or three times and then stop. As you witnessed in the previous section, timelines loop on their own without any help. The trouble is that they do it forever. It's easy enough to add a quick stop method to the very last frame of the Actions layer. That would keep the timeline from looping at all. But what if you want to control the looping?

To loop a timeline three times (a popular number for banner ads, but it could be any number), declare a counting variable in frame 1 (call it loop if you like), and initialize it to 0. Then increment that value in the last frame, and use an if statement to decide when to quit. Here's how:

> 1. Open the LoopTimeline.fla file in your exercise folder.

240

2. Select frame 1 of the Actions layer and open the Actions panel. Add the following new variable declaration:

   ```
   this.loop = 0;
   ```

   This just introduces a variable, loop, whose value is currently 0. Notice that we scope the variable to this? That enables us to access it across all frames of the timeline.

3. In the Actions layer, add a keyframe at frame 28. Select that frame, and enter the following new code. Then save and test the movie.

   ```
   this.loop++;
   if (this.loop < 3) {
           this.gotoAndPlay(1);
   } else {
           this.stop();
   }
   ```

In the first line, the loop variable is incremented by one. That's what the increment operator (++) does. If you prefer, you can swap the expression loop++ with its longhand equivalent—loop = loop + 1—but that's the nice thing about operators: JavaScript and ActionScript have tons of them, and they make light work of your efforts. In fact, the code provided in this example will work on either platform.

Next is an if statement that checks if the value of loop is less than 3. Naturally, this is true during the first pass (you declared loop as 0 in step 3). It was just incremented, so at this point, its value is 1, but that's still less than 3. Therefore, Animate sends the playhead back to frame 2 (expressed as frame 1 in CreateJS), where it plays through the tweened animation (complete with scripted pauses) until it hits frame 28 again.

Why go back to frame 2 instead of 1? Frame 1 declares the value of loop as 0, so if the playhead enters frame 1 again, you negate the increment gained at frame 28. Going back to frame 2 leaves the value of loop as is. On the playhead's second visit to frame 28, the value of loop increments again. Now its value is 2. That's still less than 3, so it loops for a third pass. This time, when it increments, its value climbs to 3. At that point, the if statement's condition no longer evaluates as true (3 is not less than 3), which means the else clause tells the playhead to stop.

Using Movieclips to Control the Timeline

Movie clips, as you know, can be thought of as Animate movies with timelines independent of the main timeline. The interesting aspect of this concept is you can use actions in a movieclip to kick off actions outside of their timeline on the main timeline or another movieclip's timeline. Here's how:

1. Open the carRace.fla file in your Chapter 4 exercise folder. When the file opens, you will see a truck on the stage. If you scrub across the timeline a car on the right side of the stage replaces the truck on the left side of the stage.

2. Test the movie. The truck moves from left to right, and then the car takes over and moves, from right to left, across the stage. If you close the browser and look at the main timeline, there is nothing to indicate the motion of either vehicle. In fact, open the code in frame 1 of the actions layer, and you will see a this.stop(); action, which essentially stops the playhead of the main time dead in its tracks. So, where does the motion come from?

CHAPTER 4 ■ INTERACTIVITY BASICS

3. Open the car1 movieclip in the Library. The motion tween between frames 1 and 35 solves the mystery of the moving truck but offers no clue as to how that car roars across the stage.

4. Open the code in frame 35 of the actions layer. When it opens you will see:

```
this.parent.gotoAndStop(9);
```

This line says when the truck hits the last frame of the animation in this movieclip, go to frame 10 (remember, in CreateJS, the timeline starts at 0) of the main timeline—the parent—and stay put. So, where does the car come into the picture?

5. Click the Scene 1 link to return to the main timeline. The car is sitting in frame 10. If you test the movie, the truck roars across the stage and then the car, thanks to the code in the previous step, keeps moving across the stage. Let's loop this animation and have the truck roar across the screen.

6. Open the car2 movieclip, select the last frame in the actions layer, and open the Actions panel.

7. Click once in the Script pane and enter the following code:

```
this.parent.gotoAndStop(0);
```

8. Test the movie. The animation now loops. The truck zooms across the stage, and the car zooms across the stage in the opposite direction.

Using Code Snippets

The wait is over. Here's how use a snippet, add one to the panel, and delete one that you no longer need:

1. Open the Snippets.fla file in your Chapter 4 exercise folder. You will see one of the images from the Pause and Loop exercise is on the stage.

   In the previous exercise exercise, you essentially had to reenter this same code three different times within a switch statement:

   ```
   startTimer();
   root.stop();
   createjs.Ticker.paused = true;
   ```

   That's a lot of typing. The Code Snippets panel allows you to save code for subsequent reuse. In this case, we want the image on the stage to fade in, and when it is clicked, the playhead advances to the next frame. On the surface, especially if you are new to JavaScript, this could be a daunting challenge. Code snippets to the rescue.

2. Click the Images layer to select it and open the Code Snippets panel either by clicking the Code Snippets button, as shown in Figure 4-27, in the panel strip on the right side of the Actions panel or by selecting Window ➤ Code Snippets to open the panel.

CHAPTER 4 ■ INTERACTIVITY BASICS

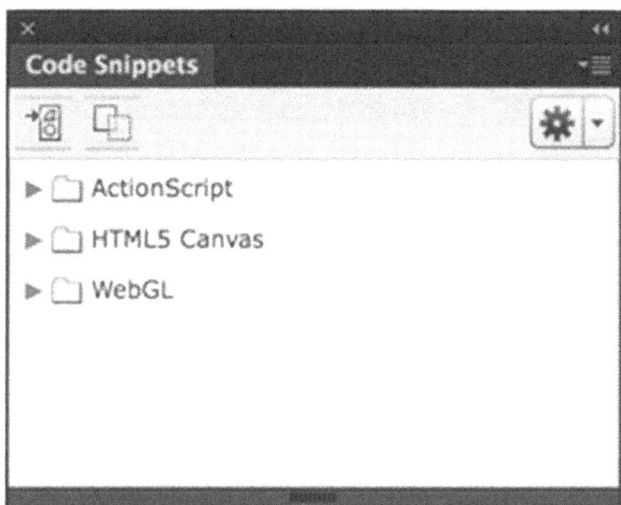

Figure 4-27. *The Code Snippets panel*

When the panel opens, it is not terribly difficult to figure out what snippets are available for each platform and the purpose of the buttons in the upper-right corner. The button on the far left, Add to current frame, is how a snippet is added to the timeline, and the one beside it copies the snippet to the clipboard and allows you to paste the code into the Script pane, if this is what you need to do.

In this case, you need to do a couple of things:

- Stop the timeline
- Fade the image in
- Allow the user to click the image and go to the next frame in the movie

To accomplish this, follow these steps:

1. Select the image on the stage (it is the Skull movieclip in the Library and has the instance name skull). Then open the Code Snippets panel, open the HTML5 Canvas folder, and twirl down the Timeline Navigation folder. You will see a list of code snippets specifically for that platform.

2. Click the Stop at this Frame snippet within the HTML5 Canvas folder to select it, and click the Add to current frame button. When you click the button, an Actions layer will be added to the timeline, the code will appear in frame 1 of the Actions layer, and the Actions panel will open, as shown in Figure 4-28.

243

CHAPTER 4 ■ INTERACTIVITY BASICS

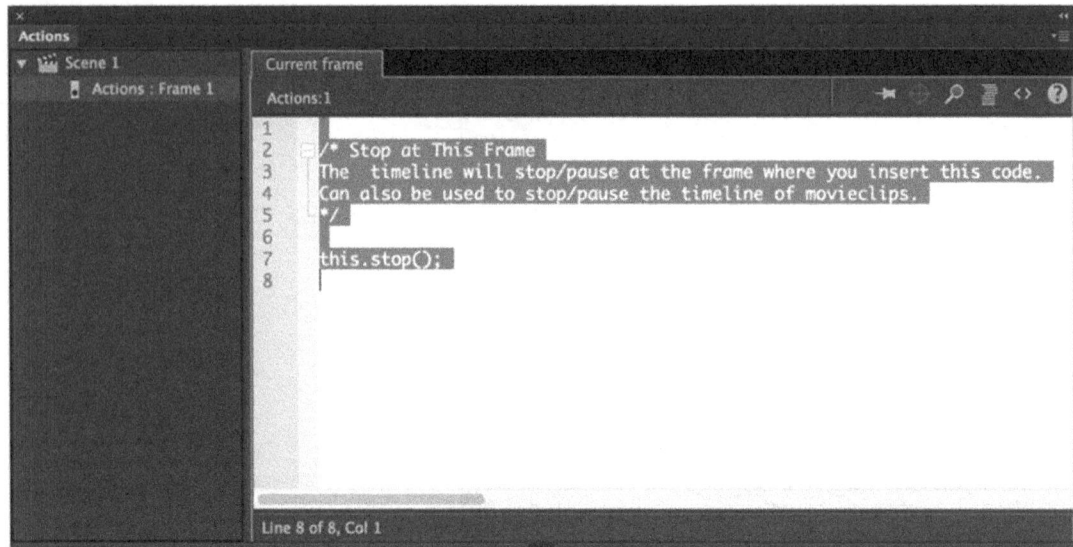

Figure 4-28. *A code snippet is added to the movie*

If you don't first select the instance on the stage which the snippet is intended to reference, you will be prompted to make the selection before applying the snippet. This does not apply the code directly to the selected object but in reference to the instance of the selected object on the stage within the Actions panel.

---

3. Remove any of the comments that have been applied to this code.
4. With the instance selected, open the Code Snippets panel and twirl down the Animation folder within the HTML5 Canvas folder. Select the Fade In a Movieclip snippet and click the Add to current frame button. If you check out the code, you will see that an alpha fade has been applied to the instance.
5. With the instance still selected, twirl down the Timeline navigation folder and apply the Click to Go to Frame and Stop snippet. Modify the code so we stop at frame 2—expressed in CreateJS as frame 1—so, gotoAndStop(1).
6. Test the movie. The image will fade in, and when you click it, the playhead is sent to the next frame of the movie and stops dead thanks to the snippet that sent it there. Note the visible numbers added to the upper-right corner of the stage on each frame.

Now that you have discovered how to use code snippets, you need to know that developing a reliance on them is not exactly going to help you learn how to use JavaScript. In fact, those who develop Animate projects using a blank stage and nothing but code are not exactly thrilled with this feature because it does not foster "best coding practices." We agree. Use code snippets as a way of learning how JavaScript works, not as the way to code a movie.

Adding a Snippet to the Code Snippets Panel

Though we have said a reliance on snippets in the last section is not exactly a best practice, within the world of coders, "snippets" are a fact of life. These are blocks of code that developers realize they can reuse, or need, and instead of entering them into the Actions panel, they save them to the Code Snippets panel for reuse. Here's how:

1. Open the AddSnippet.fla file found in your Chapter 4 exercise folder. If you test the file, you will see it does nothing more than add 60 randomly placed balls on the stage. You can refresh the browser to verify this!

2. Select the first frame of the Actions layer and open the Actions panel. Select all of the code in the Script pane.

3. Open the Code Snippets panel, click the Options button, and select Create New Code Snippet from the drop-down menu. This will open the Create New Code Snippet dialog box shown in Figure 4-29.

4. Enter CreateJS - Random Balls into the Title area, and in the Description area enter Creates a series of random balls on the stage.

5. Click the Auto-fill button where it says Use code selected in Actions panel? The code will appear in the Code area. Click OK to accept the snippet and close the dialog box.

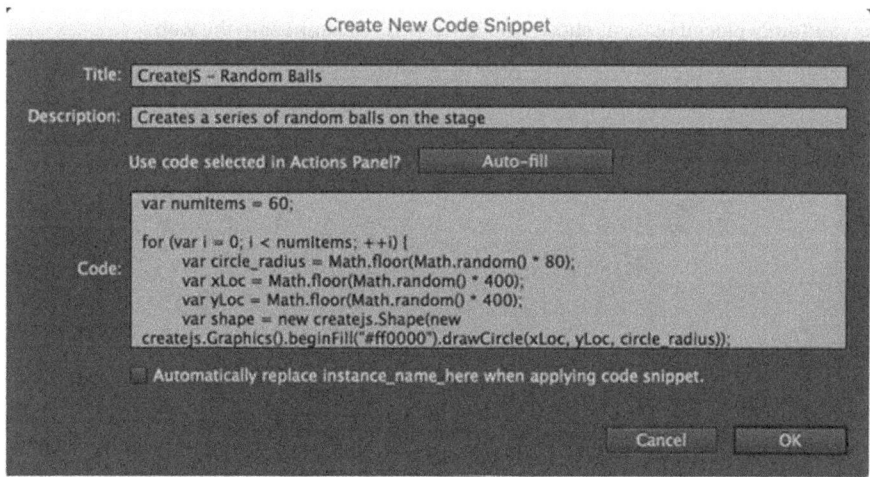

Figure 4-29. *A code snippet is created*

6. Open the Code Snippets panel and you will see that a folder named Custom has been created. Your snippet is in the folder (see Figure 4-30).

CHAPTER 4 ■ INTERACTIVITY BASICS

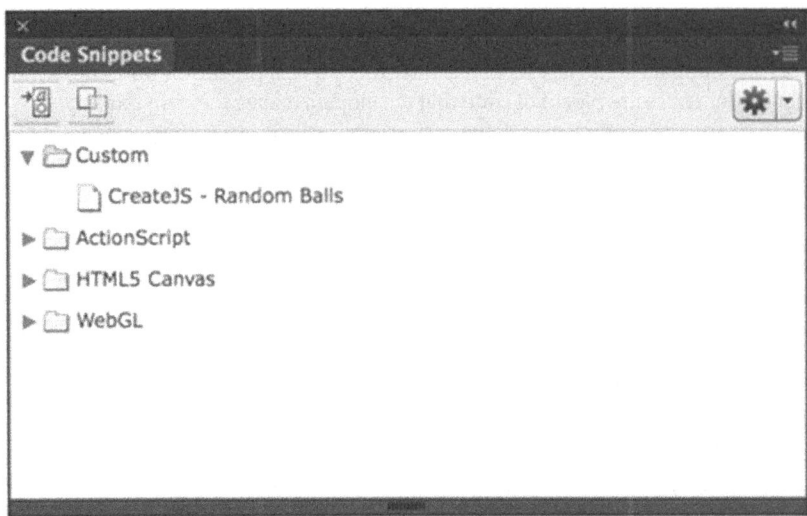

Figure 4-30. *An new snippet has been added to the panel*

7. Delete the selected code in the Script pane and close the Actions panel.
8. Select the new snippet, add the snippet to the timeline, and test the movie. A series of randomly placed balls, as shown in Figure 4-31, will appear in the web browser.

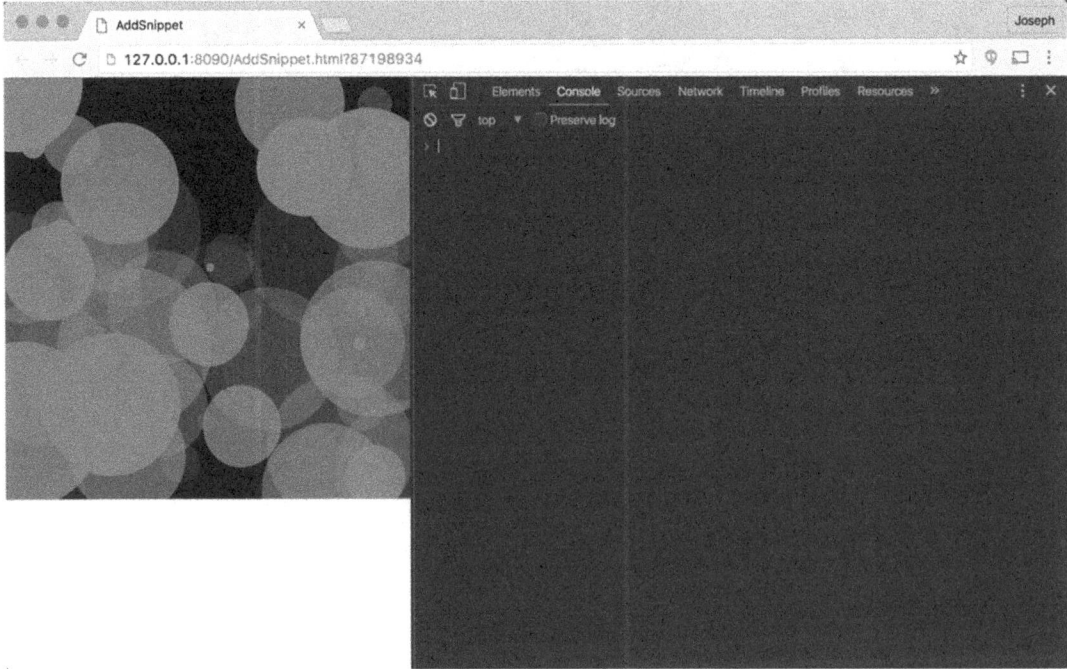

Figure 4-31. *The new snippet plays in the web browser*

246

What if you no longer need the snippet? Here's how to remove it:

1. Open the Code Snippets panel and select the snippet you just created.
2. Click the Options button and select Delete Code Snippet from the menu.
3. A dialog box will open asking whether you really want to do this. Click OK, and the snippet is gone.

What You Have Learned

In this chapter, you learned the following:

- The basics of JavaScript and ActionScript
- The anatomy of the Actions panel
- Why objects are so important and what a class is
- The roles of properties, methods, and events
- Why instance names are needed to reference objects on the stage
- Some syntax rules of thumb
- How to comment your code
- How dot notation and scope help you locate objects
- How to strongly type your variables in ActionScript
- How precedence affects operators
- How to use conditional statements
- How to check syntax
- Tips on using the ActionScript 3.0 Language and Components Reference

A lot of ground has been covered in this chapter. We hope that you are eager to start learning how to use ActionScript and JavaScript code in your everyday workflow.

In fact, every chapter from here on out will use it, so feel free to keep returning here to refresh your knowledge. Also, we recommend that you continue to learn about ActionScript in other reference books.

In Chapter 1, we told you we would get you deep into using audio in Animate CC. With the basics of writing code under your wing, let's see what we can do with audio in Animate projects and how code and audio make an ideal pairing.

CHAPTER 5

Audio in Animate CC

If you're one of those who treat audio in Animate CC as an afterthought, think again. In many respects, audio is a major medium for communicating your message. In this chapter, we dig into audio in Animate CC: where it comes from, what formats are used, and how to use it in a project. Regardless of whether you are new to Animate CC or an old hand with Flash Professional, you are about to discover the rules regarding audio in Animate CC have changed—for the better.

We'll cover the following in this chapter:

- Audio file formats used in Animate CC
- Adding and previewing audio in Animate CC
- Playing audio from the Library
- Playing remote audio files
- Using JavaScript to control audio

If you haven't done so already, download the chapter files. You can find them at `http://www.apress.com/us/book/9781484223758`.

The following are the files used in this chapter (located in `Chapter05/Exercise Files_CH05/`):

- `FrogPan.fla`
- `FrogLoop.fla`
- `Bang.fla`
- `Kaboom.mp3`
- `ButtonSound.fla`
- `CodeButtonSound.fla`
- `LibraryLinkage.fla`
- `Drowning_Past_the_Sky.wav`
- `Alice.mp3`
- `6Threads.jpg`
- `RemoteSound.fla`
- `RemoteSound2.fla`
- `RemoteSound3.fla`

T. Green and J. Labrecque, *Beginning Adobe Animate CC*, DOI 10.1007/978-1-4842-2376-5_5

- Pukaskwa.jpg
- RainStorm.mp3

Animate CC and Audio Formats

When it comes to sound, Animate CC is a robust application in that it can handle many of the major audio formats, including the more common formats listed here:

- **MP3 (Moving Pictures Expert Group Level-2 Layer-3 Audio):** This cross-platform format is a standard for web and portable audio files. In many respects, the growth of this format is tied to the popularity of Apple iOS, Google Android, and other mobile operating systems and devices that handle personal audio playback. Although you can output these files in a stereo format, you really should pay more attention to bandwidth settings for your MP3s when publishing for the web. *(ActionScript 3.0 and HTML5 Canvas)*

- **WAV:** If you use a computer to record a voice-over or other sound, you are familiar with the WAV format. WAV files have sample rates ranging from 8 kilohertz (the quality of your home phone) up to 48 kilohertz (DAT tapes) and beyond. These files are also available with bit depths ranging from 8 bits right up to 32 bits. Just keep in mind that a file with a sample rate of 48 kilohertz and a 32-bit depth will result in a massive file size that simply shouldn't be used with Animate CC. *(ActionScript 3.0 and HTML5 Canvas)*

- **AIFF (Audio Interchange File Format):** AIFF is the standard for the Macintosh and offers the same sample rates and bit depths as a WAV file. Many purists will argue that the AIFF format is better than the WAV format. This may indeed be true, but to the average person, the difference between this format and WAV is almost inaudible. *(ActionScript 3.0)*

- **AAC (Advanced Audio Coding):** AAC is the new "audio kid on the block" when it comes to working with audio in Animate CC. It is another lossy codec but is regarded as being far superior to its MP3 cousin. In fact, AAC was developed as the successor to the MP3 standard. Although you may not be familiar with the format, if you have ever downloaded a song from iTunes, used the Sony PlayStation, the Nintendo Wii, or even iPhone, you have "heard" an AAC-encoded audio file. *(ActionScript 3.0)*

- **ASND (Adobe Sound Document):** In very simple terms, an ASND file is a stereo audio file that you can use in Premiere Pro, After Effects, or Animate CC. The format was introduced way back in Adobe Soundbooth CS4 as a way of easily moving audio between Premiere Pro, After Effects, and Animate CC while at the same time saving audio edits in a nondestructive manner. For example, you can launch Audition from the ASND file in the Animate CC project library and not only make changes to the stereo audio but get an entire "multitrack environment" as well as the ability to save multiple versions of your audio edits and move between them. *(ActionScript 3.0)*

- **AU, SND (Sun AU):** A simple audio file format introduced by Sun Microsystems and used across a variety of applications. *(ActionScript 3.0)*

- **SD2 (Sound Designer II):** This format was originally developed by Digidesign for the Macintosh and is a widely accepted standard for transferring audio files between different applications. *(ActionScript 3.0)*

CHAPTER 5 ■ AUDIO IN ANIMATE CC

- **OGG, OGA (Ogg Vorbis):** An open source patent-free audio compression format, developed as a replacement for proprietary digital audio encoding formats, such as MP3 and AAC. *(ActionScript 3.0)*
- **FLAC (Free Lossless Audio Codec):** A format similar to MP3, but without any loss in quality. The compression used is similar to ZIP compression, but is designed specifically for audio. *(ActionScript 3.0)*

Take this obscure fact to a trivia contest, and you will clean up: AIFF also has a sample rate of 22,254.54KHz. Why the odd sample rate? This was the original Macintosh sample rate and was based on the horizontal scan rate of the monitor in a 128KB Mac.

Bit Depth and Sample Rates

We traditionally visualize sound as a sine wave—when the wave rises above the vertical, the sound gets "higher"; where it runs below the vertical, the sound gets "lower." These waves, shown in Figure 5-1, are called the waveform. The horizontal line is silence, and the audio is "measured" from the top of one "blip" to the top of the next one along the waveform. These blips are called *peaks*, and the sampling is done from peak to peak.

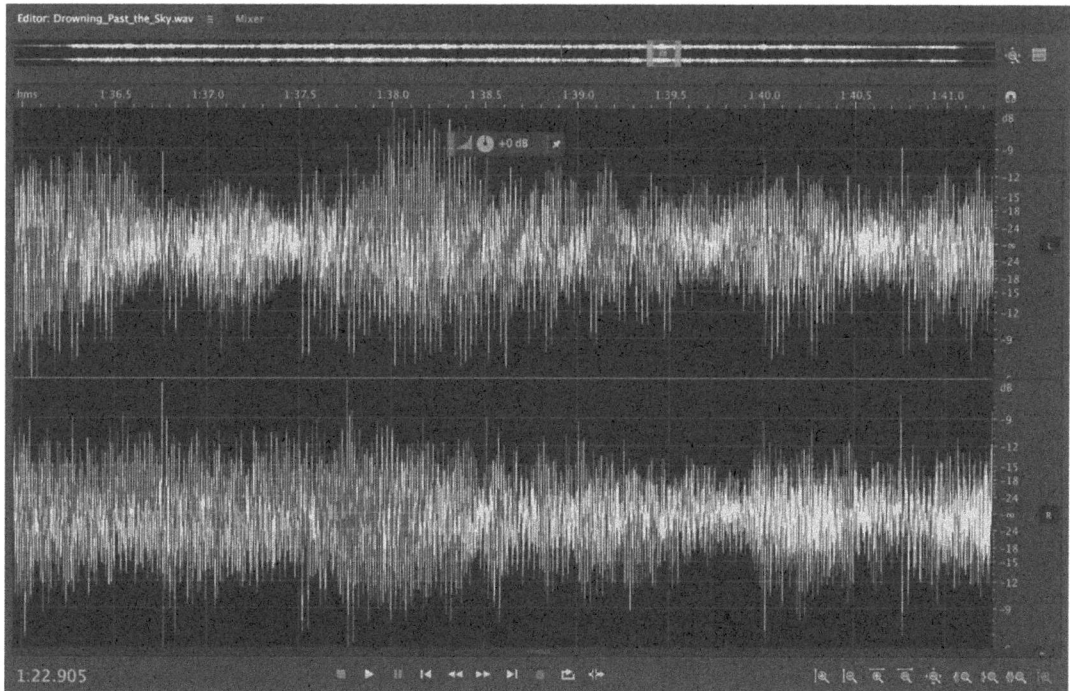

Figure 5-1. A typical stereo waveform from Audition

251

CHAPTER 5 ■ AUDIO IN ANIMATE CC

For any sound to be digitized, like a color image in Illustrator or Photoshop, the wave needs to be sampled. A sample is nothing more than a snapshot of a waveform between peaks at any given time. This snapshot is a digital number representing where, on the waveform, this snapshot was taken. How often the waveform is sampled is called the *sample rate*.

Bit depth is the resolution of the sample. A bit depth of 8 bits means that the snapshot is represented as a number ranging from –128 to 127. A bit depth of 16 bits means that the number is between –32,768 to 32,767. If you do the math, you see that an 8-bit snapshot has 256 potential samples between each peak, whereas its 16-bit counterpart has just over 65,000 potential samples between the peaks. The greater the number of potential samples of a wave, the more accurate the sound. The downside to this, of course, is the more samples on the wave, the larger the file size. These numbers represent where each sample is located on the waveform. When the numbers are played back in the order in which they were sampled and at the frequency they were sampled, they represent a sound's waveform. Obviously, a larger bit depth and higher sample rate mean that the waveform is played back with greater accuracy—more snapshots taken of the waveform result in a more accurate representation of the waveform. This explains why the songs from an album have such massive file sizes. They are sampled at the highest possible bit depth.

One wave cycle in one second is known as a hertz, which can't be heard by the human ear, except possibly as a series of clicks. Audible sound uses thousands of these waves, and they are crammed into a 1-second time span and measured in that span. A thousand waveform cycles in one second is called a kilohertz (KHz), and if you listen to an audio CD, the audio rate is sampled at the frequency of 44.1 thousand waves per second, which is traditionally identified as 44.1KHz. These waves are the sample rate.

The inference you can draw from this is the more samples per wave and the more accurate the samples, the larger the file size. Toss a stereo sound into the mix, and you have essentially doubled the file size. Obviously, the potential for huge sound files is there, which is not a good situation when dealing with Animate CC. Large files take an awfully long time to load into a browser, which means your user is in for a painful experience. One way of dealing with this is to reduce the sample rate or number of waves per second.

The three most common sample rates used are 11.025KHz, 22.05KHz, and 44.1KHz. If you reduce the sample rate from 44.1KHz to 22.05KHz, you achieve a significant reduction, roughly 50 percent, in file size. You obtain an even more significant reduction, another 50 percent, if the rate is reduced to 11.025KHz. The problem is reducing the sample rate reduces audio quality. Listening to your Beethoven's Ninth Symphony at 11.025KHz results in the music sounding as if it were playing from the inside of a tin can.

As an Animate CC project designer or developer, your prime objective is to obtain the best quality sound at the smallest file size. Though many audio-focused developers tell you that 16-bit, 44.1KHz stereo is the way to go, you'll quickly realize this is not necessarily true. For example, a 16-bit, 44.1KHz stereo sound of a mouse click or a sound lasting less than a couple of seconds—such as a whoosh as an object zips across the screen—is a waste of bandwidth. The duration is so short that average users won't realize it if you've made your click an 8-bit, 22.05KHz mono sound. They hear the click and move on. The same holds true for music files. The average user is most likely listening through the cheap speakers that were tossed in when they bought their computer. In this case, a 16-bit, 22.05KHz soundtrack will sound as good as its CD-quality rich cousin.

Animate CC and MP3

The two most common sound formats imported into an Animate CC project are WAV and AIFF. Both formats share a common starting point—they are both based on the Interchange File Format proposal written in 1985 by Electronic Arts to help standardize transfer issues on the Commodore Amiga. Like video, sound contains a huge amount of data and must be compressed before it is used. This is the purpose of a codec. Codec is an acronym for enCODer/DECoder, and the format used by Animate CC to output audio is the MP3 format, although you can import both AIFF and WAV files (and others) into Animate CC.

As Animate CC is generally a platform-agnostic application—certain audio file formats cannot be imported across all project types. You will generally be safe with WAV or MP3... but anything else can get strange. If you want to create a project that is as trouble-free as possible, stick with WAV and MP3.

Let's take WAV files versus MP3 files as an example. From your perspective, the need to compress audio for web delivery makes the use of WAV files redundant. The MP3 format is the standard, which explains why WAV files are converted to MP3 files on playback. If you are working with an audio-production facility, you will often be handed a WAV file. Even if you have the option of receiving an MP3, you are better off with the WAV file, for the same reason that you wouldn't want to recompress a JPG file: because they are both lossy compression schemes.

Why are MP3 files so small but still sound so good? The answer lies in the fact that the MP3 standard uses perceptual encoding. All Internet audio formats toss a ton of audio information into the trash. When information gets tossed, there is a corresponding decrease in file size. The information tossed when an MP3 file is created includes sound frequencies your dog may be able to hear but you can't. In short, you hear only the sound a human can perceive (and this sort of explains why animals aren't huge fans audio playback through iPhones).

All perceptual encoders allow you to choose how much audio is unimportant. Most encoders produce excellent-quality files using no more than 16Kbps to create voice recordings. When you create an MP3, you need to pay attention to the bandwidth. The format is fine, but if the bandwidth is not optimized for its intended use, your results will be unacceptable, which is why applications that create MP3 files ask you to set the bandwidth along with the sample rate.

So much for theory; let's get practical.

Adding Audio to Animate CC

Knowing that you can bring all of these formats into Animate CC for certain project types and that MP3 is the output format for your project is all well and good. But how do they get into Animate CC, and, more importantly, how does an WAV file get converted to an MP3 file when it plays in Animate CC? Let's explore that right now starting with an import.

Importing an Audio File

To see what happens when you import an audio file, create a new HTML5 Canvas document and import `Drowning_Past_the_Sky.wav` (in the exercise folder of this chapter) to the Library. Because of the unique manner in which sound files are added to an Animate CC movie, they simply cannot be imported to the stage.

If you select Import to Stage when importing an audio file, it won't be placed on the stage. Instead, it will be placed directly into the Library.

When you open the Library and select the file, you will see the file's waveform in the preview area, as shown in Figure 5-2. You can click the Play button, which is the triangle located above the waveform in the preview area, to test the sound file.

CHAPTER 5 ■ AUDIO IN ANIMATE CC

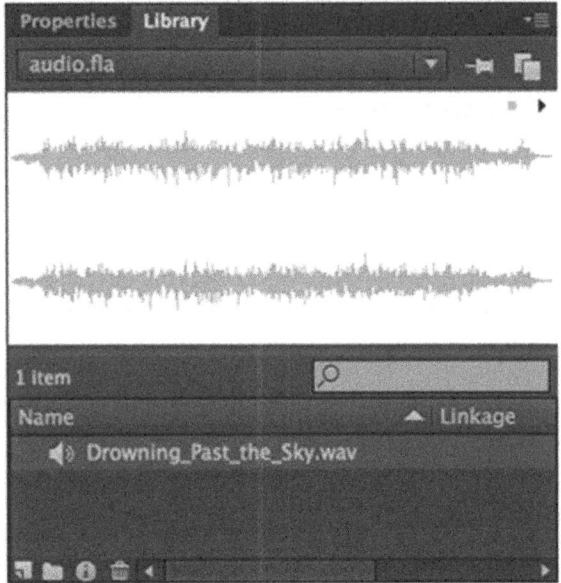

Figure 5-2. Select an audio file in the Library, and its waveform appears in the preview area

Setting Sound Properties

To set the sound properties for an audio file, double-click the speaker icon next to the audio file's name in the Library. Figure 5-3 shows the Sound Properties dialog box for `Drowning_Past_the_Sky.wav`.

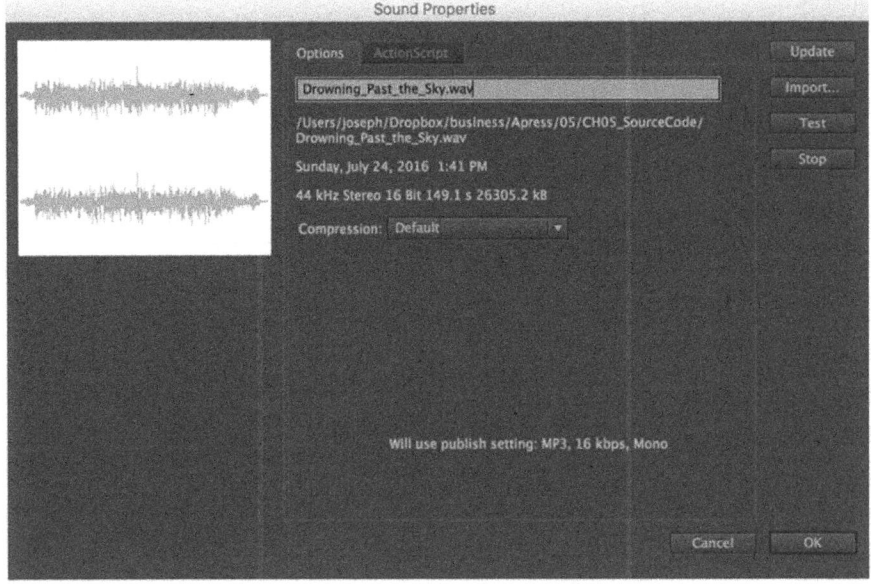

Figure 5-3. The Sound Properties dialog box is opened when you double-click an audio file in the Library

This dialog box is a really useful tool. You can use it to preview and stop an audio file: click the Test button to preview the sound file, and then click the Stop button to stop the sound playback. The Update button is also handy. If an audio file has been edited after being placed into Animate CC, you can click the Update button to replace the imported copy with the edited version—as long as its original location on your hard drive hasn't changed since the file was imported. If the file has moved, use the Import button to find it again, or replace this Library asset with a new file.

Notice the audio information under the path and date. This file—at over 2.0 minutes in duration (149.1 seconds) and around 26MB (26305.2KB)—is rather large.

From our perspective, the Compression drop-down list is of major importance. In this drop-down, you are asked to pick a codec. In Animate CC, the default is to export all sound in the MP3 format. Still, the ability to individually compress each sound in the Library is an option that shouldn't be disregarded. Your choices are as follows:

- **ADPCM:** This type of sound file is best suited for very short clips and looped sound. This format was the original sound output format in older versions of Animate CC. If, for example, you are outputting for use in Flash Player 2 or 3, ADPCM is required.
  Doc Type: (ActionScript 3.0)

- **MP3:** Use this for Flash Player versions 4 or newer, or HTML5 Canvas. MP3s are also not suited for looping sounds because the end of a file is often padded.
  Doc Type: (ActionScript 3.0 and HTML5 Canvas)

- **Raw:** No compression is applied, and it is somewhat useless if sound is being delivered over the Web. If you are creating Flash Player content for use on a DVD or CD or an Animate CC movie for incorporation into a video, this format is acceptable.
  Doc Type: (ActionScript 3.0)

- **Speech:** Introduced in Macromedia Flash MX, this codec (originally licensed by Macromedia from Nellymoser) is ideal for voice-over narrations.
  Doc Type: (ActionScript 3.0)

Once you select a codec, additional compression settings will appear. For our example, select MP3 from the Compression drop-down menu, and the settings change, as shown in Figure 5-4. Click the Test button and listen to the sound. What you may notice is how flat the audio is compared to the original version. If you take a look at the bit rate and quality settings in the Preprocessing area, you will see why. That 26MB file is now sitting at about 1 percent of its original size, or 298KB.

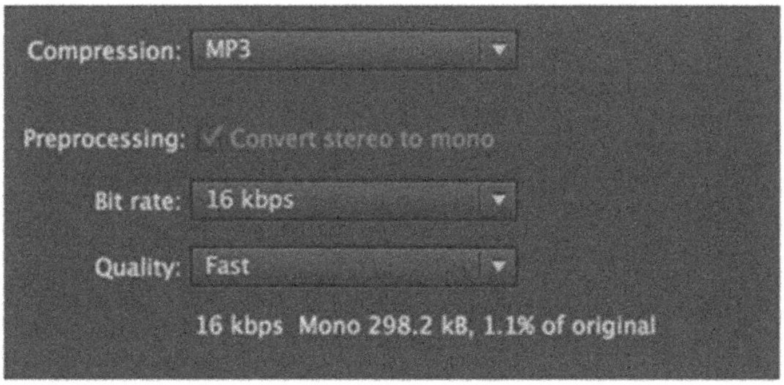

Figure 5-4. Setting MP3 compression

Change the bit rate to 48Kbps, and select Best in the Quality drop-down menu. Also make sure that Convert stereo to mono is selected. If you click the Test button, you will hear a marked improvement in the audio quality.

Unless your audio includes specialized panning or there is some other compelling reason for using stereo, feel free to convert the stereo sound to mono. The user won't miss it, and the audio file size will plummet. Animate CC even allows mono sounds to be panned.

Asking you to compare the audio quality to the original in the previous two steps is a bit disingenuous on our part. Our intention was to let you "hear" the quality differences, not compare them with the original audio. In the final analysis, comparing compressed audio against the original version is a "fool's game." Users never hear the original file, so what do they have as a basis for comparison? When listening to the compressed version, listen to it in its own right and ask yourself whether it meets your quality standard.

No, you can't "supersize" an audio file. If the original file being used has bit rate of 48Kbps when imported into Animate CC, you can never increase the bit rate above that level in Animate CC. "Up-sampling" audio will more often than not decrease, not increase, the audio quality.

If you're using an ActionScript 3.0 document, one other place where the sound output format can be set is through the Publish Settings panel. To access these settings, select File ➤ Publish Settings, and select the Flash (.swf) option in the left panel. Near the top of this panel, shown in Figure 5-5, are preferences for Images and Sounds, which include Audio stream and Audio event settings. We'll get into these two in the next section, but the important thing to note for now is the Override sound settings check box. If you select this check box, the audio settings shown for the Audio stream and Audio event areas will override any settings applied in the Sound Properties dialog box. Think of this as the ability to apply a global setting to every sound in your movie. Unless there is a compelling reason to select this choice, we suggest you avoid it. It's better to spend time with each file rather than apply a setting that may actually degrade quality for a couple of files.

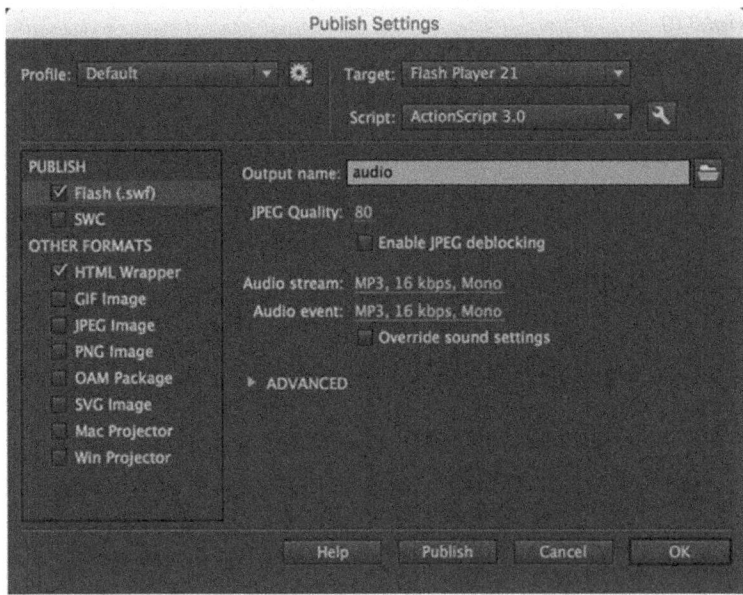

Figure 5-5. The Images and Sounds settings

If you do have a compelling reason to use these settings, click the relevant Set button, and you will be presented with the same options in the Sound Properties dialog box.

Now that you know what the properties do, let's move on to using a sound file in Animate CC. If you have been following along, close any documents you might have open and don't save the changes.

Using Audio in Animate CC

In Chapter 1, you added some crickets and wolves howling using audio files to enhance the ambience of the movie and to add a bit of realism to it. We asked you to do a couple of things in that chapter, but we didn't tell why you were doing them. The purpose was to get you hooked on Animate CC, and it obviously worked because you are now at this point of the book. The time has arrived to give you the answers to the "Why?" questions.

Choosing a Sound Type: Event and Stream

Animate CC has two primary types of sound: Event and Stream. There are also three types of Event sounds—Event, Start, and Stop—but these are all basically variations of the main Event sound type. We will make this distinction here and there, as it is important to know the differences in each. Although, as you saw, when defining sound compression options for an ActionScript 3.0 document, you can define the settings for only Event and Sync, as these are the primary. If Start is chosen, it adopts the same global compression settings as Event sound!

Event and Start sounds tell Animate CC to load a sound completely into memory—as soon as the playhead encounters the frame with this audio—before playing it. Once loaded, the sound continues to play, even if the movie's playhead stops, which means event sounds are not locked to the timeline. (Audio can be forced to stop, but that takes specific action on your part; that is where Stop comes into play.)

In a 24 fps Animate CC movie, a file like `Drowning_Past_the_Sky.wav` from the previous section takes about 3,575 frames to play completely. If you're hoping to synchronize that with animation in the same timeline, think again. If the resultant animation is played back on a slower machine than yours, it's almost certain the audio will not conclude on the frame you expect. Also, a movie would take a long time to start playing, because the project must load the sound fully before playback can begin.

Event and Start sound are ideal for pops, clicks, and other very short sounds or in situations where the audio will be played more than once or looped. These sounds will begin to play on the first frame they are encountered and will continue to play until the sound playback reaches the end, regardless of the frames provided. Start sound will behave exactly as Event sound does—with one exception—it will not play a new instance of the sound if the same sound is already playing. If you want to synchronize extended audio with timeline animation, use streaming sound. Event sound is available in both HTML5 Canvas and ActionScript 3.0 document types, but Start, Stop, and Stream sound sync are only available in ActionScript 3.0 document types.

Stop sound is more of a command then a sound type. Having this declaration on a certain frame will stop the Event or Start sound from completing playback at the point it is encountered. Stop sound commands such as this are only available in ActionScript 3.0 document types.

Stream sound is a sound that can begin playing before it has fully loaded into memory. The tradeoff is that it must be reloaded every time you want to play it. This sound type is ideal for longer background soundtracks that play only once. Because it is in lock-step with the timeline, streaming sound is the only realistic option for cartoon lip-syncing or any scenario that requires tight integration between audio and visuals. Stream sound is only available in ActionScript 3.0 document types.

CHAPTER 5 ■ AUDIO IN ANIMATE CC

Now that you know what to expect, let's work with both primary types:

1. Open the ActionScript 3.0 document Bang.fla file. We are using an ActionScript 3.0 document for this example because both main sound types—Event and Stream—can be used in it. When it opens, you will see we have included the kaboom.mp3 audio file in the Library.

2. Rename the layer in the timeline to Audio and drag the kaboom file from the Library onto the stage. Audio files are added to the Animate CC timeline by dropping them on the stage or the pasteboard where they seemingly vanish—but not by dragging them onto the timeline. When you release the mouse, you may see a line running through the middle of frame 1 in the timeline. This line is the start of the waveform.

3. Insert a frame in frame 100 of the timeline. You can now see the entire waveform on the timeline.

4. Right-click (Windows) or Control+click (Mac) the layer name and select Properties from the context menu.

5. When the Layer Properties dialog box opens, as shown in Figure 5-6, select 300 percent from the Layer height drop-down menu and click OK. When you release the mouse, the layer view is three times larger, and you can see the full waveform.

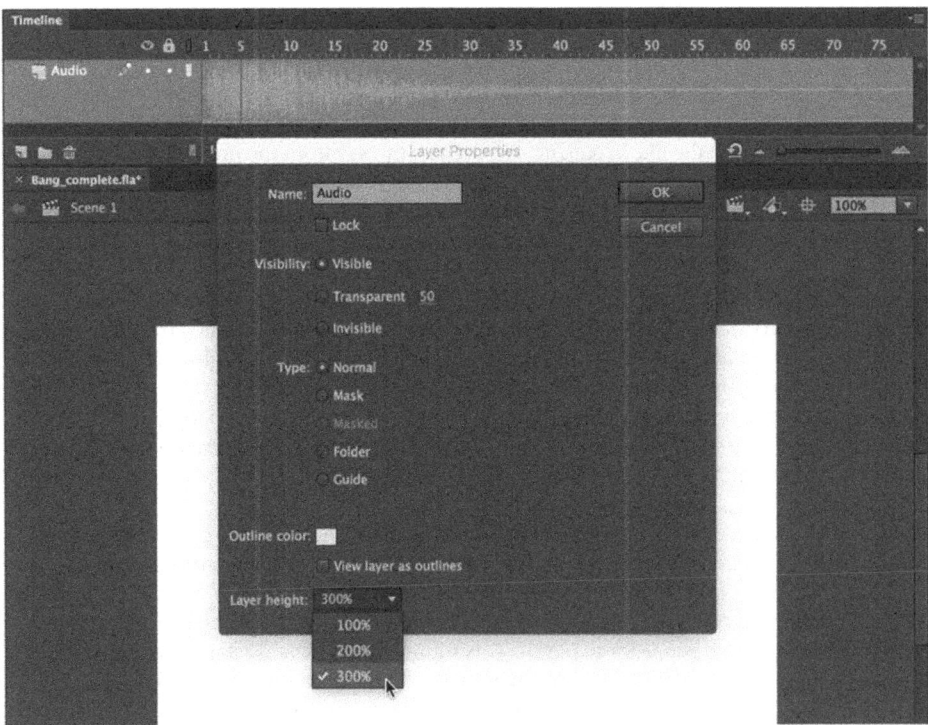

Figure 5-6. *Use the layer properties to "zoom in" on the timeline.*

258

Being able to see the waveform on the timeline is a huge advantage to you because you can now use the waveform's peaks or valleys to time animation of other events to the audio file in Stream mode.

6. Click once in the waveform on the timeline anywhere but frame 1, and in the Sync area of the Properties panel, select Event from the drop-down menu. Press Enter (Windows) or Return (Mac). The playback head moves, but the sound doesn't play. Drag the playback head to frame 1, and press Enter (Windows) or Return (Mac).

What you have just heard is a fundamental truth of an event sound: you can only preview event and start sounds by playing them in their entirety, or at least from their initial frame.

Being the nice guys we are, you can thank us for not using the Drowning_Past_the_Sky.wav audio file. If it were a Start sound, you would be sitting here listening to the full two minutes and 29 seconds of the file. Start sounds play for their entire duration, and you can't stop playback by pressing Enter (Windows) or Return (Mac). All that does is to start playing another copy of the sound over the one that is currently playing. To stop and start sound from playing on the timeline, press the Esc key.

---

7. Change the Sync setting to Stream, as shown in Figure 5-7. This time, drag the playhead across the timeline. Notice you can hear the sound as you scrub across it. Drag the playback head to frame 2 and press Enter (Windows) or Return (Mac). The sound plays from that point and, for longer audio files, pressing the Enter (Windows) or Return (Mac) key stops playback.

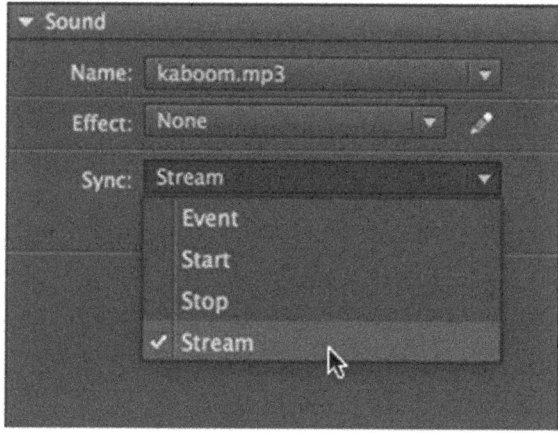

Figure 5-7. Using stream or event sound in the Properties panel

The downside is the playback is only for the frame span on the timeline. For example, the Drowning_Past_the_Sky.wav file would require 3,575 frames on the timeline to play the entire track. If the span were only 50 frames, you would be able to play only about two seconds of the file, assuming your frame rate is set to Animate CC's default rate of 24 frames per second.

We have also mentioned the Start and Stop choices in the Sync drop-down menu. As mentioned earlier, they're similar to the Event sync option with the extra ability to keep sounds from overlapping. Let's try them:

1. Add a new timeline layer and name it `audio2`. Add a blank keyframe to frame 20 of the new layer, select that frame, and drag `kaboom.mp3` from the Library to the stage. Now you have two layers associated with the explosion sound.

2. In the audio2 layer, set the Sync property to Event for the audio in frame 20. Drag the playhead to frame 1 and press Enter (Windows) or Return (Mac). You'll hear two explosions.

3. Change the Sync property in frame 20 to Stop. The first thing to notice is that the audio file in the audio2 layer disappears. Press Enter (Windows) or Return (Mac) again from frame 1, and you'll hear only one explosion. Not only that, but the explosion gets cut off right at frame 20. That's the playhead encountering the Stop keyframe. It's important to understand that a Stop keyframe doesn't halt all sounds. The halted sound must be specified.

4. Select frame 20 and choose None from the Properties panel's Name drop-down list. Now you merely have a keyframe set to Stop, but without an associated sound. Press Enter (Windows) or Return (Mac) from frame 1, and you'll hear the full explosion.

5. Select frame 20 once again. Reselect `kaboom.mp3` from the Name drop-down list.

6. Select frame 20 one last time, and change the Sync property to Start. Press Enter (Windows) or Return (Mac) from frame 1, and you might be surprised to hear only one explosion. Didn't you just tell two of the sounds to play (one as Event and one as Start)? You did, but the Start option waits until the specified sound has finished before it starts another copy of it.

7. Drag the keyframe at frame 20 until you move it past the waveform in the audio layer—frame 98 should do it. Now that the Start keyframe has moved beyond the previous sound, you should hear two explosions again when you press Enter (Windows) or Return (Mac) from frame 1. Users on a slower computer might hear only one explosion, because the first sound may not have finished by the time the playhead hits frame 100. Like the Stop option, Start relies on an explicit sound file reference in the Name drop-down list.

Before finishing with the `bang.fla`, let's get an interesting quirk out of the way.

Removing an Audio File from the Timeline

Audio files simply can't be deleted from the timeline. Go ahead, try it:

1. Hold down the Shift key and select frames 1 and 100 on the timeline to select the audio file. Press the Delete key. Nothing happens.

2. To remove an audio file from the timeline, select a frame in the audio waveform, and in the Properties panel, select None from the Name drop-down menu. The sound is removed.

3. To put the kaboom.mp3 audio file back on the timeline, open the Name drop-down menu and select kaboom.mp3. If you have a number of audio files in your Library, they will all be listed in this drop-down menu, and you can use it to add or change audio files without deleting them or dragging them onto the stage.

4. Close Bang.fla without saving the changes.

Getting Loopy

If you want to loop your audio, the Properties panel puts a couple choices at your disposal. Here's how to set up looping:

1. Open FrogLoop.fla in the exercise folder for this chapter. Press the Enter (Windows) or Return (Mac) key, and you will hear a frog croak. The waveform shows that the croaking happens only once, even though the timeline spans 60 frames. Surely, the frog has more to say than that. Let's give it something to really sing about.

2. Select anywhere inside the waveform, and change the 1 next to the Repeat drop-down list to 4, as shown in Figure 5-8. Notice that the waveform now repeats four times.

Figure 5-8. *Use the Sync area's Repeat drop-down list to configure looping*

3. Scrub the timeline to verify that, as an event sound, the audio does not preview until you press Enter (Windows) or Return (Mac) from frame 1. HTML5 Canvas cannot employ stream sound.

If you were using an ActionScript 3.0 document type, you would be able to change the Sync property to Stream and scrub again. As expected, you would now hear the audio as you drag the playhead. This tells you that streaming sound can be looped just like event sound when utilizing ActionScript.

CHAPTER 5 ■ AUDIO IN ANIMATE CC

4. Change the Sound Loop property value to Loop. The x 4 value next to the drop-down list disappears, and the waveform changes visually to what looks like a single play-through. In spite of its looks, this sound will repeat forever unless you stop it with a Stop Keyframe later in the timeline—or until your user closes your project or flees the web page out of desperation. The Loop setting repeats a sound indefinitely once published.

5. Close the file without saving the changes.

Be very careful with the Loop setting! If a sound is set to Event and Loop, you can accidentally cause instant psychosis if the timeline has more than one frame. Timelines naturally loop when they hit the end of their frame span. If the timeline cycles back to frame 1 while the audio is still playing, you can quickly produce an unwanted echo torture chamber.

Adjusting Volume and Pan

Animate CC lets you adjust the volume of audio files even after they've been imported to the Library. Because of the way Animate CC outputs its internal audio mix, this also means you can pan your sounds by adjusting each speaker's volume separately. In effect, you can bounce audio back and forth between the two speakers, even if those audio files were recorded in mono.

Ideally, you'll want to set a file's overall volume with audio-editing software, such as Adobe Audition. Animate CC can't magnify a file's volume; it can only reduce the volume. So, the volume of your file as recorded is the volume it plays back in Animate CC when the settings are turned all the way up.

You'll be surprised how easy it is to slowly pan the frog serenade from left to right in the timeline. You can only set custom sound effects if targeting an ActionScript 3.0 target in your Animate CC document. Here's how:

1. Open the `FrogPan.fla` file in the Chapter 5 exercise folder. Click into frame 1 of the audio layer, and verify that the Sync property is set to Event and Repeat x 4.

2. Select Fade to right in the Effect drop-down list in the Properties panel, as shown in Figure 5-9. Test the project so far.

CHAPTER 5 ■ AUDIO IN ANIMATE CC

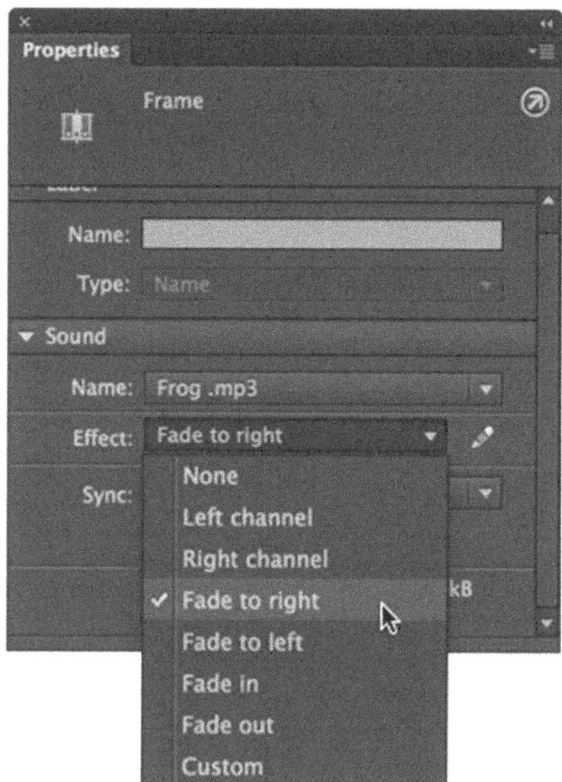

Figure 5-9. *The Effect drop-down list lets you change volume and panning*

You'll hear that the effect works, but the panning moves to the right almost immediately, rather than spread over the four "ribbits." This happens because Animate CC evaluates the actual length of an audio file when assigning one of its effects presets. It's easy enough to tweak.

3. Click the Edit button, which looks like a pencil, next to the Effect drop-down list. This opens the Edit Envelope dialog box, as shown in Figure 5-10.

263

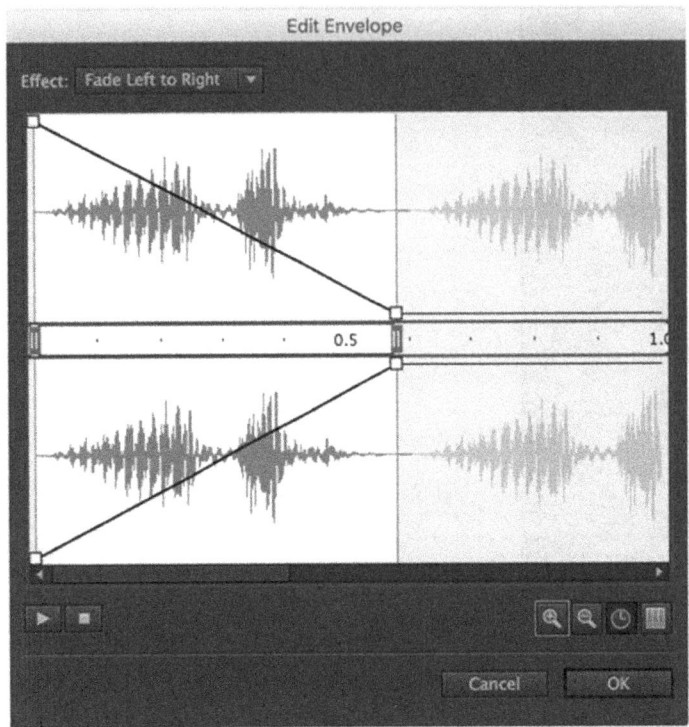

Figure 5-10. The Edit Envelope dialog box lets you apply volume changes to audio files

In the Edit Envelope dialog box, the diagonal lines represent a change in volume in the left (top) and right (bottom) speakers. The volume steadily decreases on the left (moves down) while increasing on the right (moves up), which gives the illusion that the croaking sweeps across the screen. Note that the effect applies to only the first occurrence of the waveform.

Notice the series of buttons along the bottom of the dialog box. You can preview your effect settings by clicking the Play and Stop buttons on the left. On the right, you can zoom in and out to show less or more of the waveform span. The Seconds and Frames buttons affect how the horizontal number line in the middle looks: seconds or timeline frames.

4. Click the Zoom Out button until all repeats of the waveform are visible. Drag one of the right-side squares on the diagonal lines toward the end of the fourth repeat, as shown in Figure 5-11. It doesn't matter if you drag in the top or bottom—both will move. The Effect field in this dialog box changes to show Custom, because you've altered one of the presets.

CHAPTER 5 ■ AUDIO IN ANIMATE CC

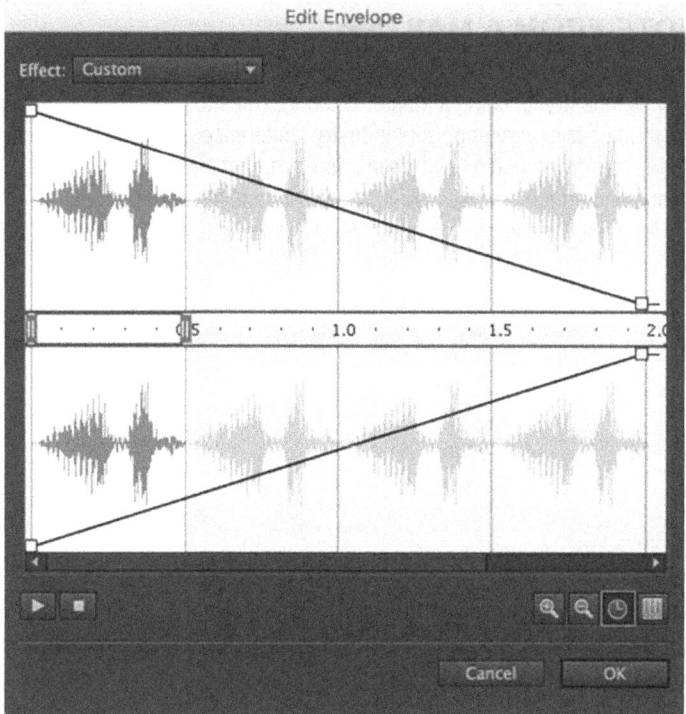

Figure 5-11. *The Edit Envelope dialog box lets you apply custom audio effects*

5. Click the Play button to preview the updated effect. Now the panning happens more slowly, arriving fully in the right speaker only after the fourth "ribbit" ends.

6. Experiment with other Effect drop-down presets. Play around with altering them. Here's a hint: You can add new draggable white squares by clicking anywhere along one of the diagonal lines. Remove white squares by dragging them off the dialog box.

7. Click OK and save your movie.

Splitting Stream Audio Along the Timeline

When working with Stream sound in Animate CC, you sometimes need to split the audio at certain frames and resume later on. You can split the stream audio embedded on the timeline using the Split Audio context menu. When using Stream sound within an ActionScript 3.0 document, right-click on the waveform to summon the context menu and choose Split Audio to create a new keyframe. You can perform this action at multiple points along the timeline, and selecting the sound as none across certain segments will, in effect, pause the audio for the duration of those frames, resuming the Stream audio playback once it is enabled through subsequent frames.

This is a really useful feature for lengthy audio segments you must sync to specific frames, or for extending pauses within your Stream sounds. Again, this is only available in ActionScript 3.0 document types.

265

CHAPTER 5 ■ AUDIO IN ANIMATE CC

A NOTE FROM A MASTER

Dave Shroeder is regarded by many in this industry as being a master when it comes to the use of audio in Animate CC. He has spoken at a number of very important industry conferences, and his company, Pilotvibe (www.pilotvibe.com), has developed a solid international reputation for supplying the industry with high-quality sound loops and effects for use in Animate CC. In fact, his home page, shown in Figure 5-12, can be regarded as a master class in the effective use in audio to set the "mood" in an Animate CC movie.

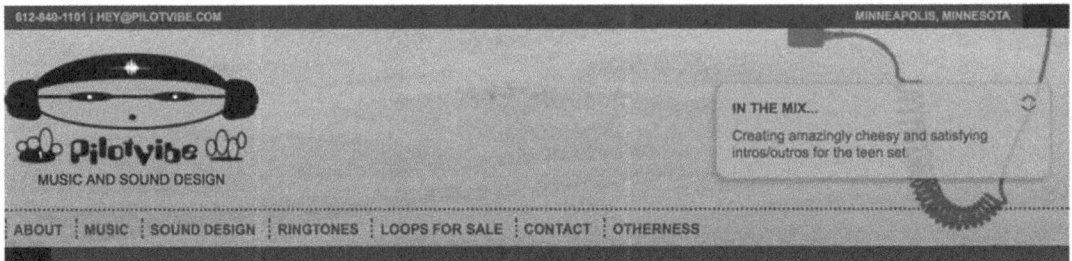

Figure 5-12. *The Pilotvibe home page is a master class in the effective use of sound in Animate CC*

Who better to talk to you about the use of audio in Animate CC than the guy who lead in setting the standard?

"Once you start to play around with adding sound to Flash (Animate CC) files, you'll probably realize that it can add an incredible dimension to your project. Sound can really tie an experience together. It can bring an animation to life. It can create a mood or suggest characteristics that reinforce your message. It can be entertaining or informative or both.

If sound is an option for your project, start with some simple planning. First determine why adding sound makes sense. What purpose does it serve? Does voice-over communicate a story? Do button sounds make the site easier to navigate? Do sound effects make a game more fun or easier to play? Does music give it a cool character? Use answers to these questions to generate a short "sonic mission statement" that outlines why and how you plan to use sound. Do this early in project planning, not after the Animate CC work is done.

Sourcing sounds is easier and cheaper than ever before, thanks to the Internet. There are many web sites that will allow you to search and download files for reasonable fees. Once you've found sounds, use audio-editing software to adjust them to have similar sonic qualities. You want them to sound like they're in the same room or in the same canyon or the same secret underground lair, and so on. Adjust their volumes and equalization (EQ) to achieve this. Use your ears, listen, and you'll do fine. Do they sound close or far, light or heavy, fast or slow? Also, trim the heads and tails of the sound files to be as short as possible without cutting the sound off. The shorter the file, the better it syncs, and the smaller the file size.

CHAPTER 5 ■ AUDIO IN ANIMATE CC

When you're picking music, try to find a piece that fits the mood or reinforces the story. Don't just use death metal because you like death metal or techno for techno's sake. Music has emotional power that transcends genre, and you want to leverage it to make your project as engaging as possible. If you're working with loops, trying to use as long a loop as possible given your file size considerations. Anything under 10 seconds gets old pretty fast unless it's something minimal like a drumbeat. Look into layering loops to create the illusion of a longer track with more variation.

A sound on/off button is a courtesy I always recommend. Compress your sounds so they sound good. A little bit bigger file is worth it if it means people will listen to it. A tiny file that sounds lousy is worse than no sound. Also, compress each sound so it sounds good by itself and in relation to the other sounds. A combination of hi-fi and lo-fi sounds wrecks the illusion of the sounds existing together."

Thanks, Dave, and also thank you for supplying our readers with the Pilotvibe clips in the exercise folder.

Your Turn: Adding Sound to a Button

Let's what you have learned to practical use and blow some stuff up. Follow these steps to accomplish this task:

1. Open the `ButtonSound.fla` file in your exercise folder and import the `kaboom.mp3` file into your Library.

2. Double-click the Blam button symbol in the Library to open it in the Symbol Editor.

3. Add a new layer named Audio and add a keyframe to the Down area of the Audio layer.

4. With the keyframe selected, drag a copy of the kaboom audio file to the stage. Your timeline should now resemble that shown in Figure 5-13.

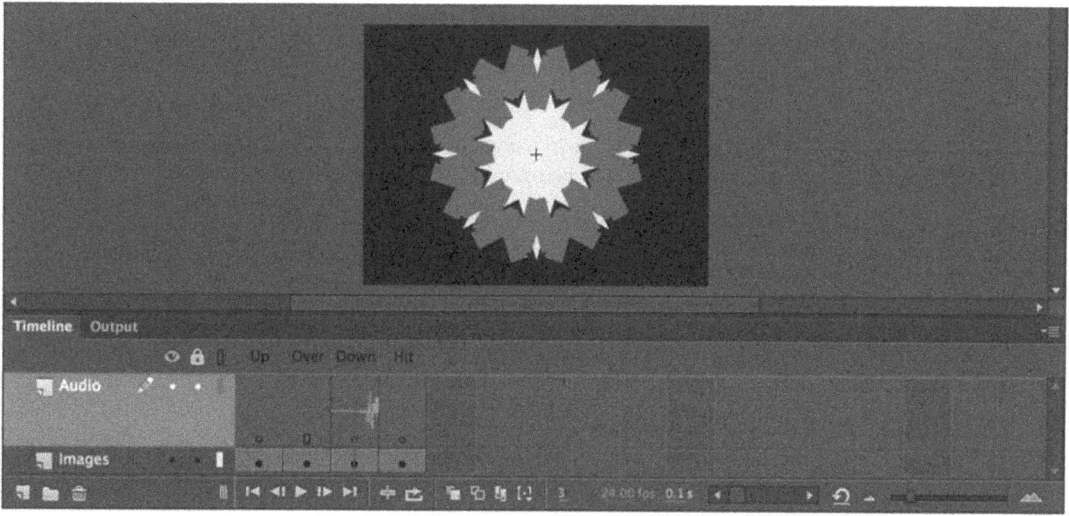

Figure 5-13. *You can add sound to buttons*

267

5. Click in the waveform, and in the Properties panel, select Event in the Sync drop-down menu.

This may seem like an odd instruction because all sounds added to the stage are event sounds by default. We have been around this silly business long enough to embrace the wisdom of the following rule: trust no one and nothing, especially yourself. Get into the habit of double-checking everything and never assuming everything is correct.

6. Click the Scene 1 link to return to the main timeline.
7. Test the file. When the browser opens, click the button. You will hear an explosion every time you click the button.

Now that you understand how audio files can be used in Animate CC, let's take that knowledge to the next level and actually control sound using JavaScript. This is where the full power of audio in Animate CC is handed to you.

Controlling Audio with JavaScript

Before we start, let's really get clear on the following: you aren't going to be fully exploring the nuances and features of audio controlled by code. We are going to give you the basics in this section. These include:

- Playing a sound in the Library without adding it to the timeline
- Using movieclips and buttons to turn audio on and off
- Using movieclips and buttons to load sound dynamically—from your HTTP server—into your Animate CC movie

Things work a little differently when using ActionScript, but are similar enough that you should be able to get a good grasp of the differences in syntax. We'll highlight these differences where it is useful or necessary.

Playing a Sound from the Library

This technique is ideal for sounds that need to play in the background. Be aware that any sound played through JavaScript is always treated similar to an Event sound, but with a bit more control.

1. Open a new HTML5 Canvas document and import the `Drowning_Past_the_Sky.wav` file into the Library. The plan is to have this sound play as background audio, when the movie starts.
2. Select the `Drowning_Past_the_Sky.wav file` in the Library. Note the Linkage column just to the right of the Name column. This is where we will enter the Linkage identifier.
3. Double-click in the Linkage column and enter the Linkage identifier `BG_Music`, as shown in in Figure 5-14. If you are going to play audio files contained in the Library and control them through JavaScript, they must be given this special identifier property to let CreateJS find them in the Library.

In ActionScript 3.0, "linkage" is accomplished in a different way from JavaScript. You need to create a custom class that extends the native Sound class. Fortunately, Animate CC handles the entire process for you, al though advanced developers may, if they want, go to the expense of writing the actual external class file normally needed. You can find this Class field in the ActionScript tab of the Sound Properties dialog box when utilizing ActionScript 3.0.

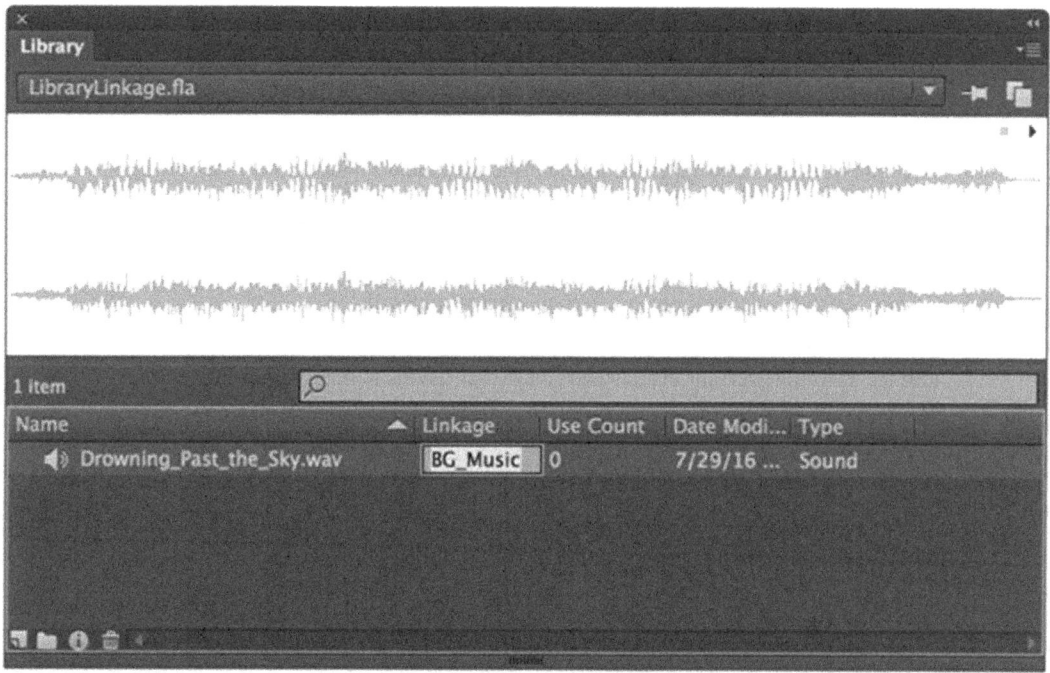

Figure 5-14. Establishing a linkage identifier

4. Click anywhere outside of this field to set the Linkage identifier for your sound file.

5. Rename Layer 1 to Actions, select the first frame in the layer, and open the Actions panel. Enter the following code:

    ```
    createjs.Sound.play("BG_Music");
    ```

This line of the code tells CreateJS to play a sound from the Library and uses the BG_Music Linkage identifier to determine which sound to play.

6. Save the file as LibraryLinkage.fla, and then test the movie by pressing Ctrl+Enter (Windows) or Cmd+Return (Mac). When the browser opens, the sound will play. To stop the audio, close the browser.

So where does the sound file end up? Have a look in the directory that you saved LibraryLinkage.fla and you will see a sounds directory. Enter this directory and you will find that Drowning_Past_the_Sky.wav has been converted by Animate CC to Drowning_Past_the_Sky.mp3 and placed in this directory. Animate CC certainly does a lot of the work for us!

Using a Button to Play a Sound

In an earlier example, you added the kaboom sound directly to the timeline of the button symbol. This time, you are going to use a button—although you can just as easily use a movieclip. Also, instead of embedding a sound in the button, you will have the sound play from the Library. Follow these steps:

1. Open the CodeButtonSound.fla file in this chapter's exercise folder. In the Library, you will see a button and the kaboom.mp3 audio file.

2. Select the kaboom.mp3 audio file in the Library. Use the Linkage column in the Library, as in the previous exercise, to give this audio file a linkage identifier of Blam.

3. Click the button symbol on the stage and give it the instance name of btnPlay. (Remember that symbols controlled by JavaScript need an instance name.)

4. Add a new layer named Actions to the timeline. Lock the scripts layer, select the first frame, and open the Actions panel. Enter the following code:

    ```
    this.btnPlay.on("click", playClicked);
    function playClicked(e){
        createjs.Sound.play("Blam");
    }
    ```

    The first line binds an event handler to listen for click events on the btnPlay button. When this event is detected, the playClicked() function will execute. In turn, the playClicked() function invokes the CreateJS Sound.play() method, which accepts the argument "Blam"—identifying the Blam sound in the Library through the Linkage identifier. The result is that you hear an explosion when you click the button.

5. Save the file and test the movie.

While simple event-level sound playback works wonderfully within HTML5 Canvas, audio playback in the web browser is woefully crippled beyond that. Many browsers have widely varying support for the standards dealing with audio. As a result, you never really know what might work and what might fail beyond simple event playback. An interesting thing to note is that the CreateJS Sound class can actually fall back to use the robust audio control in Adobe Flash Player if audio support for the browser in question is… questionable.

Playing a Sound from Outside of Animate CC

You know that embedding sound into the project library adds to overall package size for distribution. Is there a way to play a sound that isn't inside the project library? Perhaps from a curated online repository? The answer is absolutely.

One of your authors is an active member of the *An Early Morning Letter, Displaced* darkambient studio recording project—and also the *Shivervein* side project. There also exists a set of three community compilation albums of free music in the *Emergent Collective* series. You are encouraged to explore the catalog of music available though these projects, as published by Fractured Vision Media, LLC, at `http://fracturedvisionmedia.com/music`.

The best use for this technique is to play any audio file that is longer than a couple of seconds. In this case, we will be using a lengthy music track entitled "Alice". This was originally an atmospheric composition for a haunted house type event composed by the darkambient studio recording artist *An Early Morning Letter, Displaced*. A shorter, more concise (5:45) version titled "Alice (the bones)" was featured on the 2009 *Shudderflowers* LP release, and in 2010, the full 7 minute 23 second track was released as part of the *6Threads* retrospective EP. The longer, original version of this track is included within the exercise files as an `.mp3` file.

1. Open the `RemoteSound.fla` file in this chapter's exercise folder. You will notice we already have a number of assets on the stage, including some artwork, text, and what appear to be buttons. Ignore that for now.

2. Add a new layer named Actions, select the first frame in the Actions layer, open the Actions panel, and enter the following code (we will review it after you test the movie):

    ```
    createjs.Sound.on("fileload", handleLoad);
    createjs.Sound.registerSound("alice.mp3", "alice");
    function handleLoad(e) {
        createjs.Sound.play("alice");
    }
    ```

3. Test the movie to view your published content in a web browser. The audio starts to play.

The second line of the JavaScript you entered handles the external sound. In CreateJS, you can't simply tell Animate CC, "There's an audio file in this folder that you need to play." Instead, you need to register it with CreateJS to specify the file's location and assign it an ID. That ID, named `alice`, gets passed as a parameter to the `play()` method of the Sound class within the `handleLoad()` function once the load is completed.

If the MP3 is in the same folder as the HTML document, you can simply name the MP3 without a file path. Of course, you can just as easily use an absolute path to a folder on your server. In that case, the syntax would be something like this:

```
createjs.Sound.registerSound("http://some.server.com/audio/alice.mp3", "alice");
```

CHAPTER 5 ■ AUDIO IN ANIMATE CC

In recent years, web browsers have become very picky regarding cross-domain server permissions. Most browsers will not allow any data—images, video, audio, or even raw text data—to be transferred across domains unless the headers of the originating server allow it. For more information on this, have a look at the CORS specification at `http://www.html5rocks.com/en/tutorials/cors/` (it's messy business).

Turning a Remote Sound On and Off

The previous exercise contained a rather nasty usability flaw. The audio file played, and there was no way, other than closing the browser, to turn it off. Let's address this oversight. In this exercise, you will code up two buttons: one button will play the sound, and the other will turn it off. The really neat thing about these buttons is that they aren't buttons. You are about to learn how movieclips can be used as buttons instead. Let's get started:

1. Using the modified `RemoteSound.fla` file. Again, we have provided you with the raw material, as shown in Figure 5-15. The Start button with the instance name `playMC` will be used to turn the sound on. The Stop button, `stopMC`, will be used to turn the sound off.

The choice of instance names is deliberate. Many Animate CC designers and developers try to use contractions that tell the developer what type of object is being used. This explains why you may see code elsewhere and the instance names somehow contain an indication of exactly what object is being used. For example, `playMC` could also be written as `Play_mc` or `mcPlay`. The key is the `mc`, which indicates it is a movieclip.

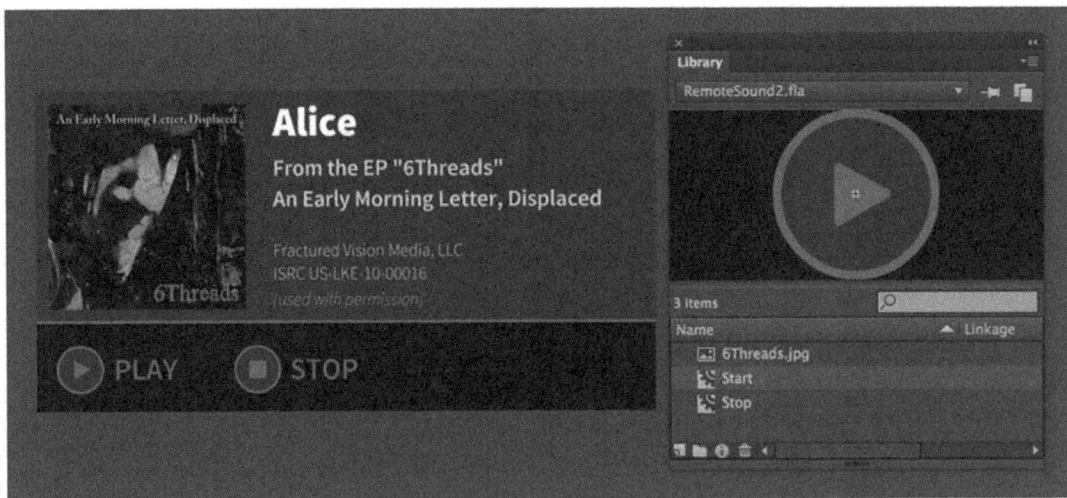

Figure 5-15. *Two movieclips are used to turn a sound on and off*

The plan for this project is to have the user click the Start button to have the audio file play and then click the Stop button to turn off the audio.

2. Remove the previous JavaScript from the Actions layer and save the file as RemoteSound2.fla.

3. When the save is complete, open the Actions panel. Within the Script pane, enter the following code:

```
stage.enableMouseOver();

this.playMC.cursor = "pointer";
this.stopMC.cursor = "pointer";

createjs.Sound.registerSound("alice.mp3", "alice");

this.playMC.on("click", function(e){
    createjs.Sound.play("alice");
});

this.stopMC.on("click", function(e){
    createjs.Sound.stop();
});
```

4. Save and test the movie by clicking the Start and Stop buttons.

The first thing to notice is that we invoke the `enableMouseOver()` method of our stage. This will allow us to change the cursor for the `playMC` and `stopMC` movieclip instances. Without this function call, the cursor cannot be changed. For both `playMC` and `stopMC`, we set the cursor property to `pointer`. What this does is to turn the cursor to the "Pointing Finger" icon, which tells the user, "Hey, you can click this to make stuff happen."

Other than that, the only major difference between this code and that used in the previous example is the addition of event listeners on each movieclip.

When the Play button is clicked, it invokes the CreateJS `Sound.play()` method and passes through the audio file ID that's already been registered with JavaScript. This will begin sound playback just as the `handleLoad()` function did in the previous example. The Stop button, when clicked, will use the CreateJS `Sound.stop()` method to stop playing all sounds in the movie.

Adjusting Volume with Code

What if you don't want to stop the audio but simply allow the user to temporarily mute it? Providing your users with this option is a courteous thing to do. Fortunately, it's not very hard to do.

To see how muting is accomplished, open the `RemoteSound3.fla` file in this chapter's exercise folder. By this point, you should be feeling a sense of déjà vu. The code will look very similar to what you saw in the previous two exercises, but the instance names have changed. The buttons now have instance names `muteMC` and `unmuteMC`. The code has also changed, but not by too much.

1. Click into frame 1 of the Actions layer and take a look in the Actions panel. You'll see the following code:

   ```
   stage.enableMouseOver();

   var s;

   this.muteMC.cursor = "pointer";
   this.unmuteMC.cursor = "pointer";

   createjs.Sound.on("fileload", handleLoad);
   createjs.Sound.registerSound("alice.mp3", "alice");

   function handleLoad(e) {
        s = createjs.Sound.play("alice");
   }

   this.muteMC.on("click", function(e){
        s.volume = 0;
   });

   this.unmuteMC.on("click", function(e){
        s.volume = 1;
   });
   ```

   This time, you set a variable s which you assign as a reference to our audio playback instance when we use the CreateJS Sound.play() method within the handleLoad() function. No button click is needed to play this song; it just plays.

   With a direct reference to the sound being played, you can modify many of the properties of this sound through CreateJS. The Sound class features a volume property, and this property is referenced in terms of the s instance. When muteMC is clicked, t is given a value of 0 (silence). When unmuteMC is clicked, it is given a value of 1 - that's all there is to it.

   Want to turn down the volume instead of muting it? That's easy.

2. Inside the muteMC click handler function, change the 0 to 0.5. Your code should now look like this:

   ```
   this.muteMC.on("click", function(e){
        s.volume = 0.5;
   });
   ```

3. Test the movie and click the buttons. Then close the browser. Change the 0.5 back to a 0 and test again. Neat stuff!

For those of you wondering why we stop with this exercise and don't get into using a slider to adjust the volume, the reason is simple: you need a bit more programming experience before you tackle that and there is no native slider component when using HTML5 Canvas documents. That means you would have a lot to build and program!

Your Turn: Storm Over Lake Superior

One of the really neat aspects of being an Animate CC designer is that you get to bring otherwise static media to life. A great example of this is turning a photograph into a motion graphics piece and then using audio to "seal the deal" and bring it to life. You are going to do just that in this exercise.

One of the authors is an avid hiker and camper. Living in Canada, he has lots of opportunities to indulge in his passion. On the North Shore of Lake Superior is a National Park named Pukaskwa (pronounced "puck-ah-squaw"). In this exercise, you are going to stand with him on the top of a cliff and "experience" a thunderstorm that rolled in off of the lake during his hike. Let's get started:

1. Create a new HTML5 Canvas document and import the Pukaskwa.jpg image in the Chapter 5 exercise folder to your Library. Save the file to your Chapter 5 exercise folder.

2. Add two more layers to the movie and name them Rain and Actions. Rename Layer 1 to Image.

3. Select the first frame of Layer 1 and drag the image from the Library to the stage. Select Modify ➤ Document to open the Document Properties dialog box and select Match Contents. Click OK, and the stage resizes to fit the image. Lock the Image layer.

   The rest of this project will be assembled "over" the image on the stage. The next step will involve adding the rainstorm to the movie. You'll generate the rainstorm through the use of JavaScript and CreateJS.

4. The first task is to create a raindrop shape within the Rain layer. Use the line tool with Object Drawing mode enabled and draw a line that's 24 pixels in height with a stroke size of 3. Use width profile 5 to create a raindrop shape and a stroke color of #FFFFFF at 20% alpha.

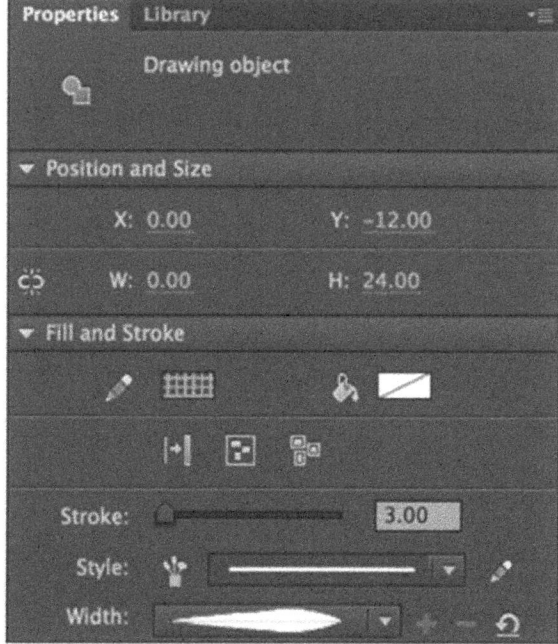

Figure 5-16. *The RainDrop movieclip properties*

5. Select the object and create a MovieClip symbol from it with the name of RainDrop. You will also need to provide a Linkage ID of "RainDrop" in the Library panel once the movieclip has been created. You will be reminded of this later on, once you begin writing code.

    With the RainDrop movieclip created and the photographic image on stage, it's time to begin writing the code that will generate the rainstorm.

6. Select the Actions layer and open the Actions panel. Type the following lines of code into the Script pane.

    ```
    var stageHeight = stage.canvas.height;
    var stageWidth = stage.canvas.width;
    ```

    This will allow you to determine the width and height of the stage and preserve these values within variables to access across our movie later on. The stage.canvas object can be used to access both width and height when writing JavaScript.

7. Next, you need to create a container to hold and manage the raindrops. Enter the following two lines.

    ```
    var rainField = new createjs.Container();
    this.addChild(rainField);
    ```

    The rainField is a type of object called a Container in CreateJS. Note that you instantiate a new Container by stating createjs.Container() directly. A Container is useful for grouping a number of additional visual objects within it. You add the rainField object to the stage so that its children will be visible within the project. Using the Container, you can treat all the child objects as a group, and even wipe them all out with a single command. It's good to be organized!

8. You will next establish a small utility function that allows you to get a random value between a chosen set of numbers. This is a useful function for all sorts of projects.

    ```
    function random(min, max) {
            return Math.floor(Math.random() * (max - min + 1) + min);
    };
    ```

9. Next, go ahead and type in the following function block. This will generate the individual raindrops for your storm.

    ```
    function generateRain(raindrops) {
        for (var i = raindrops-1; i >= 0; i--) {
                var rainDrop = new lib.RainDrop();
                rainDrop.x = random(0, stageWidth);
                rainDrop.y = random(-1000, stageHeight);
                rainField.addChild(rainDrop);
        }
        createjs.Ticker.on("tick", downpour);
    }
    ```

For the generateRain() function, note that the number value being passed in as an argument is exposed through this function with the identifier of raindrops, since it signifies the amount of raindrops for the function to produce. Based on this number, you use a for loop to basically count down from that number until you hit 0. The loop then no longer runs.

Within the loop itself, create a temporary variable (renewed with each iteration of the loop) named rainDrop. This is set to a new instance of the RainDrop movieclip symbol from our project library by invoking lib.RainDrop(). Note that you must set a Linkage identifier within the Library panel for this to work!

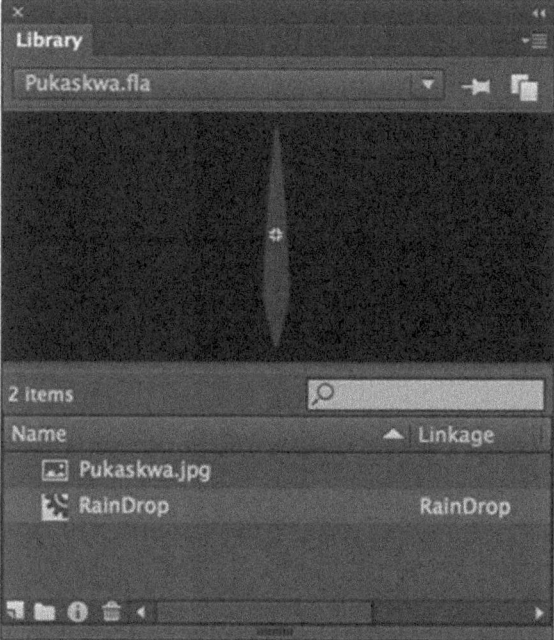

Figure 5-17. *The RainDrop movieclip with a Linkage ID of "RainDrop"*

The last line of code in this function sets up an event listener for the CreateJS Ticker. To use the Ticker, set it to fire on tick, which is actually the frames-per-second (FPS) of our Animate CC project. Since our project is set to 24FPS, the ticker will "tick" 24 times every second. When a tick fires, we want the function named downpour() to run.

10. Enter the following code to build the downpour() function. This function will cause the rainstorm to Animate CC continuously.

```
function downpour(e) {
    for (var i = rainField.numChildren-1; i >= 0; i--) {
        var rainDrop = rainField.getChildAt(i);
        rainDrop.y += 100;
        if (rainDrop.y > stageHeight + 50) {
            rainDrop.y = random(-1000, stageHeight);
        }
    }
};
```

Within the downpour() function, we run through a for loop and move each individual raindrop per loop iteration. What makes this really simple to perform is the use of the rainField Container object. There is a numChildren property inherent to this object type that will report the exact number of child objects within the Container. Using the value of this property, we know exactly how many raindrops we have to move and how many times to iterate our loop.

Within the loop itself, we create a temporary variable named rainDrop for each specific raindrop and increase its position along the y axis by 100 pixels. Seeing as how this function runs 24 times per second, the rain appears to fall very quickly!

The final thing we do is check the position of each raindrop against the height of the stage, adding a 50-pixel buffer to be sure the raindrop is no longer visible. Once a raindrop moves past this point, we reset its position, creating a never-ending rainstorm.

11. Finally, add a call to the generateRain() function to kick everything off. You are passing in a value of 500 to specify the number of raindrops for the function to generate.

    ```
    generateRain(500);
    ```

12. Run the movie in your browser to see a massive rainstorm overlay the imported photo!

Figure 5-18. *The full rainstorm over Lake Superior*

Now that you are standing on a cliff overlooking Lake Superior and getting wet, let's add that last little bit of realism: rain and thunder.

13. Select the first frame of the Actions layer and open the Actions panel once again. When it opens, enter the following code into the Script pane:

```
createjs.Sound.on("fileload", handleLoad);
createjs.Sound.registerSound("RainStorm.mp3", "storm");
function handleLoad(e) {
    createjs.Sound.play("storm");
}
```

14. Save and play the movie. As you may have noticed, the simple addition of an audio track makes this project much more powerful.

What You Have learned

In this chapter, you learned the following:

- How to add audio to an Animate CC project
- The difference between an Event, Start, Stop, and Stream sound types
- How to set the preferences for sound output in Animate CC
- Various approaches to playing a sound in the Animate CC Library and one located outside of the published document
- The various mechanics JavaScript uses to control and manage sound in Animate CC

As you discovered, there is a lot more to audio in Animate CC than simply tossing in some sort of electronica beat and becoming a "cool kid." Audio in Animate CC is a powerful communications tool, and savvy Animate CC designers and developers who realize this are leveraging audio in Animate CC to its full potential. Speaking of communications tools, text is no longer that gray stuff that goes around your animations. To find out more, turn the page, because text is the focus of the next chapter.

CHAPTER 6

Text in Animate CC

"Letterforms that honor and elucidate what humans see and say deserve to be honored in their turn. Well-chosen words deserve well-chosen letters; these in their turn deserve to be set with affection, intelligence, knowledge, and skill. Typography is a link, and it ought, as a matter of honor, courtesy and pure delight, to be as strong as the others in the chain."

—Robert Bringhurst

This quote from Bringhurst's master work, *The Elements of Typographic Style, Second Edition* (Hartley and Marks, 2002), sums up the essence of type in Animate CC. The words we put on the stage and subsequently put into motion on devices, tablets, and computer screens are usually well chosen. They have to be, because they are the communication messengers, providing the users with access to understanding the message you are trying to communicate. In this chapter, we focus on using type to do just that.

There seems to be a notion that type "is that gray stuff that goes around your cool images or interfaces". This is just plain wrong. The words are how you or your client are communicating with your users and if you make those words hard to read, illegible, or otherwise "play" with them the users are barred from understanding. To provide your users with that understanding you need to understand the role of type in Animate CC. To start that exploration, you need to understand what type is in Animate and, just as importantly, what you can do with it to honor the communication messengers of your content.

We'll cover the following in this chapter:

- The basics of type
- Using the Text properties
- Adding Typekit fonts and Google fonts
- How to format text
- Using JavaScript to create, format, and present text
- Using ActionScript to create, format, and present text
- Creating scrollable text blocks

© Tom Green and Joseph Labrecque 2017
T. Green and J. Labrecque, *Beginning Adobe Animate CC*, DOI 10.1007/978-1-4842-2376-5_6

The following files are used in this chapter (all found in `Chapter06/Exercise Files_CH06`):

- `TextFormat.fla`
- `TextJS.fla`
- `TextAS3.fla`
- `ScollableJS.fla`
- `ScollableAS3.fla`

The source files are available online at `http://www.apress.com/us/book/9781484223758`.

Fonts and Typefaces

Before we define what a font is and what a typeface is, let's get really clear on one point: type is not that gray stuff that fits around your "whizzy" Animate CC projects. It is your primary communications tool.

Reading is hardwired into us. If it wasn't, you wouldn't be looking at this sentence and assimilating it in your brain. You have a need for information, and the printed word is how you get it. The thing is, the choice of font and how you present the text not only affects the message but also affects the information. You can see this in Figure 6-1. The phrase "Animate CC Rocks" takes on a different meaning in each instance of the phrase. Using the same Times typeface but with the bold and italic variants, the message "changes" depending on the style applied.

Animate CC Rocks

Animate CC Rocks

Animate CC Rocks

Animate CC Rocks

Figure 6-1. *It is all about the message*

You can take this to the next level and see that not only variants but typeface has an effect on the message. Figure 6-2 shows five examples of the same information presented using different typefaces. You can see how the message changes even more dramatically.

Times … Animate CC Rocks

Roboto … Animate CC Rocks

Marker Felt … Animate CC Rocks

Futura … Animate CC Rocks

Rockwell … Animate CC Rocks

Figure 6-2. *It is all about the message and the typeface chosen*

When choosing your fonts, you also have to be aware of their impact on readability and legibility. Both are achieved by an acute awareness of the qualities and attributes that make type readable. These attributes include the typeface, the size, the color, and so on.

To illustrate this point, take a look at a small exercise one of the authors uses in his classes. What word is shown in Figure 6-3? Don't be too hasty to say *legibility*. What are the sixth, seventh, eighth, and ninth characters? Which letters are the first and second letters? Suddenly things become a bit disorienting.

Figure 6-3. *What word is this?*

This disorientation is important for you to understand. Our visual clue to legibility and readability, as shown in Figure 6-4, is the flow along the tops of the letters. This is why text that consists of all capital letters is so hard to read.

Figure 6-4. *We get our clues to letterforms from the tops of the letters*

CHAPTER 6 ■ TEXT IN ANIMATE CC

We include this exercise because there is a huge temptation on the part of people new to Animate CC to prove they're one of the "cool kids" and use font and color combinations that make otherwise legible text impossible to read. A good example of this is Figure 6-5. The word is set in a medium gray color on a dark gray background. The text is very difficult to read, and yet somehow the "cool kids" think this is some sweet action. Wrong! They just killed all access to the information contained in the text. The next figure, Figure 6-6, goes in the opposite direction. Type is used as a clear communications vehicle for the message.

Even though paying attention to design is critical, from a type perspective, font-rendering technology in Flash Player was a huge issue until the introduction of CoolType in Flash Professional CS4.

Figure 6-5. It is all about the message and the font you choose

Figure 6-6. The message—"Opel drives on natural gas"—comes through loud and clear

Adobe CoolType

There is a significant technology under Animate's hood and we suspect that not a lot of people will pay much attention to it. The technology is CoolType.

Designers are an odd bunch. They can pick out something that doesn't "look quite right" with what seems to be a cursory glance at the page or the screen. For years, designers have noted that type on screens just didn't "look right," and as strange as this may seem, they were correct. This was an odd situation because Adobe has always been in the lead with font technologies, and yet one of its flagship applications seemed to be lagging in this important area. We won't get into the reasons why—they are complex and tediously technical—but font rendering and management has always been a sore point with designers. CoolType may have just put that one to rest.

To understand how big a deal this is, you have to go back into the gray mists of time to around 1984 and the introduction of the Macintosh. For many of you, 1984 is a murky year in your childhood. For some of us, especially one of the authors, it was the year that graphic layout started its move from art boards, waxers, and X-Acto knives to the computer screen. Two players—Apple and Adobe—made this possible. Apple supplied the computer and the LaserWriter printer, while Adobe supplied PostScript.

To that point, layout on a computer was interesting, but the problem was that stuff called **type**. A letter would show up on the computer screen, but it would be blocky. There was essentially no way to differentiate a capital letter *A* using Garamond from its Times counterpart. This was because of the way computers rendered on-screen type. Essentially, the letters were constructed in a grid of pixels that gave them the rather blocky, pixelated look we have come to call the **jaggies**. PostScript, developed by Adobe, somewhat solved this problem by creating a language—PostScript—that, in very simple terms, "drew" the letter over the pixels and gave designers what they wanted: Garamond *A*s that actually looked like Garamond *A*s on the screen. The fact that they looked even crisper when run through the LaserWriter was also a huge factor in moving the graphics industry to computers.

Still, designers spent a lot of time complaining about on-screen resolution and font crispness. They had a point because, no matter how you cut it on the screen, text had some serious readability issues because pixels were still being lit up to create letters. As the Web took hold and devices took off, designers noticed the fonts they used still didn't look "quite right" because the text was being displayed on-screen and subject to the lingering problems inherent in on-screen text.

As we have stated, the relatively poor readability of text on-screen compared to its paper counterpart has been a significant sticking point with designers almost from the word "Go." The source of the problem is low-resolution computer screens. While the resolution of the typical printer is often 600 dots per inch (dpi) or more, the resolution of the average laptop, smartphone, tablet, or desktop screen is significantly lower. This means type that looks crisp and smooth on paper appears coarse and jagged on-screen.

To combat the jaggies, traditional grayscale font **anti-aliasing** (also called **font smoothing**) buffs out the corners in text by filling in the edges of bitmapped characters with various shades of gray pixels, which can make text at small point sizes appear blurry. Animate CC's predecessor, Flash Professional, attempted to address this issue when it introduced a number of anti-aliasing features in 2004. Though a huge improvement, designers were still unhappy because their text still didn't look "quite right." They looked at the introduction of CoolType to Acrobat in 2000 and asked, "Uh, what about us?" The thing is, a lot of our work was in color, and adding fuzzy gray pixels around colorful letters wasn't making life easier for either party.

CoolType to the Rescue

What CoolType does is create clearer, crisper type using a font-rendering technique Adobe calls **color anti-aliasing**, which works on digital liquid crystal display (LCD) screens such as those in laptops, handheld devices, and flat-panel desktop monitors. Unlike conventional anti-aliasing, which manipulates only whole pixels, CoolType controls the individual red, green, and blue subpixels on a digital LCD screen. The key word here is *subpixels*. The hundreds of thousands of squares on the screen, which are the pixels, are actually further subdivided into even more squares. These are the subpixels, which are something like quarks in the realm of the formerly indivisible atom.

According to Adobe, by adjusting the intensity of the subpixels independently, the strokes of a character can be aligned on any subpixel boundary, thus achieving sharper, more precise smoothing along the edges of characters. Using this subpixel technique, CoolType can dramatically increase horizontal resolution for improved readability. Again, the keyword in that last sentence is *horizontal*. We read text across the page, which means the characters are even sharper, which, in turn, makes them even more legible and readable.

What's the big deal with subpixels? If you have a tablet or smartphone the screen most likely uses a proprietary technology to render subpixels on an LCD screen. The result is the crisp text you are looking at every day.

Typefaces and Fonts

What is a typeface, and what is a font? Technically speaking, a **typeface** is an organized collection of glyphs (usually letters, numbers, and punctuation) that shares stylistic consistency. A **font** is one particular size or variety of a typeface. So, Arial 10 and Arial 12 represent two distinct fonts but belong to the same typeface. The same goes for Arial and Arial Bold or the fonts—Times, Times Italic, Times Bold, Times Bold Italic—used in Figure 6-1: separate fonts that belong to the same font family. In everyday talk, for better or worse, most people simply use the word *font* for all the of preceding.

Animate CC offers an interesting advantage when it comes to typography: although HTML is capable only of displaying fonts that are installed on the viewer's computer or available as a web font, Animate CC can display whatever font you like. Want to use some zany dingbat characters or an extravagant cursive font you designed yourself? Have at it. Even input text fields—the sort typed into by the user—can be displayed in whatever font suits your fancy.

Does this sound too good to be true? Well, everything has a price. Fonts can add to a project's overall file size—the more ornate, the greater the penalty. Take a moment to consider what fonts are, and you'll see that this makes sense. Most fonts store a mathematical description of the lines and curves that define each glyph. Simple shapes require less description than complex shapes.

Does that sound oddly familiar? It should because most fonts today are drawn in a PostScript drawing application. In fact, Illustrator CC is rapidly becoming the tool of choice among the type design community.

Animate CC supports the following font formats: TrueType, OpenType, PostScript Type 1, bitmap (Macintosh), and device fonts.

Using Adobe Typekit

Choosing a font is a decision driven by personal preference or the requirements of the project where a particular font is used by your client for branding purposes. In many cases, the odds are pretty good that you won't have the font in your computer and will have to obtain it. This is not as big a deal as it used to be. Back then one would have to purchase the font for a couple hundred dollars and a common complaint was the purchase would only be used once for that particular project. With the introduction of Typekit into the Creative Cloud you now have access to one of the most extensive font libraries out there and, best of all, the cost to download and use any font in the Typekit Library is included in your annual Creative Cloud subscription.

Even better is the fact you can download and install Typekit fonts from within Animate CC. Here's how:

1. Open a new HTML5 Canvas document and, when it opens, select the Text tool and click on the stage. A text field will appear and the Properties panel will light up to show you the Text options.

2. Underneath the Instance name area in the Properties panel is a drop-down offering you two choices: Static Text and Dynamic Text. Think of static text as simply being text that won't change and dynamic text as being text that will change either through the use of JavaScript or some sort of user interaction such as a touch or click event. Another way of looking at it is Static Text is limited to the fonts installed on your computer and Dynamic Text uses live web fonts. Select Dynamic Text.

CHAPTER 6 ■ TEXT IN ANIMATE CC

3. Click the Globe button aside the Family property area of the Character section in the Properties panel. You have two choices: Typekit or Google Fonts. Click Typekit and the dialog shown in Figure 6-7 appears. You may need to click through the Typekit intro screen to see this.

What has happened is you are, thanks to your Creative Cloud subscription, handed what could at first seem to be an overwhelming font selection list. If you are looking for a particular font, you can enter its name in the Search box. You can also cut back on the list by filtering what you are looking for, as shown in Figure 6-7.

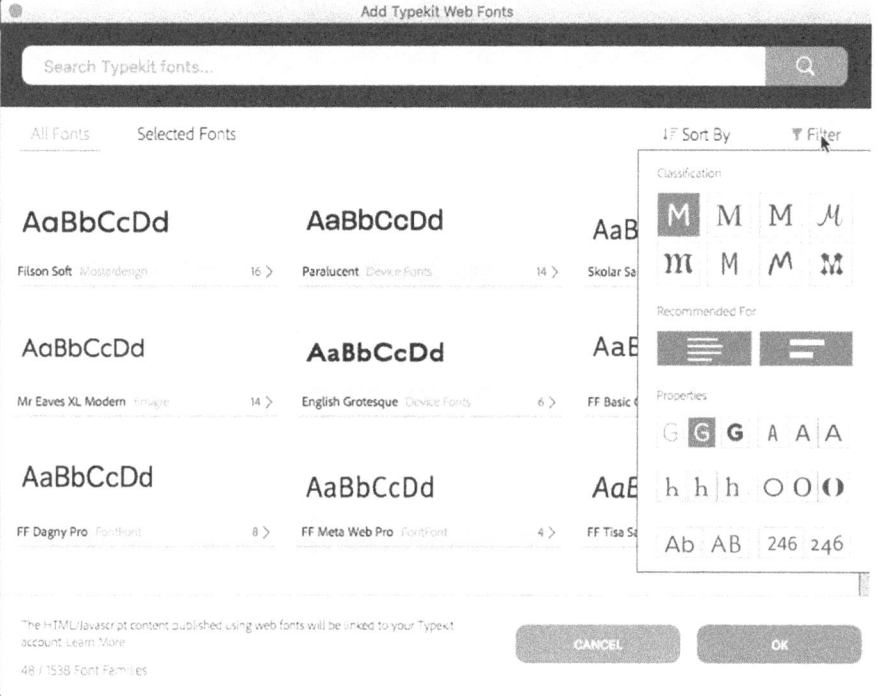

Figure 6-7. *The Add Typekit Web Fonts dialog box lets you refine your search through use of the Filter menu*

287

4. Click on the gray area at the bottom of a font and you will see all of the variations and weights that will be included in the download. If you open your Font Family drop-down, the font will be there in the Web fonts area at the top of the Font list.

If you desire to change the type from Dynamic to Static, you will see that Static has now been grayed out. There is a workaround:

1. Open a web browser, head over to typekit.com and log into Typekit using your Adobe ID. The difference here is the inclusion of an Availability area with a Sync button on the right side of the web page (see Figure 6-8).

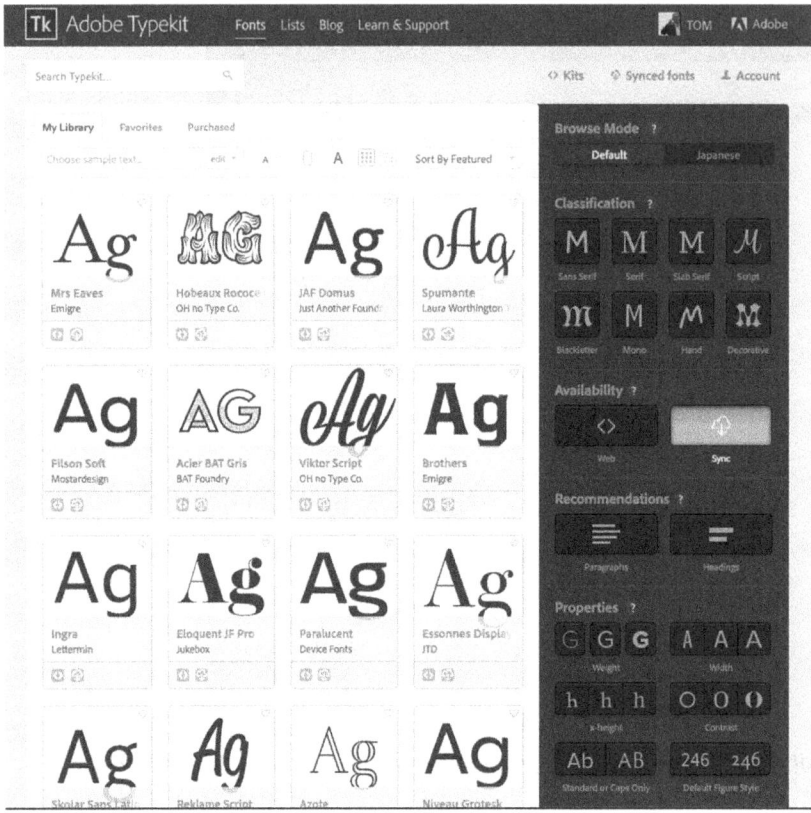

Figure 6-8. *Select Sync to download and install a font on your computer*

2. Select Sync and search for the font you need.

3. Click on the font name. This will open the weights and styles of your selected font. The Web and Sync icons you see beside each style tell you the font can be used as a web font and Sync tells you can be installed on your computer and used as a static text.

4. Click the green Use Fonts button and you can select the members of the Font family you wish to install, as shown in Figure 6-9.

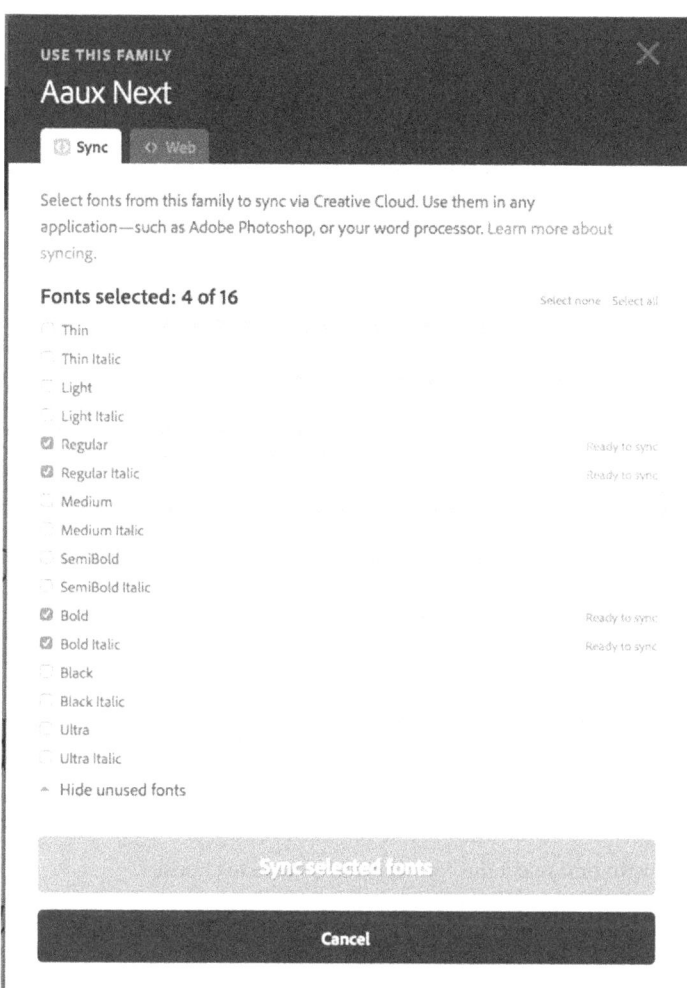

Figure 6-9. *Choose the members of the Font Family to be synced with your computer*

5. Click the Sync selected fonts button and, providing you have your Creative Cloud Desktop app running, the font will be downloaded and installed. You will be notified via the desktop app when this process has completed.

6. Return to Animate CC, select the text box, and choose Static Text. When you open your Family list, your font, as shown in Figure 6-10, will appear.

CHAPTER 6 ■ TEXT IN ANIMATE CC

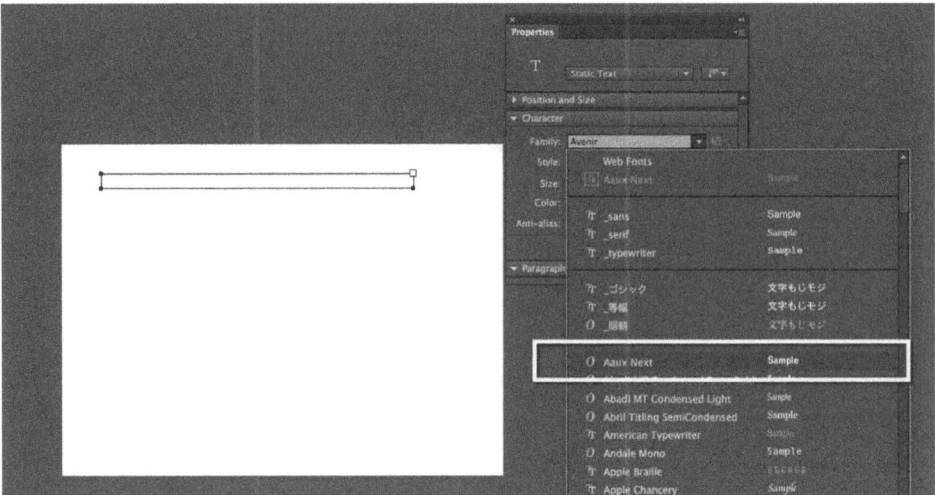

Figure 6-10. The Aaux Next font has been downloaded and installed for use as static text

Using Google Fonts

It should come as no surprise that Google Fonts are available as a Dynamic Text option for HTML5 Canvas documents through Animate CC. Since the introduction of this royalty-free font service in 2010, the collection has grown to over 800 fonts and has become a sort of de facto go-to service when web designers and developers are looking for high-quality fonts for use in the web and app development projects. Follow these steps to add a Google Font:

1. Open a new HTML5 Canvas document, select the Text tool and be sure to choose Dynamic in the Text Type drop-down. Now draw out a text box.

2. In the Properties panel, click the Globe icon beside the Family and select Google Fonts from the drop-down. This will open the Google Fonts dialog box shown in Figure 6-11. If you want to refine your search, select a Category in the Category drop-down menu.

3. Choose the Fonts you want to use and if you want to see the Styles contained in the font click Show All Styles.

4. To add the font, click the Done button and the fonts will appear in the Web Fonts listing.

CHAPTER 6 ■ TEXT IN ANIMATE CC

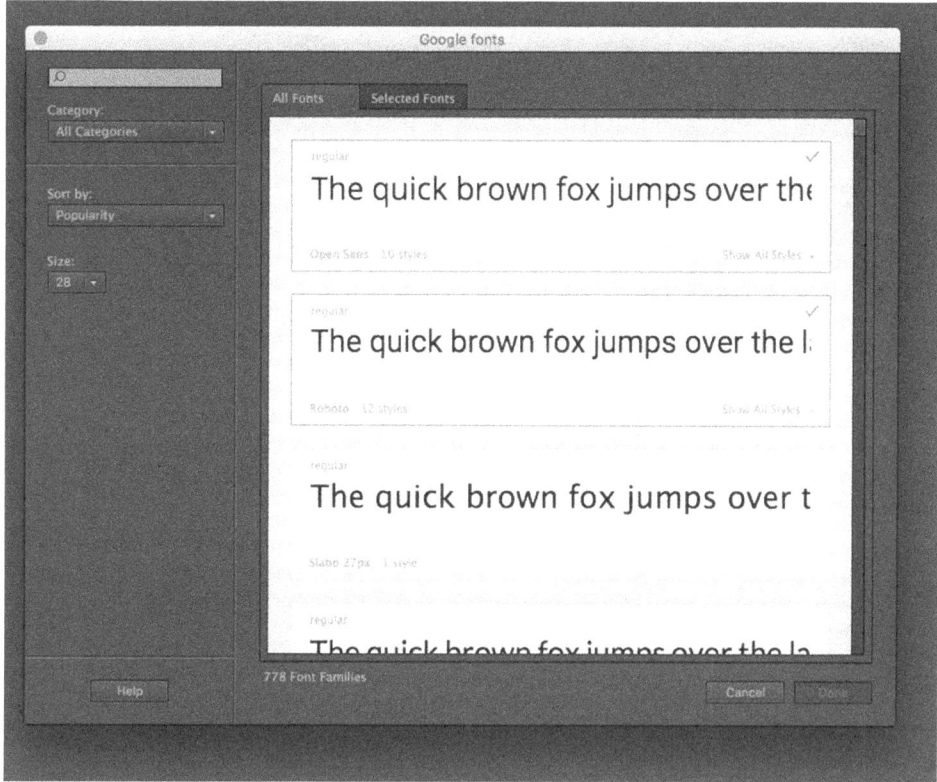

Figure 6-11. The Google Fonts dialog box

Working with Device Fonts

If you want, you certainly can go with fonts that are installed on the user's machine, just like HTML does. The benefit is that your project's weight will be completely unaffected by text content. The drawback is that you have to count on your audience having the same font(s) installed as you do (not a good idea) or choose among three very generic font categories: _sans (sans-serif), _serif, and _typewriter (monospace). These are the device fonts, and they are ideal for use on mobile devices.

In the Properties panel, take a look at your font choices in the font drop-down list. The top three, shown in Figure 6-12, are preceded by an underscore. That's the tip off. If you select one of these fonts, Animate CC will choose on your behalf whatever it thinks is the closest fit on the viewer's computer. _sans will probably be Arial or Helvetica, _serif will probably be Times New Roman or Times, and _typewriter will probably be Courier New or Courier—but who knows for sure?

CHAPTER 6 ■ TEXT IN ANIMATE CC

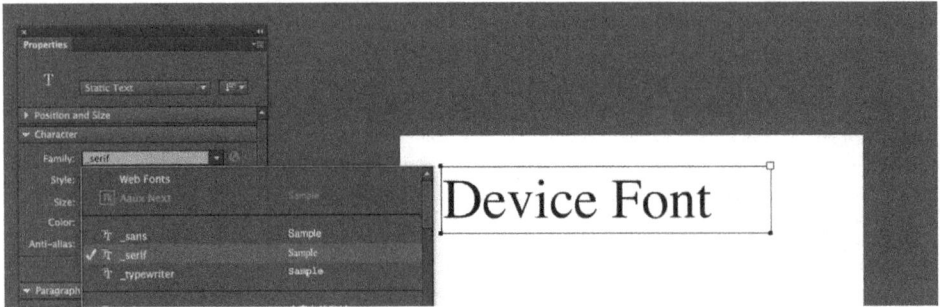

Figure 6-12. *The device fonts work everywhere but have limitations*

Another place where you can use device fonts is in those situations where you choose a font, such as Helvetica, and you aren't sure whether the user has the font. As shown in Figure 6-13, you can select Use Device Fonts in the Anti-alias drop-down menu, and the fonts will be substituted at runtime. This option is only available for ActionScript 3.0 documents.

Figure 6-13. *Device fonts can be used to override the fonts in the movie at runtime*

Currently Animate CC can't treat device fonts as graphics. Tweening stuff containing a device font is going to be unpredictable.

Also realize the term *device font* is a "weasel word" for "pick the closest approximation." This means you lose all control over the spacing and length of the text on the screen at runtime. Depending on the font chosen by the user's machine, you may wind up having the user view your work through a font that has a bigger x-height than your font. If you need an exact match, device fonts aren't the way to go.

X-height? What's that? It is the height of the letter *X* in the font, and this proportional characteristic can vary widely in different typefaces of the same size. Tall x-heights are two-thirds the height of a capital letter and short when they are one-half the height of a capital letter. Staying with our useless information theme, the trend to the larger x-height in the sans category was sparked by a Swiss typographer, Adrian Frutiger, when he released Univers 55.

Embedding Fonts

We need to deal with this subject before we move on because it is an option when working with an ActionScript 3.0 document.

As you have learned, fonts are PostScript outlines of the letters and glyphs contained in a font. You buy fonts, and as such, it is a copyright violation if you were to hand the user the opportunity to install a font in order to see your amazing work. This is one of the reasons Matthew Carter designed the classic web fonts. They were automatically installed on practically every computer on the planet in order to give designers a bit of typographic variety and to keep them out of court. Apart from the web fonts, device fonts are one solution and embedding is the other.

Matthew Carter may have designed the web fonts—Arial, Verdana, Georgia, and so on—but it was Microsoft that put them into play when they asked Matthew to design them. The fonts were released when Microsoft introduced Internet Explorer 4 in 1997.

How does embedding work? Let's assume you are creating a rather grunge-looking design for a skateboard company and the design specification calls for the use of a font named Confidential and the Anti-alias option chosen is Readability. You click the Text tool and enter "Ride The Pipe". Just the letters in those three words will get embedded into the SWF. Duplicates, in this case *i*, *e*, and *p*, will be ignored, which means a smaller SWF. Let's try it:

1. Open a new ActionScript 3.0 document and select the Text tool. Click the stage and open the Properties panel.

2. Choose Dynamic Text from the Text Type drop-down.

3. Choose a font in the family drop-down. We chose Confidential, but you can use any font in your list. Set the size to 48 points and the color to black (#000000). Make sure the Anti-alias drop-down shows Use Device Fonts.

4. Click and enter Ride The Pipe, as shown in Figure 6-14.

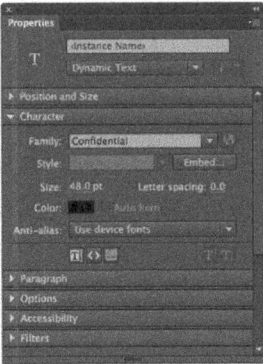

Figure 6-14. We start with a simple line of text that uses a grunge-type font

5. With the text box selected, choose anti-alias for readability from the Anti-alias drop-down menu. The alert shown in Figure 6-15 will appear. You actually have a couple of choices. Clicking the Not Now button will dismiss the alert, and Animate CC won't embed anything into the SWF. Click the Embed button, and the characters will be embedded into the SWF once you finish with the Font Embedding dialog box that will open. Click the Embed button.

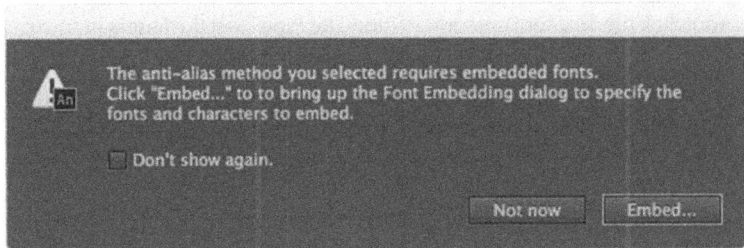

Figure 6-15. You make the decisions regarding embedding

The Font Embedding dialog box that opens, as shown in Figure 6-16, may at first appear to be a bit overwhelming. Let's go through various bits and pieces of this dialog box.

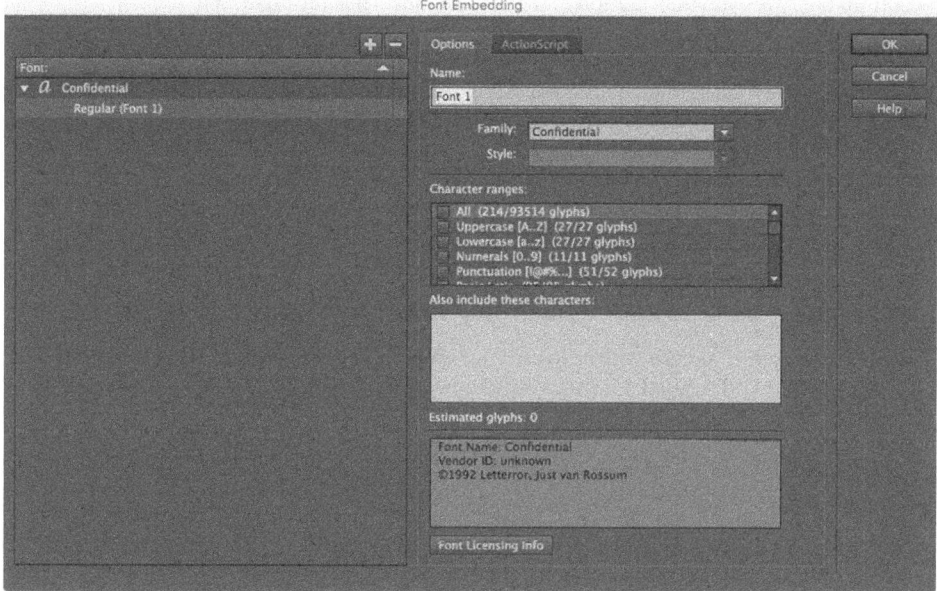

Figure 6-16. *The Font Embedding dialog box*

On the left side of the dialog box is the name of the font. Click it, and everything on the right side grays out. This is because, as we pointed out earlier, the name of the font is the family name. The fonts in the family or style—Regular (Font 1)—are listed underneath. Select it, and the right side lights up.

The Options area allows you to give the font a name. Do this, and that name will be used in the resulting font symbol in the Library. Your Character range choices allows you to control which glyphs are embedded into the font symbol. The more glyphs added, the larger the SWF. As you make your choices, the number in the Estimated Choices area will change.

Glyph? Each character in the font is called a **glyph**. In some fronts, the number of characters can range into the hundreds for bitmap, PostScript, and TrueType fonts, whereas OpenType fonts can have several thousand characters. A good example of this concept are these two glyphs: e and é. Notice the accent? The letter with the accent is a variation on the letter *e* and is a character in the font set.

You can skip the selections and include only selected letters. For example, if you use the contents of the text just entered, you would type `ridethp`, which, according to the estimated glyphs total, would add only seven characters to the embedded font.

The bottom box gives you information regarding the font. This information is pulled from the font's metadata. Clicking the Font Licensing Info button will launch the browser, take you to the Adobe site, and open a Font License page. This page gives you a bit of information regarding the end user license agreement (EULA) of the font. This would include whether the font can or cannot be embedded into a SWF. This works really well for Adobe fonts, but some fonts may result in the page telling you, in a nutshell: "We can't find the font, so you make the licensing call." Why this legal reminder? It is there to remind you to remain purer than pure when it comes to copyright.

If you click the ActionScript tab, a rather familiar area opens. The Linkage area should tell you that the resulting font symbol can be used by ActionScript.

6. Click OK to accept the changes and close the Font Embedding dialog box. Open your Library, and you'll see that a font symbol containing the name (the default is Font 1) has been added to your Library. See Figure 6-17.

Figure 6-17. *A font symbol in the Library tells you a font has been embedded*

Your Turn: Working with Text

We covered a lot of "techie" stuff to this point and there is more to come. This would be a good time to take a break and put some of that knowledge to work. In this exercise, you will be formatting text for a screen that will appear on an Android device.

This may strike you as a bit odd but when it comes to mobile—either smartphone or tablet—interactive prototypes have become an integral part of the workflow. These prototypes are used to demonstrate motion and, more often than not, are subjected to rigorous user testing before the project moves into production. Although there is a new class of interactive software—UX prototyping—making an appearance don't overlook the many advantages and features of Animate CC that make is a great UX/UIU prototyping tool.

Let's get started:

1. Open the `TextFormat.fla file` found in this chapter's source file folder. When it opens you will see, as shown in Figure 6-18, a typical Android screen. Your job will be to format the headline and the body text.

CHAPTER 6 ■ TEXT IN ANIMATE CC

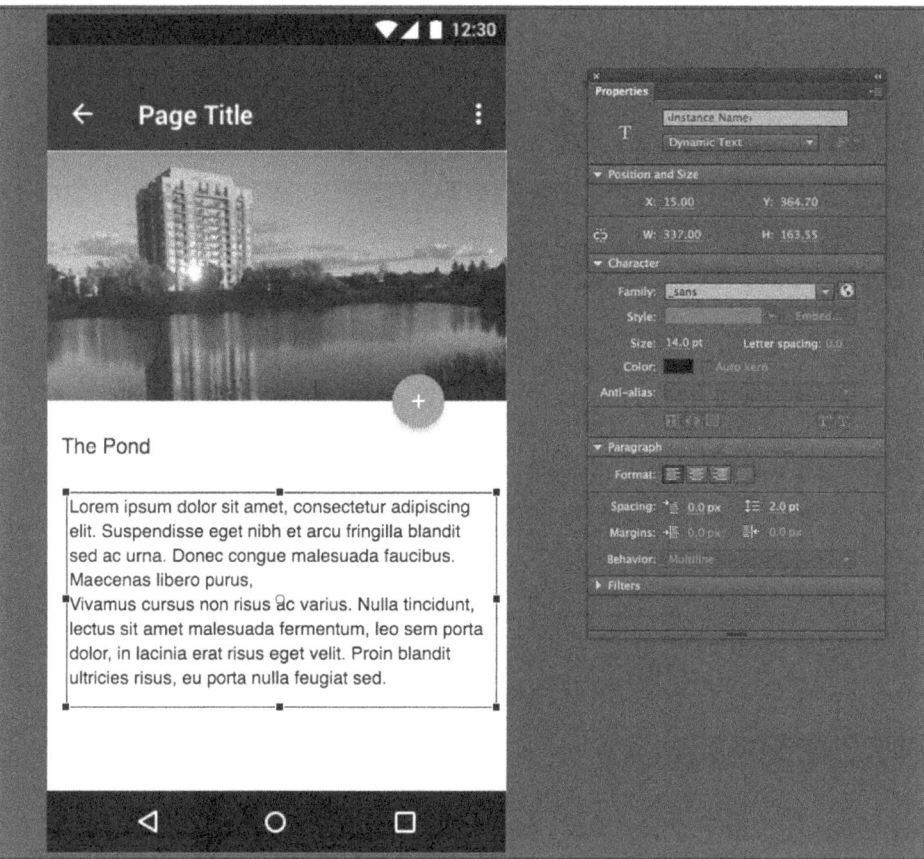

Figure 6-18. *We start with an Android screen and unformatted text*

2. Select each of the text boxes on the screen. You will notice, in the Properties panel, that each block uses the _Sans font.

3. Select the headline and, in the Properties panel, set it to Roboto Medium 20 pt. If you don't have the Roboto font, you can get it either through Typekit or Google Fonts.

4. Select the body text and set it to Roboto Regular 14 pt.

5. Twirl down the Paragraph properties and set the text to Align Left and the Line Spacing to 2 pts. By adding Line Spacing you are adding some "air" to the lines of text. You can think of this as being comparable to leading.

6. The Material Design specification suggest 16 pixels of space between the edges of the screen and the text. A quick way of accomplishing this is to do a bit of math. The screen is 340 pixels wide. Simply set the width of the text box to 328 pixels. (360- 32 = 328).

297

CHAPTER 6 ■ TEXT IN ANIMATE CC

7. To provide even spacing on either side of the text box open the Align panel, select Align to Stage and click the Align Horizontal Center button.

8. Repeat this with the headline. You have now completed the task, as shown in Figure 6-19.

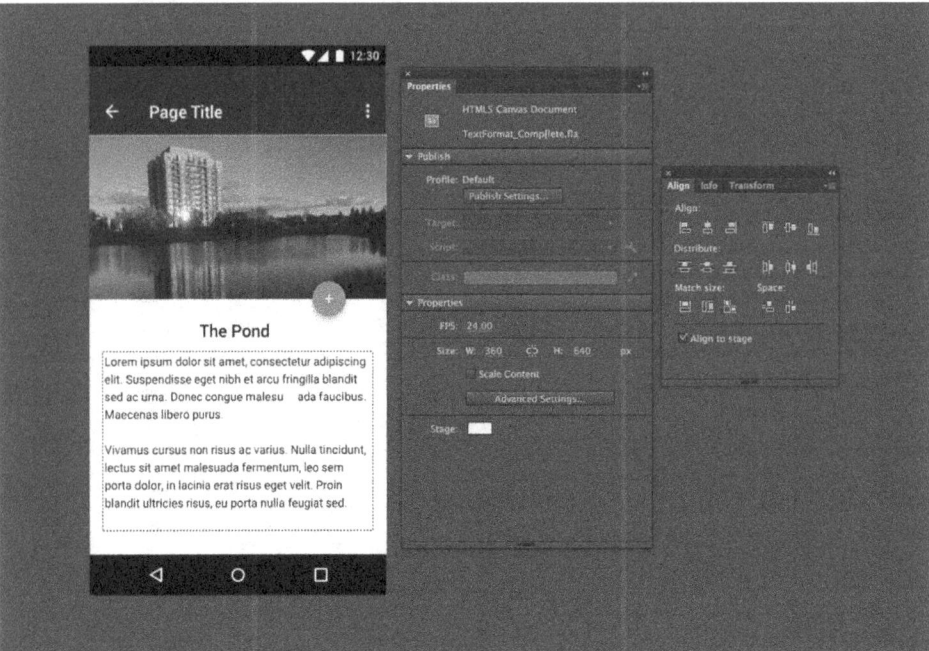

Figure 6-19. *The text is formatted and aligned*

With the fundamentals out of the way, let's turn our attention to working with text through code. Our first stop will be something many Flash developers used quite extensively and has somehow disappeared from Animate CC: The Text Layout Framework.

A Word About TLF Text in Animate CC

Back when Animate CC was known as Adobe Flash Professional CS5, a new text engine was introduced that supported typographic features like ligatures, character formatting, text flow, and other nuances that were relatively important for designers who understood the importance of typography. This new text engine was called the Text Layout Framework (TLF) engine and was put to use across projects that required such a deep level of typographic control.

However, when the application was rewritten as Flash Professional CC, this text engine was removed altogether and hasn't yet made its way back into the program. Considering this engine is only supported in ActionScript-based documents, the authors assume that the only way we would see a feature like this implemented in this era is if Adobe could develop something to work across all document types that support text. This will not likely happen anytime soon.

Dealing with Older Documents Using TLF

You might be wondering what happens when you open an older .fla document that used TLF within Animate CC. If you are a long-time Flash designer, you may even have a good pool of files that employ this text engine. So what happens? The text is automatically converted to make use of the classic text engine—that's all. So if you want to preserve TLF information within your older files, it's best to keep a copy of Flash Professional CS6 around!

Interestingly enough, even though TLF is deprecated within Animate CC, if you are using MXML and ActionScript 3.0 via Apache Flex, TLF is still available to implement through Flash Player or AIR. Of course, with no tooling behind it, you'll need to write all of the TLF instructions using ActionScript 3.0—by hand and in another editor apart for Animate CC. See http://flex.apache.org/ for more details and the latest version of the framework, if you're interested!

> ### THE HISTORICAL COMPLEXITIES OF USING TLF
>
> To give you a basic idea of what exactly is involved when creating TLF text in ActionScript (and dissuade you from attempting to use it), let's go over exactly what would be involved.
>
> Most projects will start with you creating a Configuration() object, which is used to tell the document there is a container on the stage and how to manage the Text Layout Framework for the stuff in the container. The actual appearance is handled by the TextFlow() class, which takes its orders, so to speak, from the Configuration() object.
>
> The Configuration() object needs to be told exactly how to manage the text in the container. The default format is set through a property of the Configuration class called textFlowInitialFormat. To change it, you simply use the TextlayoutFormat() class to set the fonts, colors, alignment, and so on, and then tell the boss—Configuration— that its textFlowInitialFormat has changed to the ones you set using TextLayoutFormat().The boss will get that, but he isn't terribly bright, so you next need to tell him to hand the actual work to another member of the management team, the TextFlow() class. This class has overall responsibility for any words in a container.
>
> Being just as dim as the boss, TextFlow() needs to be told what a paragraph is (ParagraphElement), how wide the paragraph is (SpanElement), whether any graphics are embedded in the paragraph (InLineGraphicElement), whether any of the text contains links (Link Element), and so on. Not only that, but it needs to be told what text is being added to the container so it can handle the line length and to add any children (addChild) that contain that formatting so the user can actually see it.
>
> The TextFlow() class, again not being too terribly bright, will then hand the job over to another member of the management team, the IFlowComposer() class, whose only job is to manage the layout and display of the text flow within or among the containers. The flow composer finishes the process by deciding how much text goes into a container and then adds the lines of text to the sprite. This is accomplished through the use of the addController() method, which creates a ContainerController() object whose parameters identify the container and its properties.
>
> The usual last step is to tell the FlowComposer to update the controllers and put the text on the stage according to how the other members of the team have told the Configuration() object how their piece of the project is to be managed.
>
> This should give you a pretty good of idea of what it takes to use TLF in a project, and why Adobe didn't include it as a feature of Animate CC.

CHAPTER 6 ■ TEXT IN ANIMATE CC

Creating Text with JavaScript

Earlier in this chapter, you learned how to visually create text on the stage with the Animate CC tooling and adjust it if different ways with the Properties panel. Remember when we said that most anything that can tweaked in the Properties panel can also be adjusted and managed through code? You can also create text objects with CreateJS and JavaScript, which is what we'll have a quick look at now.

We'll be using the HTML5 Canvas document type for this example.

1. First, open the file named `TextJS.fla` from the exercise folder for this chapter.

    You will notice that a number of things, as shown in Figure 6-20, have been set up for you here.

Figure 6-20. *The project already has a number of layers and assets present*

300

There are three layers present; the bottom-most layer contains an image of Ernest Hemingway and the layer named Shade simply contains a semi-transparent shape, which helps obscure the layer below it so that the text will be more readable. At the very top of the layer stack is our Actions layer where we will be writing all of our JavaScript.

2. Select frame 1 of the Actions layer and open the Actions panel.

   We will be creating this text object using only JavaScript and adding it to the stage dynamically.

3. Create the Text object by adding the following line of code to the Script pane of the Actions panel.

   ```
   var dynamicText = new createjs.Text("", "22px Arial Black", "#B0D575");
   ```

   This creates a new CreateJS Text instance using Arial Black as a typeface at 22px in a light-green tint.

4. Now we can add some text content to our object using the text property.

   ```
   dynamicText.text = "Got tight last night on absinthe and did knife tricks. \n\nGreat success shooting the knife into the piano. The woodworms are so bad and eat hell out of all furniture that you can always claim the woodworms did it.\n\n - Ernest Hemingway";
   ```

   Note that we could have actually included the text content as the first argument within our createjs.Text() initialization, but since we have so much text to include, it is more clear to add it in this way, as a separate property.

5. Now for the various properties of our Text object. Include the following six lines of code, each of which adjusts an important property of our text instance.

   ```
   dynamicText.lineWidth = 360;
   dynamicText.lineHeight = 28;
   dynamicText.x = 200;
   dynamicText.y = 30;
   dynamicText.snapToPixel = true;
   dynamicText.textAlign = "center";
   ```

   The lineWidth property will determine how wide the Text object is on the stage, while lineHeight specified the leading between lines of text. The next two properties, x and y, do exactly as you would expect—determining the position of the Text object on the stage, relative to its registration point. We then set snapToPixel to true, which is always important when dealing with text to be sure it renders as sharp as possible. The last property, textAlign, we set to string of "center", which aligns all text within this Text object to the center. We could additionally choose "left" or "right".

6. The next thing we will do is add a drop shadow to our text to help it really stand out against the background image. Add the following line of code after the existing properties.

   ```
   dynamicText.shadow = new createjs.Shadow("#000000", 4, 4, 12);
   ```

   What this does is creates a new Shadow filter with its own specific properties and assigns it to the shadow property of our Text instance. The properties of our shadow, in the order assigned in the constructor function, are as follows; color, offset, offset, and blur amount. You can play with these properties to adjust the Shadow effect to your liking.

   Even with all of this code written, if you test the movie now you will not see any text at all. That is because we need to add any visual instance that we create in code to the display list of our project in order for it to appear. Let's do this now.

7. Add a final line of text to the Actions panel Script Editor, below everything else we have already written.

   ```
   this.addChild(dynamicText);
   ```

   We always use the `addChild()` function to add a display object to the display list. Since we are adding our Text instance directly to the current timeline, we can simply use `addChild()` on this for it to take effect.

8. With that last piece of code written, go ahead and perform a test movie command to witness your creation, as shown in Figure 6-21.

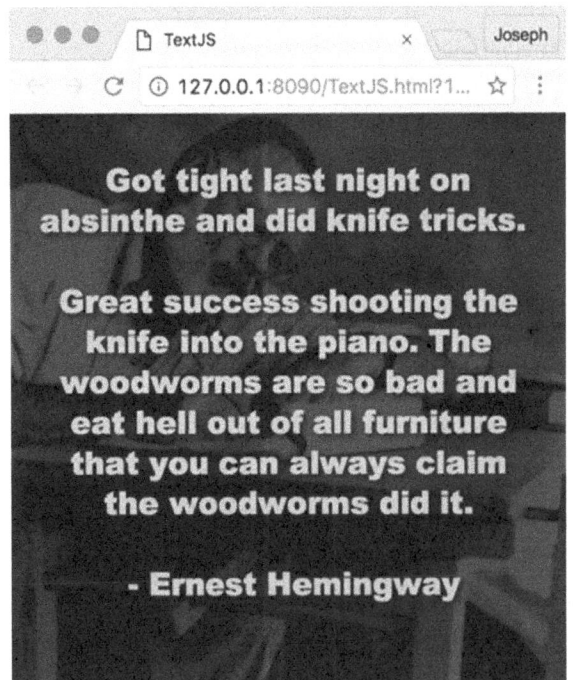

Figure 6-21. The completed HTML5 Canvas project

Ernest Hemingway had a strong affinity for absinthe and had some rather humorous things to say about the mysterious spirit. He isn't off the hook quite yet—we will be using his quotes as an example in the next exercise as well. It's an ActionScript version of this same activity!

The full code for this exercise follows:

```
var dynamicText = new createjs.Text("", "22px Arial Black", "#B0D575");
dynamicText.text = "Got tight last night on absinthe and did knife tricks. \n\nGreat success shooting the knife into the piano. The woodworms are so bad and eat hell out of all furniture that you can always claim the woodworms did it.\n\n - Ernest Hemingway";
dynamicText.lineWidth = 360;
dynamicText.lineHeight = 28;
dynamicText.x = 200;
dynamicText.y = 30;
dynamicText.snapToPixel = true;
dynamicText.textAlign = "center";

dynamicText.shadow = new createjs.Shadow("#000000", 4, 4, 12);

this.addChild(dynamicText);
```

Creating Text with ActionScript

Okay, so we just saw how to create text with JavaScript, but what if you are working on an ActionScript 3.0 based document? Since we can't effectively use TLF and likely wouldn't want to—is there any other way? Well, yes, there is!

As you've already seen, TLF has been deprecated by Adobe (even though Apache Flex still makes use of it) and thus is not available in Animate CC. However, that does not mean we cannot employ classic text creation using raw AS3. In fact, for most projects—this is really all you need. As you will see next, while using ActionScript to create text objects in Animate CC is a bit more complicated than performing the same action using CreateJS and JavaScript; it is nowhere near as complex as constructing text using TLF!

   1. First, open the file named `TextAS3.fla` in the exercise folder for this chapter (Figure 6-22).

CHAPTER 6 ▪ TEXT IN ANIMATE CC

Figure 6-22. *This example is nearly identical to the previous one, initially*

As we move through this example, do note that the Animate document we are starting with is set up exactly the same as the HTML5 Canvas example; three layers with the bottom-most layer containing an image of Ernest Hemingway and the layer named Shade containing a semi-transparent shape which helps obscure the photo. Finally, above these two contents layers is the Actions layer, within which we will be writing all of our code.

1. Select frame 1 of the Actions layer and open the Actions panel.

   We will be creating a text object using only ActionScript and adding it to the stage dynamically.

2. Add the following initial lines of code to the Script pane of the Actions panel. These are the import statements we must include for this project.

   ```
   import flash.text.TextField;
   import flash.text.TextFormat;
   import flash.filters.DropShadowFilter;
   ```

   When using various classes in ActionScript, we must import them first for them to be made available to us. Here, we are importing the TextField class, which is our visual text object, the TextFormat class which allows us to control text formatting and visual styles, and finally the DropShadowFilter class, allowing us to create a drop shadow effect for the text.

304

3. The next thing to do is to create and configure our `TextFormat` object. Notice that we do this before even touching the actual `TextField` class. Add the following two lines after the previous import statements.

   ```
   var textFormat:TextFormat = new TextFormat("Arial Black", "18", 0xB0D575);
   textFormat.align = "center";
   ```

   This creates a new `TextFormat` definition using Arial Black as a typeface at 18px in a light-green tint. The align property is then set to "center", which aligns all text that this `TextFormat` object is applied to the center. We could additionally choose "left" or "right".

   We create the `TextFormat` object first so that is is available to assign onto the `TextField` instance once we create that in the next step.

4. Skip a few lines in your code and type in the following to both create a new `TextField` instance and apply the previously created `TextFormat` configuration to it.

   ```
   var dynamicText:TextField = new TextField();
   dynamicText.defaultTextFormat = textFormat;
   ```

   Now, any text that is assigned to this `TextField` will be styled through the `TextFormat` object we created.

5. Add the following line of code to assign the text content to our `TextField` using the text property of that instance.

   ```
   dynamicText.text = "My decision was reached on a consideration of
   my physical ineptitudes, on the welcome advice of my friends and
   from the fact that it became increasingly harder as I grew older to
   enter the ring happily except after drinking three or four absinthes
   which, while they inflamed my courage, slightly distorted my
   reflexes.\n\n - Ernest Hemingway \n(on why he quit bullfighting)";
   ```

   Another brilliant quote from Hemingway!

6. Now to set the various properties of our `TextField` to determine things like positioning on the stage, height, width, and so on. Add the following code to the Script Editor.

   ```
   dynamicText.width = 360;
   dynamicText.height = 360;
   dynamicText.x = 200-180;
   dynamicText.y = 30;
   dynamicText.wordWrap = true;
   dynamicText.multiline = true;
   ```

   The properties of `width` and `height` determine the size of our `TextField`. The x and y properties will determine positioning on the stage. You can see here that x is actually calculated based on the width of the stage divided by 2 minus the width of our `TextField` divided by 2. This could be calculated dynamically, if desired!

The final two properties, wordWrap and multiline, likely do exactly as you would expect. Notice both are set to true. This will enable words to wrap across multiple lines of text since multi-line text is also enabled.

7. Next, we will apply a nice drop shadow filter to our text so it stands out against the background in a more pronounced way. Add the following line of code.

```
dynamicText.filters = [new DropShadowFilter(4, 45, 0x000000, 0.8, 12, 12)];
```

The filters property of a TextField accepts an array of filters. Here, we are only concerned with a single DropShadowFilter. We create this filter with the following properties; distance, angle, color, alpha, blurX, and blurY.

As the filter is created, it is assigned to the filters property of our TextField by including it within straight brackets [ ] – signifying an array.

8. The only bit of the code left is the instruction assigning our TextField to the display list for rendering. Add in the following line of code to complete this project.

```
this.addChild(dynamicText);
```

The TextField is now visually assigned to the stage and will appear when we publish or test this movie.

9. Finally, go ahead and perform a test movie to see the results, as shown in Figure 6-23.

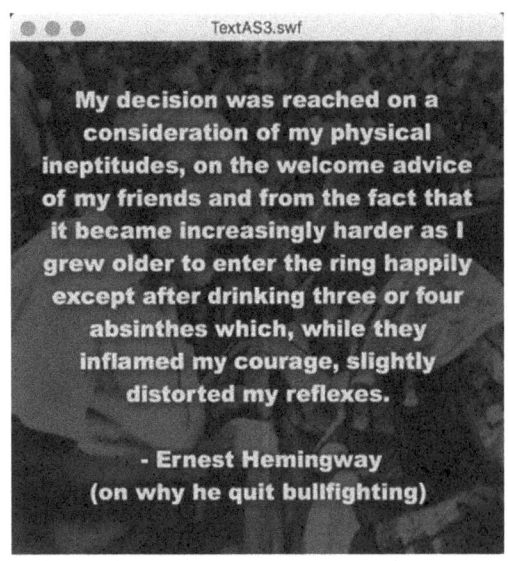

Figure 6-23. *The completed HTML5 Canvas project*

The full code for this exercise follows:

```
import flash.text.TextField;
import flash.filters.DropShadowFilter;
import flash.text.TextFormat;

var textFormat:TextFormat = new TextFormat("Arial Black", "18", 0xB0D575);
textFormat.align = "center";

var dynamicText:TextField = new TextField();
dynamicText.defaultTextFormat = textFormat;
dynamicText.text = "My decision was reached on a consideration of my physical ineptitudes, on the welcome advice of my friends and from the fact that it became increasingly harder as I grew older to enter the ring happily except after drinking three or four absinthes which, while they inflamed my courage, slightly distorted my reflexes.\n\n - Ernest Hemingway \n(on why he quit bullfighting)";
dynamicText.width = 360;
dynamicText.height = 360;
dynamicText.x = 200-180;
dynamicText.y = 30;
dynamicText.wordWrap = true;
dynamicText.multiline = true;

dynamicText.filters = [new DropShadowFilter(4, 45, 0x000000, 0.8, 12, 12)];

this.addChild(dynamicText);
```

Okay, that's enough picking on poor Mr. Hemingway, although he does present some sound advice here. We'll find someone else for this final exercise.

Your Turn: Scrollable Text in HTML5 Canvas

The final exercise in this chapter deals with one of the more frequently asked questions regarding text: "How do I scroll a large amount of text?" In fact, there are several ways of approaching this one. We'll look at the most straightforward—"roll your own"—scroller using JavaScript.

Rolling Your Own Scroller

In this exercise, you are going to wire up a scroller using JavaScript. Just keep in mind that there are several hundred ways of doing this, and the method you are going to use is a very basic example of creating scroll buttons. In this example, you use a simple Button symbol created in Animate CC that can be used to control the scrolling behavior. This button is found in the Library.

In this example in which the whole process is managed by JavaScript, the text moves up or down a short distance with each mouse press. Others may have the text move up or down until the mouse is released. Regardless, the text is scrolling, which is the point of this exercise. Let's get busy:

1. Open the `ScrollableJS.fla` file in this chapter's exercise folder and examine the different layers, shown in Figure 6-24, in the timeline. Note the various assets on the stage and within the project library.

CHAPTER 6 ■ TEXT IN ANIMATE CC

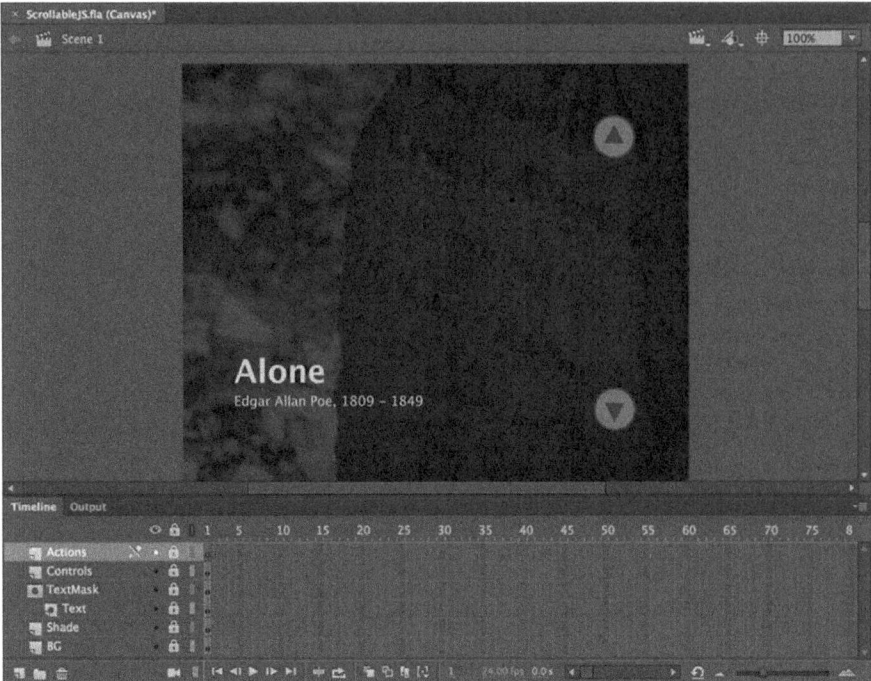

Figure 6-24. *Scrollable poem project starter*

Let's look at how things have been organized. Everything is basically already set up in terms of the layer structure and various text blocks, symbol instances, and so on. We only need to add some code to wire it all together.

Starting at the bottom of the layer stack, we have an image—a photograph taken by one of the authors some years ago—along with a Shade layer that obscures it. This is very similar to what we have seen in the preceding exercises.

The next two layers are a mask layer called TextMask, with a Text layer nested within it. The Text layer contains a MovieClip symbol with an instance name of scrolling_text, which holds a basic text field containing the poem "Alone" by Edgar Allen Poe. This is all obscured by the mask layer so that we can only see a portion of the text on-screen at any time.

Above this layer is our Controls layer, containing two instances of the ScrollControl Button symbol, which can be found within the project library. One is given the instance name of up_btn and the other is called down_btn. These are the buttons a user will be able to click to scroll the text one way or the other.

Finally, at the top of our layer stack, we have our Actions layer, which will contain all of the JavaScript code for this project. Let's move ahead and wire it all together!

2. Select frame 1 of the Actions layer and open the Actions panel.

We will be adding a bit of JavaScript to allow scrolling of the present text content through user interaction.

CHAPTER 6 ■ TEXT IN ANIMATE CC

3. Add the following code to the script pane to provide interactivity to the up_btn Button symbol instance.

```
this.up_btn.addEventListener("click", function(){
     exportRoot.scrolling_text.y += 27;
});
```

This bit of code adds an event listener to our up_btn Button instance, which responds to a click event from the user. When this event is detected, the scrolling_text MovieClip symbol instance has its y position adjusted by 27 pixels—scrolling it behind the mask.

4. Now, we can add the code to provide interactivity to the down_btn Button symbol instance right after the previous JavaScript.

```
this.down_btn.addEventListener("click", function(){
     exportRoot.scrolling_text.y -= 27;
});
```

In this block of code, we are basically doing the same thing as in the previous block, except that we are binding our event listener to the down_btn Button instance and scrolling the scrolling_text MovieClip symbol instance in the opposite direction.

5. Go ahead and test the movie. You should be able to click on each of these Button instances, shown in Figure 6-25, to scroll the text up and down.

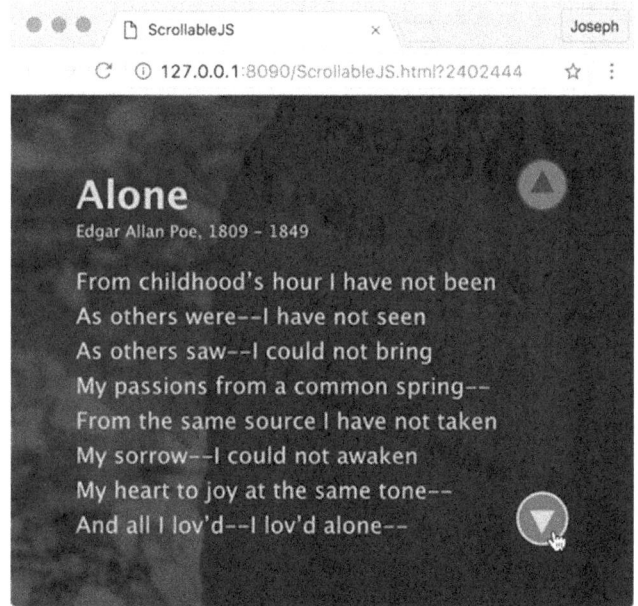

Figure 6-25. *The completed scrollable poem project*

309

Here is all the JavaScript you need for this project:

```
this.up_btn.addEventListener("click", function(){
      exportRoot.scrolling_text.y += 27;
});

this.down_btn.addEventListener("click", function(){
      exportRoot.scrolling_text.y -= 27;
});
```

Scrolling Text Using ActionScript

Okay, but what if you're working in ActionScript and want to scroll your text on that platform? Not a problem—the same thing you saw previously can be done in ActionScript document types using the following code. Go ahead and open the `ScrollableAS3.fla` file and have a look!

```
import flash.events.MouseEvent;

up_btn.addEventListener(MouseEvent.CLICK, scrollUp);
function scrollUp(e:MouseEvent){
      scrolling_text.y += 27;
};

down_btn.addEventListener(MouseEvent.CLICK, scrollDown);
function scrollDown(e:MouseEvent):void {
      scrolling_text.y -= 27;
};
```

You only need to use the exact same layer structure and assets from the HTML5 Canvas version of the project and change the code from JavaScript to the ActionScript code provided previously. When you perform a test movie, the result, shown in Figure 6-26, is nearly identical.

CHAPTER 6 ■ TEXT IN ANIMATE CC

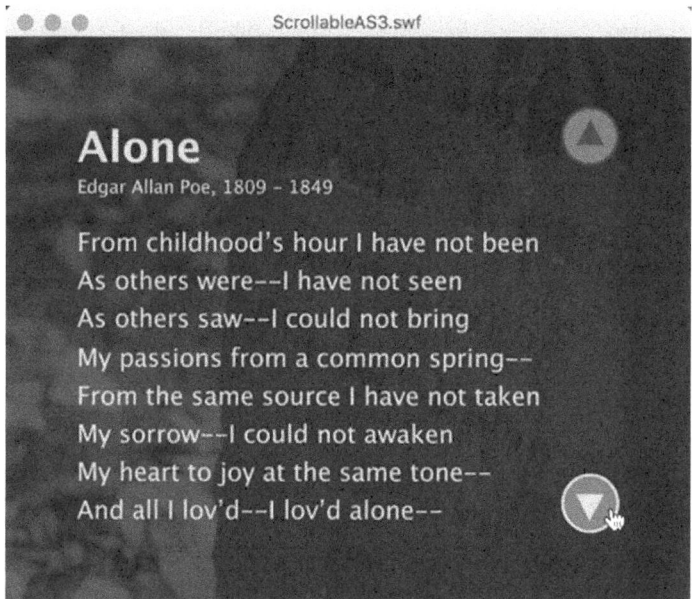

Figure 6-26. *The completed scrollable poem project using ActionScript*

The main differences in the ActionScript version are that we must import our MouseEvent class in order to add our event listeners to each button instance, that we create specific functions to handle each of the click actions (although we could have handled it this way in JavaScript as well), we have no need to use a scope proxy such as exportRoot, and we can strictly type all of our functions and objects. Conceptually, all functionality is exactly the same.

See? Very similar!

What You Have learned

In this chapter, you learned the following:

- How to add text to an Animate CC document
- The various text-formatting features available to you in Animate CC
- The code necessary to create, format, and provide interactivity through the use of text
- When to embed font outlines into a project and how to accomplish that task
- How to create scrolling text in a project

We suspect you are more than a little confounded at the possibilities open to you when it comes to using text in Animate CC. If you are one of those who saw text as the gray stuff hovering around your animations, we hope you have seen the error of your ways. And, if you are one of those who want to get going and turn out really cool motion graphics pieces, we hope you paid close attention to what Bringhurst was saying in the quote that opened this chapter. Regardless of which camp you fall into, we know that you are now aware that adding text to an Animate CC animation doesn't stop with a click of the Text tool and the tapping of a few keys on the keyboard.

Now that you know how to work with text and put it in motion, the time has arrived to put objects in motion. Animation is covered in the next two chapters, and to find out more, turn the page.

CHAPTER 7

Animation

Ah, animation! Where would we be without the likes of Disney, Warner Bros., Walter Lanz, Hanna-Barbera, and dozens more like them? For many people, animation is *the* reason to get involved with Animate CC as a creative outlet. This makes perfect sense, because Animate CC began life more than a decade ago as an animation tool. Supplemental features like ActionScript, JavaScript, XML parsing, and video integration—every one of which is a tremendous addition—all followed. What hasn't changed in all these years is Animate CC's increasingly productive ability to help you create high-quality, scalable animation for the Web, mobile devices, and even for television and film.

You caught the faintest whiff of tweening in Chapters 1, 2, and 3. It gets considerably more complex—read *considerably more fun!*—because Animate CC gives you a double-dose of animation apparatus. You now have two independent tweening models to work with, the newer of which will make users of Adobe After Effects feel right at home. Each of these tweening models gets its own chapter in this book.

The original approach to tweening, now called *classic tweening*, is covered here in Chapter 7. Chapter 8 delves into the newer stuff. To get the most out of animation in Animate CC, you should read both chapters, starting with this one. As you'll discover, you can use both models in the same movie. You'll learn enough in these chapters to help you comfortably choose which approach, or combination of approaches, works best for your particular needs.

Here's what we'll cover in this chapter:

- Shape tweening
- Shape hinting
- Classic motion tweening
- Easing
- Using the Custom Ease In/Ease Out Editor
- Animating symbols
- Combining timelines
- Applying motion tween effects
- Using ActionScript and JavaScript to create and manage animations

CHAPTER 7 ■ ANIMATION

The following files are used in this chapter (located in Chapter07/ExerciseFiles_Ch07/Exercise/):

- 01_PepperShape.fla
- 02_Ripple.fla
- 03_Ant.fla
- 04_LogoMorphNoHints.fla
- 05_FlowerWeed.fla
- 06_GradientTween1.fla
- 07_GradientTween2.fla
- 08_BitmapFillTween.fla
- 09_PepperSymbol.fla
- 10_MalletNoEasing.fla
- 11_CustomEasingComparison.fla
- 12_MalletCustomEasing.fla
- 13_CustomEasingMultiple.fla
- 14_PhotoAppCuriousRabbit.fla
- 15_RabbitSwap
- 16_CombineTimeline.fla
- 17_Grotto.fla
- 18_MotionGuide.fla
- 19_MaskTween.fla
- 20_MaskTweenMotionGuide.fla
- 21_BlueMoon.fla
- 22_CopyMotionAS3.fla
- 23_KeyboardControl.fla
- 24_RandomMotion.fla

The source files are available online at http://www.apress.com/us/book/9781484223758.

Before We Start

Keep in mind that animation is nothing more than putting the inanimate into motion. Also, motion is nothing more than moving stuff from here to there or the change of any other property. For example, moving, say, a circle from one location to another means we have to determine where the end point is—Here—and where it ends—There. It is that simple. Where the fun starts is our controlling exactly what happens between Here and There.

You can gather from this there are three elements to motion or animation: Here, There, and between Here and There. You can see them on the Animate timeline. There are always two keyframes—Here and There—and the space between them.

It is the space between that is so much fun because we can use that space to determine:

- How long the change takes to complete.
- How an object changes shape.
- The direction an object moves.
- The change in other visual properties over time.
- The path it takes to move.
- How an object changes color.

… and a host of other possibilities available to you in those frames between the Here frame and the There frame. Keep this in mind as you move through this chapter.

Because this chapter has a lot of moving parts, let's cut straight to the "without further ado" and jump directly into the fray and explore what you can do with that space between Here and There!

Shape Tweening

As useful as symbols are, both in organizing artwork and reducing file size, they shouldn't overshadow the importance of shapes. After all, unless a symbol is the result of text or an imported image file, chances are good it was constructed from one or more of Animate CC's most basic of visual entities: the shape.

Shapes differ significantly from symbols, although many of their features overlap. Like symbols, shapes are tweened on keyframes. Tweening may be finessed by something called **easing** and can affect things such as position, scale, distortion, color, and transparency. The difference comes in how these changes are achieved. In addition, shapes can do something symbols can't: they can actually morph from one form to another!

Scaling and Stretching

Let's start with the basics and build a loading animation for Peter Piper's Prepared Peppers:

1. Open the `01_PepperShape.fla` file in the Chapter 7 exercise folder. You'll notice that there is nothing in the Library other than the bits and pieces that make up the interface. That pepper you see is not there. This is because the hot pepper on the stage is composed entirely of shapes.

2. Select Insert ➤ Timeline ➤ Keyframe to insert a keyframe at frame 10 of the Pepper layer. This effectively produces a copy of the artwork from frame 1 in frame 10 and makes the copy available for manipulation. Any changes you make to frame 10 will not affect the shapes in frame 1, so you can always remove that second keyframe (Modify ➤ Timeline ➤ Clear Keyframe) and start again from scratch if you desire.

If you prefer, you can insert a blank keyframe at frame 10 (Insert ➤ Timeline ➤ Blank Keyframe) and then copy and paste the artwork from frame 1 using the Paste in Place command. It makes no practical difference, but clearly the approach in Step 2 requires less effort. You may even draw completely new shapes into frame 10, and Animate CC will do its best to accommodate—but that's skipping ahead. There's more on that in the "Altering Shapes" section.

All of these menu choices have right-click (Windows) or Control+click (Mac) equivalents, available from the context menu of any timeline frame.

CHAPTER 7 ■ ANIMATION

3. With frame 10 selected, choose the Free Transform tool and drag the right side of the pepper's bounding box to the right. As you do this, you'll see a live preview of the shapes—stem, leaves, and pepper—in their new stretched size, as shown in Figure 7-1.

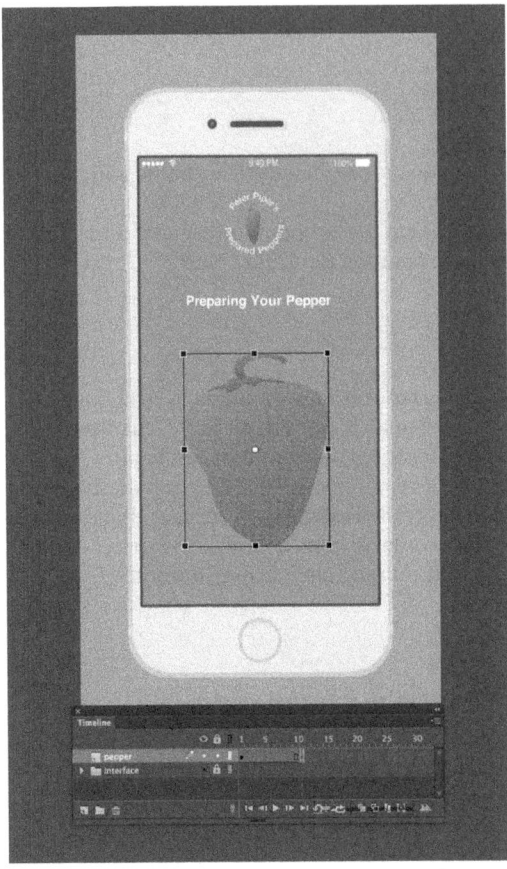

Figure 7-1. Changing a shape's shape in preparation for a shape tween

You might find that you have accidentally selected either only the pepper or only its cap. The Free Transform tool's bounding box will let you know at a glance which shape(s) you have selected, because either it will encompass the full surface area of the artwork or it won't. To ensure you've grabbed all the shapes, use the Selection tool to first draw a marquee (that is, a selection) around the whole pepper. An even simpler technique is to click the keyframe at frame 10, which selects everything on that layer in that keyframe.

4. Select Edit ➤ Undo Scale to undo. (You might need to undo twice: once to reselect and once to remove the widen transform.)

CHAPTER 7 ■ ANIMATION

5. Reapply the transform and hold down the Alt (Windows) or Option (Mac) key while dragging to the right. Notice how the artwork now scales out the side you are dragging.

This feature often comes in handy, but it's important to understand what's really going on. When the Alt (Windows) or Option (Mac) key is used, it's not the center of the artwork that becomes the pivot, but rather the **Transform point**, which is that small white circle in the middle of the pepper. You can drag this circle where you like, even outside the confines of the shape's bounding box. With or without the Alt (Windows) or Option (Mac) key, the transformation point acts as the fulcrum of your modifications, but using the modifier key changes how the fulcrum is applied.

Because you're dealing with shapes, you can even use the Free Transform tool's Envelope and Distort options (shown in Figure 7-2), which aren't available for symbols. Right-click (Windows) or Control+click (Mac) the object selected by the Transform tool, and the options are shown in the Context menu. If you do, just be aware that things can quickly fall apart with such transformations unless you use shape hints, which are covered later in the chapter.

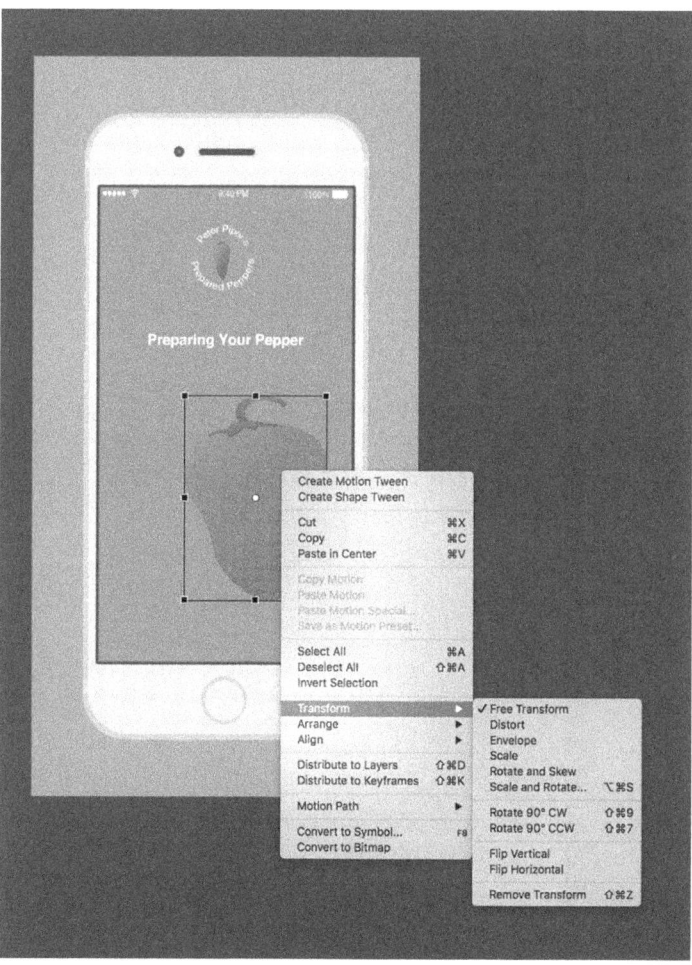

Figure 7-2. Shape transformations include Envelope and Distort

317

CHAPTER 7 ■ ANIMATION

6. Now that you have two keyframes prepared, it's time for the magic. Make sure the pepper is changed in frame 10 (for example, the widening applied in step 5). Right-click (Windows) or Control+click (Mac) anywhere in the span of frames between both keyframes, and select Create Shape Tween from the context menu (see Figure 7-3). Two things will happen:

    - The span of frames will turn green, which indicates a shape tween.

    - They will also gain an arrow and solid line pointing to the right, which tells you the tween was successful.

    - The pepper will update to reflect a visual state between the artwork in either keyframe, depending on where the playhead is positioned.

7. Drag the playhead back and forth to watch the pepper seem to breathe.

Figure 7-3. Applying a shape tween

If you applied the tween while in frame 1—a perfectly legal choice, by the way—you wouldn't immediately see the pepper change. Why? Because the tweening is applied between the two keyframes, and frame 1 still represents the artwork as it was before tweening changed it. Drag the playhead back and forth, and you'll see the tween.

8. Right-click (Windows) or Control+click (Mac) anywhere between the two keyframes and choose Remove Tween. The tween goes away.

9. Let's try another tween. Right-click (Windows) or Control+click (Mac) your frame span, and choose Create Motion Tween. Motion tweening is not supported for shapes, and Animate CC gives you an unmistakable sign that you've gone wrong. You'll see an alert box that offers to convert your shape into a symbol, as shown in Figure 7-4. Click OK, and you'll see most of your frame span turn blue, along with the appearance of a new movieclip in the Library.

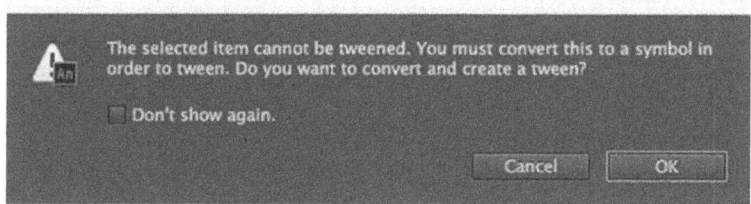

Figure 7-4. Tweens other than the shape variety require symbols

It's nice that Animate CC does this for you, but generally speaking, you'll want to decide on your own what sort of symbol to create: movieclip, graphic, or button. Unfortunately, this automated process does the choosing for you.

Motion tweens are part of the new After Effects–like tweening model you'll learn about in Chapter 8. Motion tweens are nothing like shape tweens; they are an altogether different concept.

10. Select Edit ➤ Undo Create Motion Tween to step back until the changes are removed. That sets the frames back and automatically removes the Library's movieclip.

11. Time for another mistake. Right-click (Windows) or Control-click (Mac) your frame span and choose Create Classic Tween.

Instead of green, the span of frames will become purple, and you'll see *two* new symbols in the Library (this time, graphic symbols)—without even a warning! Purple frames indicate a classic tween, which you'll learn about later in this chapter. These, too, are nothing like shape tweens.

12. Perform an undo, and the frames will revert to a nontweened state. You'll need to delete the graphic symbols by hand, though. Go ahead and do that by selecting them in the Library and clicking the Trash Can icon at the bottom of the Library panel.

13. Reapply a shape tween and scrub to frame 10.

14. Select the Free Transform tool, click on the pepper, and drag around one of the bounding box corners to change both the horizontal and vertical scales. If you like, hold down Shift to constrain the aspect ratio, and Alt (Windows) or Option (Mac) to apply changes from the transform point. Make the pepper a good bit bigger than the original size. This shows that it's possible to adjust keyframes even after they're already part of a tween.

Another way to apply shape tweens is to click between two keyframes and select Insert ➤ Shape Tween. To remove a shape tween, select Insert ➤ Remove Tween. You'll see that you can do the same with motion and classic tweens.

Modifying Shape Tweens

There are a couple ways to refine a shape tween once it's applied. These are shown in the Properties panel when you click in a tweened span of frames: Ease and Blend.

Easing tends to make tweens look more lifelike because it gradually varies the amount of distance traveled between each frame. Think about driving a car. The car is not doing the speed limit from the instant you touch the gas. The accelerates. This acceleration is called *easing in*. When you brake the car does not instantly stop. It decelerates as it comes to a complete stop. This deceleration is called *easing out*.

Click anywhere between two keyframes of a tween, and adjust the Ease hot text in the Properties panel to see how easing affects the shape tween applied to the pepper in the previous exercise. Supported values range from 100 (strong ease out), through 0 (no easing), to -100 (strong ease in). As shown in Figure 7-5, easing can have a profound effect on an object in motion. One thing to note about Figure 7-5 is the playhead is in the middle of each 10-frame timeline. Thus you can see each easing type. We'll cover easing in greater detail in the "Classic Tweening" section.

If you don't see much of a difference after experimenting with easing, try lengthening the duration of your shape tween. To do so, click somewhere in the tween span between the two keyframes and then press the F5 key several times to insert new frames.

CHAPTER 7 ■ ANIMATION

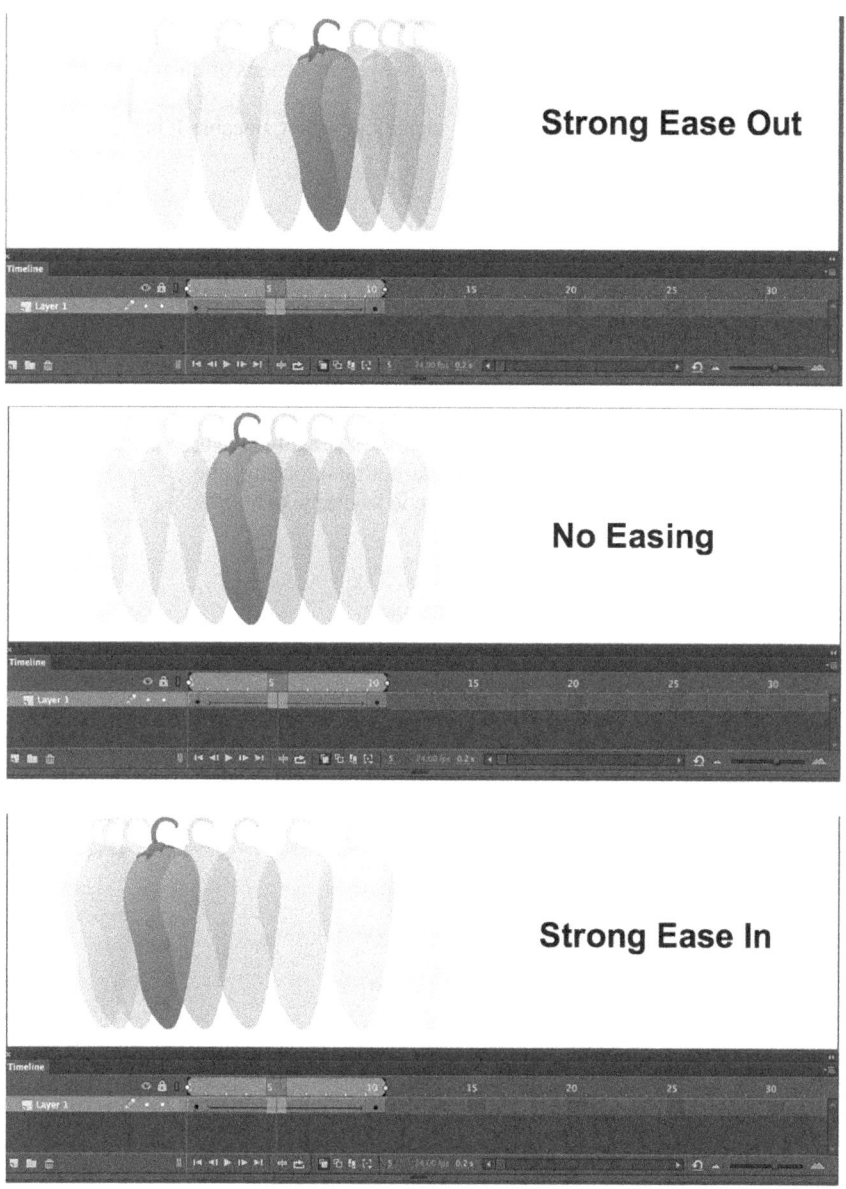

Figure 7-5. *Examples of easing*

The Blend drop-down, directly under the Ease hot text, is a much subtler matter. There are two Blend settings: Distributive (the default) and Angular. According to Adobe, Distributive "creates an animation in which the intermediate shapes are smoother and more irregular," and Angular "creates an animation that preserves apparent corners and straight lines in the intermediate shapes." In actual practice, the authors find this distinction negligible at best. In short, don't worry yourself over this setting. Feel free to use the one with which you are most comfortable. We're willing to bet you won't be able to tell one from the other.

CHAPTER 7 ANIMATION

So far, so good. These tweens have been pretty straightforward. In fact, as you'll find later in the chapter, everything you've seen to this point can be accomplished just as easily with classic tweens. This raises a good question: what makes shape tweens so special? Why not just use classic tweens or the motion tweens you'll learn about in Chapter 8?

The answer comes in two parts: gradients and shape. Let's tackle shape first, because it has the potential to set your teeth on edge if you aren't prepared for it.

Altering Shapes

The compelling reason to use shape tweens is their ability to manipulate the actual form of the artwork itself, beyond scaling and stretching. Let's keep playing:

1. Continuing with PepperShape.fla, use the Free Transform tool at frame 10 to rotate the pepper about 90 degrees in either direction.

2. You should still have a shape tween applied (if not, add one). Drag the playhead back and forth to see a result that may surprise you. Rather than rotating, the pepper temporarily deforms itself as it changes from one keyframe to another (see Figure 7-6).

Figure 7-6. *Sometimes shape tweens perform unexpected transformations*

322

What on Earth is going on here? Though it may look like an absolute mess, what you are seeing is the key distinction between shape tweening and the other kinds of tweening. Believe it or not, this behavior can be a very useful thing. You'll see an example in just a moment. First let's take a quick field trip to frame 10 in order to illustrate a point.

In case you're worried, this isn't such a big deal: it is entirely possible to rotate artwork with tweens in Animate CC. In fact, it's easy. In contrast to shape tweens, classic and motion tweens maintain a strict marriage between the vector anchor points of one keyframe and the next. We'll show you why later in this chapter and in Chapter 8. When you understand what each approach does best, you'll know which one to use for the task at hand.

3. Choose the Subselection tool, and click the edge of the pepper in frame 10. You'll see dozens of tiny squares—see Figure 7-7—that act as anchor points among the various lines and curves that make up the pepper's shape. All those points exist in frame 1 as well, of course, but they're in different positions relative to one another.

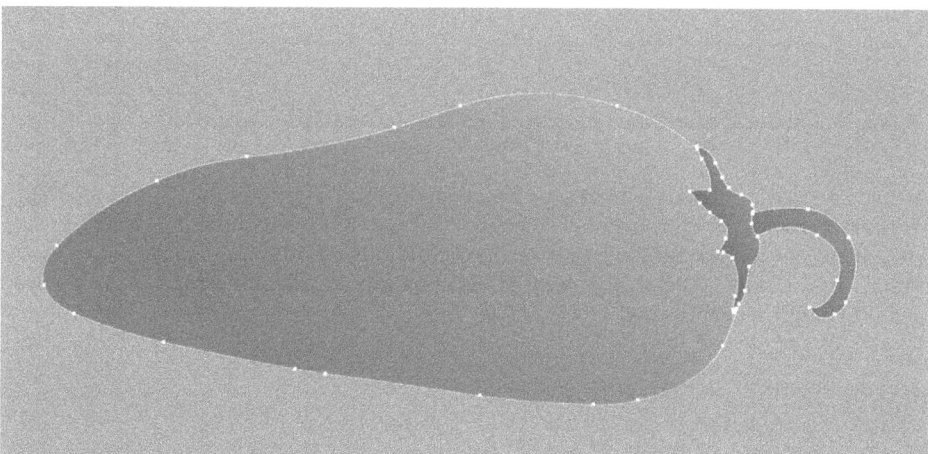

Figure 7-7. *A shape tween is based on anchor points*

With shape tweens, Animate CC does not think of artwork in terms of a whole; instead, it manipulates each anchor point separately. What seems like a rotation to you is, to a shape tween, nothing more than a rearrangement of anchor points—sometimes a chaotic one, at that!

Think of it like a square dance. If a particular point happens to be in the upper-left corner on frame 1, it has no idea that its corresponding point may be in the upper-right corner on frame 10. It simply changes a partner—do-si-do!—and moves to a new spot during the tween. Like square dancing, there are sophisticated rules at play, and movement across the dance floor may appear unpredictable. It's possible, for example, that two keyframes may even present a completely different number of anchor points. Let's look at that next.

CHAPTER 7 ■ ANIMATION

Examining Anchor Points

1. Open the `02_Ripple.fla` file in this chapter's exercise folder and examine the 22-point star in frame 1. Use the Subselection tool, if you like, to see the individual anchor points (there are 44).

2. Click in frame 20 to see a Plus Sign (12 anchor points). Note that a shape tween has already been applied between these two keyframes.

3. Drag the playhead back and forth to watch the promenade (shown in Figure 7-8). Animate CC handles the reduction in anchor points in a neat, organized way. In this case, by the way, the star in the second keyframe was drawn as new artwork into frame 20.

Figure 7-8. *The 44 anchor points artfully become 12*

4. Now drag the playhead from frame 20 to frame 40 to watch the circle expand in size.

These are some nifty transformations that are simply not possible with classic tweens. This is especially useful when prototyping a Ripple Effect for a mobile interface. This example is a basic demonstration of a Ripple Effect in which the icon in the button changes and the button expands to fill the screen.

This opens up a whole avenue of vector-morphing possibilities, from sunshine gleams to water ripples to waving hair and twitching insect antennae.

Shape Changing

For anything where you need the actual shape of an item to change—where anchor points themselves need to be rearranged—shape tweens are the way to go. Keep in mind that tweens happen on a keyframe basis, and timeline layers are distinct. If you have a complex set of shapes and you want to tween only some of them, move those shapes to a separate layer. In fact, you may want to put every to-be-tweened shape on its own layer, because that reduces the number of anchor points under consideration for each keyframe. Let's try it by setting some antennae in motion:

1. Open the `03_Ant.fla` file in this chapter's exercise folder and insert a keyframe in frames 15 and 30 of the antenna1 layer.

2. Select the Subselection tool and change the shape of the antenna in frame 30 of the antenna 1 layer.

3. Add a shape tween between the keyframes and scrub through the timeline. The antennae move around (see Figure 7-9).

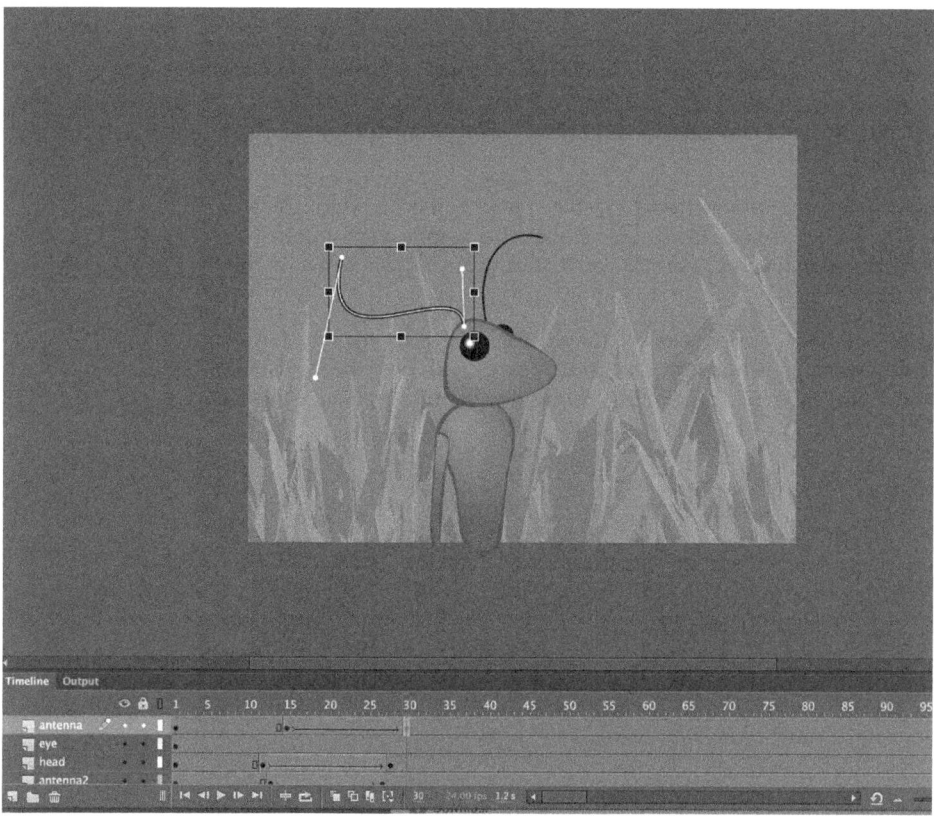

Figure 7-9. *Need to change the shape of those antennae? Shape tweens to the rescue!*

As you've seen, Animate CC can make some fairly stylish choices of its own in regard to the repositioning of anchor points. Well, that's true most of the time. The earlier pepper rotation demonstrates that Animate CC's choices aren't always what you might expect. Fortunately, Animate CC provides a way to let you take control of shape tweens gone awry. The solution is something called **shape hints**.

CHAPTER 7 ■ ANIMATION

Shape Hints

What are shape hints? Often overlooked or misunderstood, these useful contraptions allow you to specify a partnership between a vector region of your choosing from one keyframe to the next. They are a means by which you can guide an anchor point, curve, or line toward the destination you've determined is the correct one. Let's take a look.

   1. Open the `04_LogoMorphNoHints.fla` file in this chapter's exercise folder. Take a look at frame 1 to see a lowercase *i* that has been broken apart from a text field into two shapes. In frame 55, you'll see an abstract shape that represents a hypothetical logo.

   2. The aim here is to morph between the shapes in an appealing way, but something has gone horribly wrong (see Figure 7-10). Drag the playhead along the timeline, and note the atrocities committed between frames 20 and 35.

Figure 7-10. Something has gone horribly wrong

This looks as bad as (if not worse than) the hot pepper rotation, but why? On the face of it, this should be a basic shape tween. Seemingly, the letter and logo shapes aren't especially intricate, and yet, the timeline doesn't lie.

At this point, the authors look deftly side to side, and with a sly, "Hey, pssst," invite you to step with them into a small, dimly lit alley. (Don't worry, we're here to help.) "The thing is," begins the first, "honestly, there's often a bit of voodoo involved with shape tweens, and that's the truth." "That's right," chimes in the other, lowering his voice. "To be frank, if I may"—you nod—"we don't know why these anchor points sometimes go kablooey. It's just a thing, and you have to roll with it." There is a slight pause, and suddenly a cappuccino machine sploshes in the distance. The first author draws a finger across his nose. "Keep that in mind as we continue," he says. Another pause. "You wanna see the shape hints?" You nod again.

---

3. Click in frame 20 and select Modify ➤ Shape ➤ Add Shape Hint (see Figure 7-11). This puts a small red circle with the letter a in the center of your artwork. Meet your first shape hint.

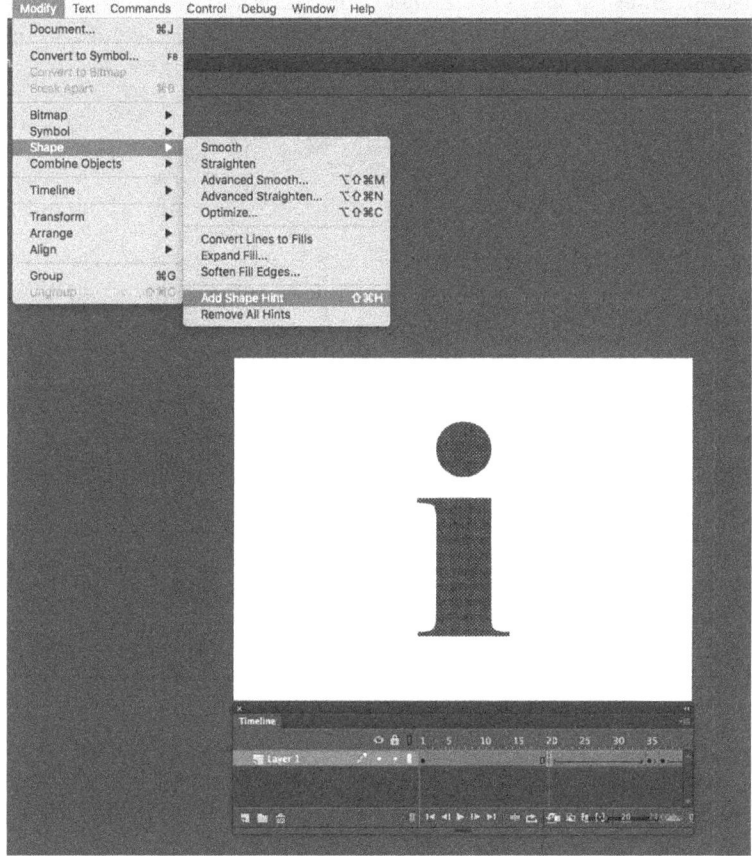

Figure 7-11. Inserting a shape hint

CHAPTER 7 ■ ANIMATION

4. You can check to ensure object snapping is on, either by selecting Snap to Objects in the Tools panel or by ensuring that a check mark is present under View ➤ Snapping ➤ Snap to Objects. Snapping helps the placement of shape hints significantly.

5. Drag and snap a circle to the lower-left corner of the letter's upper serif, as shown in Figure 7-12. If you are a stickler for detail, feel free to zoom the stage before you try snapping the circle.

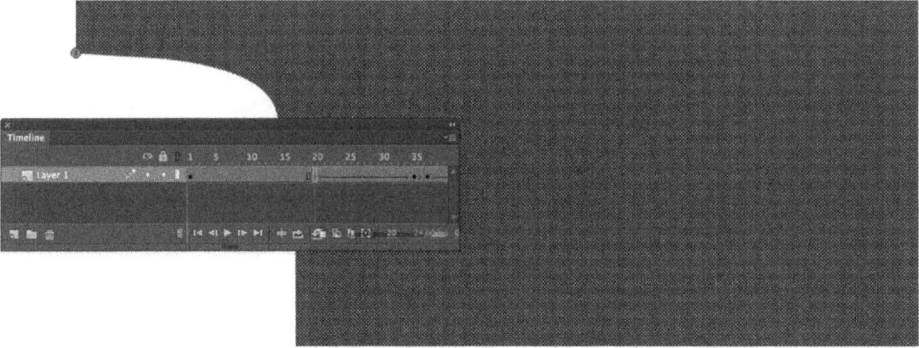

Figure 7-12. Positioning a shape hint

This next point is important: what you've done is placed *one half* of a shape hint *pair*. The other half—the partner—is on the next keyframe, frame 35.

Drag the playhead to frame 35 and position the second a circle on the corresponding serif on this keyframe's shape, as shown in Figure 7-13.

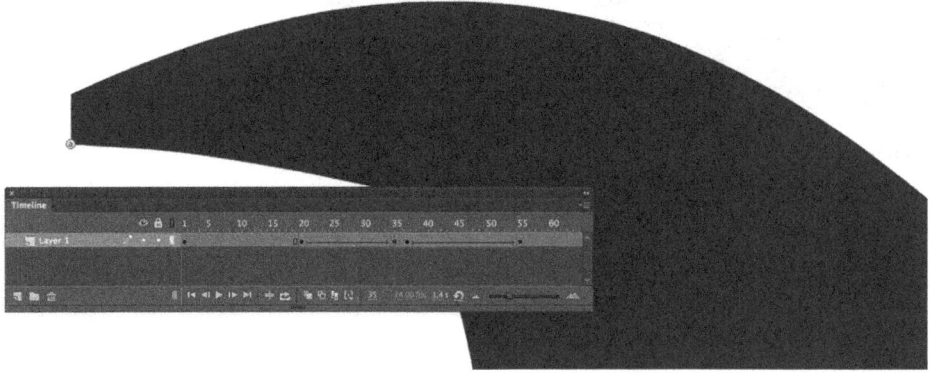

Figure 7-13. Positioning the shape hint's partner

328

When this partner snaps into place, it will turn green. Return to frame 20 and notice that the original shape hint has turned yellow. It's a dramatic improvement, but there are still a few trouble spots.

It may be that shape hints have a thing for stoplights (not that there's anything wrong with that), but the point is that the color change indicates something. It tells you that this shape hint pair has entered into a relationship. You have now indicated to Animate CC your intentions that these paired regions now correspond to each other. Going back to the start of this chapter, the red dot (now yellow) indicates the Shape Hint starts here and the Green dot indicates the Shape Hint ends there.

Slide the playhead along the timeline again, and you'll see a remarkable improvement (as shown in Figure 7-14).

Figure 7-14. *It's a dramatic improvement, but there are still a few trouble spots*

The improvement is so remarkable, in fact, that the authors look deftly side to side, wink, and silently mouth the word "voodoo." To be frank, if we may, the placement of shape hints often makes a noticeable difference, but the decision on placement is something of a dark art. We encourage you to reposition your first shape hint pair at other corners to see how the remaining trouble spots ripple to other areas.

You should get the idea by now that shape hints are a bit like cloves (you know, the star-shaped things you poke into your ham during the holidays)—a little goes a long way. Let's add a few more, but do so sparingly.

CHAPTER 7 ■ ANIMATION

6. To get rid of the kink in the upper curve, add a new shape hint to the upper-right corner of the i on frame 20. This time, you'll see a small b in a circle. Snap its b partner to the upper-right corner of the logo at frame 35, and drag the playhead again to see your progress.

7. Add shape hints c and d to the lower-left and-right corners, and you should see a very smooth morph along this span of frames.

8. The only problem remaining, if you're a perfectionist, is a slight wrinkle along the bottom of the "egg" between keyframes 37 and 55. Remedy this by adding a new shape hint at frame 37. It will start again at a, because this is a new pair of keyframes, and snap in place to the corresponding curve at frame 55.

Compare your work with the LogoMorph.fla file in this chapter's Complete folder, if you like. When you open a file that already contains shape hints, you'll need to take one small step to make them show, because they like to hide by default. To toggle shapes hints on and off, select View ➤ Show Shape Hints.

Even with the benefit of shape hints, we caution you to keep simplicity in mind. Certain collections of shapes are simply too intricate to handle gracefully. Remember that not every web site visitor or user with a smartphone in their pocket will have as powerful a computer as yours. It is entirely possible to choke Flash Player through the use of an overwhelming number of anchor points.

To see what we mean, open the 05_FlowerWeed.fla file in this chapter's exercise folder and drag the playhead along the timeline. The morph isn't especially polished (see Figure 7-15), but it certainly doesn't count as a complete eyesore. Test the SWF (Control ➤ Test Movie), and—depending on the power of your computer—you may see that playback slows or skips during the most complex portions of the tween. If that doesn't happen for you, count yourself lucky! But generally speaking, try to avoid asking this much of your users.

Why do we mention this? The reason is because it is a "bad experience" for the user. In the case of this exercise, you are the only user. Now extrapolate this out to the flower being in a banner ad and your bad experience is now being shared by thousands of others.

Figure 7-15. *Moderation in all things! Although this transformation doesn't look awful, it may nearly choke upon playback*

Altering Gradients

If you want to animate gradients, shape tweens are the only way to do it. You may not immediately think of gradients as shapes, but when you select the Gradient Transform tool and click into a gradient, what do you see? You see the handles and points shown in Figure 7-16.

That center point, to Animate CC, is not much different from an anchor point. The resize, radius, and rotate handles are not much different from Bézier control point handles. In effect, you are manipulating a shape—just a special kind. When animating a gradient, you simply change these gradient-specific features from keyframe to keyframe, rather than a shape's corners, lines, and curves.

CHAPTER 7 ANIMATION

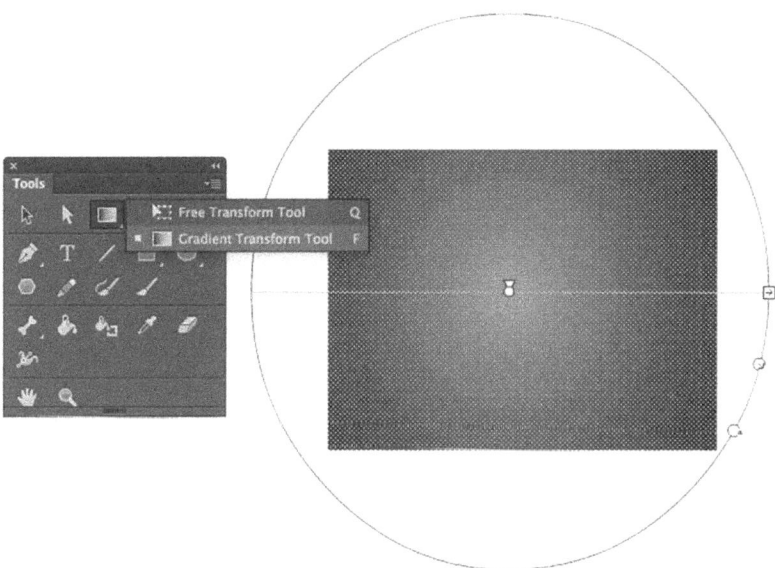

Figure 7-16. *Gradients, like anything else, can be edited on keyframes, and those keyframes are tweenable*

Open the `06_GradientTween1.fla` file in this chapter's exercise folder and drag the playhead along the timeline to see an example in action. Frame 1 contains a solid red fill. Frame 10 contains the built-in rainbow gradient, which is rotated 90 degrees in frame 20. Frames 20 through 30 provide a bit of interest because they demonstrate a limitation of gradient shape tweens: it is not possible to tween one type of gradient to another. Well, we take that back. You certainly can, but the results are unpredictable. Animate CC tries its best to convert a linear gradient into a radial one, but between frames 29 and 30, the gradient pops from one type to the other.

Next, open the `07_GradientTween2.fla` file in this chapter's exercise folder. This example shows a combination of a gradient and a shape change at the same time. Not only does the gradient fill transform, but anchor points move, and even stroke color (and thickness!) changes from keyframe to keyframe. Experiment with solid colors as well as the Color panel's Alpha property. When you finish, close the file without saving the changes.

Even bitmap fills are tweenable, which makes for some interesting visual possibilities, as shown in Figure 7-17. Open the `08_BitmapFillTween.fla` file in this chapter's exercise folder and press the Enter (Return) key to see some roller-coaster camera work using an image of a sculpture sitting on a window sill in Bern, Switzerland. As with other types of gradients, use the Gradient Transform tool to manipulate gradient control handles at each keyframe, and then let the shape tween handle the rest. Easing works the same way.

Figure 7-17. *Shape tween your bitmap fill transformations for some real zing!*

331

CHAPTER 7 ■ ANIMATION

Classic Tweening

When we left that hapless hot pepper hanging, it had been hoping to rotate. It didn't and instead found its molecules tumbling in a frenzied jumble. We told you there was a much easier way to handle that rotation, and classic tweening is one of them. Shape tweens are for rearranging anchor points and animating gradients. Classic tweens and motion tweens are for everything else, from enlivening text and imported photos to animating vector artwork drawn directly in Animate CC or imported from another application like Illustrator CC or Sketch 3 from Bohemian Coding. As we've said, we'll cover motion tweening in Chapter 8. Here, we'll continue with classic tweens only, but keep in mind that you'll have additional choices.

In contrast to shape tweens, classic tweens require self-contained entities. These include symbols, primitives, drawing objects, and grouped elements, which many designers find easier to work with than raw shapes. Open 09_PepperSymbol.fla in this chapter's exercise folder, for example, and you'll see that it's easier to select the whole pepper without accidentally omitting the cap.

Be aware that primitives and drawing objects blur the lines somewhat between what constitutes a shape and what constitutes a symbol. It is possible to apply both shape tweens and motion tweens to primitives and drawing objects. However, many properties, such as color, alpha, and the like—and in primitives, shape—are properly animated only with shape tweens. These "gotchas" tend to steer the authors toward a path of least resistance: use shapes for shape tweens and symbols for classic tweens. Within those symbols, use whatever elements you like.

One fundamental point: when it comes to classic tweens, always put each tweened symbol on its own layer. If you apply a classic tween to keyframes that contain more than one symbol, Animate CC will try to oblige—but will fail. It's a simple rule, so abide by it, and you'll be happy.

Rotation

Let's pick up with that rotation, shall we?

1. Open the 09_PepperSymbol.fla file in this chapter's exercise folder. You'll see a pepper symbol in the Library (the shapes from the earlier PepperShape.fla example have been placed inside a graphic symbol).

2. Add a keyframe in frame 10. Then select the Free Transform tool and rotate the artwork 90 degrees in either direction in that keyframe you just added in frame 10. Sounds familiar, right? Here comes the difference.

3. Right-click (Windows) or Control+click (Mac) and select Create Classic Tween from the context menu. There it is!

4. Drag the playhead back and forth to see a nice, clean rotation of the pepper. As you saw with shape tweens, the span of frames between the two keyframes changes color (to purple this time), and a solid arrow appears within the span to indicate a successful tween, as shown in Figure 7-18.

CHAPTER 7 ■ ANIMATION

Figure 7-18. *Classic tweens, indicated by purple and an arrow between the keyframes, make rotations a snap*

Now, let's think about *real* rotation: topsy-turvy—a full 360-degree spin. How would you do it? (Hint: This is something of a trick question.) In a full spin, the pepper ends up in the same position at frame 10 as it starts with in frame 1, so there's not really a transformation to tween, is there?

Rotation is set through the Rotate drop-down menu in the Tweening area of the Properties panel. Click anywhere in the tween and notice that the Rotate drop-down is currently set to Auto, as shown in Figure 7-19. This is because you have already rotated the pepper somewhat by hand. The choices are CW (clockwise) and CCW (counterclockwise). The hot text immediately to the right of the drop-down menu specifies how many times to perform the rotation.

333

CHAPTER 7 ■ ANIMATION

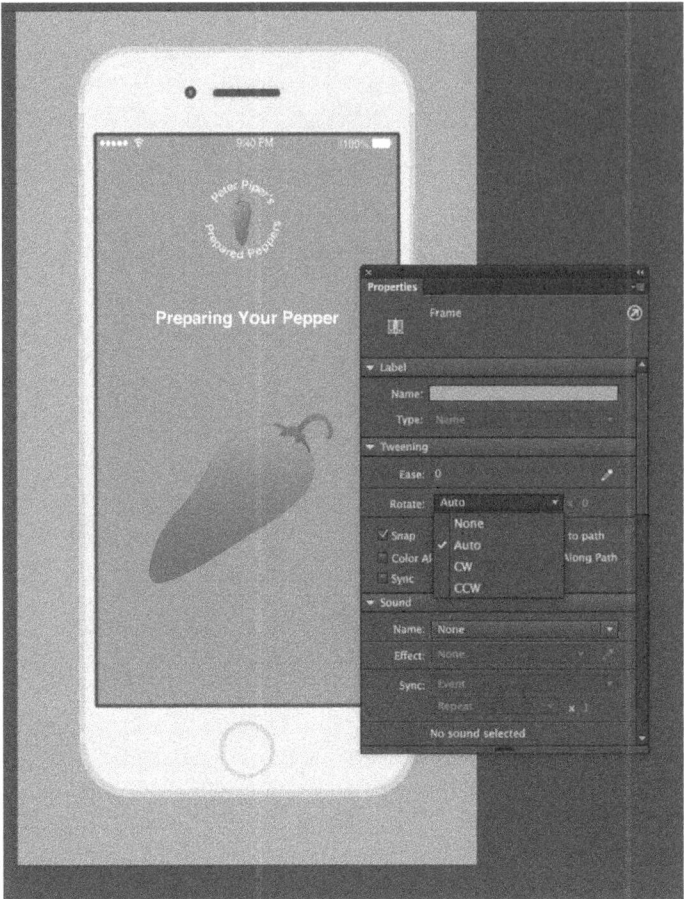

Figure 7-19. *The Rotate property makes quick work of rotations*

5. Click the pepper in frame 10 and select Modify ➤ Transform ➤ Remove Transform to reset the symbol's rotation.

6. Click once in frame 1. In the Rotate drop-down menu, change the setting to CW (clockwise), and drag the playhead back and forth. Pretty neat!

Classic Tween Properties

While we're looking at the Tweening area of the Properties panel, let's go through the other settings. Here's a quick overview of classic tween properties:

- **Ease and Edit:** These settings apply a range of easing to the tween. The Edit button (a pencil icon) allows for advanced, custom easing. More on this in the "Easing" section of this chapter.

- **Rotate and × [number]:** These settings control the type of rotation and the number of times the rotation occurs. Only CW and CCW support the × [number] setting.

- **Snap**: This Snap check box helps position a symbol along its motion guide (discussed in the "Motion Guides" section later in this chapter).

- **Orient to path**: This check box applies only to tweens along a motion guide. It determines whether a symbol points toward the direction in which it moves.

- **Scale:** If a check mark is present, tweening for the current span of frames will include a transformation in scale (size), *if such a transformation exists*. If you haven't scaled anything, it doesn't matter what state the check mark is in. If scaling and other transformations are combined in a given classic tween, only the other transformations will show if the check mark is deselected.

- **Scale Along Path:** This choice will scale an object based on the thickness of the stroke in the path.

- **Color Along Path:** If the path the object is following changes color the object's color properties will change to match those of the path segment it is following.

- **Sync**: In our experience, most people don't even realize this property exists, but it can be a real time-saver when you're dealing with graphic symbols. Unlike movieclips, which have their own independent timelines, graphic symbols are synchronized with the timeline in which they reside. Even so, there is a bit of flexibility: graphics can be looped, played through once, or instructed to rest on a specified frame of their own timeline. If a particular graphic symbol has been tweened numerous times in a layer, the presence of the Sync check mark means you can update these timeline options for all keyframes in that layer simply by making changes to the first graphic symbol in the sequence. In addition, Sync allows you to swap one graphic symbol for another and have that change ripple through all the synced keyframes in that layer. More on this feature in the "Editing Multiple Frames" section of this chapter.

Scaling, Stretching, and Deforming

We visited this topic in the "Shape Tweening" section, and honestly, there's not a whole lot different for classic tweens. The key thing to realize is that scaling, stretching, and deforming a symbol is like doing the same to a T-shirt with artwork printed on it. Even if the artwork looks different after all the tugging and twisting, it hasn't actually changed. Shake it out, and it's still the same picture. Shape tweening, in contrast, is like rearranging the tiles in a mosaic. For this reason, the Free Transform tool disables the Distort and Envelope options for symbols. These transformations can't be performed on symbols and therefore can't be classic tweened.

Symbol distortion can be performed with the 3D tools (Chapter 9) and can even be animated, but the animation requires motion tweens (Chapter 8), not classic tweens.

Let's take a quick look at the other transform options:

1. Return to the `09_PepperSymbol.fla` file, select frame 1, and set the Rotation setting for the tween to None.

2. Use the Free Transform tool to perform a shear transformation at frame 10.

CHAPTER 7 ■ ANIMATION

3. Shear? What's that? Something you do with sheep, right? Well, yes, but in Animate CC, shearing is also called **skewing**, which can be described as tilting.

4. With the Free Transform tool active, click the Rotate and Skew option at the bottom of the Tools panel, and then hover over one of the side transform handles (not the corners) until the cursor becomes an opposing double-arrow icon. Click and drag to transform the pepper (see Figure 7-20).

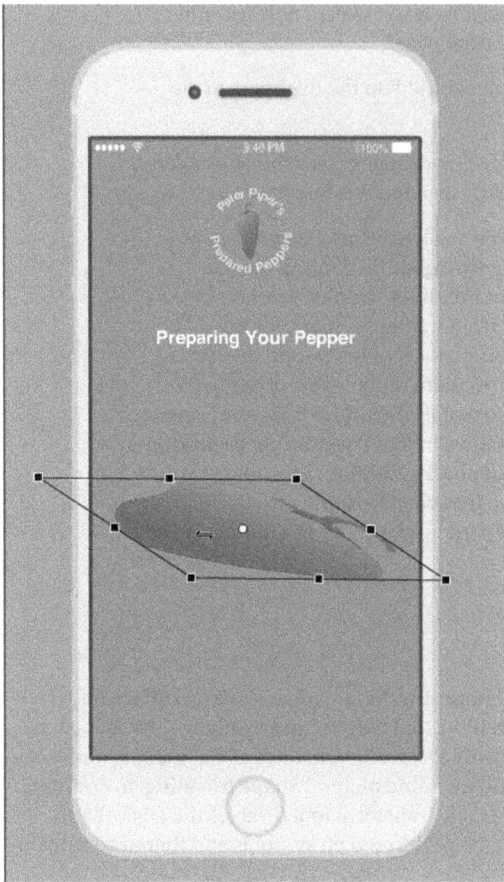

Figure 7-20. *Classic tweening a symbol transformation. The "shear" cursor is just to the left of the transformation point.*

The live preview gives you an idea what the symbol will look like before you let go of the mouse. Note that the skew occurs in relation to the transformation point, indicated by the small white circle.

336

CHAPTER 7 ANIMATION

5. Drag the white circle around inside or even outside the bounding box of the pepper, and then skew the pepper again to see how its placement affects the transformation. Hold down Alt (Windows) or Option (Mac) while skewing to temporarily ignore the transformation point and skew in relation to the symbol's opposite edge.

We've been using the Free Transform tool quite a bit, so let's try something different.

1. Open the Transform panel (Window ➤ Transform) and note its current settings. You'll see the skew summarized near the bottom and, interestingly, the change in scale summarized near the top (see Figure 7-21). From this, it becomes clear that skewing affects scale when applied with the Free Transform tool.

2. To see the difference, select Modify ➤ Transform ➤ Remove Transform or click the Remove Transform button in Figure 7-21 at the bottom right of the Transform panel to reset the symbol. The scale area of the Transform panel returns to 100 percent horizontal and 100 percent vertical.

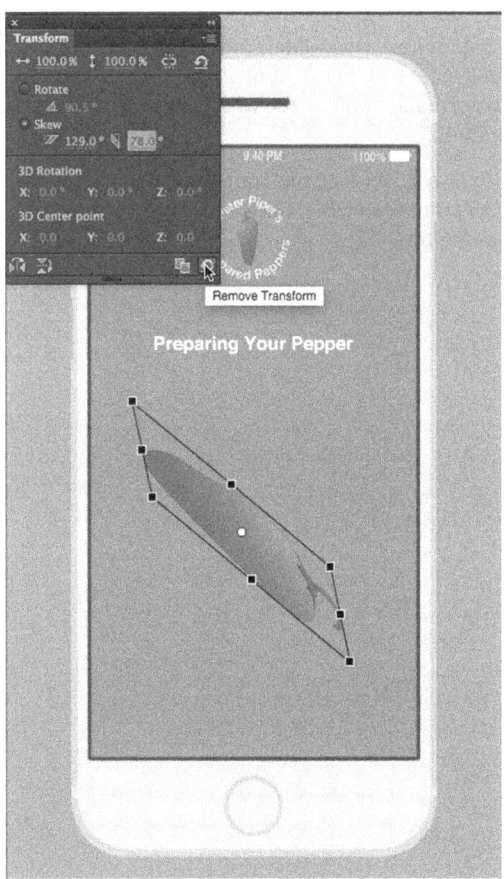

Figure 7-21. *The Transform panel provides access to precision measurements*

337

3. Click the Skew radio button and scrub the hot text of either skew value to 38. Notice that the scaling stays at 100 percent, which subtly changes how the skew looks.

4. Enter 200 into the scale input fields at the top. (The Constrain Lock icon means you need to enter this number into only one of them.) Slide the playhead back and forth to see two transformations tweened at once.

Easing

The "secret sauce" for any motion is the correct application of easing. We briefly talked about it at the top of this chapter when we talked about modifying shape tweens. The time has arrived to take a deeper look at easing and how it adds that necessary dash of "realism" to any motion.

Here's where classic tweening begins to pull ahead of shape tweening. Easing is much more powerful for classic tweens, thanks to the Custom Ease In/Ease Out Editor. Before we delve into that, though, let's look at a sample use of the standard easing controls for a classic tween, so you can see how much easier things are with the custom variety. To explore this we are going to bang a rubber hammer around. Let's get started:

1. Open the 10_MalletNoEasing.fla file in this chapter's exercise folder. You'll see a hammer graphic symbol in the Library and an instance of that symbol on the stage. Select the hammer and note that the transformation point—the white dot in the handle—is located in the center of the symbol.

2. We're going to make this hammer swing to the left, so select the Free Transform tool. Selecting this tool makes the transformation point selectable. Click and drag that point to the bottom center of the mallet (see Figure 7-22).

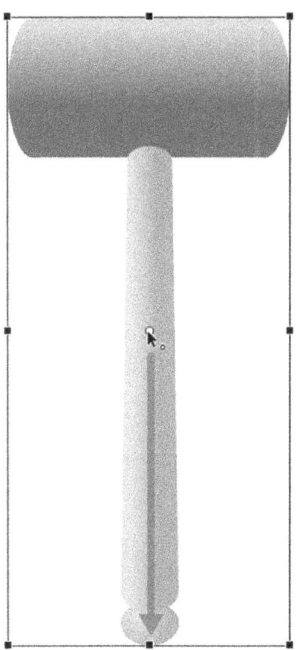

Figure 7-22. *You'll need to move that transformation point to make the movement realistic*

3. Insert a keyframe at frame 10 (Insert ➤ Timeline ➤ Keyframe) and rotate the mallet at frame 10 to the left by 90 degrees.

4. Apply a classic tween to the span of frames between 1 and 10 and scrub the timeline to see the effect. That's not bad but not especially realistic. How about some easing and bounce-back?

5. In the Tweening area of the Properties panel, scrub the Ease hot text all the way to the left to specify a full ease in. The number should be -100. This causes the hammer to fall slowly as it begins to tip and increase speed as it continues to fall (see Figure 7-23).

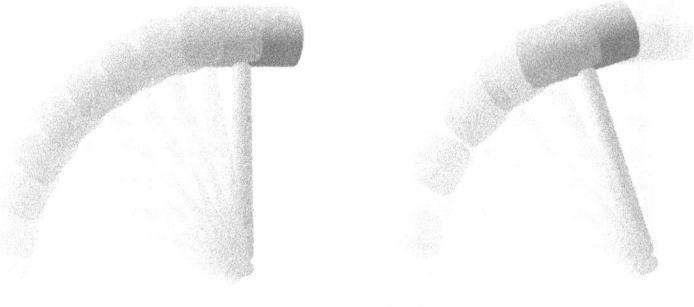

Figure 7-23. *Ease in (right) vs. no easing (left). On the right, the hammer falls in a more natural manner.*

This is a good start. To push the realism further, let's embellish the animation. We're going to provide some tweening that makes the hammer rebound on impact and bounce a few times.

6. Add new keyframes at frames 15, 20, 23, and 25. At frame 15, use the Free Transform tool or the Transform panel to rotate the hammer to approximately northwest; in the Transform panel, this could be something like -55 in the Rotate area. At frame 23, set the rotation to roughly west-northwest (something like -80 in the Rotation area). A storyboard version of the sequence might look like Figure 7-24.

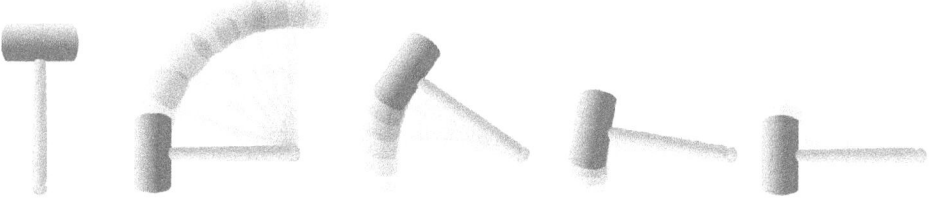

Figure 7-24. *Using several keyframes to make the hammer bounce*

The fading image trails—visual echoes of the mallet—are the result of something called *onion skinning*, which is very helpful in animation work. It's used here for illustrative purposes and is covered later in the chapter.

7. Now that the mallet has been positioned, it just needs to be tweened and eased. You can click separately into each span of frames and apply a classic tween, or you can click and drag across as many spans as you need (as shown in Figure 7-25). That way, you can apply the tweens all in one swoop.

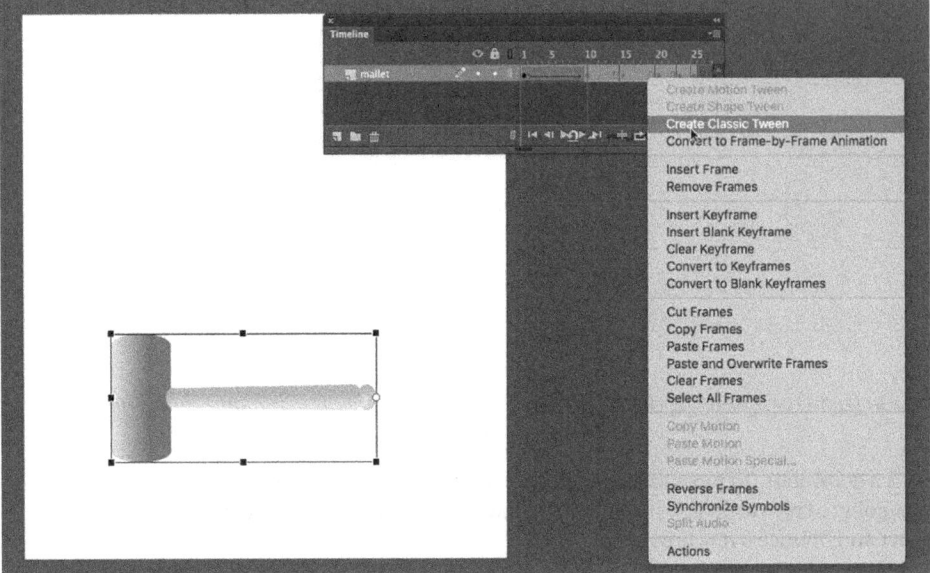

Figure 7-25. Tweens can be applied to more than one frame span at a time

8. Click into each span of frames to apply easing, for the final touch. Remember that span 1 through 10 already has -100. Apply the following easing to the remaining spans:

    - Span 10 to 15: 100 (full ease out)
    - Span 15 to 20: -100 (full ease in)
    - Span 20 to 23: 100
    - Span 23 to 25: -100

9. Drag the playhead back and forth to preview the action, and then test the movie to see the final presentation. If you like, compare your work with 10_MalletNormalEase.fla in the Complete folder.

This exercise wasn't especially arduous, but wouldn't it be even cooler if you could perform all the preceding steps with a single classic tween?

Custom Easing

Introduced in Flash 8, the Custom Ease In/Ease Out dialog box unleashes considerably more power than traditional easing. Not only does it provide a combined ease in/out—where animation gradually speeds up *and* gradually slows down, or vice versa—but it also supports multiple varied settings for various kinds of easing, all within the same classic tween. Let's take a look.

To perform custom easing, select a span of motion-tweened frames, and then click the Edit button (a pencil icon) in the Tweening area of the Properties panel. You'll see the Custom Ease In/Ease Out dialog box, as shown in Figure 7-26. This dialog box contains a graph with time along the horizontal axis, represented in frames, and percentage of change along the vertical axis.

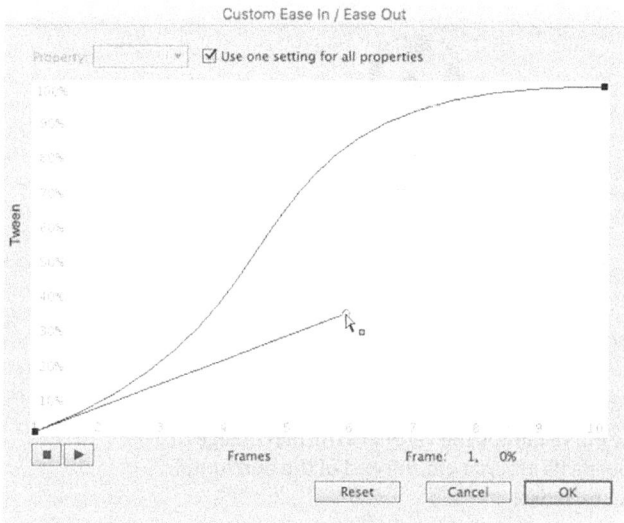

Figure 7-26. *The Custom Ease In/Ease Out dialog box*

Here's a quick rundown of the various areas of the dialog box:

- **Property**: By default, this is disabled until you deselect the check mark next to it. If the check mark is present, custom easing—as specified by you on the grid—applies to all aspects of the tween symbol. If the check mark is absent, this drop-down menu lets you distinguish among Position, Rotation, Scale, Color, and Filters.

- **Use one setting for all properties:** When deselected, this allows multiple properties to be eased individually.

- **Grid**: The Bézier curves on this grid determine the visual result of the custom easing applied.

- **Preview**: Click the two buttons in this area to play and stop a preview of the custom easing.

- **OK, Cancel, and Reset**: The OK and Cancel buttons apply and discard any custom easing. Reset reverts the Bézier curves to a straight line (no easing) between the grid's opposite corners.

- The X-axis, along the bottom, shows the number of frames in the tween.

- The Y-axis along the side, shows the strength of the tween.

CHAPTER 7 ANIMATION

So, how does the grid work? Let's look at a traditional ease in to see how the Custom Ease In/Ease Out dialog box interprets it.

1. Open the 11_CustomEasingComparison.fla file in the Chapter 7 exercise folder and set the Ease property to -100 (a normal full ease in) for the tween in the top layer.

2. Scrub the timeline to confirm that the upper symbol starts its tween more slowly than the lower one but speeds up near the end. The lower symbol, in contrast, should advance the same distance each frame (see Figure 7-27).

Figure 7-27. *An ease in causes the upper symbol to start slower and speed up (artwork by Steve Napiersk)*

3. Click the Edit button in the Tweening area of the Properties panel to see what an ease out looks like on the grid. The curve climbs the vertical axis (percentage of change) rather slowly and then speeds its ascent near the end of the horizontal axis (time in frames). Hey, that makes sense!

4. Click Cancel, apply a full ease out (100), and then click the Edit button to check the grid again. Bingo—the opposite curve.

   It follows that a combination of these would produce either a custom ease in/out (slow, fast, slow) or a custom ease out/in (fast, slow, fast). Let's do the first of those two.

CHAPTER 7 ANIMATION

5. Click the upper-right black square in the grid to make its control handle appear. Drag it up to the top of the grid and about two-thirds across to the left, as shown in Figure 7-28.

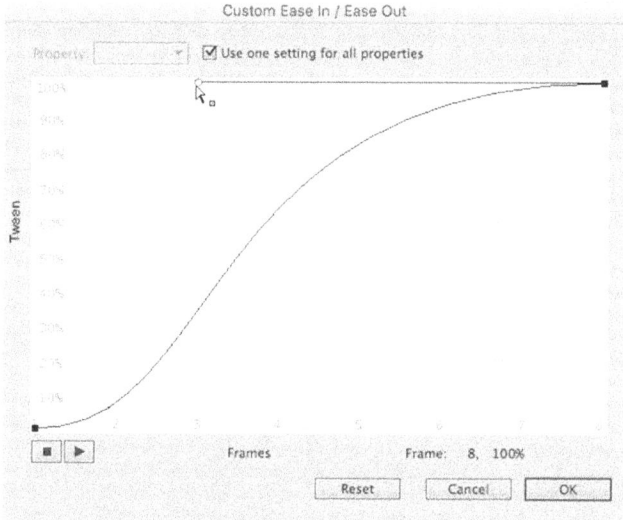

Figure 7-28. *Dragging a control handle to create a custom ease*

6. Click the bottom-left black square, and drag its control handle two-thirds across to the right. The resulting curve—vaguely an *S* shape—effectively combines the curves you saw for ease in and ease out (see Figure 7-29).

7. Click OK to accept this setting and scrub the timeline or test the movie to see the results.

343

CHAPTER 7 ANIMATION

8. Let's inverse this easing for the lower symbol. Select the lower span of frames, and click the Edit button. This time, drag the lower-left control handle two-thirds up the left side. Drag the upper-right control handle two-thirds down the right side to create the inverted *S* curve shown in Figure 7-30. Click OK and compare the two tweens.

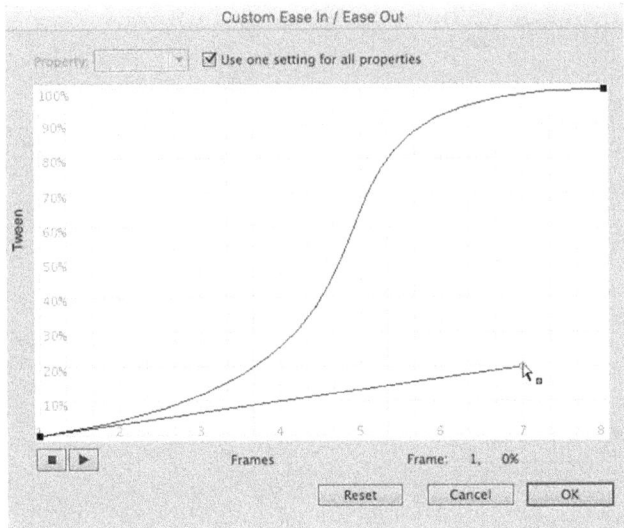

Figure 7-29. *An S shape produces an ease in/out (slow-fast-slow) tween*

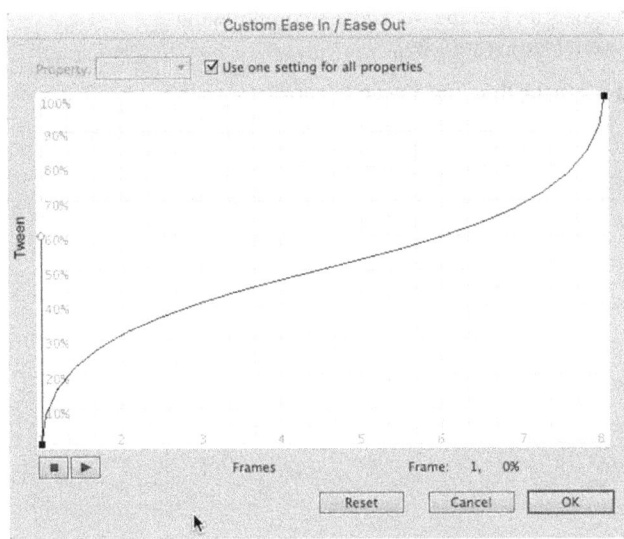

Figure 7-30. *An inverted S shape produces an ease out/in (fast-slow-fast) tween*

Think this is cool? We're just getting started!

Adding Anchor Points

By clicking anywhere along the Bézier curve, you can add new anchor points. This is where you can actually save yourself a bit of work.

1. Open the `12_MalletCustomEasing.fla` file in this chapter's exercise folder. again.

2. Confirm that the mallet's transformation point is positioned at the bottom center of its wooden handle. Now add a new keyframe at frame 25, and apply a classic tween to the span of frames between 1 and 25.

3. Using the Free Transform tool at frame 25, rotate the mallet 90 degrees to the left. Because a tween is already applied, you can preview the falling mallet by scrubbing the timeline.

    This may seem like déjà vu, but things are about to change. You're going to emulate the same bounce-back tween you did earlier, but this time, you'll do it all in one custom ease.

4. Click in frame 1—or anywhere inside the tween span—and click the Edit button in the Tweening area of the Properties panel.

5. In the Custom Ease In/Ease Out dialog box, click the Bézier curve near the middle, and you'll see a new anchor point with control handles. Click that new anchor point and press the Delete key—it disappears. Add it again and straighten the control handles so that they're horizontal, as shown in Figure 7-31.

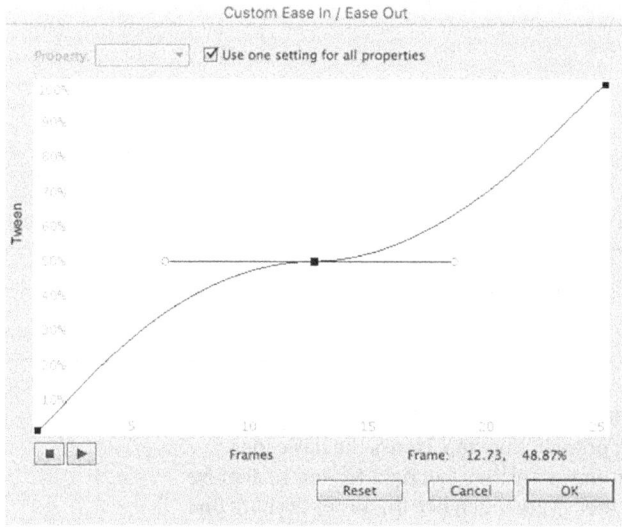

Figure 7-31. Starting a more complex custom ease

CHAPTER 7 ■ ANIMATION

Repeat this process three more times, up the hill, as shown in Figure 7-32. This prepares the way for the sawtooth shape you'll create in the next step.

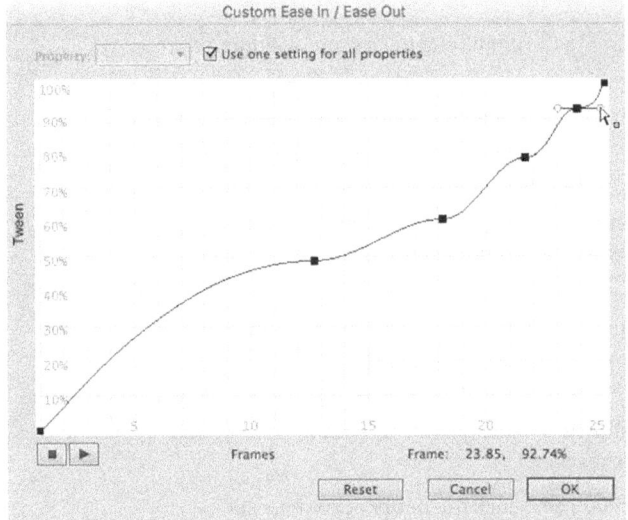

Figure 7-32. *Continuing to add anchor points for a sawtooth curve*

Leave the corner anchor points where they are. Position the four new anchor points as follows:

- 100%, 10
- 60%, 15
- 100%, 20
- 85%, 23

You'll notice that the anchor points gently snap to the grid while you drag. To temporarily suppress this snapping, hold down the X key.

You've probably heard of certain procedures described as more of an art than a science. Well, we've come to that point in this step. Here's the basic idea, but it's up to you to tweak these settings until they feel right to you. To achieve the sawtooth curve we're after—it looks very much like the series of shark fins shown in Figure 7-33—click each anchor point in turn and perform the following adjustment:

- If it has a left control handle, drag that handle in toward the anchor point.
- If it has a right control handle, drag that handle out a couple of squares to the right.

You should get something like the shape shown in Figure 7-33.

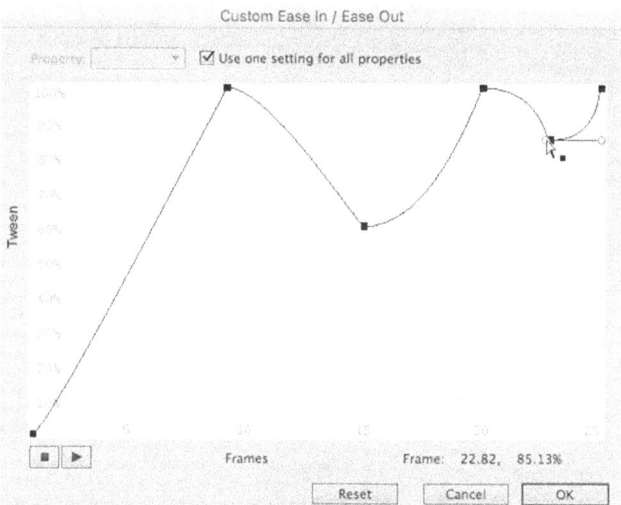

Figure 7-33. *Shark fins produce a bounce-back effect*

6. Click the Preview play button to test your custom ease. It should look similar to the original series of mallet bounce-back tweens, but this time you saved yourself a handful of keyframes.

How does this work? As depicted in the grid and following the horizontal axis, you have an ease-in curve from frames 0 to 10, an ease-out curve from 10 to 15, an ease-in curve from 15 to 20, and so on—just like your series of keyframes from earlier in the chapter. The mallet moves from its upright position to its leaned-over position in the very first curve. From frames 10 to 15, the vertical axis goes from 100 percent down to 60 percent, which means that the mallet actually rotates clockwise again toward its original orientation, but not all the way. With each new curve, the hammer falls again to the left, and then raises again, but never as high. Compare your work with `12_MalletCustomEasing.fla` in this chapter's `Complete` folder.

Easing Multiple Properties

On the final leg of our custom easing expedition, let's pull out all the stops and examine a tween that updates multiple symbol properties at once. You'll be familiar with most of what you're about to see, and the new parts will be easy to pick up.

1. Open the `CustomEasingMultiple.fla` file in this chapter's exercise folder. Select frame 1, and note that a movieclip symbol of an apple shape appears in the upper-left corner of the stage. It is solid green. Scrub across to frame 55, and note the changes to the starting state of the apple that occur as you move the playhead.

   At this point, frame 55, the apple is positioned in the center of the stage, is much larger and more naturally colored, and has a drop shadow (see Figure 7-34). From this, you can surmise that color and filters are tweenable—that's the new part.

CHAPTER 7 ■ ANIMATION

Figure 7-34. *You are about to discover that it isn't only rotation that can be tweened*

2. In frame 1, select the apple symbol to see that a Tint has been applied in the Properties panel, which is replaced by None in the other keyframe. Next, twirl down the Filters at frame 55, and click the apple to see that a drop shadow has been applied that is not present in frame 1. The Filters properties are no different from Position and Scale as far as tweens are concerned.

3. Click into the span of tweened frames, and note that a CW (clockwise) rotation has been specified for Rotation and Scale is enabled (without it, the apple wouldn't gradually increase in size). The Ease property reads ---, which means custom easing has been applied. That's what we're after. Click the Edit button.

4. Thanks to the empty Use one setting for all properties check box, the Property drop-down menu is now available. Use the drop-down menu to look at the grid curve for each of five properties, all of which are depicted in the tween: Position, Rotation, Scale, Color, and Filters. Each property has its own distinct curve, which translates into five individual custom ease settings for their respective properties (see Figure 7-35).

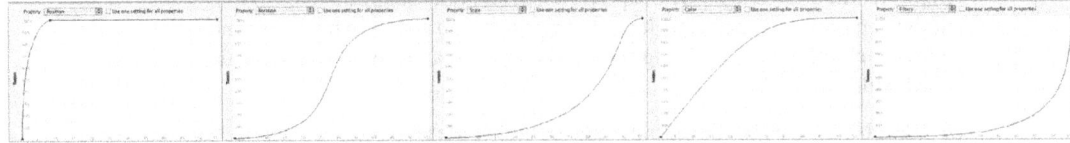

Figure 7-35. *The Custom Ease In/Ease Out dialog box lets you specify distinct easing for five different tweenable properties*

5. Click the Use one setting for all properties check box to disable the drop-down menu.

6. Ack! Have you lost your custom settings? Thankfully, no. Animate CC remembers them for you, even though they're hiding.

7. Click the Preview play button to preview the tween with no easing (the default lower-left to upper-right curve).

8. Click the check box again to see that the custom ease settings are still intact. Preview the tween again, if you like.

Using Animation

So far, we've shown you a hefty animation toolbox. We've opened it up and pulled out a number of powerful tools to show you how they work. In doing so, we've covered quite a bit of ground, but there are still a handful of useful animation features and general workflow practices to help bring it all together. Let's roll up our sleeves, then, shall we?

A Closer Look at the Timeline Panel

Whether you use shape, classic, or motion tweens, the Timeline panel gives you a pint-sized but important dashboard (see Figure 7-36). Don't let its small size fool you. This strip along the bottom of the timeline helps you quickly find your bearings, gives you at-a-glance detail on where you are, and even lets you time travel into both the past and the future, to see where you've been and where you're going.

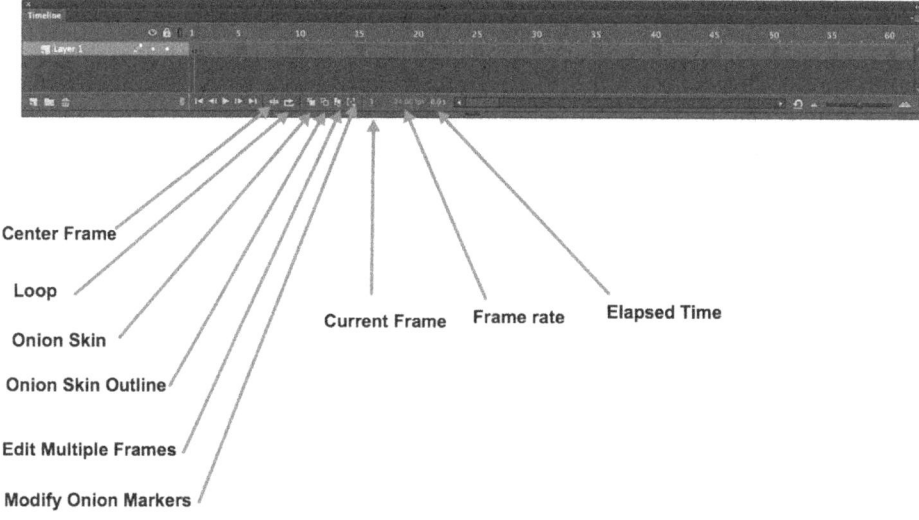

Figure 7-36. *The bottom edge of the timeline provides a collection of useful tools*

Let's take an inventory of this useful, if small, real estate.

- **Center Frame:** In timelines that are long enough to scroll, this button centers the timeline on the playhead.
- **Onion Skin and Onion Skin Outlines:** These buttons toggle two different kinds of onion skinning, which give you a view of your work as a series of stills.
- **Edit Multiple Frames:** This button allows you to select more than one keyframe at the same time, in order to edit many frames in one swoop.
- **Modify Markers**: Click this button to see a drop-down menu that controls the functionality of the onion skin buttons.
- **Current Frame:** This indicates the current location of the playhead. Scrub or enter a value to move the playhead to that frame.
- **Frame Rate:** This indicates the movie's frame rate.
- **Elapsed Time:** Given the current frame and the movie's frame rate, this indicates the duration in seconds of the playhead's position. For example, in a movie with a frame rate of 24 fps, this area will say 1.0s at frame 24. Scrub or enter a value to move the playhead to the frame that closely matches your specified elapsed time.

Onion Skinning

Traditional animators—those wonderful people who brought us Mickey Mouse and Bugs Bunny—often drew the motion of their characters on very thin paper over illuminated surfaces called **light boxes**. This paper, called **onion skin**, allowed the artist to see through the current drawing to what had occurred in the previous drawings or frames. In this way, animators could control the motion of someone's head or the speed and shape of the anvil about to land on a coyote's head.

Animate CC offers you this same capability with a lot more flexibility than flipping through sheets of paper. In Animate CC, you can choose to see through as many frames as you want, moving backward and forward looking at solids or outlines. Let's take a look at how you do this:

1. Open the 14_PhotoApp.fla file in this chapter's exercise folder. Pay particular attention to the movie's frame rate of 24 fps.
2. All of the animation happens on the main timeline. Drag the playhead to frame 20 where the image starts to grow. Take a look at the Elapsed Time indicator at the bottom of the panel. It should, as shown in Figure 7-37, read about .6 seconds. This makes sense: 30/20 = 0.6.

CHAPTER 7 ANIMATION

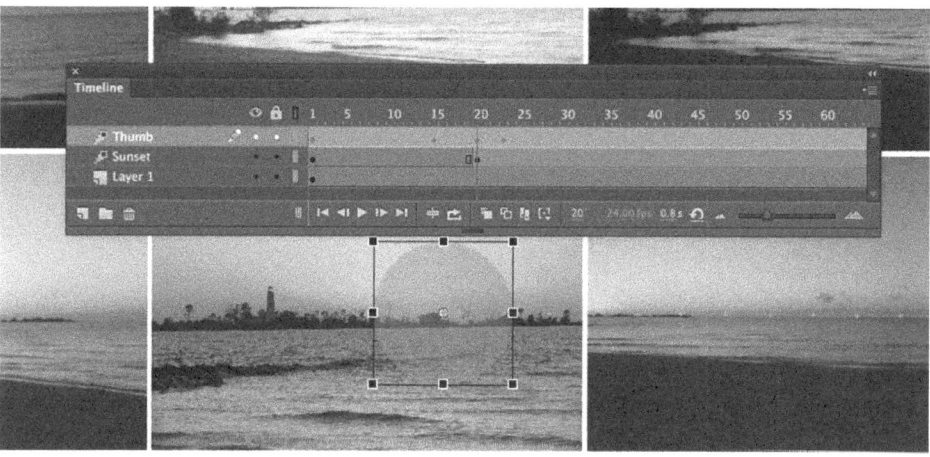

Figure 7-37. *Now you know why it is called a timeline*

3. In the Properties panel change the movie's fps to 60, and note the Elapsed Time changes, as expected, to 03 second. Now change the frame rate to 15 fps. The fps shows 1.3 seconds. Change the time back to the original 30 fps.

4. Place the playhead at frame 80, and, using the bar at the bottom of the timeline, scroll all the way to the left until you see frame 1 and the playhead may be hidden. If your display is wide enough in resolution, it may not be hidden. Take note in either way—this is a common issue faced by Animate CC designers. You have a long timeline, and it suddenly hits you: where's the playhead? Click the Center Frame button (shown in Figure 7-36), and you will pop right over to frame 60. This is a great "you are here" panic button that's really shines with especially long timelines.

5. Position the playhead at frame 20 and click the Onion Skin button. This puts two markers on frames 18and 22 on either side of the playhead, as shown in Figure 7-38. If you aren't seeing them, return to the Modify Onion Markers menu, and select Always Show Markers.

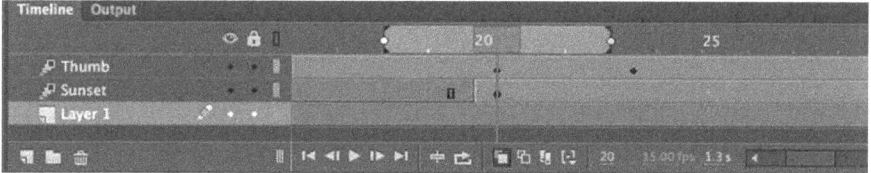

Figure 7-38. *Onion skinning adds markers to either side of the playhead*

These markers extend two frames back from and ahead of the current position. What they show are semitransparent views of those frames fading as they get farther from the playhead—just like artwork on thin paper! Not only do they let you see back in time at previous frames, but they also show artwork on future frames, which provides practical sequential context for any moment in time.

CHAPTER 7 ■ ANIMATION

6. To actually see these onion skins, pull the two colored handles to either side of the keyframes shown in Figure 7-39. In this case, you're seeing 11 "sheets," including the one under the playhead (which is the darkest) and then five ahead and behind.

Figure 7-39. You determine the range for the Onion Skin "sheets"

7. Click the Onion Skin Outlines button. Note that the same sort of onion skinning occurs, but that the tweened areas are shown in wireframe format (see Figure 7-40). This makes it even clearer to see what's moving and what isn't.

Onion skinning is just as relevant to shape and motion tweens as it is to classic tweens. Use it to help you whenever you get the notion.

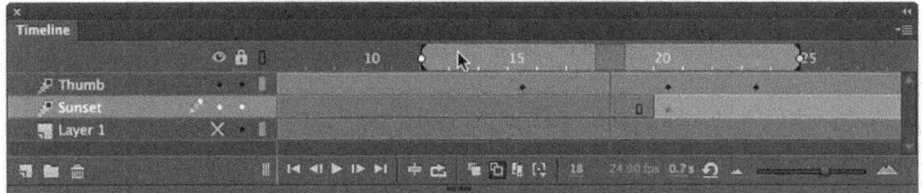

Figure 7-40. Onion skin outlines show tweened artwork in a wireframe format

352

Modifying Multiple Frames

Timeline animation can be painstaking work, no doubt about it. Even if you're using onion skinning, chances are good that you're focused on only a handful of frames at a time. There's nothing wrong with that, just as long as you remember to keep your eye on the big picture, too. Sooner or later, it happens to everyone: artwork is replaced, your manager changes her mind, or you find that you've simply painted yourself into a corner and need to revise multiple keyframes—maybe hundreds—in as few moves as possible.

Fortunately, the timeline has a button called Edit Multiple Frames, which allows you to do just what it describes. That's the obvious answer, of course, and we'll cover that in just a moment, but it's worth noting that the concept of mass editing in Animate CC extends into other avenues.

Because of the nature of symbols, for example, you can edit a Library asset and benefit from an immediate change throughout the movie, even if individual instances of that symbol have been stretched, scaled, rotated, and manipulated in other ways. For example, if an imported graphic file, such as a BMP, has been revised outside Animate CC, just right-click (Windows) or Control+click (Mac) the asset in the Library, select either Update (if the location of the external image hasn't changed) or Properties, and then click the Import button to reimport the image or import another one.

Sometimes it's not that easy. Sometimes you will have finished three days of meticulous classic tween keyframing only to learn that the symbol you've tweened isn't supposed to be *that* symbol at all. Time to throw in the towel? Well, maybe time to roll the towel into a whip. But even here, there's hope if you're using graphic symbols.

Swapping Graphic Symbols

It's easy enough to swap out symbols of any type for any other type at a given keyframe, but the swap applies only to the frames leading up to the next keyframe. With graphic symbols, it's possible to apply a swap across keyframes, but you need to know the secret handshake. Let's try it.

1. Open the 15_RabbitSwap.fla in this chapter's exercise folder. You have decided to get in touch with your inner "Looney Tunes" and drop an anvil on the rabbit's head. Your co-workers all think this is rather cool except for the guy who is a "comic book" fan. He points out that the animation doesn't do a thing for him. "In fact," he says, "shouldn't the rabbit react to an anvil dropping on its head?" Tell him to give you a minute to fix that oversight, and you'll call him back. He wanders off to his cubicle at the other side of the office.

2. Scrub over to frame 30 and click the rabbit's head on the stage.

3. Open the Properties panel and click the Swap button to open the Swap Symbol dialog box shown in Figure 7-41. A list of all the symbols in the movies appears; the selected symbol is indicated with a dot, and a preview of the selected rabbit head appears on the left.

Figure 7-41. *Swapping symbols is a great way to create animation effects*

4. Select the Head4 graphic symbol and click OK. The new symbol, as shown in Figure 7-42, appears on the stage. Move it into position.

Figure 7-42. *One rabbit head has been swapped for another in the Library*

5. Select the rabbit head in Frame 33 and swap the Head1 graphic symbol with the Head3 graphic symbol. Scrub across the timeline to see the rabbit wince, close its eyes, and then open them as the anvil leaves the stage.

This technique a great productivity booster, and once you get the hang of it, you can make changes like these well before the "comic guy" makes it back to his cubicle. When he asks how you did it, look knowingly at him with a faint smile and say, "magic."

Combining Timelines

Pat your head. Good! Now rub your tummy. Excellent. Now do those both at the same time. Until the undertaking snaps into place, it might seem an impossible feat, but once you manage to pull it off, you know you've done something pretty snazzy. Animate CC animations get interesting in the same way when you combine techniques and timelines. This is where the distinction between graphic symbols and movieclip symbols really comes into play. Both types of symbols have timelines, but each behaves in a different way. Understanding this paves the way toward good decision making in your animations.

Movieclip Timelines versus Graphic Symbol Timelines

Movieclips operate independently of the timelines they occupy. You can create a 500-frame animation on the main timeline and then transfer all those frames into a movieclip symbol, and everything will run the same, even if that movieclip occupies only a single frame on the main timeline. This is not so with graphic symbols. Graphic symbols are synchronized with the timelines that contain them. So if you transfer all those frames into a graphic symbol, that symbol will need to span a length of 500 frames in the main timeline in order for its own timeline to play fully.

Although movieclips can be instructed by ActionScript or JavaScript to stop, play, and jump to various frames, graphics can only be told to hold their current position, play through once, or loop. This instruction comes not from code used, but from the Properties panel settings. Any code placed within the timelines of graphic symbols is not performed by a containing timeline. Sound in graphic symbols is also ignored by parent timelines. Let's see this in action:

1. Open the `16_CombineTimeline.fla` file in this chapter's exercise folder and select the symbol at frame 1.

2. Look in the Properties panel's Looping area, and you'll see that the Options drop-down menu is set to Single Frame. Below it, the First field is set to 1, which refers to the timeline of this graphic symbol. Change this number to 20 and press Enter (Return). Doing so changes the graphic. The rabbit's eyes close, as shown in Figure 7-43.

CHAPTER 7 ■ ANIMATION

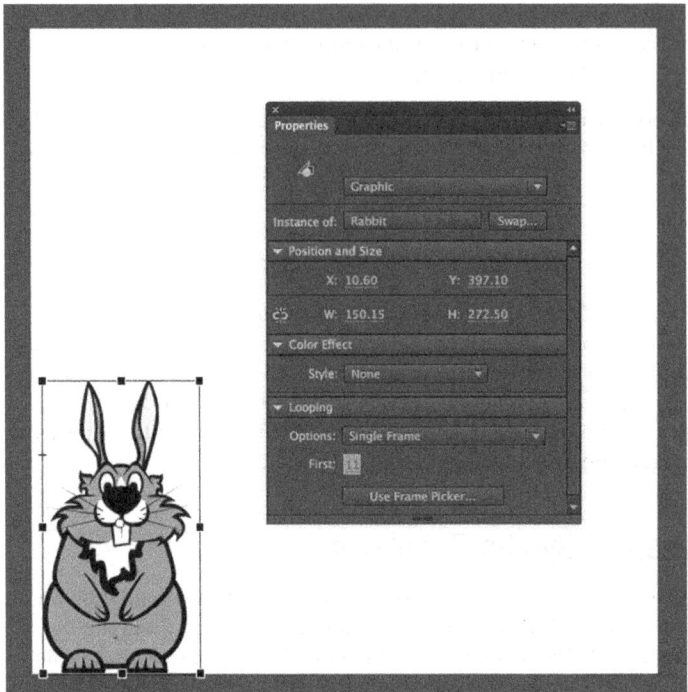

Figure 7-43. *Changing the displayed frame of a graphic symbol*

3. Double-click the Rabbit symbol in the Library, and you'll see why this change occurs. The Rabbit symbol has a timeline, and the Head symbol changes every 10 frames. You can see this by selecting the head on the stage in frame 1. The instance name in the Properties panel is Head1. Scrub over to frame 10, click the head on the stage, and the instance name changes to Head2.

4. Select the symbol again in the main timeline. Change the Single Frame setting to Play Once, and change the First input field to 10. This changes the rabbit's head and instructs the graphic symbol to play through the end of its timeline a single time.

5. Drag the playhead slowly to the right to see the heads change while the symbol moves across the stage. At the top, the symbol continues to move but no longer updates the rabbit head. The reason for this is that the symbol's timeline has reached its end but does not repeat.

6. Change the Play Once setting to Loop and change First to 1. Scrub again, and you'll see the heads change.

You might also want to select Sync in the Looping properties. When Sync is selected for the various spans in a multiple-keyframe classic tween, Looping properties are applied to all spans. When Sync is deselected, Looping properties apply to only the current span. Selecting this option for a nested animation ensures the nested frames in the graphic symbol will be synchronized with the main timeline.

CHAPTER 7 ■ ANIMATION

Nesting Symbols

Designer and animator Chris Georgenes (http://keyframer.com/) has lent his talents to numerous cartoons on television and the Web, including *Dr. Katz, Professional Therapist*, Adult Swim's *Home Movies*, and, well, more online animation than either of us could shake a stick at. One of the giants in the field, Chris uses combined timelines to great effect in practically all of this Animate CC work. From walk cycles to lip-syncing, Chris builds up elaborate animated sequences by organizing relatively simple movement into symbols nested within symbols. The orchestrated result often leaves viewers thinking, "Wow! How did he do that?" Luckily for us, Chris was kind enough to share one of his character sketches, which provides a simplified example.

 1. Open the 17_Grotto.fla file from the example folder for this chapter. Note that the main timeline has only one frame and only one symbol in that frame (see Figure 7-44). This base symbol is a movieclip, because Chris wanted a slight drop shadow effect on the friendly monster, and graphic symbols don't support filters.

Figure 7-44. *Nested symbols allow you to take the most useful features of each symbol type*

357

CHAPTER 7 ANIMATION

2. Double-click this movieclip to enter its timeline. Even with a basic example like this one, you may be surprised by the number of layers inside. Try not to feel overwhelmed! The layers are neatly labeled, as shown in Figure 7-45. (Now that you see how a pro does it, start labeling your layers as well.) Also, although there are many of them, they all have a purpose. If you like, temporarily hide a number of layers to see how each layer adds to the complete picture. What we're interested in is the mouth.

Figure 7-45. *Complex images and animations are built up from simple pieces*

3. Double-click the mouth symbol to enter its timeline. Here, too, there is a handful of layers, comprising the lips, teeth, and a few shadows on this monster. There are 115 frames of animation here—mostly classic tweens, but also a shape tween at the bottom. If you scrub the timeline, you'll see the mouth gently move up and down. This is Grotto breathing (see Figure 7-46). Because the mouth itself is a graphic symbol, its movement can be made to scrub along with the timeline of its parent.

Figure 7-46. Nesting timelines is a way to compartmentalize complexity

4. Return to the Grotto timeline by clicking the Grotto movieclip icon in the breadcrumbs area of the Timeline panel (shown above the monster in Figure 7-46). Drag the playhead to a keyframe, such as 11, and click the mouth symbol. Note that it's set to Loop in the Properties panel and starts at frame 11. Because the mouth symbol loops, the mouth itself can be tweened to various locations and rotations during the course of the Grotto symbol's timeline. The complexity of the mouth's inner movement is neatly tucked away into the mouth symbol.

At any point, you can pause this breathing movement by adding a keyframe in the Grotto symbol's timeline and changing the mouth symbol's behavior setting from Loop to Single Frame.

The phenomenon you've just seen can be nested as deeply as you like. Even limited nesting, like that in 17_Grotto.fla, can, for example, be used to animate a bicycle—the wheels rotate in their own timeline while traveling along the parent timeline—or twinkling stars. Just keep in mind that if a given graphic symbol's timeline is, say, 100 frames long, and you want *all* of those frames to show, the symbol will need to span that many frames in the timeline that contains it. Of course, you may purposely want to show only a few frames.

Graphic Symbols as Mini-Libraries

Between the rabbit and Grotto, we are sure you are slowly coming to the conclusion that animation projects can get rather complicated, rather quickly. There are a lot of tweens and symbols, and the odds for becoming quickly entangled in a project seem to be rather significant. Our answer is, "Not really." The graphic symbol's timeline is your life ring.

1. To understand what we are getting at, open TalkingPanda found in File ➤ New ➤ Templates ➤ Sample Files ➤ Lip Synch.

    Lip syncing, when one is first introduced to Animate CC, is one of those techniques one will avoid because…well…because it looks so hard. Let's get over that right now.

2. To start, simply press the Return/Enter key to see the project in action. As the playhead moves, the panda says: "Sweet and sour chicken." This is accomplished through the use of the ten graphic symbols you see on the pasteboard and in the Mouth shape with graphic symbols folder in your Library. Each symbol represents a sound or range of sounds, which means you won't need one symbol for each letter of the alphabet.

    As you have seen, there are a couple of methods of swapping out the symbols. If you look at the mouth layer, the first conclusion you may come to is that each keyframe in the layer represents a symbol from the collection on the pasteboard. This looks complicated because just the word *sweet* looks like you need to use three of the symbols. You could if you are into beating yourself in the head with a board.

3. Click the first mouth symbol on the stage and open the Properties panel. The first thing you will notice, as shown in Figure 7-47, is it isn't one of the symbols on the pasteboard. It is the mouth symbol. Twirl down the Looping parameter in the Properties panel, and you will immediately see why this example falls smack into the category of "Work smart. Not hard." The Looping Option is set to Single Frame, and each keyframe or swap is accomplished by shooting the playhead to a specific frame in the mouth symbol and letting it play from there.

Figure 7-47. *Graphic symbols can be used as mini-libraries to keep the real Library from overcrowding*

This is a perfect example of how a graphic symbol's timeline can be used to reduce clutter in the Library. Sure, you can use the Swap button to replace any symbol with another at any keyframe, but it is much less hassle to update the First field in the Properties panel for graphic symbols. This technique is one of those hidden gems that becomes a favorite once you realize it, and we thank Chris Georgenes for sharing such a useful trick.

For more information about character design, advanced tweening, and lip-syncing techniques, search *Chris Georgenes* on the Adobe web site (http://www.adobe.com/). You'll find a number of Chris's articles and Macrochats (recordings of live tutorial presentations).

Motion Guides

Tweening in a straight line is effortless, and we've shown how easing can make such movement more realistic. But what if you want to tween along a curve? Wouldn't it be great if we could tell you that it's only marginally more difficult? Well, we can, and we'll even show you. The trick is to use something called a **motion guide**, which requires its own layer. You were first introduced to this feature at the end Chapter 1, but now is the time to really look at it. When you get to Chapter 8, you'll see an even easier way to do this for motion tweens, but for classic tweens, motion guides are the way to go.

1. Open the 18_MotionGuide.fla file in this chapter's exercise folder. You'll see a butterfly graphic symbol in one layer. If you scrub the timeline at this point, you'll see the butterfly tween in a straight line. Butterflies don't really fly like that, so let's fix the flight pattern.

2. Select the Path layer and switch to the Pencil tool. Draw a meandering path across the stage. This will be the path the butterfly will follow. Turn off the visibility of the Image layer to see the path and the butterfly.

3. Right-click (Windows) or Control+click (Mac) the Path layer and choose Guide from the context menu, as shown in Figure 7-48. Its icon turns from a folded page to a T-square.

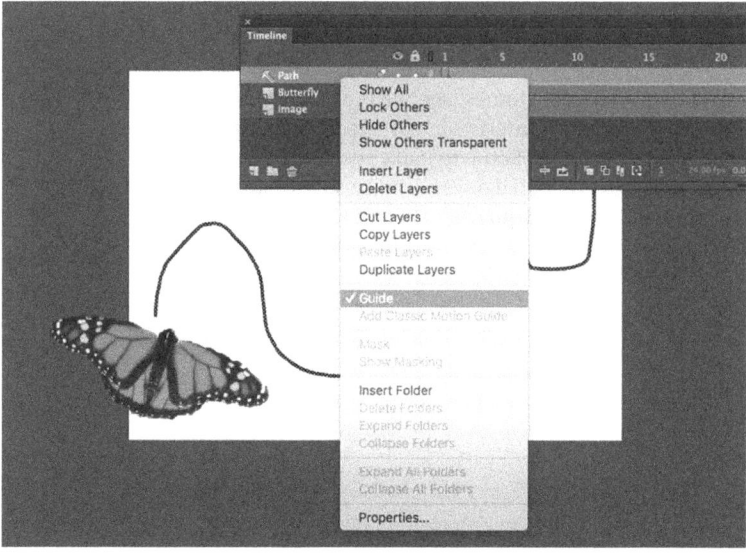

Figure 7-48. Changing a normal layer into a guide layer

You've changed the path layer into a guide layer, which means anything you put into it can be used as a visual reference to help position objects in other layers. Depending on your snap settings (View ➤ Snapping), you can even snap objects to drawings in a guide layer. Artwork in guide layers is not included in the published output and does not add to file size. In this exercise, the squiggle is your guide—but setting its layer as a guide layer isn't enough. It must become a motion guide. Let's make that happen.

4. Gently drag the butterfly layer *slightly up* and then to the right, as shown in Figure 7-49. Drag too high, and you simply swap layer positions. Do it right, and the T-square icon changes into a shooting comet.

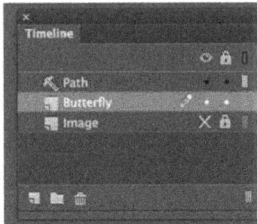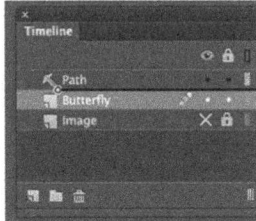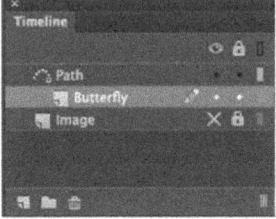

Figure 7-49. *Changing a guide layer into a motion guide layer by dragging a layer slightly up and to the right*

To undo this association, simply drag the butterfly layer slightly down and to the left again. Practice this a few times, and when you're finished, make sure the butterfly layer is reassociated (the T-square has turned into the comet).

Motion guides must have a clear beginning and end point, as does the squiggle shown. Guides that cross over each other may cause unexpected results, so take care not to confuse Animate CC. Also, make sure your motion guide line extends the full length between two keyframes, including the keyframe at either end.

---

5. Thanks to the Snap setting in the tweened frames (see the Properties panel while clicking anywhere inside the tween), the butterfly should already be snapped to the closer end point at the last keyframe. Scrub to make sure. The butterfly should follow the squiggle along its tween. If it doesn't, make sure to snap the butterfly symbol's registration point to the squiggle's left end in frame 1 and snap it again to the right end in frame 75.

CHAPTER 7 ANIMATION

6. Click anywhere inside the tween, and put a check mark in the Orient to Path check box in the Tweening area of the Properties panel (as shown in Figure 7-50). Scrub the timeline to see how this affects the butterfly's movement. The butterfly now points in the direction described by the squiggle.

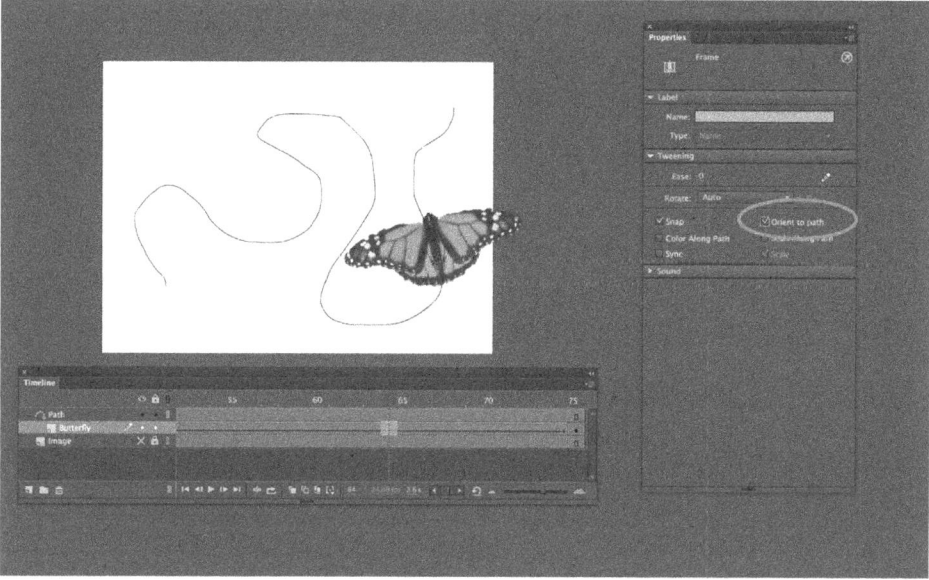

Figure 7-50. *A motion guide affects the tweened path of a symbol*

For more realism, let's add some complexity, as described earlier in the "Combining Timelines" section.

7. Double-click the Butterfly asset in the Library to enter its timeline. Add a keyframe to the LeftWing and RightWing layers in frames 10 and 20.

8. In the Body layer, click in frame 20 and extend the frames to that point (Insert ➤ Timeline ➤ Frame).

9. Select both wings symbols at frame 10 and use the Free Transform tool to reduce their width by about two-thirds.

10. Add classic tweens to the LeftWing and RightWing layers, as shown in Figure 7-51. Make sure to add your tweens between keyframes 1 and 10 and also between keyframes 10 and 20.

CHAPTER 7 ■ ANIMATION

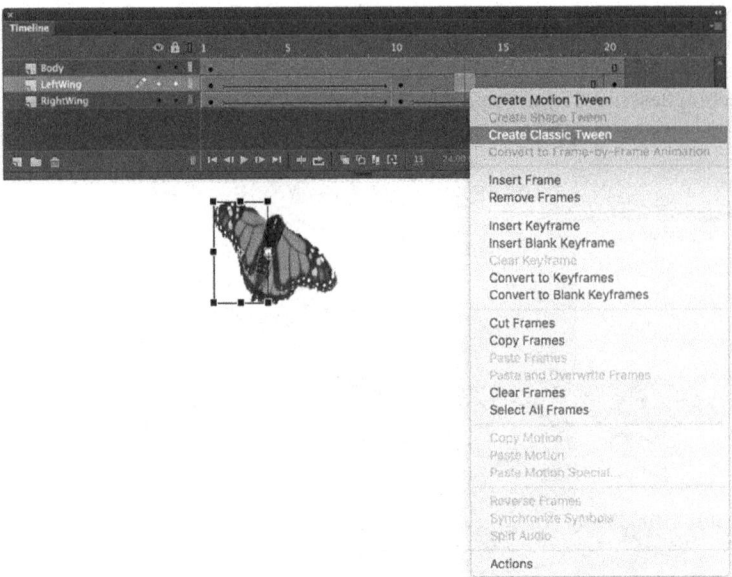

Figure 7-51. Tweening a timeline inside the butterfly graphic symbol

11. Return to the main timeline, turn on the visibility of the Image layer, and test your movie to see the combined effect.

Did you notice an alternate way to create a motion guide in Figure 7-51? The context menu features a selection called Add Classic Motion Guide just beneath the Guide selection discussed in Step 2. If you choose that instead, Animate CC handles the gentle dragging described in Step 3 for you.

Tweening a Mask

Animating masks is no more difficult than animating normal shapes or symbols. In fact, the only difference is the status of the layer that contains the mask.

Animating a Mask

In Chapter 3, you used text to create a mask. In this exercise, you'll use a shape for a mask, and you'll apply a shape tween to it to produce an iris-wipe transition, like in the old movies.

1. Open the `19_MaskTween.fla` file in this chapter's exercise folder. You'll see three layers: a photo of a doorway in Guangzhou, China, plants in a garden to provide some background texture, and a small yellow dot.

2. Use the Free Transform tool to increase the size of the dot in the keyframe in frame 30 so that it covers the photo.

CHAPTER 7 ANIMATION

3. Because the dot is a shape, apply a shape tween between the keyframes in the dot layer.

4. Right-click (Windows) or Control+click (Mac) and select Mask to convert the dot layer to a mask layer.

5. Scrub the timeline to see the result, as shown in Figure 7-52. Easy as pie!

Figure 7-52. *Masks can be tweened just as easily as regular shapes or symbols*

365

CHAPTER 7 ANIMATION

Using Motion Guides with Masks

Often, once new designers get comfortable with motion guides and masks, they come to the realization that a layer can be converted to either a guide or mask layer, but not both. Naturally, the question arises, "Is it possible to tween a mask along a motion guide?" The answer is yes, and yet again, combined timelines come to the rescue. Let's see how it's done:

1. Open the 20_MaskTweenMotionGuide.fla file in this chapter's exercise folder. The setup here is very similar to the MaskTweenk.fla file, except that the dot layer is now named guide mask.

2. Double-click the DotMotion symbol to enter its timeline. Confirm that a dot symbol is classic tweened in association with a motion guide. Return to the main timeline.

3. Right-click (Windows) or Control+click (Mac) the GuideMask layer and select Mask from the context menu. This nested combination gives you a motion-guided mask!

Tweening Filter Effects

It may come as a bit of a surprise, but not only can objects—graphic symbols, text, and movieclips—be tweened but so can filters. Just keep in mind that filters can be applied only to movieclips or text.

In this example, we visit a lounge in Las Vegas and, using filter tweens, fix an obviously broken neon sign. What we are going to do is to have that broken tube flicker on and off as neon is wont to do on occasion. Here's how:

1. Open the 21_BlueMoon.fla file in your exercise folder and take a gander at the timeline. It is quite obvious from Figure 7-53 that the M in the sign is not working. To fix it, we started by using the Pen tool to trace out the shape of the tube, filled it with a 2-point white stroke, and converted the shape to a movieclip.

CHAPTER 7 ■ ANIMATION

Figure 7-53. *We start with a broken neon sign*

2. Click the movieclip on the stage and apply a Glow filter with these settings:
   - Blur X: 5
   - Blur Y: 5
   - Strength: 100%
   - Quality: High
   - Color: F0FDF8

How did we know what color to use? We zoomed in on the lights, clicked the filter's Color chip to open the Color Picker, and, when you move the cursor over the image, it changes to the Eyedropper. We found a color we liked, clicked it, and that became the color for our glow.

3. Add a keyframe in frame 60 of the M layer and add a classic tween between the two keyframes.
4. Add eight more randomly placed keyframes between the two keyframes.

5. Select each new keyframe and change the Blur and Strength values of the filter. The objective here is to create the effect of a flickering neon sign.

   When finished, return to frame 1, and press the Return/Enter key to see your attempt, as shown in Figure 7-54, at a neon repair. If you really want to "rock" this sign, try tweening the alpha from the Color effect drop-down to fade the letter in and out.

Figure 7-54. Repairing a neon sign is easy with filter tweens

Programmatic Animation

To this point in the chapter, we have explored physically moving things from "here" to "there" using tweens. In this, the final section, we are going to let both ActionScript and JavaScript shove things around. This is a rather large subject because, as you have discovered, animation involves a lot more than motion. Most everything you have done to this point—move, distort, swap, change—can just as easily be done using code.

Our intention is to show you how this is accomplished. That's the good news. The bad news is we can't cover the subject in any great depth because it is massive. Still, once you understand, in broad terms, how code moves stuff around, you can start to fully explore how games are created, slide shows are pulled together, and interface elements such as sliders are constructed.

You may recall that we've actually already accomplished a bit of animation in Chapter 5: Audio. Remember the final exercise that involved generating rain droplets which continually animated across the stage – creating a rain storm? That was an additional taste of programmatic animation you may want to review after completing this chapter.

Additionally, Animate CC contains code snippets and templates focused around programmatic animation that are ideal learning tools, and we strongly urge you to fully explore them and to take from what you learn with them and apply it to your projects.

In this section, you are going to do the following:

- Let Animate CC convert motion to data.
- Create a small game that uses the keyboard to control an object's motion.
- Create random motion that simulates particles jiggling around in a suspension.

Again, these are very simple projects, using very simple code to accomplish some very basic tasks. Even so, if you are new to this, you have to start somewhere, and this is as good a place as any. Let's start by bouncing that rabbit around the screen.

Copying Motion as Data

You'll start with a really neat option that fits this chapter like a glove. The option is called Copy Motion. Here's how it works:

1. Open the `22_CopyMotionAS.fla` file in the Chapter 7 exercise folder. You will see that we have added an animated ball and that rabbit to the stage (see Figure 7-55).

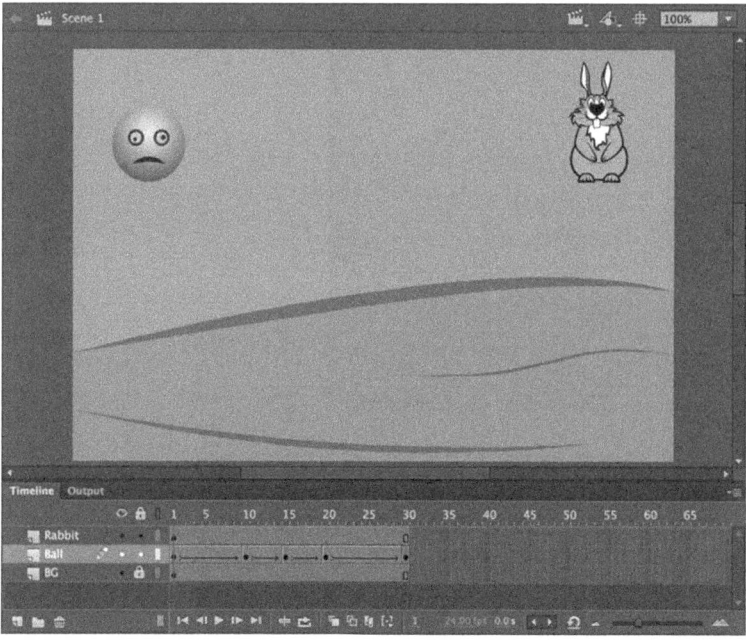

Figure 7-55. *We start with a confused ball and one really dumb rabbit*

369

CHAPTER 7 ■ ANIMATION

2. Scrub the playhead across the timeline. You will see the ball fall to the bottom of the stage, squash, stretch, and bounce back up to the top of the stage. Let's apply that animation to the rabbit.

3. Select the first frame of the ball layer, press the Shift key, and then select frame 29. This selects all but the last frame of that layer. Why all but the last? Because only the first 29 frames will contain a classic tween.

4. With the frames selected, either select Edit ➤ Timeline ➤ Copy Motion, as shown Figure 7-56, or right-click (Windows) or Control+click (Mac) and select Copy Motion from the context menu.

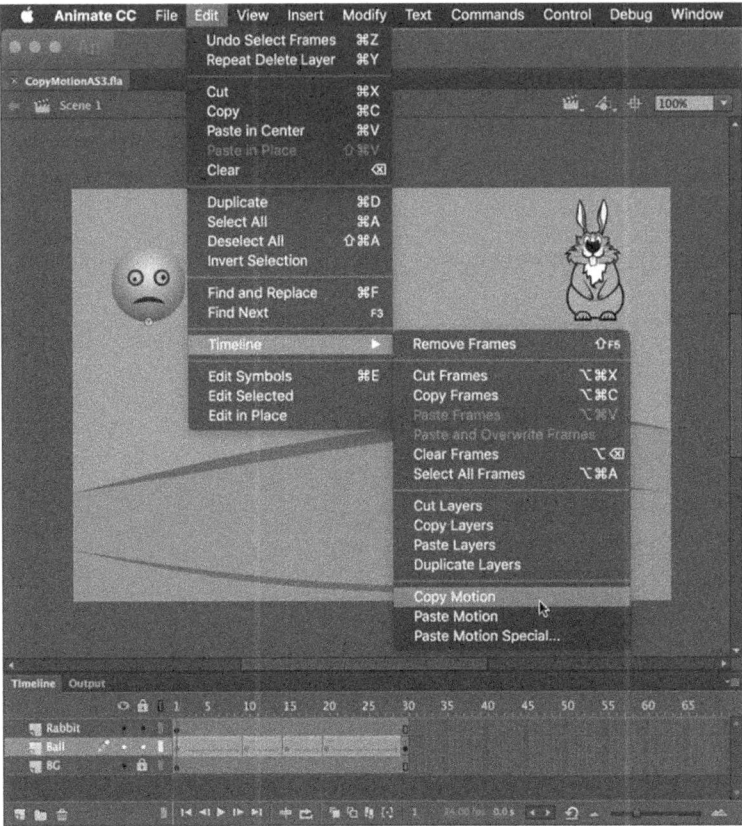

Figure 7-56. *You can access the command through the Edit menu item or the context menu*

What you have done is ask Animate CC to translate the motion of the ball into raw data so that we can then apply that same motion to the rabbit.

5. Select the Rabbit MovieClip symbol instance on the stage and right-click to summon the context menu. Choose Paste Motion and the exact same motion will be applied to the rabbit. Just as when the motion was copied, this option can be accessed from Edit ➤ Timeline ➤ Paste Motion as well.

370

6. Save and test the movie. The rabbit, Figure 7-57, takes on the animation and distortion of the ball in the published project.

Figure 7-57. *Only stupid rabbits enjoy being squashed*

Now that you know how this works, there are obviously some rules. The motion must be a classic or motion tween using a symbol (any symbol will do; the ball happens to be a movieclip, as is the rabbit). The great thing about this feature is that the tween can contain the following properties and features (many of which we've talked about in this chapter):

- X position
- Y position
- Horizontal scale
- Vertical scale
- Rotation and skew
- Color
- Filters
- Blend mode

In fact, you may have noticed that directly beneath the Paste Motion menu option is the similarly named Paste Motion Special. This option will summon the Paste Motion Special dialog box (Figure 7-58), which allows you to select which properties of the copied motion data you want to apply to the instance that has been selected.

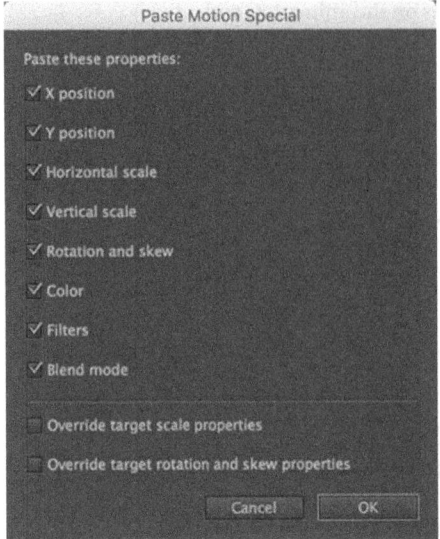

Figure 7-58. *It is easy to select exactly which motion properties you want to use*

The bottom line is that you can create, transfer, and reuse some pretty amazing scripted animation effects without writing a single line of code.

Using the Keyboard to Control Motion

In this very simple example, we are going to use the arrow keys on your keyboard to move a ball across the stage. Though a very simple example, it is a starting point for many games requiring a user to move something from here to there using the keyboard.

Let's get started:

1. Open the `KeyboardControl.fla` file found in your exercise folder. This is an HTML5 Canvas document, and as such, we will be using JavaScript for any interactivity.

   When it opens, you will see, as shown in Figure 7-59, a number of layers and assets have been assembled for this project:

   - The Actions layer is where all of our code will exist.

   - The Text layer includes a set of dynamic text fields. One, named `keyNotice`, exists to output the various key codes generated by our keyboard interactions. The second text field, named `wallNotice`, is available to provide a status or alert to the user, when appropriate.

   - The Player layer contains a MovieClip symbol instance with the instance name of `player`. This is the asset we want to respond to our keypresses by moving across the stage.

   - Next, we have a Mask layer named `FloorMask` and nested within this are layers containing our static background assets, which appear as a rough map.

CHAPTER 7 ANIMATION

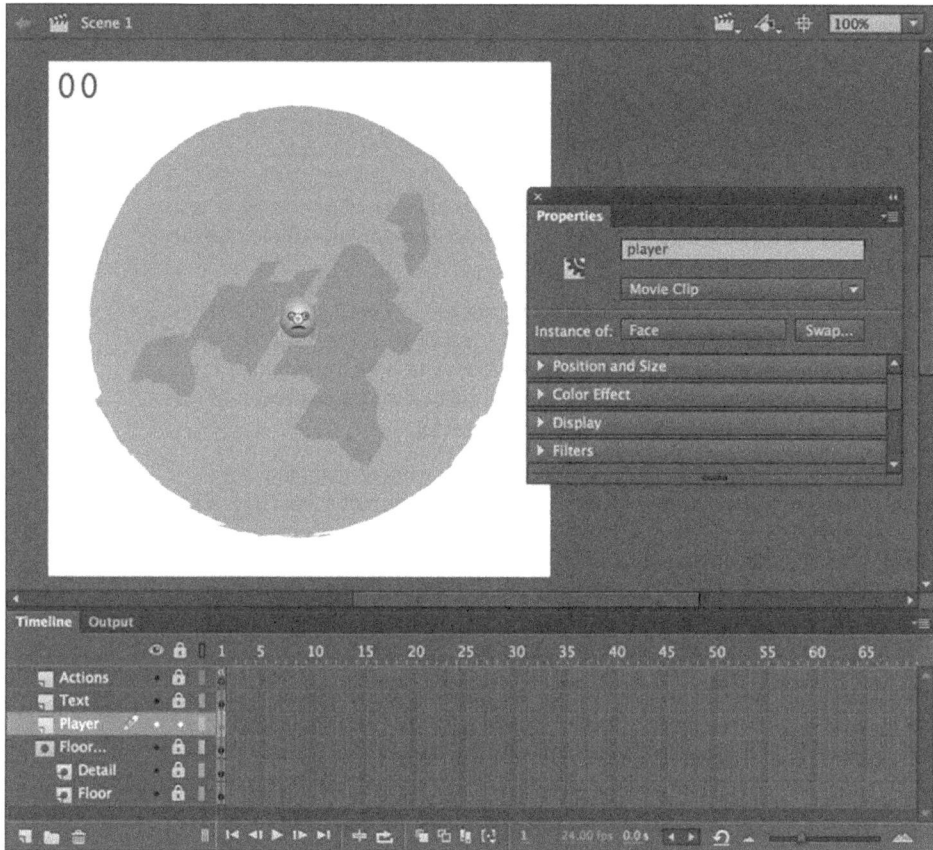

Figure 7-59. *The keyboard control document includes a number of layers*

2. With a basic project overview out of the way, it is time to enter some code. Select the Actions layer and open the Actions panel. Type the following code snippet into the script pane:

```
window.addEventListener("keydown", handleKeyPress);
function handleKeyPress(e) {
	exportRoot.keyNotice.text = e.keyCode;
	var p = exportRoot.player;
	switch (e.keyCode) {
		case 37:
			p.x = p.x -= 20;
			break;
		case 38:
			p.y = p.y -= 20;
			break;
		case 39:
			p.x = p.x += 20;
			break;
		case 40:
```

373

```
                    p.y = p.y += 20;
                    break;
        }
        e.preventDefault();
}
```

The code block starts by having the project listen for keyboard input and, when it detects it, executes the `handleKeyPress()` function. That function makes up the remainder of our code for now.

The remainder of the code essentially tells Animate CC: "Don't do a thing unless one of the four arrow keys—UP, DOWN, RIGHT, or LEFT—is pressed." The use of the `switch` statement makes life easier for you because it tests for a condition—Is the UP arrow pressed? —and, if it is, to do something. The `break` statement tells the project that there are no other conditions to test for.

Every keypress is assigned a unique key code. This is what we feed into the `switch` statement as an argument to test against in the form of `e.keyCode`. A key code is numeric and if you are curious as to the key code value of any key on your keyboard... when this project is run in the browser, it will actually tell you which key has been pressed - even if it is a key we are not responding to in this project. We do this by simply outputting the value of `e.keyCode` to the dynamic text field on the stage via `exportRoot.keyNotice.text = e.keyCode;`.

Each of the keypresses is contained in a `case` statement, which is how things are done when a `switch` statement is in play. The beauty of `case` statements is they replace what would otherwise be your sitting down and writing out a separate function for each keypress, or using a series of `if/else` conditionals. It puts all of that in one tidy package.

The magic is found in how the `player` instance moves—`p.x += 20` or `p.y-= 20`. Remember, all on screen motion can occur on only two axes: the X-axis for left to right motion and the Y-axis for up and down. The operator (+= or - =) tells Animate CC which direction to move. If a minus sign is used, the instance moves to the left or up. Use the plus sign, and the opposite occurs. The number, 20, tells your project how many pixels the instance will move each time a key is pressed.

You may be curious about the `exportRoot` variable. This is a special variable in CreateJS that will always refer to the root stage scope. So anytime we need to refer to objects that exist on the stage from within JavaScript functions, we can always employ `exportRoot` to access them.

We are also creating a bit of a coding shortcut with the p variable. The line of code which reads `var p = exportRoot.player;` is assigning a reference to the actual player instance on the root stage to a variable named p. It is a convenience feature and just makes your code quicker to type and less verbose!

3. Save and test the movie. You will be told which key has been pressed (see Figure 7-60).

CHAPTER 7 ■ ANIMATION

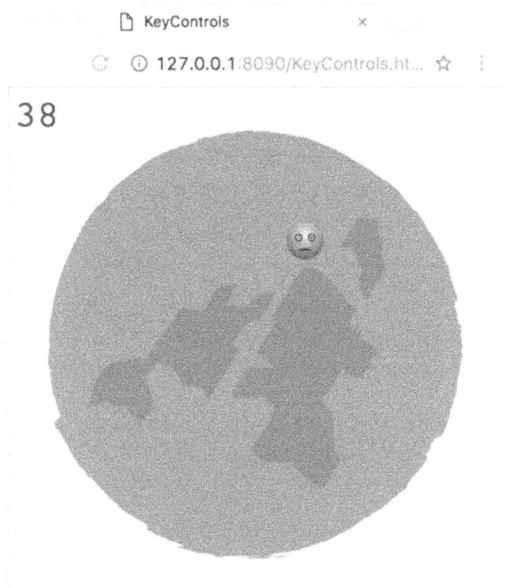

Figure 7-60. *The key code is output as you press each key*

Adding Simple Movement Constraints

We now have an interactive Animate CC project that allows control of a MovieClip symbol instance through keypresses using JavaScript and CreateJS. You may have noticed that if you move the player instance in any one direction for too long; it will exit the stage completely. That's no good! Let's employ a system of constraints to make sure our little fellow can never leave.

1. Go ahead and select the Actions layer again and open up the Actions panel if it's not already visible.

2. Add the following function directly below all existing code in this project:

```
function checkBounds() {
        var p = exportRoot.player;
        if(p.x < 60){
                p.x = 60;
                exportRoot.wallNotice.text = "NO ESCAPE";
        }else if(p.x > 340){
                p.x = 340;
                exportRoot.wallNotice.text = "NO ESCAPE";
        }
        if(p.y < 60){
                p.y = 60;
                exportRoot.wallNotice.text = "NO ESCAPE";
        }else if(p.y > 340){
                p.y = 340;
                exportRoot.wallNotice.text = "NO ESCAPE";
        }
}
```

375

This function will effectively check to see whether the player instance moves too close to any of the four edges of our world by checking its X and Y position against certain stage X and Y coordinates. To accomplish this, we employ a series of `if/else` statements.

We cannot use a `switch` statement as we did before, since we are checking a number of differing properties and values. `switch` statements are generally quicker to execute and simpler to read, but, as this example shows, they are not always the best solution.

Take for instance the X position of our instance. If the user presses the up key too much, the instance will eventually arrive at the top of the stage. We check to see whether the X position of our player instance is less than 60. If that is the case, we simply force the instance back to a position of 60 along the X axis—thus never allowing it to escape the bounds of our stage.

We also go ahead and alert the users that they are not able to proceed in the current direction by outputting a message of NO ESCAPE to the `wallNotice` dynamic text field on the stage.

1. We now have our function to constrain the movement, but we need to invoke this after each keypress. In order to do this, add the following code to the `handleKeyPress()` function, right after our `switch` statement:

    ```
    checkBounds();
    ```

    This function will now be invoked at every keypress.

2. We also want to clear out our status to an empty string at each keypress. Add the following line of code to the top of the `handleKeyPress()` function, just before the `switch` statement:

    ```
    exportRoot.wallNotice.text = "";
    ```

    This will set the value of this text field to an empty string.

3. Test your project. Note that the player instance can never get near the bounds of the project stage any longer, and when it does, a NO ESCAPE alert is shown to the user, as seen in Figure 7-61.

CHAPTER 7 ■ ANIMATION

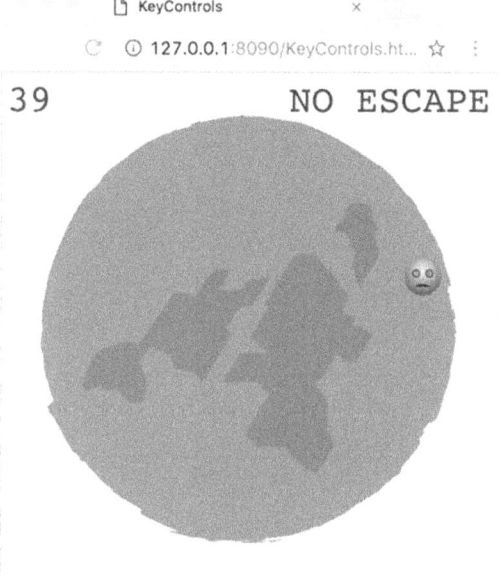

Figure 7-61. *No escape. Sorry!*

The complete code for this project is as follows:

```
window.addEventListener("keydown", handleKeyPress);

function handleKeyPress(e) {
	exportRoot.wallNotice.text = "";
	exportRoot.keyNotice.text = e.keyCode;
	var p = exportRoot.player;
	switch (e.keyCode) {
		case 37:
			p.x = p.x -= 20;
			break;
		case 38:
			p.y = p.y -= 20;
			break;
		case 39:
			p.x = p.x += 20;
			break;
		case 40:
			p.y = p.y += 20;
			break;
	}
	e.preventDefault();
	checkBounds();
}
```

377

```
function checkBounds() {
        var p = exportRoot.player;
        if(p.x < 60){
                p.x = 60;
                exportRoot.wallNotice.text = "NO ESCAPE";
        }else if(p.x > 340){
                p.x = 340;
                exportRoot.wallNotice.text = "NO ESCAPE";
        }
        if(p.y < 60){
                p.y = 60;
                exportRoot.wallNotice.text = "NO ESCAPE";
        }else if(p.y > 340){
                p.y = 340;
                exportRoot.wallNotice.text = "NO ESCAPE";
        }
}
```

Keyboard Control Using ActionScript

In the preceding section, we saw an example of how to perform keyboard control using JavaScript in an HTML5 Canvas document. It is also possible to perform the same actions with an ActionScript document. In fact, Adobe provides a code snippet for this very thing within the Code Snippets panel!

You can easily convert the previously used HTML5 Canvas document to employ ActionScript 3.0 by choosing Commands ➤ Convert to Other Document Formats from the application menu with that document open and selected. Choose Flash ActionScript 3.0/AIR as the new document type from the selector, provide a location and name to save the new file as, and save it to your machine. The new ActionScript 3.0 document will then open up with all of the assets and timelines preserved and with all the JavaScript commented out.

With the ActionScript 3.0 document prepared, you can now perform the following steps:

1. Be sure the Player layer is unlocked and select the player MovieClip symbol instance on the stage.

2. With that instance selected, open the Code Snippets panel from Window ➤ Code Snippets.

3. Open the ActionScript folder within the Code Snippets panel and then the Animation folder within that. Select the first item in that list named Move with Keyboard Arrows.

4. With our intended snippet selected, click the Add to current frame icon at the top left of the Code Snippets panel. The snippet will be added to the Actions layer on frame 1, below the commented JavaScript code.

5. Open the Actions panel and have a look.

The following code is what will be placed on the selected frame in your Actions layer:

```
/* Move with Keyboard Arrows
Allows the specified symbol instance to be moved with the keyboard arrows.

Instructions:
1. To increase or decrease the amount of movement, replace the number 5 below with the
number of pixels you want the symbol instance to move with each keypress.
Note the number 5 appears four times in the code below.
*/

var upPressed: Boolean = false;
var downPressed: Boolean = false;
var leftPressed: Boolean = false;
var rightPressed: Boolean = false;

player.addEventListener(Event.ENTER_FRAME, fl_MoveInDirectionOfKey);
stage.addEventListener(KeyboardEvent.KEY_DOWN, fl_SetKeyPressed);
stage.addEventListener(KeyboardEvent.KEY_UP, fl_UnsetKeyPressed);

function fl_MoveInDirectionOfKey(event: Event) {
        if (upPressed) {
                player.y -= 5;
        }
        if (downPressed) {
                player.y += 5;
        }
        if (leftPressed) {
                player.x -= 5;
        }
        if (rightPressed) {
                player.x += 5;
        }
}

function fl_SetKeyPressed(event: KeyboardEvent): void {
        switch (event.keyCode) {
                case Keyboard.UP:
                        {
                                upPressed = true;
                                break;
                        }
                case Keyboard.DOWN:
                        {
                                downPressed = true;
                                break;
                        }
```

```
                case Keyboard.LEFT:
                    {
                            leftPressed = true;
                            break;
                    }
                case Keyboard.RIGHT:
                    {
                            rightPressed = true;
                            break;
                    }
        }
}
function fl_UnsetKeyPressed(event: KeyboardEvent): void {
        switch (event.keyCode) {
                case Keyboard.UP:
                    {
                            upPressed = false;
                            break;
                    }
                case Keyboard.DOWN:
                    {
                            downPressed = false;
                            break;
                    }
                case Keyboard.LEFT:
                    {
                            leftPressed = false;
                            break;
                    }
                case Keyboard.RIGHT:
                    {
                            rightPressed = false;
                            break;
                    }
        }
}
```

We will not get into every line of code here, but you should immediately recognize a number of structures and logical conditions that also exist in the JavaScript example. For instance, we are using the exact same key codes across both languages, along with a number of `switch` statements. Being ActionScript, certain items are more verbose and include strict data types.

If you test this movie, you'll notice that the key codes do not print out on the stage and the constraints we added in JavaScript are not accounted for within this snippet. Since we have the custom JavaScript commented out, it would be fairly simple to convert the instructions which feed key code values into the text field and constraint logic into ActionScript.

Want to test your ability to convert such structures across programming languages? This is a great opportunity to try your hand at it!

Creating Random Motion

The final exercise in this section has its roots with a Scottish botanist named Robert Brown who worked out the math around the random movement of particles suspended in a solution such as water or air. When ActionScript arrived in Flash/Animate CC, it was only a matter of time before such wizards as Jared Tarbell (http://levitated.net/) and James Patterson (http://presstube.com/project.php?id=259) started using math to create particles and jaw-dropping programmatic art. See Jared's example in Figure 7-62.

Figure 7-62. *Gathering line from levitated.net.*

Random Motion Using Templates

In this example, we are going to move into the realm of design heresy and actually use a template that comes packaged with Animate CC. Many regard these things with disdain, claiming "real designers don't use templates." Though there is some truth to this, we also might add the templates that ship with Animate CC are invaluable teaching and learning tools—similar to how one would use code snippets as seen previously in this chapter. Let's get started:

1. Select File ➤ New and click the Templates tab in the New Document dialog box.

2. Select the Animation category, and select Random Movement Brownian (Figure 7-63) in the Templates area. On the right side, you will see a preview of the template's stage and a brief description of what the template does underneath it. Click OK to open the template.

CHAPTER 7 ■ ANIMATION

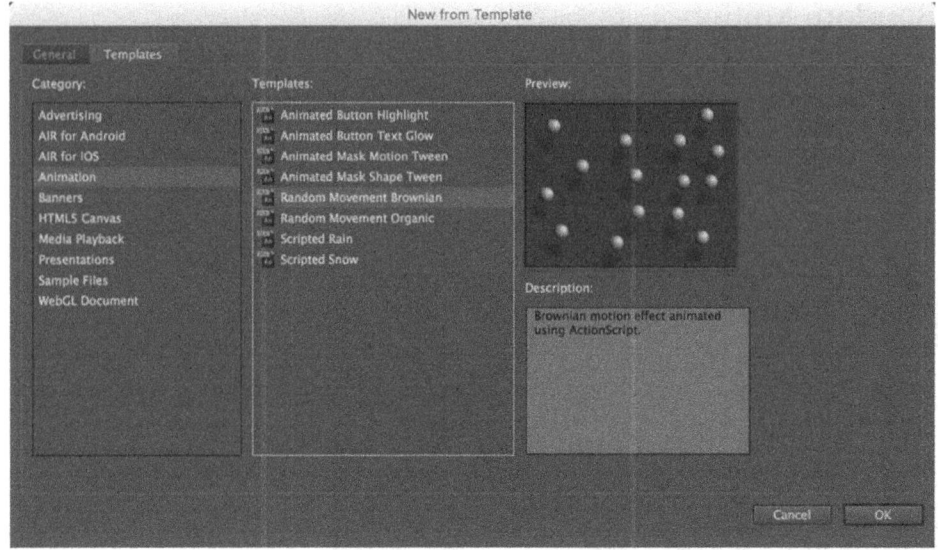

***Figure 7-63.** Choosing a template in Animate CC*

All templates open as an Untitled document. When the template opens, feel free to save it to your exercise folder. In this case, Adobe has told us how to check out the code by putting the instruction in a guide layer, which will be ignored when the SWF is created. See Figure 7-64.

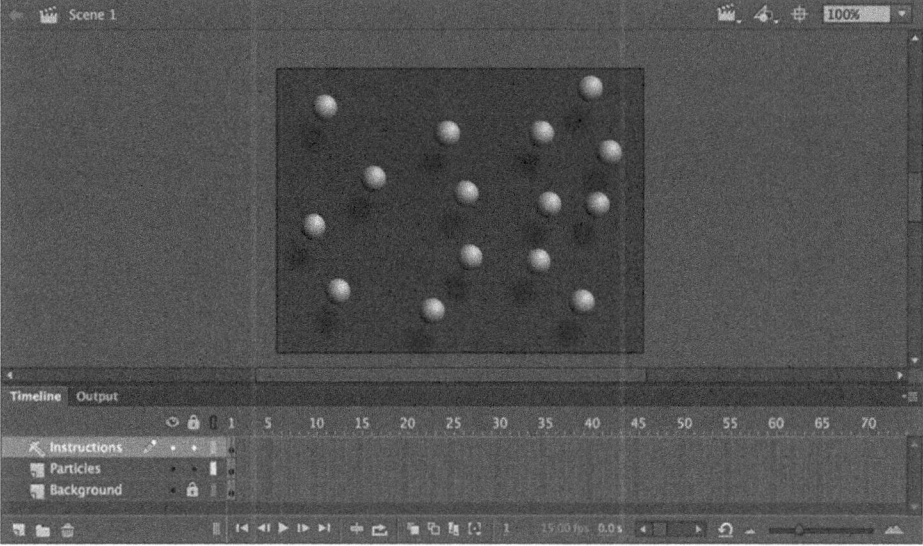

***Figure 7-64.** The open template document*

382

3. To start, test the movie. You will see the little green balls jiggling and moving around on the stage. Close the SWF and let's see how that happens.

4. Double-click any of the balls on the stage to open the Particle MovieClip symbol found in the Library.

5. Select the first frame of the Actions layers and open the Actions panel. When it opens, you will see this code:

```
var moveAmount:Number = 12;
addEventListener(Event.ENTER_FRAME, fl_randomParticleMove);
function fl_randomParticleMove(evt:Event):void {
        var xChange:Number = Math.round( Math.random()*moveAmount - (moveAmount/2) );
        var yChange:Number = Math.round( Math.random()*moveAmount - (moveAmount/2) );
        x += xChange;
        y += yChange;
        if(x > 550) { x = 0; }
        if(x < 0) { x = 550; }
        if(y > 400) { y = 0; }
        if(y < 0) { y = 400; }
}
```

Your first reaction to the code most likely was "Come on, there's got to be more to this." That is quite understandable considering you saw all of those balls jittering around the stage in the SWF. What you need to understand is that each ball on the stage is a copy of this MovieClip symbol, and the ball in the MovieClip is managed by this simple code. Let's go through it.

The code starts off by setting a number for how far the ball will move. In this case, the distance is 12 pixels. To change the effect, feel free to play a "what if?" game and change the number. "What if?" games are wonderful ways of learning how things work in ActionScript. In this case, it would be "What if I change the number to 24. What would that look like?" Do that, and the balls, when you test the SWF, move into jitter overdrive. Reduce the number to 6, and things slow down. The rest of the code explains how that happens.

This is a one-frame movie, so the next line listens for the playhead to come back into the frame—ENTER_FRAME—and when it does, the function is executed. This is a way of looping a one-frame timeline.

The function uses math to change the X and the Y position of the ball, each time the playhead comes back into the frame. This is accomplished by first using the `Math.round()` method to strip off any decimal points that result from the calculation between the bracket. The calculation creates a random number between 0 and 1, multiplies it by the moveAmount set in line 1, and multiplies that result by half of the moveAmount variable. To wrap your mind around this, let's walk through the math assuming the random number chosen is .92:

```
var xChange:Number = Math.round( .92*12 - (12/2) );
var xChange:Number = Math.round( .92*12 - (6) );
var xChange:Number = Math.round( 11.04 - (6) );
var xChange:Number = Math.round(5.04);
var xChange:Number = 5;
```

That result is then used to move the ball over and down on the X- and Y-axes by 5 pixels.

The if statement keeps an eye on the location of the ball on the stage. Obviously there is a potential for the number to eventually move the ball off the stage. This statement checks its location and, if it does indeed move outside of the stage's 500 by 450 boundary, yanks it back on to the stage.

CHAPTER 7 ■ ANIMATION

Advanced Random Motion Using JavaScript

Let's now move on from the use of a template and write our own code to enable Brownian motion using JavaScript in an HTML5 Canvas document. Some of the structural mechanics behind this are a bit different than what we have seen with the ActionScript template, but a lot of the concepts will be similar. We will be writing all of our code on a single frame in our Actions layer.

1. Open the HTML5 Canvas file named `24_RandomMotion.fla` from this chapter's exercise folder. The first thing to notice is that there is really nothing on the stage or the timeline at all. There exists a single Actions layer and that is that!

2. Open the Library panel and you will see a single MovieClip symbol named `Face`. We will generate a great number of instances from this one MovieClip and place them on the stage.

   To enable this functionality, we must provide a linkage identifier to this symbol. Notice (as seen in Figure 7-65) that a linkage identifier of `Face` has been supplied already.

Figure 7-65. *The Face MovieClip is assigned a Linkage identifier of Face*

   While we have simply duplicated the name of the MovieClip symbol as the linkage identifier, it would also be completely fine to use a different value for each. The important thing is that the linkage identifier is present because that is the only way we can address Library objects using JavaScript.

3. Select frame 1 of the Actions layer and open the Actions panel to begin writing the code necessary to get things moving. In the script pane, enter the following code:

```
var numFaces = 100;
var moveAmount = 12;

function random(min, max) {
        return Math.random()*(max-min+1)+min;
};
```

Here, we set a variable numFaces, which will determine how many symbol instances are generated. A second variable, moveAmount, determines the amount of movement which feeds the Brownian movement calculations.

Additionally, we establish a small utility function named random(), which accepts a minimum and maximum number and returns some number between these two. We'll use this in a number of places in our code to help randomize various properties of our Face instances.

4. The next piece of code will create a CreateJS Container object and add it to the stage. We will populate this Container with our dynamically generated Face instances.

```
var faceContainer = new createjs.Container();
this.addChild(faceContainer);
```

Using a Container will allow us to perform actions like counting the number of children within, move all internal instances as one object, or even completely remove all instances with a single command.

Even if you're not explicitly using any of this Container functionality, it's often a good idea to employ a Container when dealing with many objects, just in case you need to use it down the road.

5. Next is the code to generate all of our Face instances. Include this for loop directly following the previous code snippet.

```
for(var i=0; i<numFaces; i++) {
        var face = new lib.Face();
        var fs = random(0.5, 2.0);
        face.x = random(0, 400);
        face.y = random(0, 400);
        face.alpha = random(0.2, 0.9);
        face.scaleX = face.scaleY = fs;
        faceContainer.addChild(face);
}
```

CHAPTER 7 ANIMATION

This for loop exists apart from any other function in our code, and thus will only execute once. It will perform the actions within it a certain number of times and then stop. The number of times that our loop will run is determined by the numFaces variable we declared a few steps back—instructing our loop to run 100 times generating 100 MovieClip symbol instances from the Library.

Upon each iteration of the loop, we first declare a variable face, which references a new instance of our Face MovieClip symbol by referencing lib.Face() - remember that Face, in this case, is our linkage identifier. The lib object is the way in which CreateJS references the project Library.

With our new instance created, we then make use of the random() function established earlier to set a number of properties determining X and Y position, scale, and alpha of each instance. Once that is complete, the new instance is added to our Container object and thus made visible on the stage displaying the properties provided.

6. Now to handle instance movement. We will employ the CreateJS Ticker to execute the same exact code we saw in the template exercise (but adapted to JavaScript). Enter the following code at the end of the current JavaScript code:

```
createjs.Ticker.addEventListener("tick", onTick);
function onTick(e) {
	for(var i=0; i<numFaces; i++) {
		var face = faceContainer.getChildAt(i);

		var xChange = Math.round( Math.random() * moveAmount - (moveAmount/2) );
		var yChange = Math.round( Math.random() * moveAmount - (moveAmount/2) );

		face.x += xChange;
		face.y += yChange;

		if(face.x > 400) { face.x = 0; }
		if(face.x < 0) { face.x = 400; }
		if(face.y > 400) { face.y = 0; }
		if(face.y < 0) { face.y = 400; }
	}
}
```

Compare this JavaScript code snippet with the Brownian movement code from the ActionScript template. Apart from language differences such as data types and how we reference our object to move, the code is basically identical. JavaScript and ActionScript are really not so different at a fundamental level.

7. With our code complete, go ahead and test your project (Figure 7-66) in the browser. You will see 100 Face MovieClip symbol instances generate with varying properties which employ Brownian movement to wriggle across the screen. Additionally, the resulting animation will be different every time that this project is run.

CHAPTER 7 ■ ANIMATION

Figure 7-66. *The resulting advanced Brownian motion in Canvas*

The full code for this example is included here:

```
var numFaces = 100;
var moveAmount = 12;

function random(min, max) {
        return Math.random()*(max-min+1)+min;
};

var faceContainer = new createjs.Container();
this.addChild(faceContainer);

for(var i=0; i<numFaces; i++) {
        var face = new lib.Face();
        var fs = random(0.5, 2.0);
        face.x = random(0, 400);
        face.y = random(0, 400);
        face.alpha = random(0.2, 0.9);
        face.scaleX = face.scaleY = fs;
        faceContainer.addChild(face);
}
```

```
createjs.Ticker.addEventListener("tick", onTick);
function onTick(e) {
        for(var i=0; i<numFaces; i++) {
                var face = faceContainer.getChildAt(i);

                var xChange = Math.round( Math.random() * moveAmount - (moveAmount/2) );
                var yChange = Math.round( Math.random() * moveAmount - (moveAmount/2) );

                face.x += xChange;
                face.y += yChange;

                if(face.x > 400) { face.x = 0; }
                if(face.x < 0) { face.x = 400; }
                if(face.y > 400) { face.y = 0; }
                if(face.y < 0) { face.y = 400; }
        }
}
```

Brownian Bonus Round

If you are new to writing code, this is a great place to start the process of understanding that, when it comes to code, you usually play with numbers. Just because this is the code you were given doesn't mean you don't have permission to change it. Try the following and see what happens in your project when you make the change:

- Change the moveAmount number.

- Change the moveAmount/2 calculation to moveAmount*.3 or any other number or operator such as -, * and +.

- Reduce the values in the if statement to see how a more confined space will affect the movie.

- Add a few more copies of the MovieClip symbol to the stage by manipulating the numFaces value.

What You Have Learned

In this chapter, you learned the following:

- The difference between a shape tween and a classic tween
- Various methods of using easing to add reality to your animations
- How to use the timeline and the Properties panel to manage animations
- How to create and use motion guides in animation
- How to animate a mask
- How to translate an animation into raw data
- How to create programmatic animation

This has been a busy chapter, and we've covered one side of the Animate CC animation coin. The path so far has led from tweening shapes to turning animations into raw data. In many respects, this is an important chapter, because whether you care to admit it, Animate CC is quite widely regarded as an animation program first—all that other cool stuff it does is secondary. Many of the techniques and principles presented in this chapter are the fundamentals of animation in Animate CC. If there is one message you should get from this chapter, it is pay attention to how things move.

Thanks to the motion tweening model, that concept—how things move—has been flipped on its head, just like a coin, in a really cool way. The new approach doesn't negate any of the techniques you've seen here. It's just that your kitchen has gotten bigger, and there are a lot of new gadgets! Whenever you're ready to continue cooking, just turn the page.

CHAPTER 8

The Motion Editor and Inverse Kinematics

What you saw in the previous chapter was a compendium of traditional animation techniques—traditional not in the Flash animation pioneer John Kricfalusi sense, but in the sense that they represent the basic tools animators working in Animate CC have used since time out of mind. Some tools don't change simply because they don't have to; *they're that useful.* The exciting part is that Adobe introduced a new set of tools back in the Flash Professional CS4 era in addition to the time-tested tools. This double-whammy puts you in charge of the workflow that makes the most sense to you. Use one set or the other or combine them—the choice is yours. The best part is that because this is animation, you pretty much have to drink a broth of lukewarm poisonwood oils to not have fun while you're working.

Here's what we'll cover in this chapter:

- Motion tweening, using the Motion Editor and the Timeline panel
- Advanced easing with the Motion Editor's graphs
- Manipulating motion paths
- Using motion presets and copying motion from one symbol to another
- Applying inverse kinematics (IK), including the Bone and Bind tools
- IK tweening

The following files are used in this chapter (located in Chapter08/ExerciseFiles_Ch08/Exercise/):

- 01_Map.fla
- 02_EasePin.fla
- 03_CustomEasePin.fla
- 04_MultipleEasePin.fla
- 05_PixelDisposal.fla
- 06_MotionGuideSimple.fla
- 07_MotionGuideComplex.fla
- 08_MotionPreset.fla
- 09_Bones.fla
- 10_Springs.fla

CHAPTER 8 ■ THE MOTION EDITOR AND INVERSE KINEMATICS

- 11_BonesRigged.fla
- 12_Poses.fla
- 13_BadBind.fla
- 14_Worm.fla
- 15_Penelope.fla

The source files are available online at http://www.apress.com/us/book/9781484223758.

Animating with the Motion Editor

Before there were websites like Digg and Delicious and before the term *viral marketing* became a cliché, people actually emailed hyperlinks to each other. Some of the earliest must-share Flash animations include Alex Secui's "Nosepilot" (http://animation.nosepilot.com/) and JoeCartoon.com's "Frog in a Blender" (http://joecartoon.atom.com/cartoons/67-frog_in_a_blender), shown in Figure 8-1. These are classics that still entertain after more than a decade, and they were created with shape tweens and what are now called classic tweens, along with a good dose of elbow grease.

Clearly, the existing animation tool set—the Timeline panel and its trusty sidekicks, the Free Transform tool, the Transform panel, and a handful of others—is perfectly adequate to get the job done. But just as it can be good in a relationship to agree on acceptable word pronunciations *(toe-may-toe* and *toe-mah-toe* come to mind), it will be good for your relationship with Animate CC to consider other ways to animate content. You're about to start flirting with the Motion Editor.

Figure 8-1. *A scene from Joe Cartoon's infamous "Frog in a Blender" from 2000, which was among the first Flash animations to go viral*

Introduced in Flash Professional CS4, the Motion Tweens provided a second non-ActionScript paradigm for moving things from here to there. It's an alternate mechanism to the classic tweens and shape tweens that are carried out in the Timeline panel. In Chapter 1, we gave you a drive-by Motion Editor overview, and you've seen glimpses of it in a handful of other chapters. Now that you have read Chapter 7 and have experimented with the various details and nuances of the traditional tweening model, the differences between the old and the new will become abundantly clear.

Since that time, there has been a huge surge of interest in the new-style motion tweens—and there's good reason for that, as you'll see. People have begun to ask, "Which approach is better?" We're compelled to reply with the only legitimate answer there is: the best approach depends entirely on whatever works best for the project at hand.

Think of it like this: you've been using a conventional oven for years, when suddenly a newfangled microwave shows up on your doorstep. It's small and sleek and even has a rotating platter. Grinning, you carry it into the kitchen, plug it in, and slide in some of the goulash leftovers from last night. Two minutes and 20 seconds later—*ding!*—you have an instant lunch. "Let's try that again," you think, and put in a glass of milk with Hershey's syrup—45 seconds later, instant hot chocolate. Does it get any better? From this day forward, it takes you only 3 minutes to get fresh popcorn. In many ways, life has gotten easier, but you can bet your bottom BBQ that the conventional oven isn't leaving its venerable perch. There's no way the microwave bakes a loaf of homemade bread, for example. Then again, a medium rare steak done on the BBQ is far better than one done in a skillet.

Clearly, you'll want the best of both worlds. And your kitchen is big enough for it.

Getting Acquainted: Scaling and Moving

Let's take a comprehensive tour of the Motion Editor, covering all the basics. Portions of this will feel like a review after Chapter 7, but it's important to understand how the mechanics of motion, scaling, and distortion are distinct from the machinery of classic tweens. You won't be seeing any shapes, by the way, until much later in the chapter. The Motion Editor deals exclusively in symbols and text fields, just as is the case with classic tweens.

In this case, you'll be creating **motion tweens**, which look and behave like their classic cousins. The differences come in how they're made and how you can edit them, as you'll see in the following steps:

1. Open the `01_Map.fla` file found in the Chapter 8 Exercise folder. When it opens, you will notice a pin on a map. The pin you see on the stage is the Pin graphic symbol found in the Library.

2. Right-click on Frame 1 of the Pin Layer and select Create Motion Tween. This converts the layer into a tween layer and makes it available to the Motion Editor. (Alternatively, you can click frame 1 of the Pin layer and select Insert ➤ Motion Tween.)

    When you apply the motion tween, several things happen at once: the single frame stretches out to a 24-frame span and the span turns light blue when deselected. Why 24 frames? The default length is 1 second, so what you are seeing is one second of animation on the timeline. If you need more time, roll the mouse pointer to the end of the span. When the mouse pointer changes to a double-arrow, click and drag to the right, extending the tween to frame 70.

3. With the playhead at Frame 70, drag the pin down and to the right where the two big white streets intersect. What you have is a Pin, Figure 8-2, that moves in a straight line. Let's change that, shall we?

CHAPTER 8 ■ THE MOTION EDITOR AND INVERSE KINEMATICS

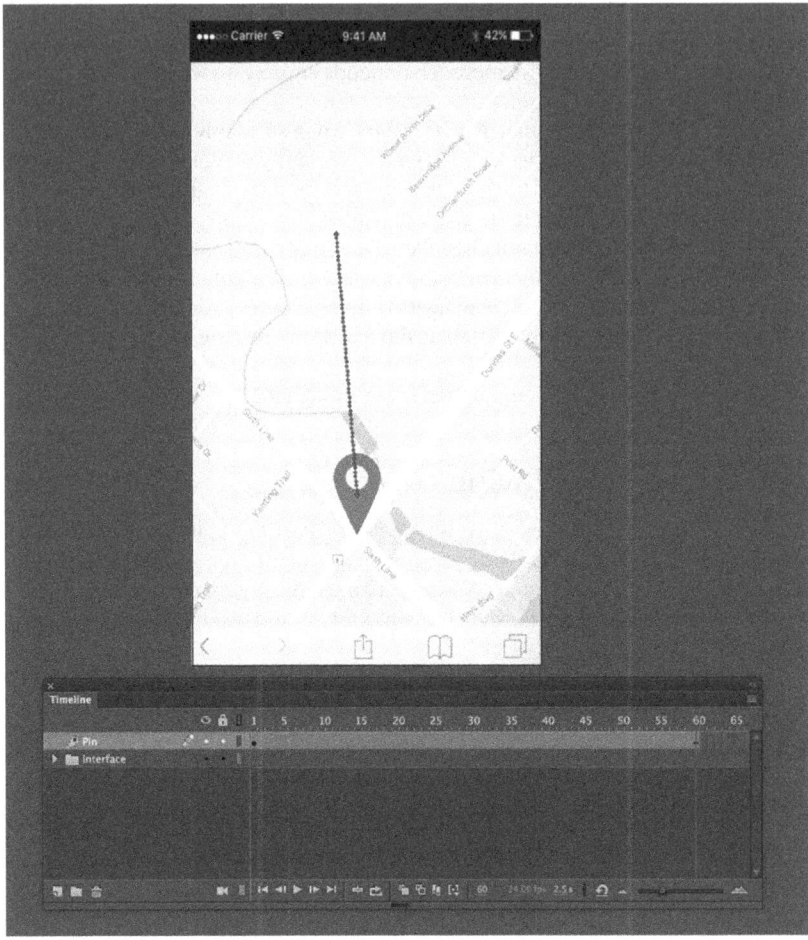

Figure 8-2. A motion tween has been applied to the Pin symbol

At this point we have played with the Motion Path by dragging a point on the path. There is another method. Here's how:

1. Open the Motion Editor by double-clicking anywhere between the two keyframes. This time—provided you haven't deselected the tween layer—you'll see the various grids and input controls shown in Figure 8-3.

CHAPTER 8 ■ THE MOTION EDITOR AND INVERSE KINEMATICS

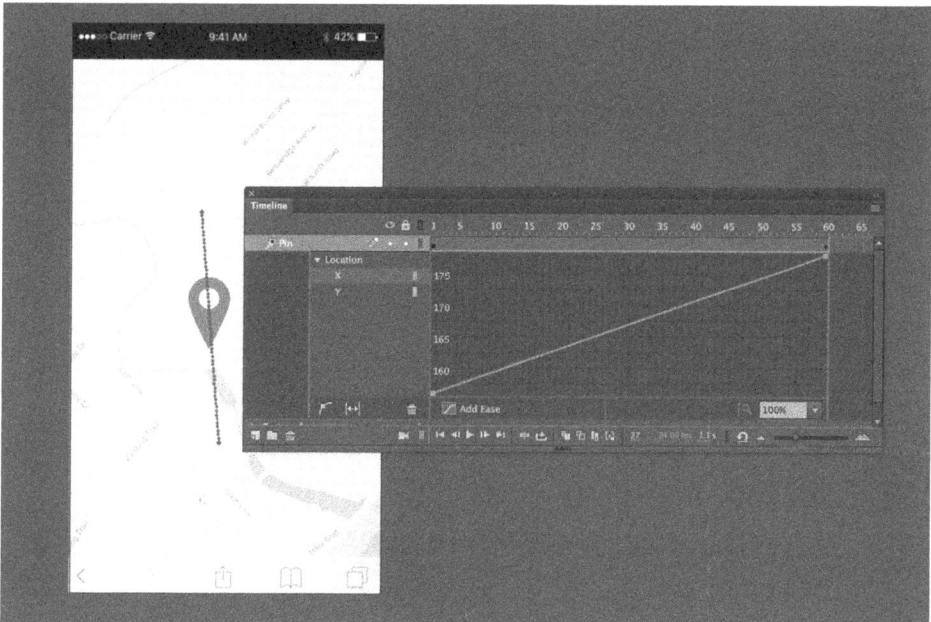

Figure 8-3. *Applying a motion tween activates the Motion Editor for that layer*

2. Removing a motion tween is as easy as applying one. Right-click (Windows) or Control+click (Mac) the tween layer. Select Remove Tween, and the layer turns gray again. If you have removed the tween, undo it.

It's time to take a look at the some of the differences between motion tweens and classic tweens. The key is to be aware the Timeline and Motion Editor are so integrated in Animate CC that they are actually fond of each other. You might even say they're connected at the hip. When you apply changes to a tween layer in one view, you'll see the changes are instantly reflected in the other.

3. In the Timeline panel, drag the playhead to frame 20. Use the Free Transform tool or the Transform panel to make the symbol much wider than it should be.

When you widen the symbol, you'll see a black diamond appear under the playhead in frame 20, as shown in Figure 8-4. Notice the diamond is a tad smaller than the dot that represents the default keyframe in frame 1. The difference in shape and size tells you this is a *property keyframe*, which is just "tween-layer-speak" for a keyframe.

395

CHAPTER 8 ■ THE MOTION EDITOR AND INVERSE KINEMATICS

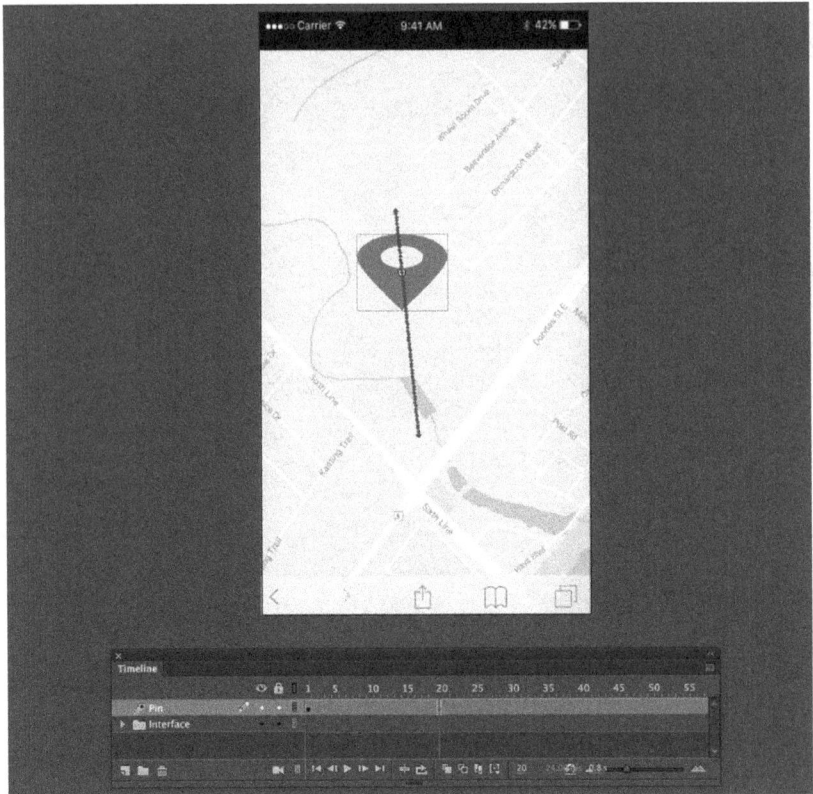

Figure 8-4. *Tween layer changes are stored in property keyframes*

4. Open the Motion Editor by double-clicking anywhere in the tween span. Scroll vertically until you find the Scale X grid, as shown in Figure 8-5, and then scroll horizontally until you find the property keyframe that was automatically added when you changed the symbol's width in the Timeline panel.

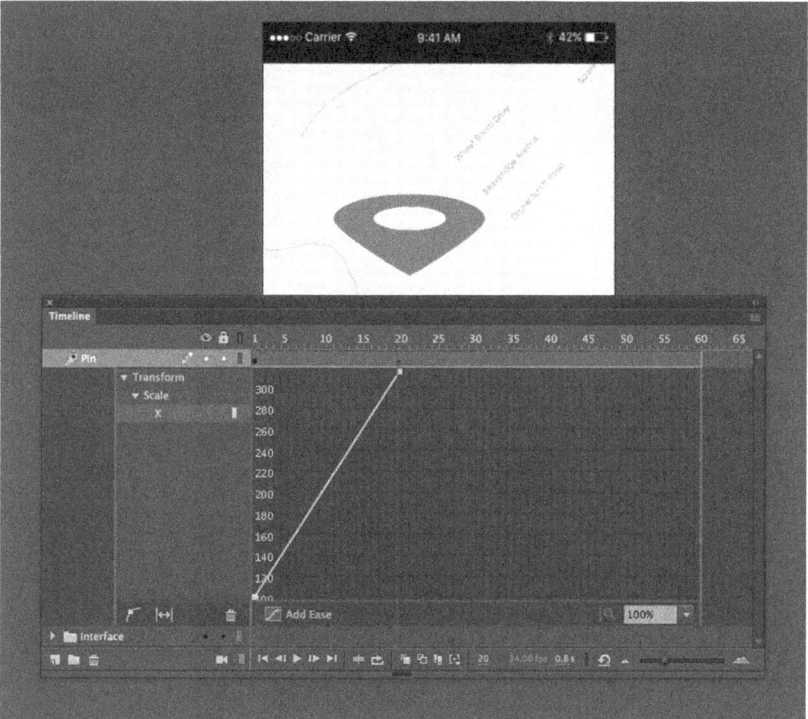

Figure 8-5. *The Motion Editor shows property changes in detailed, collapsible graphs*

5. In the Motion Editor and select Transform ➤ Scale ➤ X.

    The graph depicted shows a change in x-axis scale; that is—assuming the symbol isn't rotated—the width. The numbers along the left side stacked vertically show values that pertain to this property, which are percentages of scale. The numbers along the top show frames, which equate to changes over time.

    Follow the slanted line in the graph from bottom left up toward the upper right. It shows that the selected symbol began at a 100 percent width—the 100 is partially obscured by the slanted line's left point—and was stretched to over 200 percent over a span of 20 frames

    This is considerably more detail than you get with classic tweens. We'll come back to this graph concept in just a moment. First, back to the kissin' cousin.

6. In the Timeline and with the playhead still in frame 20, drag the Pin symbol to the upper-right corner of the stage, as shown in Figure 8-6. At this point, you've tweened three distinct properties: Scale X, the X position, and the Y position.

CHAPTER 8 ■ THE MOTION EDITOR AND INVERSE KINEMATICS

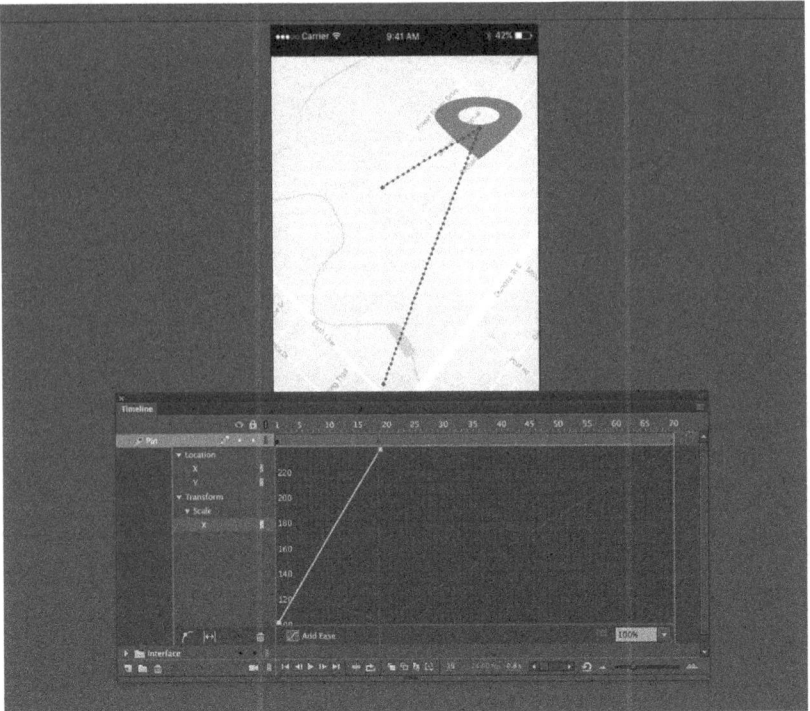

Figure 8-6. *Expanded graphs in the Motion Editor can make motion data easier to see*

Note that the property keyframe, from this view, is still just a small diamond at frame 20 in the timeline. All you can tell at a glance is that something has changed. But even if there's less detail here, the two views are in agreement, and the Timeline view does give you a summary. Later in this chapter, in the "Changing Duration Nonproportionally" section, you'll see how the Timeline panel's abridged view actually makes it easier to update numerous property keyframes at once.

Naturally, you can *see* the changed properties directly on the stage, not only because the symbol itself is stretched and moved but also because of that dotted line that connects the current position of the symbol (specifically, its transformation point) to the position it held in frame 1. If you count them carefully, you'll see 20 dots along the line, which represent the 20 frames in this tween span. The dots are all evenly spaced apart, which tells you the tween has no easing applied.

The vertical values in these graphs, along with the tooltips, change depending on the property represented. For example, the Location X graph starts just under 160 on the left side (not 100, like the Scale X graph), because the symbol is positioned at 156.95 pixels on the x-axis in frame 1. On the right side of the slanted line, the Properties panel shows a value of 291.95, because that's where the symbol is positioned on the x-axis in frame 20. The point to take away from this is that these graphs are adaptable, and they change to suit the values of the property at hand. The X graph shows pixels, Scale X shows percentages, Rotation Z and Skew X show degrees, and so on.

Applying Easing

It is a fact of life, when it comes to objects in motion in Animate CC, that easing needs to be applied. Objects in motion don't automatically stop and start. Instead they accelerate and decelerate, which is the purpose of easing. The really neat aspect of the Motion Editor is that you can apply eases from the Properties panel or right in the Motion Editor. Here's how:

1. Open the Timeline panel and select the keyframe at frame 20 of the timeline.

2. In the Properties panel; twirl down the Ease twirlie, if necessary; and scrub the hot text value—0, by default—slowly toward the left. Scrub it to approximately -10, and then let go. Scrub again to -20 or so, and then let go. Scrub again to -30, -40, and so on, until -100, which is a full ease-in.

   As you scrub and release in small increments, you'll see that the dots, which were evenly distributed after Step 12, begin to cluster toward the lower left, as shown in Figure 8-7, which represents the beginning of the tween. You just applied an ease in, so it makes sense that the dots are packed more closely at the beginning of the tween.

In classic tweens, easing takes effect only between keyframes. In motion tweens, easing is distributed over the frame span of the whole tween, independent of property keyframes. This is a significant departure from the classic model.

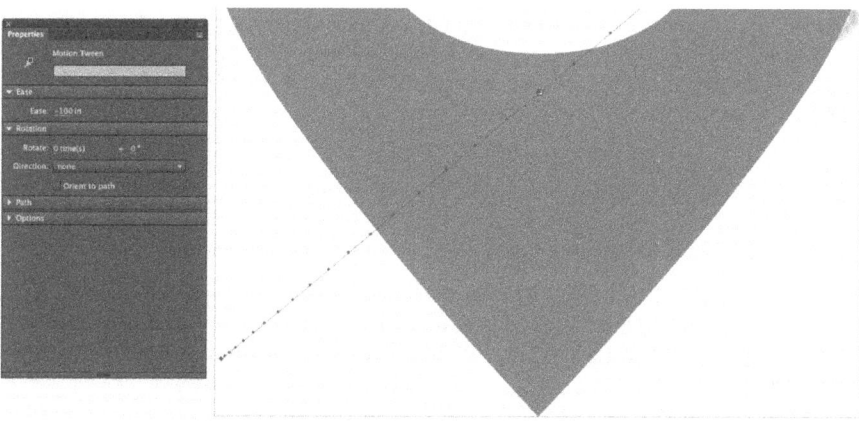

Figure 8-7. *Easing can be applied using the Properties panel*

3. Close your file without saving it.

Easing applied to a motion tween with the Properties panel is the same sort of easing applied to classic tweens, excluding the special-case Custom Ease In/Ease Out dialog box, discussed in Chapter 7. To get to the exciting stuff, you'll need the Motion Editor, and advanced easing merits its own section.

Easing with Graphs

When it comes to the Motion Editor, the concept of easing ascends to a whole new level. For classic tweens, the Custom Ease In/Ease Out dialog box is the only thing that came close to sharing similar functionality, yet it provides little more than an introduction. The Custom Ease In/Ease Out dialog box associated with a classic tween is a good place to start but the real power of easing is found in the Motion Editor.

A powerful feature of the Motion Editor is that it overcomes a subtle, but significant, limitation of the Custom Ease In/Ease Out dialog box: classic easing, for whatever property is under consideration, begins at a starting point of 0 percent and ends at a destination point of 100 percent. If you're moving a symbol from left to right—for example, from 25 pixels to 75 pixels—a classic tween begins at its starting point of 25 pixels (0 percent of the destination) and ends at 75 pixels (100 percent of its destination). Normal easing lets you adjust the acceleration and deceleration between those two immutable points. The Custom Ease In/Ease Out dialog box lets you adjust the velocity with greater control, thanks to Bézier curve handles. In fact, by adding anchor points, you can even opt to arrive at the destination point early, then head back out again and return later, as demonstrated in Chapter 7 with the bouncing mallet exercise. But in the end, there must always be a final anchor point. With classic easing, the final anchor point is always tethered to the 100 percent mark (see Figure 8-8).

Unimpeded in this regard, the graphs of the Motion Editor can end up where you like. A custom ease can start at its beginning point of 0 percent, travel three quarters of the way to its destination, dance around a bit, and then return all the way to the beginning.

This freedom within the property graphs is a powerful tool, which is generally a good thing. But as anyone into *Spider-Man* will tell you, "With great power comes great responsibility." Everything comes at a cost, and the price here is that the banished 100 percent restriction can occasionally be disorienting, especially when eases continue past the last property keyframe in a tween span. Let's take a look.

Built-In Eases

If you'll pardon the pun, we're going to *ease* into this. Let's start with the built-in eases:

1. Open the 02_EasePin.fla file in the Chapter 8 exercise folder. Our Pin is back, and this time the symbol has been given a 60-frame motion tween that moves it from the left side of the stage (frame 1) to the right side (frame 30) and then lets it sit in place until frame 60.

2. Select the tween layer or the symbol by clicking it, and then open the Motion Editor. Find the X graph and notice the straight line from the beginning point (bottom left) to the destination point (upper right), as shown in Figure 8-8. Because no other X changes occur after frame 30, there are only two property keyframes in the graph.

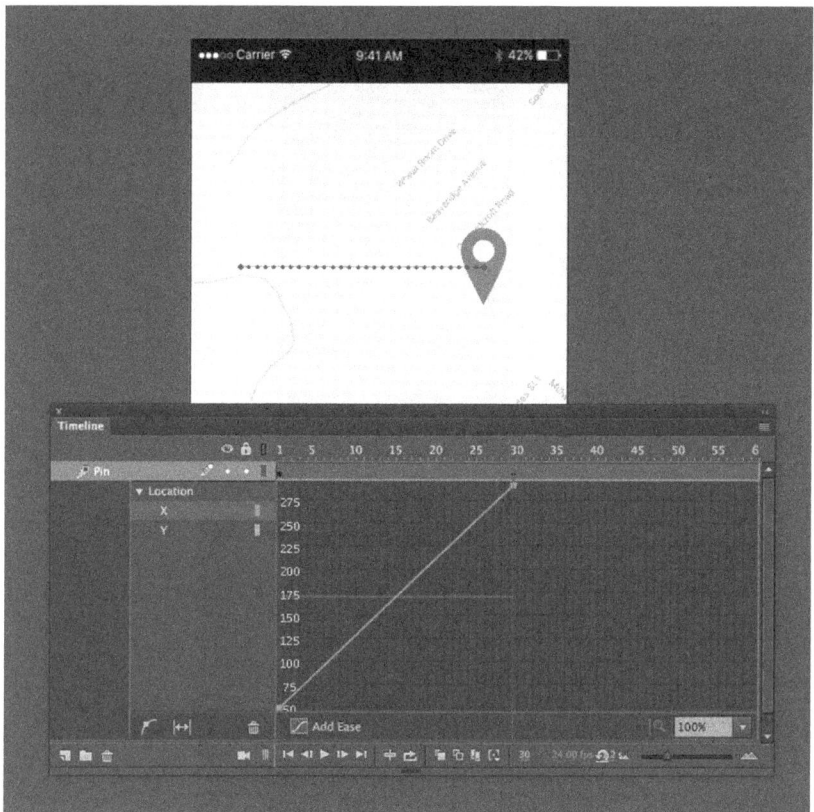

Figure 8-8. *Without easing, the graph shows a straight line*

3. Notice the button at the bottom of the graph that says Add Ease? Click it to enable easing, and from the drop-down list select Simple ➤ Slow. At this point, you've applied an ease, which is the dashed line on the graph shown in Figure 8-9.

CHAPTER 8 ■ THE MOTION EDITOR AND INVERSE KINEMATICS

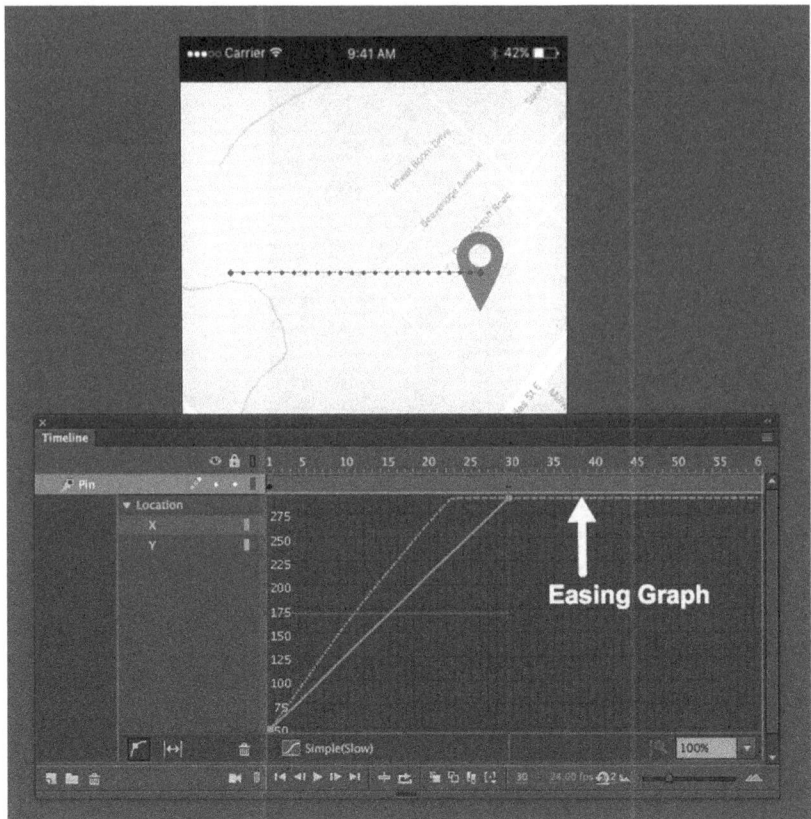

Figure 8-9. Apply an ease and the Motion Editor shows it to you

4. Press Enter (Windows) or Return (Mac) and watch the Pin move from left to right.

   If that doesn't look like easing to you, you're right. Selecting Simple (Slow) isn't enough. You need to choose a percentage for that ease, which affects its strength. Think of it as a faucet—applying the ease means you've paid the water bill, but you won't see water until you turn on the faucet.

5. Scroll down to the bottom of the Motion Editor and click the Ease button. When the panel opens, you'll see the reason why Simple (Slow) appeared in the X graph's easing drop-down list.

6. Scrub the hot text as far right as it will go, changing the default 50 to 100. As you scrub, you'll see a solid line, representing the ease, begin to curve in the graph, as shown in Figure 8-10.

CHAPTER 8 ■ THE MOTION EDITOR AND INVERSE KINEMATICS

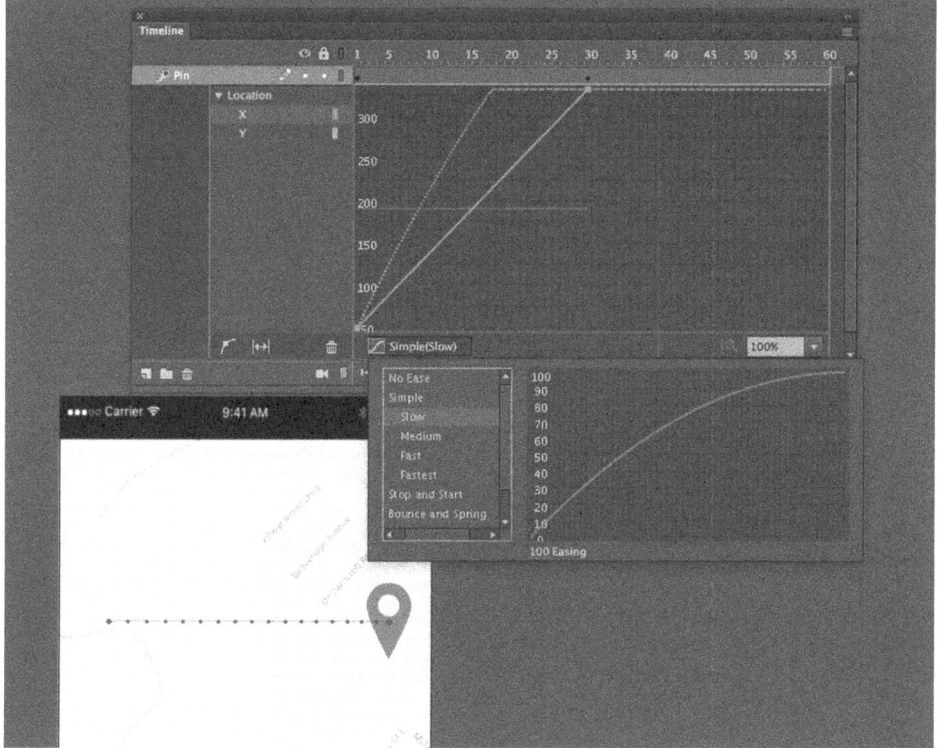

Figure 8-10. *Change the default from 0 to 100, and the curve appears*

This particular graph changes the Simple (Slow) ease itself, which is comparable to changing a symbol inside the Library. As you learned in Chapter 3, changing a Library symbol means that every instance of it is changed on the stage. The same goes for these eases. You also might have noticed the mascot shift around on the stage as the ease is applied to the motion.

Scroll back up to the X graph, and you'll see that the ease is now superimposed over the line that represents the symbol's x-axis movement. To get a better view, click the left side of the X graph, and click the fit to view button. All 60 frames are displayed in the graph.

7. Press Enter (Windows) or Return (Mac) again to preview the movement, but prepare yourself for disappointment: it still doesn't look like much of an ease.

    The reason for this is that motion tween eases are applied to the full span of the tween. In this case, the full span is 60 frames, while the only visible change occurs between frames 1 and 30.

8. Click the upper-right red property keyframe in the Motion Editor graph and, holding down the Shift key, drag the keyframe to the right until you hit frame 60. Doing so turns the dashed line to a gentle curve, as shown in Figure 8-11. The tooltip lets you know which frame you're on, and the Shift key constrains your movement.

CHAPTER 8 ■ THE MOTION EDITOR AND INVERSE KINEMATICS

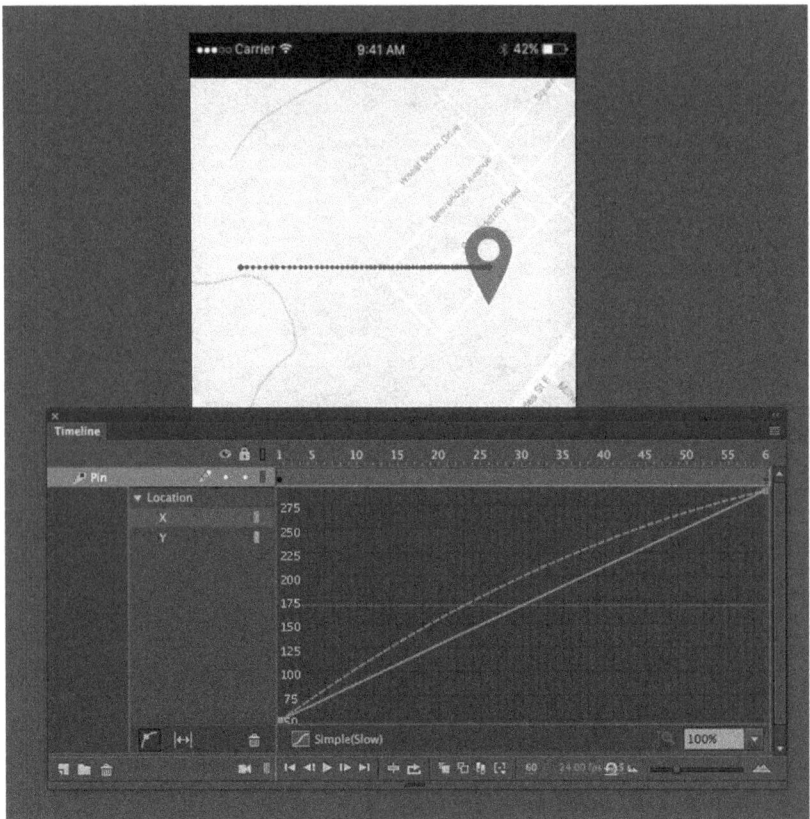

Figure 8-11. Keyframes can be moved from inside a graph

If you don't use the Shift key while you drag, it's easy to slide the keyframe up and down, even if you intend to move only to the right, which increases the duration between this keyframe and the one before it. Why is it a bad thing to slide up and down? Actually, it isn't. Sometimes, you might *want* to do that, and it's good to know you have the option. Sliding up and down changes the property's destination point. In this case, because you're dealing with x-axis movement, it means that even from this graph, you could push the symbol farther to the right on the stage (slide the keyframe higher) or back toward the left (slide the keyframe lower).

The visual result of a property's destination point depends entirely on what the property represents. In the Y graph, the destination point affects the symbol's vertical position. In the Rotation Z graph, it affects the symbol's rotation. If you add a color effect or filter, the destination point determines how much of that effect is applied.

---

9. Press Enter (Windows) or Return (Mac) again. Because the solid and dashed lines' final anchor points meet, you'll see the full Simple (Slow) ease.

10. Using the Shift key again, drag the right property keyframe back to frame 30.

CHAPTER 8 ■ THE MOTION EDITOR AND INVERSE KINEMATICS

11. Open the Eases area in the Motion Editor, and let's add a bounce to the Pin. Choose Bounce and Spring ➤ Bounce, as shown in Figure 8-12.

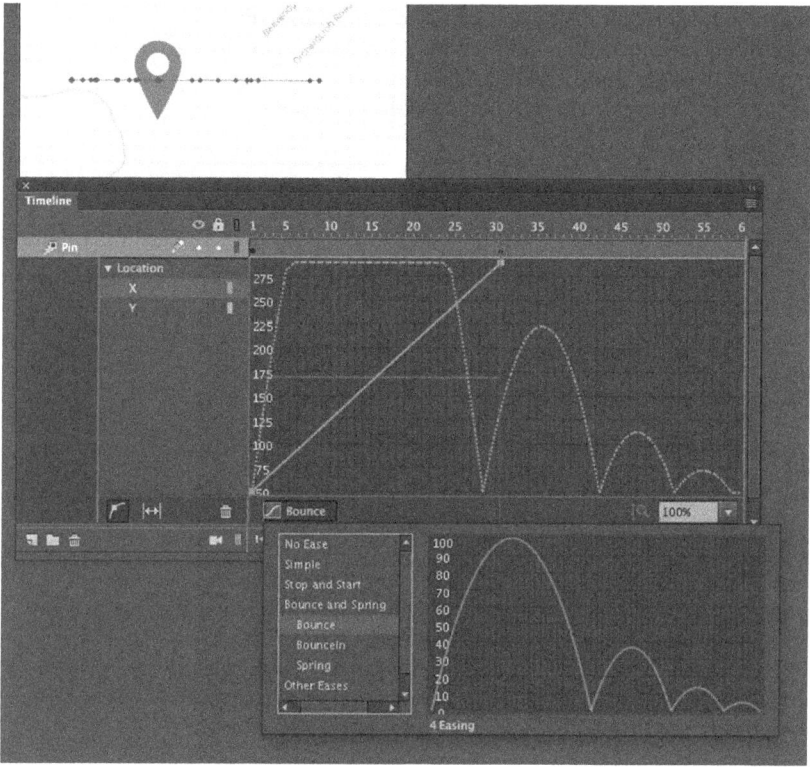

Figure 8-12. *Animate CC lets you change the ease to meet your needs*

12. By default, the Bounce ease's hot text is set to 4, which makes the four bounces depicted in its graph. Change the hot text at the bottom of the Ease pane to 3 to reduce the number of bounces to three.

   Adding an ease to the Eases area makes that ease available to all the property graphs in the Motion Editor. Eases can be applied and changed for each property individually by using that property's drop-down menu and/or check mark. Eases can be applied and changed for whole groups of properties. Add as many eases as you like, including multiple custom eases.

   As you may have guessed, you can use the No Ease button at any time in the Eases area to remove an ease from consideration for all drop-downs.

   By adding the Bounce, three interesting things happen when you make this change. First, because you moved the property keyframe back to frame 30, part of the Bounce ease is clipped, as you can see in the flattened hump of the first bounce—between frames 6 and 27—in Figure 8-12. The second interesting thing is, though the graph may have developed "bumps," they are only on the x-axis, meaning the bumps represent lateral movement, which explains why the motion path on the stage doesn't change. The third interesting thing becomes apparent when you preview the ease.

405

CHAPTER 8 ■ THE MOTION EDITOR AND INVERSE KINEMATICS

13. Press Enter (Windows) or Return (Mac), and watch the Pin slam to the right side, pause for a moment (that's the clipped first bounce), then resume its rebounding course, and finally end up back on the left side of the stage!

   With motion tweens, easing can completely override the actual property represented by the solid line in the graph. Without the ease, this is a simple left-to-right movement. With easing, this *could be that*, but as you've seen, it can just as easily change the destination point to one quite outside of Kansas.

We chose physical movement to illustrate the mechanics of motion tween easing, because a change in position correlates well with the lines and curves on the graph. Be aware that this concept applies in exactly the same way to rotation, scaling, skewing, color effects like alpha and tint, and filters like Drop Shadow and Blur.

---

14. Shift-drag the right property keyframe back to frame 60. Verify that all three bounces are now visible in the X graph.

15. Press Enter (Windows) or Return (Mac) to view the full, smooth three-bounce easing of the Pin.

Creating Custom Eases

Even after seeing more than a dozen built-in eases, you might be wondering whether you can create your own. The answer is yes, and it's pretty easy. Best of all, custom eases are saved with the FLA, which means you don't need to commit all your easing finagling to memory. Your custom eases will be there when you reopen your files in the morning, and even better, once they are added to the Eases area, you can apply (and reapply) custom eases to any property, just like built-in eases. Here's how:

1. Open 03_CustomEasePin.fla in this chapter's exercise folder. Again, we start you with a basic left-to-right motion tween, this time over a full 60 frames.

2. Click the tween layer (layer 1) or the symbol, and then open the Motion Editor. Scroll down to the Eases area, click the + button, and select Custom from the context menu. This creates a Custom graph for you, so let's take a look.

   What you see is a line with run-of-the-mill Bézier curve handles. The anchor points and handles operate very much like those for normal drawings with the Pen tool, and we encourage you to experiment.

3. To create a custom ease click the "Add Anchor Point on Graph" button. When you move the cursor over the graph it changes to a Pen Tool and, to add the anchor point, click the mouse. To remove an anchor, just roll the mouse over the anchor point to be removed. You will see a small box appear under then cursor. This technique removes any anchor point but the first and last (there must always be a beginning and destination point). Use the Alt (Windows) or Option (Mac) key while clicking to convert a curve anchor point to a corner anchor point and vice versa. See Figure 8-13.

CHAPTER 8 ■ THE MOTION EDITOR AND INVERSE KINEMATICS

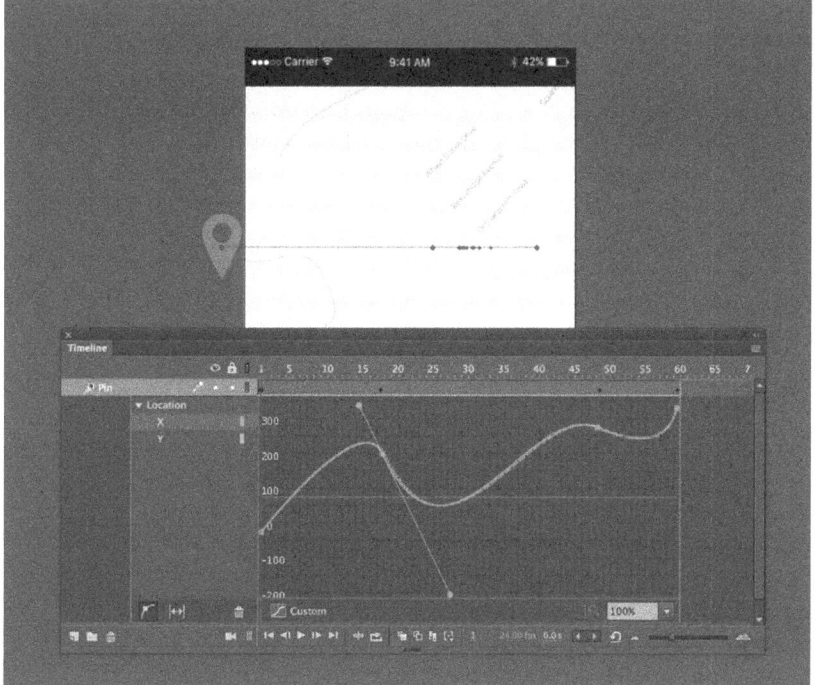

Figure 8-13. *Use the pen to create custom eases in the Motion Editor*

4. When you finish, scroll to the X graph, and select your custom ease from the X property's drop-down menu. Press Enter (Windows) or Return (Mac) to preview the effect.

5. Close your file without saving the changes.

Applying Multiple Eases

It may not immediately sound ambiguous, but the phrase "applying multiple eases" can actually be interpreted in a variety of ways. To be sure, you can apply numerous eases to a given motion tween—one separate ease for each tweenable property is perfectly acceptable. Give your X a bounce, your Y a Simple (Slow), your Rotation Z a custom ease, and so on, down the line. What you can't do is to apply more than one ease between property keyframes. If you've used previous versions of Animate CC or Flash, this may take some getting used to, which is why we've stressed that motion tween easing applies to the full tween span, not to the span between property keyframes.

To follow one sort of easing with another sort within the same tween layer, you'll need to use more than one tween span. Here's how:

1. Open 04_MultipleEasePin.fla in this chapter's exercise folder. This time, to mix it up, we prepared a vertical motion tween for you.

2. Open the Motion Editor and, with the X Location graph selected, add a Stop and Start (Medium) ease. When its graph appears, scrub its hot text to the right until it says 100.

407

CHAPTER 8 ■ THE MOTION EDITOR AND INVERSE KINEMATICS

3. Select the Y graph, and select Stop and Start (Medium) in the easing drop-down menu. Press Enter (Windows) or Return (Mac) to preview the ease, which makes the Pin look as if it were being dragged downward with two heaves of a rope.

4. Select the Timeline layer. Right-click (Windows) or Control+click (Mac) the tween span, and select Copy Frames from the context menu. Now right-click (Windows) or Control+click (Mac) frame 31, and select Paste Frames. Just like that, you've created a twin of the original animation, complete with its easing.

5. Right-click (Windows) or Control+click (Mac) the second tween span, and select Reverse Keyframes. Preview the animation again, and this time, the Pin gets heaved up and then heaved down again. Even though the motion is reversed, the tween is still the same for both tween spans.

6. Open the Motion Editor, and change the second span's Y easing from Stop and Start (Medium) to Spring. Preview the animation, and you'll see the Pin getting heaved up and then suddenly fall and "sproiiing" to a halt.

Same tween layer, two tween spans—that's how you get two or more types of easing in the same layer. As an aside, notice that the Pin doesn't come to a rest at the bottom of the stage. That's because the Spring ease is one of those whose destination point doesn't stop at 100 percent.

Managing property keyframes

Before we turn you loose on a rather interesting project, there is one final issue to cover: property keyframes. The small diamonds you see on a motion layer are called **property keyframes**, and they can be managed in one of two areas: through the Timeline or through the Motion Editor. The thing you need to know is that each one has its own way of handling the details. When it comes to exercising fine control of keyframes, the Motion Editor is your best bet, but there are a few circumstances where using the Timeline panel definitely makes your life simpler. We'll get to that in a moment, but let's start with a diamond:

1. Open the 05_PixelDisposal.fla file from the Chapter 8 exercise folder. When it opens, you will see a character on a sign tossing a red pixel into the trash. If you scrub across the timeline, the property keyframe at fame 35 is where the pixel changes direction, rotates, and starts to shrink.

2. While you are in the Timeline panel, the only way to move from keyframe to keyframe is to scrub the playhead. Go ahead and scrub to frame 40.

3. Right-click the tween layer at frame 40, and select Insert Keyframe ➤ Position from the context menu, as shown in Figure 8-14. A property keyframe will appear at frame 40.

CHAPTER 8 ■ THE MOTION EDITOR AND INVERSE KINEMATICS

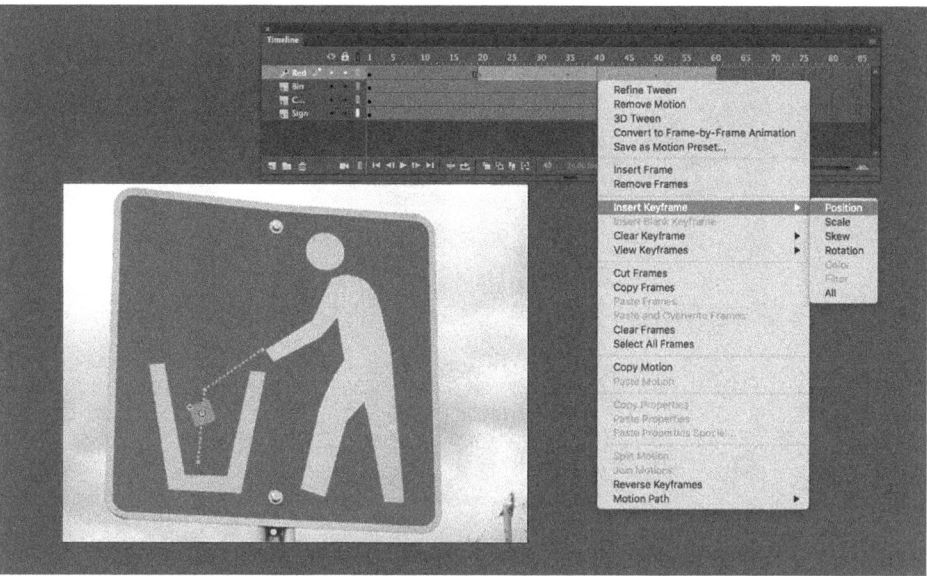

Figure 8-14. Property keyframes can be added from the Timeline panel

4. Select the Red cube symbol, and move it downward. As you saw earlier in the chapter, property keyframes are created for you automatically in the current frame when you change a symbol's position, scale, rotation, or the like. What you learned from step 3 is that it's still perfectly OK to create your keyframe first.

5. Switch back to the Timeline panel, and right-click (Windows) or Control+click (Mac) again on frame 40. Note that you have options for clearing keyframes and also determining which property keyframes to display in the Timeline panel.

    Don't be fooled by the Clear Keyframe choice! You would think, because Insert Keyframe inserts the desired keyframe(s) in the current frame, that Clear Keyframe would, like its Classic Tween brother, follow suit and remove only keyframes in the current frame. This is not so. By choosing Clear Keyframe, you're removing *all property keyframes* in the current tween span. If you select Clear Keyframe ➤ Rotation, for example, you remove all property keyframes in the Motion Editor's Rotation Z graph, regardless of in which frame they appear.

    Once you see these features and understand them for what they are, you'll surely find them useful, but the Motion Editor does more.

6. Open the Motion Editor, and scrub the playhead along the Motion Editor's timeline. You get the same sort of preview as the Timeline panel. The difference is that the Motion Editor, Figure 8-15, also gives you the ability to change properties ... by the numbers.

409

CHAPTER 8 ■ THE MOTION EDITOR AND INVERSE KINEMATICS

Figure 8-15. In the Motion Editor, keyframes can navigated, added, and removed with this widget

7. Scrub to frame 40, and click the Y Location point on the graph. Keep an eye on the cursor. It will change to a box when over the keyframe. That change tells you that you can move this keyframe.

8. Drag the keyframe upwards to about 360 on the graph. Notice how the location changes on the stage?

9. Select the Add Anchor Point button and move your mouse elsewhere in the Y graph. The cursor changes to the pen and you can add an anchor point (Keyframe) when you click the mouse, and then hold down the Ctrl (Windows) or Cmd (Mac) key while you hover over one of the line segments. As shown in Figure 8-16, the cursor turns into a pen with a plus sign, which indicates you can click to add a new keyframe.

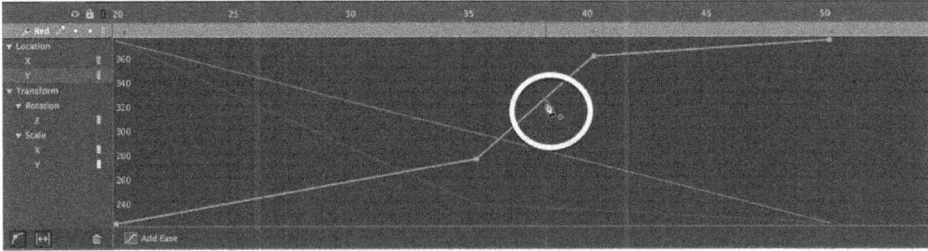

Figure 8-16. Keyframes can also be added and removed with the mouse

10. With the keyframe selected, switch to the Pen tool, hold down the Alt (Windows) or Option (Mac) key, and hover over the new keyframe. The cursor turns into an upside down V. Click, and this converts the anchor point into a curve anchor, which can be adjusted with Bézier handles. Just drag the cursor to see the handles. The effect of these handles on the X and Y graphs isn't always obvious, but for many properties, it gives you a "quick-and-dirty" custom ease.

CHAPTER 8 ■ THE MOTION EDITOR AND INVERSE KINEMATICS

11. Switch to Transform ➤ Rotation and select the Z-Axis. The middle keyframe up and to the right. As you drag the point watch the rotation of the cube as you move the anchor point up or down on the graph and as you move the handles on the curve.

12. Press Enter (Windows) or Return (Mac) to preview the animation, and you'll see that the symbol rotates farther than it did before—you've pushed it past its original destination, to approximately 160 percent—and then eases back the Rotation Z setting in the property keyframe at frame 50. Don't close this file just yet; we are going to work some further "magic" on it in the next exercise.

As helpful as the Motion Editor is, sometimes less is more. When you want to compress or expand the duration of a tween span, for example, the Timeline panel is the only way to do it, if you want to do it proportionally. If not, you could use either panel, but the Timeline panel makes it easier.

Changing Duration Proportionally

The animation in the `PixelDisposal.fla` you were just using spans 60 frames. At 24 fps, that's approximately 2.5 seconds, which may or may not be what you want. To change a tween span's duration proportionally, you'll need to use the Timeline panel. Here's how:

1. Move your mouse to the right edge of the tween span. You'll see the cursor turn into a double-headed arrow, as shown in Figure 8-17. Click and drag toward the left. For example, shorten the tween span so that it ends at frame 50. Notice that all four property keyframes are still in place, and, proportionately speaking, are the same relative distance from each other as before.

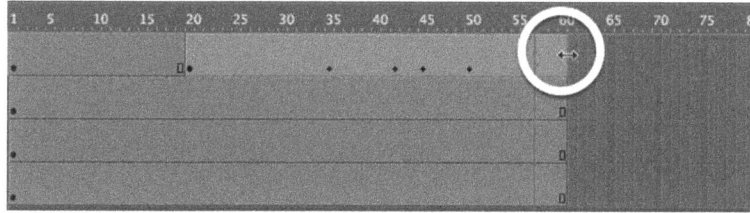

Figure 8-17. *Drag the tween span to shorten or increase a tween's duration*

2. Click and drag the right edge tween span so that it ends at frame 59. Now release and drag the right edge of the tween span to frame 60.

This time, the property frames are *nearly* back to their original places, but some are slightly off. That makes sense, because frame 59 is an odd number, and Animate CC had to make a decision on how to shift the frames to compensate.

To get the property keyframes back to frames 30, 40, 45, and 50 exactly, you'll need to use a different approach. If you're into tedium, you could switch to the Motion Editor and visit every property graph in turn, sliding numerous anchor points while holding the Shift key. The middle keyframe, especially, would give you a headache, because it affects the X, Y, Rotation Z, Scale X, and Scale Y graphs. There's an easier way, and we describe it in the very next paragraph.

Changing Duration Nonproportionally

Sometimes you'll want to change the duration *between* property keyframes, which may or may not incorporate a change in span duration. You could do this with the Motion Editor, visiting each relevant graph and moving property keyframes individually, or you can update the keyframes in several graphs at the same time. For that, use the Timeline panel. Here's how:

1. Continuing with 05_PixelDisposal.fla file you have been working on and still in the Timeline panel, hold down the Ctrl (Windows) or Cmd (Mac) key and click the keyframe closest to frame 35. Notice that holding down Ctrl (Windows) or Cmd (Mac) allows you to select a single frame in the tween span, rather than the whole span.

2. Now that you have a single property keyframe selected, release the Ctrl (Windows) or Cmd (Mac) key, and then click and drag the selected keyframe left or right along the timeline. Doing this effectively selects all the anchor points for the current frame in the Motion Editor and lets you move them as one.

Motion Paths

In Chapter 7, we showed you how to animate a butterfly along a special kind of layer called a **motion guide**. As you discovered, it was a path that could be as intricate as you wanted and allows a symbol to appear to meander around the screen following loops and curves that you drew with the pen tool. This capability is also possible in the Motion Editor. When you go this route, you don't use a guide, you use a path that is hardwired right into the motion layer. In fact, you have already seen this feature but never really got a chance to use it. Your opportunity has arrived.

Manipulating Motion Paths

The most fascinating thing about this feature of the Motion Editor is you don't need to use the Motion Editor. Motion paths are best manipulated through the Timeline panel. Here's how:

1. Open the 06_MotionGuideSimple.fla file from this chapter's exercise folder. When it opens, you will see that our pixel disposer has three pixels to toss into the trash bin. Turn off the visibility of the Green and Blue layers by clicking the eyeball icon on the layer strip.

2. Scrub through the timeline, and you will see that red cube fall to the bottom of the wastebasket. Did you catch the problem? The cube seems to move over the bin before hitting the bottom. You can see this in Figure 8-18 if you follow the motion path. Let's fix that.

CHAPTER 8 ■ THE MOTION EDITOR AND INVERSE KINEMATICS

Figure 8-18. *The motion path shows you the "line" an object in motion will follow*

3. Drag the playhead somewhere between the two keyframes and switch to the Selection tool. Hover near the motion path, and a curve will appear under the arrow. Click and drag the path to the left. As you do, the path will curve, as shown in Figure 8-19.

Figure 8-19. *Motion paths can be manipulated on the stage*

413

CHAPTER 8 ■ THE MOTION EDITOR AND INVERSE KINEMATICS

4. Turn on the visibility of the Green layer and switch to the Subselection tool.

5. Click on either anchor point and drag the Bézier curve handles, as shown in Figure 8-20 to increase the range of the curve. As you can see, motion paths can be treated as vector objects.

This technique works only if the path has a curve.

Figure 8-20. *Use the Subselection tool to treat the path as a vector line*

Not only can you reshape the motion path, but you can also move it, rotate, skew it, and treat it like any other shape or object on the stage. Let's keep experimenting.

6. Turn on the visibility of the Blue layer and select it. Now turn your gaze to the Properties panel. Twirl down the Path options. Scrub across the X, Y, W, and H values, and you will see that you can move and resize the path. Impressed? Hang on—it gets better.

7. Open the Transform panel. Get your hand off the mouse because this one is a bit trickier. You need to select the path here, not the object, or Animate CC will think it has to transform the blue cube instead.

8. Use the Selection tool to click anywhere along the path. Now scrub across the Transform panel's Rotate value. The path will, as shown in Figure 8-21, rotate around its start point.

9. Experiment with the Width, Height, and Skew properties in the Transform panel.

414

10. If you want to do it yourself and not use numbers, switch to the Free Transform tool and select the path. As shown in Figure 8-21 you can manipulate the path just as you would with a movieclip of graphic symbol. If you don't want to switch tools and do this strictly with the mouse, select the path with the Subselection tool and press Ctrl (Windows) or Cmd (Mac).

Don't forget the Alt (Windows) or Option (Mac) key while you make these transformations with the mouse. Without it, transformations pivot around the bounding box's center. With Alt (Windows) or Option (Mac), transformations pivot along the opposite corner or edge. In either case, the Ctrl (Windows) or Cmd (Mac) key is required to produce the bounding box.

Figure 8-21. Use the Free Transform tool, Transform panel or press Ctrl (Windows) or Cmd (Mac) to transform a motion path with your mouse

Using Advanced Motion Paths

In Chapter 7, the butterfly went on a pretty wild ride—nothing like the tame Bézier curves you've seen so far in this chapter. You can do the same thing with the new tweening model, and you still don't need a motion guide layer. Here's how:

1. Open 07_MotionGuideComplex.fla in this chapter's exercise folder. You'll see a slightly different finished version of the butterfly MotionGuide.fla exercise from Chapter 7, including a classic tween directed by a motion guide layer. Your job—and it's an easy one—is to convert that complex motion guide into a motion path.

2. Right-click (Windows) or Control+click (Mac) the flutter by (motion guide) layer, and deselect Guide from the context menu. This converts that layer back to a normal layer.

3. Using the Selection tool, double-click the wavy line to select the whole thing, and then cut the curves to the clipboard (Edit ➤ Cut).

4. Right-click (Windows) or Control+click (Mac) the classic tween and select Remove Tween from the context menu.

5. Right-click (Windows) or Control+click (Mac) again and select Create Motion Tween.

6. With the tween layer selected, paste the wavy line into the layer by selecting Edit ➤ Paste in Place. That's all there is to it! If you like, delete the now-empty flutter by layer.

7. Click the tween layer again. Use the Properties panel to select or deselect Orient to path, which behaves as it did for the classic tween version.

Motion Tween Properties

As you've seen throughout this book, the Properties panel is the most versatile panel in your arsenal, simply because it changes to reflect whatever object is selected. When you're dealing with motion tweens, there are two things the Properties panel lets you manipulate: the symbol and the tween itself (that is, the motion path). Some of these properties are the ones you see for classic tweens, but they don't all apply for motion tweens.

Let's take a look. Open any of the files you've used to far, and make sure a motion tween is applied to at least one symbol. Select the tween span, and you'll notice the following properties in the Properties panel:

- **Ease:** This applies the Motion Editor's Simple (Slow) ease to the full frame span selected. You can adjust this ease's hot text to a value from -100 (ease in) through 0 (no ease) to 100 (ease out).

- **Rotate [x] time(s) + [y]°:** This is comparable to the Rotate drop-down for classic tweens and manages symbol rotation. The two hot text values let you specify the number of full rotations ([x]) and degrees of partial rotation ([y]).

- **Direction:** Once rotation numbers are configured with the previous property, you can choose clockwise (CW), counterclockwise (CCW), or none to determine the direction of those settings or cancel them.

- **Orient to path:** This check box applies only to orientation along a motion path.

- **X, Y, W (Width) and H (Height):** These reposition or transform a tween span's motion path.

- **Sync graphic symbols:** Human beings still have an appendix, but modern science still hasn't definitively figured out what it's good for, and the same goes for this property. Given its name, it's presumably the motion tween equivalent to the classic tween Sync property discussed in Chapter 7. With motion tweens, symbol synchronization happens automatically, whether or not this property is selected. As you'll see in the next section, this feature is moot in any case, because motion paths can be reassigned to any symbol you like.

The other motion tween–related Properties panel settings depend on the symbol itself. For movieclips, your configuration options for motion tweens are the same as those for classic tweens. Some properties—such as position, scale, and rotation, and even color effects such as alpha—are tweenable. Others, such as blend modes, are not. These are consistent across the board when you're dealing with movieclips. It's when you're using graphic symbols that you need to be aware of a few limitations.

The limitations involve the Loop, Play Once, Single Frame, and Frame options in the Properties panel's Looping area. These properties apply to classic tween keyframes as discussed in Chapter 7. For motion tweens, they apply only to the tween span's first keyframe. They're ignored for property keyframes. The long and short of it is that you can set the Loop, Play Once, and Single Frame drop-down options and Frame input field once for a given motion tween—and Flash will obey your command—but only once for that tween span. Change these settings at any frame along the span, and the settings are changed for the whole span.

Even though we're focusing on symbols in these paragraphs, bear in mind that motion tweens can also be applied to text fields.

One final note. Like classic tweens, motion tweens can accommodate only one symbol per tween span. In fact, motion tweens are a bit stricter about this constraint. Once you've applied a classic tween between two keyframes, Animate CC won't let you draw a shape or add a symbol to any of the frames between the keyframes. Interestingly enough, it will let you draw or add symbols to tweened *keyframes*, but doing so breaks the classic tween, whose "I'm a tween" indicator line then becomes a dashed line. With motion tweens, Animate CC won't let you draw or add a symbol to *any frame* of the tween span, keyframe or not. The moral of this story is that you should give each of your tween spans its own layer.

Motion Presets

Here's another good example of letting the computer do the work for you. Animate CC takes advantage of one of the major facets of motion tweens—that you can copy and paste motion paths—by providing you with a panel with more than two dozen prebuilt *motion presets*. These are reusable motion paths, complete with motion changes, transformations, and color effects, which you can apply to any symbol or text field. Here's how:

1. Open 08_MotionPreset.fla from the Chapter 8 exercise folder. You'll see our two Pins on a map.

2. Select the Red Pin on the stage and open the Motion Presets panel (Window ➤ Motion Presets).

3. Open the Default Presets folder, if it is not already open, and click among the various choices to see a preview of the animation in the Motion Presets panel's preview (see Figure 8-22). You'll see wipes and zooms, blurs and bounces, and all manner of helter-skelter. When you find a preset you like—we chose bounce-smoosh, the third one—click the panel's Apply button to copy that motion path to the RedPin symbol.

CHAPTER 8 ■ THE MOTION EDITOR AND INVERSE KINEMATICS

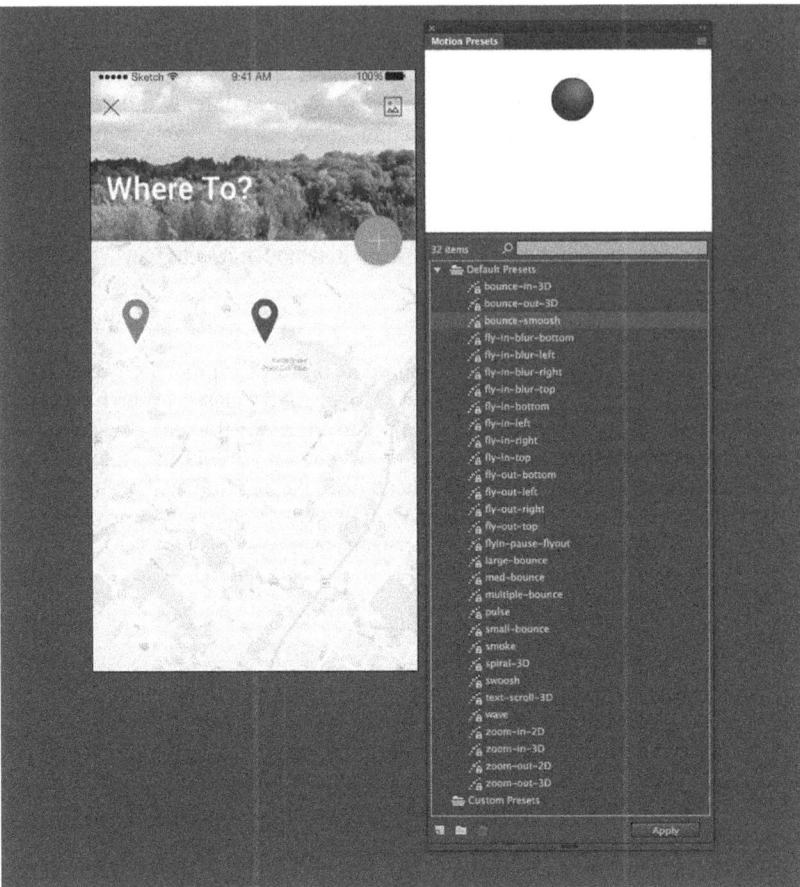

***Figure 8-22.** The Motion Presets panel gives you 30 stock motion paths*

Applying the motion preset automatically inserts a motion tween on the RedPin layer and then adds the relevant property keyframes to reproduce the animation in question

4. Using the Subselection tool, click the motion path, and then use the Align panel to center the animation vertically on the stage.

    As you may have guessed, it's just as easy to apply the same (or different) motion preset to the other symbol, but we would like to draw your attention to a related feature instead. That related feature is that motion paths can be edited, or created completely from scratch, and then saved to the Motion Presets panel. How? Glad you asked.

5. Shorten the duration of the RedPin animation by dragging the right edge of the tween span slightly to the left. In our file, we shortened the tween span from 75 frames to 50. Drag the playhead to one or more of the property keyframes and use the Properties panel, Transform panel, or Free Transform tool to alter the symbol's antics along the existing motion path. Also, the Move the Pin, at the last frame to a street intersection to the left of the pin. Notice how the Pin's path shows a bounce to that location?

418

CHAPTER 8 ■ THE MOTION EDITOR AND INVERSE KINEMATICS

6. Click the tween span, and in the Motion Presets panel, click the Save selection as preset button (Figure 8-23). You'll be prompted to give the new preset a name. Enter whatever you like (we used altSmoosh), and click OK. Scroll to the Custom Presets folder to find your preset.

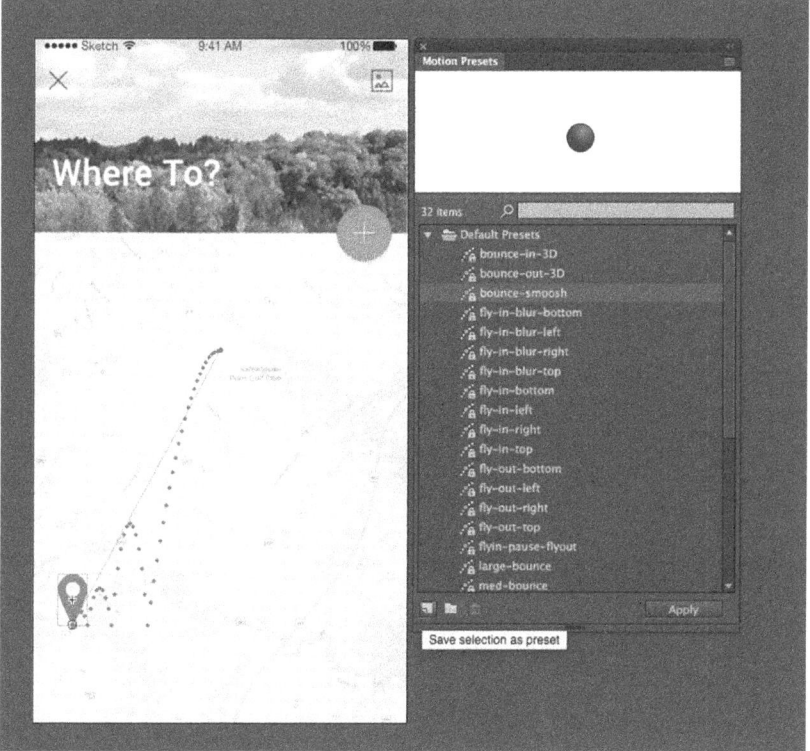

Figure 8-23. *Motion paths, whether made from scratch or based on presets, can be saved for later reuse*

The other buttons in the Motion Presets panel let you create new folders and delete folders or presets.

Naturally, you could select the BluePin symbol and apply your newly minted custom preset, but there's another way you can share motion paths.

7. Right-click (Windows) or Control+click (Mac) RedPin's tween span and select Copy Motion from the context menu. Now right-click (Windows) or Control+click (Mac) frame 1 of the BluePin layer and select Paste Motion.

Because you used the Align panel to change the position of the original motion path, you'll need to do the same for the copied path, assuming you want the lunatic and the mascot to fall in sync. It's easy as pie. Although you could certainly use the Edit Multiple Frames workflow discussed in Chapter 7—that does still work here—you've learned in this chapter that motion tweens can be repositioned by way of their motion paths.

419

8. Using the Subselection tool, click the BluePin's motion path to select it. Drag the BluePin's last position to a street intersection on the right.

9. Preview the animation. You'll see that both symbols perform the same movements (see Figure 8-24).

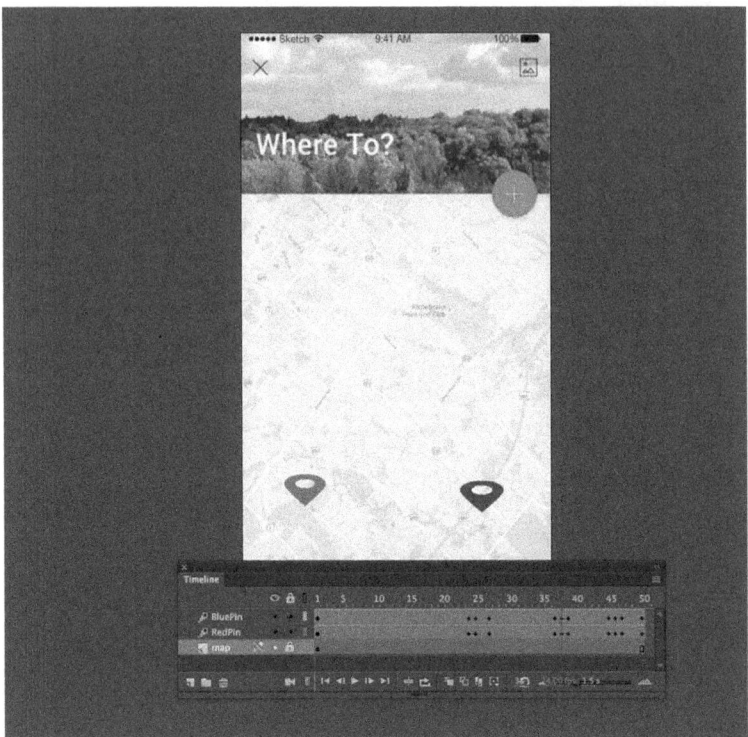

Figure 8-24. *Motion paths can be shared even without the Motion Presets panel*

That's impressive enough, but let's redo the last demonstration in a more dramatic way. These last few steps should drive home the notion that, in Animate CC, motion tweens—specifically, motion paths—are entities that stand on their own, distinct from the symbol.

10. Select the RedPin symbol at any point along its tween span and delete the symbol.

When you delete the symbol, the tween span remains, along with all its property keyframes. Visually speaking, the only difference in the tween span is that its first frame, usually a black dot, is now an empty white dot.

11. Click the empty tween span to select it.

12. Drag a copy of the RedPin symbol from the Library, and drop it somewhere on the stage. Location doesn't matter—it can even be on the right side of the BluePin symbol on the stage.

Because you selected the tween span first, the symbol will immediately adopt that span's motion path when you release the mouse to drop the symbol. You can't do that with a classic tween!

Inverse Kinematics (IK)

In one of the happiest sequences in Disney's 1940 classic, *Pinocchio*, the wooden-headed puppet, once freed from the apparatus that formerly helped him move, bursts into song, proudly declaring, "I got no strings on me!" In Animate CC, the authors suspect that you, too, will burst into song—but for the opposite reason—when you see the tools for a feature introduced in Adobe Flash Professional CS4 called inverse kinematics (IK).

What is this academic, vaguely sinister-sounding term? In simple words, IK lets you string up your artwork like a train set, like sausages, or, if you prefer, like a marionette. And when you pull the strings, so to speak, or move one of the connected symbols, your artwork responds like a bona fide action figure. You can use IK to make poseable models and then animate them.

As stated on Wikipedia:

> *"Inverse kinematics refers to the use of the kinematics equations of a robot to determine the joint parameters that provide a desired position of the end-effector. Specification of the movement of a robot so that its end-effector achieves a desired task is known as motion planning."*

Seriously, this feature is way cool, and we think you're going to love playing with it. That said, it's one of the more complicated feature sets in Animate CC. Stringing up your symbols is easy enough. The official terminology calls for creating an armature and populating it with bones, which can then be dragged around. Adobe engineers have made this dead simple.

The tricky part is a question of how. To a certain extent, you'll find armatures and bones immediately intuitive, but just when you think they make sense, they'll behave in a way that might just strike you as utterly wrong. You'll see what we're talking about in the following exercises, and we'll show you an approach that should give you what you expect.

It all starts with something called the Bone tool.

When Flash Professional was updated from the CS6 version to CC – it was completely rewritten to modernize the codebase and make the program more powerful than ever. Unfortunately, certain features such as the Bone tool were not rewritten along with the core application. Thus, for a few years, the program did not include this tool. However, Adobe had always stated that features that were left out would be added back in if there was enough of a desire for them. In 2015, we saw Flash Professional receive a revamped and reintegrated Bone tool and inverse kinematics system of animation – and this is now all available in Animate CC as well.

Using the Bone Tool

The Bone tool is your key to the world of poseable armatures in the authoring environment. Using it will give you an inkling of the satisfaction experienced by a certain famous Victor Frankenstein, without anywhere near the hassle he went through or the illegal outings. You won't be visiting any actual graveyards, for example.

Let's see how the Bone tool works.

1. Open the `09_Bones.fla` file from the exercise folder for this chapter. You'll be greeted by a more or less anatomically correct hand, sans flesh. Go ahead and wave! The wrist and hand bones are all part of the same graphic symbol, named "hand" in the Library. The knuckles are also graphic symbols, named by finger and knuckle number—for example, ring1, ring2, and ring3. All of these symbols happen to be on the same layer, but that doesn't need to be the case.

CHAPTER 8 ■ THE MOTION EDITOR AND INVERSE KINEMATICS

2. Select the Bone tool from the Tools panel. It's the one in Figure 8-25 that looks like a bone, just above or to the left of the Paint Bucket, depending on your Tools panel configuration.

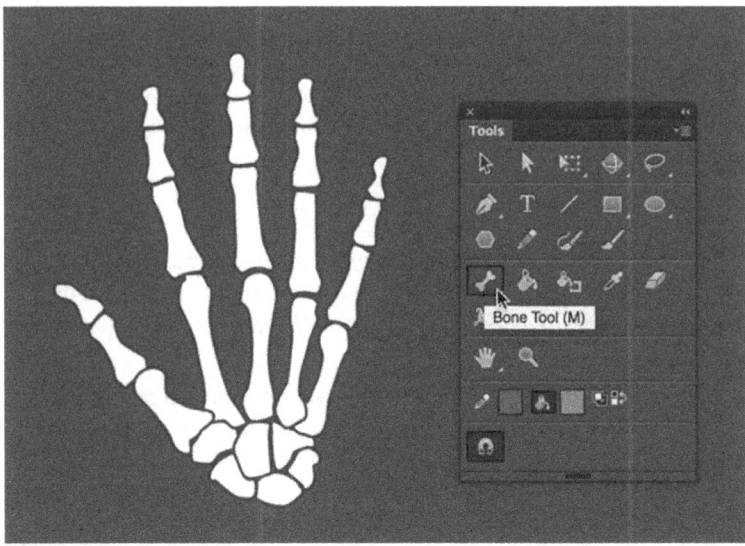

Figure 8-25. *The Bone tool lets you connect symbols the way bones are connected in real life*

3. Click over the bottom-center portion of the skeleton's wrist, and drag toward the bottom of the thumb's first knuckle, as shown in Figure 8-26. When you release the mouse, you'll see your very first armature, which includes a single IK bone.

Bones can only be rigged between graphic symbols, movieclips, or artwork that has been broken apart. Trying to run a bone, for example, from one photo to another will result in an error message telling you, essentially, "Nope you can't do that!"

Notice the new layer in the Timeline panel, called Armature_1. The layer icon is also noticeably different, resembling a stick figure. That's your armature, and as you continue to connect your symbols together with IK bones, those symbols will automatically be pulled to this new layer. Just like a motion tween layer, this layer has distinctive properties. For example, you can't right-click (Windows) or Control+click (Mac) an armature layer to tween it, even though IK poses can be tweened (more on this later in the chapter, in the "Animating IK poses section"). You can't draw shapes on or drag symbols to an armature layer.

Bones have two ends, and it's helpful to know their anatomy. The larger end of the bone, where you started to drag, is called the head. The smaller end of the bone, where you released the mouse, is called the tail. The tail is pointing up and to the left in Figure 8-26. A string of connected bones is called an IK chain or a bone chain.

CHAPTER 8 ■ THE MOTION EDITOR AND INVERSE KINEMATICS

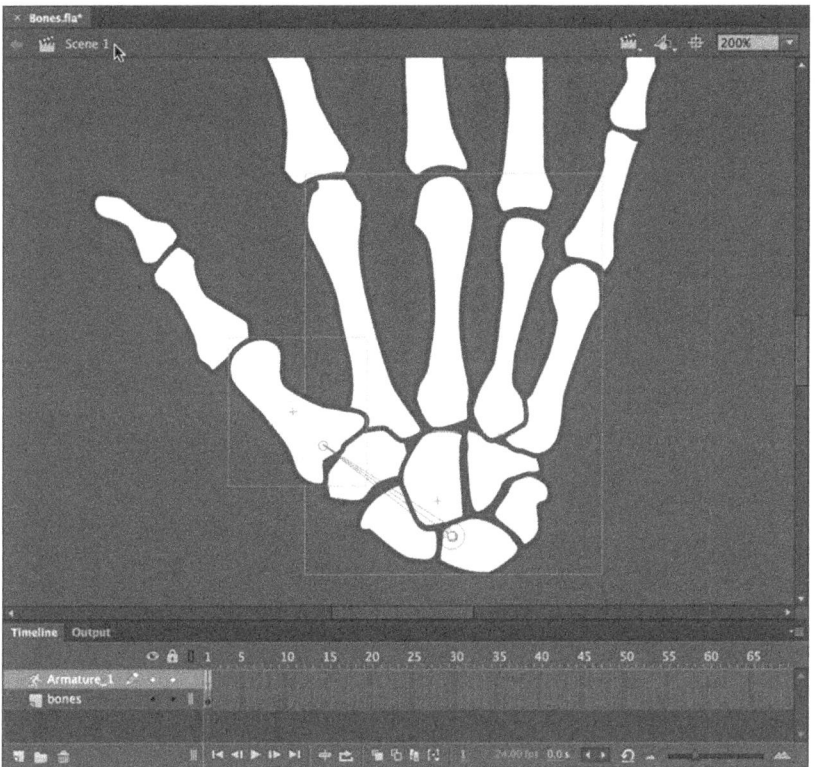

Figure 8-26. *Drawing your first bone creates the armature*

4. Still with the Bone tool, hover somewhere inside the symbol that represents the first knuckle on the thumb. You don't need to be exact—just within the symbol's bounding box. Then click and drag toward the bottom of the second knuckle. You'll notice that even if you don't begin the second drag directly over the tail of the first armature bone, Animate CC will automatically snap it into place for you. Release when you're over the bottom of the second knuckle.

5. To finish the thumb, hover anywhere inside the second knuckle's symbol. Click and drag upward to the bottom of the third knuckle. When you release, you'll have the simple bone rigging shown in Figure 8-27.

423

CHAPTER 8 ■ THE MOTION EDITOR AND INVERSE KINEMATICS

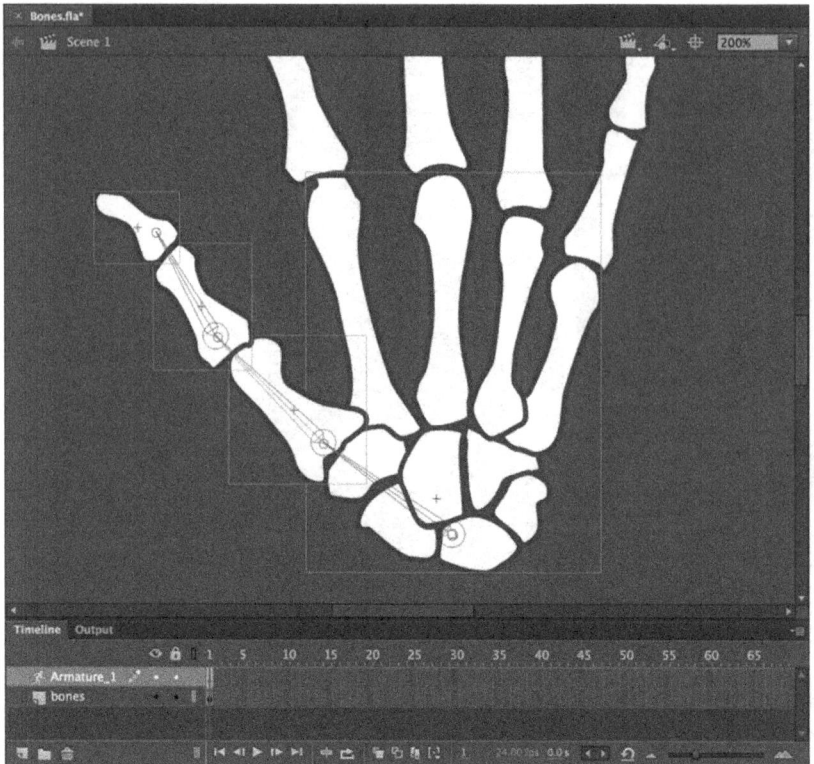

Figure 8-27. *As you connect symbols with bones, the symbols are pulled to the armature layer*

If you're anything like the authors, you're just dying to try these bones, so let's take a quick break and do just that.

6. Switch to the Selection tool, grab that third knuckle, and give it a shake.

We fully expect you'll have fun, but all the same, you'll also see that it's also pretty easy to arrange the hand into what looks like an orthopedic surgeon's dream (see Figure 8-28). It may surprise you, for example, that the wrist pivots, and those knuckles are bending into contortions that make even our yoga buddies wince. We'll fix those issues in just a moment. First, let's get acquainted with the Bone tool properties.

CHAPTER 8 ■ THE MOTION EDITOR AND INVERSE KINEMATICS

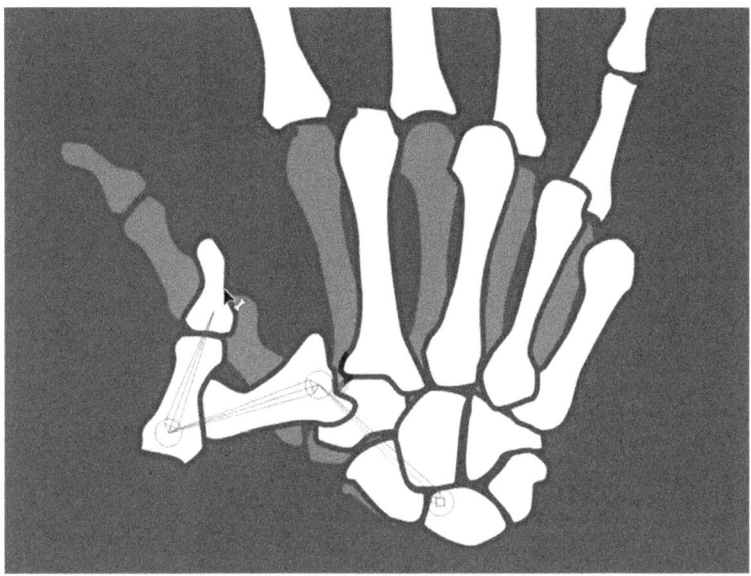

Figure 8-28. *Ouch! Bones are easy to connect, but the results aren't always what you might anticipate*

Bone Tool Properties

There are two ways to nudge the Properties panel into showing bone-related properties: by clicking an IK bone on the stage and by clicking the armature itself, which is represented by an armature layer. Let's start with the armature.

1. Continuing with the Bones.fla file, click frame 1 of the Armature layer. When you do, the Properties panel updates to show three twirlies:

    - **Ease**: In this area, you'll find a drop-down list for selecting easing from a list of prebuilt choices and a Strength value that lets you specify intensity, just as you saw in the Properties panel for motion tweens. These settings configure easing for the span of an armature layer (you can drag out an armature span to encompass as many frames as you like). Armature layers provide their own tweening capability, which is discussed in the "Animating IK Poses" section and again in the last exercise of this chapter. For now, just note that this is where you can apply easing.

    - **Options**: The area gives you something to see even without tweening. The Style drop-down list lets you specify how you want the IK bones to look. You have three choices: Wire (the default), Solid, Line, and None, which are illustrated in Figure 8-29 from left to right. When working with numerous or very small symbols, consider using the Wire or Line styles. Why? Because the Solid view can obscure symbols that appear under the IK bones.

    - **Springs**: Allows you to enable or disable springs for the entire armature. Springs are enabled by default.

425

CHAPTER 8 ■ THE MOTION EDITOR AND INVERSE KINEMATICS

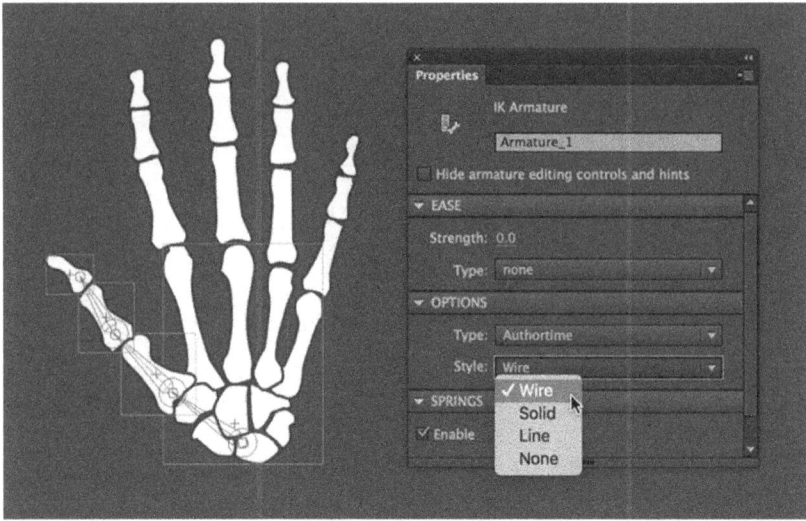

Figure 8-29. Bones can be configured as Wire, Solid, Line, and None

2. Change the Type drop-down selection from Authortime to Runtime. You'll see the warning message shown in Figure 8-30.

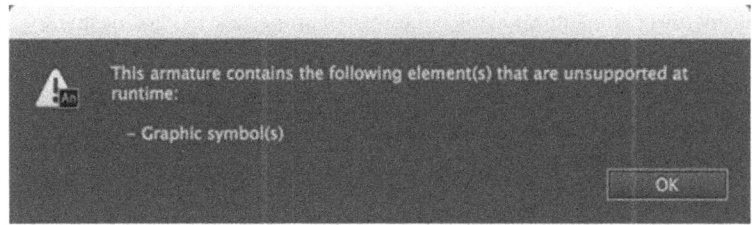

Figure 8-30. Only MovieClip bones can be interactive at runtime

The reason for the warning is that, although bones can be made interactive for the user, Animate CC requires that the boned symbols be movieclips when Type is set to Runtime. Fortunately, this is easy to change, even if there are numerous symbols in play.

3. Click OK to close the warning dialog box.

4. Open the Library, and click the first symbol, named hand, to select it. Press and hold the Shift key, and then select the last symbol. Now everything in your Library is selected.

5. Right-click (Windows) or Control+click (Mac) any one of the symbols and choose Properties from the context menu.

What you get is a feature introduced way back in Flash Professional CS4, which is an incredible time-saver. The Symbol Properties dialog box opens—not just for the symbol you clicked, but for all selected symbols.

CHAPTER 8 ■ THE MOTION EDITOR AND INVERSE KINEMATICS

6. In the Symbol Properties dialog box, place a check mark in the Type property, and change the drop-down choice to Movie Clip, as shown in Figure 8-31. Then click OK.

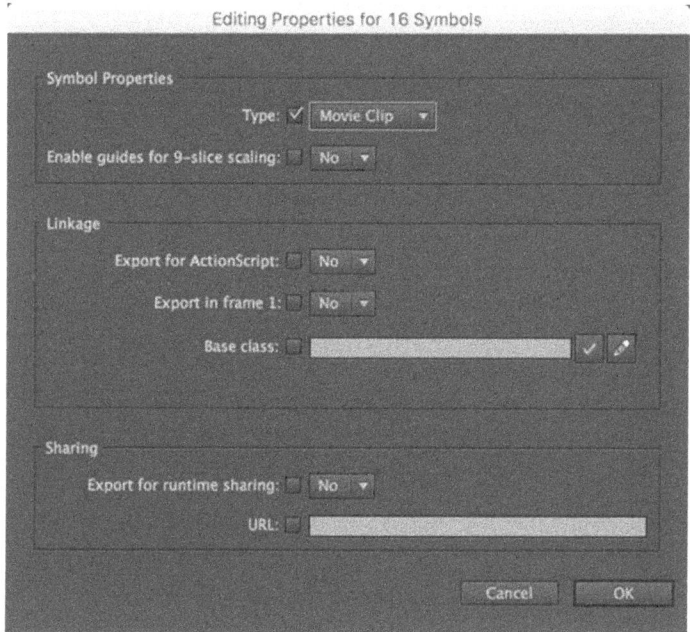

Figure 8-31. *Animate CC lets you change multiple symbol properties at once in the Library*

All of your Library's graphic symbols become movieclips simultaneously. This used to take a separate visit to each asset. However, you still need to let the stage know what you've done.

7. Click the stage to select it. Select Edit ➤ Select All. In one swoop, you just selected all your symbol instances on the stage.

8. Click any one of the symbol instances to update the Properties panel, and then select MovieClip from the drop-down list at the top of the Properties panel.

9. Click frame 1 of the Armature layer and change the Type drop-down selection to Runtime.

10. Test the movie and wiggle those thumb knuckles inside Flash Player. Pretty neat!

11. Close the SWF and click one of the IK bones to update the Properties panel.

RUNTIME ARMATURES IN HTML5 CANVAS

As you've seen, in order to manipulate IK at runtime, your armature must be composed of MovieClip symbol instances. There is another restriction to consider when dealing with armatures—target document type, as shown in Figure 8-32.

CHAPTER 8 ■ THE MOTION EDITOR AND INVERSE KINEMATICS

Figure 8-32. *When targeting HTML5 Canvas, you cannot select Runtime as an Armature Type*

12. With the properties updated, double-click one of the bones on the stage (not the symbol instance) and in the Properties panel you now see bone-specific properties. Let's go over those:

    - **Position X, Y, Length, and Angle**: These are read-only properties, which means you can look, but don't touch. Thankfully, the names are self-explanatory.

    - **Speed**: Think of this as friction, or how much "give" the selected bone has in the armature. A higher number means faster movement, and your range is 0 (no movement) to 200 (fast movement). You can also select the Pin check box here to pin the tail of the selected bone to the stage.

    - **Joint: Rotation**: Here, you have the following choices:

        - **Enable**: Selecting this check box allows the bone to pivot around its head. In contrast, deselecting it means the bone won't act like a hinge.

        - **Constrain, Min, and Max**: Selecting Constrain activates the Min and Max hot text values, which allow you to determine how wide an arc your hinge can pivot on.

    - **Joint: X and Y Translation**: The choices for this property are as follows:

        - **Enable**: Selecting this check box allows the bone to effectively pop in and out of its socket, in the X- or Y-axis.

        - **Constrain, Min, and Max**: Selecting Constrain activates the Min and Max hot text values, which allow you to determine how far the bone can move.

    - **Spring**: This property integrates dynamic physics into the Bones IK system. The two properties allow easier creation of physics-enhanced animation.

        - **Strength**: Think of a car spring and a Slinky. The car spring is rigid, whereas the Slinky is totally bendable. The Strength property stiffens a spring. If the Slinky has a value of 0, then a car spring has a value of 100.

        - **Damping**: The rate of decay of the spring effect. Higher values cause the springiness to diminish more quickly. A value of 0 causes the springiness to remain at its full strength throughout the frames of the pose layer

Of the properties available, Rotation, Translation, and Spring will give you the biggest bang for your buck. Let's see how easy it is to fix that misshapen hand! While we're at it, you'll learn some helpful subtleties on manipulating the symbols in an armature.

428

Constraining Joint Rotation

IK bone rigs are as much an art as a science. The science facet derives from the Properties panel, which gives you have some configuration settings. The art facet depends on your sense of the appropriate range of motion for a given armature. Let's jump in:

1. Continuing with the Bones.fla file, use the Selection tool to drag the hand itself—not any of the fingers or the thumb—and carefully pivot the hand so that it realigns again under the fingers.

2. Select the first IK bone (the one closest to the wrist), and deselect the Enable check box in Properties panel's Joint: Rotation area.

3. Drag the thumb's third knuckle again, and note that the wrist no longer moves.

   If you ever change your mind, just reselect the first IK bone, and put a check mark back in the Enable property. Now let's make sure the thumb doesn't look so double-jointed.

4. Select the second IK bone and, in the Properties panel, enable the Constrain check box in the Joint: Rotation area, as shown in Figure 8-33.

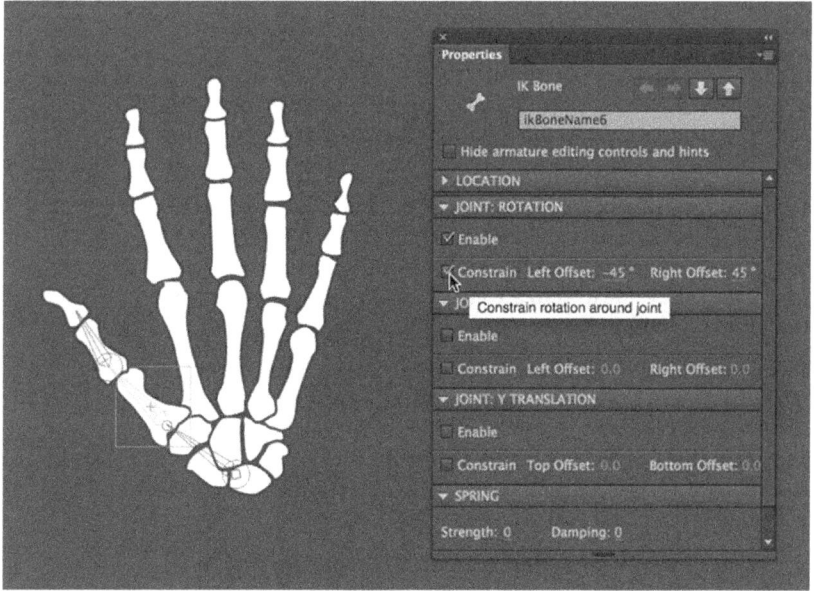

Figure 8-33. *The Constraint check box lets you constrain a joint's range of motion*

Choosing Constrain adds a new component to the IK bone, which you can see in Figure 8-34. Suddenly, the bone's head sprouts a wedge shape, with a line in the middle that separates the wedge into two pie pieces. The line has a square handle on its outside end. (If you're in a Robin Hood mood, it may look like a bow and arrow.) This wedge represents the joint's range of movement. By default, you get a 90-degree sweep.

CHAPTER 8 ■ THE MOTION EDITOR AND INVERSE KINEMATICS

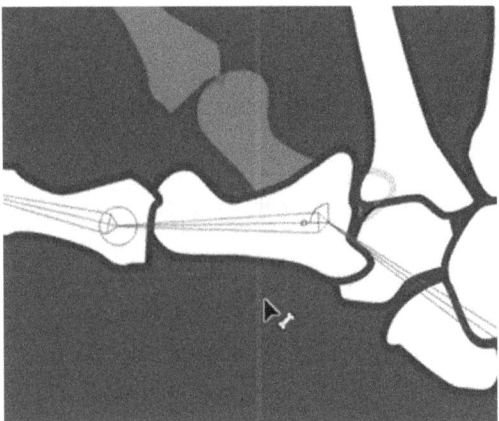

Figure 8-34. *Select Constrain in the Joint: Rotation area of the Properties panel, and joints sprout a range-of-movement icon*

5. Drag the third knuckle downward. The line with the square handle moves counterclockwise until it rests against that side of the wedge. Drag the knuckle up, and the handle moves to the other side—clockwise—until it meets the opposite side of the wedge.

   Adjusting this range of movement is easy. The workflow we prefer is to pivot the IK bone into position first and then scrub the Min or Max hot text as necessary to meet that position.

6. Drag the third knuckle upward until the thumb moves as far in that direction as you like. If you need more room, select first knuckle's IK bone, and scrub the Max value toward the right to increase its value. Readjust the thumb, and when you like how it sits, scrub the Max value toward the left again to bring the edge of the wedge toward the square-handled line.

7. Drag the third knuckle all the way down, and repeat this process for the other extreme. You'll notice that the first knuckle appears above the bones of the wrist. That may or may not be what you want. If you want to send the knuckle behind the wrist, use the Selection tool to select that knuckle's symbol and select Modify ➤ Arrange ➤ Send to Back. The first knuckle is done. You can now move onto the second, which isn't any harder to manage.

8. Add a Joint: Rotation constraint to the second knuckle and configure the Min/Max values in whatever way suits you.

   As you move the skeleton bones around, you can use the Shift key to temporarily change the way the IK bones respond. For example, drag the third knuckle up and down, and then hold down Shift and drag again. When Shift is pressed, only the third knuckle moves. This works with any other bone. Drag the second knuckle with and without Shift to see what we mean.

   While you're at it, experiment with the Ctrl (Windows) or Cmd (Mac) key as well. If you ever want to reposition a symbol without having to redo an IK bone from scratch, hold down Ctrl (Windows) or Cmd (Mac) while you drag. This temporarily releases the dragged symbol from its IK chain. When you release the key, the IK bones are reapplied.

CHAPTER 8 ■ THE MOTION EDITOR AND INVERSE KINEMATICS

The third knuckle is the interesting one, because although it's attached to an IK bone, it's only associated with that bone's tail. This means you can't constrain its rotation. (Give it a try!) So, what to do? Since we're dealing with so many kinds of bones, we think it's fitting that the answer relies on the presence of a ghost—not a real ghost, of course, but a stand-in "ghost" movieclip.

9. In the Timeline panel, select the non-armature layer (the one labeled bones).

10. Use the Oval tool to draw a small circle—say, 20 pixels by 20 pixels—no stroke, and color doesn't matter.

11. Convert that circle to a MovieClip. Name the symbol Ghost and position it just past the thumb's third knuckle.

12. Using the Bone tool, add a fourth IK bone between the third knuckle and the ghost handle movieclip, as shown in Figure 8-35.

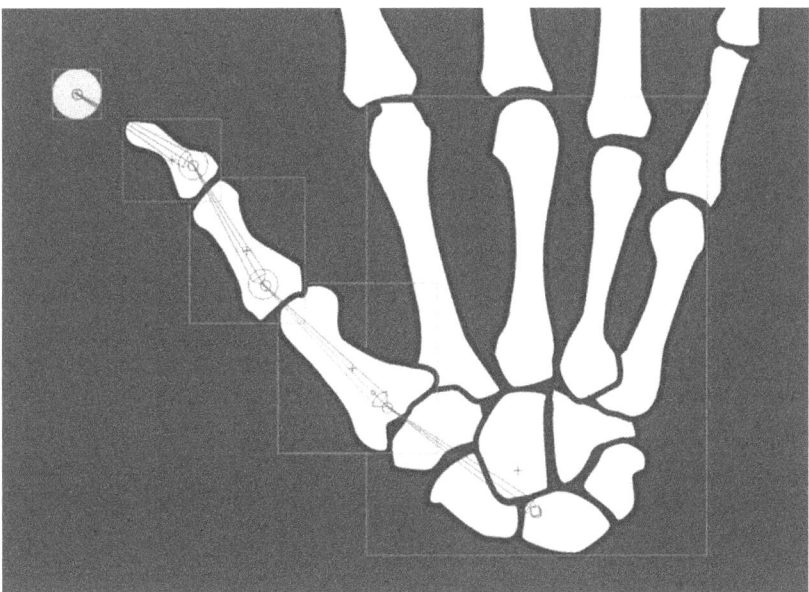

Figure 8-35. *Use a stand-in movieclip to let you constrain the previously end-of-the-line IK bone*

13. Select the newest IK bone and constrain its Joint: Rotation property.

14. Save your file.

Sure, the ghost movieclip may look a little silly, but its presence allows you to configure your IK bones from start to finish.

Here's the best part: whenever you need another stand-in IK bone, make sure to keep reusing that same Ghost MovieClip. Why? Because when you're ready to publish the project, all you have to do is open that symbol in the Library and change its fill color to 0% Alpha. Just like that, your extra handles become invisible, and they still do their job.

431

Deleting Bones

We showed you how to create IK bones, but you'll also want to know how to delete them. It couldn't be easier:

1. After saving your Bones.fla file, use the Selection tool to select the fourth IK bone from the previous exercise. Press the Delete key. Badda bing, badda boom...the bone is gone.

2. Skip the third IK bone and select the second one. Press the Delete key.

   This time, both the second and third bones disappear. This tells you that deleting an IK bone automatically deletes any other bones attached to its tail.

3. Right-click (Windows) or Control+click (Mac) frame 1 in the Armature layer and select Remove Armature from the context menu.

   As expected, the last IK bone disappears. If you had made this selection in step 1, all of the IK bones would have disappeared from the start.

4. Select File ➤ Revert and then click the Revert button in the alert box to undo all the deletions.

Putting Some "Spring" in Your Bones

In addition to general IK properties such as Rotation and Translation, there is a Spring option for bones. Adobe calls it a "physics engine for Inverse Kinematics" and, regardless of what you call it, we think it's a pretty neat way of bending stuff in an animation.

You may notice in this exercise that we are using IK on shapes and not symbol instances. The IK tooling can be used on either Animate CC object type!

Okay, let's take a look:

1. Open the 10_Springs.fla file in your exercise folder. When it opens, you will see two trees on the stage, and if you scrub across the timeline, you will see them bend in a gust of strong wind.

2. Springiness works best when the object containing the bones is put into motion. This is done using poses, which we will get into later in this chapter.

3. Click the tree on the left, and click the bone at the bottom to select it.

4. Open the Properties panel, and you will notice the bone has a Strength value of 100 and a Damping value of 5. Strength is the stiffness of the spring (see Figure 8-36). Higher values create a stiffer spring effect. Damping is the rate of decay of the spring effect. Higher values cause the springiness to diminish more quickly. A value of 0 causes the springiness to remain at its full strength throughout the frames of the pose layer.

CHAPTER 8 ■ THE MOTION EDITOR AND INVERSE KINEMATICS

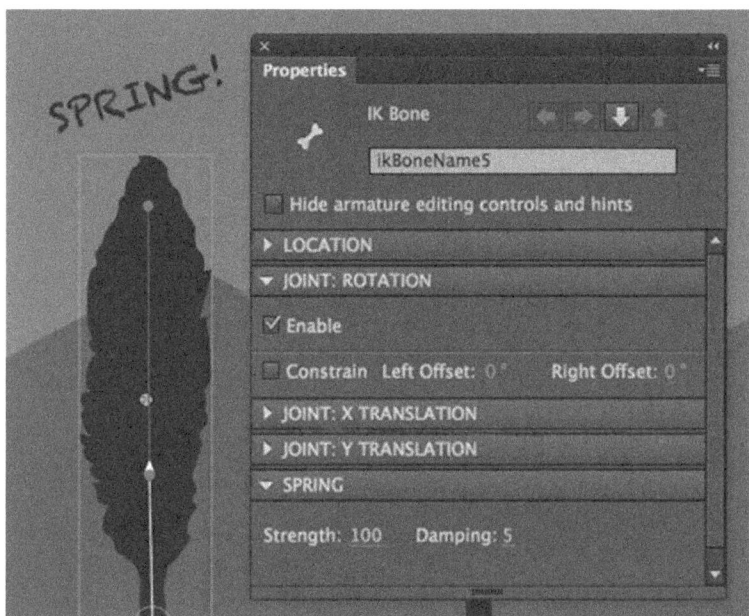

Figure 8-36. *Adding spring to a bone using the Strength and Damping properties*

5. Now that you know what the values mean, scrub across the timeline to the first keyframe and compare the shapes of the trees. The tree on the right does not have springiness applied to it. As shown in Figure 8-37, the tree that has been "stiffened" looks a lot more natural than its counterpart on the right which has had springiness disabled.

There is something else you need to know: Spring properties are applied to bones. Springiness is applied to layers. If you click any frame of the NoSpring layer and open the Properties panel, you will see that the Enable check box for springs is deselected.

433

CHAPTER 8 ■ THE MOTION EDITOR AND INVERSE KINEMATICS

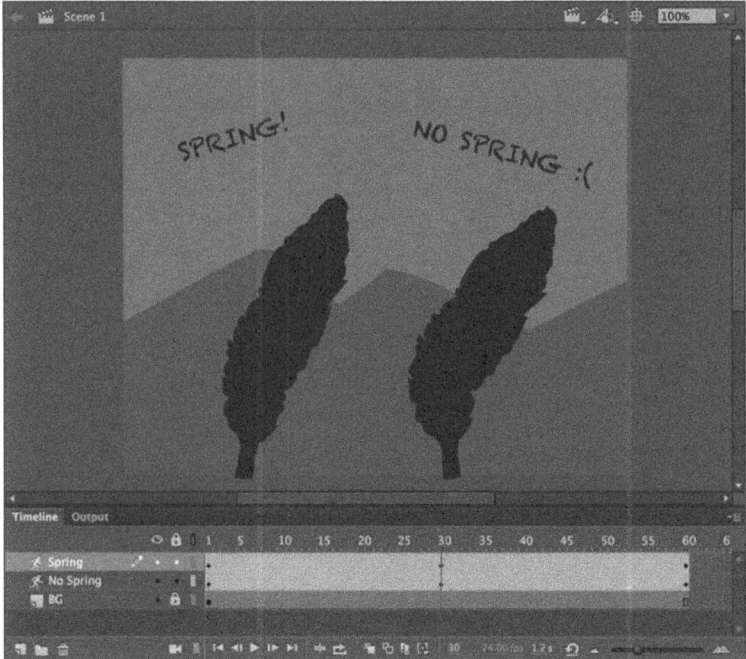

Figure 8-37. *Springs, used in the tree on the left, add realism to objects in motion*

Applying Joint Translation

Another way to control the movement of joints is called joint translation—generally meaning a change in position or movement. This affects movement of an IK bone along its X- or Y-axis (or both). To illustrate, we'll leave our skeleton at the chiropractors for a while and turn our attention to a vampire.

> *"Sava Savanović was said to have lived in an old watermill on the Rogačica river, at Zarožje village in the municipality of Bajina Bašta. It was said that he killed and drank the blood of the millers when they came to mill their grains."* – Wikipedia

It was in November of 2012 that the authorities of the Serbian village of Zarozje issued a warning to the world after the vampire's mill (the place he would reside in) collapsed. The local mayor even stated "People are worried, everybody knows the legend of this vampire and the thought that he is now homeless and looking for somewhere else and possibly other victims is terrifying people. We are all frightened." Truly frightening. Let's build Sava a new mill.

1. Open the `Mill.fla` file from the Chapter 8 exercise folder. The symbols are already in place for you and there is much additional artwork to help attract Sava back to his refuge.

    In Figure 8-38, we've labeled the mill wheel assembly's anatomy to assist you in the next steps, so you can focus your attention entirely on the IK rigging. You're going to connect three horizontal symbols from left to right. Ignore the actual wheel for the time being.

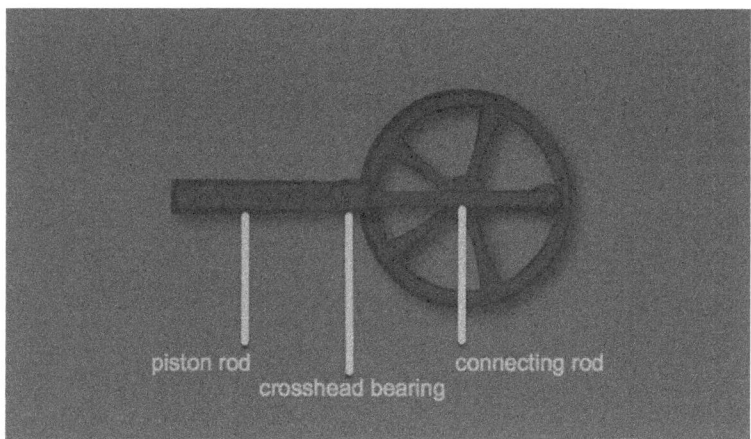

Figure 8-38. *The movement of this mill wheel will include joint translation*

2. Select the Bone tool and then add a bone that starts on the left side of the piston rod symbol and ends on the crosshead bearing symbol (the center symbol).

3. Add another bone from the crosshead bearing symbol to the right side of the connecting rod symbol, as shown in Figure 8-39. This is no different from the bone rigging you did for the knuckles.

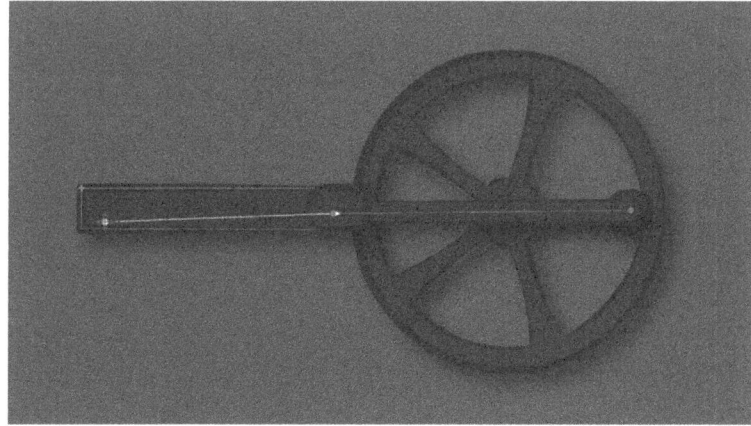

Figure 8-39. *Two bones connect three symbols*

Joint translation doesn't require ActionScript, but we're going to use some programming to demonstrate it in this particular case. Because we'll be using ActionScript, let's give the bones and armature meaningful instance names.

4. Using the Selection tool, select the bone on the right, and use the Properties panel to give it the instance name `connectingRod`, as shown in Figure 8-40.

CHAPTER 8 ■ THE MOTION EDITOR AND INVERSE KINEMATICS

Figure 8-40. *Bones and armatures support instance names, just like movieclip symbols*

Pay close attention to the Properties panel when making your selections. It's easy to accidentally click the symbol to which a bone is applied, rather than the bone itself. In this context, the symbol is listed as an IK Node in the Properties panel. If you select an IK node, this exercise won't work properly. Figure 8-41 shows the correct selection of a bone, which displays IK Bone in the Properties panel.

5. Select the other bone and give it the instance name `pistonRod`.

6. Select the armature itself by clicking frame 1 of its layer in the Timeline panel. Use the Properties panel to give the armature the instance name `engine`. The armature's layer name will update to the same name.

    Now it's time for the joint translation, but first, let's keep this bone from rotating. It's possible for bones to translate and rotate, but that isn't what we want here. Our aim is to let the piston rod slide left and right when the armature moves.

7. Select the `pistonRod` bone and use the Properties panel to disable its rotation (that is, deselect the Enable check box in the Joint: Rotation area).

8. To achieve the left-and-right motion, select the Enable check box in the Joint: X Translation area. The bone's head gets a horizontal double-headed arrow, as shown in Figure 8-41.

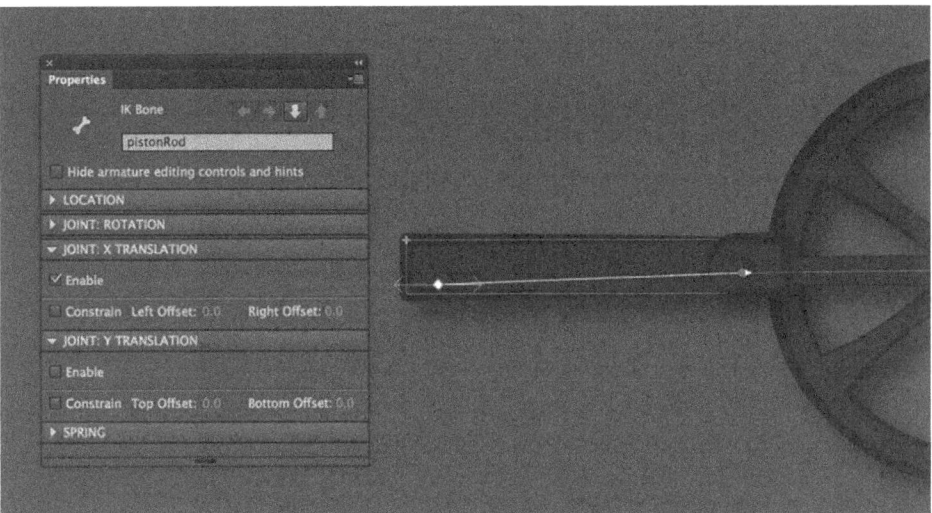

Figure 8-41. Joint translation is indicated by a double-headed arrow along the relevant axis

You could optionally constrain this translation by selecting the Constrain check box and configuring Min and Max values, just as with joint rotation, but that isn't necessary here. Note, too, that you could optionally translate (and constrain) along the y-axis, but we'll also omit that step.

Time to get Sava's wheel moving!

9. Click frame 1 of the armature's layer (engine) to select the armature. In the Options area of the Properties panel and change the Type drop-down selection to Runtime. Now this rigging is ready for ActionScript.

10. Select frame 1 of the Actions layer and open the Actions panel. Type the following ActionScript:

```
import fl.ik.*;

var pt:Point = new Point();
var arm:IKArmature = IKManager.getArmatureByName("engine");
var bone:IKBone = arm.getBoneByName("connectingRod");
var tail:IKJoint = bone.tailJoint;
var pos:Point = tail.position;

var ik:IKMover = new IKMover(tail, pos);
```

The first line imports all the classes in the fl.ik package, which includes classes necessary for identifying and manipulating armatures created in the authoring tool. The next line declares and instantiates a variable, pt, set to an instance of the Point class. (The Point class doesn't reside in the fl.ik package, but in just a moment, you'll see that something called the IKMover class needs a Point instance.)

437

CHAPTER 8 ■ THE MOTION EDITOR AND INVERSE KINEMATICS

From the third line on, the code unfolds like the lyrics in that old catchy tune, "Dry Bones" ("the knee bone's connected to the...thi-i-igh bone"). How so? A variable, arm, is declared and set to an instance of the IKArmature class. This variable takes its value from a method of the IKManager class, which connects it to the armature whose instance name is engine.

After that, a bone variable—an instance of the IKBone class—is connected to the bone whose instance name is connectingRod. Then a tail variable (IKJoint class) is connected to the tailJoint property of the bone instance. Finally, a new Point instance (pos) is connected to a pair of coordinates from the position property of the tail instance.

The tail and pos variables are passed as parameters to a new instance of the IKMover class, which is stored in the variable ik. That ik variable allows you to move the armature with code.

11. Add the following new ActionScript after the existing code:

```
wheel.addEventListener(Event.ENTER_FRAME, spin);
function spin(evt:Event):void {
  wheel.rotation += 5;
  pt.x = wheel.crank.x;
  pt.y = wheel.crank.y;
  pt = wheel.localToGlobal(pt);
  ik.moveTo(pt);
}
```

The basic premise here is something you've already seen in other chapters: a custom function, spin(), is associated with the Event.ENTER_FRAME event of an object with the instance name wheel. In this case, wheel is the instance name of the wheel-shaped movieclip symbol. (We've already configured the instance name for you in the sample file, and the wheel symbol contains another movieclip inside it with the instance name crank.)

So, what's going on in this event handler? First, the MovieClip.rotation property of the wheel instance is incremented by five. That gets the wheel rolling continuously. After that, it's just a matter of updating the pt variable declared earlier. Being an instance of the Point class, the pt variable has x and y properties, which are set to the crank movieclip's x and y properties, respectively. Because crank resides inside wheel, the object path to the desired x property is wheel.crank.x. The same goes for y.

This updates pt's properties to the current position of crank, but that isn't quite enough. From the wheel symbol's point of view, crank never actually moves—it's wheel that does the rotating!—so the coordinates need to be considered from the point of view of the stage. That's what the second-to-last line does by invoking the DisplayObject.localToGlobal() method on the wheel instance. In plain English, it tells pt to reset itself in from crank's local coordinates inside wheel to the crank's global coordinates shared by all objects on the stage.

Finally, pt is passed as a parameter to the IKMover instance represented by the ik variable.

12. Test your movie so far to see the result.

    It's close to being correct, and the `pistonRod` bone does perform its horizontal joint translation, but if you look carefully, you'll notice that the armature occasionally "slips" from the `crank` movieclip. That's easy to fix, and it's nothing more than a matter of priorities.

    The armature isn't updating as quickly as the wheel turns, so let's fix that by tweaking the number of calculations it has to make.

13. Use the Actions panel to insert the following two lines after the `ik` variable declaration and before the event listener (the new code is shown in bold):

    ```
    ...
    var ik:IKMover = new IKMover(tail, pos);
    ik.limitByIteration = false;
    ik.iterationLimit = 5;

    wheel.addEventListener(Event.ENTER_FRAME, spin);
    function spin(evt:Event):void {
    ...
    ```

14. Test the movie again. As you can see in Figure 8-42, everything should run fine.

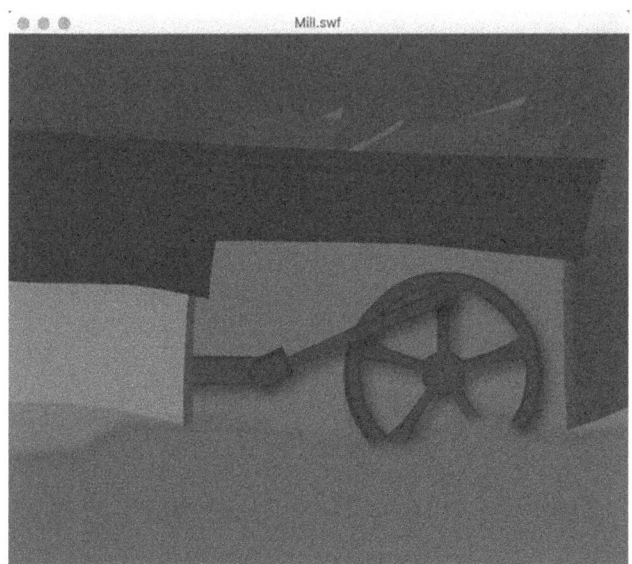

Figure 8-42. *The completed mill—you've saved Serbia from the vampire's wrath!*

We've used ActionScript to wire up the code for this example. What if you needed to use JavaScript instead? Sorry, you're out of luck and Sava has you for an early breakfast. JavaScript and CreateJS simply do not allow the sort of control over armatures that ActionScript does so you must be targeting either Flash Player or AIR for the above to work correctly. Of course, you can always perform the same sort of animation without code when targeting HTML5 Canvas. It's a matter of choice and approach.

A Note About Bone Preferences

Let's return to our friendly skeleton hand. We mentioned earlier in this chapter that IK poses can be animated, even without the use of a motion tween layer. You'll see how in the next section. First, it's time for a quick field trip.

1. Open the 11_BonesRigged.fla file in this chapter's exercise folder. You'll see the fingers and thumb pointing upward, and the thumb has a ghost handle.

2. Use the Selection tool or the Free Transform tool to click the first knuckle of the pointer finger. As Figure 8-43 shows, the symbol's transformation point (the small white circle) is dead center.

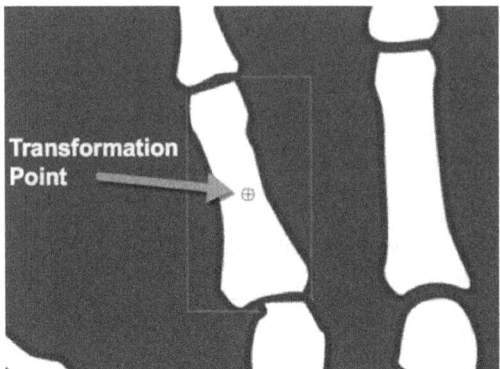

Figure 8-43. *This symbol's transformation point is horizontally and vertically centered*

3. Noting the transformation point, select Edit (Animate CC) ➤ Preferences, and click the Drawing choice in the Category area. Find the IK Bone tool: Auto Set Transformation Point check box and deselect it, as shown in Figure 8-44. Click OK to close the Preferences dialog box.

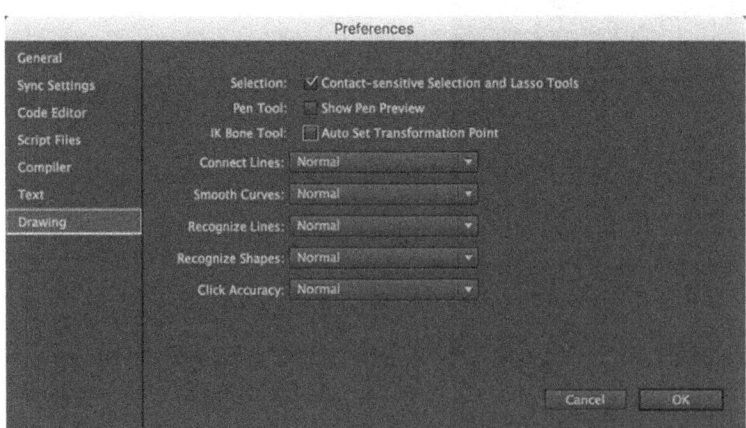

Figure 8-44. *The Auto Set Transformation Point setting affects how bones are applied to symbols*

CHAPTER 8 ■ THE MOTION EDITOR AND INVERSE KINEMATICS

4. Using the Bone tool, hover over the hand symbol, and then click and drag a new IK bone toward the first knuckle of the pointer finger. As you do, notice that the tail of the IK bone snaps to the transformation point of the first knuckle. Note, also, that the armature is perfectly capable of handling more than one chain of bones.

5. Repeat this process to rig up the remaining knuckles of the pointer finger.

6. Using the Selection tool, grab the third knuckle and give the finger a wiggle. As shown in Figure 8-45, the pivots occur on the transformation points, which just doesn't work for this scenario. We want the knuckles to line up end to end.

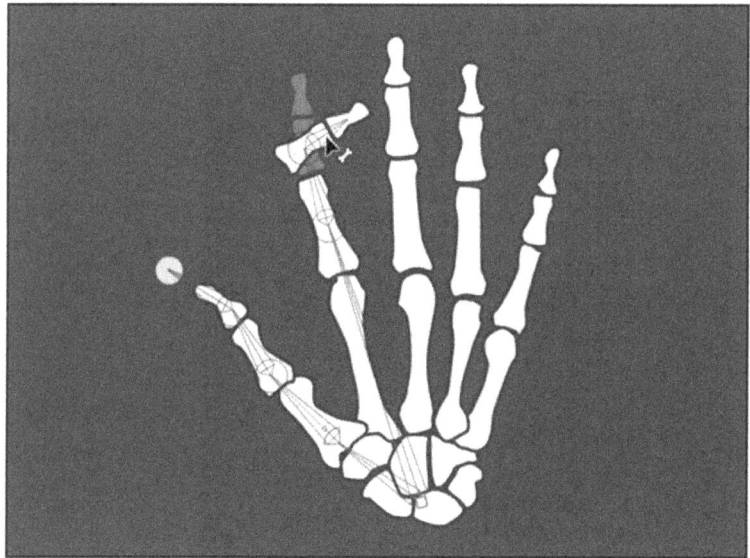

Figure 8-45. *If you want, IK bones can snap to a symbol's transformation point*

7. Return to the Preferences dialog box and reselect the IK Bone tool check box.

8. Select File ➤ Revert and then click the Revert button to roll the file back to its original state.

    We brought up the IK Bone tool preference setting because it's hard to spot unless you happen to be poring through the Preferences dialog box. We chose a silly example because silly visuals tend to stick.

By leaving the Auto Set Transformation Point check box selected in the Preferences dialog box's Drawing section, you're telling Flash to move a symbol's transformation point for you automatically. If you prefer to maintain that control on your own, deselect that check box, and then use the Free Transform tool to make your symbol selections. When selected with the Free Transform tool, a symbol lets you move its transformation point with an effortless click-and-drag operation. If the symbol already belongs to an IK chain, any heads or tails connected to it will reposition themselves to the new location of the symbol's transformation point.

441

CHAPTER 8 ■ THE MOTION EDITOR AND INVERSE KINEMATICS

Animating IK Poses

As you saw earlier with the springs example, to get those trees to bend in the wind, we needed to animate the IK poses. In this section, we show you how to do that but rather than bend trees, let's slip on our hard hats and visit a construction site.

1. Open the 12_Poses.fla file in your exercise folder. You will see we have placed a Steam Shovel on the stage. The image started life as a multilayer Photoshop image imported into Animate CC. Each layer of the Photoshop image was placed in a graphic symbol, and each symbol has its own layer on the main timeline.

2. Select the Magnifying Glass tool and zoom in on the machine. You are going to need a closer view of the pieces to place the bones.

3. Select the Bone tool and draw a bone from the back of the MainArm symbol to the top joint of the ShovelArm symbol. Keep in mind that Bones only link symbols to each other. Bones within a symbol will kick out an error message. In this case, run the bone between the MainArm and ShovelArm symbols, as shown in Figure 8-46.

Figure 8-46. *The bones used in the animation are in place*

4. Draw another bone from the top of the ShovelArm symbol to the joint where the shovel is attached to the ShovelArm. The three symbols have been moved from their respective layers to the armature layer.

5. Right-click (Windows) or Control+click (Mac) frame 70 of the Cab layer and select Insert Frame. The Cab symbol now spans 70 frames. Lock the Cab layer.

6. We are going to start the animation by establishing its finish position. Right-click (Windows) or Control+click (Mac) frame 70 of the armature layer, and, as shown in Figure 8-47, select Insert Pose from the context menu.

   That green strip across the armature layer tells you that you have created a pose layer. Pose layers are quite different from motion layers. They can only be created by adding a pose at a frame and they only work with armature layers. The little keyframe icon in the pose layer tells you where the poses are located.

CHAPTER 8 ■ THE MOTION EDITOR AND INVERSE KINEMATICS

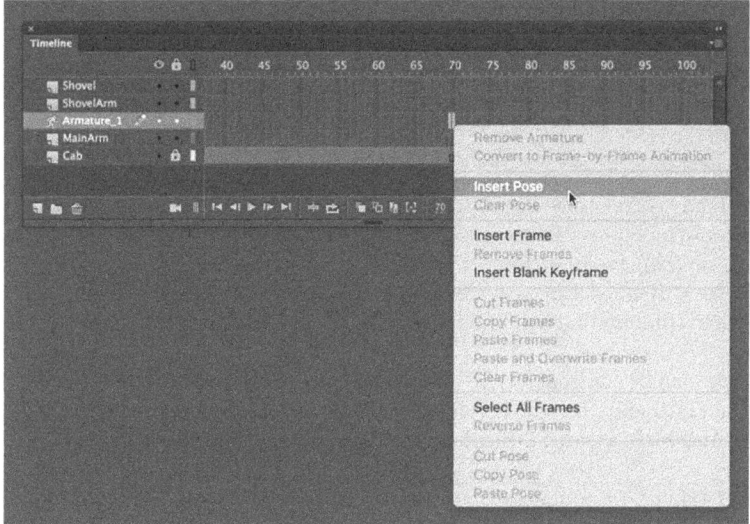

Figure 8-47. *Poses are added through the context menu*

7. Scrub back to frame 1. Switch to the Selection tool, and move the arms and the shovel to the position shown in Figure 8-48. If you scrub across the timeline the two arms and the shovel lower to the ground. This tells you that poses in an armature layer can be tweened only in the armature layer.

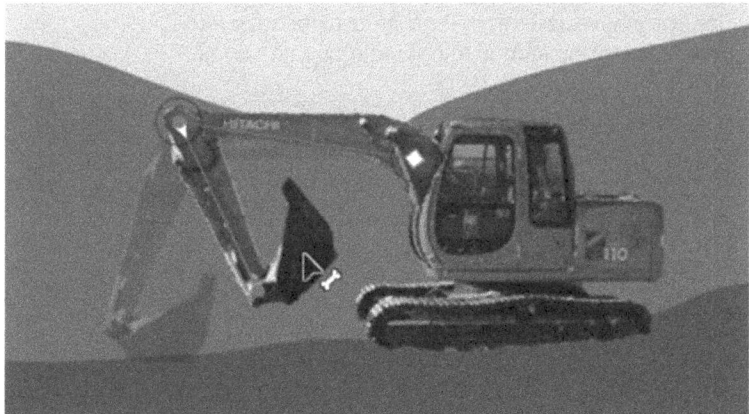

Figure 8-48. *Use the Selection tool to change a pose*

8. Move the playhead to frame 15. Switch to the Selection tool, and extend the shovel arms. What you need to know about this is that by changing the positions of the bones in an armature layer, a keyframe is automatically added. There is no need to insert a pose. This may sound rather familiar because this is exactly what happens when you change the properties of an object in a motion layer.

443

CHAPTER 8 ■ THE MOTION EDITOR AND INVERSE KINEMATICS

9. At this point you can continue moving through the timeline and having the machine scoop up and dump some dirt however you wish. When finished, go ahead and close this example and don't save the changes.

Using the Bind Tool

We expect that IK has sparked the creative center of your brain enough to keep you happily busy for weeks. Believe it or not, you still have one more tool to see. The team at Adobe has made IK available not only to symbols but also to shapes! You'll be using the Bone tool for this exercise, but the Bind tool will make an appearance as an important sidekick. The best way to describe IK for shapes is to consider it a super-advanced evolution of shape tweens in combination with the shape hinting discussed in Chapter 7. Let's jump right in.

When it comes to IK, the distortion to be controlled is in both the stroke and fill areas of a shape. Depending on the configuration of an IK shape, you may find that the stroke of the shape does not distort in a pleasing way or joints move around when moving the armature. This is where the Bind tool comes into play.

By default, the control points of a shape are connected to the bone that is nearest to them. The Bind tool allows you to edit the connections between individual bones and the shape control points. The upshot is you control how the stroke distorts when each bone moves.

Before we start, it might not be a bad idea to simply take a look at what effect "binding" has on a drawing. This way, you can see in a rather dramatic fashion what it does and learn what to look for.

1. Open the `13_BadBind.fla` file in your exercise folder. When it opens, you will see a girl resting her arm.

2. Click the girl's left arm to see the bones.

3. Switch to the Selection tool and move the arm. You will notice two things, as shown in Figure 8-49. First, the elbow moves from the bottom of the stage and some rather disturbing distortions occur around the elbow joint.

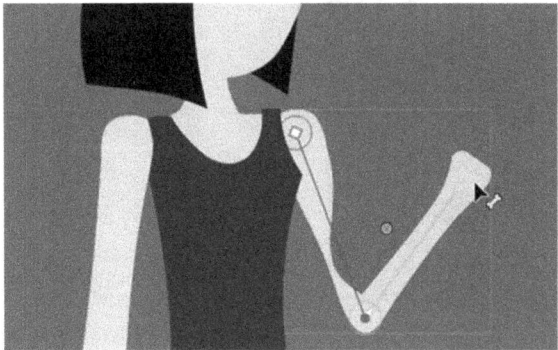

Figure 8-49. *Moving a bone in a shape causes distortions and artificial movement*

4. Open the `GoodBind.fla` file in your exercise folder and give the arm a wiggle. As you can see the distortions are not nearly as severe.

Now that you have seen how binding can affect an armature, let's get to work and start learning how to use the Bind tool.

1. Open the 14_Worm.fla file in the exercise folder for this chapter and say hello to a smiling worm, as shown in Figure 8-50. (The correlation between a worm, bones, steam shovels, and graveyards is purely coincidental, we assure you.) The Library for this FLA is empty, because the worm is nothing more than a handful of shapes.

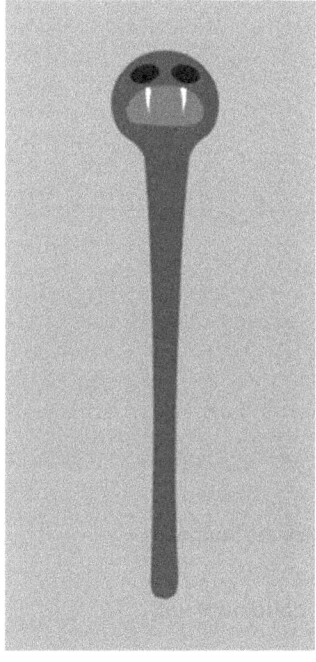

Figure 8-50. *IK for shapes is brought to you by a worm*

2. Assuming you want to drag the worm around by its head, you'll want to draw the bones of your armature from the opposite side of the worm. Select the Bone tool and starting from the bottom of the shape, drag a small IK bone upward.

3. With that first bone in place, hover over the tail of the IK bone. When the tiny white bone icon inside the mouse cursor turns to black, you'll know you've hit the right spot. Click and drag upward to add another bone.

   In this manner, keep adding small IK bones until you reach the top of the worm (see Figure 8-51).

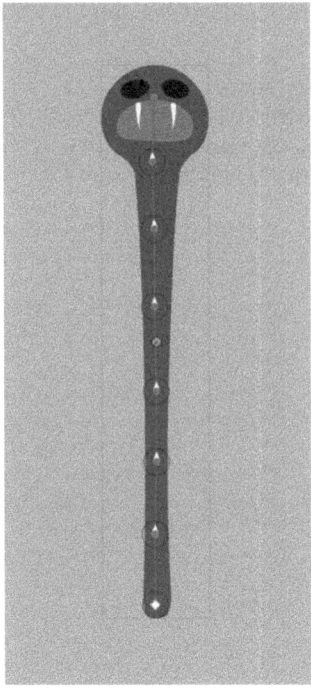

Figure 8-51. *IK bones can easily be applied to shapes*

4. Before you give the worm a wiggle, switch to the Bind tool, and click the bottom-most IK bone.

5. This is where it gets interesting. Using the Bind tool, marquee the bottom several bones in the tail. Now you're ready for action.

    Using the Bind tool is a bit like using the Subselection tool in that it reveals a shape's anchor points. In Figure 8-52, you can see anchor points represented in three different ways. At the top of the figure, they look like the sort you've seen in previous chapters—just small squares. At the bottom, they're considerably larger and thicker and appear in the form of triangles as well as squares.

CHAPTER 8 ■ THE MOTION EDITOR AND INVERSE KINEMATICS

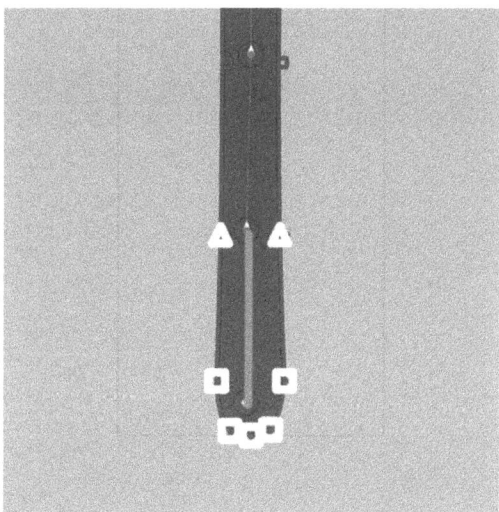

Figure 8-52. *The Bind tool lets you manipulate anchor points*

When you select an IK bone with the Bind tool, Animate CC shows you which of the shape's anchor points are associated with that particular bone. Squares indicate an association with a single bone; triangles indicate an association with many bones.

In this case, the bottom four anchor points—the heavy squares—are associated with the bottom-most bone only. The upper two anchor points—the heavy triangles—are associated with the bottom-most bone and with the bone immediately above it. The triangle anchor points are affected when either of their associated bones moves.

Click any of the other IK bones in this armature, and you'll see that Animate CC has done a great job of automatically deciding which associations to make. This won't always be the case. Thankfully, you can override these decisions.

6. Hold down the Ctrl (Windows) or Cmd (Mac) key, and click one of the bottom four heavy squares. This makes it look like a normal anchor point (smaller and not bold). Still holding Ctrl (Windows) or Cmd (Mac), click one of the heavy triangles, which also becomes a normal anchor point.

7. Select the next IK bone, and you'll see that the triangle anchor is back. but now it's a heavy square. That makes sense: before step 6, this anchor was associated with two bones (triangle), but now it's associated with only this one (square).

8. Select the bottom-most bone again, and, without holding down Ctrl (Windows) or Cmd (Mac), click the anchor point that was previously a heavy square. Drag it toward the bone (see Figure 8-53) and release. That anchor point is now reassociated with the bone.

CHAPTER 8 ■ THE MOTION EDITOR AND INVERSE KINEMATICS

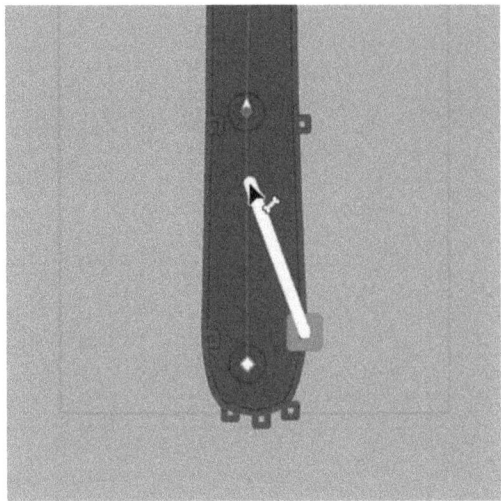

Figure 8-53. *Click and drag an anchor point to associate it with a bone*

9. Click another bone, and then click this one again. You'll see the heavy square as it originally was, along with its companions.

10. To reassociate the formerly triangle anchor point, use the Bind tool to select the appropriate anchor, and then press and hold Ctrl (Windows) or Cmd (Mac) while you drag it to the bottom-most bone. As you do, you'll see an association line in the upper bone as well as the diagonal association line created by your dragging (see Figure 8-54).

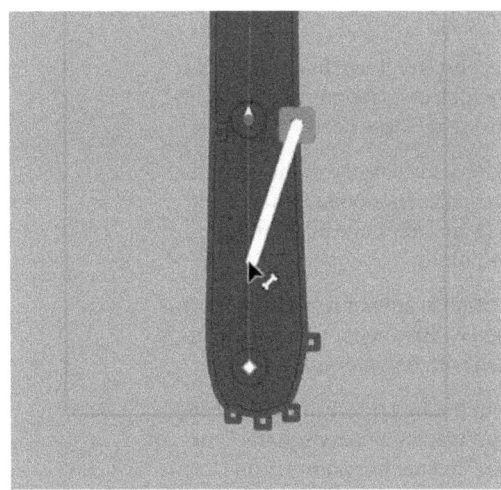

Figure 8-54. *Press Ctrl (Windows) or Cmd (Mac) while dragging to associate an anchor point with more than one bone*

11. Save the file. (You're going to continue with it in the next exercise.)

Use the Bind tool to fine-tune your shape armatures, just as you would use shape hints to fine-tune a shape tween. Any anchor points not associated with an IK bone are ignored when the armature is manipulated.

Your Turn: Animate a Fully Rigged IK model

We figure you appreciate worms, bending trees, steam shovels, and skeleton hands as much as the next designer (and so do we!). But surely, your thoughts have already wandered toward more complex implementations. We suspect you're wondering if the IK tools are useful for more than a few fingers. What about a whole body? The answer to these questions is yes, and you're about to find out firsthand. In this final exercise of the chapter, you'll expand on what you learned in previous sections by rigging up a character with arms and legs and then animating it. Let's do it.

1. Open the `15_Penelope.fla` file from the exercise folder. You'll see an assembled collection of symbols in human form. Let's name her Penelope (see Figure 8-55).

Figure 8-55. *Let's bring Penelope to life!*

2. Select Edit (Animate CC) ➤ Preferences and click the Drawing choice in the Category area. Deselect the IK Bone tool: Auto Set Transformation Point check box. Click OK to confirm the changes. As described in the "A Note About Bone Preferences" section earlier, this means you'll be the one deciding where to place your bone heads and tails, and you'll adjust them afterward.

3. Select the Oval tool and, in the Penelope layer, draw a small circle about 22 pixels × 22 pixels near one of the character's hands. Select the shape and convert it to a MovieClip symbol named Ghost. This is going to be your "ghost handle," which lets you constrain the hands, feet, and head.

4. Drag additional instances of the handle symbol from the Library to the stage, positioning them near the Penelope's other hand, her feet, and her head, as shown in Figure 8-56. In this exercise, Penelope's chest will act as the starting point for every new chain of bones, just as the skeleton's palm did in earlier exercises.

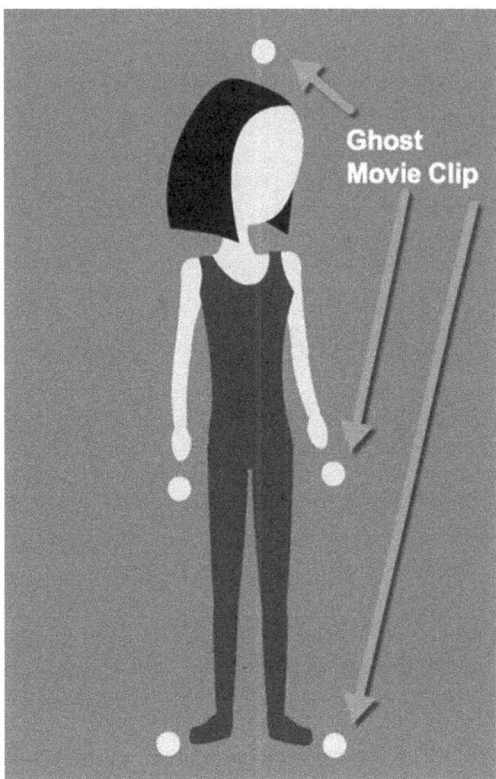

Figure 8-56. *Make sure to include extra symbols to allow for rotation constraints*

5. Select the Bone tool and then click and drag a bone from the torso symbol to the pelvis symbol.

6. Now drag a bone from the pelvis to one of the legs. Be sure to release the bone's tail low enough on the upper leg that it clears the bounding box of the torso (see the bounding box in Figure 8-57, and note how the bone tail falls below it). Even though this puts the bone tail lower than it should on the leg symbol—effectively moving the "hip" into the thigh—you'll be able to readjust it in just a moment.

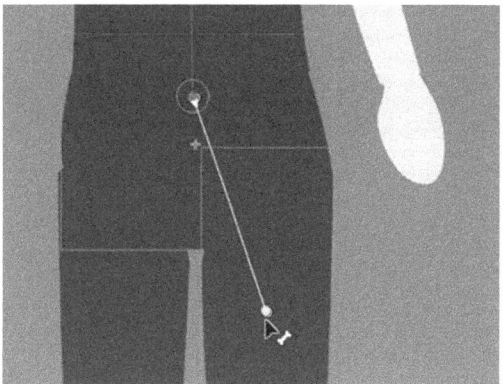

Figure 8-57. *Make sure the bone's tail clears the bounding box of the pelvis symbol*

The fact these symbols overlap is part of the reason we had you deselect Auto Set Transformation Point in step 2. Although not always a problem, in this case, the obscured symbol rotation points make it harder for Animate CC to decide on its own where new chains of bones should begin.

7. Just as you did earlier for the knuckles, continue adding a new bone that connects the upper leg to the lower leg, the lower leg to the foot, and finally the foot to the foot's ghost handle. Feel free to zoom the stage—particularly for the foot!—if necessary.

8. Select the Free Transform tool and then click the stage to deselect the armature itself.

9. Click each symbol in turn, from the ghost handle back up to the torso, and adjust the transformation point so that it sits over the symbol's registration point. To do this, click the white circle (transformation point), drag it to the small plus sign (registration point), and then release. Selecting Snap to Objects in the Tools panel will make this task easier for you.

10. After you've adjusted the transformation point for each boned symbol, select the Bone tool again, and click the head of the torso's existing bone to begin a new chain of bones down the other leg. Follow this with a repeat of the Free Transform tool adjustments of the relevant symbols' transformation points.

11. Obviously, the arms need the same treatment, as does the head. Starting from the same gathering of torso bones each time, use the Bone tool to create new bone chains from the torso to upper arm, lower arm, hand, to ghost handle on both sides, and then from torso to head to ghost handle at the top of the character. When you're finished, revisit all relevant symbols with the Free Transform tool to reposition transformation points over their corresponding registration points. Your armature should look like the one shown in Figure 8-58.

CHAPTER 8 ■ THE MOTION EDITOR AND INVERSE KINEMATICS

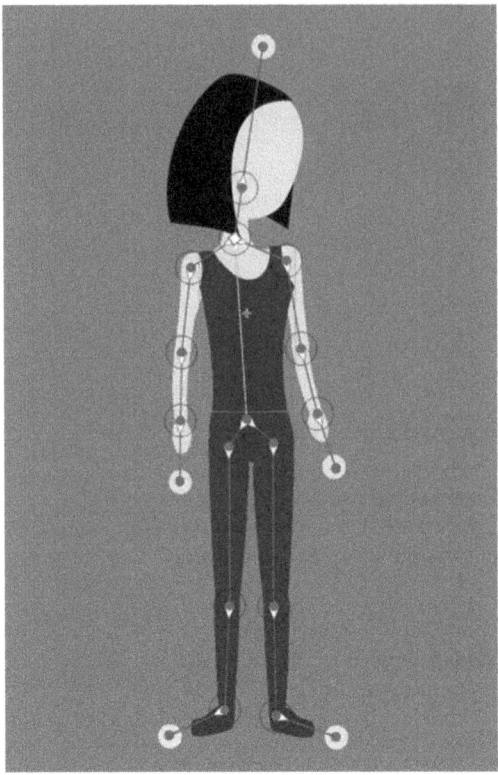

Figure 8-58. *A complete IK rig*

Go ahead and adjust the Alpha property value to 0 in the Properties panel Color Effect area with each Ghost instance selected to render them all invisible. You can still select them for various adjustments, even if not they aren't visible!

At this point, Penelope is nearly ready for her stretches. First, we need a few rotation constraints.

12. Using the Selection tool, click any of the torso bones and deselect the Enabled option in the Joint: Rotation area of the Properties panel. Because all the torso bones share the same head, this action will disable rotation for the whole body.

13. Add rotation constraints to the remaining bones according to your preferences. For example, select the lower leg's bone, and in the Properties panel, select the Constrain option and adjust the Min and Max values to keep the knee from bending backward.

When you're finished, the Timeline's original Penelope layer will have long since been emptied, because every symbol was moved to the automatically created armature layer as it was associated with a bone.

14. Create a new layer named Poses and move it below the layer containing your armature.

15. Select File ➤ Import ➤ Import to Stage and import the jumping.jpg file in this chapter's exercise folder. This JPG features a number of hand-drawn poses you can use as guides to manipulate the armature. Position the imported JPG slightly to the right, so that it appears behind Penelope, and then lock the armature layer.

16. Select the imported image and adjust its size until the initial drawn pose matches the height of Penelope, as shown in Figure 8-59. You will use this as a guide to position the armature.

Figure 8-59. *Resize the hand-drawn guides to match Penelope, and you're set*

Penelope's jump should take about one second. Because the movie's frame rate is 24 fps, that means 24 frames is fine.

17. Hover near the right edge of the of the armature's single frame until the icon turns into a double-headed arrow. Drag out the armature span until it reaches frame 24.

18. Right-click (Windows) or Control+click (Mac) the poses layer at frame 24, and select Insert Frame from the context menu. This matches up the JPG to the time span of the armature layer.

19. We're about to cut you loose, so here's the basic gist of what you'll repeat until the sequence is finished:

    a. Unlock the poses layer and slide the JPG to the left in order to position the next pose under the armature. Once the JPG is moved, lock the poses layer again.

    b. Drag the playhead six frames to the right (one-fourth of the armature span, because there are four poses after the first drawing).

c. Use the Selection tool to manipulate the character's body parts so they match the hand-drawn pose.

Here are two important tips:

- Depending on how you might have constrained your joints, you may not be able to match the drawing perfectly. Treat the drawings as rough guides. You may have noticed, for example, that our elbows don't match the pose at all—they're bent in the opposite direction! Just have fun with it.

- You will often need to move the whole armature at once. To accomplish this, hold down the Ctrl (Windows) or Cmd (Mac) key, and click the current frame of the armature layer. Doing so simultaneously selects all the armature's symbols in the chosen frame. At this point, slowly tap the keyboard's arrow keys to move the armature. If you hold down Shift while pressing the arrow keys, you can move in 10-pixel increments, which makes it go faster.

20. After you've finished posing the armature at frames 6, 12, 18, and 24, right-click (Windows) or Control+click (Mac) the poses layer and convert it to a guide layer. This will keep it from showing when you publish the project. (Alternatively, you could hide the poses layer and configure your preferences to omit hidden layers from the published project—or simply delete the poses layer.)

21. Save your file and test the movie.

What You Have Learned

In this chapter, you learned the following:

- How to use the Motion Editor
- That even though the new tweening model is intended for the Motion Editor, the Timeline continues to be useful for motion tweens
- How to use and configure advanced easing graphs and how to create your own
- How to navigate property keyframes in the Motion Editor and Timeline
- How to change the duration of a tween span
- How to manipulate and reuse motion paths, with or without the Motion Presets
- How IK works in Animate CC
- How to use the Bone and Bind tools
- How to use the Spring feature
- Tips on improving your IK bone rigging workflow
- How to animate an IK armature

This has been a rather intense chapter, but, you have to admit, there is some seriously cool animation stuff in Animate CC. We started by walking you through the Motion Editor, including motion paths. Up to this point in the book, the Motion Editor was something you "visited." Now you have learned how valuable a tool it will be as you strengthen your Animate skills.

From there, we took you deep into the inverse kinematics features of Animate CC. Starting with the Bone tool and a skeleton, we guided you through this subject. By animating trees in a wind storm, steam shovels, steam engines, and an honest-to-goodness real cartoon character, you discovered the power of inverse kinematics and quite a few of the gotchas and workarounds being developed as the Motion Graphics industry adjusts to this new animation capability.

As you went through this chapter, you were probably thinking, "This is all well and good in a flat space, but where's the 3D?" Great question. Why don't you turn the page and find out.

CHAPTER 9

Animate CC and the Third Dimension

Designers had been asking for 3D manipulation tools in its Flash predecessors for a long time. In fact, this feature has been requested in some form or another since the beginning of the product line. That makes sense if you consider that the mid-1990s promise of Virtual Reality Modeling Language (VRML) gave web surfers a taste of 3D before Flash ever hit the market. VRML was a great idea, but it was ahead of its time and, sadly, didn't go very far. In any case, it was more of a programmer's pursuit than something a designer would want to grapple with.

Then came Flash, which sparked an explosion of stylish 2D designs that began to reshape what the web experience meant. Over the years, intrepid designers began experimenting with ways to simulate three dimensions in their SWFs. They used centuries-old techniques to accomplish these goals—for example, increasing the size of an object to "move it forward"—which were the same practices used in real-life painting and sketching. Nothing in the Flash interface provided direct assistance. This all changed in Flash Professional CS4, with the arrival of the new Camera tool in Animate CC, a whole new dimension in creative and storytelling potential is open to you.

Here's what we'll cover in this chapter:

- Understanding the 3D environment
- Using the 3D tools
- Positioning symbols in 3D space
- Using the Camera tool

The following files, located in Chapter09/ExerciseFiles_Ch09/Exercise/, are used in this chapter:

- 01_Ulab.fla
- 02_Doors.fla
- 03_AirheadMail.fla
- 04_Space.fla

The source files are available online at http://www.apress.com/us/book/9781484223758.

A Brief Lowering of Expectations

Before we get started, it is important to understand there are three levels of "wow" when it comes to 3D:

- Good ("Hey, this is dope!")
- Better ("Get out of here. This isn't happening")
- Best ("Bring me oxygen!")

CHAPTER 9 ANIMATE CC AND THE THIRD DIMENSION

The absolute gold standard for 3D is the movies. There is hardly an action film that doesn't contain a Computer Generated (CG) character such as Rocket and Groot from Guardians of the Galaxy. Watching how these characters are created is what requires the call for oxygen. Game consoles such as Xbox One and PlayStation are the gold standard for 3D interactivity and are solidly in the Better category. So, let's get this out of the way right now: This simply isn't available in Animate CC.

What you'll learn about in this chapter is the super-cool stuff—the Good level—and a great place to start if you're new to nonscripted 3D in Animate CC. We won't be covering 3D in terms of ActionScript and Stage3D. What you are about to discover, though, is a bunch of tools that give you direct three-dimensional manipulation of your symbols. But first, we need to cover a bit of theory.

Understanding the Vanishing Point

When you open your eyelids and cast your gaze ahead, even if all you can see are the tweed walls of your cubicle, you have a horizon in front of you. Turn your head, and it's still there. The horizon might be hidden, but the principles of perspective still apply, just as gravity still applies even when you climb a tree or take a dive in the swimming hole. In a theoretical sense, this horizon holds something called a **vanishing point**, which is a special location, usually off in the distance, where the parallel lines in your view seem to converge. It's a natural optical illusion, and you see it every time you stare down a length of railroad tracks. In linear perspective drawings, you can have as many as three vanishing points, but Animate CC keeps things manageable for you by providing one vanishing point. Here's how it works.

Imagine you are walking along a boardwalk through a marsh. The marsh looks really interesting and you take a picture from where you are standing. If you draw lines along either side of the boardwalk, those lines will eventually intersect at a place, as shown in Figure 9-1, called the *vanishing point*.

Figure 9-1. *The vanishing point is the location where parallel lines appear to converge on the horizon*

That vanishing point is your key to understanding how the 3D Rotation and 3D Translation tools, coupled with the Transform panel and Properties panel, give you access to 3D manipulation in Animate CC. Without this concept, you can still experiment with these tools and have plenty of fun. But if you want to actually wallpaper a three-dimensional cube with movieclips or project a photo on to a wall that isn't displayed head-on, you should keep a firm grip on the notion of those perspective lines. By actually drawing them as temporary guides over your artwork, you'll find the 3D tools quite easy to use and a ton easier to work with.

CHAPTER 9 ■ ANIMATE CC AND THE THIRD DIMENSION

Before we start working with perspective and vanishing points, let's turn our attention to those 3D tools.

If you are authoring for HTML5, then you are simply out of luck. The tools mentioned here aren't available in HTML5 documents. You need to start with an ActionScript 3.0 document. To ensure that your changes convert properly across document types, right-click on any motion tween containing 3D tweens and choose Convert to Frame-by-Frame Animation from the options that appear.

Using the 3D Rotation Tool

There are two 3D tools available to you: the 3D Rotation tool and the 3D Translation tool. If you have never used them before, they will take a bit of getting used to because, instead of the usual Up/Down and Left/Right movement on the X- and Y-axes, they add a third axis. This Z-axis moves objects forward and backward or toward or away from the viewer. On top of that, this Z-axis also appears in the Properties and Transformation panels when the tools are in play. These two tools, as shown in Figure 9-2, are found just under the Free Transform tool and they are used for two separate purposes. As well, they can be used to manipulate movieclip symbols in 3D space. Let's start with the 3D Rotation tool.

1. Open a new ActionScript 3.0 document and, when it opens, draw a rectangle on the stage and convert it to a movieclip.

2. Select the 3D Rotation tool and click on the movieclip on the stage. Your movieclip is now sporting two lines and two circles. They are your rotation axes.

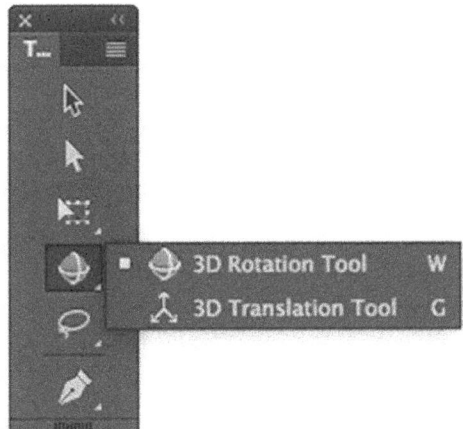

Figure 9-2. *The 3D Rotation and Translation tools are found just under the Free Transform tool*

Figure 9-3 shows the purpose of those circles and lines with the mouse pointer moving from area to area. The key here is to pay attention to how the mouse changes because each of those shapes has a specific meaning. The image on the left shows the mouse hovering over the red vertical line, which means the symbol can be rotated on its X-axis. The next one over rotates the symbol on the green Y-axis. The inner blue circle rotates the symbol on the Z-axis and the outer, orange, circle doesn't have a letter because it affects all three axes at the same time. That tiny circle in the middle is, essentially, the pivot for all four rotation methods.

CHAPTER 9 ■ ANIMATE CC AND THE THIRD DIMENSION

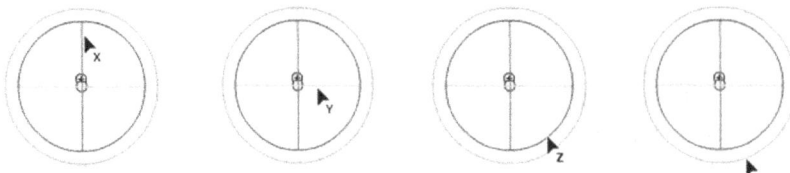

Figure 9-3. *Four views of the 3D Rotation tool's four axes of rotation*

3. To see what an X-axis rotation does, hover over the vertical red line and then click and drag, slowly, to the right and to the left. What you will see is a pie chart wedge, as shown in Figure 9-4, appear and the movieclip rotates. That wedge gives you an approximation of the rotation amount, which is about 45 degrees. The other reference you will see is a "ghosted" view of the start position of the movieclip.

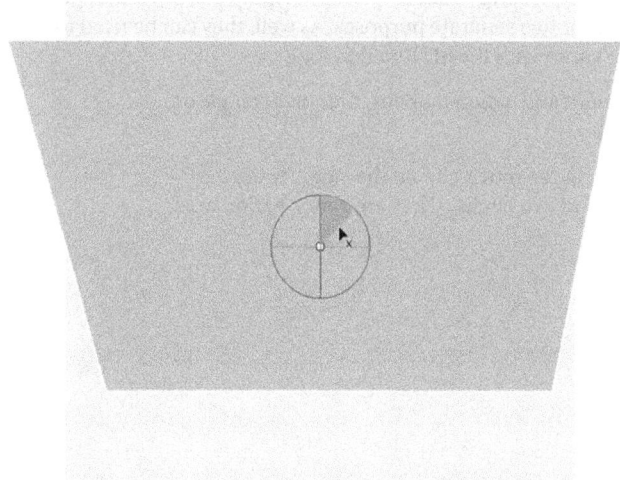

Figure 9-4. *The wedge and the ghost give you a visual clue as to how far the object is rotating*

4. Now do the same thing with the Y-axis, only this time slowly dragging up and down.

5. Drag along the blue circle and the object rotates around the Z-axis. It doesn't get closer or farther because it is rotating at the origin point—that pivot point—of the Z-axis.

6. The fun really kicks in with that outer circle. Click it and drag your mouse all over the stage. The shape rotates on all three axes at the same time.

CHAPTER 9 ■ ANIMATE CC AND THE THIRD DIMENSION

7. Open the Transform panel and check the 3D Rotation values after you rotate your movieclip on all three axes. If things are totally out of control, click the panel's Remove Transform button (Figure 9-5) to return the symbol to its original flat appearance.

8. In the 3D Rotation area of the Transform panel, scrub the hot text numbers or double-click a number and enter your own value. The symbol rotates to the values set.

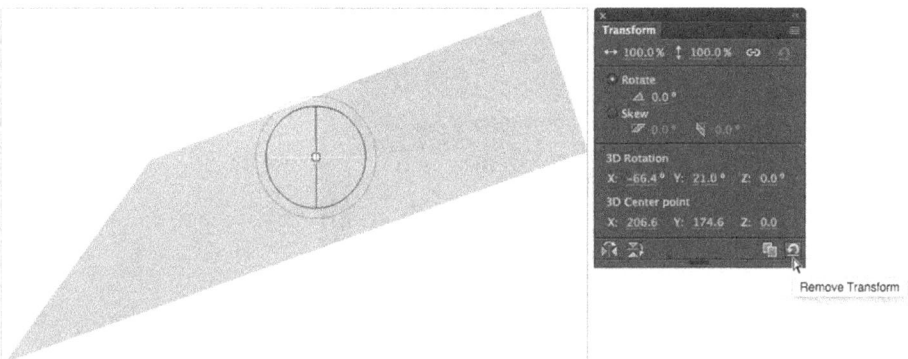

Figure 9-5. *Use the Transform panel to rotate by the numbers or to return the symbol to its original state*

Now that you understand rotation in a 3D space, let's move on to positioning objects in a 3D space in Animate CC. This form of movement is called *translation* and it has its own tool.

The 3D Translation Tool

If you have primarily used Animate CC to position objects in the traditional 2D flat space, the 3D Translation tool will also take a bit of getting "used to," but once you get it, the odds are it will become one of your "Go To" tools. Without the context of a vanishing point, this tool may seem to be nothing more than a fancy selection tool. It lets you move stuff into position, but the way it works is more restrictive than yanking stuff from here to there. What's with that? To answer that question let's put a dancing horses screen saver in a monitor. Before we do that we need to provide the 3D Translation with some context: A vanishing point. Let's get started.

How to Set a Vanishing Point

Follow these steps to set a vanishing point:

1. Open the `01_Ulab.fla file` in this chapter's exercise folder. When it opens you will see an image of four monitors on a wall. If you open the Library, you will see the DancingHorses movieclip, as shown in Figure 9-6. The plan is to put those dancing horses into the screen of the second monitor from the left.

461

Figure 9-6. *It is time to put some dancing horses on a screen*

Prior to the introduction of the 3D Translation tool, getting the dancing horses to fit on a screen was a laborious process involving a lot of scaling and skewing to match the dimensions of the screen. This is no longer the case because the 3D Translation tool works with the vanishing point. To find it and set it, we need to find out where it is in this image. Here's how:

2. Add a new layer to the timeline and name it Perspective. Right-click (Windows) or Control+click (Mac) the layer's name and, from the context menu, select Guide. This converts the layer to a guide layer, which means anything added to it will be seen when authoring but will disappear when the project is published to the SWF format.

3. Select the Line tool and, in the Properties panel, make sure Object Drawing Mode is off, the stroke width is one pixel, the stroke color is white or any other color, and the Style is set to hairline.

4. With the Perspective layer selected, draw two lines along the inner edges of the screens. Be sure to go well off of the stage. At some point those two lines will intersect (see Figure 9-7). That intersection is the vanishing point. We will be using it shortly.

CHAPTER 9 ■ ANIMATE CC AND THE THIRD DIMENSION

Figure 9-7. *Use a Guide layer to identify the vanishing point*

5. Add a new layer named DancingHorses and drag the DancingHorses movieclip to the stage.

6. Switch over to the Free Transform tool and scale the movieclip to the height of the two lines using the left inside edge of the screen as your edge. You might want to move the transform point of the movieclip to the bottom-left corner to make the scaling easier.

7. This is where those two lines are put to work. With the movieclip selected, open the 3D Position and View area of the Properties panel and note the vanishing point values found just above the Reset button, as shown in Figure 9-8. Those two numbers currently show the location of the center of the stage.

Figure 9-8. *The vanishing point can be set in the Properties panel*

463

8. Scrub the X and Y values of the vanishing point hot text. As you do this, a faint horizontal and vertical guide will move across the screen. Move those guides to the intersection point of those two white lines. You have just set the vanishing point for the movieclip and the vanishing point is the key to the 3D Translation tool. Without it, the 3D Translation tool is nothing more than a fancy selection tool.

How to Use the 3D Translation Tool

Follow these steps to use the Translation tool:

1. Switch over to the 3D Translation tool and click on the movieclip instance. The movieclip instance will, as shown in Figure 9-9, sport a red horizontal arrow, a green vertical arrow, and what looks like a big black dot. Those are the three axes. If you hover the mouse over that black dot, you will see you are over the Z-axis because the letter "Z" appears under the cursor.

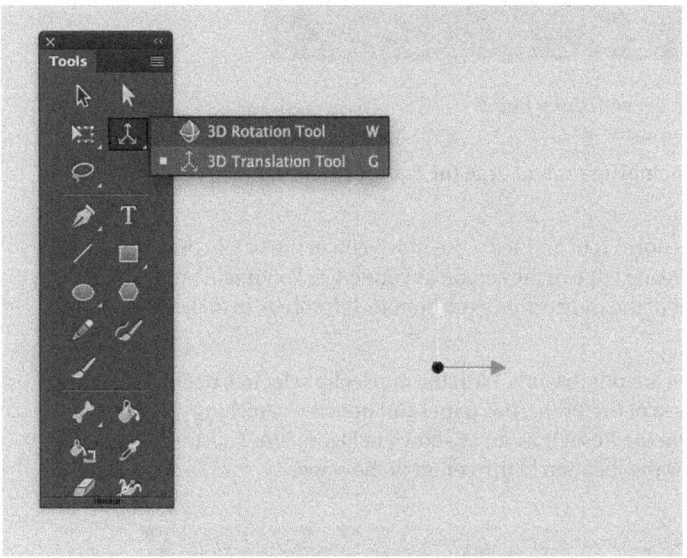

Figure 9-9. The 3D Translation tool allows movement along three axes

2. To move (translate) the movieclip along the Y-axis, click on the tip of the green arrow and drag upward or downward. It is the same technique for movement on the X-axis.

3. Moving along the Z-axis is somewhat similar. Click and drag the mouse when you see that Z appear. The movieclip follows the perspective set when you set the vanishing point. Move the movieclip into position over the monitor.

If dragging the mouse is not to your liking, scrub the Z value in the 3D Position and View area of the Properties panel.

CHAPTER 9 ■ ANIMATE CC AND THE THIRD DIMENSION

The movieclip is still in flat space. This is where the Transform and Properties panels come into play to put the DancingHorses "into" the screen.

4. Open the Transform panel and, with the movieclip selected, scale the image to fit its left edge between the two perspective lines.

5. With the movieclip in position, scrub the Y value in the Transform panel's 3D Rotation area. A negative value will rotate the movieclip into alignment with the screen.

6. To nudge the movieclip to the left edge of the screen scrub the Z value (Figure 9-10) in the 3D Position and View area of the Properties panel.

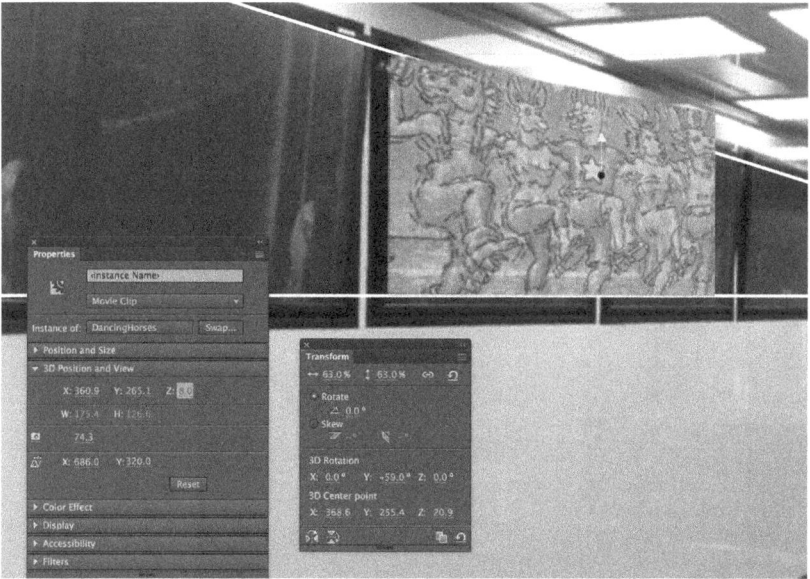

Figure 9-10. *Use the Transform and Properties panels to "nudge" the content into place and into perspective*

Although the image is following the correct perspective and is in its proper position, it still spills out across the screen. Let's fix that with a mask.

7. Turn off the visibility of the perspective and DancingHorses layers.

8. Add a new layer named Mask and, using the Pen tool, draw a shape that matches the screen.

Using the 3D Center Point to Your Advantage

If there is an underlying theme throughout this book it is: "Pay attention to the world around you." This is especially true when it comes to working with the 3D tools in Animate CC. Door don't just "flop" open over a bitmap. Icons in banner ads don't just "jiggle" around as they move across the screen. It is the prudent Animate CC artist who takes the time to "sweat the details" and get it just right. The last thing we want to hear from a user is," That just doesn't look right."

This brings us to the 3D center point feature of the Transform panel that you may have noticed and asked yourself, "What does it do?". In very simple terms, it is the pivot point for any 3D rotation. It is how doors swing open, hatches close, and icons smoothly rotate when they are in motion. Use it properly and doors swing open. Don't use it properly and doors just flop open. Let's see how it works:

1. Open the 02_Doors.fla file. When it opens, you will see a pair of doors on a New York brownstone.

2. Before moving on, let's look at the layering order. You will note there are two door layers—the building and a Guide layer named Layer 1. That Guide layer is critical because for a door opening to look natural, there absolutely needs to be a vanishing point. If you turn on the Guide layer's visibility, you will see the vanishing point is found, roughly, at the center of the two doors (see Figure 9-11). Remember, it is the doors that are in motion, not the building.

Figure 9-11. *Set a vanishing point before opening or closing doors*

3. Select the left door and click once on the 3D Rotation tool. Roll the mouse over the black dot and, if you don't see a Z appear under the cursor, drag the center to a point where you think there may be a door hinge. Move it back to where it was when it first appeared. That's the hard way of doing it. There is an easier, and more precise, method.

4. With the 3D Rotation visible, open the Transform panel and scrub the X area of the 3D center point area (see Figure 9-12). Doing it by the numbers is far more accurate than using "Mark One Eyeball". Place the center point where you think the center hinge would be on the door.

CHAPTER 9 ■ ANIMATE CC AND THE THIRD DIMENSION

5. Scrub the 3D Rotation Y-value and the door opens and closes. Close the door.

Figure 9-12. *Open doors with the Transform panel*

Now that you know how doors open, let's take that knowledge and actually have the doors open using a motion tween.

6. Right-click on the Left layer and select Create Motion Tween from the context menu. Drag the right edge of the tween strip out to frame 72.

7. Open the Transform panel and open the door in the 3D Rotation area.

8. Add a frame in Frame 72 for the Building and Perspective layers.

9. Repeat Steps 6 and 7 for the Right layer. Both doors, as shown in Figure 9-13, now swing open on their own.

467

Figure 9-13. *Use motion tweens to put the doors in motion*

Animate CC also reminds you the tween is a 3D tween. If you right-click the tween span, the context menu tells you that very fact. Deselect that notification; the motion tween remains but the 3D tween is gone.

---

10. Just because you added a 3D tween, that doesn't mean all of the other properties that can be tweened are unavailable. Move the playhead to frame 25, select a door, and add a Color keyframe. Scrub over to the end of the timeline and reduce the brightness of the selected door in the Properties panel. Repeat this step for the other door.
11. Save and test the movie.

Be Aware of Depth Limitations

As cool as the 3D tools are, they do have a limitation in terms of how three-dimensional depth (generally the Z-axis) corresponds to the stacking order of your layers, and even the stacking order of numerous symbols inside a single layer. In short, stacking order overrides 3D depth. If you drag the layer of one 3D movieclip above the layer of another 3D movieclip, the movieclip on the higher layer will always appear on top, no matter how you adjust its Z index.

CHAPTER 9 ■ ANIMATE CC AND THE THIRD DIMENSION

There are pros and cons to everything, and the pro here is that layers and in-layer symbol stacking continue to operate the way they always have. For longtime Flash users, this will feel familiar and comfortable. If you're new to Animate CC, this behavior may throw you for a loop, but you can work around it. The challenge arises when you want to perform a 3D tween that moves one object in front of another, when its original position was behind (and therefore obscured). Let's look at a hands-on example:

1. Open the 03_AirheadMail.fla file from the Chapter 9 exercise folder. You'll see an envelope with a couple postage stamps above it, one stacked behind the other, as shown in Figure 9-14. There's another stamp in a hidden layer behind the envelope, but we'll get into that in a moment. Just be aware that both of the visible stamps are located in the same timeline layer.

Figure 9-14. *Depth is determined more by layer and stacking order than by Z index (envelope photo by Cris DeRaud)*

2. Select the 3D Translation tool and click the unobscured stamp (the one on top) to select it. Adjust its Z index to scale the stamp smaller and larger.

   In terms of 3D space, a higher Z-index value seems to "push the stamp away," making it smaller. No matter how far you "push," you'll find that you cannot move the upper stamp behind the lower one. To do that, you'll have to use the old-fashioned approach.

469

CHAPTER 9 ■ ANIMATE CC AND THE THIRD DIMENSION

3. Right-click (Windows) or Control+click (Mac) the upper stamp, and select Arrange ➤ Send Backward (or Send to Back). You'll see the upper stamp pop behind its partner.

4. Unhide the bottom timeline layer (named stamp, just like the top timeline layer). This reveals a third stamp partially obscured by the envelope.

5. Using the 3D Translation tool again, adjust the Z index of either stamp in the upper stamp layer. As in Step 2, nothing you do moves either stamp behind the envelope or the stamp in the bottom stamp layer.

6. To bring the lowest stamp above the other two, you'll need to move its layer. Click the lower stamp layer and drag it above the other stamp layer, as shown in Figure 9-15.

Figure 9-15. *Drag layers to move lower content above higher content*

This is all well and good for still compositions, but how does it work for animation? You can't very well drag layers around in the middle of a tween. The trick is to split your animation over two layers, as shown in Figure 9-16. Check out `AirheadMailAnimated.fla` in this chapter's `Complete` folder to see the animation in action.

CHAPTER 9 ■ ANIMATE CC AND THE THIRD DIMENSION

Figure 9-16. *Splitting an animation between separate layers*

In what appears to be one smooth motion, the stamp emerges from behind the envelope, flies in front of it, and settles into place for mailing. In actuality, the magic happens at frame 14, where the movieclip abruptly ends in the lower stamp layer and reappears in the upper stamp layer to continue its above-the-envelope movement.

The Camera Tool in Animate CC

A new addition to the Animate CC tool collection is the Camera tool. This nifty tool turns the stage into a virtual camera, letting you pan and zoom in on the stage, crop out contents that are offstage, rotate the camera and, if you are using an ActionScript 3.0 document, you can even manipulate the color properties of object in the camera's frame. This tool is a much-needed addition to the toolset because it addresses a major complaint users had with Animate. In order to create smooth camera-like motion, they had to rely on third-party tools whose quality and ability to work with various releases of Animate CC was, to put it gently, spotty at best.

Due to the fact this is Adobe's first "kick at the can" with this tool, don't think you are being handed the power of the camera in After Effects or that you can start cranking out high-end Hollywood-like results. Having said that, there is some pretty neat stuff you can do with this tool. Let's take a look:

1. Open the 04_Space.fla file found in the exercise folder. You will notice the astronaut drifts off into space and that the planet below him is slowly rotating. Let's try out a new camera to see what it can do.

If you want to see how this was set up, we included Space.psd in the chapter's exercise folder.

471

CHAPTER 9 ■ ANIMATE CC AND THE THIRD DIMENSION

2. Select the Camera tool and you will notice that a Camera layer has been added to your timelines and a camera controller appears on the stage, as shown in Figure 9-17.

Figure 9-17. *Select the camera and a layer is added to the timeline and the camera controls appear*

Before we get into playing with the camera, it is important that you understand a couple of things about this new Camera layer:

- The camera layer must be the top layer. You have no control over this. Any new layers are added below it.
- You can add motion tweens and classic tweens to a camera layer as well as easing to the tweens. In fact, Adobe recommends adding some simple easing to all Camera motion.
- You can't add anything to the Camera layer.
- You can't copy and paste a camera layer into a symbol.
- You can't add a camera layer to a symbol's timeline.

3. The Controller allows you to do two things: rotate the camera or zoom. If you find using a slider a bit imprecise, you can "do it by the numbers".

4. Select the Camera layer and open the Properties panel. The Camera properties, shown in Figure 9-18, will appear. You can either scrub the Zoom and Rotate numbers or enter your own values.

472

CHAPTER 9 ■ ANIMATE CC AND THE THIRD DIMENSION

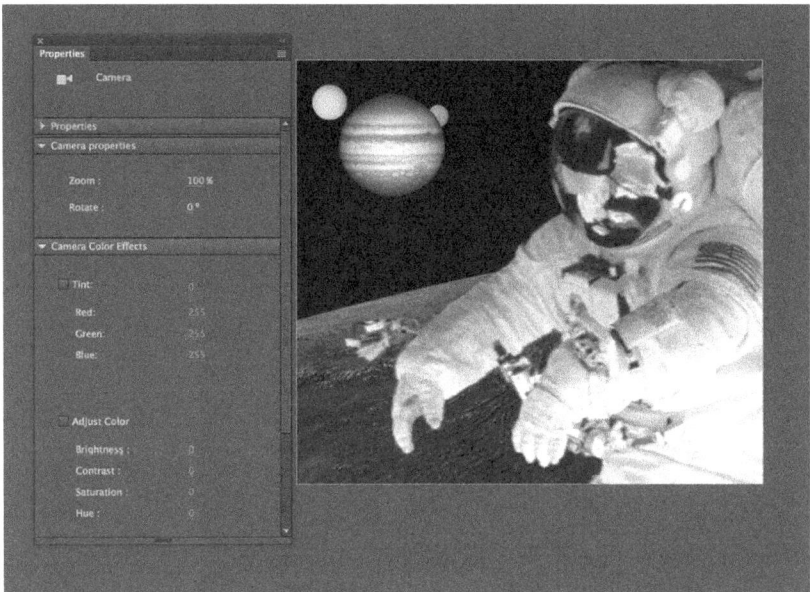

Figure 9-18. *The Camera properties give you granular control over the camera movement*

5. To remove the Camera layer, you can either select the Camera layer and delete it or click the Camera button to the right of the Trash icon in the timeline. Clicking the Camera button also adds a Camera layer if one is not present.

How to Use the Camera

Follow these steps to use the camera:

1. To zoom the camera, select the Zoom feature of the controller and drag the slider to the right or left to zoom out or in. Alternatively, scrub the Zoom value in the Properties panel.

2. To rotate the camera, select the Rotate feature of the controller and drag the slider to the left or the right to rotate the contents of the frame. Alternatively, scrub the Rotate value in the Properties panel.

3. To pan across the stage, hover the cursor on the stage. The cursor will change to a camera, as shown in Figure 9-19. Click and drag in any direction and the stage will follow the panning motion. You can also press the Shift key to constrain a pan to horizontal or vertical movement.

473

CHAPTER 9 ■ ANIMATE CC AND THE THIRD DIMENSION

Figure 9-19. *Drag the cursor to pan the camera*

None of these camera movements will be applied to anything but the Camera layer. Zooming will not affect any objects with a 3D translation or rotate any objects with a 3D rotation. You are only modifying the view of the Camera itself and not individual objects.

How to Move the Camera

To start, camera movement is accomplished with a tween. You can use a motion tween or a classic tween. In the case of this exercise, we will be using classic tweens.

1. In the 04_Space.fla file, drag the playhead to frame 140 of the Camera layer, and insert a keyframe.

2. Return to frame 1 and, using the Properties panel, set the Zoom amount to 250%. You should just see the surface of the planet on the stage.

3. Right-click anywhere between the two keyframes and add a classic tween.

4. Press the Return/Enter key to preview the motion. The full scene becomes revealed as the camera zooms out, as shown in Figure 9-20.

CHAPTER 9 ■ ANIMATE CC AND THE THIRD DIMENSION

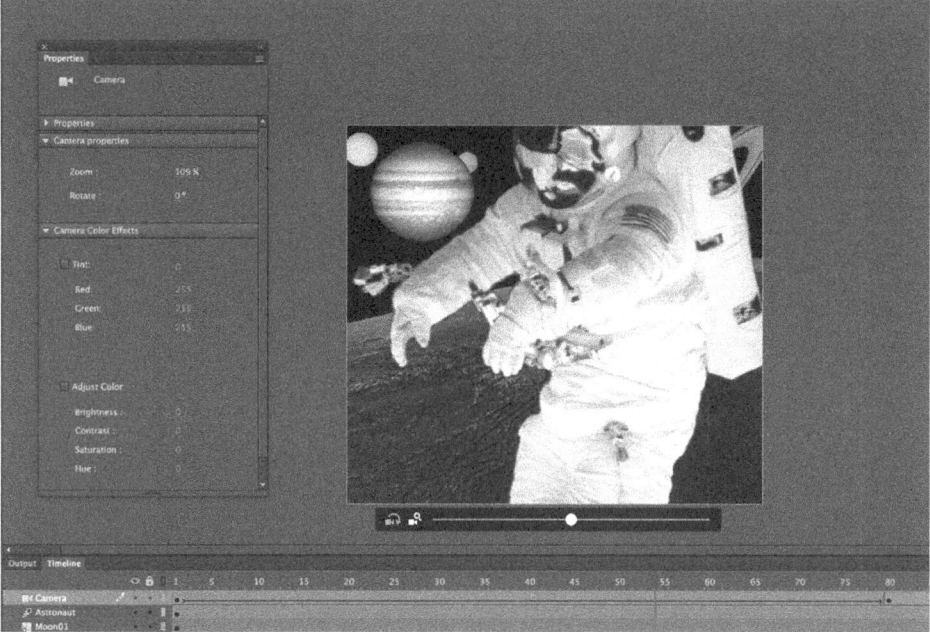

Figure 9-20. *Zooming using a classic tween*

Tweens need easing and easing can be applied to the camera motion.

 5. Now let's rotate the camera. Add keyframes at frames 240 and 270 of the Camera layer. In frame 270, rotate the camera -20 degrees. Add a classic tween and don't forget to add an ease to the tween.

 6. Next, let's pan the camera. Add keyframes at frames 300 and 450. Making sure you have the Camera tool selected, pan to the left until the astronaut is visible. Create a classic tween and add an ease.

 7. Let's put it all together. Add keyframes at frames 500 and 600. Select the keyframe at frame 600 and set the zoom to 25%, Rotate to -11. Pan upward until the two planets are in the lower half of the stage and our lonely astronaut is lost in space.

 8. Still on that last keyframe, select Adjust Color in the Properties panel and, as shown in Figure 9-21, reduce the brightness to -100. One of the more interesting aspects to this step is the planets and moons are also in motion, darkening as the camera pulls back, even though they are in static timeline layers.

Remember that list of things you can't do with the camera? Here are a couple more: You can't apply color or tint changes if you are using an HTML5 Canvas document. Color and tint only work with ActionScript 3.0 and WebGL documents. You can't hide, lock, or add a guide or mask to a Camera layer either.

475

CHAPTER 9 ■ ANIMATE CC AND THE THIRD DIMENSION

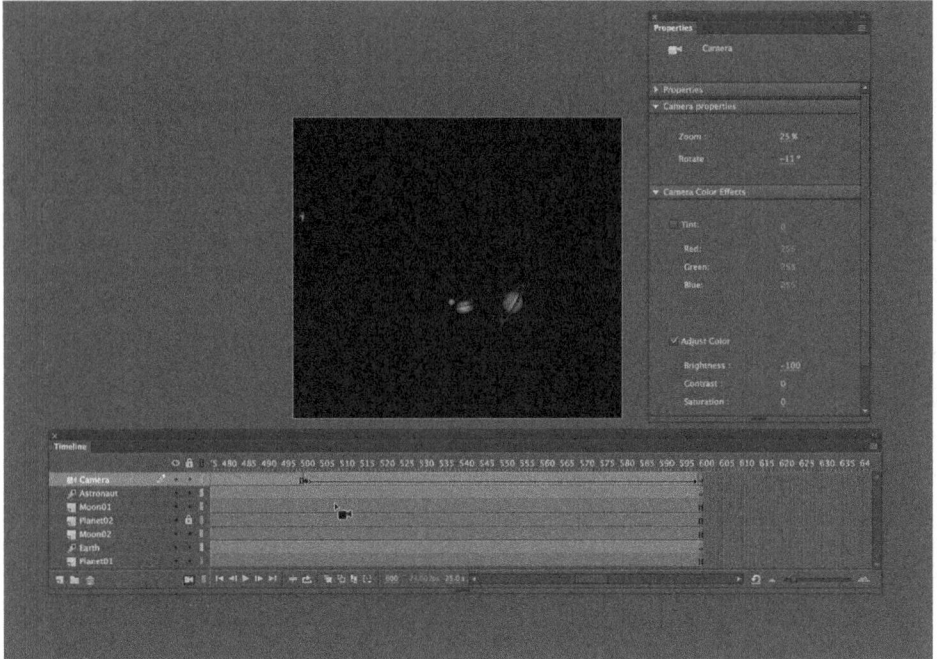

Figure 9-21. *You can create some very interesting motion effects with the camera*

Bonus Round: Select File ➤ Export ➤ Export Video. When the Export Video dialog box opens, browse to the folder where you want to place the video and click Export. We have included a copy of the video in this chapter's Complete folder. Yes, you can export your Animate CC movies as video files. Welcome to Hollywood, kid!

What You Have Learned

In this chapter, you learned the following:

- The rudiments of perspective drawing with an emphasis on the all-important vanishing point
- How to use the 3D Rotation and 3D Rotation tools
- How to use the Properties panel and the Transform panel in conjunction with the 3D tools
- How to use the Camera tool to tell a story

You may have noticed that you can output your Animate movie as an MP4 video. In fact, Animate CC has the ability to play video. We get into all of that and what you need to know to create video for Animate CC in the next chapter. We'll see you there.

CHAPTER 10

Video

When it comes to video in Animate CC, the Grateful Dead had it right when they named one of their earlier albums, "A Long Strange Trip".

For Animate CC, video has indeed been a long, strange trip. Between 2005 and 2011, the best video platform on the web was Flash Player-based. In fact, YouTube videos were primarily delivered through Adobe Flash Player. This was understandable because, around that time, Flash Player was available on over 90% of all of the computers on the planet. Then mobile arrived, the market started to fracture, and Apple banned Flash Player from the iPhone. At that point, Flash video declined into obscurity until the arrival of the <video> tag in HTML5. The odd thing about that was even though Animate CC offered an HTML5 Canvas document, it wasn't until November 2016 that video components made their way back into Animate for that particular platform.

In many respects, this is unsurprising. Video has made quite the resurgence on the web and on mobile. There is hardly a web page or app—either Android or iOS—that doesn't include a video or motion based on video. We have seen everything from video used as backgrounds in full-screen web pages to a rather marked interest in cinemagraphs, which are hybrids of video and GIF. The fascinating aspect of all of this is that Animate CC is up to the task.

It has indeed been a long, strange trip.

Here's what we'll cover in this chapter:

- Streaming video
- Encoding video
- Playing video
- Using the Animate CC Video components

The following files, located in Chapter10/ExerciseFiles_Ch10/Exercise/, are used in this chapter:

- video/Stockhorn.mov
- video/Stockhorn.mp4
- video/Waterfall.mp4
- video/Raid.mp4
- video/Zombies.mp4
- video/Zombies.vtt
- 01_AS3Captions.fla

CHAPTER 10 ■ VIDEO

- 02_AS3Captions.fla
- 03_CustomVideoControls.fla

The source files are available online at http://www.apress.com/us/book/9781484223758.

Video on the Web and Beyond

Before we turn you loose with creating and playing video in Animate CC, it is very important that you understand how video is delivered from a server to a web page or app.

First off you would be highly mistaken if you thought MP4 was the universal-play-anywhere-and-on-anything video format. Not quite. If you are including video to be played through an HTML5 Canvas document, you would be sadly mistaken. You have the W3C, the body that sets the HTML standard, and the browser manufacturers to thank for that one.

There can be no dispute that the W3C adding the <video> element made video universally playable on the web. Where they "missed the boat" was leaving the choice of video format to the browser manufacturers—Opera, Firefox, Google, Microsoft, and Apple. The first three embrace open source and the 'Hacker Precept" that "Information must be free." The remaining two, in very simplistic terms, believe in a common, closed video format. Although .mp4 may, on the surface, appeal to both factions, the fact that it wasn't royalty-free hindered agreement. Google, in an effort to break the impasse, developed a royalty-free format called WebM and, at the time, made it very clear Chrome would move to that standard. Firefox embraced the format and Opera added it to its royalty-free lineup of OGV and WebM. Google dragged its feet for a couple of years before before announcing MP4 as its preferred video format with the result that, today, MP4 is the common browser format. That's the good news.

The bad news is an internet fact of life: You have no control over the user's browser. If a user in Europe opens the video in Opera or a user in South Africa opens the video in Firefox, there is an excellent chance that the poor user will be looking at a blank screen where the video should be located. This is because there are still browser versions in use that can't play an .mp4 video. It has become a common best-practice, until further notice, to include WebM and OGV copies of the content in the <source> element of the HTML5 code.

This whole video discussion can get very deep, very quickly. If you want to learn the ins and outs of working with HTML5 media, we suggest you pick up a copy of *Beginning HTML5 Media* from Apress.

The MP4 and WebM Video Formats

What you need to first understand about these two formats is they are container formats. If this is the first time you have encountered the term substitute the word "container" with the words "shoe box". Inside that box are two shoes—a right shoe and a left shoe. Keep the image of that shoe box in mind when you encounter a video container. Instead of finding shoes when you open the box, you will see two tracks—an audio track and a video track. Here's what you need to know about them:

- MPEG 4 usually has the .mp4 or .m4v file extension. This container holds an H.264 or H.265 encoded video track and an AAC (Advanced Audio Codec). This format is based on Apple's older .mov format and is the most common format output for the video camera in your smartphone or tablet.

- WebM uses the .webm extension. This is a royalty-free open source format designed specifically for HTML5 video. This container holds a VP8 or VP9 encoded video track and a Vorbis or Opus encoded audio track. This format is supported by all modern browser with the exceptions of Safari from Apple and Internet Explorer from Microsoft.

There is a third universal format out there.

- Ogg, which uses the .ogg or .ogv extensions. Ogg is another open source format. It contains the Ogg video (Theora codec) and the Ogg audio (the Vorbis or Opus codec). This format is supported by every browser out there, including Linux distributions. The quality of the files is rather poor and, with the move to MP4 by Opera, this format can, in many respects, be regarded as a legacy video format.

For the purposes of this chapter, we are going to concentrate on the MP4 format. You also may be wondering if .AVI, .MOV, or even .DivX videos can be use in Animate CC. Absolutely. All you need to do is to transcode them to the MP4 or WebM formats.

Encoding Video

Getting video to run smoothly through a browser is, in many respects, a "black art". If you have ever encountered a video that stops and starts, looks fuzzy, looks blocky, or seems to take forever to load and start playing, you can't blame Animate CC, the browser, or even the application that output the video in the first place. Instead, blame the individual who encoded the video. Encoding video as an .mp4 or .webM video involves a lot more than simply selecting a preset and clicking an OK button.

Here are just a few considerations:

- If you're targeting the web, you need to create the .mp4 and .webM versions of the video.

- If any connected device can play the video, then you need to be deeply concerned with the user's bandwidth.

- File size is a huge issue because load times, especially on mobile devices, can be enormous.

- Is the audio track mono or stereo?

- What data rate is appropriate for audio?

- What data rate is appropriate for the video?

- What bit rate should you use: constant or variable?

All of these decisions are made when you encode the video.

Using Adobe Media Encoder

Before we start, we need to tell you we are using Adobe Media Encoder because it is part of the Creative Cloud and is installed on your computer when you installed Animate CC. It is a pretty robust piece of software that asks you to make the same encoding decisions you would make using the majority of video creation software out there. If you find Adobe Media Encoder to be a bit daunting, there are a number of other, very simple-to-use encoders available to you. One of the more popular ones is the Miro Video Encoder, which is available in Apple and Windows versions. Best of all, it is free.

With that out of the way, let's encode a video and discover to some of the important decisions you have to make along the way.

CHAPTER 10 ■ VIDEO

1. To begin, launch Adobe Media Encoder and drag a copy of the Stockhorn.mov file into Queue area in the upper-right quadrant. When you release the mouse, you will see that a preset has been applied, as shown in Figure 10-1. The plan here is to create an MP4 video that will play on devices and web pages. Instead of producing a number of versions of the video for a variety of situations, the plan here is to create a single source file.

Be wary of presets in the Adobe Media Encoder. By their very nature, they are designed to appeal to a broad spectrum of needs and may not fit your specific encoding goal.

Figure 10-1. Encoding starts with adding a video to the Adobe Media Encoder queue

2. To launch the Export settings, double-click the format (H.264). This will open the Export window shown in Figure 10-2. This is where the "magic" happens.

CHAPTER 10 VIDEO

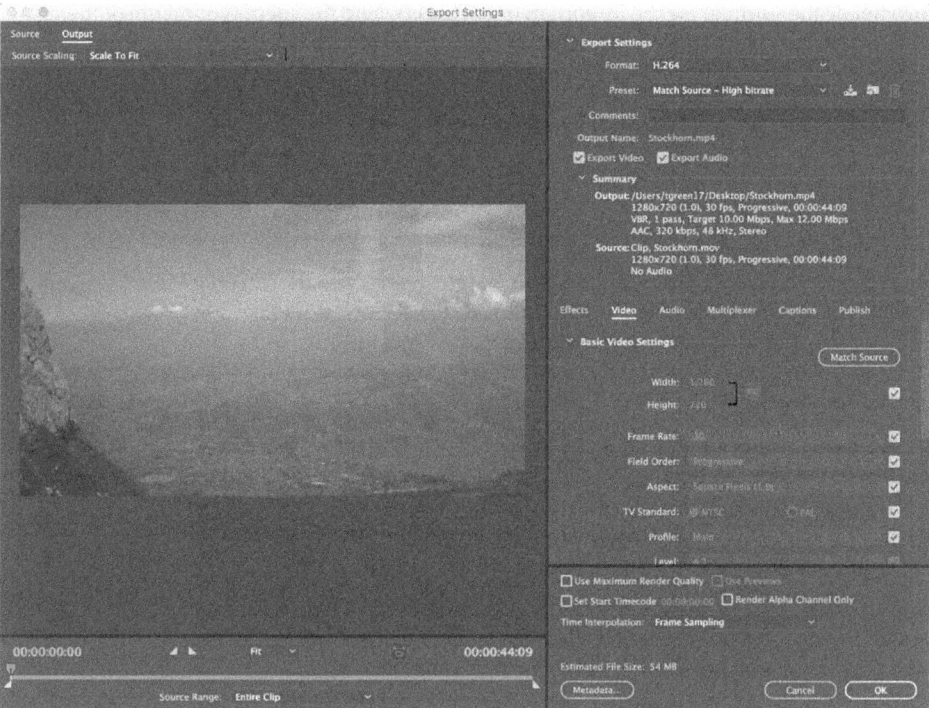

Figure 10-2. *The Export Settings window is where the critical decisions are made*

Let's take a moment and explore this window.

- The area to the left shows you a preview of the video. Under the video is where you can trim the video by setting the In and the Out points.

- Over on the right, the area is divided into two areas. At the top are the Export Settings. If you open the Format drop-down, you will be presented with a list of 26 formats ranging from AAC Audio to Wraptor DCP (Digital Cinema Package). For the purposes of this exercise, there really are only two formats you need to know: H.264 (.mp4) and WebM. There is an MPEG4 format, which could be confused with the .mp4 file extension. This format creates a 3GP file, which is a format normally used by mobile devices.

3. The preset drop-down is rather extensive and designed for a variety of devices, frame rates, and playback situations. They are a good starting point, more than anything else, and for the purposes of this exercise, let's start with the Match Source-Medium Bitrate setting.

4. Double-click the output name to change the name of the file and indicate where to save it.

5. The Export Video and Export Audio check boxes ensure both the audio and the video tracks will be added to the file. If your video doesn't contain a sound track, you can deselect Export Audio. Still always check to ensure both are selected.

481

The next area below the summary is the important one. This is where the success or failure of the process is set. Let's take some time to review the decisions you will need to make. Keep in mind, our intention here is to create a single source file to be used in everything from smartphones to the computer on your desk.

How to Use the Basic Video Settings

The next step in the process is to "tweak" the video settings to ensure the video will play smoothly.

1. Select the video tab and twirl down the Basic Video Settings and deselect the check box beside the Width and Height setting. By deselecting this check box, you can resize the video. If you do, be sure not to deselect the link. This way the video will always resize in proportion and maintain its 16:9 aspect ratio. Change the width value to 720.

2. Deselect frame rate and open the drop-down. The items in the list shown are the common frame rates. For example, 29.97 frames per second (fps) is the standard for NTSC broadcast, 25 is the PAL standard for European TV, 30 fps is common for digital video and 15 fps is common for digital video that doesn't have a lot of motion. We'll stay with 30 fps.

3. Deselect Aspect and open the drop-down. These values are the pixel aspect values for a variety of outputs. We have it easy because we are using a digital display and only need to ensure that square pixels are selected.

4. Deselect Profile and choose High from the drop-down. What are these profiles? The video codec we are using is H.264 and its primary purpose is to provide a single codec for anything from a smartphone (low bandwidth, low CPU) to a large computer monitor (high bandwidth, high CPU). To accommodate this broad range, the codec is broken into a series of profiles, each of which is designed to trade off complexity for file size. The ones you see in the profile list are the three most common:

    - **Baseline**: Use this if you are targeting iOS devices.

    - **Main**: This one is mostly an historic profile used on Standard Definition (SD with a 4:3 aspect ratio.) TV.

    - **High**: Think of this as a Swiss Army Knife profile, which can be used for the Web, SD, and HD video publishing.

If your settings match those shown in Figure 10-3, let's now turn our attention to the all important bitrate settings.

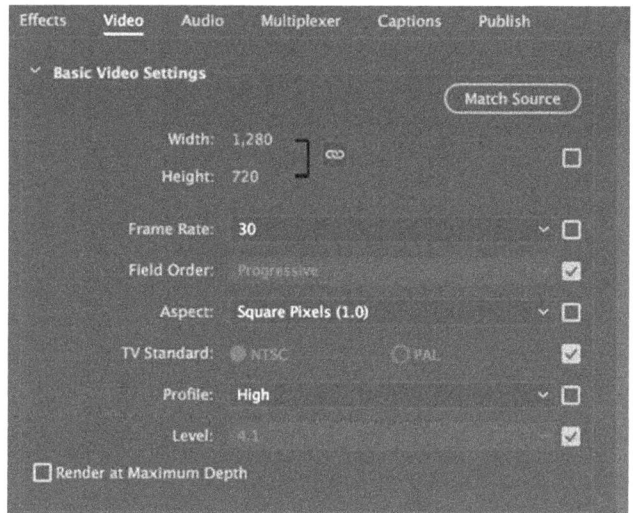

Figure 10-3. *The video settings are in place*

What do all those numbers in the Levels drop-down mean? Profiles address the problem of code complexity and processing power. Levels address the problem of *bandwidth*, *max resolution*, and *memory issues* on the decoder side. Any given device supports a profile depending on the memory and the maximum resolution of the device. Lower levels mean lower resolutions, lower allowed maximum bitrates and less memory to store reference frames. An obvious question is: What level should I use? The Media Encoder's Level 4.1 is perfect for SD and HD videos.

How to Set the Video Bitrate

The bitrate settings are where "the rubber hits the road". We wish we could present you with a magic number, but it simply doesn't exist. Even so, studies have shown the average U.S. broadband speed is 12.6 megabits per second (Mbps). To a resident of Seoul, South Korea, that number is a joke because their average is 20.5Mbps. Whereas to a resident of China, with an average of 3.6Mbps, South Korea's rate is a dream. To put this in perspective, your work can be seen by anyone, anywhere, at any time, which means your video can be viewed in Korea, the United States, and China but the users will have inconsistent experiences. Target a video for Korean consumption and those viewing it in the United States will experience it stopping and starting as the data overwhelms their devices. Thus, if consistency is the goal, you need to target the lowest common denominator. The Bitrate settings are where you do this.

The Akami State of Connectivity report is rather eye-opening. Each year they publish a global report and the 2015 Connectivity Visualization tends to support our "lowest common denominator" observation. You can see it here: https://www.akamai.com/uk/en/our-thinking/state-of-the-internet-report/state-of-the-internet-connectivity-visualization.jsp.

1. Twirl down the Bitrate Encoding and you will be presented with three choices that will determine both the quality and compression of the video. Select VBR, 2 Pass. The choices are:

   - **CBR: Constant Bitrate.** This method uses a single value to encode the video. The problem here is this value will be used to compress motion and with a single value the assumption is all motion is the same. If the video is being sent out through a streaming server then CBR is acceptable. Otherwise, ignore it.
   - **VBR, 1 Pass**: Essentially each frame of the video regardless of whether there is motion is compressed. This method is more efficient than the CBR method.
   - **VBR, 2 Pass:** The way to go if there is motion. Essentially, the compressor, in the first pass, detects motion and other major changes. On the second pass, the compression is done based on the changes detected.

2. Reduce the Target Bitrate to 2 and set the Maximum Bitrate value to 4.

The Target Bitrate value is that "lowest common denominator," whereas the Maximum Bitrate sets the ceiling or acts as a speed delimiter. If your settings match those in Figure 10-4, you can now turn our attention to the Audio settings.

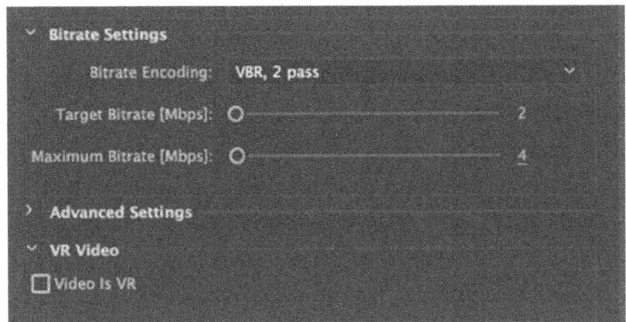

Figure 10-4. *The video bitrate is set*

Before we move on, take a look at the estimated files size just above the Metadata button. This video started at 2.2GB because it was uncompressed. The current file size is 11MB, which shows you the dramatic file size reduction obtained with the H.264 codec. This has no effect on the final quality of the video that one would expect with that serious drop in file size.

How to Encode the Audio Track

Next up is the audio track. It, too, needs to have AAC compression applied to it. Let's get started:

1. Click the Audio tab to open the Audio settings for the video.
2. The H.264 codec has to have an AAC audio track. This is usually set by default. Select AAC from the Audio Format drop-down.

CHAPTER 10 ■ VIDEO

3. Choose AAC from the Audio Codec drop-down.

4. Reduce the sample rate to 32,000Hz. For you audio purists, this is equal to 32kHz.

5. Choose Mono from the Channels drop-down. We choose Mono because we are targeting a variety of devices and Stereo adds nothing more than a hit on bandwidth.

6. Set the Audio Quality to Medium. This will affect the quality but if the user is watching this on a smartphone and listening to the audio through a pair of ear buds, the loss of quality won't be noticeable.

7. Select 80 as the audio bitrate. Two things will happen. The first is you just shaved 1MB off the file size. The second is the bitrate for a video is the sum of the Video and the Audio bitrates. This explains why the video bitrate was set to 2Mbps. With the current value of 2.8Mbps, this file will play rather smoothly anywhere in the world. If your audio settings match those shown in Figure 10-5, click OK to be returned to the queue.

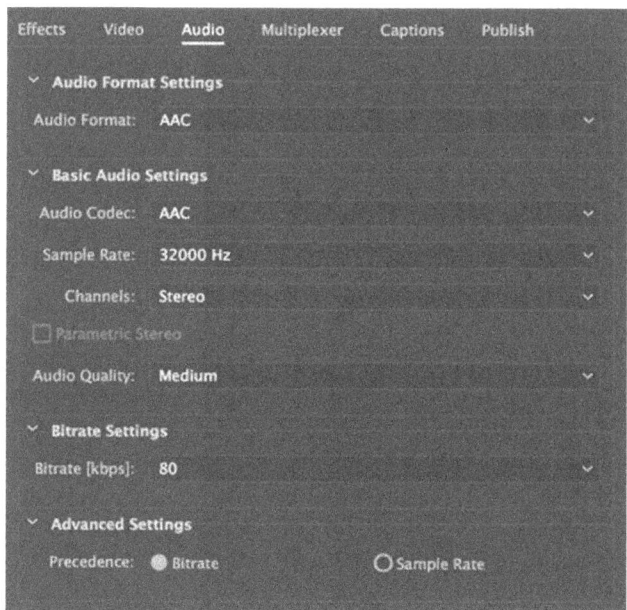

Figure 10-5. *The audio encoding settings*

8. Click the Green Start Queue button to encode the MP4. You will see a progress bar and actually see the two encoding passes. When finished, your file will sport a green check mark.

The Advanced settings ask you to tell the encoder what is important when compressing the audio track. Choosing Bitrate means getting the audio to play smoothly is important to you. Choosing Sample Rate means audio quality is your prime consideration.

Using the Animate CC Video Wizard

Now that you have a shiny new MP4 file on your hands, you're probably just itching to play it. There are a number of ways of accomplishing this and we will deal with them for the balance of this chapter. In this part of the chapter, let's start with the easy way of doing things and use the Video Wizard.

Essentially the wizard walks through the process in a rather uncomplicated manner and lets you choose what type of video player will be used. Just keep in mind this feature can only be used with ActionScript 3.0 documents. Here's how:

1. Open a new ActionScript 3.0 document and set the stage width to 700 pixels and the height to 600 pixels.

2. Select File ➤ Import ➤ Import Video. This opens the Import Video Wizard.

3. The first question the wizard is asking is where your file is located. As shown in Figure 10-6, there are only two possible locations: your computer or a web server. Click the Browse button and navigate to the MP4 you created earlier or use the Stockhorn.mp4 file found in the chapter's exercise folder.

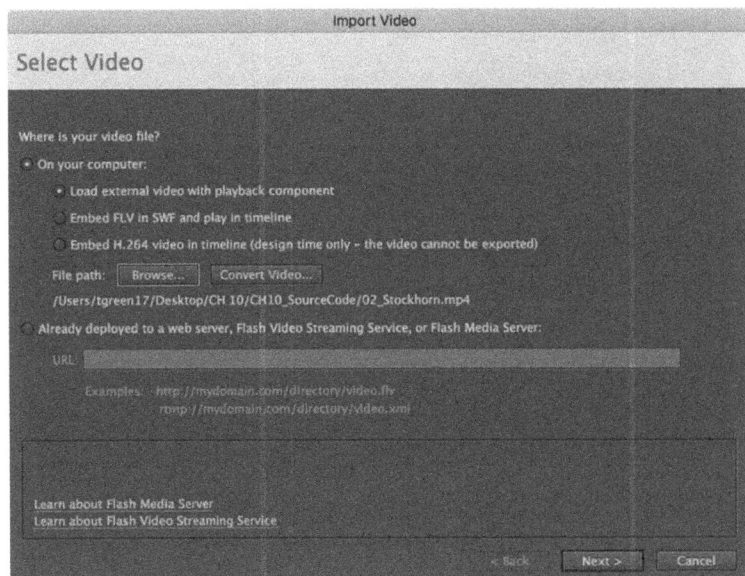

Figure 10-6. *Setting the path to a video using the wizard*

4. Click the Load External Video with Playback Component button. This tells Animate you intend to stream the video into the Flash Player. Click the Next button, which moves you to the Skinning screen of the wizard.

You may have noticed a couple of other options for handling the video. The two embed options are to be avoided at all costs because it embeds the entire video into the player or on to the timeline. Do that and your file size will increase to that of the video file. In fact, the Embed FLV option shouldn't even be there because the FLV file format has been dead for quite a few years. If you don't believe us, try finding that format in the Adobe Media Encoder.

5. Click the Skin drop-down to see the choices available to you. Click a skin style and the preview will change to show you the skin (see Figure 10-7).

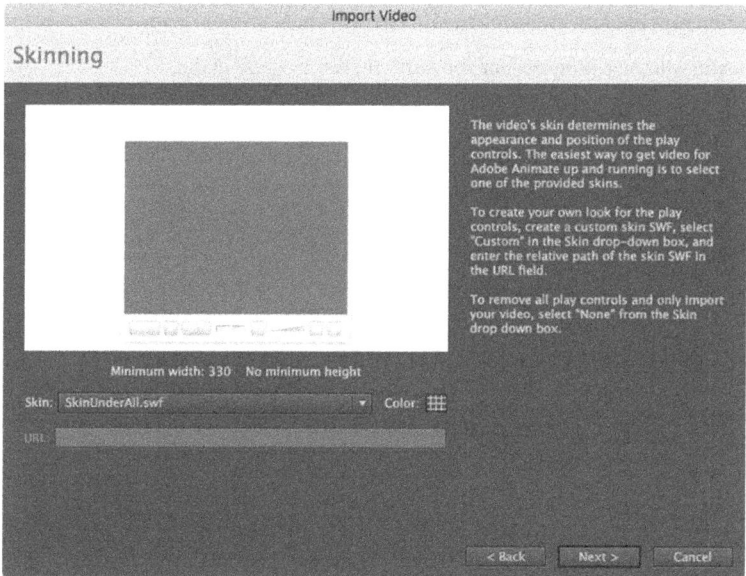

Figure 10-7. What skin or control style will be used?

"Skin" may strike you as a rather odd word. Think of it as a techie word for video controls.

The skin choices available to you can be broken into two major groupings: Controls that appear over the video and controls that appear under the video. If you choose an "over" skin, those controls will only appear when the user hovers over the video. The remaining choices in each group basically let you determine which controls will be added to the skin.

CHAPTER 10 ■ VIDEO

The color choice may trip you up. You can have any color you wish for the controls. The problem is the default color is an Alpha value of 0 meaning unless you increase the Alpha value the controls will essentially be transparent. To fix this "nasty" gotcha, click the color chip, choose a color, and increase the Alpha value in the Color Picker to 100%. You also get a choice of None when setting the skin. This is a dangerous choice and should be used only if you intend to create your own custom controls, use the Video components, which we will get to later in this chapter, or play the video with no user interaction. That last decision is not regarded as a best practice unless there is no audio associated with the video and it is being used as a graphic element.

6. Select `MinimalFlatCustomColorAll.swf` and choose a color for your controls.

7. Click the Next button to move to the Finish Video Import screen. All this screen does is tell you what will happen when you click the Finish button.

8. Click the Finish button. You will see a progress bar showing you the progress of the video being added to the Animate stage. When it finishes, the video and the controls will be placed on the Animate stage, as shown in Figure 10-8. Go ahead, test the file.

Figure 10-8. Your video is "good to go"

You need to know there is another "gotcha" when the video and controls hit the Animate stage. If you change the stage height to 405 in the Properties panel you will see what we are talking about. The video is on the stage but the controls are below the stage. This means when you publish this file, the controls are gone. This only applies, for obvious reasons, to any of the Under controls. Keep this in mind if, for any reason, you need to reduce the stage height.

CHAPTER 10 ■ VIDEO

Although we called the skin controls, in fact, what you are looking at is the FLV Playback component that comes packaged with Animate CC. Let's turn our attention to this nifty component.

Video Playback with ActionScript 3.0 Documents

For the longest time, when you wanted to write a fully customizable video playback solution for the Web, it was as straightforward as firing up Animate CC (Flash Professional back then) and creating a new ActionScript 3.0 project. In fact, without Flash Player and the video capabilities it provided, we would not have services like YouTube or Vimeo today!

Of course, in the modern age of HTML5 and the ability to play video content directly within the web browser, things have changed. It cannot be overstated just how much the current web platform owes to Flash Player in light of these advances over the past few years. We will look at video playback with HTML5 Canvas documents later in this chapter.

Using the ActionScript 3.0 FLV Playback 2.5 Component

In this exercise, you'll be connecting a video file to the FLV Playback 2.5 component manually. Alternatively, you could also use the FLV Playback component. There are not significant functional differences when considering what tasks we are looking to complete. Follow these steps to wire it up:

1. Create a new ActionScript 3.0 document and save it.

2. In the Components panel (Window ➤ Components), click the Video category. Drag a copy of the FLV Playback 2.5 component onto the stage, as shown in Figure 10-9.

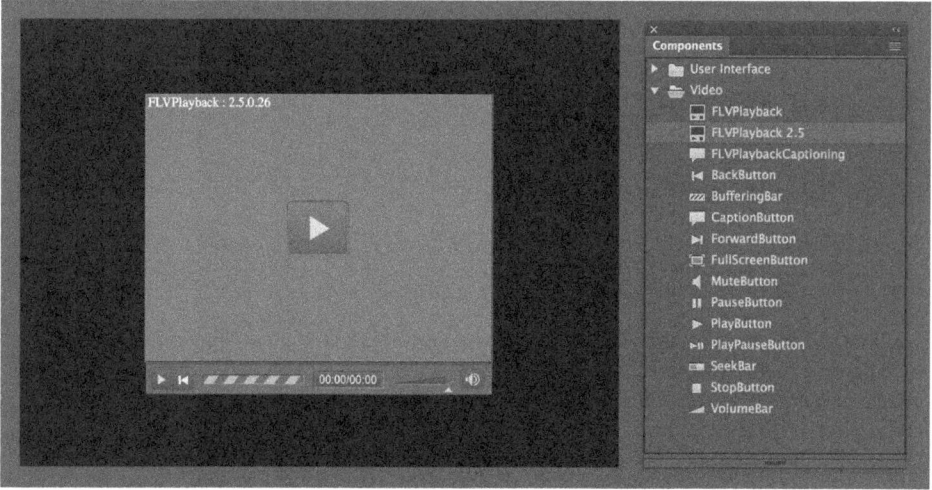

Figure 10-9. *The FLV Playback 2.5 component is found in the Video section of the Components panel*

489

CHAPTER 10 ■ VIDEO

Note that if you open the Library, you will see a copy of the component has been added there. This is a handy feature, because you can use the Library, rather than the Components panel, to add subsequent copies of the FLV Playback 2.5 component to the movie.

3. Click the component on the stage and open the Properties panel. The parameters for the component are set there, as shown in Figure 10-10. These parameters allow you to determine how the component will function:

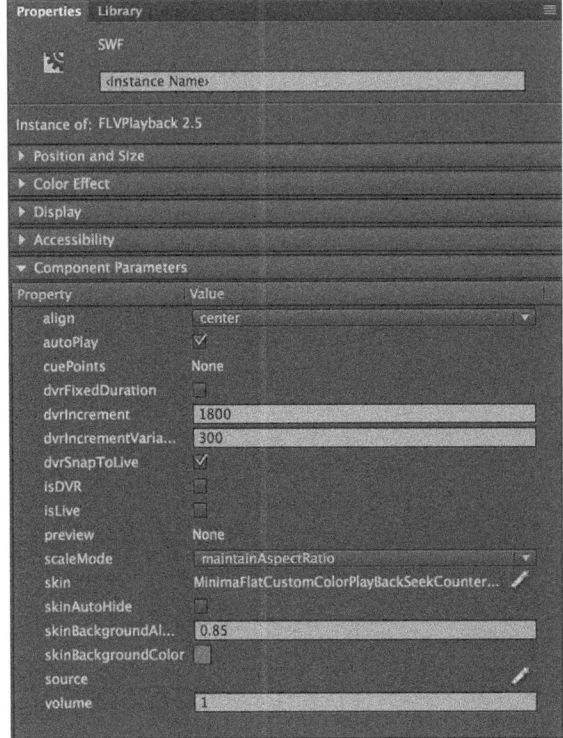

Figure 10-10. The FLV Playback 2.5 component relies on the Properties panel to determine its look and functionality

- **align**: The choices in this drop-down list have nothing to do with the physical placement of the component on the Flash stage. The choices you make here will determine the position of the video in the playback area of the component if the component is resized.

- **autoPlay**: When the check box is selected, the default, the video plays automatically. Deselect it, and the user will need to click the Play button in the component to start the video.

- **cuePoints**: If cue points are embedded in an FLV, they will appear in this area. Using cue points is only available in FLV files.

- **DVR and Live options**: These options are strictly for use with RTMP streaming through the Adobe Media Server.

490

- **preview**: If you select this and a file is connected to the component, you can see the video without needing to test the movie. This feature, you discovered, is a bit redundant. It is ideal for capturing a frame of the video.

- **scaleMode**: Leave this at the default value—`maintainAspectRatio`—if video is to be scaled.

- **skin**: Select this by clicking the pencil icon and the Select Skin dialog box will appear.

- **skinAutoHide**: Adding a check to this means the user will need to place the mouse over the video, at runtime, for the skin to appear.

- **skinBackgroundAlpha**: Your choice is any two-place decimal number between 0 to 1. 0 means the background is totally transparent, and 1 means there is no transparency.

- **skinBackgroundColor**: Select this, and the swatch selector appears.

- **source**: Double-click this area, and the Content Path dialog box opens. From here, you can either set a relative path to the video file or enter an HTTP or RTMP address path to the video.

- **volume**: The number you enter—any two-place decimal number between 0 and 1—will be the starting volume for the video.

4. With the component selected on the stage, set autoPlay to false by deselecting it, and change the `skinBackgroundColor` to #999999 (medium gray).

5. Double-click the `source` parameter to open the Content Path dialog box, as shown in Figure 10-11.

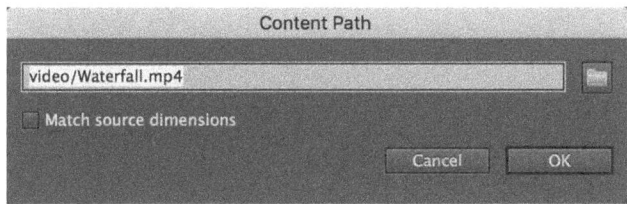

Figure 10-11. Setting the content path to the video file to be played in the component

6. In the Content Path dialog box, click the Navigate button—the file folder icon—to open the Browse for source file dialog box. Navigate to the video folder, select the `Waterfall.mp4` file, and then click the Open button.

7. The relative path to the MP4 will appear in the Content Path dialog box. Then click OK.

If you select the Match Source Dimensions check box, the component will size to the exact dimensions of the video file. You can always resize if the resulting video is too large for the stage.

---

8. Save the project.

9. Test the movie in Flash Player. When you have finished, close the SWF to return to the Animate CC stage.

In the Video components area of the Components panel, you'll find a bunch of individual buttons and bars. They are there for those situations when you look at the skin options available to you and think, "That's overkill. All I want to give the user is a play button and maybe another one to turn off the sound." This is not as far-fetched at it may sound. There are a lot of web sites that use custom players that are nothing more than a series of the individual controls.

Playing Video Using Raw ActionScript

So far in this chapter, you have seen different ways of getting a video file to play through the FLV Playback 2.5 component. In this exercise, you won't be using the component; instead, you'll let ActionScript handle everything. Playing video using ActionScript is a lot like connecting your new television monitor to the receiver in an empty room. There are essentially three steps involved: connect, stream, and play.

When you walk into the room where you are about to hook up the monitor to the receiver, the monitor is sitting on a stand or mounted to a wall, and there is an HDMI (or some other cable) ready to make the connection. When you insert and secure the HDMI cable into the receiver port, you are establishing a connection between the cable or satellite signal provider and your home. When you insert the other end of the cable into the monitor, it is now connected to the service provider. When you turn on the monitor and receiver, the programming that is flowing from the service provider to your monitor starts to play. Let's connect our monitor to a video source:

1. Create a new ActionScript 3.0 document and save it as a new .fla file on your local machine in the parent directory just above your video subdirectory from the exercise files. Set its stage dimensions to 845 × 480.

2. Rename Layer 1 to Actions and lock the layer.

3. Open the Actions panel by selecting Window ➤ Actions if it's not already open.

4. In the script pane of the Actions panel, we are going to create a Video object using pure ActionScript. Enter the following code:

    ```
    import flash.media.Video;
    import flash.net.NetConnection;
    import flash.net.NetStream;

    var myVideo:Video = new Video(712, 400);
    this.addChild(myVideo);
    ```

    So what does this code do? It first imports the Video class from the flash.media package so that we can create instances of that class in our project. We also import the NetConnection and NetStream classes from the flash.net package for use later on.

    The next step is to create a new Video object named myVideo and pass in the values of 712 for width and 400 for height. You can set the width and height when you create the Video object like this, which is pretty convenient. Finally, we have to add our Video object to the display list by invoking addChild and passing a reference to myVideo through as an argument.

You can also create a visual Video object like this from the project Library. Just open the Library panel and choose the panel options drop-down menu in the upper-right corner. From there, you select New Video to open the Video Properties dialog box and create a Video object (a sort of a "physical" manifestation of the AS3 Video class).

5. With that out of the way, enter the following code:

```
var nc:NetConnection = new NetConnection();
nc.connect(null);

var ns:NetStream = new NetStream(nc);
myVideo.attachNetStream(ns);
```

The first line declares an arbitrarily named variable, nc, and sets it to an instance of the NetConnection class. This provides the network connection between the player and the server.

The second line, nc.connect(null);, tells the player this is an HTTP connection, not an RTMP connection, which requires Adobe Media Server installed on your system. Any requested video files—such as the SWF itself or typical web page assets like JPEGs or GIFs—will download progressively and no streaming will take place.

The third line declares another variable, ns, and sets it to an instance of the NetStream class. This establishes the stream—that is, the flow of video data.

The fourth line connects the Video object, with the instance name myVideo, to the stream that is connected to the server.

6. Press Enter (Windows) or Return (Mac) twice and enter the following code:

```
ns.client = {};
```

The client is the object that will hold such stuff as the metadata inside the video file. If this isn't there, you are going to see some rather bizarre messages in the compiler.

7. Press Enter (Windows) or Return (Mac) twice and enter the remaining bit of code:

```
ns.play("video/Waterfall.mp4");
```

This line uses the NetStream.play() method to actually stream the video content into the Video object on the stage. The important thing to note here is that the name of the video is a string (it falls between quotation marks) and the .mp4 extension is added to the name of the video. The important thing you need to know here is the file extension—.flv, .f4v, .mp4, or .mov—must be included in the file's name, as well as the full path to the video file.

8. Save and test the movie. When Flash Player opens, the video starts to play, as shown in Figure 10-12.

Figure 10-12. *A few simple lines of ActionScript code drive the playback of this HD video*

To recap, if you want to play video using ActionScript, here is all of the code you will need to get started:

```
import flash.media.Video;
import flash.net.NetConnection;
import flash.net.NetStream;

var myVideo:Video = new Video(712, 400);
this.addChild(myVideo);

var nc:NetConnection = new NetConnection();
nc.connect(null);

var ns:NetStream = new NetStream(nc);
myVideo.attachNetStream(ns);

ns.client = {};
ns.play("video/Waterfall.mp4");
```

The only thing you will ever need to do to reuse this code is change the name of the FLV, F4V, or MP4 file in the last line. Of course, there is a *lot* more to be learned about video playback and streaming. That's how it's done with an ActionScript 3.0-based project; let's now learn how to go about this when using HTML5 Canvas.

Video with HTML5 Canvas Documents

Even though Animate CC—and Flash Professional CC before it—has had the ability to target HTML5 and the native browser for years now, only recently has Animate CC gotten the ability to integrate video into a project in the proper sense. In this section, we'll look at how to use video in HTML5 Canvas document types through use of the Video Component, which first became available in Adobe Animate CC 2017.

You'll find a bit of this to be similar to what we saw with the FLV Playback component, but it is important to note that ActionScript 3.0 and HTML5 Canvas documents both handle video playback very differently. Read on to find out how.

Using the HTML5 Canvas Video Component

In the previous section of this chapter, we saw how easy it is to play video in an ActionScript 3.0 document using the FLV Playback component. In this section, we will explore a similar workflow when using HTML5 Canvas documents. Here we go.

1. Create a new HTML5 Canvas document and save it to your file system.

2. In the Components panel (Window ➤ Components), click the Video category. Drag a copy of the Video component onto the stage, as shown in Figure 10-13.

Figure 10-13. *The Video component is found in the Video section of the Components panel*

Just as with ActionScript 3.0 components, if you open the Library, you will see that a copy of the Video component has been added to the Library.

3. Click the component on the stage and open the Properties panel. The parameters, as shown in Figure 10-14, are set here. These parameters allow you to determine how the component will function:

   - **Source**: Double-click this area and the Content Path dialog box opens. From here, you can set a path to the video file.
   - **autoPlay**: When the check box is selected, the default, the video plays automatically. Deselect it, and the user will need to click the Play button in the component to start the video.

- **Controls**: Leave this at the default value to enable default browser controls. Disable it to write your own controls.
- **Muted**: Enabling this will mute the sound upon playback.
- **Loop**: Select this to enable automatic replay as the file ends playback.
- **Poster image**: Allows you to browse to a still image file to use as a poster image before playback begins.
- **Preload**: When this is enabled, the video will attempt to preload even before the user clicks play.
- **Class**: The HTML class name to bestow upon the actual video tag, allowing you to add style rules via CSS, if desired.

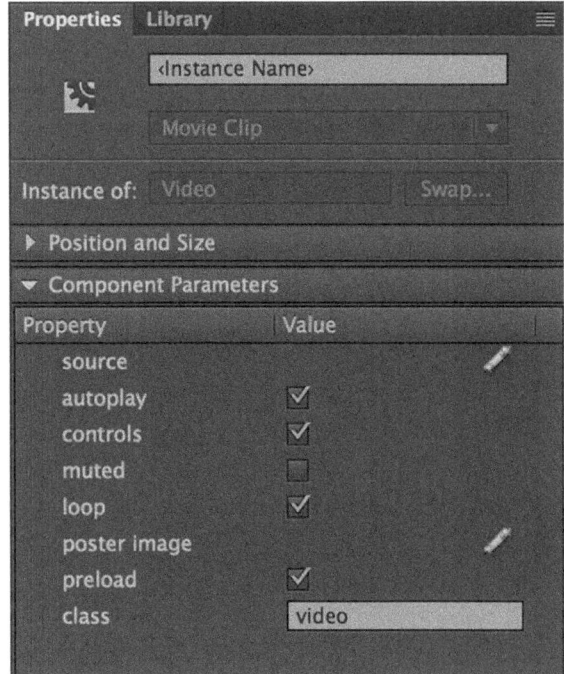

Figure 10-14. The Video component relies on the Properties panel to determine its basic functionality

4. With the component selected on the stage, set autoPlay to false by deselecting it.

5. Double-click the source parameter to open the Content Path dialog box, as shown in Figure 10-15.

CHAPTER 10 ■ VIDEO

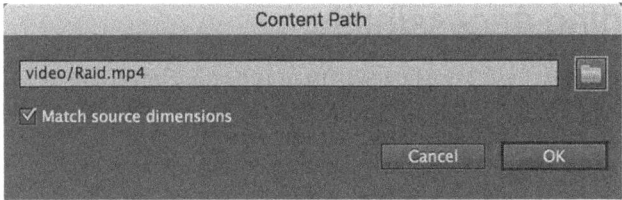

Figure 10-15. Setting the content path to the video file to be played in the component

6. In the Content Path dialog box, click the Navigate button—the file folder icon—to open the Browse for Source File dialog box. Navigate to the video folder, select the 03_Raid.mp4 file, and then click the Open button.

7. The relative path to the MP4 will appear in the Content Path dialog box. Select the Match Source Dimensions check box. This will allow the component to adjust its size to match the exact dimensions of the video file. Now click OK.

8. The video is likely now larger than your given stage. If you like, go ahead and use the Free Transform tool or the Properties panel to adjust the size and position of your video component instance. When you finish, save the project.

9. Test the movie in your web browser to see real video playback within an HTML5 Canvas project. See Figure 10-16.

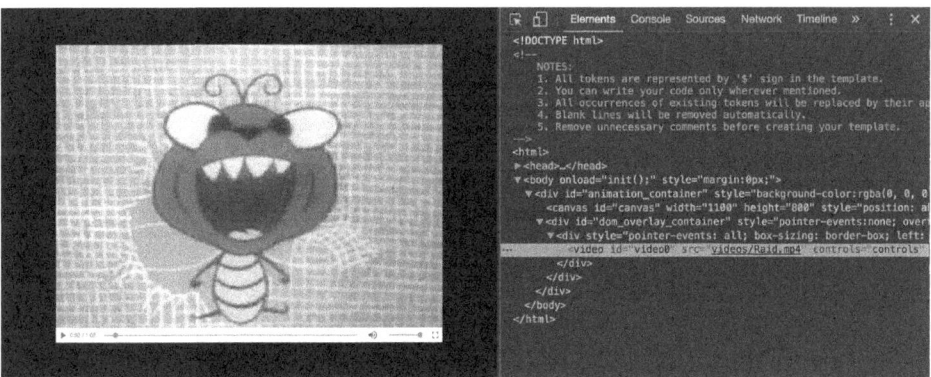

Figure 10-16. Inspect the project within your web browser and see that Animate CC is truly using an HTML5 <video> tag for playback

As you can likely tell, the Video component is just one of many components you can use within an HTML5 Canvas document. The next chapter will explore some of the additional components that are available and will go deeper into how the components work. We are keeping this strictly video-based for now.

497

CHAPTER 10 ▪ VIDEO

Creating Captions and Adding Accessibility

Accessibility is hugely important for the Web—not just for those who have visual or hearing impairments, but also for those who benefit from being able to both hear the audio and read the associated text in order to better digest the material. If you think these exercises are nothing more than "mildly interesting," you would be making a profound error in judgment. One of the reasons video rarely appears on government or other publicly funded/subsidized web sites is that video was, for all intents and purposes, inaccessible. The ability to easily add captioned video and to turn the captions on and off has opened up a market that was otherwise closed to many designers and developers.

WebVTT and HTML5 Canvas Documents

In past versions of Animate CC (when it was named Flash Professional), there were a number of mechanisms to include various timed text segments throughout a video in the form of cue points. You could either set these cue points manually or ingest an XML file containing the data which could be then used in your project. These methods have been deprecated as standards have moved forward and it now seems as though most have settled on the WebVTT standard for representing timed subtitle and caption data for the web.

So how do you assign a WebVTT file to a video for playback? A simple version of this can be seen here:

```
<video src="video.mp4">
  <track kind="captions" src="video.vtt"></track>
</video>
```

Note that we have an HTML `<video>` tag with a `src` attribute pointing to the video file. There is also a nested HTML `<track>` tag that points to the captions file, in the form of the WebVTT standard.

Here is what a WebVTT caption file looks like:

```
WEBVTT

00:00:01.000 --> 00:00:04.000 A:middle
Let's prepare some absinthe.
I have some Jade PF 1901 here.

00:00:06.000 --> 00:00:10.000 A:middle
We'll pour 1 ounce of the absinthe
into our absinthe glass.

00:00:15.000 --> 00:00:17.000 A:middle
There we are. Very nice color!
```

It begins with the WEBVTT declaration and then includes certain time-based markers defining the span of time a specific portion of text should be visible during playback. There is also the alignment option, defined as `A:middle` in our sample. The only thing left for each item is then to populate each with the text you want to appear.

You can view all options when dealing with the WebVTT file format at WC3: `https://w3c.github.io/webvtt/`. Mozilla also has a concise guide to WebVTT on its developer network: `https://developer.mozilla.org/en-US/docs/Web/API/Web_Video_Text_Tracks_Format`.

When dealing with video using HTML5 Canvas components in Animate CC, you do not have the ability, as shown in Figure 10-17, to include a reference to files to be used as track data within the resulting HTML5 video element rendered by the component. Perhaps in future versions of Animate CC, we will have the ability to define track data using the HTML5 Canvas Video component.

So you may be screaming, "Is there no way to include captions in an HTML5 Canvas-based Animate CC project? Why even tell me this if I cannot use it?" Hold on a sec, there is most definitely a way we can do this, although it involves a bit of a hack. Let's see how.

1. Create a new HTML5 Canvas document and name it CanvasCaptions.fla. Save it to your local machine.

2. Open the Components panel by choosing Window ➤ Components from the application menu.

3. Ignore everything else but for the Video category for now. Open the Video category to expose the Video component and drag an instance of the Video component onto the stage.

4. Use the Selection tool to select the new Video component instance and look to the Properties panel. You will see a section called Component Parameters.

5. There is a source property with a small pencil beside it, as seen in Figure 10-17. Click the pencil to open the Content Path dialog box. Click the folder icon to browse to the location of Zombies.mp4 within this chapter's exercise files.

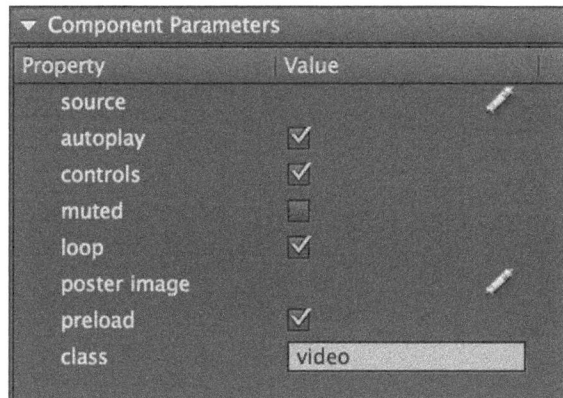

Figure 10-17. *In Animate CC 2017, the HTML5 Canvas Video component has no mechanism to include subtitles and caption tracks*

6. Select the Match Source Dimensions check box (see Figure 10-18) to allow Animate CC to read the width and height of the video and apply those attributes to the component instance on the stage. It may be too big for the stage right now, but we actually only care about the aspect ratio at this point.

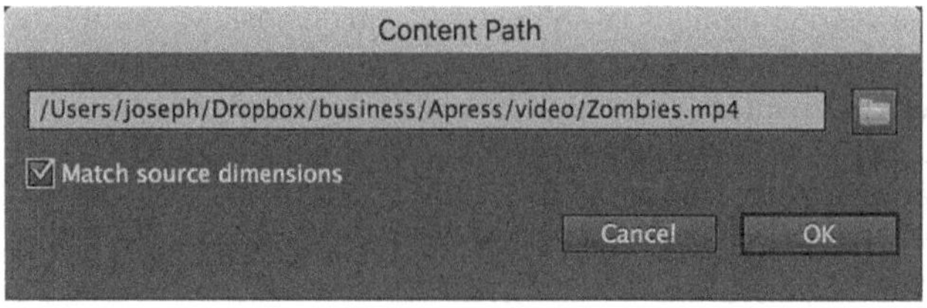

CHAPTER 10 ■ VIDEO

Figure 10-18. *Setting the content path in the HTML5 Canvas Video component instance*

7. The video is now likely larger than the stage. To resize it, be sure the video component instance is selected and look to the Properties panel once more. Set the X and Y positions to 0 and then ensure the small chain toggle to the left of the width is toggled on (an unbroken linked chain). Set the width of the component instance to the stage width. Mine is 550 pixels, as shown in Figure 10-19.

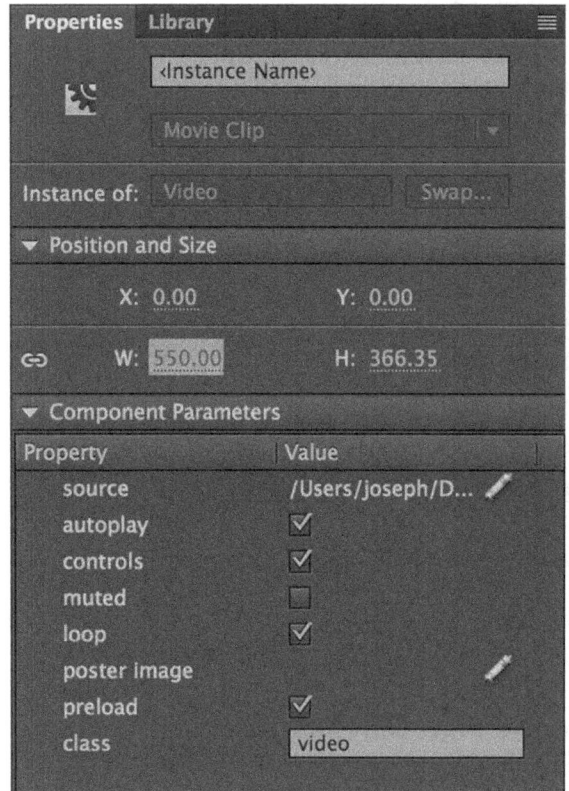

Figure 10-19. *Constrain the width and height by using the lock width and height values together option*

This linked chain visual toggle is the Lock Width and Height Values Together option and will allow us to preserve the aspect ratio of our video as it is resized to match our stage width.

8. With that done, go ahead and deselect everything in the project and look at the Properties panel. It should now display the document properties. Change the height of your document to match the height of the Video component instance. If the width of your stage is 550 pixels, the height will be 337 pixels.

9. We will now look at our Publish Settings from within the Properties panel. Clicking on Publish Settings will open the Publish Settings dialog box (see Figure 10-20). Select the Advanced tab and choose Include JavaScript in HTML.

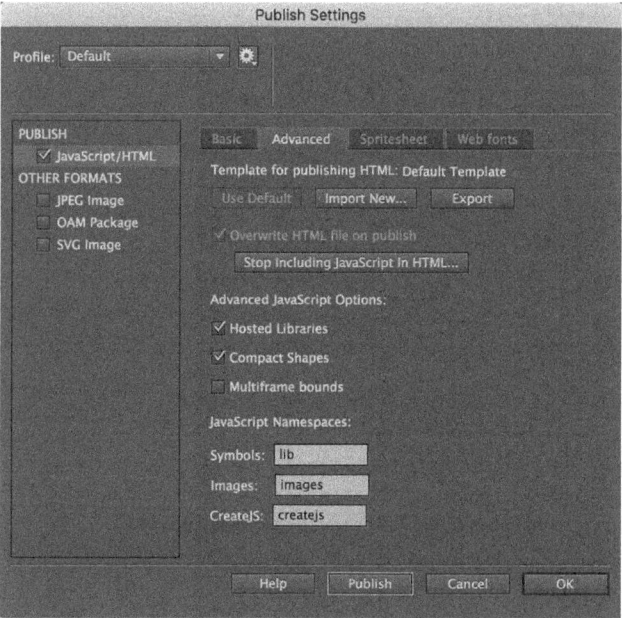

Figure 10-20. *Include the JavaScript in the published HTML file*

This will allow you to make changes to the JavaScript and HTML that is published all within a single document. Once the button has been clicked, it will read Stop Including JavaScript In HTML. Be careful though, as each time you publish from here on out, the entire file will be overwritten!

10. You will find a Publish button at the bottom of this panel. Click this button to publish the project and then click the OK button to dismiss the dialog box.

    We will have a much more in-depth look at publishing Animate CC projects in Chapter 12.

11. With our project published, locate the folder on your local machine where you saved `CanvasCaptions.fla`. You will find an HTML file alongside it named `CanvasCaptions.html`. Open this file within your text editor of choice.

Dreamweaver CC, Brackets, Visual Studio Code, or even Notepad are all fine choices for this. Additionally, you may want to make a copy of this HTML file just to ensure it will never be overwritten if your project is published again.

12. Locate the line of code that provides setup of the video component. The easiest way is to perform a search for lib.an_Video. You will locate a chunk of code that appears as follows:

```
(lib.an_Video = function(options) {
        this._element = new $.an.Video(options);
        this._el = this._element.create();
        var $this = this;
        this.addEventListener('added', function() {
                $this._lastAddedFrame = $this.parent.currentFrame;
                $this._element.attach($('#dom_overlay_container'));
        });
})
```

This is the code generated by Animate CC to create our video component. We will want to focus on the function that fires off when the component instance is added to the DOM overlay layer.

13. Modify the body of the event listener function to include an additional line of code:

```
this.addEventListener('added', function() {
        $this._lastAddedFrame = $this.parent.currentFrame;
        $this._element.attach($('#dom_overlay_container'));
        $("video").append('<track kind="captions" src="videos/Zombies.vtt" default></track>');
});
```

All HTML5 Canvas components within Animate CC use jQuery to manipulate the DOM. All we are doing here is leveraging this fact to inject a <track> tag within the <video> tag after it is inserted by the code generated by Animate CC.

14. With these small tweaks now complete, we can run the HTML and see the captions overlaying our video. Inspect the video element and you will see that the <track> tag (see Figure 10-21) has been dynamically added.

Figure 10-21. *The completed HTML5 Canvas Video component with captions*

Now, depending on how you are serving the files, and which browsers you are attempting to view them in, you may need to provide additional hacks in order for everything to work properly. This is simply the nature of web development, with every browser implementing the standards in their own way. You also must worry about Cross-Origin Resource Sharing (CORS) and all sorts of browser-based security nightmares.

For instance, to get the captions to display properly using Google Chrome, we needed to add the following CSS styles to our HTML document:

```
<style>
video::-webkit-media-text-track-display {
    -webkit-transform: translateY(-3em);
    transform: translateY(-3em);
}
</style>
```

It may also be necessary to run the files from an actual web server and not simply from your local file system. Don't we live in fun times?

If you intend to do any long-term work with web browsers, this is an unfortunate reality you must come to grips with. One of the great things about Flash Player in its glory days was that you generally didn't have to worry about specific browsers—it just worked. These typical issues just prove once again that Flash Player is more of a standard than the standards—even still!

CHAPTER 10 ■ VIDEO

WebVTT and ActionScript 3.0 Documents

We mentioned before that there was once a dedicated format for captioning ActionScript 3.0 documents using a cue point system or specially formatted XML data. Since that mechanism has been deprecated, wouldn't it be great if you could use the same exact WebVTT files in an ActionScript 3.0 document as we have seen work with HTML5 Canvas document? Well, using a certain set of open source third-party AS3 utility classes, such as the one shown in Figure 10-22, you can!

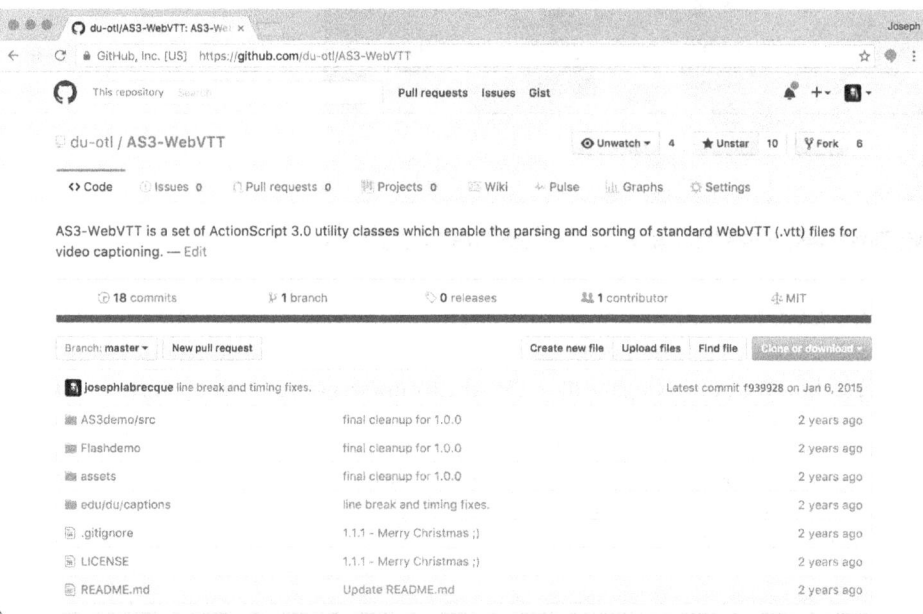

Figure 10-22. *The AS3-WebVTT GitHub repository allows you to access and contribute to the Library*

AS3-WebVTT is a set of ActionScript 3.0 utility classes that enable the parsing and sorting of standard WebVTT (.vtt) files for video captioning. Yep, the same exact files used in HTML5 Canvas. Before proceeding with this project, visit https://github.com/du-otl/AS3-WebVTT/ and familiarize yourself with the source files. Note that you can even contribute to and extend this codebase! When you are ready to proceed, follow these steps.

1. First, open the 02_AS3Captions.fla file from the AS3Captions subfolder within the chapter's exercise files. The AS3-WebVTT utility source files are already included in this project folder.

2. Reveal the Actions panel (Window ➤ Actions), and you will see some code that should appear very familiar:

   ```
   import flash.media.Video;
   import flash.net.NetConnection;
   import flash.net.NetStream;

   var myVideo:Video = new Video(712, 400);
   this.addChild(myVideo);
   ```

504

```
var nc:NetConnection = new NetConnection();
nc.connect(null);

var ns:NetStream = new NetStream(nc);
myVideo.attachNetStream(ns);

ns.client = {};
ns.play("video/Absinthe.mp4");
```

Yep. This is nearly the exact same code that we put together in the previous exercise titled "Playing Video Using Raw ActionScript". We are using a video that demonstrates the preparation of a glass of absinthe this time (see Figure 10-23), in place of the previous waterfall video. If you have any questions about this code, go back a bit and review that exercise! All set? Okay—moving along.

Figure 10-23. *We will be using a video (MP4) of fine French absinthe being prepared in the traditional manner*

Look in the AS3Captions folder and the nested video subfolder in the exercise files for this chapter and you will find two files. The one we want to pay attention to first is named Absinthe.mp4 and if you play it, you'll see a short video of a glass of absinthe being prepared. If you don't know a lot about absinthe, some of what you see may be a mystery. We are going to use the other file named Absinthe.vtt to include some descriptive captions to the video, thereby providing some context to the actions presented and a bit of education around the mysterious spirit.

Now that we are clear on the purpose of this project, let's get cracking. This will be a very code-heavy project and we will explain everything bit by bit.

CHAPTER 10 ■ VIDEO

3. The thing to do now is import the classes we need to get this all wired up. We'll be importing both our AS3-WebVTT classes and a few native AS3 classes. Enter the following code after your existing code:

    ```
    import flash.utils.Timer;
    import flash.text.TextField;
    import flash.text.TextFormat;
    import edu.du.captions.utils.CaptionsHandler;
    import edu.du.captions.events.CaptionLoadEvent;
    import edu.du.captions.events.CaptionParseEvent;
    ```

    We are importing the Timer, TextField, and TextFormat classes, which are native to Flash Player. We also import the CaptionsHandler, CaptionLoadEvent, and CaptionParseEvent classes from the edu.du.captions package.

4. The first of those classes we will take advantage of is Timer. Add the following after your new import statements:

    ```
    var captionsTimer: Timer;
    captionsTimer = new Timer(200);
    captionsTimer.addEventListener(TimerEvent.TIMER, checkCaptionTime);
    ```

    Here, we declare captionsTimer as a new Timer instance that runs every 200 milliseconds. Additionally, add an event listener function named checkCaptionTime, which will execute at every iteration.

5. We will now enter the lines of code that establish a new instance of the CaptionsHandler class named captionsHandler, and then add some event listeners to that class.

    ```
    var captionsHandler:CaptionsHandler = new CaptionsHandler();
    captionsHandler.captionsParser.addEventListener(CaptionLoadEvent.
    LOADED, onCaptionsLoaded);
    captionsHandler.captionsParser.addEventListener(CaptionLoadEvent.
    ERROR, onCaptionsError);
    captionsHandler.captionsParser.addEventListener(CaptionParseEvent.
    PARSED, onCaptionsParsed);
    captionsHandler.captionsParser.addEventListener(CaptionParseEvent.
    ERROR, onCaptionsError);
    ```

    We can monitor and respond to when the captions file is loaded, when it has been parsed correctly, and respond to any errors which may occur during the load or parse procedures.

6. A TextFormat instance allows us to define how text will visually appear. We can set the font, size, color, alignment, and much more.

    ```
    var captionFormat:TextFormat;
    captionFormat = new TextFormat("Arial", 16, 0xFFFFFF);
    captionFormat.align = "center";
    ```

This `captionFormat` instance can then be assigned to any `TextField` in our project.

7. The next step is to instantiate a `TextField` instance to apply our `captionFormat` instance to.

   ```
   var captionDisplay:TextField = new TextField();
   captionDisplay.defaultTextFormat = captionFormat;
   captionDisplay.width = stage.width;
   captionDisplay.y = stage.height-40;
   this.addChild(captionDisplay);
   ```

   To do this, we create a new `TextField` named `captionDisplay` and set its `defaultTextFormat` property to the previously created `captionFormat` `TextFormat` instance. We'll then set the `width` and `y` position of the `TextField` instance and add it to the Display List.

8. Remember establishing a `Timer` class instance a few steps back? Let's write the function that is called upon each iteration of that `Timer`.

   ```
   function checkCaptionTime(e:TimerEvent):void {
       var t:Number = ns.time;
       captionsHandler.renderCaptions(t, captionDisplay);
   }
   ```

   What we are doing here is reading the `time` property from our `NetStream` class instance and then invoking the `renderCaptions()` method of our `CaptionsHandler` instance. We pass in both the current video time and the `TextField` with which to display any captions associated at that specific time.

9. The last bit is to write the functions that have been bound to various event listeners added to our `CaptionsHandler` instance.

   ```
   function onCaptionsLoaded(e:CaptionLoadEvent):void {}
   function onCaptionsError(e:*):void {}
   function onCaptionsParsed(e:CaptionParseEvent):void {
           captionsTimer.start();
           captionsHandler.captionsParser.removeEventListener(CaptionLoa
           dEvent.LOADED, onCaptionsLoaded);
           captionsHandler.captionsParser.removeEventListener(CaptionPar
           seEvent.PARSED, onCaptionsParsed);
           captionsHandler.captionsParser.removeEventListener(CaptionLoa
           dEvent.ERROR, onCaptionsError);
           captionsHandler.captionsParser.removeEventListener(CaptionPar
           seEvent.ERROR, onCaptionsError);
   }
   ```

   Basically, once our captions file is loaded and parsed, we start our `Timer` to continually check for captions at specific times along the `NetStream` as previously established. Note that we have one function to catch errors and another for intercepting the captions load event. We are doing nothing to respond to these events in this example, but you certainly could.

Here is the full WebVTT file for your perusal:

WEBVTT

00:00:01.000 --> 00:00:04.000 A:middle
Let's prepare some absinthe. I have some Jade PF 1901 here.

00:00:06.000 --> 00:00:10.000 A:middle
We'll pour 1 ounce of the absinthe into our absinthe glass.

00:00:15.000 --> 00:00:17.000 A:middle
There we are. Very nice color!

00:00:19.000 --> 00:00:23.000 A:middle
Next, we grab our iced water...

00:00:26.000 --> 00:00:32.000 A:middle
and place our dripper upon the glass. (you could also use a carafe or fountain)

00:00:36.000 --> 00:00:39.000 A:middle
Now, a measure of water is poured into the dripper. (4-5 ounces)

00:00:40.000 --> 00:00:44.000 A:middle
We can see the trails begin to form in the absinthe as the water is introduced.

00:00:45.000 --> 00:00:50.000 A:middle
The absinthe louche forms. Cloudy, milky... we can watch it rolling within the glass.

00:01:05.000 --> 00:01:10.000 A:middle
When the line of unlouched absinthe is gone it is a sign that the absinthe is ready to enjoy.

00:02:05.000 --> 00:02:10.000 A:middle
Delicious - enjoy!

10. One more line of code to write. This is the gatherCaptions() method, which is part of our CaptionsHandler instance. It accepts the path to the VTT file as a string and sets everything else into motion once it's called.

captionsHandler.gatherCaptions("video/Absinthe.vtt");

You should see the video play, along with time-synced captions, as shown in Figure 10-24.

Figure 10-24. *WebVTT captions appear at specified points within our ActionScript 3.0 video project*

You should take note that using the methods and formats outlined in this book, you will be able to use a single MP4 video file alongside a single VTT files across both ActionScript 3.0 and HTML5 Canvas projects. True cross-platform video playback and accessibility support!

The completed code for this project is included here:

```
import flash.media.Video;
import flash.net.NetConnection;
import flash.net.NetStream;

var myVideo:Video = new Video(712, 400);
this.addChild(myVideo);

var nc:NetConnection = new NetConnection();
nc.connect(null);

var ns:NetStream = new NetStream(nc);
myVideo.attachNetStream(ns);

ns.client = {};
ns.play("video/Absinthe.mp4");

import flash.utils.Timer;
import flash.text.TextField;
import flash.text.TextFormat;
import edu.du.captions.utils.CaptionsHandler;
import edu.du.captions.events.CaptionLoadEvent;
import edu.du.captions.events.CaptionParseEvent;
```

```
var captionsTimer: Timer;
captionsTimer = new Timer(200);
captionsTimer.addEventListener(TimerEvent.TIMER, checkCaptionTime);

var captionsHandler:CaptionsHandler = new CaptionsHandler();
captionsHandler.captionsParser.addEventListener(CaptionLoadEvent.LOADED, onCaptionsLoaded);
captionsHandler.captionsParser.addEventListener(CaptionLoadEvent.ERROR, onCaptionsError);
captionsHandler.captionsParser.addEventListener(CaptionParseEvent.PARSED, onCaptionsParsed);
captionsHandler.captionsParser.addEventListener(CaptionParseEvent.ERROR, onCaptionsError);

var captionFormat:TextFormat;
captionFormat = new TextFormat("Arial", 16, 0xFFFFFF);
captionFormat.align = "center";

var captionDisplay:TextField = new TextField();
captionDisplay.defaultTextFormat = captionFormat;
captionDisplay.width = stage.width;
captionDisplay.y = stage.height-40;
this.addChild(captionDisplay);

function checkCaptionTime(e:TimerEvent):void {
    var t:Number = ns.time;
    captionsHandler.renderCaptions(t, captionDisplay);
}

function onCaptionsLoaded(e:CaptionLoadEvent):void {}
function onCaptionsError(e:*):void {}
function onCaptionsParsed(e:CaptionParseEvent):void {
    captionsTimer.start();
    captionsHandler.captionsParser.removeEventListener(CaptionLoadEvent.LOADED,
    onCaptionsLoaded);
    captionsHandler.captionsParser.removeEventListener(CaptionParseEvent.PARSED,
    onCaptionsParsed);
    captionsHandler.captionsParser.removeEventListener(CaptionLoadEvent.ERROR,
    onCaptionsError);
    captionsHandler.captionsParser.removeEventListener(CaptionParseEvent.ERROR,
    onCaptionsError);
}
captionsHandler.gatherCaptions("video/Absinthe.vtt");
```

The video and text objects are completely under your control. Experiment with text positioning and format to get the desired results. You can see an example of all of this in the demo project.

Your Turn: Custom HTML5 Canvas Video Controls

All right, now that you have a good grasp on what is available to you when it comes to using video in Animate CC project, let's integrate video playback with a number of the specific workflow concepts you've already learned in this book.

CHAPTER 10 ■ VIDEO

Animate CC is the intersection of design and development. We hope that you have gotten an understanding of this fact from reading this book so far, and that these concepts are beginning to solidify within your mind into a realization of the wide potential Animate CC holds when combining design and creativity with programming and development practice.

1. A document has been prepared for you named `03_CustomVideoControls.fla`. You will find this in the chapter's exercise files. Open it in Animate CC and have a look (see Figure 10-25).

Figure 10-25. *The HTML5 Canvas project already includes background graphics and a Button symbol*

Note that this file already has a number of items prepared and configured. We have visual assets on the stage contained within the Assets layer, a Components layer which is currently empty, and an Actions layer for our JavaScript code. Additionally, you will find a Button symbol has been prepared and exists within the project library.

2. Open the Components panel (Window ➤ Components) and drag an instance of the Video component onto the stage.

3. Tweak the position and size so that it fits within the rough blue rectangle in the lower left of the stage.

4. Give it an instance name of `nightVideo` so that we will be able to interact with it through use of JavaScript.

5. With the Video component instance selected, look in the Properties panel and focus on Component Parameters. Use the `source` parameter to select the video called `Night.mp4`. Be sure the Match Source Dimensions option is not selected.

6. Now open the project library and drag an instance of the PressButton symbol onto the stage, positioning it to the side of the video component instance. Give it the instance name of `playBtn`.

511

7. Create another instance of PressButton and position this one below the first so they appear stacked. Give this new instance the instance name of pauseBtn.

You will note by examining the PressButton Button symbol instance, that it contains a dynamic text field with the instance name of dyn, as shown in Figure 10-26. This is an important point to remember as it will allow us to provide a unique text label to each instance through JavaScript.

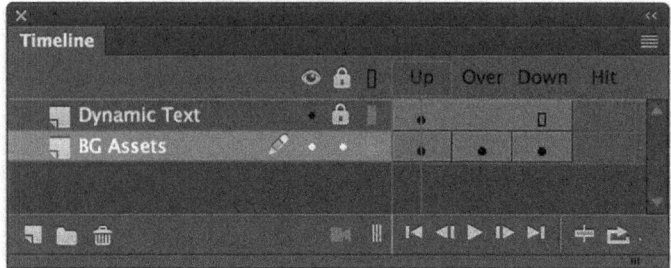

Figure 10-26. Our Button symbol includes a dynamic text field with the instance name of "dyn" across all states

8. Open Actions panel (Window ➤ Actions) and be sure that frame 1 of the Actions layer is selected.

9. We will now assign unique labels to each of our Button instances. We will target the dynamic text field named dyn, which exists within each instance and provide a new value for each. playBtn should read Play and pauseBtn should read Pause.

    ```
    this.playBtn.dyn.text = "Play";
    this.pauseBtn.dyn.text = "Pause";
    ```

10. We will now wire up the playBtn code to allow video playback when pressed by the user. Note that we bind the event listener to our playBtn instance, which targets the nightVideo component and invokes its play() method.

    ```
    this.playBtn.addEventListener("click", playClicked.bind(this));
    function playClicked() {
         $("#nightVideo")[0].play();
    }
    ```

11. The pauseBtn code is very similar, except we invoke pause() on our Video component instance in place of play().

    ```
    this.pauseBtn.addEventListener("click", pauseClicked.bind(this));
    function pauseClicked() {
         $("#nightVideo")[0].pause();
    }
    ```

12. All that is left is to test our project to see it in action (see Figure 10-27).

CHAPTER 10 VIDEO

Figure 10-27. *The completed custom video control using HTML5 Canvas*

Of course, you can do this project using an ActionScript 3.0 document as well. The main differences are that you would use an AS3 Video object or FLV Playback component, and ActionScript in place of JavaScript. The additional assets can generally stay exactly as they are.

The completed code for this project is included here:

```
this.playBtn.dyn.text = "Play";
this.pauseBtn.dyn.text = "Pause";

this.playBtn.addEventListener("click", playClicked.bind(this));
function playClicked() {
	$("#nightVideo")[0].play();
}

this.pauseBtn.addEventListener("click", pauseClicked.bind(this));
function pauseClicked() {
	$("#nightVideo")[0].pause();
}
```

Bonus Round: Create a Cinemagraph in Animate CC

The really interesting thing about working in the digital universe is that technologies are here one day and then wink out of existence. The FLV format for what was then known as "Flash Video" is a classic example of that. One day it was everywhere and then, with the iOS ban of Flash Player in the mobile Safari browser, the rise of HTML5's <video> element and the ubiquity of the MP4 format—it was gone. Then there is the lowly animated GIF.

We cannot begin to count how many times this format has been declared dead only see it rise, yet again, from the ash heap of history. The latest reincarnation involves its use in the production of *cinemagraphs*. These things are all over the Internet. They are, essentially, still images that also have a motion aspect contained in them. For example, a still of a busy street city where nothing, including the people on the sidewalk, are moving except the cars. Cinemagraphs are a recent phenomenon and their invention is attributed to the U.S. photographers, Kevin Burg and Jamie Beck, in 2011.

513

CHAPTER 10 ▪ VIDEO

Essentially, a cinemagraph is a series of still images composited into a short loop and then one of the images from that loop is placed over the others and the motion area in the still image has a mask applied to it. What makes this technique so ubiquitous is that it is normally output as an animated GIF, which means it will play anywhere without the processor and bandwidth strains posed by short video clips.

Before you get rolling on creating cinemagraphs, there are a couple of things you need to know:

- They are short. No more than 10 to 15 seconds or less.
- The video camera must be on a tripod.
- The still images are output either from the Adobe Media Encoder or video editing software as a JPG or PNG sequence.
- You can't add audio to a cinemagraph.

In this exercise, we will be creating a cinemagraph from a short clip of a river in Northern Ontario shot by one of the authors. The clip was run through the Adobe Media Encoder and output as a PNG sequence. Let's get started:

1. Open a new HTML5 Canvas or ActionScript 3.0 document and, when it opens, set the stage size to 720 pixels wide by 405 pixels high.

2. Select File ➤ Import ➤ Import to Stage and navigate to the CinemagraphSequence folder in your Chapter 10 exercise folder.

3. Select all of the images in the folder and click Open. You will see a progress bar showing you the import press and, when it closes, you will see what looks to be a single image on the stage. It isn't. All 50 images are stacked up under it. Let's fix that.

4. Switch to the Selection tool and marquee that one image. Select Modify ➤ Timeline ➤ Distribute to keyframes. When that process finishes, each image in the sequence, as shown in Figure 10-28, is now sitting on its own keyframe.

Figure 10-28. *The images have all been distributed to keyframes*

CHAPTER 10 ■ VIDEO

You may notice the first keyframe is blank. If this is the case, delete that frame.

If you press the Return/Enter key, you will see the water flowing. The plan is to only have moving water between the bottom of the photo to the point where it curls over that big rock in the middle of the photo.

5. Click once on the image in the first frame and copy it to the clipboard. This will be our still image that will be masked.

6. Add a new layer to the timeline and, with this new layer selected, select Edit ➤ Paste in Place. The image will be pasted into the new layer and span the 50-frame duration.

7. Add a new layer and name it Mask.

8. Select the Pen tool and draw the mask to cover the water area that won't contain the motion. Feel free to use Figure 10-29 as a guide. When you're finished, convert the content in the Mask layer to a mask.

Figure 10-29. *The mask is drawn*

Before we create the animated GIF, scrub across the timeline. Did you happen to notice that around frame 40 there is a very slight camera movement? It could have been the wind or some other cause but that sort of thing is quite noticeable. Feel free to remove frames 41 to 50. Keep this in mind when creating these things. Even the slightest camera movement will be noticed, which is why we told you at the start to use a tripod.

515

How to Create an Animated GIF

With the mask in place and the water moving, let's now turn our attention to creating the animated GIF.

1. Select Export ➤ Export Animated GIF. The Export Image dialog box, shown in Figure 10-30, will open.

Figure 10-30. The Animated GIF dialog box

Let's take a moment to talk about this dialog box.

If you take a look in the bottom-left corner, you will see the final file will be about 9MB. This dialog box will help you to trim off some of the excess file size.

- **Color reduction algorithm**: There really are only three choices that apply here—Perceptual, Selective, and Adaptive. What they do is create a 256 color palette for the image. Perceptual creates a palette based on colors the eye is sensitive to. Selective creates a color table like the Perceptual color table, but is more concerned with broad areas of color and a web palette. Adaptive uses the predominant colors in the image to build the color table. We favor Selective but make you choice based on the image you see in the preview and the file size.

- **Colors**: If you look at the image there are not a lot of distinctive colors. If you reduce the colors to 128 or 64 you will see a file size reduction. The problem is the degree of banding that will appear on the rock face on the right side of the image. We went with 128 colors.

- **Dither**: This slider controls how the colors in the palette will combine to approximate the original colors in the image. The lower the dithering value, the less the colors are approximated.

- **Image Size**: The current image is 720 pixels wide. If you really want to reduce the file size then reduce the image size. If you reduce it by 50% the file size drops to about 2MB.

- **Looping**: You have two choices here. One loop or forever.
- **Playback controls**: These let you preview the animation.

2. Use these settings: Perceptual, 128 Colors, 100% Dither, and Forever.
3. Click the Preview button. This will open the animated GIF in a browser and, as shown in Figure 10-31, it gives you some more information and suggested HTML. Close the browser to return to Animate CC.

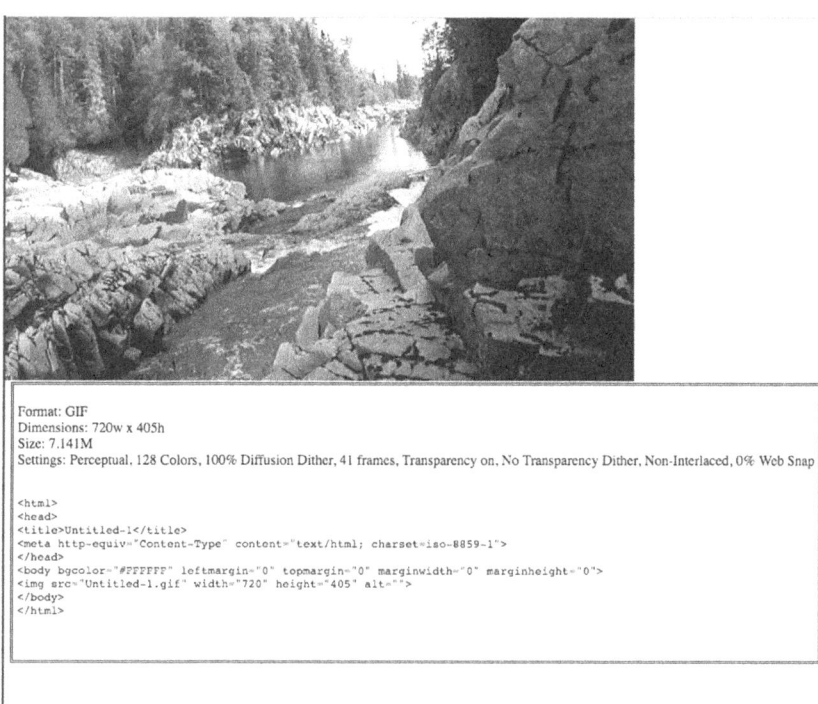

Figure 10-31. The browser preview

4. Click the Save button to save the animated GIF. Clicking the Done button simply saves the current settings.

Here's something we bet you never considered. If you create the cinemagraph you can then import it into an Animate document. The animated GIF lands in the Library as a movieclip symbol with the same timeline and assets as the original.

One final note The physical dimensions of this exercise are overly large simply to give you a big area to work with and to give this technique a try. The key is file size and quality and, as you saw, there are a few tools available to you to meet both goals. We can't tell you what the "magic numbers" are because any decision you make is subjective, not objective. Still, this is a rather interesting way of getting video into an Animate movie without having to use code or a wizard.

CHAPTER 10 ■ VIDEO

What You Have Learned

In this chapter, you learned the following:

- How video can be played from your web server
- How to use the Adobe Media Encoder
- How to encode video
- Several methods of embedding and playing video
- How to display video content in Flash Player
- How to add captions to a video using WebVTT
- An alternate captioning approach
- Controlling video through custom symbols
- Creating a Cinemagraph

This has been quite the chapter, and we suspect you are just as excited about the possibilities of video in Animate CC as we are. The key to the use of video is really quite simple: keep an eye on the pipe. The Adobe Media Encoder is one of the most powerful tools in the video distribution arsenal, and mastering it is the key to video success. From there, as we showed you in several exercises, the only limit to what you can do with video in Animate CC is the one you put on your creativity. Just don't overdo it. Video need to be regarded as content not entertainment and just because "I can do it" is no reason to use it.

As you started working with the Animate CC video components, we just know you were wondering, "How do those user interface components work?" Great question, and we answer it in the next chapter.

CHAPTER 11

Components and External Media

Up to this point in the book, you have created quite a few projects using images, text, audio, video, and other media. We bet you're feeling pretty good about what you've accomplished (you should!), and, like many who have reached your skill level, you are wondering, "How does all of this hang together?"

For user-facing applications, you need user interface (UI) elements, plain and simple—something to receive input from the person viewing your content or display information in a specific way, such as in a grid, drop-down selection, check box, radio button, etc.

In this chapter, we will bring together the various skills and knowledge you have developed, and use them to create some rather interesting projects. We are going to start slowly and first provide an overview of Animate CC user interface Components for both ActionScript and HTML5 Canvas, and then move through a video player, image slideshow, and finish with an MP3 player. Some of these are quite complicated projects, but if you have reached this point in the book, you are ready to develop some Animate CC "chops" and explore what you can do with your newfound skills.

Here's what we'll cover in this chapter:

- ActionScript 3.0 components
- HTML5 Canvas components
- Loading and parsing XML
- Loading and parsing JSON
- Loading external media
- Controlling playback and display with components

Building Content with UI Components

Since early in its life, Animate CC has proven itself the leader in web animation. In recent years, that dominance has nudged into the realm of online applications as well. For user-facing applications, you need user interface (UI) elements, plain and simple—something to receive input from the person viewing your content or display information in a specific way, such as in a grid or check box. Sure, you've already seen how button symbols work, and you're aware that input text fields accept hand-typed content.

Anyone familiar with HTML development knows how easy it is to add a check box, radio button, or other form element into a document. These are usually used in "contact us" pages, online surveys, and other application scenarios. Animate CC components provide you the same set of "widgets," but you also get a whole lot more, including components not possible in a browser alone when dealing with Flash Player. A smidgen of ActionScript or JavaScript is required to wire up components, but for the most part, adding them is a drag-and-drop operation.

CHAPTER 11 ■ COMPONENTS AND EXTERNAL MEDIA

Animate CC allows the use of both ActionScript and JavaScript based components, which are accessible depending on the specific document type being used in any given project. We will look at both sets of components here.

Working with ActionScript 3.0 UI Components

When working in an Animate CC project that targets Flash Player or AIR, you'll have access to a large number of ActionScript-based components (see Figure 11-1). Some of the more familiar components include check boxes, combo boxes, lists, data grids, numeric steppers, and more. These components are normally used for highly interactive projects, which are designed for eLearning or for any other type of general user feedback or data acquisition.

Figure 11-1. *ActionScript 3.0 UI components*

Additionally, as you learned in Chapter 10, we have a good number of video playback components and controls that can be used in our projects. With Flash Player being such a driving force for video playback on the web over the past decade, it is only to be expected that Animate CC would include such a wide variety of components to allow designers to easily wire up their own custom video playback experiences (see Figure 11-2).

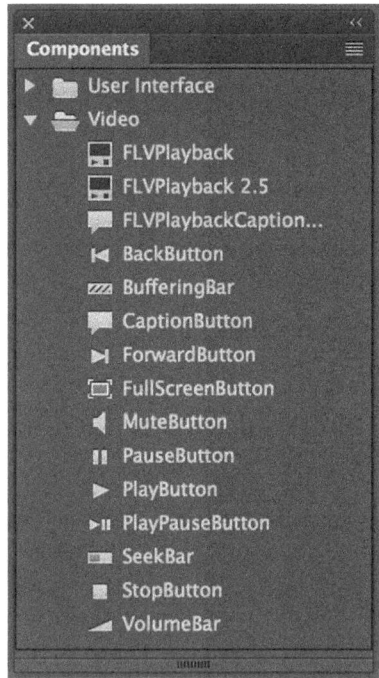

Figure 11-2. *ActionScript 3.0 video components*

Out of the box, the Animate CC components are styled in a modest, attractive manner that comfortably fits a broad range of designs. Of course, Animate CC being what it is—a highly creative, visual tool—you may want to customize their appearance, and you can. Designers and developers familiar with older versions of Animate CC might warn you with a shudder that you're in for a barrel of headaches. Tell the old-timers they can breathe easy. Things have improved considerably in the past few years.

Skinning ActionScript 3.0 Components

What you're about to see can be achieved with most of the UI components, not just the button, as shown in the forthcoming example. (Some components have little or no visual element, so there are exceptions.) This is good news, because it means you'll get the basic gist right off the bat.

There are two ways to alter a UI component's appearance:

- *Skinning*, which generally deals with the material *substance* of the component, such as the shape of the clickable surface of a button or the drag handle of a scrollbar. Think of how the component "looks" and you will have a handle on the term skinning.

- *Styling*, which generally deals with text, style, and padding.

At first glance, the Button component could be regarded as just another button symbol, but the two shouldn't be confused. As discussed earlier, button symbols have a specialized timeline, made of Up, Over, Down, and Hit frames. As such, button symbols are very flexible: Over artwork can be made to spill over the button's Up shape, paving the way for quick-and-dirty tooltips and other tricks. Assets on the Hit state can make the button invisible—but still clickable—if it is the only frame with content. In contrast, the Button

CHAPTER 11 ■ COMPONENTS AND EXTERNAL MEDIA

component has no discernable timeline. It's a self-contained component and is much more conservative (at first glance) than its wild, partying cousin the Button symbol. Figure 11-3 shows an example of the Button component.

We also need you to prepare yourself. We spend what may seem, to you, an inordinate amount of time on something so simple. In actual fact, much of what we are going to talk about applies to all of the components. It is time well spent.

Before Flash Professional CS3, the practice of skinning UI components was an exercise in alchemy. Only the wisest and purest of wizards would trust themselves to toss mysterious ingredients into the frothing cauldron. All of that changed when the components were rewritten for ActionScript 3.0, and the improvement remains intact in Animate CC. In fact, it couldn't get much easier. Here's how:

1. Create a new ActionScript 3.0 document and open the Components panel using Window ➤ Components. Locate the Button component within this User Interface section of this panel.

2. Drag an instance of the Button component to the stage. Double-click the button and you'll see a convenient "buffet table" of the various visual states available to the button, as shown in Figure 11-3.

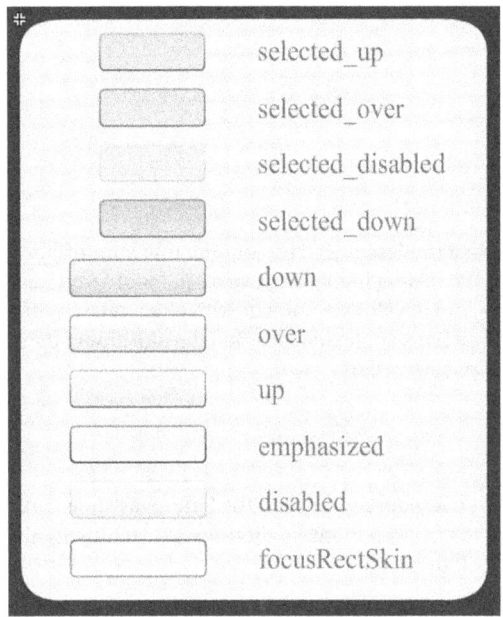

Figure 11-3. *Skinning UI components is really easy*

3. The Up skin is the button's default appearance. Double-click that, and you'll come to the symbol that represents the Up skin for this component, complete with 9-slice scaling, as shown in Figure 11-4. This particular skin happens to be made of three layers.

CHAPTER 11 ■ COMPONENTS AND EXTERNAL MEDIA

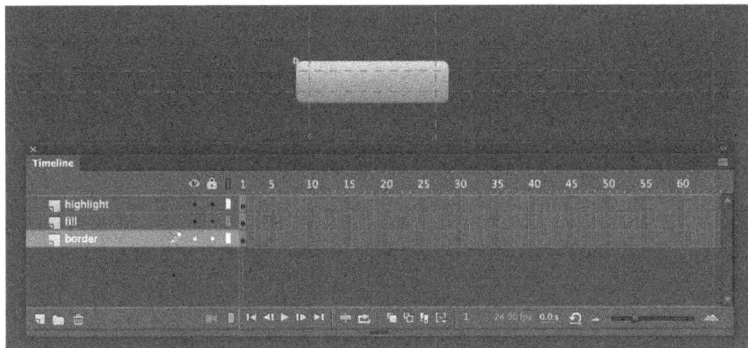

Figure 11-4. *A mere two levels in, and you're ready to change the appearance of the button*

4. Select an area in one of these layers and change the button's appearance—perhaps like Figure 11-5, but the choice is yours. Make sure that the existing shapes, or any new ones, align to the upper left (0,0) of the symbol's registration point. Adjust the 9-slice guides as necessary.

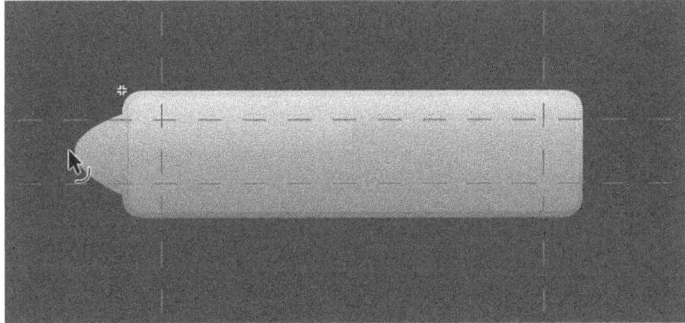

Figure 11-5. *Adjust the existing shapes or create new ones*

5. Select Edit ➤ Edit Document to return to the main timeline. What the...? In the authoring environment, your button hasn't changed. Folks, this is a fact of life with ActionScript 3.0-based skins in Animate CC: there is no preview mode for skinning.

6. Test your movie to see how your alteration appears.

To reskin a component completely, every skin symbol must be edited or replaced.

Styling ActionScript 3.0 UI Components

As you've seen, components are easy enough to customize, even if a complete job takes some effort. You may have noticed an important omission, however, while poking around the skin symbols. Even though the Button component features a text label, none of the skins contains a text field. What if you want a different font in there, or at least a different color? ActionScript to the rescue.

523

Each component has its own list of styled elements. Many overlap, but you can see the definitive list for each in the class entry for that component. For example, find the Button class entry in the ActionScript 3.0 Language and Components Reference, then browse the Styles heading, as shown in Figure 11-6. Don't forget to click the Show Inherited Styles hyperlink to see the full listing. Remember, the Button class gives you details on the Button component; the SimpleButton class gives you details on button symbols.

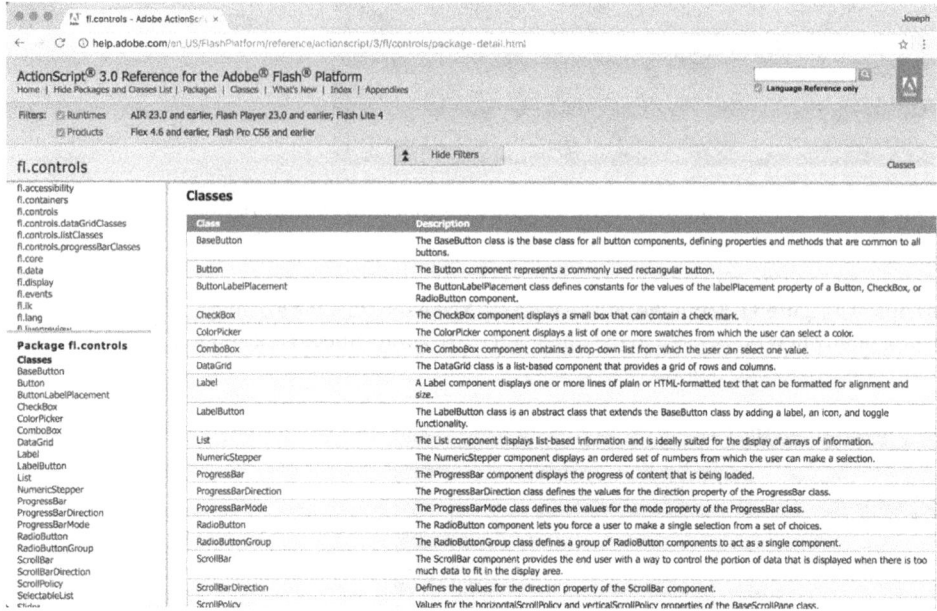

Figure 11-6. The fl.controls package within the ActionScript 3.0 Reference

Components that include text elements, such as the Button component, support the inherited UIComponent.textFormat style, which lets you make changes to the button's text label. Other button styles include the inherited LabelButton.icon, which lets you specify an optional image for the button in addition to text.

You can view the entire list of ActionScript 3.0 Component classes (as seen in Figure 11-6) along with all the classes they inherit by accessing the ActionScript 3.0 Reference for the Adobe Flash Platform: http://help.adobe.com/en_US/FlashPlatform/reference/actionscript/3/fl/controls/package-detail.html.

For this sort of styling, ActionScript allows you to affect the following:

- All components in a document
- All components of a certain type (for example, all Button components)
- Individual component instances

CHAPTER 11 ■ COMPONENTS AND EXTERNAL MEDIA

Let's see it in action:

1. Open the StyleComponents.fla file in Chapter 11's exercise folder. You'll see three instances of the Button component and one of the CheckBox component, as shown in Figure 11-7. Note that each has its own label.

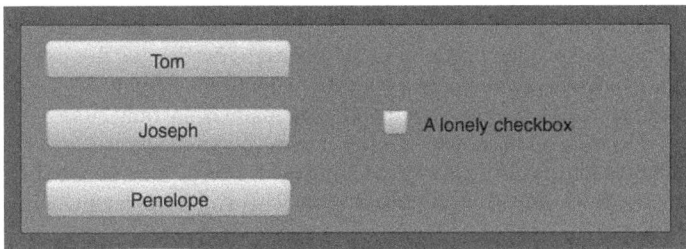

Figure 11-7. *Styling is about to change these components*

2. Click once in the first frame of the Actions layer. Open the Actions panel and type the following ActionScript into frame 1 of the Actions layer:

   ```
   import fl.managers.StyleManager;
   import fl.controls.Button;
   
   var fmt1:TextFormat = new TextFormat();
   fmt1.bold = true;
   fmt1.color = 0xFF0000;
   
   var fmt2:TextFormat = new TextFormat();
   fmt2.bold = false;
   fmt2.color = 0x0000FF;
   
   StyleManager.setStyle("textFormat", fmt1);
   StyleManager.setComponentStyle(Button, "textFormat", fmt2);
   btn2.setStyle("icon", "star");
   ```

3. Test the movie.

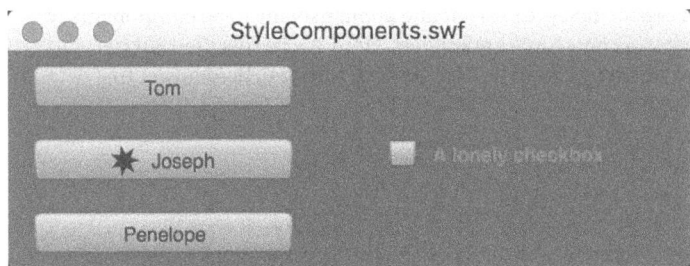

Figure 11-8. *Styling is applied at runtime to targeted component instances*

525

You'll notice the following changes:

- The check box's label is red and bold.
- The buttons' labels are blue and not bold.
- The second button contains an icon.

So what's going on here to actually make this happen?

First up are the opening two lines, which use the `import` statement. We've been sidestepping this one so far because the `import` statement isn't often necessary in timeline code. In ActionScript 3.0 class files—that is, code that can be written outside Animate CC altogether—the `import` statement is not only more prevalent, it's actually *required* in order let the compiler know which other classes you intend to use. In contrast, Animate CC takes care of this for you—for the most part—in frame scripts. This just happens to be an exception. Without those first two lines, Animate CC will get confused about what you mean later when you mention `StyleManager` and `Button` directly.

These hierarchical class arrangements are called *packages*. To find the package for other components, so that you can carry the preceding styling knowledge to other scenarios, look up the component's class in the ActionScript 3.0 Language and Components Reference. When you're looking at the component's class entry, you'll see a number of headings immediately beneath the name of the class, including Package, Class, and Inheritance. The Package heading is the one you want. Most components, including Button, belong to the `fl.controls` package. As an example of the oddball, `ScrollPane` belongs to the `fl.containers` package. In keyframe scripts, you only need to import classes outside the Flash package, such as `fl.managers`, `fl.controls`, `fl.containers`, and the like.

Two variables, `fmt1` and `fmt2`, are declared and set to instances of the `TextFormat` class, and each is given its own styling. Here's where it gets interesting.

The `StyleManager` class has two methods you can use to apply styling to components. Both methods are static, which means they're invoked on the class itself, rather than an instance. The first of these, `StyleManager.setStyle()`, applies formatting to all components. In this case, we're setting the `textFormat` style of all components—specifically, all components that have a `textFormat` property—to the `fmt1` instance of the `TextFormat` class. We programmed this style to make text red (0xFF0000) and bold, and it is indeed applied to all three buttons and the check box. You can specify any styling you like, and the `textFormat` style is common to many components.

"Wait a minute, guys," you may be saying. "Only the check box is red!" This is true. The reason for this is the other method, `StyleManager.setComponentStyle()`. That one applies styling to all components *of a certain type*, which explains the fact that it accepts three parameters. Here, we've specified `Button`, and then set the `textFormat` style of all `Button` instances to `fmt2`. This overrides the red, bold formatting of fmt1 applied in the previous line. Comment out the second `StyleManager` line:

```
StyleManager.setComponentStyle(Button, "textFormat", fmt2);
```

And now test your movie again to prove it.

A good way to tell which style will take effect is to remember this: the more specific the style—for example, `Button` components versus all components—the higher priority it takes. If you holler to everyone in the room (`StyleManager.setStyle()`), giving instructions to wear green scarves, then everyone will do so. If you holler a second time, telling only the tall people to change their scarves to purple (`StyleManager.setComponentStyle()`), then only the tall people will comply. The instruction you've given the tall people

CHAPTER 11 ■ COMPONENTS AND EXTERNAL MEDIA

is *more specific*—it only applies to people over six feet in height—and because of that, you can rest assured that, given the choice between two sets of instruction, the tall folks will follow the more specific set and wear purple.

This precedence goes a step further: the UIComponent.setStyle() method is invoked directly and specifically on *a particular instance* of the Button class—in this case, the component whose instance name is btn2. It works just like StyleManager.setStyle() in that it accepts two parameters: the style to change and its new setting. Here, the LabelButton.icon style, which Button inherits, is set to "star", which refers to the linkage class of the star asset in the Library. Right-click (Ctrl+click) the star asset and choose Properties to verify this.

And now you've had a quick tour of the lobby and one of the rooms here at the UI Component Hotel. There are other rooms, of course, some more elaborate than others, but the layout for each is basically the same. Explore at your leisure!

Code Snippets for ActionScript 3.0 UI Components

There are no code snippets that explicitly target the components of an ActionScript 3.0 document type (see Figure 11-9), because we are dealing with the same exact concepts and structures across anything we create. This is a huge benefit though, as it means we can use just about any of the existing code snippets with our component instances.

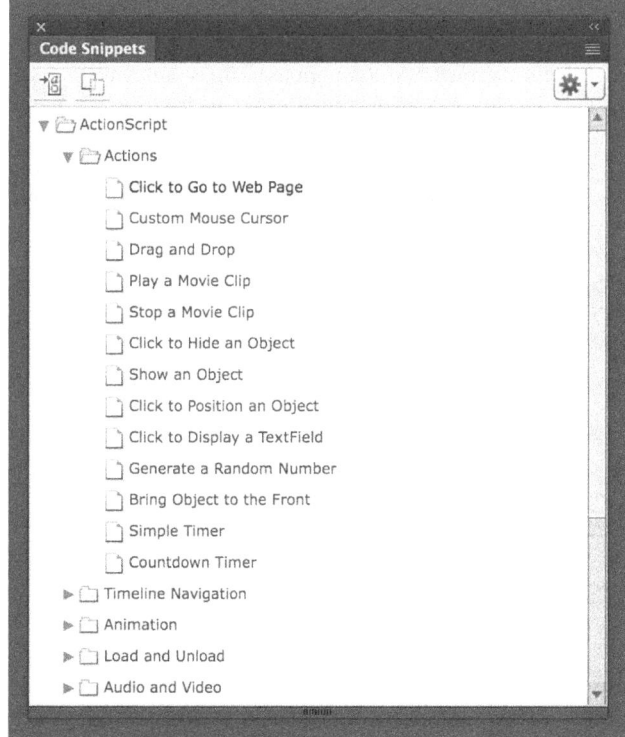

Figure 11-9. *Code snippets for ActionScript documents*

Want to see how to use code snippets on component instances? Sure, you do!

1. With the StyleComponents.fla file still open, click on the Button component instance with the label of Tom.

2. You can open the Code Snippets panel through the application menu by choosing Window ➤ Code Snippets.

3. Open the ActionScript category within the Code Snippets panel and then twirl down to Actions.

4. If you choose the Click to Go to Web Page snippet while the component instance is selected on the stage, and then click the Add to Current Frame button (the icon looks like a frame with code) in the upper left, the code snippet will be added to our Actions layer on frame 1 and will bind to the selected component instance using the instance name (btn1) previously given:

    ```
    btn1.addEventListener(MouseEvent.CLICK, fl_ClickToGoToWebPage);
    function fl_ClickToGoToWebPage(event:MouseEvent):void
    {
            navigateToURL(new URLRequest("http://www.adobe.com"), "_blank");
    }
    ```

5. Test your movie and click on the Tom button to visit Adobe.com.

Of course, there are various properties of each ActionScript 3.0 component that can be adjusted through the Properties panel just like any other symbol instance. You will find these specific attributes by clicking on the component instance on the stage and then observing the Component Parameters section of the Properties panel, as seen in Figure 11-10.

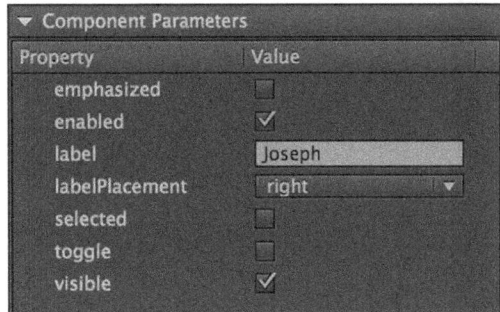

Figure 11-10. Component parameters for a Button component instance

---

These properties can also be accessed and changed through ActionScript as well. Details for the specific properties of each component type can again be accessed through the ActionScript 3.0 Reference for the Adobe Flash Platform: http://help.adobe.com/en_US/FlashPlatform/reference/actionscript/3/fl/controls/package-detail.html.

CHAPTER 11 ■ COMPONENTS AND EXTERNAL MEDIA

Working with HTML5 Canvas UI Components

Since the release of Animate CC 2017, we are also able to use UI components within HTML5 Canvas document types. This is absolutely huge for those working in eLearning and the interactive web space as it means that common component types such as check boxes, combo boxes, numeric steppers, and the like can now be used within native web projects where the Flash Player runtime may not be desired.

To access these components, you must be using a HTML5 Canvas document type within Animate CC. With the document open, choose Window ➤ Components from the application menu. The Components panel, shown in Figure 11-11, will then appear.

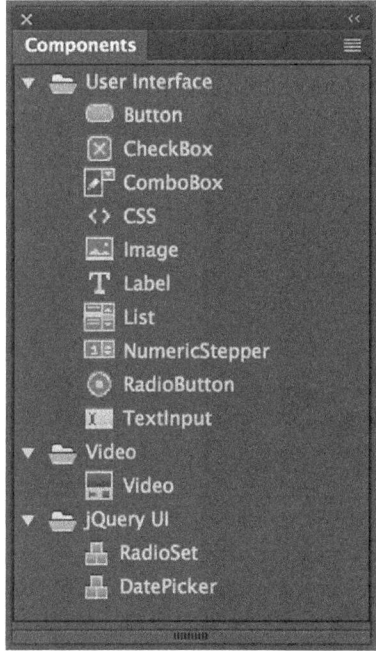

Figure 11-11. *HTML5 Canvas Components panel*

You'll notice we have several categories to explore within the Components panel. In this chapter, we are only concerned with those that exist under the User Interface category. To make use of any of these components, simply click and drag from the Components panel onto the stage. You can provide an instance name to each of the component instances created and can access the various settings, as shown in Figure 11-12, for each instance through the Properties panel, just as we saw with ActionScript 3.0 based components earlier in this chapter. In fact, the process is exactly identical!

529

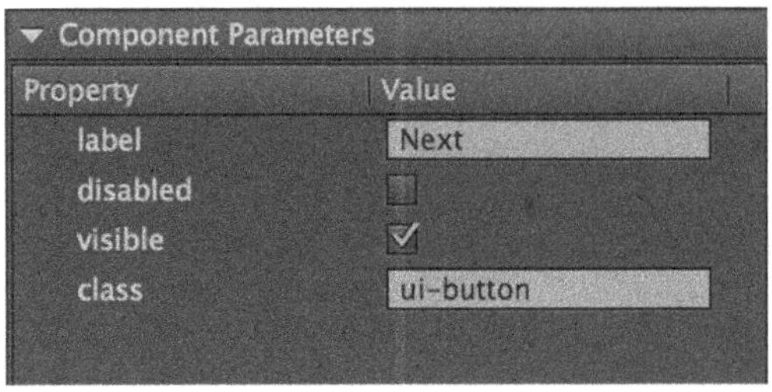

CHAPTER 11 ■ COMPONENTS AND EXTERNAL MEDIA

Property	Value
label	Next
disabled	
visible	✓
class	ui-button

Figure 11-12. *HTML5 Canvas Button component instance parameters*

Although the process of accessing and using components are identical between target platforms, you may notice that we do not have access to the same components on each platform, while there is a set of similar component types, many are unique. Additionally, the parameters that can be accessed and set between like components across each platform may differ considerably, as can be seen when examining the parameter differences in the Button component across both ActionScript 3.0 and HTML5 Canvas document types.

Styling HTML5 Canvas UI Components

The styling of HTML5 Canvas components is done through the use of CSS. These components, even though usable within a canvas based project, are entirely DOM based. When using components in this way, they function as additional elements overlaying the canvas itself. Because of this, we can use the full extent of CSS to style these components however we want.

Let's look at a simple of example that illustrates how this all works.

1. Open the file called HTML5style.fla from this chapter's exercise folder. This is an HTML5 Canvas document. You'll see, as shown in Figure 11-13, a minimal stage with three different component instances on it. Two of these are Button component instances, and the third is an instance of the CSS component.

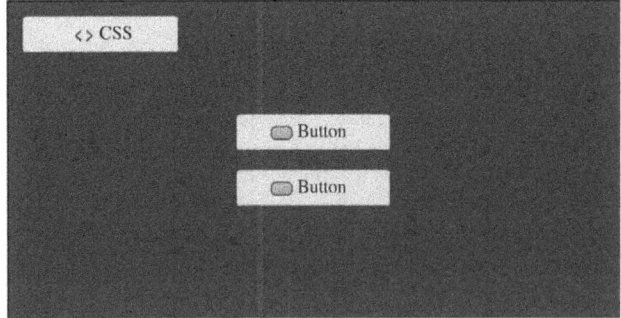

Figure 11-13. *The stage with UI component instances prearranged*

CHAPTER 11 ■ COMPONENTS AND EXTERNAL MEDIA

2. Using the Selection tool, select each one and view the Properties panel (see Figure 11-14) to verify that each is given a unique instance name and is an instance of certain component types. Select the top-most Button component instance first (not the CSS component instance).

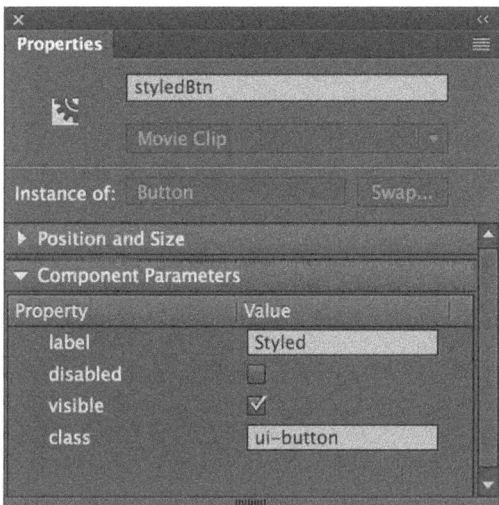

Figure 11-14. Instance with the class of "ui-button" applied

3. Now select the Button component instance directly beneath. Notice that the class of ui-button-unstyled has been applied to this instance. This is very important to realize—even though each is an instance of a Button component, they each will inherit different CSS style rules due to completely different class names.

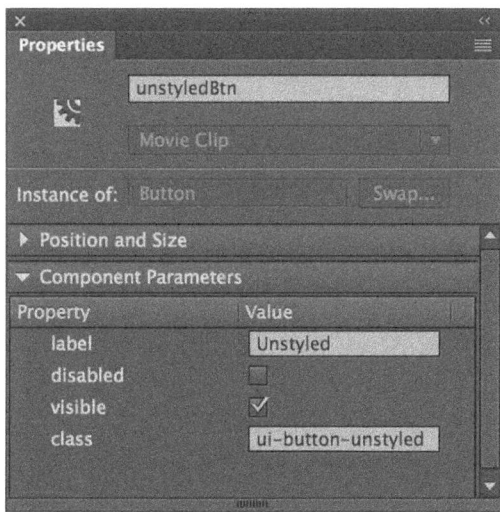

Figure 11-15. Instance with the class of "ui-button-unstyled" applied

531

CHAPTER 11 ■ COMPONENTS AND EXTERNAL MEDIA

4. Finally, select the CSS component instance. A CSS component instance like this will actually not be visible when we publish our project. It only exists to include an external, custom CSS file that supplies CSS style rules to our other component instances. Pay particular attention to the source attribute (Figure 11-16) and how it points directly to a local CSS file. This file contains all of our stylistic rules that determine the look of specific component instances based on their given class names.

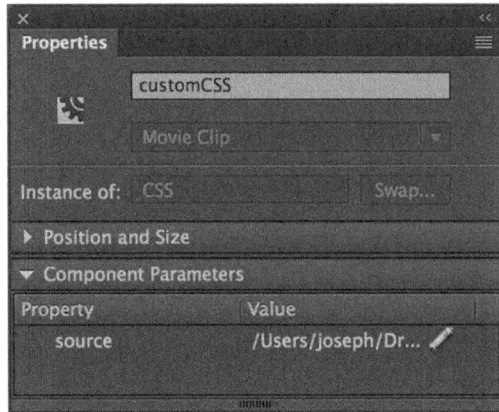

Figure 11-16. CSS component that includes our custom CSS file

5. Open the file called HTML5style.css in your text editor of choice. Notepad, TextEdit, Brackets, Dreamweaver CC, Visual Studio Code, or any number of other editors will be able to open a CSS file like this. You will see the following CSS rule defined:

```
.ui-button {
    font-family: sans-serif;
    background-color: #ed7600;
    border: 1px solid #c75d24;
    color: #003838;
    font-size: 28px;
}
```

6. This rule of .ui-button provides information to Animate CC as to how any instance with the specific class of ui-button should appear in terms of background color, text color, size, font used, etc. Only one of our Button component instances has this class applied through the Properties panel and, as a result, only one of our instances will have these rules applied while the other will retain a default appearance.

7. Test the project to see the CSS applied. It should resemble that shown in Figure 11-17.

532

CHAPTER 11 ■ COMPONENTS AND EXTERNAL MEDIA

Figure 11-17. *Only the one instance with a matching class is affected by the CSS styles*

You should now have a good understanding of how to style HTML5 Canvas components with CSS. If you have previous experience using HTML and CSS for general web pages, this should be nothing new. For those who haven't dealt with such a thing before, there are plenty of resources out there to learn the basics of CSS. You can easily locate and apply specific styles by investigating the source code from your favorite web sites as well for use within Animate CC projects.

There is no "skinning" capability with HTML5 Canvas components similar to what we've seen in ActionScript 3.0 components, as skinning in this way is also accomplished through CSS rules.

Code Snippets for HTML5 Canvas UI Components

Unlike the code snippets for ActionScript 3.0 documents, when using code snippets in an HTML5 Canvas document, you actually do have a set of dedicated snippets! Why? This again has to do with the nature of HTML5 Canvas document components—that they are actually HTML DOM elements overlaying the canvas element. In fact, these code snippets actually use the jQuery Code Library to target and manipulate the component instances.

You access HTML5 Canvas code snippets (Figure 11-18) from the same exact Code Snippets panel you've seen with ActionScript 3.0 documents. Just choose Window ➤ Code Snippets from the application menu and twirl down the HTML5 Canvas category to see the variety of snippets at your disposal.

CHAPTER 11 ■ COMPONENTS AND EXTERNAL MEDIA

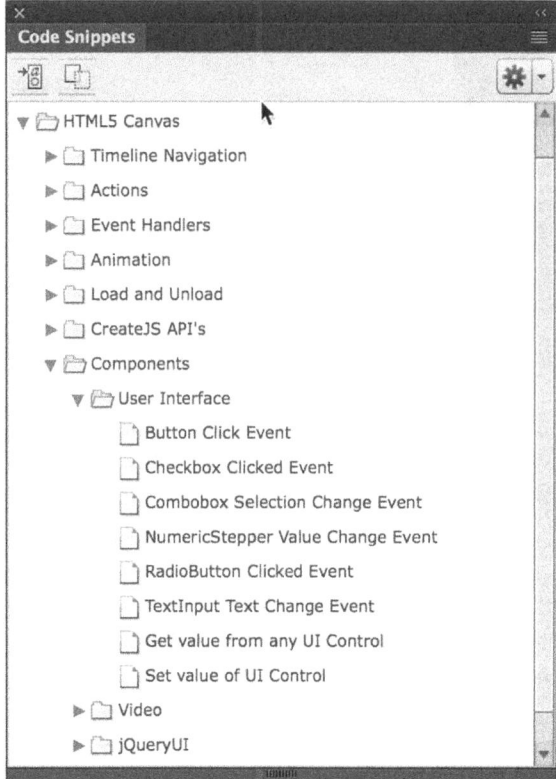

Figure 11-18. UI component code snippets

For the remainder of this chapter, we will be building two HTML5 Canvas projects that take full advantage of UI components, code snippets, and more, so let's move on and take full advantage of these tools!

Building a Slideshow with XML

The popularity of web sites like Instagram, Flickr, Behance, and even Facebook prove that people like to share photos. Of course, this was true even before the Internet. But modern technology makes it easier than ever to whip out that tumbling, unfolding wallet and proudly show off all the children, aunts, uncles, cousin Absalom, and even distant Guillaume Couture, not only to friends, but to every human on the planet. At the rate most people take pictures, photo collections just keep growing. So, if you were to make a photo slideshow in Animate CC, you would want to be sure it was easy to update. With components and XML, that goal is closer than you may think.

To explore the concept, we'll start in an interesting location: the Quanjude Roast Duck Restaurant in Beijing, China. Some time ago, one of the authors was in Beijing. One night, he was enjoying dinner in the company of a couple of Adobe engineers, John Zhang and Zhong Zhou. Naturally, one of the dishes was duck (It's Tom who ate the poor duck! Joseph is a vegetarian!) and, because of the restaurant's history, there was a particular way in which the duck was served and to be consumed. The author was struggling, and Zhong Zhou called the waitress over to demonstrate the proper (and complex!) procedure. It involved a wafer-thin wrap, duck meat, sauces, scallions, and a couple of other treats, which were to be added in a particular order. It took a couple of tries, but the grimacing author finally nailed it. When he thanked Zhong Zhu for the lesson, Zhong said, "It's really simple if you first master the process."

Mastering the creation of an Animate CC slideshow is a lot like preparing that duck dish: it is all about process. In fact, you'll be using some of the same processes learned here for the MP3 player later in the chapter.

Image Files and XML Structure

Whether working in an ActionScript 3.0 or HTML5 Canvas document type, you are going to want to keep a reign on the overall file size of your project. You'll also likely want to keep a project such as a slideshow easy to update—allowing the addition and subtraction of image files, and manipulation of the associated data which defines each image. The process we use here will allow you to have complete control over these aspects of the project and will not even require that you even publish the Animate CC authoring file any more than a single time. This can be done thanks to the modular integration of external media and data sources.

Image Files Overview

Keeping the image files in a separate location allows us to switch them out whenever we like, without having to modify the Animate CC project directly. This is a great process to use when creating a project for a client, as once it is delivered, you can be completely hands-off and they won't be bothering you with every little change they want to make.

Let's a have a quick look at the image files we've prepared for this project. Have a peek at the chapter's exercise files and you'll find a directory named `slideshow`. Within it are a number of files and subdirectories. Open the folder named `photos` and you will see the files in Figure 11-19.

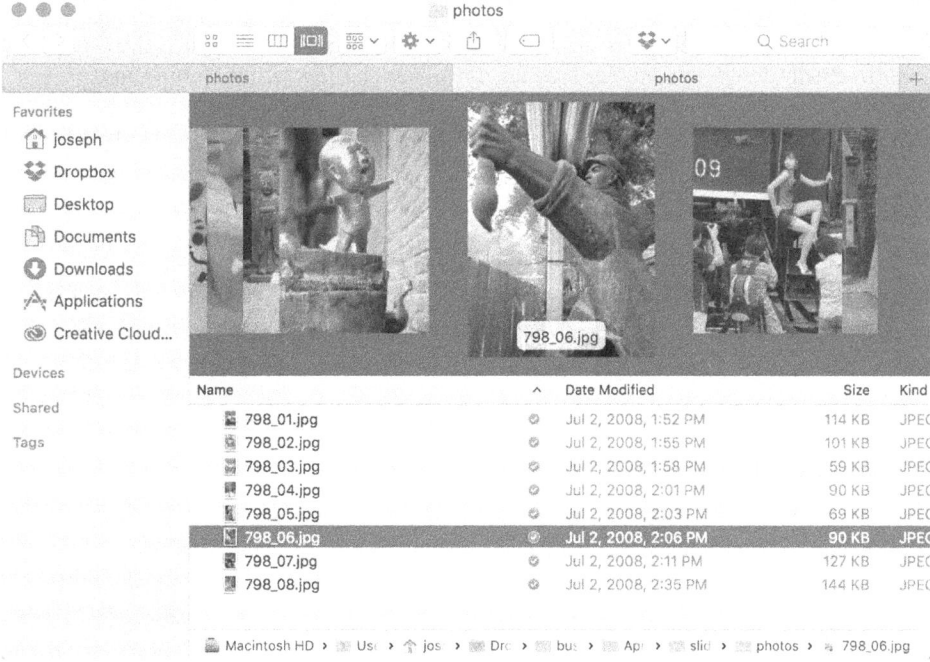

Figure 11-19. *The photographic images for this project*

In truth, these files could be named whatever you like. The project we build needs to know the names of these various files. We'll supply this information through a data file which specifies not only the filename of each photograph, but additional display data as well. How do we do this you may ask? Through the use of XML, of course!

Understanding XML

If you haven't already worked with XML, we bet our next single malt Scotch or glass of fine Absinthe you've at least heard of it. The letters stand for eXtensible Markup Language, and extensibility—the ability to create your own HTML-like tags—is almost certainly the reason XML has become a towering champ in data communication. Countless markup languages and file formats are based on XML, including SMIL, RSS, XAML, MXML, RDF, WAP, SVG, SOAP, WSDL, OpenDocument, XHTML, and so on—truly more than would fit on this page. We'll leave the letter combinations to a Scrabble master.

Even the Animate CC .xfl file format includes project document data, which is defined with XML. Curious? Save your file as .xfl in place of .fla, then open the directory that format created and have a look. Alternatively, take any old .fla document, rename it to .zip, and extract its contents. Voila—XML!

"That's fine and dandy," you might be saying, "but, guys, *what is XML?*" Fair enough. The remarkable thing about this language is that it can basically be whatever you want it to be, provided you stick by its rules. The W3C defines the syntax recommendation for XML (XML 1.0, fifth edition, which is the latest at the time this book was written) at https://www.w3.org/TR/xml/.

The main purpose of XML is to let you share data. In fact, XML is so flexible that newcomers are often baffled about where to even begin. On paper—or rather, on the screen—XML looks a lot like another famous W3C specification: HTML. However, rather than using the predetermined tags and attributes supplied by HTML, XML lets you organize your content into descriptive tags of your own design. While HTML structures data for display, XML actually describes data. The combination of familiar, hierarchical format and completely custom tags generally makes XML content easy to read, both to computers and to humans. By separating your data from the movie, you give yourself the opportunity to change content from the outside, affecting SWFs without needing to republish them.

While we are using XML within a HTML5 Canvas document for this example, you can absolutely use XML within an ActionScript 3.0 document as well. In fact, ActionScript 3.0 includes a special API for traversing XML structures known as E4X! You can read up on using XML in ActionScript 3.0 and the E4X approach to node traversal here: http://help.adobe.com/en_US/FlashPlatform/reference/actionscript/3/XML.html.

Assembling XML Structures

Every XML document must have at least one tag, which constitutes its root element. The root element should describe the document's contents. In this case, we're dealing with image slides, so let's make an entire slideshow the root:

```
<slideshow></slideshow>
```

CHAPTER 11 ■ COMPONENTS AND EXTERNAL MEDIA

The rest of our elements will stack themselves inside this first one. Every image is its own slide, so we'll add eight custom <slide> elements:

```
<slideshow>
        <slide></slide>
        <slide></slide>
        <slide></slide>
        <slide></slide>
        <slide></slide>
        <slide></slide>
        <slide></slide>
        <slide></slide>
</slideshow >
```

Again, these tag names aren't things that exist in XML. It's up to you to decide which elements make sense for the data at hand, to name those elements accordingly, and then to use them.

Let's add some data that describes each of our images in the slideshow. We will add attributes for data (to describe the actual image filename) and caption (which provides a descriptive label to inform the user).

```
<slideshow>
        <slide data="798_01.jpg" caption="Lazy day on the street." />
        <slide data="798_02.jpg" caption="Wall art." />
        <slide data="798_03.jpg" caption="Angry and cute." />
        <slide data="798_04.jpg" caption="The modern and the ancient!" />
        <slide data="798_05.jpg" caption="Not sure what to make of this." />
        <slide data="798_06.jpg" caption="The power of the artist?" />
        <slide data="798_07.jpg" caption="Fashion shoot at a steam engine." />
        <slide data="798_08.jpg" caption="A street in the district." />
</slideshow>
```

The necessary file and caption information for each slide is conveyed here as tag attributes, or attribute nodes, rather than nested tags, just as you would see in standard HTML elements. This exact structure can be found in the XML prepared for the project in the slideshow directory as slideshow.xml. Go ahead and open it in your text editor of choice to view the data for yourself.

Working with and structuring an XML document follows the first principle of web development: "No one cares how you did it. They just care that it works." Find what works best for you, because in the final analysis, your client will never pick up the phone and say, "Dude, that was one sweetly structured XML document you put together." Having said that, if you are part of a collaborative workgroup, be sure that everyone involved agrees on terminology before you start.

Folks, this is a bit like a ceramics class. As long as you're careful around the kiln, no one can tell you whose vase is art and whose isn't. Just work the clay between your fingers, let a number of shapes mull around your mind, and then form the clay into a structure that appeals to you. While you're at it, keep a few rules in mind:

- If you open a tag, close it (<tag></tag>).
- If a tag doesn't come in two parts—that is, if it contains only attributes, or nothing at all—make sure it closes itself (<tag />).

CHAPTER 11 ■ COMPONENTS AND EXTERNAL MEDIA

- Close nested tags in reciprocating order (`<a><b><c /></b></a>` is correct, but `<a><b><c /></a></b>` will "blow up").

- Wrap attribute values in quotation marks or single quotation marks (`<tag done="right" />`, `<tag done=wrong />`).

Feel free to use a text editor such as Notepad on Windows or TextEdit on macOS to create your XML files. Just be sure you add the .xml extension to the file's name. If you have Adobe Dreamweaver CC, that's even better, because it automatically writes the document declaration for you at the top, and it offers tools such as code completion to speed up your workflow. Also, keep in mind that manually writing XML is just one approach. As you start becoming more comfortable with using XML, you will eventually find yourself drifting toward server-side scripting—such as PHP—to handle complex data management.

With our images within a subdirectory named photos and our data structure organized as slideshow.xml, we can now proceed with building our slideshow with UI Components.

Assembling the UI Components

We will now start working within Animate CC to build a project that pulls in both the data from our XML file and the image files specified by that data for display to the user. We will provide additional controls to the user through the user interface components present in Animate CC.

Visual Component Layout

Within the same slideshow directory, you'll find the .fla file called slideshow.fla. Go ahead and open it using Animate CC (see Figure 11-20).

CHAPTER 11 ■ COMPONENTS AND EXTERNAL MEDIA

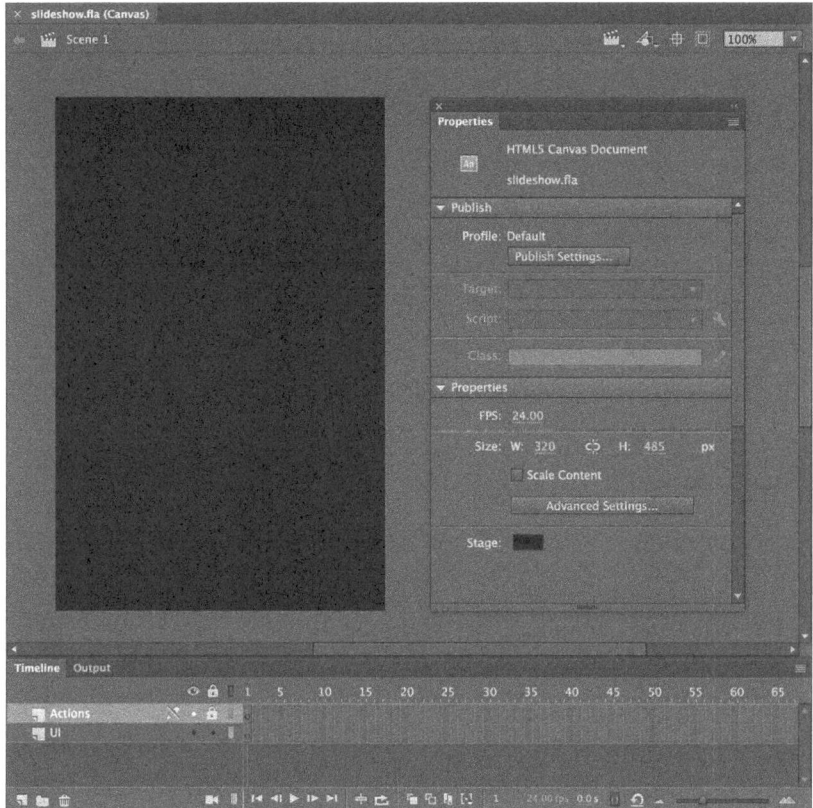

***Figure 11-20.** The prepared slideshow document*

Not much to it, is there? We have a stage set to 320 by 485 with an Actions layer to contain any JavaScript, and a UI layer within which to assemble our visual component instances. So let's get cracking.

1. Be sure that you have the UI layer selected, as this is where we will be placing our component instances.

2. Open the Components panel by choosing Window ➤ Components.

   We are now going to drag a variety of components from the Components panel onto the stage, and provide a number of properties including the position, width and height (be sure to disable the Lock width and height values together button), and will be providing a unique instance name for each instance. The instance name will allow us to target these specific instances through JavaScript later on in this project.

3. Locate the Image component and drag an instance onto the stage.

4. Select the Image component instance and adjust its properties to reflect the following: x:10, y:10, width:300, height:400, and instance name:photoHolder.

5. Locate the Label component and drag an instance onto the stage.

539

CHAPTER 11 ■ COMPONENTS AND EXTERNAL MEDIA

6. Select the Label component instance and adjust its properties to reflect the following: x:10, y:420, width:300, height:22, instance name:captionLabel. Additionally, change the `label` component parameter to read ... as a placeholder.

7. Locate the ComboBox component and drag an instance onto the stage.

8. Select the ComboBox component instance and adjust its properties to reflect the following: x:10, y:452, width:190, height:22, instance name:photoSelect.

9. Locate the Button component and drag an instance onto the stage.

10. Select the Button component instance and adjust its properties to reflect the following: x:210, y:452, width:100, height:22, instance name:nextBtn. Additionally, change the `label` component parameter to read Next.

You should now have four separate component instances on the stage, each bearing a unique instance name, and correctly positioned and sized to reflect what is represented in Figure 11-21.

Figure 11-21. The slideshow document with a variety of component instances

CSS Component Usage

Our component instances are now set up exactly as we want them, however, there is one more component to use in this project—the CSS component. As we saw in the previous section of this chapter, including a bit of external CSS will allow us to provide custom styles to our component set for HTML5 Canvas. Let's go ahead and wire this up.

We've already prepared a .css file that can be used in this project. Look in the same directory as the .fla file and you'll find a file called slideshow.css. Open this file in your text editor of choice and you will see the following CSS style rules:

```css
.ui-button, .ui-combobox {
    font-family: sans-serif;
    background-color: #525252;
    color:azure;
    font-size: 1rem;
}
.ui-label {
    font-family: sans-serif;
    color:azure;
    font-size: 1.2rem;
    text-align: center;
}
.ui-image {
    border: 1px solid #bebebe;
}
```

This CSS isn't very complicated. You can see that we are using the various default "class" component parameter values which Animate CC provides, binding certain rules to change the fonts used, the text color, element background, and so on. If you are unfamiliar with CSS syntax, tweaking some of these values and previewing your documents afterwards can be a worthwhile exercise.

You'll note in the CSS that we are using relative units to specify font size. This is a tricky thing because different display hardware (retina/hiDPI versus non-retina/lowDPI) operating systems, and browsers can all have an effect on how a particular font displays. Using simple rem units like this should make things fairly straightforward, but you are encouraged to tweak the values as you see fit!

With this understanding, let's complete our component setup by linking the slideshow.css file to our project using a CSS component instance.

1. Locate the CSS component and drag an instance onto the stage or the pasteboard. The CSS component will not be visible when published so either is fine—I normally set it off to the side, using the pasteboard.

2. Select the CSS component instance and change the source component parameter by clicking the small pencil icon (Figure 11-22) and locating the slideshow.css file for this document.

CHAPTER 11 ■ COMPONENTS AND EXTERNAL MEDIA

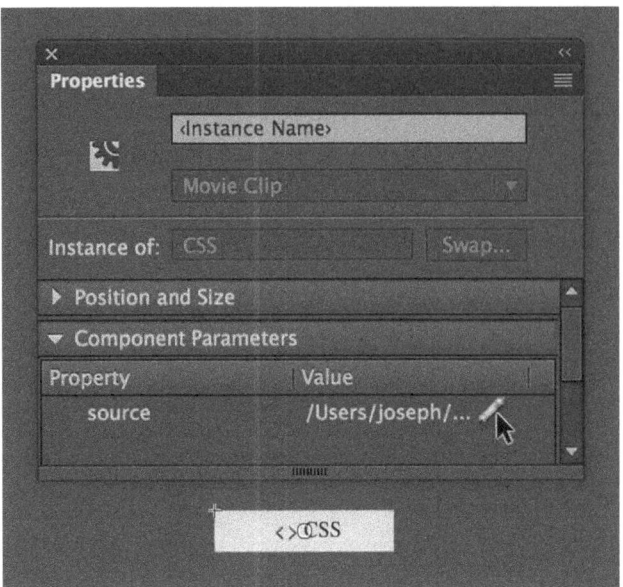

Figure 11-22. Binding a .css file to the document using the CSS component

3. With this done, save your project.

All that is left to do now is write some code to get everything working as a functional slideshow.

Slideshow Functions

This part might get a little dry for some of you. We are writing a bit of JavaScript and will be doing so in a step-by-step manner. If you want to just see what the finished code looks like while referring to the explanations provided in each step—that's a completely valid workflow. For others, taking it all piece by piece will work better—and that's all right too. This book is a resource for you to take and learn in whatever way makes sense to you. With that said, let's get our hands dirty with some JavaScript.

1. The first thing is often the simplest. We will set two variables in our code—an Array to hold information about each photo slide, and a numeric index to keep track of which slide is currently active. We set photoArray to an empty array and initially set the value of currentImage to a value of 0:

   ```
   var photoArray = [];
   var currentImage = 0;
   ```

2. Next, we will invoke the jQuery AJAX function. Since HTML5 Canvas UI Components rely on jQuery, the JavaScript Library is already available in our project. We tell it to retrieve slideshow.xml as data type xml using GET. We can also stub out a function to run upon success, which is currently empty:

   ```
   $.ajax({
           type: 'GET',
           url: 'slideshow.xml',
   ```

```
            dataType: 'xml',
            success: function (xml) {
                    //code to execute with success event
            }
});
```

3. So, what should we do upon success? We'll use jQuery once again to find all the slide nodes within our loaded XML. For each one, we need to create a temporary photo object and supply it with the data and caption attributes from each slide node. We then add that object to our array with the push() method, which simply adds it to the end of the array.

   We also need to target the photoSelect ComboBox component instance to add the object caption attribute as an option the user will be able to choose from. We do this by creating a temporary variable named select which (again) uses jQuery to target our ComboBox instance, adding each new option using the add() method.

   Outside of our jQuery each() loop, after everything else has executed, we invoke a function called changePicture() and pass in the first index (0) of our photoArray. We will create this function in the next step.

   Wow! That's a lot of JavaScript! Place the following code, as described above, directly within the success function code block defined as success:function(xml){}:

```
$(xml).find("slide").each(function () {
        $slide = $(this);
        var photo = new Object();
        photo.data = $slide.attr("data");
        photo.caption = $slide.attr("caption");
        photoArray.push(photo);

        var select = $("#photoSelect")[0];
        select.add(new Option(photo.caption));
});
changePicture(0);
```

4. Let's write the changePicture() function now. This will be called whenever we need to switch out the current slide for another and it accepts a numeric index as a single argument. This index receives the identifier of slide within the function body and is used to determine the index of photoArray that we retrieve the data and caption values from. We change the src parameter of the photoHolder component instance and the inner text of our captionLabel Label component instance based on the data received. Go ahead and add the following function below the code we just entered:

```
function changePicture(slide) {
        $("#photoHolder")[0].src = 'photos/'+photoArray[slide].data;
        $("#captionLabel").text(photoArray[slide].caption);
}
```

CHAPTER 11 ■ COMPONENTS AND EXTERNAL MEDIA

> For the next few steps we will take advantage of the Code Snippets panel. If it's not already open, you can access this panel from the application menu by choosing Window ▶ Code Snippets. Be sure and open the HTML5 Canvas category and then Components ▶ User Interface to reveal the snippets we require. Using code snippets like this will allow us to easily wire in interactions across the various components such as ComboBox and Button, which are used in this project!

5. We now want to program the nextBtn Button component instance to respond to user interaction via a simple click event. Select the nextBtn Button component instance on the stage and then look to the Code Snippets panel. Locate the snippet named "Button Click Event" and choose Add to Current Frame. The following code is added to frame 1 of the Actions layer:

```
if(!this.nextBtn_click_cbk) {
        function nextBtn_click(evt) {
                // place your code here
        }
        $("#dom_overlay_container").on("click", "#nextBtn", nextBtn_click.bind(this));
        this.nextBtn_click_cbk = true;
}
```

6. Now we need to tell the function what we want to have happen when a user clicks the Button component instance. We need to increment our currentImage variable since we want the next slide in the photoArray to be active. We should also ensure that currentImage is now equal to the length of photoArray and reset currentImage to a value of 0 if this is the case.

   Next, we will tell the photoSelect ComboBox component instance to switch to the selectedIndex represented by currentImage and then invoke our changePicture() function as previously defined.

   Insert the following code into the body of our nextBtn_click() function to accomplish this:

```
currentImage++;
if (currentImage == photoArray.length) {
        currentImage = 0;
}
$("#photoSelect")[0].selectedIndex = currentImage;
changePicture(currentImage);
```

7. We now want to program the photoSelect ComboBox component instance to respond to user interaction via a change event. Select the photoSelect ComboBox component instance on the stage and then look to the Code Snippets panel. Locate the snippet named "Combobox Selection Change Event" and choose Add to Current Frame. The following code is added to frame 1 of the Actions layer, directly below all existing JavaScript:

```
if(!this.photoSelect_change_cbk) {
        function photoSelect_change(evt) {
                // place your code here
        }
```

```
            $("#dom_overlay_container").on("change", "#photoSelect", photoSelect_
            change.bind(this));
        this.photoSelect_change_cbk = true;
    }
```

8. To complete this project, we only need to provide a few more instructions within the photoSelect_change() function that was just created to handle our change event. We will set the currentImage to the selectedIndex of our photoSelect ComboBox component instance, and then once again invoke changePicture(), passing the new index through as an argument. Insert the following JavaScript into the body of our photoSelect_change() function to complete this portion of the project:

```
currentImage = evt.target.selectedIndex;
changePicture(currentImage);
```

9. All done! Select Control ➤ Test from the application menu to interact with your custom photo slideshow application, as shown in Figure 11-23.

Figure 11-23. *The completed slideshow*

You might be asking, "Could I do this same thing with ActionScript as well and just target Flash Player?" Sure you could! Honestly though, if you're targeting the web with a project like this—a project that functions completely well on the native web without an external browser plugin—why wouldn't you do so? Flash Player is excellent technology for certain projects, but for a case like this, HTML5 Canvas makes way more sense.

Completed Code

Here is the full, completed JavaScript code for this example:

```
var photoArray = [];
var currentImage = 0;

$.ajax({
        type: 'GET',
        url: 'slideshow.xml',
        dataType: 'xml',
        success: function (xml) {
                $(xml).find("slide").each(function () {
                        $slide = $(this);
                        var photo = new Object();
                        photo.data = $slide.attr("data");
                        photo.caption = $slide.attr("caption");
                        photoArray.push(photo);

                        var select = $("#photoSelect")[0];
                        select.add(new Option(photo.caption));
                });
                changePicture(0);
        }
});
function changePicture(slide) {
        $("#photoHolder")[0].src = 'photos/'+photoArray[slide].data;
        $("#captionLabel").text(photoArray[slide].caption);
}

if(!this.nextBtn_click_cbk) {
        function nextBtn_click(evt) {
                currentImage++;
                if (currentImage == photoArray.length) {
                        currentImage = 0;
                }
                $("#photoSelect")[0].selectedIndex = currentImage;
                changePicture(currentImage);
        }
        $("#dom_overlay_container").on("click", "#nextBtn", nextBtn_click.bind(this));
        this.nextBtn_click_cbk = true;
}

if(!this.photoSelect_change_cbk) {
        function photoSelect_change(evt) {
                currentImage = evt.target.selectedIndex;
                changePicture(currentImage);
        }
        $("#dom_overlay_container").on("change", "#photoSelect", photoSelect_change.
        bind(this));
        this.photoSelect_change_cbk = true;
}
```

The associated file and folder structure is as follows:

- slideshow.fla
- slideshow.css
- slideshow.xml
    - photos
        - 798_01.jpg
        - 798_02.jpg
        - 798_03.jpg
        - 798_04.jpg
        - 798_05.jpg
        - 798_06.jpg
        - 798_07.jpg
        - 798_08.jpg

Building a MP3 Player with JSON

You are likely already familiar with the use of audio in Animate CC projects from our explorations in Chapter 5 of this book. You learned how to import audio files into the project library and then make audio playback available along the timeline through both regular animated playback and also through the use of interactive event sounds. When people get around to working with audio within the timeline in Animate CC, one of the more common requests is, "Can I make my own MP3 player? Can the audio files exist apart from and completely external to my project?" The answer to these questions, of course, is YES.

Like photo sharing, audio playback has exploded as evident from the success of services like SoundCloud, Spotify, Google Music, and more. Using Animate CC, it's a fairly easy task to build a small MP3 player for the native web that can be used on any web site you like. This project will be somewhat similar to the previous slideshow project, except that we are using sound files in place of images and a different set of components. That's a little too similar though, right? Let's mix things up a bit more and use JSON data in place of the XML structures used in the Slideshow project.

Just as with the Slideshow project, a lot of this code relies heavily on the jQuery JavaScript Library. Many developers tend to avoid jQuery and would rather do everything using plain old vanilla JavaScript, which is a completely valid approach. The thing is, Animate CC is leveraging jQuery anyhow to get these components working. We might as well take advantage of a tool that's just lying there to make things easier for ourselves and to be in closer synchronization with what is happening under the hood.

MP3 Files, Image Files, and JSON Structure

Many of the concerns around image files in Animate CC projects apply to audio files as well. We will still want to keep the overall size of our project file bundle as small as possible. It's also great to have a project that is completely driven by external data. This way, we can easily swap out different files so long as the data which feeds our project is updated accordingly. In this project, similar to the last, we have a set of media files and a text file which contains all of the data associated with these files. Let's explore both of these resources now.

Audio and Art Files Overview

The benefits of keeping our audio files separate from the actual Animate CC project are evident. In order to get acquainted with the media associated with this overall project, let's a have a quick look at the audio files we've prepared. Have a peek at the chapter's exercise files and you'll find a directory named musicplayer. Within this are a number of files and subdirectories. Open the folder named music and you will see the set of .mp3 files shown in Figure 11-24.

Figure 11-24. *The audio files for this project*

The audio files supplied for this project have been composed, recorded, and produced under the name of either **An Early Morning Letter, Displaced**, or **Shivervein**. You are encouraged to explore the full catalogue of music published by Fractured Vision Media, LLC, by visiting http://fracturedvisionmedia.com/music.

Additionally, we have a folder named covers which, as shown in Figure 11-25, contains .png images of the album art for each track of music. While it is fairly easy to pull embedded cover art from the ID3 tags of an .mp3 file using ActionScript, when targeting the native web with HTML5 Canvas and JavaScript, the path we are about to take is the simpler approach.

CHAPTER 11 ■ COMPONENTS AND EXTERNAL MEDIA

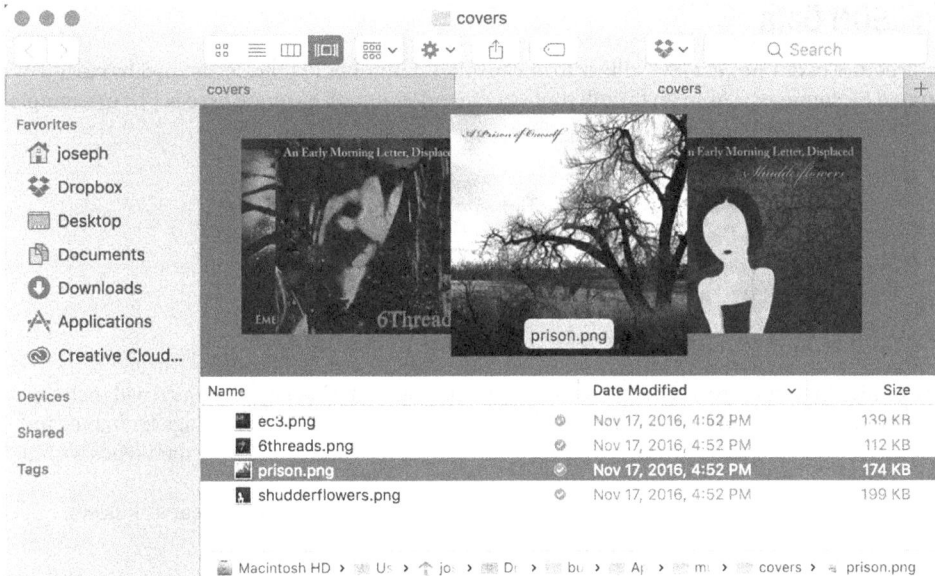

Figure 11-25. *The cover images for this project*

The data file we construct will include entries for each piece of audio and will refer to both the .mp3 file for playback and the .png file for visual identity and display. As mentioned previously, we will be using the JSON data format to structure and deliver this data to our project.

Understanding JSON

JSON is conceptually very similar to XML in that its purpose is to define data and make the transport of such data a simple affair—whether being read by humans or machines. The term itself is an acronym for "JavaScript Object Notation" and is based on a subset of the JavaScript Programming Language, Standard ECMA-262 3rd Edition. Just about any modern programming language supports JSON, including both JavaScript and ActionScript.

So what kind of data can be stored within JSON data structures? JSON supports `string`, `number`, `object`, `array`, `boolean`, and `null` data types. This set of data types cover just about anything you'd like to do in terms of storing and representing data. In this project, we'll be storing all of our data as name:value pairs within a series of `object` data types. The actual values stored will be simple `string` data.

As with XML, no one interacting with your project really cares how it was done. In fact, you could easily use XML to structure this same data if you wanted to. Looking back at the Slideshow project, that could have just as easily used JSON, instead.

For a lot more information on the nuances of JSON, pay `http://json.org/` a visit.

CHAPTER 11 ■ COMPONENTS AND EXTERNAL MEDIA

Assembling JSON Data

The most basic structure of our project JSON file is to encapsulate a number of objects, defined by curly braces {}, separated by commas, within an overall root structure defined with square braces []. An example of this basic structure can be seen here:

```
[
        {},
        {},
        {},
        {}
]
```

Each object within this structure, for the purposes of defining audio tracks in our project, will include three unique property:value pairs. We will include the `title` of the track, the `cover` art image filename, and the `audio` filename. These values are all strings, in this case, though JSON allows multiple data types within such structures.

The completed JSON file structure with all properties and values defined would appear as follows:

```
[
    {
        "title":"Razorpalm",
        "cover":"ec3.png",
        "audio":"Razorpalm.mp3"
    },
    {
        "title":"To Lead You Down",
        "cover":"6threads.png",
        "audio":"ToLeadYouDown.mp3"
    },
    {
        "title":"Drowning Past The Sky",
        "cover":"shudderflowers.png",
        "audio":"DrowningPastTheSky.mp3"
    },
    {
        "title":"Condemnation",
        "cover":"prison.png",
        "audio":"condemnation.mp3"
    }
]
```

The necessary information for each audio track is conveyed here within each separate object. These objects are then contained within a simple array index as a root element. This exact structure can be found in the JSON prepared for the project in the `musicplayer` directory as `musicplayer.xml`. Go ahead and open it within your text editor of choice to view the data for yourself.

CHAPTER 11 ■ COMPONENTS AND EXTERNAL MEDIA

Assembling the UI Components

We will now start working within Animate CC to build our music player project. This HTML5 Canvas document will pull in both the data from our JSON file and the associated audio and image files specified by that data for display to the user. We will provide additional controls to the user through the user interface components present in Animate CC.

Visual Component Layout

Within the same musicplayer directory, you'll find the .fla file called musicplayer.fla. Go ahead and open it within Animate CC, as shown in Figure 11-26.

Figure 11-26. *The prepared music player document*

Again, very simple to start things off. We have a stage set to 320 by 385 with an Actions layer to contain any JavaScript, and a UI layer within which to assemble our visual component instances. Moving along:

1. Be sure that you have the UI layer selected, as this is where we will be placing our component instances.

2. Open the Components panel by choosing Window ➤ Components.

551

We are now going to drag a set of components from the Components panel onto the stage, and provide some adjustments to various properties including the position, width and height, and will be providing a unique instance name for each instance. The instance name will allow us to target these specific instances through JavaScript. This should all be second-nature for you by now.

3. Locate the Image component and drag an instance onto the stage.

4. Select the Image component instance and adjust its properties to reflect the following: x:10, y:10, width:300, height:300, and instance name:coverHolder.

5. Locate the Video component (within the Video category) and drag an instance onto the stage.

6. Select the Video component instance and adjust its properties to reflect the following: x:10, y:318, width:300, height:22, and instance name:audioPlayer. Disable `autoplay` and `loop` within Component Parameters.

7. Locate the ComboBox component and drag an instance onto the stage.

8. Select the ComboBox component instance and adjust its properties to reflect the following: x:10, y:352, width:300, height:22, and instance name:musicSelect.

You should now have three separate component instances on the stage, each bearing a unique instance name, and correctly positioned and sized to reflect what is represented in Figure 11-27.

Figure 11-27. *The music player document with its set of component instances*

CSS Component Usage

Our component instances are now set up exactly as we want them, but we want to add some custom CSS just as in previous projects. We do this, once again, through the combination of a custom .css file and the CSS component.

We've already prepared a .css file that can be used in this project. Look in the same directory as the .fla file and you'll find a file called musicplayer.css. Open this file within your text editor of choice and you will see the following CSS style rules:

```
.ui-combobox {
    font-family: sans-serif;
    background-color: #525252;
    color:azure;
    font-size: 1rem;
}
.ui-image {
    border: 1px solid #bebebe;
}
```

This CSS isn't very complicated. You can see that we are using the various default "class" component parameter values which Animate CC provides for both Image and ComboBox, binding certain rules to change the fonts used, the text color, element background, and so on.

We are once again using relative rem units to specify font size. Just as with the slideshow project, you are encouraged to tweak these values to see what works best for you. 1rem should provide a good baseline no matter what your particular configuration.

Let's now complete our component setup by linking the musicplayer.css file to our project using a CSS component instance.

1. Locate the CSS component and drag an instance onto the stage or the pasteboard. The CSS component will not be visible when published so either is fine—a common best practice is to normally set it off to the side, using the pasteboard.

2. Select the CSS component instance and change the source component parameter by clicking the small pencil icon and locating the .css file for this document (see Figure 11-28).

CHAPTER 11 ■ COMPONENTS AND EXTERNAL MEDIA

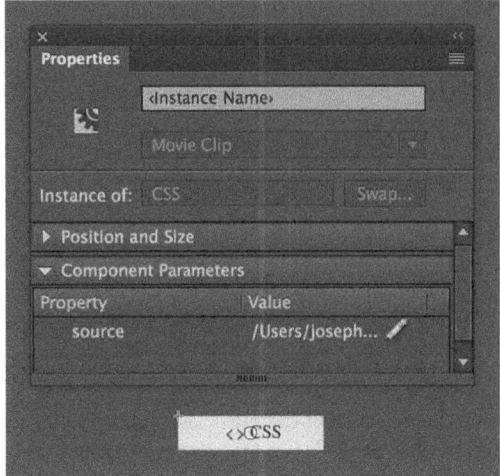

Figure 11-28. Binding a .css file to the document using the CSS component

   3. With this done, save your project.

All that is left to do now is write the functional JavaScript to pull in the JSON data, parse through each object, and supply the user with some elements to interact with through event listeners.

Sound Playback Functions

Now is time to write the JavaScript necessary to ingest the data and make the component instances work with the retrieved data and associated media files. Because we are using HTML5 components, which we've already seen in action, this will be a fairly straight-forward process. To make things even simpler, we'll be employing code snippets here and there to supplement our own JavaScript and jQuery instructions.

   1. This should look very familiar. We create an empty array to hold our music tracks called musicTracks and a numeric variable called currentTrack to keep track of the current position within this array across our project.

   ```
   var musicTracks = [];
   var currentTrack = 0;
   ```

   2. Next is an AJAX call, via jQuery, which will retrieve and parse our JSON data. We tell it to retrieve slideshow.xml as data type xml using GET. We can also stub out a function to run upon success, which is currently empty:

   ```
   $.ajax({
           type: 'GET',
           url: 'musicplayer.json',
           dataType: 'json',
           success: function (json) {
                   musicTracks = json;
                   populateSelect();
           }
   });
   ```

3. The populateSelect() function loops through all the indexes of the assembled musicTracks array and adds an option to the musicSelect ComboBox component instance for each one. After this has been assembled, we invoke a function called changeTrack() and pass in the track index we want to switch to. We will pass in a value of 0 to begin, as this is the initial index of our musicTracks array. We will write our changeTrack() function to handle this in the next step.

```
function populateSelect() {
        for(var i=0; i<musicTracks.length; i++){
                var select = $("#musicSelect")[0];
                select.add(new Option(musicTracks[i].title));
        }
        changeTrack(0);
}
```

4. We will invoke a function named changeTrack() whenever we need to switch to a different piece of music. This function accepts a number as an argument that is exposed to this function body with the identifier of track. Using this index, we can change our cover art image file and audio file for playback by adjusting the src parameter of both the coverHolder Image component and audioPlayer Video component instances.

```
function changeTrack(track) {
        $("#coverHolder")[0].src = 'covers/'+musicTracks[track].cover;
        $("#audioPlayer")[0].src = 'music/'+musicTracks[track].audio;
}
```

For the next step we will make use of the Code Snippets panel. If not already open, you can always access this panel from the application menu by choosing Window ➤ Code Snippets. Be sure and open the HTML5 Canvas category and then Components. We will be using snippets located under the User Interface sub-category.

5. Now for the ComboBox component instance change event listener. This event will fire whenever the user changes the selected item within our musicSelect component instance. We'll use a code snippet to wire this up.

Select the musicSelect ComboBox component instance on the stage and then look to the Code Snippets panel. Locate the snippet named "Combobox Selection Change Event" and choose to Add to Current Frame. The following code is added to frame 1 of the Actions layer, directly below all existing JavaScript:

```
if(!this.musicSelect_change_cbk) {
        function musicSelect_change(evt) {
                // add code here
        }
        $("#dom_overlay_container").on("change", "#musicSelect",
        musicSelect_change.bind(this));
        this.musicSelect_change_cbk = true;
}
```

6. We need to make some additions within the musicSelect_change() function that was just created to handle our change event. We will set currentTrack to the selectedIndex of the musicSelect ComboBox component instance and then pass this as an argument through to our changeTrack() function to switch the selected piece of music as selected by the user. Place this code directly below the line that reads function musicSelect_change(evt) {:

   ```
   currentTrack = evt.target.selectedIndex;
   changeTrack(currentTrack);
   ```

7. That's all the JavaScript we need to write for this one. Select Control ➤ Test from the application menu to interact with your custom music player application in the native web browser, as shown in Figure 11-29.

Figure 11-29. The completed music player

One additional note about audio file playback in web browsers—there will always be circumstances in which certain file formats are not supported based on certain configurations. MP3 is supported across most all browsers per http://caniuse.com/#feat=mp3. However, there are always caveats! For instance, playback of an MP3 file in Firefox is dependent on the host operating system providing a decoder.

Completed Code

Here is the full, completed JavaScript code for this example:

```
var musicTracks = [];
var currentTrack = 0;

$.ajax({
        type: 'GET',
        url: 'musicplayer.json',
        dataType: 'json',
        success: function (json) {
              musicTracks = json;
              populateSelect();
    }
});
function populateSelect() {
      for(var i=0; i<musicTracks.length; i++){
            var select = $("#musicSelect")[0];
            select.add(new Option(musicTracks[i].title));
      }
      changeTrack(0);
}
function changeTrack(track) {
      $("#coverHolder")[0].src = 'covers/'+musicTracks[track].cover;
      $("#audioPlayer")[0].src = 'music/'+musicTracks[track].audio;
}
if(!this.musicSelect_change_cbk) {
      function musicSelect_change(evt) {
            currentTrack = evt.target.selectedIndex;
            changeTrack(currentTrack);
      }
      $("#dom_overlay_container").on("change", "#musicSelect",  musicSelect_change.bind(this));
      this.musicSelect_change_cbk = true;
}
```

The associated file and folder structure is as follows:

- musicplayer.fla
- musicplayer.css
- musicplayer.json
    - covers
        - 6threads.png
        - ec3.png
        - prison.png
        - shudderflowers.png

- music
  - Razorpalm.mp3
  - condemnation.mp3
  - DrowningPastTheSky.mp3
  - ToLeadYouDown.mp3

Additional Customization Options

As mentioned, we are using the Video component to playback audio rendering the regular video playback controls within the native browser. Which works just fine, but there are other ways to further customize the audio playback experience. The browsers also have a native audio tag that we could write a custom component for, for instance. Additionally, we could hide the default controls and use our own custom controls for playback. While these methods are beyond the scope of a book like this, the authors believe they are worth mentioning so that you have a basic understanding of the possibilities and know which direction to explore if a nagging desire to pursue such customization keeps you up at night.

Creating Custom HTML5 Components

When Adobe built out the functionality to include components within HTML5 Canvas documents, they did so in a very forward-looking and extensible manner. As hinted at here and there, These components are written in basic HTML and JavaScript, with the assistance of jQuery here and there as needed. So what does this mean for users of Animate CC? It means that anyone can write custom components for use in their projects, as shown in Figure 11-30. A good example of this would be to copy and modify the current Video component and switch it out to use the HTML5 Audio element in place of the Video element.

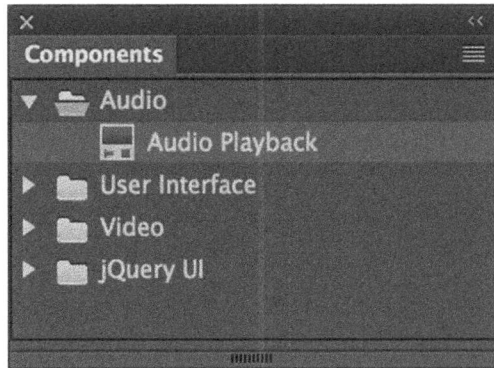

Figure 11-30. *A basic custom Audio Playback component within Animate CC*

CHAPTER 11 ■ COMPONENTS AND EXTERNAL MEDIA

If you'd like to experiment with creating your very own components, Adobe has a number of resources that you can read up on, available at the following address:

https://helpx.adobe.com/animate/using/custom-html5-component-development.html.

Creating Custom Interface Controls

Across many of the previous chapters of this book, you've learned how to use the variety of tools and techniques which are available in Animate CC to design all manner of animated, static, and interactive elements. Just because we are using some Components in a project does not preclude the use of MovieClip, Graphic, and Button symbols that you create on your own. In fact, the mixture of components and symbols in an Animate CC project is just another example of the versatility of this platform!

If designing your own custom controls, you'll first need to disable the present controls on the Video component instance being used, as shown in Figure 11-31. When using audio in such a case, we could alternatively just move the instance over onto the pasteboard to obscure it from view. It's really up to you regarding which option you choose to employ.

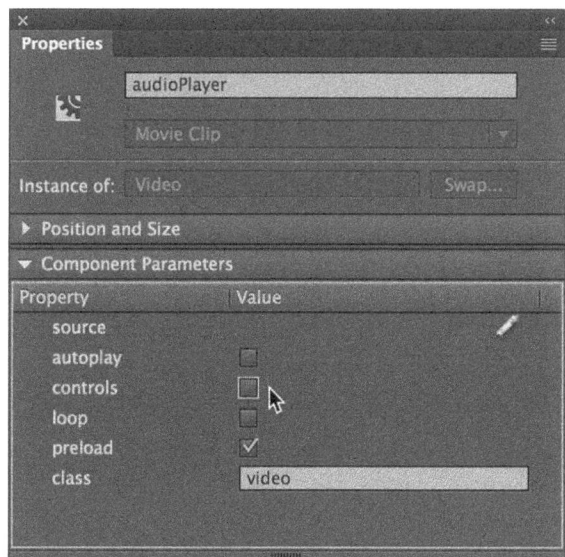

Figure 11-31. *Turning off the default component controls*

We then need to build the replacement elements, since our default playback controls have been disabled. Here is where we can get really creative and design a set of MovieClip or Button symbols that replace the default controls that have been hidden, as shown in Figure 11-32.

559

CHAPTER 11 ■ COMPONENTS AND EXTERNAL MEDIA

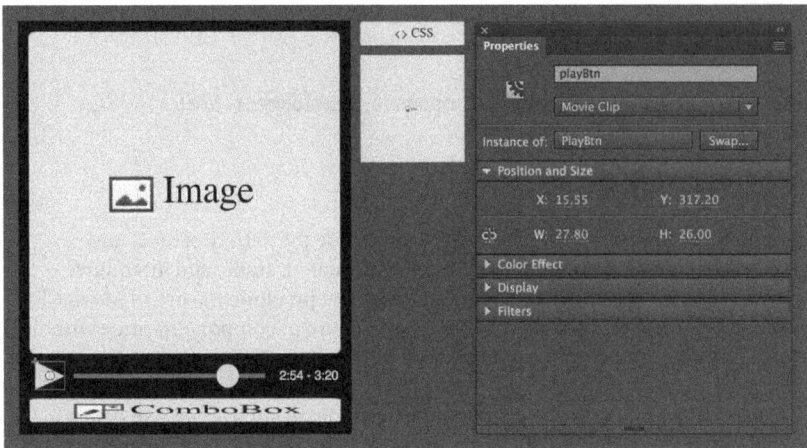

Figure 11-32. Wiring up a symbol instance for custom controls

Using the Code Snippets panel, it's simple enough to cobble together a click event for our playBtn MovieClip symbol instance to control our audioPlayer Video component instance playback.

```
this.playBtn.addEventListener("click", fl_MouseClickHandler.bind(this));
function fl_MouseClickHandler()
{
        $("#audioPlayer")[0].play();
}
```

Using this sort of workflow, we can additionally wire up other controls like a scrubber to seek to specific times, and a display to track the current and elapsed playback time of the current audio file. Using Animate CC, you can make these visual elements appear however you want!

To review the full extent of available media events available in the native browser, look at a resource such as the "HTML5 Video Events and API" page supplied by the World Wide Web Consortium (W3C): https://www.w3.org/2010/05/video/mediaevents.html.

What You Have Learned

Rather than list what we covered in this chapter, we think it is more important to take a broader view of that statement. Step back for a moment and think about what you knew when you first laid this book on your desk and flamed up Animate CC. The answer, we suspect, is "Not a lot."

Now think about your working through this chapter. The odds are pretty good you were able to follow along, and we are willing to bet there were a couple of points where you may have asked us to "move along a little quicker." This says to us that we have done our job, and that you may just know a lot more than you are aware of. Congratulations.

We were also a little sneaky with this chapter. If you follow the flow from the start to the end, you will see it actually follows the structure of this book: each exercise is designed to add to your knowledge base by building on what you learned in the preceding exercise and, as we kept pointing out, in preceding chapters.

Finally, this chapter expanded on practically every concept presented in this book. If you have completed the exercises, then you have quite a bit of practical experience using Animate CC.

Now that you've learned the ropes and have practiced numerous techniques, let's concentrate on the end game of the design and development process: publishing your file.

CHAPTER 12

Optimizing and Publishing Animate CC Projects

When it comes to publishing Animate CC projects for the Web, a common user experience is sitting around waiting for the project to start. From your perspective, as the artist who designed the piece, this may seem odd. After all, when you tested the movie in the authoring environment, it was seriously fast and played flawlessly. What happened? To be succinct, the Web happened. Your project may indeed be cool, but you made a fundamental mistake: you fell in love with the technology, not the user. In this chapter, we'll talk about how to improve the user experience.

Here's what we'll cover in this chapter:

- Understanding how Animate CC projects are delivered to a web page
- Using bandwidth-monitoring tools to optimize projects
- Choosing publish formats
- Publishing for Flash Player and AIR
- Publishing for HTML5 Canvas

Animate CC, Flash Player, and the Internet

Back in the early days of Flash Player, when we really didn't know better, Flash designers would prepare these really "cool" intros to the site, which played while the rest of the site loaded. The problem was they were large; in many cases, the intro seemed to take almost as long to load as the site. The solution was the infamous Skip Intro button, as seen in Figure 12-1. The intro would start playing, and after a couple of seconds, the Skip Intro button would appear. The user would click it, only to discover the site hadn't quite loaded. Users were left to sit there, drumming their fingers on their desk. So, users began to see the button not as a Skip Intro option but as a "skip site" warning. This resulted in Flash Player (and Flash Professional) gaining a rather nasty reputation for bloat, which Animate CC is just now beginning to finally shake off. Of course, some people will take their sense of humor to outrageous levels. One of the best was a site that really was nothing more than one massive intro is http://www.zombo.com. To deal with the bloat issue, it is critical that you understand the underlying technology behind an Animate CC project, regardless of the document target format. That's right, HTML5 Canvas projects can be just as "bloated" as those targeting Flash Player.

CHAPTER 12 ■ OPTIMIZING AND PUBLISHING ANIMATE CC PROJECTS

Figure 12-1. Welcome to… Skip Intro hell

This "Internet" Thing

When publishing Animate CC projects that will end up on the Web, no matter what format you are working in, you must understand a bit of fundamental history and terminology. The Internet's roots go back to the U.S. Department of Defense's need to create a bulletproof means of maintaining communications among computers. This involved such things as file transfers, messaging, and so on. At the time, computers were a virtual Tower of Babel, which meant different computer types and operating systems rarely, if ever, could talk to each other. As well, in battle conditions, the needed system would have to carry on even if a piece of it was knocked out, and it had to be accessible to everything from portable computers to the big, honking mainframes in "clean rooms" around the world.

The solution was an enabling technology called the Internet Protocol suite, though we know it by a far sexier name: TCP/IP. This is how data moves from your computer to our computers, or from your web server to our computers, and, as you may have guessed, the slash indicates that it comes in two parts:

- **IP (Internet Protocol):** How data gets from here to there by using an address called the IP address. This address is a unique number used to identify any computer currently on the Internet. This protocol creates little bundles of information, called packets, which can then be shot out through the Internet to your computer. Obviously, the route is not a straight line. The packets pass through special computers called routers, and their job is to point those packets to your computer. Depending on the distance traveled, there could be any number of routers, which check your packets and send them either directly to your computer or to the next router along the line.

- **TCP (Transmission Control Protocol):** The technology that verifies all the data packets got to your computer. The IP portion of the trip couldn't care less if packet 10 arrives at your computer before packet 1, or even that it got there at all. This is where TCP comes in. Its job is to ensure that all of the packets get to where they are supposed to go.

Once all of this got the kinks worked out, the U.S. military had quite the communications system on its hands.

Enter the World Wide Web

Although straight data transmission was interesting, once the cool factor wore off, people started wondering how it would be possible to use this communication network to access files containing images, audio, and video. The solution was the World Wide Web—a network of networks, which is commonly seen as web pages and hyperlinks.

A web page is a simple text file, which uses HTML—a formatting language of tags and text—to define how a page should look and behave. This is important, because your Flash Player and HTML5 Canvas projects will always be found in an HTML wrapper when targeting the Web.

The concept of hyperlinks and hypertext was around long before the Internet. The gentleman who managed the atomic bomb project for the United States during World War II, Vannevar Bush, wrote an article for the *Atlantic Monthly* in July 1945 that proposed a system of linking all information with all other information. The article was entitled "As We May Think," and you can still read it at http://www.theatlantic.com/magazine/archive/1945/07/as-we-may-think/303881/.

An HTML page may be nothing more than a text file, but it can contain links to other assets, such as JavaScript files, CSS files, JPEGs, PNGs, GIFs, and potentially Flash Player SWFs if targeting that platform. These links take the form of a Uniform Resource Locator (URL) and specify the location of the assets requested by the HTML document. When Chrome, Firefox, Edge, or any other graphical browser translates the page, those addresses are used to load the external assets and display them on your computer screen. Thus, the Web is really composed of two parts: browsers that request files and servers that store files and make them available when a browser asks for them.

As you can see, the infrastructure that moves your project files from a server to thousands of browsers is already in place. Where your pain and heartache arise is from something called bandwidth.

Bandwidth

In the early days of Flash Player, around 1999, one of the authors read an article written by a New York Flash designer, Hillman Curtis, and one phrase leaped out of the article and has been glued to the front of his cerebral cortex ever since. What's that phrase? "Keep an eye on the pipe."

The "pipe" is bandwidth. Bandwidth is a measure of how much data will move along a given path at a given time or how much information can be downloaded through a modem and how fast. One of the authors, when speaking on this topic in the past, used a rather amusing analogy that will help you understand this topic. Imagine trying to push the amount of data contained in your favorite TV show through a modem. When that modem is connected to a telephone line, the effort is no different from "trying to push a watermelon through a worm."

Bandwidth is measured in bits per second (bps), usually in the thousands (Kbps) or millions (Mbps). A bit is either a one or a zero, so ultimately bandwidth is a measure of how many ones and zeros can be fed through a router or modem each second. The higher the number, the greater the bandwidth, and the faster things get from here to there. But bandwidth is not constant. It requires more bandwidth to move a video from here to there than it does to transfer a page of text. The issue is not "here to there." The issue is the modem's capacity to manage the data. This is the "pipe." Users with 56Kbps dial-up modems have a pipe that has the diameter of a garden hose. Users with fast Internet service like DSL or cable have a pipe that has the diameter of a fire hose. Connect the tiny garden hose to the fire hydrant in front of your house, and you will get a graphic demonstration of data flow and the pipe when you turn on the hydrant.

CHAPTER 12 ■ OPTIMIZING AND PUBLISHING ANIMATE CC PROJECTS

As we pointed out earlier, the data packets sent to your computer get there eventually, and the route is never a straight line. Over time, TCP/IP ensures that the transmission rate averages to a more or less constant rate, but this is technology we're dealing with here. It is the prudent Animate CC designer who approaches technology with a dose of pragmatism and does not assume a constant flow. This has implications for your design efforts, and we will get into those implications shortly.

You need to regard the pipe and data transmission in much the same manner you regard your local highway. It may have six lanes for traffic and a posted speed limit of 60 mph (or 100 kph), but all of that becomes irrelevant during rush hour. Traffic moves at the pace of the slowest car. It is no different with the Internet. Servers can become overloaded.

A powerful example of this in recent history is the infamous event known as 9/11. On that day, the Internet essentially ground to a halt as it seemed like every computer on the planet was attempting to get the latest information on the tragedy. A more recent example is the day Michael Jackson died. The chart in Figure 12-2 from Google Trends shows Google search traffic on that day. The sharp spike between 1 and 6 p.m. follows the news from the first reports around 1 p.m. and the reaction to the formal announcement a couple of hours later.

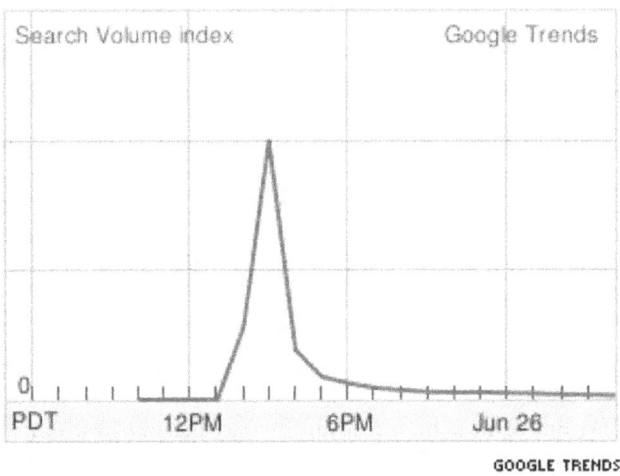

Figure 12-2. *Google search traffic when the world discovered Michael Jackson had died*

What people overlooked on both days was that a server is only a computer, and it can only reply to a finite number of requests at a set rate. If the browser can't get the information, it will assume the assets are not there. As a consequence, the requested page either will not be displayed or will be displayed with information missing. It got so bad for CNN and the BBC on 9/11 that they were forced to post a message that essentially told people "come back later." Even the people lucky enough to make a connection experienced pauses in the download and frequent disconnects, which are the hallmarks of an overloaded server.

What you need to take away from these two stories is that the time it takes to download and play your project files is totally dependent on the contents of your Animate CC document and traffic flow on the Internet. This means you need to concentrate not only on what is in your movie but also on who wants to access it. This is where you fall in love with the user and not the technology. So, what do you really need to know before putting your work out there? Here are some general guidelines:

- Small means fast. Studies show you have 15 seconds to hook the user. If nothing is happening or is appealing to your users, they're gone. Small SWFs and light HTML5 Canvas asset pools mean fast download. The days of introductory eye candy for your projects are over, especially now that we must cater to mobile browsers and cellular networks. If the content they see within that 15-second window is not relevant to the site or the experience, users leave.

- If a bleeding-edge web site isn't viewable on a two-year-old computer with a standard operating system and hardware, it's time to go back to the drawing board.

- For a commercial site, you may have to go back three years. Corporations are relatively slow to upgrade hardware because of the significant cost to do so. Old hardware means slower computers. In fact, many older machines will not be able to run projects written with current HTML5 "standards" at all.

- If your target audience is urban and in a developed country, assume they have, at minimum, a cable or DSL connection.

- If your audience is anywhere else in the world, develop to the lowest common denominator, which is a dial-up modem or remote network.

Now that we have provided some background, let's look at how your project files actually get from here to there.

Project Delivery

As you have discovered by this point in the book, simply tossing a bunch of audio, images, and video into your project is not a good thing when targeting the Web. They take an inordinate amount of time to download. In fact, toss all of that content into frame 1 of an ActionScript 3.0 document project, and you can kiss your 15-second window of opportunity good-bye.

Flash Player has the natural tendency to stream in content incrementally and HTML5 Canvas projects using the native browser will load project assets in an incremental way as well. Please understand that these facts do not make things faster. What this all does is give you the opportunity to intelligently organize the timeline and organize your assets so the project starts playing in very short order. Used wisely, delivery optimization can ensure that everything in the project is downloaded before it is needed. The result is a project that seems to start playing almost immediately and moves "as smooth as the hair on a frog's back." So, what happens when a web page requests your initial JavaScript code, media assets, or SWF file? Two things are sent to the browser:

- The project timeline, including the stuff that is not in the Library, such as code, text, and shapes that haven't been converted to symbols

- The Library, including audio, video, images, and symbols

- If employing a content delivery network (CDN) to include CreateJS JavaScript libraries, externally hosted libraries and assets, Typekit fonts, or Google Web Fonts, these will need to be delivered to the client as well

When your project is employing Flash Player and delivered via SWF file, the actual timeline is received in frame-by-frame order. If the project is split into scenes (a relatively rare practice today), the scenes will be sent in the order they appear in the Scenes panel, which is effectively in sequential order of the main timeline. The Library is also sent, but the Library items are not received in the order they appear in the Library panel. They are received in the sequence in which they appear on the timeline.

Project Profiling

When a developer or interactive designer talks about profiling their project, they will generally mean that they are using some tools to look for performance or bandwidth bottlenecks in order to make adjustments and optimizations. Animate CC has no built-in profiling tools, so if we want to perform any such profiling on our projects, we will need to look elsewhere.

Luckily, if we are targeting the native web using HTML5 Canvas documents within Animate CC, our profiling tools, such as the one shown in Figure 12-3, are only a web browser away.

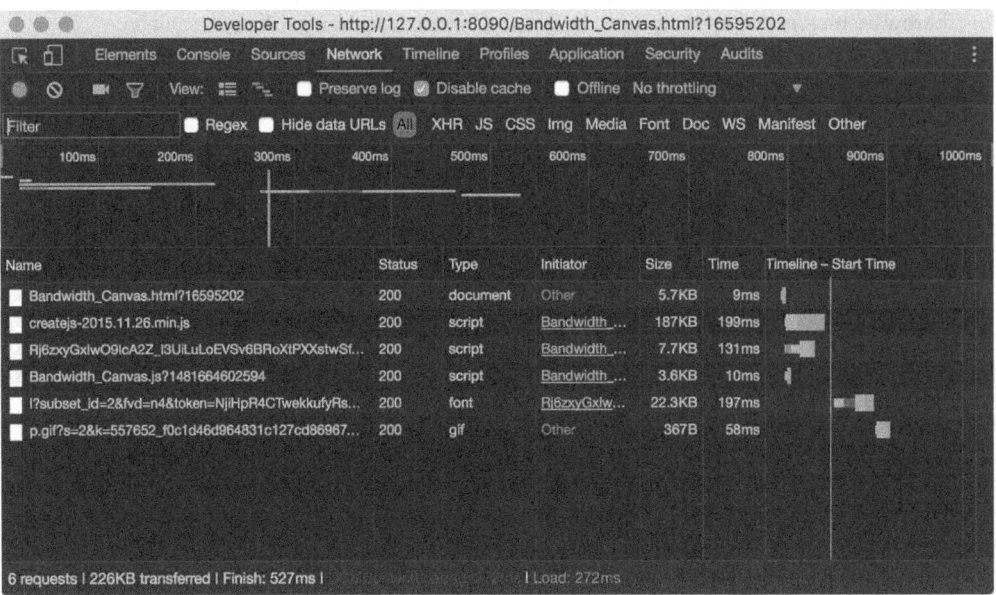

Figure 12-3. The profiling and inspections tools in browsers have come a long way

Google Chrome, Mozilla Firefox, Microsoft Edge, and all modern browsers have a set of developer tools built in that can be accessed by anyone with the inclination or curiosity to do so. Using Chrome, for instance, just right-click on any portion of a web site and choose Inspect from the menu that appears. This action will bring up a robust set of developer tools, including a Network profiler as seen in Figure 12-3. Using this tool in particular, we can monitor the current project to see how long it takes each asset to load and discover whether any might be causing problems. You can use additional tools available here to even more deeply monitor all aspects of a web-based project.

CHAPTER 12 ■ OPTIMIZING AND PUBLISHING ANIMATE CC PROJECTS

Simulating a Download

An additional, highly useful task we can accomplish is to simulate how long a project will take to download and appear to a user running at a specific bandwidth. Let's see how this works. We'll be using an HTML5 Canvas document and Google Chrome:

1. Create a basic HTML5 Canvas document within Animate CC and pull in a few image files you have on your machine. Arrange them on your stage however you want.

2. Perform a test in a web browser by choosing Control ➤ Test from the application menu.

3. If Google Chrome is not your default web browser, open Google Chrome and enter the URL of your project as taken from your default browser address bar.

4. Within Google Chrome, summon the Developer tools by right-clicking on any portion of a web page and choosing Inspect.

5. Developer tools will open. Notice, in the upper left, there is a small icon that looks like the outlines of a couple devices. Choosing this will cause the Device toolbar to appear above your web view.

6. At the upper right of the Device toolbar is a drop-down, which is likely set to No Throttling by default. Clicking this will display a number of options, as shown in Figure 12-4, which you can use to throttle your bandwidth in order to see how your Animate CC project downloads based on that choice.

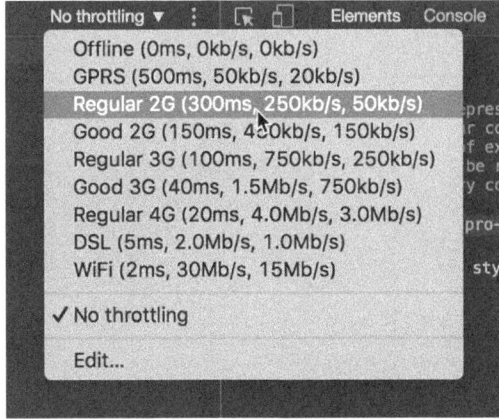

Figure 12-4. Simulating download speeds in Google Chrome

Learning and using the developer tools built into modern browsers will allow robust bandwidth testing and project profiling. We used Google Chrome as an example here since it is so popular among web developers, but you can use the tooling available in any modern browser.

569

CHAPTER 12 ■ OPTIMIZING AND PUBLISHING ANIMATE CC PROJECTS

Those of you who have used older versions of Flash Professional in the past may be asking, "What about the Bandwidth Profiler?" Sorry to be the bearers of bad news, but it's as dead as dead gets. If you want to use the old Bandwidth Profiler for ActionScript 3.0 documents, you can grab a copy of Flash Professional CS6 or use Adobe Scout CC, which allows you to profile both traditional display list and Stage3D assets.

Optimizing Elements in an Animate CC Project

Every chapter in this book has directly or indirectly made it clear that Animate CC loves "small." After your experiences with monitoring bandwidth, we think you now understand why we are so adamant on this point. Small files mean fast loads. A fast load means short wait time. A short wait time means happy users. In various chapters, we have shown you several methods of keeping things small when it comes to images, sounds, fonts, and video. What about vectors?

We know Animate CC and vectors are bosom buddies. The thing about vectors is that they can be both small and large at the same time. Huh? Every time Animate CC encounters a vector point, it must load it into memory in order to draw the shape. If you create a vector with a large number of vector points, you may have a small file on your hands, but you have also increased the demand on memory to redraw the image. The result is the inevitable spike in needed resources. Here's one way of addressing this issue:

1. Create a new Animate CC document. The particular target platform is of no concern.

2. Select the Pencil tool, and in frame 1, draw a curvy shape, like the one in Figure 12-5.

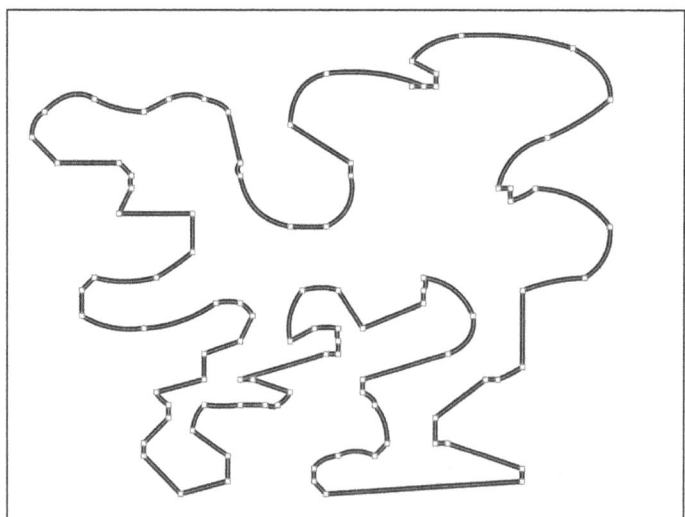

Figure 12-5. We start by drawing a shape containing a lot of vector points

3. Duplicate the current keyframe (Insert ➤ Timeline ➤ Keyframe) three times so that you have four identical keyframes on the timeline.

570

CHAPTER 12 ■ OPTIMIZING AND PUBLISHING ANIMATE CC PROJECTS

4. Select the shape in frame 2 and select Modify ➤ Shape ➤ Advanced Smooth. The Advanced Smooth dialog box, shown in Figure 12-6, opens and not a lot seems to happen. Make sure the Preview check box is selected, set the Smoothing strength to 100, and scrub across the Smooth Angle below hot text. Note the changes to the object when you change the value to one greater than 90 degrees.

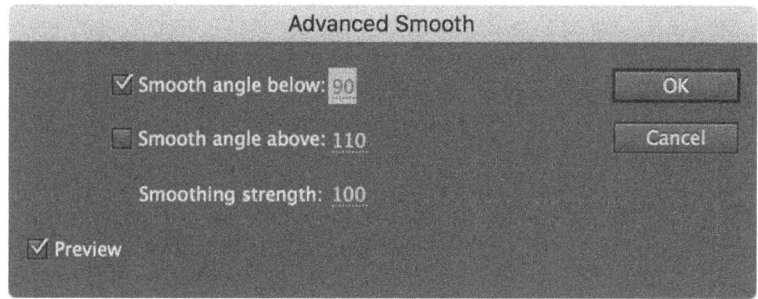

Figure 12-6. *The Advanced Smooth dialog box*

5. Select the shape in frame 3 and select Modify ➤ Shape ➤ Advanced Straighten to open the Advanced Straighten dialog box. Scrub across the Straighten strength hot text, and the curves will start to come to attention as you increase the value.

6. Select the shape in frame 4 and select Modify ➤ Shape ➤ Optimize. This time, you are presented with the Optimize Curves dialog box shown in Figure 12-7.

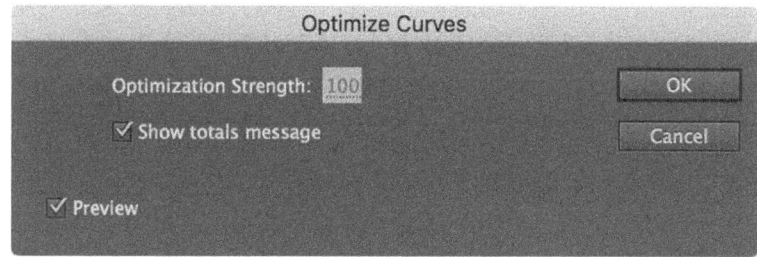

Figure 12-7. *The Optimize Curves dialog box*

7. Select Show Totals Message and Preview. Shift the value all the way to the top and click OK. The dialog box will close and be replaced by an alert box, telling you how many curves were found, how many were optimized, and the size of the reduction as a result of the optimization (see Figure 12-8).

571

CHAPTER 12 ■ OPTIMIZING AND PUBLISHING ANIMATE CC PROJECTS

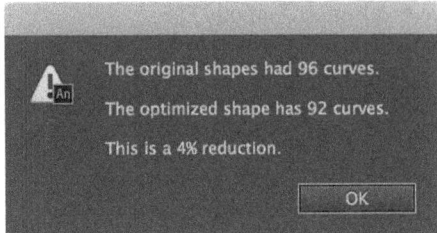

Figure 12-8. Curve optimization results

You are most likely looking at these results and thinking, "Wow, I am going to start optimizing all of my vector shapes!" Not so fast. Each of the three methods presented did a good thing and a bad thing. They did indeed reduce the complexity and thus the bandwidth load. However, they also introduced distortions into the image. If you are happy with the distortions, fine. If you aren't, then you might want to consider doing the optimization manually, by selecting the shape with the Subselection tool and manipulating the shape and the points.

If you import vector artwork from outside sources, such as Illustrator files, you may find shape optimization quite challenging. Obviously, it depends on the intricacy of the artwork, but industrial-strength tools like Illustrator CC naturally have more complex features than the drawing tools provided by Animate CC.

Just be mindful of the pipe. If elaborate vector artwork seems to weigh more than you would expect, consider exporting it from the original application as a bitmap or SVG file and compare file sizes. If you don't have the original application, import the artwork into Animate CC, situate it on the timeline of a temporary stand-in project, and then use File ➤ Export ➤ Export Image to select a suitable format.

Aren't vectors supposed to be smaller? Generally speaking, yes. But every rule has its exception, and it goes both ways. Giulia Balladore, a self-taught artist produces jaw-droppingly beautiful artwork directly in Animate CC. Her vector drawings rival the sort of detail that normally requires a camera and meticulous studio lighting. And yet, because she works in Animate CC and optimizes her vectors, images like "Sole" (see Figure 12-9) can be resized in the browser without ever getting pixelated. And the depicted SWF weighs a minuscule 23KB!

Figure 12-9. Yes, this image was drawn entirely with the Animate CC drawing tools, by Giulia Balladore

CHAPTER 12 ■ OPTIMIZING AND PUBLISHING ANIMATE CC PROJECTS

Publishing and Web Formats

Again, as we have been saying since the first page of this book: keep it small! When you publish your project, Animate CC compresses the file, removes the redundant information in the FLA, and what you are left with—especially if you've been taking this chapter to heart—is one sleek, mean project.

When it comes to Animate CC, the Web is only part of the story. You can also build and compile for Google Android, Apple iOS, AppleTV, and both Windows and macOS desktop computers. In addition, Animate CC can output to any additional target platform if Adobe or a third-party built a platform extension for it. You can find extensions of this sort on the Adobe web site: https://creative.adobe.com/addons.

Before we move into actually publishing a project, let's look at some of the more common file types used on the Web, listed here:

- Flash Player (.swf)
- HTML (.html)
- JavaScript (.js)
- CSS (.css)
- Images (.gif, .jpg, .png, .svg)
- Audio (.mp3, .aac)
- Video (.mp4, .webm)

Flash Player

Before there was Animate CC there was Flash Professional, and before Flash Professional there was Director. Though used primarily for interactive CDs, DVDs, and kiosks, it was at one time the main instrument employed to get animations to play on the Web. The technology developed by Macromedia to accomplish this was named Shockwave, and the file extension used was .dcr. Flash Professional also made use of this technology, and in order to differentiate between them, it became known as Shockwave for Flash and used the .swf file extension. Flash Player is the technology that allows the SWF to play through a user's browser. Through a series of clever moves, and in short time, Flash Player had become ubiquitous on the Web. In fact, Adobe rightfully once claimed that Flash Player, regardless of version, could be found on 98 percent of all Internet-enabled computers on the planet. This means, in theory, that you can assume your movies are readily available to anyone who wants to watch them. But the reality gets a bit more complicated.

For you trivia buffs, the first couple of iterations of Shockwave for Director used a small application named Afterburner to create the DCR files. When Director developers prepared a presentation for the Web, they didn't just create the DCR; the movie was "shocked." One of the authors happened to be around on the night Macromedia quietly released Shockwave and Afterburner to the Director community. He still remembers the excitement generated by members of the group as they posted circles that moved across the page, and he remembers the "oohs" and "ahs" that followed as the circles moved up and down.

Each new Flash Player version brings with it new functionality. Flash Player 24 was the first time spherical video support became available, Flash Player 11 introduced the GPU-accelerated Stage3D APIs, Flash Player 8 showcased filter and blend effects, which can't be displayed in Flash Player 7. FLV video can't be played in Flash Player 5. Any movie you prepare using ActionScript 3.0 can be played only in Flash Player 9 or newer. Flash Player 9 was the first to display HD video content. Though you may initially think the Flash Player version is a nonissue, you would be making a gross miscalculation. Corporations, through their IT departments, have strict policies regarding the addition or installation of software to corporate-owned computers. We personally know of one organization that isn't budging, and its Flash Player policy is Flash Player 6 or lower to this day. Shrewd media designers actually ask potential clients which versions of Flash Player are to be targeted for the project. The last thing you need is to find yourself rewriting every line of code and reworking the project, because you assumed the target was Flash Player 9, but corporate policy dictates Flash Player 7 or older.

Flash Player content is included within a web page through the use of HTML and sometimes JavaScript as well. HTML and Flash Player truly do go hand-in-hand; in fact, HTML5 is the first version of the HTML markup language that makes the tags that allow such a relationship between the two platforms part of the approved spec. Thinking about it that way, Flash Player is HTML5 approved!

HTML

HTML is short for Hypertext Markup Language. Where HTML and ActionScript part company is that HTML (even HTML5!) is a structural markup language, whereas ActionScript is a programming language. This means HTML is composed of a set of specific tags that describe the content within. Interestingly enough, HTML does not tell the browser where content is placed on a web page or what it looks like (that is in the realm of CSS). The HTML instructions, or tags, are both its strength and its weakness. HTML was originally developed to allow the presentation of text and simple graphics. As the Web matured, HTML found itself hard-pressed to stay current with a community that was becoming bored with static content on pages. JavaScript goes a long way to remedy this.

JavaScript

Ah, JavaScript, once upon a time a simple way of client-side form validation. Then it was a way to manipulate the HTML DOM and now it's a no-nonsense creative programming powerhouse. We have HTML5 to thank for this stunning transformation. We also have Flash Player to thank—perhaps even more so. What we mean is that all the great things about Flash Player: rich interactive visuals, video and audio playback, great programming libraries, and more. It's fairly obvious that the new canvas, video, and audio tags present in HTML5 are directly inspired by Flash Player. Of course, with HTML5 Canvas documents in Animate CC, the differences between developing content for one platform or another became increasingly minute.

Cascading Style Sheets (CSS)

While HTML describes the content of a web page, CSS is what dresses that content in the morning and makes sure it is presentable to the world before leaving the house. CSS styles are defined as a set of rules that determine the visual quality of specific HTML elements. Web browsers have their own internal rules for displaying content within an H1 tag versus a P tag and this is why those elements always appear so different when unstyled. It isn't HTML doing that but the browser's internal CSS rules. Of course, when working in CSS you will want to define your own set of rules for H1 and P—that's what is was made for!

Images

What can we say about images on the Web? Whether taking the form of a JPG, PNG, SVG, or animated GIF, the Web experience today would not exist without images. There was a time (back before the early 1990's) when there was no tag for displaying images in browsers—the Web consisted only of text and hyperlinks. It is interesting to note that there was actually a disagreement as to whether images should even be part of the Web experience at all—and an even larger one in terms of how images should be included in a page. In fact, Tim Berners-Lee, regarded as the inventor of the World Wide Web, was initially opposed to the IMG tag!

Audio

Audio file playback on the Web—even in the current year—is a tricky thing. While HTML5 makes AUDIO a true tag in the specification, unified support among browsers is fragmented. Yet, audio playback is an important part of the Web and services like SoundCloud, Amazon Music, Google Music, and Bandcamp would not be here for us to enjoy without it! Many providers get around native audio inconsistencies by serving different file formats at once and even by leveraging the excellent audio support in Flash Player behind the scenes.

Video

At this point in the book, you've likely read the chapter on video. It cannot be understated how important video playback on the Web really is. Everything from streaming services to ads to general web sites use video either directly or indirectly, and the growth of video shows no signs of stopping.

You have the ability to output your Animate CC animations as HD Video—using File ➤ Export ➤ Export Video—and use them in video projects or transcode to a distributable format using Adobe Media Encoder. Animate CC is heavily used as a broadcast animation technology.

Publish Settings for ActionScript 3.0 Documents

We'll start by exploring the publish settings. Create a new ActionScript 3.0 document and select File ➤ Publish Settings from the application menu to open the Publish Settings dialog box, as shown in Figure 12-10.

CHAPTER 12 ■ OPTIMIZING AND PUBLISHING ANIMATE CC PROJECTS

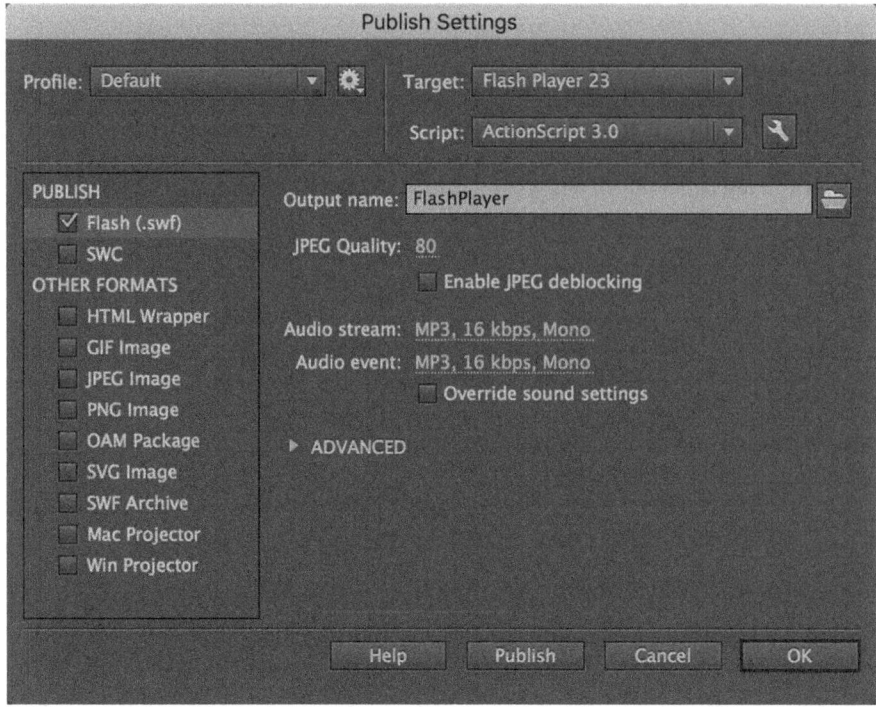

***Figure 12-10.** The Publish Settings dialog box*

You can also launch the Publish Settings dialog box by clicking the Publish Settings button in the Publish section of the Properties panel. The one thing you don't want to do, unless you have a lot of experience with publishing Animate CC projects, is select File ➤ Publish. Selecting this will publish the project using whatever default settings are in place.

Note that at the top of this dialog box is the ability to select, define, and import new publish profiles through the Profile drop-down and associated settings button. A publish profile will preserve the choices made across your Publish Settings so you can easily apply certain profiles depending on the project.

There is also the ability to choose from Target and Script drop-downs.

- **Target:** This menu allows you to choose any version of Flash Player from versions 10.3 to 23 (the currently supported version as of this writing), AIR for Desktop, AIR for iOS, and AIR for Android. If you have the Properties panel open, you will see the version chosen also appears there. It is extremely important for you understand that if you change your Flash Player version and are using features in the movie that aren't supported by the chosen Flash Player version, those features will not work!

- **Script:** There are three versions of the ActionScript language. In the current version of Animate CC, only ActionScript 3.0 is supported, so it makes your choice in this regard quite simple! However, there is a small wrench icon to the right through which you can tackle advanced parameters, which are beyond the scope of this book.

Publish Formats

The file types are as follows:

- **Flash (.swf):** Select this, and you will create a SWF that uses the name in the File area unless you specify otherwise.

- **SWC:** A SWC is a package of assets and ActionScript code that can be referenced and used in other Animate CC projects.

- **HTML Wrapper:** The default publishing setting is that the Flash and HTML settings are both selected. This does not mean your SWF will be converted to an HTML document. It means Animate CC will generate the HTML file that will act as the wrapper for the SWF.

- **GIF Image (.gif):** Select this, and the animation will be output as an animated GIF, or the first frame of the movie will be output as a GIF image.

- **JPEG Image (.jpg):** The first frame of the movie will be output as a JPEG image.

- **PNG Image (.png):** The first frame of the movie will be output as a PNG image. Be careful with this one, because not all browsers can handle a PNG image.

- **OAM Package:** A portable format for including an entire Animate CC document within other applications like Dreamweaver, InDesign, and more.

- **SVG Image:** Scalable Vector Graphics allow native vector rendering on the Web. An interesting note is that SVG (even though it is an older file format) is steadily becoming a popular method of publishing scalable, resolution-independent vector graphics to the Web.

- **SWF Archive:** This option will package each individual layer of an Animate CC project as a SWF for multi-layered use with After Effects or other application where separation of layers as SWF is important.

- **Windows Projector:** Think of this as being a stand-alone, SWF-based application that is best suited to play back from a Windows desktop or CD, not from the browser.

- **Macintosh Projector:** This is the same idea as the Windows projector. Just be aware that a Mac projector won't play on a Windows machine, and vice versa.

Exploring Flash (.swf) Publish Settings

Click the Flash (.swf) option to display the Flash Player settings, as shown in Figure 12-11.

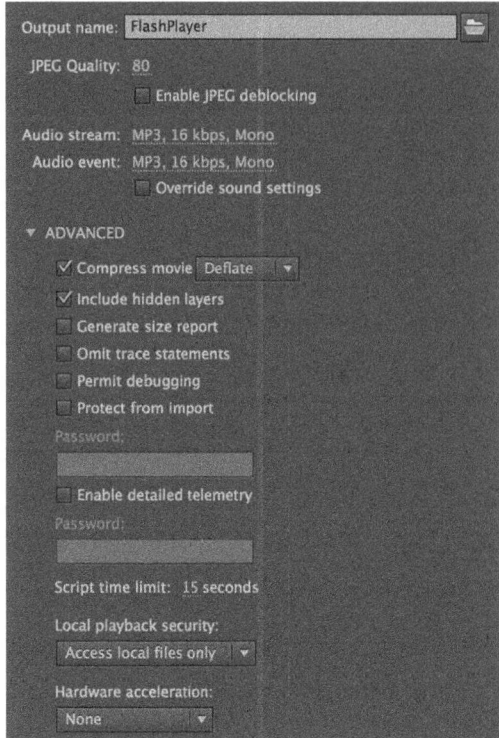

Figure 12-11. *The Flash Player settings in the Publish Settings dialog box*

Let's review each of the areas in this panel:

- **Output Name:** Allows you to specify a name and location for the published project. By default, the project will publish alongside your FLA file and use the same name aside from the file extension of .swf.

- **JPEG Quality:** This value specifies the amount of JPEG compression applied to bitmapped artwork in your movie. The value you set here will be applied to all settings in the Bitmap Properties area of the Library, unless you override it for individual bitmaps on a per-image basis.

- **Audio Stream:** Unless there is a compelling reason to do otherwise, leave this one alone. The value shown is the one applied to the Stream option for audio in the Properties panel. Stream audio is most appropriate for such uses as background music, narration, and longer pieces where synchronization with the animation is most important.

- **Audio Event:** This comes with the same warning as the previous choice but for event sounds. Examples of appropriate event sound usage are brief sounds like clicks or beeps.

- **Override Sound Settings:** Click this, and any settings—Stream or Event—you set in the Sound Properties area of the Library are, for all intents and purposes, completely ignored.

- **Compress Movie:** Even though Animate CC compresses the FLA's assets when it creates the SWF, selecting this allows it to compress the SWF itself—usually text-heavy or ActionScript-heavy—to an even greater extent during the publish process. If you are publishing to Flash Player 5 or older, you can't use this option.

- **Include Hidden Layers:** This option falls squarely in the category of "it's your call." All this means is that any timeline layer whose visibility icon is turned off will not be compiled into the SWF. Designers often like to keep reference layers handy during authoring, but in previous versions of Animate CC, such layers would show in the SWF, even if they were hidden in the FLA. An old trick to "really" hide them was to convert such layers to guide layers—but that can get tedious. If you really want those layers gone, just delete them. If you're a little lazy, use this feature instead. We tend to leave it unselected, but if there is a compelling reason to include your hidden layers, select this option.

- **Generate Size Report:** Select this, and Animate CC will generate a .txt document that shows you where potential bandwidth issues may be located. The .txt file is generated when you publish the SWF.

- **Omit Trace Statements:** Animate CC will ignore any appearances of the trace() function you may have added to your ActionScript (they will actually be removed from the SWF). You use this function to track the value of a variable and display that value in the Output window. Tracing is great for debugging, but a ton of these common statements can affect performance.

- **Permit Debugging:** Select this, and you have access to the Debugger workspace in Animate CC, even if the file is being viewed in a web browser. You really should turn this off before you make the movie public on the Web.

- **Protect from Import:** When this option is selected, the user will be prevented from opening your SWF in Animate CC. A password can be set here.

- **Enable Detailed Telemetry:** Allows the resulting SWF to be profiled within Adobe Scout CC. Most useful for debugging Stage3D. You can also set a password.

- **Script Time Limit:** Sometimes your scripts will get into a loop, sort of like a dog chasing its tail. This can go on for quite a long time before Flash Player sighs and gives up. Enter a value here, and you are telling it exactly when to give up.

- **Local Playback Security:** The two options in this drop-down menu—Access Local Files Only and Access Network Only—permit you to control the SWF's network access. The important one is the network choice. Access networks only protects information on the user's computer from being accidentally uploaded to the network.

- **Hardware Acceleration:** This needs a bit of explanation because if you make the wrong choice, your user is in for a really bad day. We'll provide that explanation immediately below this list.

For the Hardware Acceleration option, you get three choices. These choices are offered thanks to Flash Player 10.1 and newer, and the ability to do a lot more heavy lifting than any previous Flash Player version. By using hardware acceleration, Flash Player will work with the user's video card to render graphics and video more smoothly.

The first choice (None) is self-explanatory. The next one, Level 1 – Direct, tells Flash Player to look for the shortest path through the CPU from the video card to the screen. This mode must be used when employing Stage3D in a project.

The Level 2 – GPU option is a bit more complicated. The best way of wrapping your mind around it is to consider how movieclips are rendered. They are essentially drawn on the screen using software, but they are rendered with your graphics card, or GPU. Scaling is a great example of this, and full-screen HD video rendering is also done this way.

You probably read that last sentence and thought, "Well shucks, I'll do everything this way." Not so fast, bucko. Think of the frame rate for one example. The frame rate will max out to the screen refresh rate. This means if you have a movie with a frame rate of 72 fps, you have exceeded the refresh rate of 60 times per second. In this case, your movie's frame rate will downshift to 60 fps or, more realistically, 50 to 55 fps, thanks to dropped frames.

The bottom line here is that either Hardware Acceleration choice will result in a serious memory hit on the browser, to the point where the browser becomes either sluggish or unresponsive. If you must use this feature, limit yourself to one SWF per HTML page, and use Level 1 – Direct as your first choice. Both choices are tied directly to the video card manufacturers and their drivers.

It's worth noting that if using any form of Adobe AIR, all of the Flash (.swf) settings discussed here still apply. In addition to these are the AIR settings are specific to the platform AIR is targeting (Windows, macOS, Android, iOS, etc.) and can be accessed through File ➤ AIR Settings on the application menu.

Publish Settings for HTML5 Canvas Documents

You can access Publish Settings for HTML5 Canvas the same way as you did with ActionScript 3.0 documents. Create a new HTML5 Canvas document and select File ➤ Publish Settings from the application menu to open the Publish Settings dialog box, as shown in Figure 12-12.

CHAPTER 12 ■ OPTIMIZING AND PUBLISHING ANIMATE CC PROJECTS

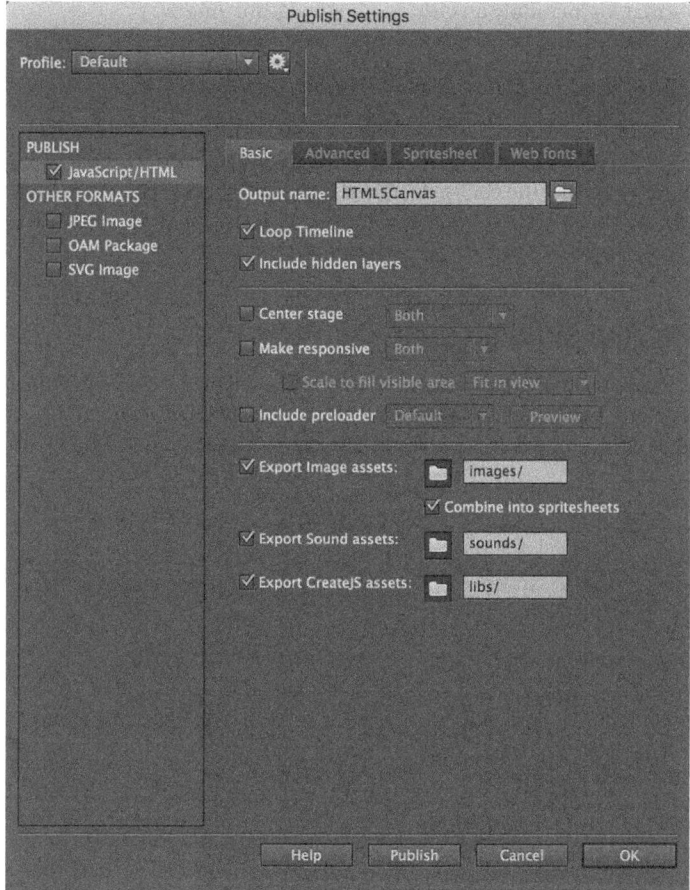

***Figure 12-12.** The HTML5 Canvas Publish Settings dialog box*

You can also launch the Publish Settings dialog box from the Properties panel. The one thing you don't want to do, unless you have a lot of experience with publishing Animate CC projects, is select File ➤ Publish. Selecting this will publish the project using whatever default settings are already in place.

Note that at the top of this dialog box is the ability to select and define new publish profiles through the Profile drop-down and associated settings button. A publish profile preserves the choices made across your Publish Settings so you can easily apply certain profiles depending on the project.

Publish Formats

The file types are as follows:

- **JavaScript/HTML:** This is the main choice which determines all of the settings for your HTML5 Canvas project in regard to the handling of the project timeline, responsive attributes, folder structure, the handling of JavaScript files and libraries, and much more. We will examine this in detail in the next section.

- **JPEG Image (.jpg):** The first frame of the movie will be output as a JPEG image.

581

CHAPTER 12 ■ OPTIMIZING AND PUBLISHING ANIMATE CC PROJECTS

- **OAM Package:** A portable format for including an entire Animate CC document within other applications like Dreamweaver, InDesign, Adobe Muse, and more.
- **SVG Image:** Scalable Vector Graphics allow native vector rendering on the Web.

You will notice that there are not nearly the same number of publish formats within HTML5 Canvas documents as are present with ActionScript 3.0 documents. This is because HTML5 Canvas documents are focused on designing content for the native web using the canvas DOM element and JavaScript. ActionScript 3.0 documents have a much wider target and so they obviously require more options: SWC, SWF, AIR, EXE, APP, iOS, Android, and the list goes on.

Exploring JavaScript/HTML Publish Settings

Let's explore these settings. If it's not yet selected, click the JavaScript/HTML option to begin. You will notice that the Publish Settings dialog box for HTML5/Canvas is now separated into a series of tabs along the top with this option selected. We'll explore the options present within these tabs, beginning with Basic (see Figure 12-13).

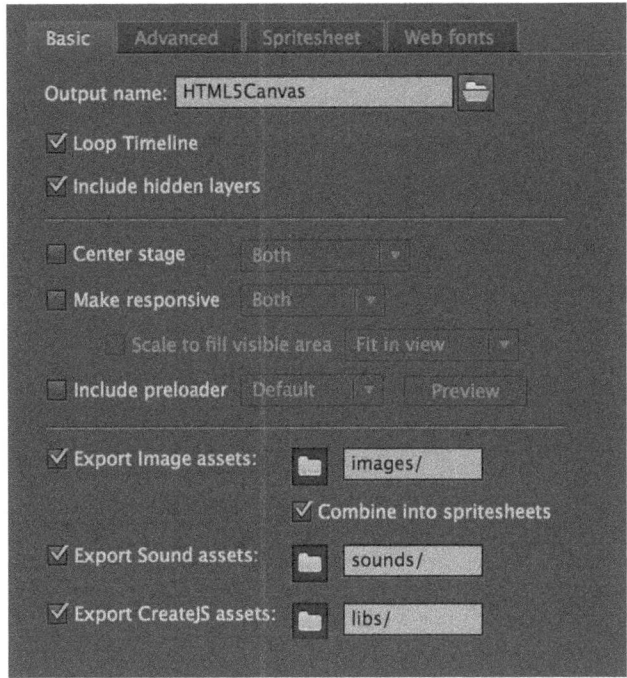

Figure 12-13. The Basic options for HTML5 Canvas Publish Settings

582

The Basic tab includes some of the more general publish options you may want to set for your project:

- **Output Name:** Allows you to specify a name and location for the published project. By default, the project will publish alongside your FLA file and use the same name excluding the extensions of the resulting files.
- **Loop Timeline:** Disabling this option will stop the playhead on the last frame of the project timeline.
- **Include Hidden Layers:** Works exactly the same way as the same option when publishing an ActionScript 3.0 document. Any timeline layer whose visibility icon is turned off will not be compiled into the published project.
- **Center Stage:** With this option enable, the stage will be centered within the browser viewport—Vertically, Horizontally, or Both —depending on the drop-down selection.
- **Make Responsive:** Enabling this option will shrink your project stage by Width, Height, or Both if the browser viewport is smaller than the stage. You can also select the Scale to Fill Visible Area option to have the stage increase in size to fill a larger viewport.
- **Include Preloader:** This option allows you to include a preloader in your project as the browser starts up your project. You can use the default preloader or browse to an animate GIF file to use as a preloader for your project.
- **Export Image Assets:** The subfolder within which to include published bitmap images.
- **Export Sound Assets:** The subfolder within which to include any audio files.
- **Export CreateJS Assets:** The subfolder within which to include CreateJS JavaScript library source files.

The next tab is the Advanced tab, shown in Figure 12-14.

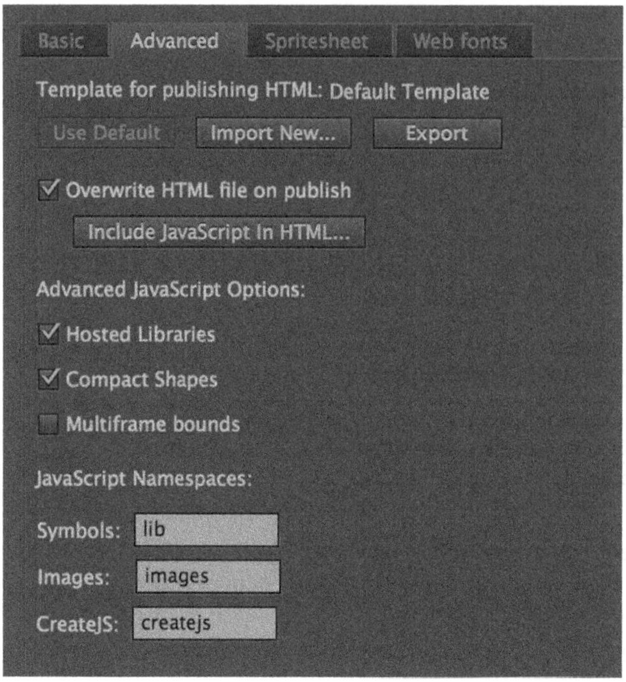

CHAPTER 12 ■ OPTIMIZING AND PUBLISHING ANIMATE CC PROJECTS

Figure 12-14. The Advanced options for HTML5 Canvas Publish Settings

Options within the Advanced tab are more obscure than those found within the Basic tab. The first set of choices to examine involve the concept of templates. When publishing to HTML5 Canvas from Animate CC, the resulting HTML file is hugely important in terms of the project's ultimate destination. Templates allow you to tweak the HTML file that is published by Animate CC in order to include custom JavaScript libraries, and to make general tweaks to how the HTML is constructed.

The options for dealing with templates are as follows:

- **Template for Publishing:** This text changes depending on whether you have the default template selected or have chosen a custom template of your own.

- **Use Default:** If you previously imported an edited template using the Import New option, this button will reset the template being used to the default template.

- **Import New:** If you have already exported and edited the default template using the Export option, clicking this will allow you to locate the edited HTML file to use it within your project. The selected template will then be clearly indicated within the dialog box in the text "Template for publishing HTML:" above.

- **Export:** The first thing to do if you want to create a template of your own is to export the default template in order to modify it to your liking. To do so, click the Export button and save the HTML file on your machine for editing. You will be prompted by Animate CC to give this file a name and location on your hard drive. With the default template exported, you will now be able to open it in Adobe Dreamweaver CC, Brackets, or any text editor of your choosing to customize the HTML, JavaScript, and CSS contained within.

HTML5 Canvas templates can be automatically applied to your content prior to publication by assigning a specific template to a publish profile, and then switching to whichever profile you want to use. This action will employ the specific template applied within that profile to the document being published.

One thing to note before we move on is the availability of special tokens with the HTML template that can be used when customizing. For instance, tokens such as $BG, $WT, and $HT can be used in conjunction with custom logic and elements to adjust for sizing and background colors in your template.

Here is a short list detailing some of these common tokens and what they represent:

- $CANVAS_ID: The ID of the Canvas element in your HTML document.
- $TITLE: The title of your project document.
- $BG: The background color of the stage defined within the FLA.
- $WT: The width of the stage defined within the FLA.
- $HT: The height of the stage defined within the FLA.

These tokens are available for use in any template and will be replaced by their appropriate values upon publication. Other tokens exist as well and can be explored within the exported HTML template file.

For a full list of Animate CC HTML5 Canvas publish tokens, look at the table Adobe provides at https://helpx.adobe.com/animate/using/html-publishing-templates.html#html_template_variables.

That's a lot of information for one small area in the Advanced tab, but it is very powerful in the grand scheme of things. Okay—on to the rest!

Additional advanced settings include:

- **Overwrite HTML File on Publish:** Having this option selected will instruct Animate CC to generate the HTML file anew upon each Publish command. Uncheck this to preserve the originally generated HTML file, in case you have made tweaks to it and do not want your changes overwritten.

- **Include JavaScript in HTML:** If this button is pressed, all project-generated JavaScript will be included in the generated HTML file and not as a separate JavaScript file. Choosing this will force the Overwrite HTML file on publish option.

- **Hosted Libraries:** Instructs Animate CC to use CreateJS libraries hosted on a Content Delivery Network (CDN) as opposed to locally generated files.

- **Compact Shapes:** Allows vector assets to be output in a more compact form.

- **Multiframe Bounds:** Instructs Animate CC to include a frameBounds property for each symbol containing data specifying the bounds, including width and height, for each frame. Selecting this option may greatly increase publish time since it must generate a lot of additional data.

- **JavaScript Namespaces:** When using multiple JavaScript libraries within a project, unique namespaces will protect libraries that may have similarly named objects from interfering with one another.

The next tab along the Publish options is Spritesheet, as shown in Figure 12-15.

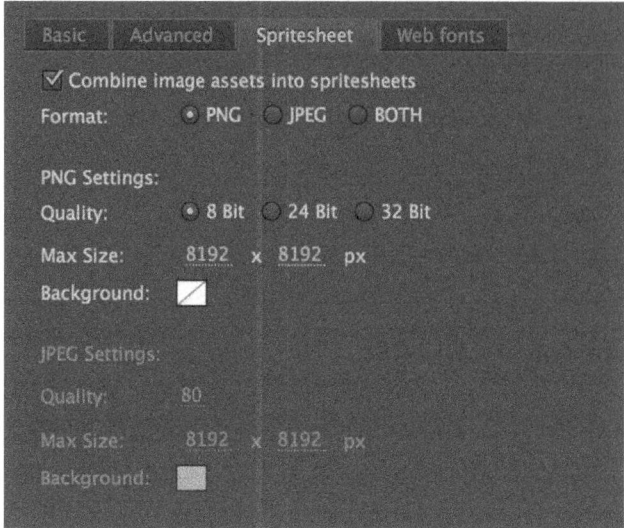

Figure 12-15. The Spritesheet options for HTML5 Canvas Publish Settings

The Spritesheet tab includes options that determine whether to compile all images into spritesheets and the parameters around this.

A *spritesheet* is a single image file that contains multiple source image files as a single "sheet" of images with specific coordinates. The idea behind it is that the browser only needs to make a single call over the server for one image as opposed to multiple calls for many images. In addition to the generated image file, there is also data that gets created by specifying coordinates and sizes of the embedded source images as they exist as layed out within the spritesheet. They allow the HTML5 Canvas project to only display the portions of the spritesheet as necessary per source image at any given time.

- **Combine Image Assets into Spritesheets:** Enabling this will instruct Animate CC to combine all bitmap images used in your project into a single image file known as a spritesheet. Deselecting this option will simply publish all bitmap images as individual files.

- **Format:** You can select to have all bitmaps compiled to a single spritesheet as a PNG, a JPEG, or Both. Note that PNG files can include a transparent background and are regularly preferred for spritesheets over JPEG.

- **PNG Settings:** If a format of PNG or Both has been chosen, this allows you to specify quality, size, and background options for the PNG version of a spritesheet.

- **JPEG Settings:** If a format of JPEG or Both has been chosen, this allows you to specify quality, size, and background options for the JPEG version of a spritesheet.

CHAPTER 12 ■ OPTIMIZING AND PUBLISHING ANIMATE CC PROJECTS

The final tab, shown in Figure 12-16, has to do with web fonts.

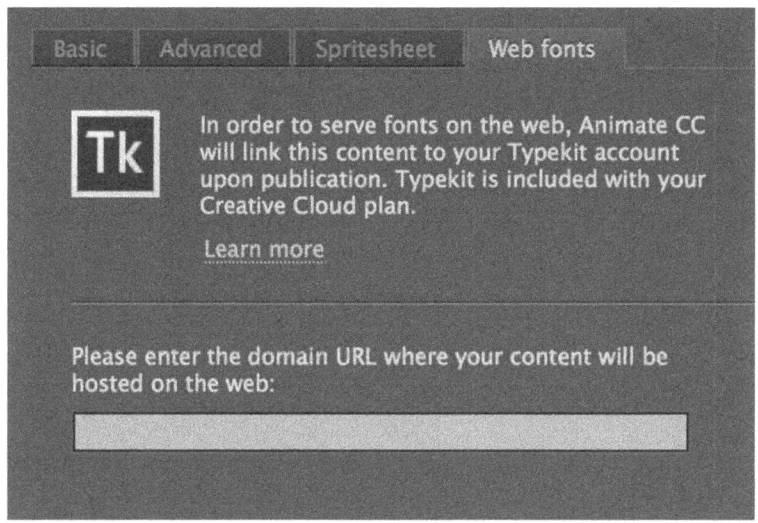

Figure 12-16. *The Web Fonts options for HTML5 Canvas Publish Settings*

The Web Fonts tab includes a single text input for the domain where your published Animate CC project will be hosted. This is only necessary if you're using dynamic text fields in your project that employ Typekit fonts. Google Web Font usage does not require this.

So, that's all there is for HTML5 Canvas Publish Settings!

You may be wondering why we don't have a section on Animate CC WebGL documents in this chapter. As of this writing, WebGL is a format that Adobe still declares as in "preview"—meaning that it is a bit experimental and things will likely change. Additionally, there are not a lot of options in WebGL Publish Settings to explain, and the few options that do exist mirror those we've already discussed for other publish targets.

What You Have Learned

There wasn't a lot of geeky or cool stuff in this chapter. Instead, the focus on this chapter was how to optimize and publish your Animate CC projects. We examined how the data in your project gets from "here to there" and in what order. We reviewed several ways of monitoring bandwidth, from identifying content bottlenecks to actually emulating the download of a bloated web based project. It wasn't pleasant, but we then showed you a number of ways to fine-tune your documents in order to let you maximize that "15-second window of opportunity" you get when a user hits your site. The chapter wrapped up with a lengthy discussion about the publishing process. Along the way, you learned the following:

- How projects are delivered to a web page
- Ways of monitoring bandwidth and performance

CHAPTER 12 ■ OPTIMIZING AND PUBLISHING ANIMATE CC PROJECTS

- How to control publish settings for Flash Player
- How to control publish settings for HTML5 Canvas

This chapter dealt with the "end game" in Animate CC. We think you are now aware that preparing your files for web output involves a lot more than simply selecting Publish in the File menu. There is a lot to consider, and those considerations range from what format will be used to output the file to a number of very important options that need to be addressed.

Speaking of the end game, we are at the end of this beginner's journey with Adobe Animate CC. We hope you had fun and that you are inspired to explore Animate CC even further. As you do, you will discover a fundamental truth about this application: the amount of fun you can have with it should be illegal. We'll see you in jail.

Index

A

ActionScript, 129, 229, 236
    Adobe Flash platform, 233
        MovieClip class, 234
        panel menu, 233
        search tactics, 234
    document class, 229
    keyboard control using, 378–380
    scrolling text using, 310–311
    syntax checking, 230
    text with, 303–307
ActionScript 3.0
    documents
        FLV Playback 2.5 component, 489, 491–492
        playing video, 492–494
        WebVTT, 504–508, 510
    publish settings, 575–576
        exploring Flash (.swf), 577–580
        publish formats, 577
    UI components
        code snippets, 527–528
        eLearning, 520
        Flash Player/AIR, 520
        HTML development, 519
        skinning UI components, 521–523
        styling, 523, 525–526
        user interface (UI), 519
        video components, 521
ActionScript tab, Flash Font Embedding dialog box, 296
Actions layers, Flash, 383
Actions panel, 182, 383
    context menu, 184
    edit and view menu items, 185
    script navigator, 183
    script pane, 183
Add Classic Motion Guide context menu item, Flash, 364
addController() method, ActionScript, 299
Add Shape Hint menu item, Flash, 327

Adobe CoolType, 284–285
    rescue, 285
    typefaces and fonts, 286
    Typekit, 286–289
Adobe Flash CS4, 421
Adobe Flash Player, 477
Adobe sound document (ASND), 250
Adobe Typekit, 286–289
Advanced audio coding/codec (AAC), 250, 478
Alpha property, Flash Color panel, 331
Always Show Markers option, Flash
    Timeline panel, 351
Anchor point, 81
Angular setting, Flash Properties panel, 321
Animate CC, 123–124
    ActionScript 3.0 documents, 96
    bitmap images, 99–100
    CC library, 119
    color palettes, 90–91, 94–95
    color picker, 90–91
    custom colors, 91, 93–94
    file importer, 115
    gradient effects, 96
    hexadecimal model, 89
    HSB model, 89
    interface. see Interface, Animate CC
    layers and paths, 116
    Looney Tunes, 97
    movie
        adding, color, 39–40
        Color Picker, 37
        Lake Nanagook, 50–51
        lighting up Lake Nanagook, 55
        MoonOverLakeNanagook.fla file, 37
        moonrise, creation, 53–54
        movie test, 52–53
        specifications, 37
        step, moon creation, 45–49
        transform panel, 44
        trees, 40–42
        twinkling star, creation, 43

movie (*cont.*)
  photoshop documents, 112–114
  PolyStar tool, 98
  reflect overflow, 96
  RGB model, 89
  sketch 3 documents, 120–121
Animate CC projects
  ActionScript 3.0, publish settings, 575–576
    exploring Flash (.swf), 577–580
    publish formats, 577
  Flash Player and Internet, 563
    bandwidth, 565–567
    "Internet" Thing, 564
    World Wide Web, 565
  HTML5 Canvas document, publish settings, 580
    exploring JavaScript/HTML, 582–587
    publish formats, 581–582
  project delivery, 567–568
  project profiling, 568
    optimizing elements, 570–572
    simulating a download, 569
  publishing and Web formats, 573
    audio, 575
    CSS, 574
    Flash Player, 573–574
    HTML, 574
    images, 575
    JavaScript, 574
    video, 575
Animation, 313–314
  classic tweening, 332
    easing, 338–340
    easing, custom, 341–343, 345–347, 349
    properties, 334–335
    rotation, 332–334
    scaling, stretching, and deforming, 335, 337–338
  combining timelines, 355
    graphic symbols as mini-libraries, 360–361
    movieclips *vs.* graphic symbols, 355–356
    nesting symbols, 357–359
  elements, 314
  filter effects, tweening, 366–368
  inverse kinematics (IK), 449
  modifying multiple frames, 353
    swapping graphic symbols, 353–355
  Motion Editor, 392–393, 400, 408
  motion guides, 361–364
  motion paths, 412, 415–417
  motion presets, 417, 420
  onion skinning, 350–352
  programmatic, 368–369
    copying motion as data, 369–372
    keyboard to control motion, 372, 374–380
    random motion, 381–388

property keyframes, 408, 411–412
shape tweening, 315
  altering gradients, 330–331
  altering shapes, 322–325
  modifying, 320, 322
  scaling and stretching, 315, 317–320
  shape hints, 326–330
Timeline panel, 349–350
tweening mask, 364
  animating mask, 364–365
  motion guides, 366
Antenna1 layer, Flash, 324
Anti-alias drop-down menu, Flash, 293–294
Anti-aliasing, 285
Anti-alias option, Flash, 293
Anti-alias pop-down menu, Flash, 292
AS3-WebVTT, 504, 506
Audio files, 249
  AAC, 250
  adjust volume and pan, 262
  AIFF, 250
  ASND, 250
  ButtonSound.fla file, 267
  event and stream, 257
  FLAC, 251
  import, 253
  Javascript
    adjust volume, 273
    Lake Superior, 275
    remote sound, 272
    sound file from outside, 271
    sound from library, 268
    using button, 270
  loop, 261
  MP3 files, 250, 253
  OGA, 251
  OGG, 251
  peaks, 251
  remove timeline, 260
  sample rate, 252
  SD2, 250
  sound properties, 254
  Split Audio context menu, 265
  Sun AU, 250
  WAV, 250
Audio Interchange File Format (AIFF), 250
Auto Set Transformation Point setting, Flash Preferences dialog box, 440

B

Bandwidth, 565–567
Banner.psd image, 113
Bitmap images, 58
  Adobe application, 100–101
  optimization, 101

Blank keyframe menu item, Flash, 315
Blend pop down menu, Flash
    Properties panel, 321
Blends, 152, 154–155, 157
Body layer, Flash, 363
Bone tool
    constraining joint rotation, 431
    properties, 425, 428
Bringhurst, Robert, 281
Brownian Bonus round, 388
Brown, Robert, 381
Butterfly asset, Flash, 363
Butterfly layer, Flash, 362
Butterfly symbol, Flash, 362
Button component, 521
Button symbols, 128–129

C

Camera tool
    camera layer, 473
    camera movement, 473
    movement, 474–476
    timeline and camera controls
        appear, 472
    usage, 473–474
Carter, Matthew, 293
Cascading Style Sheets (CSS), 574
Catalina Island
    bonus round, 179
    clouds, 175–176
    clouds in motion, 177–178
    fog bank, 173–175
Center Frame button, Flash
    Timeline panel, 350–351
changePicture(), 543
changeTrack(), 555
Character range field, Flash Font
    Embedding dialog box, 295
Cinemagraphs, 513–515
Classic tweening,
    animation, 313, 332
    easing, 338–340
    easing, custom, 341–343
        adding anchor points, 345–347
        multiple properties, 347, 349
    properties, 334–335
    rotation, 332–334
    scaling, stretching, and
        deforming, 335, 337–338
Clear keyframe menu item, Flash, 315
Cloud Libraries, 142, 144
Code Editor preferences, 187
    edit options, 188
    format code, 189
Code snippets panel, 189

Coding fundamentals, 206
    capitalization matters, 206
    comments, 207
    conditional statements, 219
    data types, 213
    dot notation, 209
    keywords, 207
    operators, 216
    scope, 211
    semicolons, 207
    syntax, 206
    variables, 212
Color anti-aliasing, 285
Color chip, Flash filter, 367
Color effect drop-down menu,
    Flash, 368
Color panel, Flash, 331
Color Picker, Flash, 367
Complete folder, 340
Configuration class, ActionScript, 299
Constrain option, Flash Properties
    panel, 430
Constraint check box, Flash Properties
    panel, 338, 429
Content delivery network (CDN), 567, 585
Content management, 157–159
    align panel, 165–166
    grid snapping, 159–160
    guides alignment, 160
    masks. *see* Masks
    objects alignment, 159
    snapping in guide layer, 161
    stacking order, 162, 164
Context menu, Flash, 317
CoolType. *See* Adobe CoolType
Copy Motion as ActionScript 3.0 option,
    Keith, 369
Create Classic Tween context menu item,
    Flash, 319, 332
Create Motion Tween context menu item,
    Flash, 319
Create Shape Tween context menu item,
    Flash, 318
Cross-Origin Resource Sharing (CORS), 503
Current Frame indicator, Flash Timeline
    panel, 350
Custom Ease In/Ease Out dialog
    box, 341, 345, 348, 400

D

Devices fonts, 291–292
Distort option, Flash, 317, 335
Distributive setting, Flash
    Properties panel, 321
Document Properties panel, 7

INDEX

Dot layer, Flash, 365, 366
Drawers, 6
Drop shadow filter, 147, 149
3D rotation tool
    four axes of rotation, 459-460
    free transform tool, 459
    transform panel, 461
    wedge and ghost, visual clue, 460
3D translation tool
    3D center point, advantage, 465-468
    depth limitations, 468-471
    usage, 464-465
    vanishing point setting, 461-462, 464

E

Ease hot text, Flash Properties panel, 320-321, 339
Ease option, Flash Properties panel, 320
Ease property, Flash, 334, 342, 348
Easing, 19, 315, 338-340
    custom, 341-343
        adding anchor points, 345-347
        multiple properties, 347-349
    easing in, 320
    easing out, 320
ECMA, 182
Edit button, Flash Properties panel, 341-342, 344-345, 348
Editing symbols, 131
Edit Multiple Frames button, Flash Timeline panel, 350, 353
Edit property, Flash Properties panel, 334
Elapsed Time indicator, Flash Timeline panel, 350, 351
Embed button, Flash Font Embedding dialog box, 294
Embedding fonts, 293-296
End user license agreement (EULA), 296
Envelope option, Flash, 317, 335
Estimated glyphs total, Flash Font Embedding dialog box, 295
Extensible Markup Language (XML)
    assembling, 536-538
    Behance and Facebook, 534
    CSS component, 540-542
    data communication, 536
    image files, 535
    Instagram and Flickr, 534
    JavaScript code, 546-547
    slideshow functions, 542-545
    UI components, 538
    visual component layout, 538-540

F

Filters
    additional perspective, 149-150
    application, 147
    drop shadow, 147, 149
    effects, tweening, 366-368
    facts, 151
    properties, Flash Properties panel, 348
First field, Flash Properties panel, 355, 356, 361
First input field, Flash Properties panel, 356
Flash CS4, 457
Flash Player, 563
    bandwidth, 565-567
    "Internet" Thing, 564
    publishing and Web formats, 573-574
    World Wide Web, 565
Flash (.swf), 577
fl.controls package, 524
Flutter by layer, 361
Font Embedding dialog box, Flash, 294-296
Fonts and typefaces, 282-284
    Adobe CoolType, 286
    smoothing, 285
Frame input field, Flash, 417
Frame menu item, Flash, 363
Frame option, Flash Properties panel, 417
Frame Rate indicator, Flash Timeline panel, 350
Frames, 4, 15-18
    Olive Seller, 135, 137
    rate, 14
Free lossless audio codec (FLAC), 251
Free Transform tool, Flash, 316-317, 320, 322, 332, 335-339, 345, 363-364, 392, 415
Frutiger, Adrian, 293

G

Georgenes, Chris, 357, 361
Ghost handle movie clip, Flash, 431
GIF Image (.gif), 109, 111, 577
Glow filter, Flash, 367
Glyph, 295
Google Fonts, 290-291
Gradient Transform tool, Flash, 330-331
Graphics
    drawing
        brush tool, 77-79
        dropping, pin, 85-88
        eraser tool, 80
        paint brush tool, 75-77
        pencil tool, 71, 73-74
        pen tool, 81-84

free transform tool, 63-65
gradient transform tool, 66-69
object drawing mode, 69, 71
selection and subselection tools, 60-63
tools panel, 58-59
types, 58
vector drawing and animation tool, 58
vector images, 58
Graphics interchange format (GIF), 516-517
Graphic symbols, 127-128
Grotto movie clip icon, Flash Timeline panel, 359
Grotto symbol, Flash, 359
Grotto timeline, Flash, 359
Guide context menu item, Flash, 361, 364
Guide mask layer, Flash, 366

H

Handles, 81
Hardware acceleration, 579
Head3 graphic symbol, Flash, 355
Head4 graphic symbol, Flash, 354-355
Hexadecimal model, 89
HSB model, 89
HTML
    JavaScript, 585
    publishing and Web formats, 574
    Wrapper, 577
HTML5 Canvas, 223, 286
    custom template, 228
    document, 494-499, 501-503
        exploring JavaScript/HTML, 582-587
        publish formats, 581-582
        publish settings, 580
    edit template, 227
    export templates, 227
    publish profiles, 228
    scrollable text in, 307
        rolling own scroller, 307-309
        using ActionScript, 310-311
    UI components
        code snippets, 533-534
        eLearning and interactive web space, 529
        panel, 529
        parameters, 530
        styling, 530-531, 533
    video controls, 510-513
HTML5style.css, 532

I

IFlowComposer() class, ActionScript, 299
IKMover class, 437

Interface, Animate CC
    components, 4
    create new, 3
    creative cloud library, 28
    docked and floating, 4
    document
        creation, 3-4
        preferences, 8-9
        settings, 9-10
    frames, 4, 15-18
    library panel, 27
    managing, workspace, 5-7
    motion editor, 19-20
    open recent item, 3
    playhead, 4
    properties panel, 21-22, 24
    scrubbing, 4
    start page, 2
    timeline, 4, 13-14
    tools panel, 25-26
    zooming, 10, 12
Internet Protocol (IP), 564
Inverse kinematics (IK)
    Bone tool, 425, 428, 431
    Spring option for bones animating IK poses, 442
    Bind tool, 444

J

Jaggies, 285
JavaScript, 129, 236
    code snippet, 242, 245
    documentation, 224-225
    in HTML, 585
    library. see HTML5 Canvas
    loop timeline, 240
    movieclips, 241
    pause timeline, 237
    publishing and Web formats, 574
    random motion using, 384-388
    text with, 300-303
    troubleshooting, 225
JavaScript Object Notation (JSON), 549
    assembling, 550
    audio and art files, 548-549
    completed JavaScript code, 557
    CSS component usage, 552-553
    custom HTML5 components, 558
    custom interface controls, 559-560
    customization options, 558
    data structures, 549
    JavaScript Object Notation, 549
    jQuery JavaScript Library, 547
    MP3 files and image files, 547

JavaScript Object Notation (JSON), 549 (*cont.*)
    sound playback functions, 554–556
    UI components, 551
    visual component layout, 551–552
JPEG image (.jpg), 108, 577, 581
    Bitmap Properties dialog box, 107
jQuery Code Library, 533

K

Keyframe menu item, Flash, 315, 339
Keyframes, 17

L

LabelButton.icon, 524
Layers
    adding content, 32
    creation, 30–31
    grouping layers, 35
    properties, 29–30
    showing/hiding and locking layers, 34–35
    timeline, 28
LeftWing layer, Flash, 363
Library panel, Flash, 27, 295–296, 307, 319
Light boxes, 350
Linkage area, Flash Font Embedding
    dialog box, 296
Liquid crystal display (LCD), 285
LogoMorph.fla file, 330
Loop drop-down option, Flash, 417
Looping area, Flash Properties panel, 355, 417
Looping option, Flash Properties panel, 360, 417
Looping parameter, Flash Properties
    panel, 360
Looping properties, Flash, 356

M

Macintosh Projector, 577
MalletNormalEase.fla file, 340
Mask context menu item, Flash, 365–366
Masks
    animation creation, 169–171, 173
    layer, 29, 365
    simple mask, 167–169
    tweening, 364
        animating mask, 364–365
        motion guides, 366
MaskTweenk.fla file, 366
Math.round() method, ActionScript, 383
MinimalFlatCustomColorAll.swf, 488
Modify Onion Markers button, Flash
    Timeline panel, 350, 351
MoonOverLakeNanagook.fla file, 37

More Font Info button, Flash Font
    Embedding dialog box, 296
Motion Editor, 408, 410–412
    easing with graphs, 400, 408
        applying multiple eases, 407–408
        built-in eases, 400
        custom eases, 406
    moving, 393, 400
    scaling, 393, 400
Motion guides, 361–364, 412
    with masks, 366
Motion paths, 413
    advanced, 415
    manipulating, 412
    properties, 416–417
Motion Presets panel, Flash, 418, 420
Motion tweens, 393
Mouth layer, Flash, 360
Mouth shape, Flash, 360
Mouth symbol, Flash, 359–360
MoveAmount variable, ActionScript, 383
Movieclips symbol, 129–130
Moving Pictures Expert Group Level-2
    Layer-3 Audio (MP3), 250
musicplayer.css., 553

N

Nesting, 129

O

Ogg video, 479
Onion Skin button, Flash Timeline
    panel, 350, 352
Onion skinning, 340, 350–352
Onion Skin Outlines button, Flash Timeline
    panel, 350, 352
Opera, 478
Optimization, 101
Options area, Flash Font Embedding
    dialog box, 295
Options drop-down menu, Flash Properties
    panel, 355
Orient to path check box, Flash Properties
    panel, 335, 363

P, Q

Packages, 526
Panel collapse, 5
Panel set, 6
Particle Movie Clip symbol, Flash, 383
Penelope's jump, 453
Pen tool, Flash, 366

Playhead, 4
Play Once drop-down option, Flash, 417
Play Once setting, Flash Timeline panel, 356
PNG Image (.png), 577
Position properties, Flash Properties panel, 348
Preferences dialog box, 7
Preview play button, Flash, 347, 349
Programmatic animation, 368–369
    copying motion as data, 369–372
    keyboard to control motion, 372, 374
        movement constraints, 375–378
        using ActionScript, 378–380
    random motion, 381
        using JavaScript, 384–388
        using templates, 381–383
Programming concepts, 191
    Animate interface, 191
    class, 192
    events, 202
    methods, 199
    properties, 193
        instance names, 194
        with code, 198
Project delivery, 567–568
Project profiling, 568
    optimizing elements, 570–572
    simulating a download, 569
Properties panel, Flash, 291, 293, 320, 333, 334, 339, 341–342, 345, 348, 353, 355–356, 359–363, 400, 416–417, 425, 430
Property drop-down menu, Flash Properties panel, 348
Property Inspector, 37
Property keyframes
    changing duration nonproportionally, 412
    changing duration proportionally, 411
    definition, 408

R

Rabbit symbol, Flash, 356
Random motion, 381
    using JavaScript, 384–388
    using templates, 381–383
Random Movement Brownian template, Flash New Document dialog box, 381
Readability, Flash Anti-alias option, 293, 294
Registration point, 38
Remove Transform button, Flash Transform panel, 334, 337
Remove Tween context menu item, Flash, 319, 320
RGB model, 89
RightWing layer, Flash, 363
River.jpg file, 102
Rotate and Skew option, Flash Tools panel, 336
Rotate area, Flash Transform panel, 339
Rotate drop-down menu, Flash Properties panel, 333
Rotation area, Flash Transform panel, 339
Rotation property, Flash bones, 348, 428
Rotation setting, Flash, 335

S

Scalable Vector Graphics (SVG) image, 577, 582
Scale check box, Flash Properties panel, 335
Scale properties, Flash Properties panel, 348
Scrubbing, 4
Selection tool, Flash, 316, 443
Shape hints, 325–326, 328–330
Shape tweening, animation, 315
    altering gradients, 330–331
    altering shapes, 322–323
        anchor points, 324
        changing shape, 324–325
    modifying, 320, 322
    scaling and stretching, 315, 317–320
    shape hints, 326–330
Shape Tween menu item, Flash, 320
Show Shape Hints menu item, Flash, 330
SimpleButton class, 524
Single Frame drop-down options, Flash, 417
Single Frame setting, Flash Timeline panel, 356, 417
Skewing, 336
Skew radio button, Flash Transform panel, 338
skinAutoHide, 491
skinBackgroundAlpha, 491
skinBackgroundColor, 491
9-Slice gotchas, 137–138, 140
9-Slice scaling, 132–133, 135
slideshow.css., 541
Snap check box, Flash Properties panel, 335
Snap setting, Flash Properties panel, 362
Snap to Objects menu item, Flash, 328
Spring ease, Flash, 408
Spring option, Bind tool, 444
Spring property, Flash bones, 428
StyleManager class, 526
StyleManager.setComponentStyle(), 526
StyleManager.setStyle(), 526–527
Subpixels, 285
Subselection tool, Flash, 323–324
Swap button, Flash, 361
Swap Symbol dialog box, Flash, 353
SWC, 577
Symbols
    button symbols, 128–129
    cloud libraries creation, 142, 144
    editing symbols, 131
    essentials, 124–127

Symbols (*cont.*)
   graphic symbols, 127–128
   movieclip symbols, 129–130
   sharing, 140–141
   types, 127
Sync property, Flash Properties panel, 335

T

Tarbell, Jared, 381
Target layer, 32
Telemetry, 579
Templates area, Flash New Document dialog box, 381
Test Movie menu item, Flash, 330
Text in Animate CC
   ActionScript, text with, 303–307
   Adobe CoolType, 284–289
   devices fonts, 291–292
   embedding fonts, 293–296
   fonts and typefaces, 282–284
   Google Fonts, 290–291
   JavaScript, text with, 300–303
   scrollable text in HTML5 Canvas, 307–311
   TLF, 298–299
   working with, 296–298
TextFlow() class, ActionScript, 299
textFlowInitialFormat property, ActionScript Configuration class, 299
TextLayoutFormat() class, ActionScript, 299
Text Layout Framework (TLF), 298
   historical complexities, 299
   using older documents, 299
Text Type drop-down menu, Flash, 293
Third dimension, vanishing point, 458
Timeline panel, Flash, 349–350, 359, 392, 398, 408, 409, 411–412
Tools panel, Flash, 328, 336
Torso symbol, Flash, 451
Tracing bitmaps
   Bunsen burner, 103–105
   optimizing, drawing, 105
Transformation point, 317
Transform menu item, Flash, 337
Transform panel, Flash, 337, 339
Transform tool, Flash, 317
Translation property, Flash bones, 428
Transmission Control Protocol (TCP), 564
Trash Can icon, Flash Library panel, 319
Tweening area, Flash Properties panel, 333–334, 339, 341–342, 345, 363
Twirlies, 20
Typefaces, 282, 286
Typekit, 286–289
Typography, 281

U

UIComponent.setStyle() method, 527
UIComponent.textFormat style, 524
Undo Create Motion Tween menu item, Flash, 319
Undo Scale menu item, Flash, 316
Uniform Resource Locator (URL), 565
Use device fonts option, Flash Anti-alias pop-down menu, 292, 293

V

Vanishing point, 458
Vector images, 58
Video
   Adobe Flash Player, 477
   Adobe media encoder, 479–481
   Animate CC video wizard, 486–489
   audio track, 484–485
   basic video settings, 482–483
   encoding video, 479
   HTML5, 477
   HTML5 Canvas document, 478
   MP4 and WebM video formats, 478
   Opera, 478
   video bitrate, 483–484
   WebM, 478
Virtual Reality Modeling Language (VRML), 457

W

Web formats, publishing and, 573
   audio, 575
   CSS, 574
   Flash Player, 573–574
   HTML, 574
   images, 575
   JavaScript, 574
   video, 575
Web Graphics Library (WebGL), 3
WebM, 478
WebVTT, 498–499, 501–503
Windows Projector, 577
Wings symbols, Flash, 363
Woodstock, 20
World Wide Web, 565

X, Y

XML. *See* Extensible Markup Language (XML)

Z

Zooming, 10, 12
Zooming square, 19

Get the eBook for only $4.99!

Why limit yourself?

Now you can take the weightless companion with you wherever you go and access your content on your PC, phone, tablet, or reader.

Since you've purchased this print book, we are happy to offer you the eBook for just $4.99.

Convenient and fully searchable, the PDF version enables you to easily find and copy code—or perform examples by quickly toggling between instructions and applications.

To learn more, go to http://www.apress.com/us/shop/companion or contact support@apress.com.

All Apress eBooks are subject to copyright. All rights are reserved by the Publisher, whether the whole or part of the material is concerned, specifically the rights of translation, reprinting, reuse of illustrations, recitation, broadcasting, reproduction on microfilms or in any other physical way, and transmission or information storage and retrieval, electronic adaptation, computer software, or by similar or dissimilar methodology now known or hereafter developed. Exempted from this legal reservation are brief excerpts in connection with reviews or scholarly analysis or material supplied specifically for the purpose of being entered and executed on a computer system, for exclusive use by the purchaser of the work. Duplication of this publication or parts thereof is permitted only under the provisions of the Copyright Law of the Publisher's location, in its current version, and permission for use must always be obtained from Springer. Permissions for use may be obtained through RightsLink at the Copyright Clearance Center. Violations are liable to prosecution under the respective Copyright Law.

CPSIA information can be obtained
at www.ICGtesting.com
Printed in the USA
LVHW10s1931161018
593811LV00007B/173/P